To Roger and Alma Williams;
the Episcopal Church; Brooklyn, New York, public schools;
Oakwood Friends School; Haverford College;
The Washington Post; and
Delise, Antonio, Rae, and Raphael.

Welcome to the University of Maryland!

Each year the University selects a book that will provide a shared intellectual experience for faculty, staff, and all first-year students. The First-Year Book Committee, which is comprised of representatives with diverse backgrounds from across campus, reviews several selections, carefully considers the issues that each will generate, and solicits community input before making its final recommendation.

The first-year book provides an opportunity for community dialogue on a topic and its impact on the lives of individuals from a number of perspectives, from the sciences to the humanities. Guest speakers, films, theater productions, and panel discussions often provide additional opportunities outside of class to generate discussion around a common theme. Our community is stronger when we are free to challenge each other and listen respectfully. The University does not shy away from challenging or controversial issues; on the contrary, free and spirited speech is at the very heart of an academic community.

I am pleased that the committee has selected *Thurgood Marshall: American Revolutionary*, by Juan Williams, as the 2005-2006 First-Year Book. A Maryland native, Justice Marshall's legal challenges on access to education provide a unique lens through which to view the history of the twentieth century. As we celebrate the 150th anniversary of the University of Maryland this year, it is my hope that the conversations generated by this book will enrich the campus community and broaden our understanding of the meaning of citizenship.

William W. Destler
Senior Vice President for Academic Affairs and Provost

ALSO BY JUAN WILLIAMS

Eyes on the Prize

THURGOOD
MARSHALL

American Revolutionary

THURGOOD MARSHALL

American Revolutionary

Juan Williams

THREE RIVERS PRESS

NEW YORK

Published by Three Rivers Press, New York, New York.
Member of the Crown Publishing Group.

Random House, Inc. New York, Toronto, London, Sydney, Auckland
www.randomhouse.com

THREE RIVERS PRESS is a registered trademark and the Three Rivers Press colophon is a trademark of Random House, Inc.

Originally published by Times Books in 1998.

Printed in the United States of America

Library of Congress Cataloging-in-Publication Data
    Williams, Juan.
      Thurgood Marshall: American Revolutionary / Juan Williams.
        1. Marshall, Thurgood, 1908–1993.   2. Judges—United States—Biography.   3. United States. Supreme Court—
Biography.   4. Civil rights workers—United States—Biography.
I. Title.
KF8745.M34W55   1998
347.73'2634—dc21   98–9735
[B]

ISBN   0-8129-3299-4

10 9 8

*For inquire, I pray of you, of bygone ages, and consider
what the fathers have found. . . . Will they not teach you,
and tell you, and utter words out of their understanding?*
—Job 8:8–10

CONTENTS

INTRODUCTION xiii

FAMILY TREE xvii

1. *Right Time, Right Man?* 3

2. *A Fighting Family* 15

3. *Educating Thurgood* 24

4. *Waking Up* 40

5. *Turkey* 52

6. *His Own Man* 61

7. *Getting Started* 75

8. *Leaving Home* 86

9. *69 Fifth Avenue* 93

10. *Marshall in Charge* 101

11. *Pan of Bones* 113

12. *The War Years* 122

13. *Lynch Mob for a Lawyer* 131

14. *Jim Crow Buster* 143

[xi

15. *Groveland*   152

16. *Lessons in Politics*   158

17. *On the Front Line*   167

18. *Direct Attack*   174

19. *Number One Negro of All Time*   187

20. *Planning a Revolt*   195

21. *Case of the Century*   209

22. *No Radical*   228

23. *Martin Luther King, Jr.*   245

24. *Machiavellian Marshall*   253

25. *The Second Civil War*   263

26. *Marshall and the Militants*   275

27. *Exit Time*   284

28. *Black Robes*   296

29. *Johnson's Man*   313

30. *Justice Marshall*   332

31. *Backlash on the Court*   353

32. *Hangin' On*   374

33. *Resurrection*   397

AFTERWORD   405

ACKNOWLEDGMENTS   413

NOTES   415

RESOURCES AND BIBLIOGRAPHY   441

PRINCIPAL CASES CITED   447

INDEX   451

INTRODUCTION

We make movies about Malcolm X, we get a holiday to
honor Dr. Martin Luther King, but every day we live with
the legacy of Justice Thurgood Marshall.

—*Washington Afro-American* editorial
after Thurgood Marshall's death

THURGOOD MARSHALL'S LIFEWORK made him one of America's leading radicals. As a suit-and-tie lawyer, however, he was the unlikely leading
actor in creating social change in the United States in the twentieth century. His great achievement was to expand rights for individual Americans. But he especially succeeded in creating new protections under law
for America's women, children, prisoners, homeless, minorities, and immigrants. Their greater claim to full citizenship in the Republic over the
last century can be directly traced to Marshall. Even the American press
has Marshall to thank for an expansion of its liberties during the century.

But for black Americans especially, Marshall stood as a colossus. He
guided a formerly enslaved people along the road to equal rights. Oddly,
of the three leading black liberators of twentieth-century America—
Thurgood Marshall, Martin Luther King, Jr., and Malcolm X—Marshall
was the least well known. Dr. King gained fame as the inspiring advocate
of nonviolence and mass protests. Malcolm X was the defiant black nationalist whose preachings about separatism and armed revolution were
the other side of King's appeals for racial peace. But the third man in this
black triumvirate stood as the one with the biggest impact on American
race relations.

It was Marshall who ended legal segregation in the United States. He
won Supreme Court victories breaking the color line in housing, transportation, and voting, all of which overturned the "separate-but-equal"
apartheid of American life in the first half of the century.

It was Marshall who won the most important legal case of the century, *Brown v. Board of Education*, ending the legal separation of black and white children in public schools. The success of the *Brown* case sparked the 1960s civil rights movement, led to the increased number of black high school and college graduates and the incredible rise of the black middle class in both numbers and political power in the second half of the century.

And it was Marshall, as the nation's first African-American Supreme Court justice, who promoted affirmative action—preferences, set-asides, and other race-conscious policies—as the remedy for the damage remaining from the nation's history of slavery and racial bias. Justice Marshall gave a clear signal that while legal discrimination had ended, there was more to be done to advance educational opportunity for blacks and to bridge the wide canyon of economic inequity between blacks and whites.

Marshall's lifework, then, literally defined the movement of race relations through the century. He rejected King's peaceful protest as rhetorical fluff, which accomplished no permanent change in society. And he rejected Malcolm X's talk of violent revolution and a separate black nation as racist craziness in a multiracial society.

Instead Marshall was busy in the nation's courtrooms, winning permanent changes in the rock-hard laws of segregation. He created a new legal landscape, where racial equality was an accepted principle. He worked in behalf of black Americans but built a structure of individual rights that became the cornerstone of protections for all Americans. Marshall's triumphs led black people to speak of him in biblical terms of salvation: "He brought us the Constitution as a document like Moses brought his people the Ten Commandments," the NAACP board member Juanita Jackson Mitchell once said.

The key to Marshall's work was his conviction that integration—and only integration—would allow equal rights under the law to take hold. Once individual rights were accepted, in Marshall's mind, blacks and whites could rise or fall based on their own ability.

Marshall's deep faith in the power of racial integration came out of a middle-class black perspective in turn-of-the-century Baltimore. He was the child of an activist black community that had established its own schools and fought for equal rights from the time of the Civil War. His own family, of an interracial background, had been at the forefront of demands by Baltimore blacks for equal treatment. Out of that unique family and city was born Thurgood Marshall, the architect of American race relations in the twentieth century.

Martin Luther King, Jr., and Malcolm X both died young, the victims of assassins. They became martyrs to the nation's racial wars. Thurgood Marshall lived to be eighty-four and was no one's martyr. He held high public office, but for those last thirty years of his life Marshall was reclusive, making few public appearances and rarely talking with reporters. The public knew him primarily as a distant figure whose voice was heard only in the legalistic language of Supreme Court dissents.

I began writing to Marshall in the early 1980s, while working on a book to accompany the Public Broadcasting documentary *Eyes on the Prize: America's Civil Rights Years, 1954–1965*. Marshall knew me as a writer for *The Washington Post* but declined my request to talk to him about his life. His family and friends persisted in asking the cloistered justice to tell his story. Eventually Marshall called and invited me to his Supreme Court chambers.

That two-hour visit in July 1989 began six months of almost weekly interviews. The result was a 1990 article in *The Washington Post Magazine*. But that article could hold only so much of the rich material Marshall had shared in the exclusive interviews. I hoped that he might agree to cooperate with a more lengthy biography. But his earlier experience with a book project had left a bad taste, and he confided that he was tired. He wanted neither to do the work required for a biography nor to defend his views to critics. He agreed, however, not to burn his personal papers, as he had always threatened to do. He let me know he had sent them to the Library of Congress, where they could be opened after his death.

I was in Japan and still hoping Justice Marshall might change his mind about doing a book when I heard that he had retired from the court. The ensuing fury over the confirmation of his successor, Clarence Thomas, made Marshall all the more gun-shy about doing a biography. He felt both out of sync with the times and forgotten.

As I persisted, Marshall gave me some tips on people to interview and I got started on the book in 1992. His wife, Cissy, refused to cooperate with the project and persuaded her children to do the same. Marshall's FBI files were shut to me for years and opened only in stages, after painstaking struggles. Even worse, the NAACP Legal Defense and Educational Fund withheld its cooperation despite Marshall's long, happy association with that group. Justice Marshall had offered to have the LDF's files opened to me while I was working on the magazine article. But later the head of the LDF, angry over a column I wrote defending the conservative Clarence Thomas's right to confirmation hearings based on his merits and ideas—and not on charges of making off-color sexual comments ten years earlier—shut the door on my efforts to see those files.

Despite a petition by more than ten leading historians, as well as requests by the Library of Congress that terms be set for legitimate research, the LDF tried to stop my work. They discarded a powerful chance to promote the LDF and advance Marshall's legacy by deciding to keep the history of the LDF's heroic struggles closed to the American people.

Ultimately other sources of documents and stories opened up and more than covered that time period. Marshall's friends, schoolmates, fellow lawyers at the LDF, and colleagues on the court provided me with more than 150 interviews.

Marshall also arranged for me to see the oral history he had contributed to Columbia University in the 1970s, and I reviewed interviews he had done for the Kennedy and Johnson presidential libraries, as well as files in archives and repositories nationwide. In addition, there was a wealth of fascinating newspaper coverage of his exploits against the worst bigots in southern courtrooms. Best of all, I had his words and memories of the work he had done.

After Marshall died, in 1993, there was still no authoritative, thorough account of his life and the impact of his work. The combination of his reclusiveness and his standing in popular culture as an elderly, establishment figure blinded much of the nation to the importance of his legacy. Young people were especially uninformed about the critical role Marshall had played in making history.

This book is intended to fill some of that vacuum. In these pages the great storyteller tells his stories. And the history, of both his family and the civil rights movement, is in one place so that future generations can understand the dynamics that created and sustained Thurgood Marshall's conception of successful race relations. Given that Marshall laid the foundation for today's racial landscape, his grand design of how race relations best work makes his life story essential for anyone delving into the powder keg of America's greatest problem. He was truly an American Revolutionary.

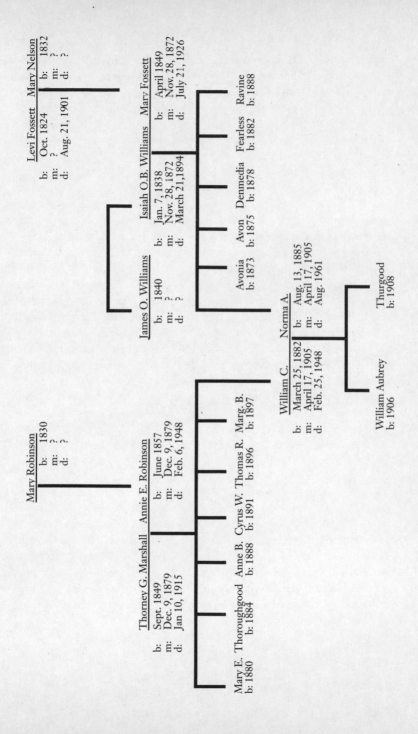

Levi Fossett   Mary Nelson
Oct. 1824   b: 1832
b:
m: ?   m: ?
d: Aug. 21, 1901   d: ?

Isaiah O.B. Williams   Mary Fossett
b: Jan. 7, 1838   b: April 1849
m: Nov. 28, 1872   m: Nov. 28, 1872
d: March 21,1894   d: July 21, 1926

James O. Williams
b: 1840
m: ?
d: ?

Avonia   Avon   Denmedia   Fearless   Ravine
b: 1873   b: 1875   b: 1878   b: 1882   b: 1888

Mary Robinson
b: 1830
m: ?
d: ?

Thorney G. Marshall   Annie E. Robinson
b: Sept. 1849   b: June 1857
m: Dec. 9, 1879   m: Dec. 9, 1879
d: Jan 10, 1915   d: Feb. 6, 1948

Mary E. Thoroughgood   Anne B.   Cyrus W.   Thomas R.   Marg. B.
b: 1880   b: 1884   b: 1888   b: 1891   b: 1896   b: 1897

William C.   Norma A.
b: March 25, 1882   b: Aug. 13, 1885
m: April 17, 1905   m: April 17, 1905
d: Feb. 25, 1948   d: Aug. 1961

William Aubrey   Thurgood
b: 1906   b: 1908

THURGOOD MARSHALL

❧

American Revolutionary

CHAPTER 1

❧

Right Time, Right Man?

Rumors flew that night. Supreme Court Justice Tom Clark had resigned a few hours earlier. By that Monday evening, Solicitor General Thurgood Marshall and his wife, Cissy, heard that the president was set to name Clark's replacement the very next morning. At the Marshalls' small green town house on G Street in Southwest Washington, D.C., the phone was ringing. Friends, family, and even politicians were calling to see if Thurgood had heard anything about his chances for the job. But all the Marshalls could say was that they had heard rumors.

As Marshall dressed for Clark's retirement party on that muggy Washington night of June 12, 1967, he looked at his reflection in the mirror. Years ago some of his militant critics had called him "half-white" for his straight hair, pointed nose, and light tan skin. Now, at fifty-eight, his face had grown heavy, with sagging jowls and dark bags under his eyes. His once black hair, even his mustache, was now mostly a steely gray. And he looked worried. He did have on a good dark blue suit, the uniform of a Washington power player. But the conservative suit looked old and out of place in an era of Afros and dashikis. And even the best suit might not be strong enough armor for the high-stakes political fight he was preparing for tonight. At this moment the six-foot-two-inch Marshall, who weighed well over two hundred pounds, felt powerless. He was fearful that he was about to lose his only chance to become a Supreme Court justice.

Staring in the mirror as if it were a crystal ball, Marshall could see clearly only that he would have one last chance to convince the president he was the right man. That chance would come tonight at Justice Clark's retirement party.

In his two years as solicitor general there had been constant rumors floating around the capital about Marshall being positioned by the president to become the first black man on the high court. However, with one exception, no one at the White House had ever spoken to him about the job. That exception was President Lyndon Johnson. Whenever Johnson talked about the Supreme Court in front of him, the tall, intense Texan made a point of turning to Marshall, thrusting a finger in his face, and reminding him there was no promise that he would ever have a job on the high court.

But Johnson was privately talking about putting Marshall on the Supreme Court. For a southern politician, Johnson had a strong sense of racial justice. As a skinny twenty-year-old, he had taught school to poor Hispanic children in south Texas and seen firsthand the disadvantages they faced. Now Johnson's fabled political instincts had drawn him to the idea that he would be hailed by history as the president who put the first black on the Supreme Court. The president had set the wheels in motion by making Marshall the nation's first black solicitor general. And he had confided to his wife, Lady Bird, that he wanted to appoint Marshall to the Supreme Court. But the president had been having second thoughts about Marshall. Was he really a good lawyer? And what about talk that Marshall was lazy? Was it realistic to think he could win enough votes to get by white racists in the Senate and be confirmed?

As he finished getting ready for the party, Marshall replayed all the rumors he had heard about why the president was reluctant to appoint him to the high court. Thinking about it, Marshall got grumpy, then angry. His chance to be in the history books as the first black man on the Supreme Court was fading, and he felt abandoned. The word around the capital was that the nomination would be announced tomorrow. Marshall had heard nothing from the White House.

Looking in the mirror, Marshall began to buck himself up. He decided that he had run this course before—and won. He remembered when, as a failing lawyer in Depression-era Baltimore, he had pressured the NAACP for a job. He had peppered Charles Houston, his former law school dean, who was then running the NAACP's legal office, with letters and phone calls detailing ideas for lawsuits to fight racial segregation. The NAACP had little money and could not afford to hire a junior lawyer. But Marshall's aggressiveness and his record of early successes in Maryland civil rights cases finally paid off. Houston offered him a small salary if he would move to New York. Marshall jumped at the chance.

Once in New York, Marshall won case after case, culminating in the landmark *Brown v. Board of Education*, desegregating America's public schools. Then a driven Marshall played his political cards with care. When the Democrat John Kennedy won the White House, the successful and persistent Marshall headed everyone's list of black lawyers deserving a top federal judgeship. However, Attorney General Robert Kennedy feared that southern segregationists would be angered by the nomination of any black man, especially the famous black lawyer who had been on the cover of *Time* magazine for having undressed them as bigots and defeated them in court.

But Marshall played tough. He refused the Kennedy administration's offer to be a judge on any lower court. He told the attorney general it was the appeals court job or nothing. Then Marshall increased the political pressure on Robert Kennedy's left by drumming up support in the black press and among civil rights leaders who had been crucial to John Kennedy's narrow election as president. Robert Kennedy weighed the price of angering the civil rights groups and decided to give Marshall the seat he wanted. The determined and willful Thurgood Marshall had won.

Marshall's forceful personality usually allowed him to get his way. He could charm a racist cop with stories and jokes, and he was also capable of intimidating black political rivals by being loud and defiant. But Marshall was full of nagging doubts about this Supreme Court job. He had a desperate need to be respected, to be seen as the equal of top white lawyers who had always looked down on black lawyers. The Supreme Court job would distinguish him for all history and make him the equal of any lawyer. Marshall's personal ambition went deeper than most because it was inextricably tied to his idea of what was best for a racially tense nation. All his life Marshall had been an integrationist. If black people could mix freely with white people, study and work together, he believed, there would be no racial problems in America. He had pushed that theory in courtrooms throughout the nation, won in the Supreme Court, and created the foundation for a modern civil rights movement that to this night still had the nation in turmoil. As a matter of principle, history, and personal ambition, Thurgood Marshall wanted to be the man to integrate the high court. This desire stirred a lifetime of passion and determination in him.

But campaigning for a seat on the Supreme Court might be self-defeating; President Johnson was the kind of man to kill a deal if his hand was being forced or someone was telling him what to do. When newspapers wrote stories in advance of his policy decisions and appointments, Johnson would change his mind just to prove the papers wrong.

Marshall had asked Louis (pronounced "Louie") Martin, the smooth, senior black political player at the Democratic National Committee and deputy chairman of the party, to speak to the president about the nomination. Martin had known Marshall since the 1940s, when Marshall was director of the NAACP Legal Defense Fund and Martin ran several black midwestern newspapers. Martin, a tall honey-brown man who spoke slow, thoughtful words in a raspy voice, was entertained by Marshall's rapid, blunt comments and his gusto for an argument or a drink. Martin often told friends how after one bout of drinking in Harlem years before, he had driven Marshall around in the early morning hours to give him some air and sober him up before taking him home.

But when Martin sat and talked with the president about Marshall, Johnson fired back, "That son of a bitch is not worth a damn; he is lazy." Martin did not tell Marshall about that conversation. He didn't want to deflate Marshall's ego, and he didn't take Johnson's outbursts all that seriously. Martin figured it was just "Lyndon being Lyndon." He continued saying a good word here and there to the president on his friend's behalf and getting Marshall into meetings so the president saw him regularly.[1]

But Martin could never give Marshall any guarantee, and Marshall realized that his friend's best efforts may not have been enough. Marshall saw other indications that Johnson was slowly moving away from giving him consideration as a nominee for the Court. The president had told Ramsey Clark, then the acting attorney general and the son of Justice Tom Clark, that Marshall's reputation as solicitor general worried him. With the keen eye of a man who had been watching the scoreboard, the president precisely noted that by the end of 1966 Marshall had lost five of fourteen cases he'd argued as solicitor general before the Supreme Court. That was not good enough. Johnson wanted a perfect record—no losses—so that even Marshall's most racist critics would have to say he was qualified.

Johnson's main worry was about the politics of putting Marshall on the Court in 1967. It was a time of a growing backlash against liberal politics. The college campuses were filled with antiwar and civil rights protests. Violent riots had shaken Baltimore, Chicago, and Los Angeles during the Black Power summer of 1966. Talking to Clark about the politics of nominating Marshall to the Court, the president had said Marshall was a man who would "just be in the liberals' pocket 100 percent of the time." A Court with Marshall, William Douglas, Hugo Black, Abe Fortas, and Earl Warren was a sure bet to be a liberal playground: "Think they'd send a man to the penitentiary for raping a woman if you had a photograph of it?" the president asked Clark. Johnson also worried that putting another liberal on the Court at that time would infuriate conservatives and might mean that his chance to be reelected in 1968 "was long gone."

Clark listened to Johnson's rant. But he did not agree. A fellow Texan and close confidant to the president, Clark was different from most of the men surrounding Johnson. He was a University of Chicago graduate who was considered by Johnson's political cronies to be an extreme liberal, even if he was from Texas. In his deep southern drawl the young Clark reminded Johnson that Marshall shared the president's core belief that the key to ending the 1960s racial strife was promoting integration. Marshall's record showed a willingness to crack down on younger, more militant blacks who could be seen on TV rioting and battling with cops. Given his record as a famed civil rights lawyer, Marshall would be a powerful man to oppose the black radicals.

The president listened to Clark but never said yes or no to putting Marshall on the Court. Clark found himself attempting to stop Johnson from ruling Marshall out. He tried to soothe the president by allaying his biggest fear—that Marshall could not be confirmed. But with southern segregationists in many key positions in the Senate, Johnson expected a fight over the first black justice. He said he could not afford to have a major nomination go down to defeat with the election so near.

Some of the president's doubts eventually got back to Marshall. In conversations with Louis Martin and other friends, he worried that the president was looking at other black lawyers—less well known and less controversial—who would be more likely to win easy Senate confirmation. *Jet*, the weekly black newsmagazine, reported that the president's list of potential black nominees to the Supreme Court included Marshall but also federal judges Wade McCree of Detroit and William Hastie of Philadelphia. They had first-rate credentials in the white legal establishment—and none of Marshall's baggage of a career in the civil rights movement. In fact, the president had asked Nicholas Katzenbach, Ramsey Clark's predecessor as attorney general, a Rhodes scholar and Yale Law School professor with impeccable establishment credentials, to identify other black candidates for the Court.

Johnson, standing toe-to-toe with the equally tall, balding Katzenbach, told him, "Marshall's not the best—he's not the most outstanding black lawyer in the country." Katzenbach grimaced as the imposing Johnson listed prominent, supposedly better-qualified black lawyers, such as William Coleman and Bill Hastie. Finally, Katzenbach, who had come to be friends with Marshall, faced up to Johnson's charge. He replied, "Mr. President, if you appoint anybody, any black to that court but Thurgood Marshall, you are insulting every black in the country. Thurgood is *the* black lawyer as far as blacks are concerned—I mean there can't be any doubt about that."

Katzenbach did agree with the president that Marshall was lazy some of the time. But he reassured Johnson that he would never regret putting Marshall on the Supreme Court. "He may not be a Felix Frankfurter, he may not be a Hugo Black, but he will never disgrace you."[2] Katzenbach wanted Marshall on the Court as a symbol of racial harmony.

Inside the White House, Marshall had asked another good friend to urge the president to put him on the high court. Clifford Alexander, one of Johnson's White House lawyers, was the chief adviser on hiring blacks for the administration. Alexander had known Marshall for years. When Alexander won the presidency of the student council at Harvard University in 1954, he asked Marshall to address the students. At that moment Marshall was world famous for his victory desegregating U.S. public schools. When he agreed to come to Harvard, it was a coup for the student council president, and Alexander never forgot it.[3]

In the Oval Office, dominated by the president's massive mahogany desk, the unassuming Alexander had walked the same path as Ramsey Clark and Nicholas Katzenbach. Sitting by the side of the desk, Alexander in a soft voice had pressed him to make history by nominating Marshall to replace the retiring Clark. Johnson, again, did not say yes or no. Later, Alexander could only tell Marshall that he had put in a good word for him and not to worry about all the rumors.

On June 12, 1967, his last day on the high court, Justice Tom Clark told reporters the president would appoint a replacement "who will fill my shoes to overflowing, possibly break them open."[4] His comment sparked a new wave of rumors. Justice Clark's comments raised

Marshall's hopes. But as his petite Hawaiian wife later told reporters, she had heard hints before, and "you can't live on hints."[5]

At the retirement party Johnson was his usual dominating self, alternately bullying and ingratiating himself with both justices and the politicians in the crowd. When Marshall made his way through the faces surrounding Johnson, the president quickly greeted him with a wide smile. The two men loved to drink bourbon and tell stories full of lies. They were the same age and had strong feelings for each other. So it was no surprise when the president threw a long arm around Marshall and briefly pulled him aside. Johnson bluntly told him not to get his hopes up because he was not going to replace Justice Clark.

Marshall played it off with a laugh. Standing to his full height, he reminded Johnson that he didn't need a job and there had never been any promise he would get to the high court. Behind his bluster, however, Marshall felt a fierce determination to argue with Johnson right there. It was Marshall's style to apply pressure and fight. But this time he bit his tongue. It didn't make sense to think he could bully Lyndon Johnson in the middle of a party and win. He drove home, cutting across the Mall, with the U.S. Capitol's magnificent white dome glowing to one side and the towering Washington Monument on the other. The nation's grand symbols made him feel small, an outsider. He had missed his chance.

The next morning, Tuesday, June 13, Marshall was in his office at the Justice Department on Pennsylvania Avenue when his secretary got a call from the attorney general. It was just before 10:00 A.M., and Clark told her he was coming down to see Marshall and to keep everyone else out. When Clark got into Marshall's office, he asked him what he was doing later that morning. Marshall replied that he was going to the White House to speak with a group of students. Clark told him to go over fifteen minutes early and stop in the Oval Office. Marshall pressed Clark to tell him what was going on. Clark said he didn't know. But given the spate of rumors over the last twenty-four hours and the disaster at the party, Marshall figured this trip was for Johnson to stroke him and tell him why he didn't get the job.[6]

Meanwhile, the president phoned Louis Martin at the Democratic National Committee that morning and asked him to come to the Oval Office. Before Martin's arrival Johnson placed another call. He told Clifford Alexander to come over as well. Alexander was the first to arrive. He found Johnson sitting in a rocking chair in front of a circular marble coffee table in the middle of the Oval Office. The president was holding handwritten notes on large white index cards. Listed were the names of key members of the Senate Judiciary Committee; the Senate leaders, including Mike Mansfield and Everett Dirksen, the majority and minority leaders; Chief Justice Earl Warren; and a tally of Marshall's record in cases argued before the Supreme Court. Highlighted on one card was the fact that Marshall had been first in his class at Howard Law School. Alexander could barely contain his glee when he realized what was going on.

With Alexander standing by, the president, using the white phone built into the coffee table, called Vice President Hubert Humphrey, informing him of the decision. Then Johnson, alternately leaning forward and pushing back as he spoke, called the man who was sure to be the leader in any confirmation fight in the Senate, James Eastland of Mississippi, a hard-line segregationist. "That conversation was mostly in monotone," Alexander recalled. "President Johnson said to him, 'I know you must agree that this is the best-qualified person.' "

Johnson then called several more senators. Alexander remembered the conversations all ended the same way: "I am sure with this distinguished record that you will support his nomination." No one, neither Republican nor Democrat, argued. There was hardly any reason for discussion. Johnson had made up his mind, and he spoke with presidential authority. He was not asking for anyone's support. "God knows by the time he finished his monologue, the people at the other end of the phone had to think about what they had agreed to," said Alexander.

Louis Martin soon came in and stood with Alexander as the president called Earl Warren, who was in San Francisco. Warren gave his approval to the nomination and later sent a note thanking Johnson for early notice of the nomination.

With the calls finished, Johnson asked Alexander and Martin to wait outside while he spoke with Marshall alone. Marshall had been next door since 10:45, talking with Marvin Watson, Johnson's appointments secretary. Watson played dumb when Marshall asked him why the president wanted to see him. When he was finally called into the Oval Office at 11:05, Marshall saw Johnson, all by himself, bent over the news service ticker-tape machine.

While Marshall waited for the president to turn around he quickly glanced about the Oval Office. In the far corner was a bronze caricature of a frenetic President Johnson running while holding a phone in one hand. On the marble coffee table Marshall could see a bunch of index cards and papers, some of which had spilled onto the green rug under the president's rocking chair. Nervously, Marshall coughed to get the president's attention. Johnson spun around, as though surprised, and said, "Oh, hi, Thurgood. Sit down, sit down." Marshall moved toward the couch and sat next to Johnson's rocking chair. Johnson made small talk with the fidgety Marshall until he abruptly turned to him and said, "You know something, Thurgood? . . . I'm going to put you on the Supreme Court." Marshall was stunned. All he could say was "Oh, yipe!" [7]

Johnson laughed and had Martin and Alexander come back into the office. They sat on the couch across from Marshall, with the president occasionally leaning forward in the rocking chair. Johnson joked with Marshall that he appointed him to the Supreme Court because "you are very much like me—brought up in poverty . . . not a Harvard boy like Cliff." Alexander later recalled thinking to himself that Marshall was not brought up in poverty, but that was the image he gave off. For nearly an hour a giddy Marshall joked around, never moving far from the president's rocking chair even as Johnson made phone calls to ecstatic civil rights leaders. Marshall shook his head and laughed at Johnson's trickery as he recalled for Martin and Alexander that just the night before, the president had told him he would not get the job. Johnson just smiled.

At noon Johnson led his new nominee out the French doors behind his desk and into the bright June sunshine. The minute the reporters in the Rose Garden saw Marshall, they knew what was coming. His nomination, while historic, somehow was expected because it had been rumored for so long.

"I have just talked to the Chief Justice and informed him that I shall send to the Senate this afternoon the nomination of Mr. Thurgood Marshall, Solicitor General, to the position of Associate Justice of the Supreme Court," Johnson said. "He has argued nineteen cases in the Supreme Court since becoming Solicitor General. Prior to that time he had argued some thirty-two cases. Statisticians tell me that probably only one or two other living men have argued as many cases before the Court—and perhaps less than half a dozen in all the history of the Nation. . . .

"I believe he has already earned his place in history, but I think it will be greatly enhanced by his service on the Court," continued Johnson. "I believe he earned that appointment; he deserves the appointment. He is best qualified by training and by very valuable service to the country. I believe it is the right thing to do, the right time to do it, the right man and the right place."

Surprisingly, there was no express mention of the fact that Marshall was black, just Johnson's singular focus on his legal record and an expression of doing the "right thing," a quick jab at critics, particularly southern senators, who might oppose the idea of putting a black man on the nation's highest court. The president, with Marshall by his side, then began a twenty-minute news conference, most of which, incredibly, had nothing to do with the nomination. Reporters asked about Vietnam, the Middle East, and riots in the big cities. Finally, a reporter asked Johnson if he had been advised to name a more conservative nominee than Marshall.

President Johnson shook his head and said, "No, I received very little pressure of any kind in this connection." The American Bar Association found Marshall "highly acceptable," Johnson added. Another reporter jumped in: "I was just going to ask Justice Marshall, if we might, how he feels about this appointment?"

Johnson, turning to Marshall, responded: "I hope the justice doesn't go into an extended news conference before his confirmation." Marshall, who was almost as tall as the president, then stepped forward, bent over the microphone, smiled, and looking out through thick, black-framed eyeglasses said: "You speak for me, Mr. President, we will wait until after the Senate acts."[8] The president and Marshall, arm in arm and smiling, then marched with long, loping strides back into the Oval Office, where Marshall asked the president for permission to tell his wife the good news before she heard it on the radio. Johnson, with a startled look, said he was surprised Marshall had not already told her. "How could I, sir?" Marshall asked. "I've been with you all the time." Marshall rang up his wife from a phone on the circular coffee table, and an eager Johnson grabbed for the receiver. "Cissy, this is Lyndon Johnson. . . . I just put your husband on the Supreme Court." The stunned wife replied, "I sure am happy I'm sitting down."[9]

To Marshall's surprise, the next morning's newspapers did not greet the nomination with high praise. It was "rich in symbolism," said *The New York Times*. But the paper did not give Marshall high marks as a legal thinker, saying he was not particularly distinguished either as a federal judge or as solicitor general.

Newsweek magazine said President Johnson did not have to mention at his press conference that Marshall would be the first black on the

Court. In a week of race riots across the nation, for the president to choose a black man to sit on the high court looked to a lot of people like a deft political move by a master politician. And there was the chance that the nomination could win back liberal white voters, who were increasingly turning away from Johnson over the Vietnam War. With a potential primary challenge from Sen. Robert Kennedy next year, Johnson had tied up the black vote, the magazine concluded. *Newsweek* did laud Marshall as a black leader who "in three decades . . . has done as much to transform the life of his people as any Negro alive today, including Nobel Laureate Martin Luther King, Jr."[10]

One faint line of praise for Marshall's nomination came from conservatives who thought it might stop wild-eyed black people from rioting. An editorial in the *Las Vegas Sun* didn't have much good to say about Marshall but celebrated the fact that his nomination "pretty much negate[s] the complaints of the Negro multitudes. . . . It is hoped the significance is not lost on the Martin Luther Kings and the Stokely Carmichaels and their rampaging followers."[11]

While cheering for the nomination was polite at best in most papers, the voices of criticism were full-blooded. The Chicago *Sun-Times* wrote that lawyers would be keeping an eye on Marshall "because he has been subject to criticism for laziness by those who dealt with him as Solicitor General and Circuit Court Judge."[12] Joseph Kraft, the preeminent Washington columnist, wrote Marshall's only qualification was that he was "a Negro, not just any Negro [but] not even the best qualified Negro."[13]

The administration quickly responded to the critics by emphasizing Marshall's strong belief in the law and racial integration. Johnson and his top aides transformed Marshall into a living symbol of racial progress and good American race relations. Two weeks after his nomination and before any Senate hearings began, the White House arranged for Marshall to be appointed to a special commission to study whether crime and violence were the cause of rioting in Harlem. The leaders of the liberal white establishment were embracing him as their answer to angry blacks who said whites never gave a black man a chance.

And yet a strong undercurrent of criticism of Marshall—he was unqualified, lazy, too liberal—continued. Marshall came under the most brutal attack from segregationists, who did not want an integrationist on the Court. President Johnson's political strategy to have Marshall quickly and easily confirmed was crumbling. And even Marshall's tough-mindedness, his amazing will to win, seemed to be overmatched.

Hearings for most Supreme Court nominees began within a week of the nomination. Byron White, President Kennedy's first candidate for the Court, had been nominated and confirmed within eight days. Abe Fortas, President Johnson's first, had to wait only fourteen days. Thurgood Marshall was different. It would be seventy-eight days before his name would come up for a vote of Senate confirmation.

In the two and a half months between the nomination and the vote on Marshall, his record as a lawyer, his writings, his drinking, the women he slept with, and his family came under the intense scrutiny of FBI and Senate investigations. Sen. Robert Byrd, Democrat of West Virginia, wrote to FBI director J. Edgar Hoover, asking if there was information about Marshall's ties to Communists. Another senator focused on uncovering evidence that Marshall hated whites; other senators loaded up on detailed legal questions, hoping to reveal gaps in Marshall's knowledge of the law that would disqualify him for the high court.

But the larger topics for Marshall's opponents were still left unanswered: Who was this man? How did a black man so despised by millions of segregationists rise past Jim Crow political power to become a federal judge, the first black solicitor general, and finally to stand at the door of the highest station of American law, the Supreme Court? Simply put, where did this Negro come from?

CHAPTER 2

❦

A Fighting Family

Thurgood Marshall's rise to power played out against the backdrop of America's tempestuous history of slavery, Jim Crow segregation, and the civil rights movement. That panorama would dwarf most people, but Marshall was raised to stand out. He grew up in an exceptional family and was rooted in an exceptional place—Baltimore, Maryland. Any attempt to know Thurgood Marshall had to start with his family and his hometown. His defiance of segregation, his willingness to stand up to powerful whites, and his insistence that he was the equal of any man were rooted in his Baltimore family.

William Marshall, his father, told Thurgood from an early age to treat everyone with respect but never to let any insult go by without standing up for himself. "If somebody calls you a 'Nigger' take it up right then and there," his father, a pale-skinned, blue-eyed man, told him. "Either win or lose right then and there."

The advice came into play one afternoon while fifteen-year-old Thurgood was delivering hats. He was on an errand for Mr. Schoen, a Jewish man who ran a women's hat and dress store. Schoen's shop was on Pennsylvania Avenue, a large, noisy street running through Old West Baltimore. The avenue was lined with street vendors and their horse-drawn wagons called Arabs, fancy clothing stores as well as butcher shops, theaters, numbers runners, and jazz clubs. It was where most of Baltimore's black people shopped, and for Thurgood it was a great place to have an after-school job.

During the five o'clock rush hour one afternoon, Mr. Schoen sent his young worker out with a tall stack of hats to be delivered to customers. As he was getting on a trolley and struggling to see around the boxes, Thurgood pushed by a white woman who was also getting onboard. He felt a hand grab at his shirt collar, and before he knew what had happened, he was being pulled backward off the trolley by a white man.

"Don't push in front of a white lady," the man told him. Marshall brashly responded, "Damn it, I'm just trying to get on the damned bus." The white man glared at the teenager and said, "Nigger, don't you talk to me like that."

Thurgood dropped the hats and started swinging. The man, trampling over the hats, grabbed Thurgood's shirt and started wrestling with him. But Thurgood, tall and awkward for his age, kept throwing wild, hard punches despite all attempts to slow him down. A crowd gathered and others gawked from the trolley. A nearby policeman ran over and pushed into the fray. To Thurgood's surprise the policeman never said a word to the man who had started the fight. Instead he arrested Thurgood, who had to phone Mr. Schoen from the precinct to tell him about the fracas and the damage to the hats. Schoen came down to the station and told the police that his young worker had been provoked.

"So they took his word and let me go," Marshall recalled. Marshall apologized to Schoen for destroying all of his expensive hats. "It was worth it if you're right," Schoen said. "Did the man really call you a nigger?" The young Thurgood responded forcefully: "Yes, sir, he sure did." Schoen stopped walking, put an arm around Thurgood, and told him he had done the right thing.

The fight was an early sign of a defiant streak that would be prominent throughout Marshall's life. But it was also the result of being the child of a proud, politically active, black, middle-class family that owned successful businesses and lived in an integrated neighborhood. Young Thurgood was accustomed to living, playing, and working with whites. His family was full of strong people who were not intimidated by the violent segregation that had spread across much of the country at the turn of the century.

Marshall's understanding of America's racial problems and his approach to attacking them in the twentieth century—the belief that changing the law was the core of any civil rights movement—did not come simply out of his fight on the trolley. It was rooted in the epic struggle of free blacks in Baltimore for equal rights, a fight in which his grandparents had taken a leading role. Attaining equal treatment for black people under the law was an issue that Thurgood Marshall's family had been involved with since the 1800s.

If Marshall's family had been from the North or Deep South, he would not have had a vision of blacks and whites living together as equals under the law. A sparse population of blacks in the North during the 1800s made racial integration uncommon. In the Deep South the realities of slavery and crass oppression kept blacks separate and silent.

But Baltimore was between North and South—a nerve center where the nation's fractured racial picture came together. Maryland's eastern and southern counties overflowed with vast communities of slaves on rural plantations. Its northern counties, however, were industrial and transportation centers that attracted free black people and runaway slaves from rural Maryland and around the nation.

Baltimore, the state's biggest city, had the largest population of free blacks of any city in the nation before the Civil War. Free blacks were well-to-do homeowners, businessmen, and religious leaders, and there were even private schools for free black children.

In fact, at the start of the Civil War, forty-seven years before Marshall was born, all four of his grandparents lived either in or near Baltimore. Among the city's free black population, his grandparents were literate, proud people, and political activists for equal rights for blacks.

One of Marshall's grandfathers, Isaiah O. B. (Olive Branch, as in a peacemaker) Williams, was a twenty-three-year-old free man as the war's first shots boomed out at Fort Sumter, South Carolina. A fair-skinned mulatto, he was living in rural Howard County, just west of Baltimore. Williams traveled to the Navy Yard in New York to sign up six months after the Civil War started. He served as the captain's steward aboard the USS *Santiago de Cuba*, a ship that successfully battled several Confederate vessels.[1]

At the outbreak of the war, Isaiah's future wife, Mary Fossett, was a twelve-year-old free black girl living in Baltimore. She could read to her mother and father the chilling newspaper accounts of Confederate sympathizers attacking Northern troops at the Baltimore train station at Camden Yards in 1861.[2]

Marshall's other grandmother, Annie Robinson, was also a free black. She was a mulatto but looked like any blue-eyed white girl. Born in Baltimore, she was just three in April of 1861, as reports of the war's first battles spread to the city.[3] Annie lived with her mother, a thirty-five-year-old widow who was working as a housekeeper in the downtown home of a rich, white merchant, who may have been Annie's father.[4]

The only one of Marshall's grandparents who was not free when the war started was the twelve-year-old Thorney Good Marshall, already a defiant and angry character. As the War Between the States began, Thorney was a slave living in Accomac County, among the rows of corn and tobacco along Virginia's Eastern Shore, in the midst of one of the largest concentrations of slaves in America. He was described as having a "yellow complexion," and later records list his race as mulatto.

During the chaos of the war, young Thorney apparently escaped slavery and ended up in Baltimore. The city was the first and closest taste of the better life in the North for any Southern black soul who could get there. Frederick Douglass, a Maryland-born slave who later gained fame as an abolitionist orator, once described Baltimore as the one place "short of a free state, where I most desired to live."[5] With the city's large population of free blacks, it was easy for Thorney Marshall to take on the life of a free black and go unquestioned in Baltimore.

A wonderful family lore grew up around Thorney's escape from slavery. As the tale was told, Thorney was bought in the Congo by a rich, white American hunter. The hunter carried the child to America, expecting him to be his lifelong servant. But as the boy grew older his dislike of slavery made him ornery and mean. The hunter finally told the young slave he would sell him—"You're so evil I got to get rid of you." But Thorney was so difficult that the hunter decided it would be unfair to sell him to an unsuspecting buyer; instead he gave Thorney his freedom on the promise that he would leave Virginia's Eastern Shore and never return. Thorney left, but he soon returned to buy land next to his former owner and torment the old man for the rest of his life.[6]

The facts tell a slightly different story. Documents show that Thorney was between thirteen and fifteen years old when he left Accomac County. He was certainly old enough to be a defiant, spirited lad, but not old enough to have become the mighty slave of the family tale.

The true story of Thurgood Marshall's other grandfather was as good as the one that was made up about Thorney. With the Civil War over and Baltimore filling with larger numbers of blacks, Isaiah Williams returned a victorious veteran. He used his navy pay to buy a house in Old West Baltimore, a thriving neighborhood filled with Irish, Russian, and German immigrants as well as free blacks. Isaiah saw himself as the equal of anyone, attending church with whites and standing up for the rights of black people in the city. He was never afraid to argue, even with the white man who lived next door. When the neighbor, a recent German immigrant[7] who was known for being mean to everyone, unexpectedly asked Isaiah to work with him repairing a broken fence that separated their property, the proud Isaiah had no problem telling him to get lost. "I'd rather go to hell," he snapped.[8]

Hungry for adventure, Isaiah reenlisted in November 1866 and worked as the captain's steward onboard the USS *Powhatan*, the flagship of the South Pacific squadron for the U.S. Navy. The ship sailed along the Pacific coast of South America, patrolling the waters from Chile to Panama.

The long stays in several exotic ports allowed Isaiah to get to know the people and their way of life. He saw carnivals, Shakespearean plays, and opera; for a black man born in the United States during slavery, this was extraordinary, and Isaiah had more than his share of good times. After shore leave during one stay in Payta, Peru, he was "confined in double irons, 'per order of Captain,' . . . for drunkenness."[9]

After three years of duty, Isaiah was honorably discharged on December 30, 1869, in Philadelphia. Back in Baltimore he began working as a baker and soon had enough money to open a successful grocery store in the basement of his house. Within a few years he opened a second store, which was even more successful, on Denmead Street.[10] It catered to some of the city's rich white families.

His prominence in business and experience as a world traveler made Isaiah a respected black leader in the city. He was well known in local politics and the Republican Party. The party of Lincoln provided a base for black activists such as Isaiah, who were trying to win equal rights. He was known to battle with white city officials over police brutality and to argue for admitting black children to public schools.

In November 1872 he married Mary Fossett, then a teacher in one of the city's black private schools. They had six children, including in 1885 Norma Arica Williams, the future mother of Thurgood Marshall. Isaiah named her after the opera *Norma*, which he had seen when his navy ship visited the town of Arica, near the border between Chile and Peru.

While Thurgood Marshall's maternal grandfather was establishing his grocery business, the former slave Thorney Marshall was making good money working as a waiter at Baltimore's popular Barnum Hotel. But the rambunctious twenty-one-year-old wanted more adventure than waiting tables.

With blacks in Congress and in southern state legislatures in the early 1870s, as part of the ballyhooed Reconstruction effort to allow newly freed slaves political power, Thorney wanted to get out of Baltimore and see the South. He signed up with the army to go out west with the all-black 24th Regiment of the U.S. Cavalry. They were called Buffalo Soldiers, a term coined by Native Americans in honor of their supposed buffalolike strength and because they wore thick buffalo hides in winter.[11] Their job was to fend off Indian and Mexican attacks and keep peace among settlers on the western frontier. Marshall was immediately sent to the deepest, most southern point of Texas, Fort Brown.

The fort was renowned as "the most unhealthful" and unpleasant U.S. Army outpost in the nation. To the north was Brownsville, a town with no drainage system. A mosquito-laden marsh sat to the east, and temperatures stayed in the high nineties for much of the year. It was not uncommon for the soldiers to come down with fevers, dysentery, and diarrhea.[12] Thorney's job was to ride shotgun for the army paymaster who traveled along the Rio Grande every other month. There was a constant threat of robbers—American, Mexican, and Indian—along the two-hundred-mile route between Fort Brown and Laredo. Thorney had to be brave and quick, with both his hands and a gun.

Thorney Marshall was described by his superior officers as a "cheerful, manly, neat soldier" for most of the assignment, but he began to suffer repeated illnesses, such as diarrhea.[13] Most of those illnesses seemed standard at Fort Brown, but then he got a puzzling ailment that army doctors called "Chronic Hepatitis."[14]

Thorney was discharged on November 30, 1874, for medical problems that had caused him to become "morose, untidy and careless, manifesting fears and melancholy," according to Capt. H. C. Corbin, head of the 24th Cavalry.[15] After his discharge he rode a train back to Baltimore wrapped in blankets. When he arrived, his eyes inflamed and half of his face paralyzed, he had to be carried to the home of a friend with whom he had waited tables at the Barnum Hotel. A year later, the twenty-five-year-old was still ailing, and doctors operated, placing a drainage tube into his right lung to relieve what they diagnosed as emphysema.

After leaving the hospital, Thorney slowly recuperated; he eventually married his neighbor Annie Robinson in 1879. He went back to work as a waiter at the Barnum Hotel while Annie began having children, seven in all. Their first son, William Canfield Marshall, was the future father of Thurgood Marshall.

Despite his marriage and new family, Thorney's long illness had damaged his spirit. There were bouts of drinking, and some remembered him as a loud, difficult, and bitter man. He was by all accounts a "tough customer."

Nevertheless, Thorney used his army disability payments and wages from his job to open a small grocery store on the bottom floor of his house, just a few blocks away from Isaiah Williams's house; it is likely that the two men knew each other. In addition, the Marshalls and Williamses were part of a tight-knit West Baltimore community with a strong focus on family and neighbors. It was in this community that Willie Marshall met his future wife, a brown-skinned, teenage girl with long, straight, jet black hair.

Norma Williams was destined to be a teacher. Her mother had taught at one of Baltimore's private academies for black students in the early 1870s. Mary had stopped teaching only when she began raising a family. But her oldest daughter, Avonia, also went into teaching, using her father's political connections to get one of the first jobs for black teachers in the black public schools. Both mother and older sister spent long hours nurturing young Norma's ambition. Most of all they impressed on her the need to do well in school. Avonia, who was twelve years older, was a powerful role model for Norma. She was a living example of a young black woman making good money and being given respect because of her job.

While she admired her older sister's academic excellence, the man Norma fell in love with was a wild boy who had dropped out after elementary school. When he did go to school, Willie was a troublemaker, quick to mouth off to teachers and principals. One day teachers complained to his father that Willie was acting up. The next day Thorney appeared in Willie's classroom and, in front of the whole class, pulled off his leather belt and began beating his son. The humiliation was too much. Willie Marshall never went back to school.

Willie did know how to read and write, however. He also worked as an errand boy, and when his father opened the family-run grocery, Willie began working at the store full-time. By 1904 the blue-eyed, light-skinned Willie had saved up enough money to move out of the family home to 1410 Ward Street and begin working at the city's big railroad station as a porter.

Somewhere in his comings and goings from the family store, his work at the railroad, and his wanderings around West Baltimore, Willie met Norma Williams. She was four years younger and still living with her mother and siblings on West Biddle Street. Norma had graduated from the Colored High School in 1904 and immediately gone on to teachers college at Coppin State in Baltimore. But before the nineteen-year-old could graduate, she became pregnant. Norma's father had died, and the family sacrificed to pay her tuition. She had been expected to finish school and begin earning income from her teaching job for the family.

But with Norma pregnant the plans had to change. Her mother insisted to Willie that Norma finish school no matter what. Willie agreed to pay the bills, and he supported the idea that Norma should be a college graduate. The couple got married on April 17, 1905,[16] and Norma Marshall graduated from teachers college a few weeks later. The couple's first child, William Aubrey, was born September 15, 1905.[17] While Willie continued to work as a porter, Norma stayed home with the baby.

Three years later, on July 2, 1908, a second child, Thurgood, was born. The family had moved from an apartment at 1127 Argyle Avenue, where Aubrey was born, into a larger apartment in the same neighborhood, 543 McMechen Street, where Thurgood was delivered.

On his birth certificate the boy's name was listed as Thoroughgood, Willie's younger brother's name. The older Thoroughgood had traveled the world as a seaman out of Baltimore's ports since he was nineteen, and Willie envied his brother's life. The brother's name was also a variation on their father's name, Thorney Good, which family lore claimed had come from prominent white slaveholders in eighteenth- and nineteenth-century Virginia. On the large Virginia plantations where young Thorney Marshall lived as a slave, census records show that there were white families named Thorogood, Thoroughgood, and Thorowgood.

The infant "Thoroughgood" was born into a town going through a wave of racially divisive politics. In 1899 the Democrats had gained political control of Baltimore with the slogan "This Is a White Man's City."[18] But such rhetoric was simply the local reflection of a national movement toward rigid segregation. In 1896 the Supreme Court handed down its decision in *Plessy v. Ferguson*, enabling a pattern of "separate but equal" to become the law of the land. Jim Crow, already a fact of life for much of the country, was now legal precedent. In the early 1900s life in the city's stores and workplaces became more racially divided. But even in the face of increased segregation and racism, Baltimore's black community remained surprisingly well organized and was able to put up resistance.

Unlike in much of the South, blacks in the city had a long tradition of owning their own businesses and holding skilled jobs. The society of free black people gave Baltimore's black community reason to expect that they could respond to threats against their rights and defy the segregationist politics of the Democratic Party. In addition, the Republican Party in Maryland gave blacks a political home—a prominent organization in which they could be allied with powerful white politicians. Black activists teamed with Republicans to block enactment of laws to segregate black travelers on trains in the city during the early 1900s.

But by 1908, when Thoroughgood was born, the Maryland legislature had passed laws requiring "white" and "colored" toilets on ships and trains. Baltimore's black community fought back, with a boycott of the rails and steamship companies, but they had little success. Even in defeat Baltimore's black community won a measure of respect, however, when the big ship lines took out advertisements to apologize to black patrons and explain that they were simply obeying Maryland's new law.[19]

The passage of laws compelling racial segregation created a climate of violence throughout the nation, particularly in the South. White fears of black political power led to efforts to intimidate blacks, and the year Thoroughgood was born, eighty-nine blacks were lynched nationally.[20] Lynchings in the South, race riots in Springfield, Illinois (the home of Abraham Lincoln), and the general increase in segregation laws across the nation prompted several prominent social reformers to start a movement to stop the abuse of blacks. Members of the Brotherhood of Liberty, a group of Baltimore activists for black rights, joined over a thousand people in New York on May 30, 1909, for a meeting of social reformers from around the nation. A year later the group took the name the National Association for the Advancement of Colored People (NAACP).[21] While its headquarters were in New York, the second oldest branch of the NAACP opened in 1912 in Baltimore.[22]

Meanwhile, Willie continued to work as a sleeping-car porter while his wife took care of their two sons. They did their best to insulate the boys from the harsh hand of Jim Crow by keeping them in Old West Baltimore, among family and friends. For all the political and racial storms raging at the start of the century, Marshall's large, extended family managed to give him a childhood full of warmth and loving comfort. The cocoon surrounding the Marshall boys gave them only passing glimpses of the Jim Crow segregation that chilled black life in most of America. But the boys were about to see more.

CHAPTER 3

Educating Thurgood

Thoroughgood took his first steps out of the cocoon when he was two. In 1910 Willie and Norma Marshall moved to Harlem at the invitation of Norma's older sister Denmedia. Her name was born out of Isaiah Williams's imagination: He christened her Denmedia Marketa in honor of the street corner market he opened on Denmead Street. Aunt Medi, as the boys called her, lured her younger sister's family to New York by telling Willie Marshall that he could get steady work with her husband, Clarence Dodson, on the New York Central while she helped Norma care for the boys.

When Norma and Willie said yes to the invitation, they became part of a wave of black families heading to New York at the turn of the century. The 1900 census indicated that Harlem was quickly becoming a center for the black population of Manhattan. By 1910 Harlem was a mecca for southern blacks eager to escape Jim Crow.

The sudden influx of blacks transformed Harlem. It was becoming world renowned for its electrifying mix of people, politics, and culture. By the time Thoroughgood arrived, black writers, religious leaders, and intellectuals were making Harlem the place for debate about the future of the race. And its many gambling joints, bars, and after-hours clubs drew both blacks and high-society whites. Harlem's streets became a magnet for black entertainers—from ragtime musicians to vaudeville actors and classically trained singers.

Norma Marshall and Aunt Medi, who was eight years older than

Norma, took the boys for walks in a city both bigger and busier than Baltimore. There was nothing in Old West Baltimore, not even Pennsylvania Avenue, that was as crowded, noisy, and vibrant as the streets around the Dodsons' apartment on Lenox Avenue. In Baltimore the immigrants were mostly whites from Europe. New York had black immigrants from the Caribbean and Africa, as well as the surge of black migrants from all parts of the Deep South. And, unlike Baltimore, Harlem had a crowded feeling to it; whereas Baltimore had row houses and alleys, Harlem had apartment buildings reaching several stories high, many divided into single rooms, all packed full of people.

While it was not the South, there was racial strife in Harlem. Some landlords, to attract white tenants, posted signs that read: "This Part of 135th Street Guaranteed Against Negro Invasion."[1] The open display of white racism in the North was a bitter lesson for many blacks who had come in the hope of escaping bigotry. The tense relationship between the races in Harlem set the stage for the emergence of Marcus Garvey's back-to-Africa movement, which soon became a rage in New York.

Willie Marshall and Clarence Dodson both worked as waiters on the New York Central, leaving their wives and the boys on their own several days every week. While the men were away Norma and Medi kept the boys under their skirts. Thoroughgood and Aubrey were not exposed to the jive or politics of Harlem's street life. Among the family's friends, Thoroughgood was known as a dainty, timid child called Goody. Aunt Medi felt that he was "nothing but a cry-baby." When he seemed to show some strength of character a few months later, she attributed it to some of the neighborhood boys, who had "slapped his head."[2]

Norma doted on her boys, dressing them like little princes, in blue Buster Brown suits with pretty white blouses. One of the family's friends later said of Thurgood, "He was too good-looking—he should have been a girl."[3] While Aubrey managed to keep his clothes clean, Goody usually came back dirty, once carrying a smelly, gray cat.

"Get that cat out of here," his mother screamed. But little Goody pleaded until his mother gave in and got a saucer of milk. That led to him regularly caring for the cat as well as a white rat and a dog. After that he did not limit his houseguests to animals. He brought Harlem's kids as well as strangers over to the house to eat and sleep. His mother later recalled, "Our home got to be known as the 'Friendly Inn.' "[4]

Although they liked New York, Norma and Willie had to return to Baltimore when Norma's mother broke her leg in 1914.[5] Thoroughgood, now six, was about to start first grade. By this time he had tired of being teased about his dainty nickname. And he was fed up with having to spell out his complicated given name. In a strike of determined independence, he began telling everyone to call him Thurgood. And he got his mother to change the name on his birth certificate.[6] "It was too damn long, so I cut it," he explained. "I didn't have nobody's permission, I did it."

On January 10, 1915, just as Thurgood was starting school, Thorney Marshall died at age sixty-six of heart failure.[7] Thorney's death marked the end of an era for the family. His powerful personality and larger-than-life stories about everything from slavery to the Buffalo Soldiers had cast a strong shadow over his son and grandsons.

The Marshall family was changing, and so was Baltimore City. Racial hostility had become more common in the five years the family had been away. The *Baltimore Afro-American*, the activist black paper that sold throughout the state, wrote an emotionally pained editorial complaining that no one could remember a time when tensions between the races were so troubled. The city's black political leaders reacted to the hostile climate by becoming more politically organized and stirring people to join the Baltimore branch of the new NAACP.[8]

The key political issue in the city was the divide between the all-white segregationists in the Democratic Party and the Republicans over the movement of wealthy blacks into white neighborhoods. The Democrats cloaked their efforts to segregate blacks with claims that they were trying to contain tuberculosis and typhoid. In fact these diseases were raging through the impoverished black sections of Old West Baltimore, not far from the Marshall family. City officials described one street, Biddle Alley, as "the Lung Block" after doctors said every house on that street held someone with TB.[9]

When George F. McMechen, a black lawyer, moved to a white part of McCullough Street in 1910, the city council's Democrats banned blacks from moving into predominantly white neighborhoods. To make it look more balanced, the Democrats offered a provision also to keep whites from moving into mostly black areas of the city.[10] "It is becoming more and more disturbing to permit . . . unrestricted invasions by Negroes into white-occupied streets," the Democrats wrote in city council records.[11]

Baltimore's black community was politically strong enough to respond to the Democrats. Harry Cummings, the first black Baltimore city council member, was able to attract wide attention for a speech in which he called the new segregation laws pure racism. He expressed black Baltimore's desire for integration with whites by saying all they wanted was "an opportunity to secure better homes, live under better conditions, be better citizens."

Cummings's passionate speech did not persuade the Democratic majority of the council. The law went into effect, the first time anyone in America had tried to compel residential segregation. A few weeks later, however, it was declared unconstitutional by the Baltimore Supreme Bench.

Even with Baltimore's racial problems boiling around them, Thurgood's family found a safe place to set up house when they returned from New York. They moved in with Norma's brother Fearless Mentor Williams at 1632 Division Street. The Williamses' house, not far from Pennsylvania Avenue, was on one of the better streets in Old West Baltimore. Families on Division Street were among black Baltimoreans with steady work or their own businesses. It was a middle-class street, and they lived next to a white, Jewish family.

The Old West Baltimore neighborhood had Russian, German, and Italian immigrants, although it was overwhelmingly black. The store owners on Pennsylvania Avenue, however, were nearly all Jewish. And in several of the stores blacks were not allowed to try on clothes; some stores would not even let blacks walk in the door unless their skin was so light they could pass for white. The segregated life in many stores on Pennsylvania Avenue had prompted increasing grumbling among Baltimore's black community by the time young Thurgood and his family returned.

While Thurgood's family was living with Uncle Fearless, his life was centered in the warmth of his grandmother's house. Thurgood's mother had to spend time with Grandma Mary as she recuperated from her broken leg, and Mary lovingly took her grandson into her kitchen to feed him and teach him to cook. As part of the protective blanket she wrapped around little Thurgood, Grandma Mary also gave him practical advice about his chances as a young black man in turn-of-the-century America. "Your mother and father want you to be a dentist or a doctor, something like that," she told him. "And I hope you make it. But just in case you don't, I'm going to teach you how to cook. And you know why? You've never seen an unemployed black cook."

While his grandmother and mother provided the strong female presence in his life, the leading male figure was Thurgood's Uncle Fearless. Fearless got his name when his father, the imaginative Isaiah Williams, decided that the infant stared at him just after birth and was "a fearless little fellow." Although Thurgood's dad was often gone working on the railroad for several days at a time, Uncle "Fee" was there every afternoon and night to play and talk about school, the family, and the neighborhood with Thurgood and Aubrey.

Uncle Fearless, who was about thirty-four when Thurgood and his family moved in, had a good job as personal attendant to the white president of the B & O Railroad. Fearless set up the president's meetings and served his lunch. He wore a suit and bow tie to work every day. He was on a first-name basis with the city's top white business and political leaders. Fearless was a "tall, broad-shouldered, wide smiling man. . . . A sort of major domo in the office of the president," the *B & O Railroad Magazine* wrote about him years later.[12] "Fearless was the most important black in the B & O Railroad," remembered Douglas C. Turnbull, Jr., executive assistant to the president of the railroad for many years. "The president talked to Fearless several times a week."[13] Uncle Fee, who had no children of his own, delighted in being a powerful influence on the young boys.

When six-year-old Thurgood began attending school, he went to Number 103 on Division Street, just three blocks from Uncle Fee's house. The segregated 103 was the best colored elementary school in Baltimore. "Everybody in the community relied on public neighborhood schools but parents . . . were especially proud of school 103 on Division Street, a model elementary school," a historian later wrote.[14] The school was an old, redbrick, two-story building with twelve makeshift classrooms. The classes were separated by sliding doors, which, when opened, made two or three rooms into an auditorium.

The academic year at the black schools was about a month shorter than it was for the city's white children. Black children were expected to get jobs, and most did leave school every spring when the strawberry crop was ready to be picked.[15]

Thurgood's classmates remembered him as an energetic boy who had to sit in the first seat of the first row. Agnes Patterson, one of his classmates, explained that Thurgood had to sit up front because "he was always playing, and so they had to keep right on top of him."[16]

His class was called "The Sissy Class," because it had few boys besides Thurgood and his best friend, Jimmy Carr, the son of a prominent black doctor. Thurgood and Jimmy took pleasure in teasing the many girls around them: "He used to drive me crazy," recalled Julia Wood-house Harden.[17]

Carrie Jackson, another classmate, portrayed the young Thurgood as annoying but never mean: "Thurgood didn't get into fights." Thurgood's mother remembered her son the same way: "Thurgood wasn't much of a street fighter—Aubrey was the tough one. He did all the fighting. Thurgood would always come home and tell me about what the boys did to him."[18]

Thurgood, a great storyteller even as a boy, told his mother and his friends about the people who lived in the alley streets and their rough-neck children. Their scary world fascinated Thurgood, but while he might venture out for a peek, he was much more comfortable at home.

After school Thurgood and his older brother went home to a house ruled by women: Norma Marshall and Aunt Flo (Fearless's wife) oversaw family affairs, with frequent visits from Grandma Mary, now in her late sixties. Willie Marshall was at work much of the time. Even when he came home, Willie was a distant father figure, an intense, introverted man who liked to drink. Aubrey was not much of a presence either. A bright student and a snappy dresser, he socialized with an older crowd and was a regular on local baseball fields.

"Aubrey was more outgoing," said Ethel Williams, one of Thurgood's classmates. She recalled that "Aubrey looked just like white, he was blond, the blondest black guy you've ever seen, with sharp features, too." "You wouldn't think that they were brothers, other than they were both fair," said Pat Patterson, who knew both boys. "The interesting thing about the family is that when they were young, Aubrey was the fair-haired boy. They just felt he had a whole lot of promise," said Elizabeth [Penny] Monteiro, who later married into the Marshall family.[19]

Thurgood, meanwhile, could be regularly seen in the late afternoons playing and working at the grocery next door to Uncle Fee's house—owned by Mr. Hale, a Jewish merchant. His job was to pick out items ordered by customers, then deliver them in his little red wagon. Thurgood started the job when he was seven, working for ten cents a day plus all he could eat. On his second day he made a neighborhood reputation for himself when he got "sick as a dog" eating pickles and candy. Mr. Hale had to take him home and later joked, "That's why I let you do that—I knew you'd break yourself out of the habit."

Thurgood moved easily among the Jews in the neighborhood. He considered the rabbis the most learned men he knew. And his best friend after school was Mr. Hale's son, Sammy, who also worked in the store. Sammy and his parents would join Uncle Fee and the Marshalls for dinner once in a while. It was rare for blacks and whites to have dinner together. Julia Woodhouse Harden said of that era: "We had no contact with anybody white." Even so, the Marshall family did not hold negative stereotypes about whites or Jews. The only racist influence in his family, Marshall later recalled, was his mother, who he said was "a little anti-Semitic because of a couple of bad deals" with Jews.

Thurgood and Sammy learned how to deal with race at the same time but out of different traditions. "We used to have fights, fusses, because he would let people call him a kike and wouldn't fight back," Marshall said later. "If anybody called me a 'Nigger' I fought 'em. He said he was always told by his father that fighting was not good."

Despite the racial tension in the city, Thurgood's father had very good white friends, including a local policeman, Captain Cook, who occasionally came by to spend some time with Willie Marshall. According to Thurgood, his dad had no hostile feelings toward whites in Baltimore. When Captain Cook knocked at the door, Thurgood knew to go get his father because the policeman would never come in without Willie Marshall's personal invitation. His father had set down a rule—if any policeman entered his house without permission, he would kill him. This rule, applying even to friends, reflected a widespread concern among black Baltimoreans about the power of the all-white police force. Willie's hard-nosed stance came from an 1875 incident. Norma's father had been the leader of a citywide protest against a policeman who shot and killed a black man after forcing his way into the man's house.

The incident began when police responded to a complaint early on the morning of Saturday, July 31, 1875. A neighbor contacted them about a loud party just blocks from Isaiah Williams's house. Officer Patrick McDonald thought it was a "Cake Walk" party, at which couples held a dance competition for a prize cake. The neighborhood police charged blacks to hold such parties, issuing permits and taking a percentage of the fees.

When Officer McDonald went to tell Brown to quiet down sometime around 2:00 A.M., events quickly turned violent. The redheaded policeman threatened to "snatch" the partygoers off to jail if they didn't immediately halt the party. Daniel Brown, a thirty-seven-year-old mulatto, shouted at McDonald: "Snatch? No, you won't." With that the short, muscular policeman jumped at Brown, hitting him on the head with his nightstick.

Brown's wife jumped in to save her husband. But the policeman pushed the screaming woman away. As the injured man began to get up, the officer pulled out his revolver. Still struggling with the woman, he shouted, "Damn your husband," then shot Brown in the head.

The murder led Isaiah Williams and several other leading black Baltimoreans to investigate what had happened and hold a public rally against police brutality. Speaking before a crowded Douglass Institute, named for Frederick Douglass, Williams said the situation cast a revealing light on larger issues plaguing Baltimore's black community: "There is little protection, if any, afforded us by the police in cases of assault where the offenders are white; second, there are frequent arrests made by officers . . . without warrant or authority by entering houses occupied by colored people."

There was no holding back the crowd's emotion as Williams spoke. His remarks reached their crescendo when he said black Baltimoreans only wanted "simple justice . . . and the same protection in life, liberty and the pursuit of our happiness which white men enjoy as a right." His speech was greeted with a loud and long outburst of applause. But he was criticized the next day in the *Baltimore Sun*, which said Williams was wrong to charge that black people were being abused by police: "We are not aware of any systematic oppression in this state or city of any class of citizens by another, nor do we believe that there is any disposition or intention on the part of the police . . . to oppress, injure or maltreat colored people. . . . There is no ground for any such assertion."[20]

Officer McDonald's trial began on November 15, 1875, with the entire city fixed on what the newspapers called "The Cake Walk Homicide." Every day drew a large crowd of blacks and whites to the courtroom. A dozen people testified in the opening round to the events that had led up to the shooting, and their testimony fit with Isaiah Williams's earlier account.

On November 22 closing arguments began. Isaiah Williams was at the front of a courtroom described by the *Sun* as "so crowded it was difficult for those concerned in the case to squeeze their persons through the compact mass." The next morning, the day before Thanksgiving, the jury reached a verdict. The *Sun* said Officer McDonald stood straight as the jury foreman read out loud: "Not guilty of murder, but guilty of manslaughter." A reporter wrote the next day that McDonald was satisfied with the jury's decision; he had "dreaded a verdict for a higher grade."[21]

The powerful role Isaiah Williams played in that celebrated case no doubt added to Marshall family folklore about abuses that stemmed from police entering private homes without permission. But Willie Marshall regularly spent hours with his white friend on the police force. Young Thurgood was often in the room with the two men, listening to their stories and debates over crimes, Baltimore politics, and race relations.

One frequent topic of conversation between Captain Cook and Willie Marshall was the war in Europe. Thurgood was nine when the United States officially entered World War I, and several of his uncles fought in the war. However, when black soldiers returned home victorious in 1918 and 1919, they were greeted by a white backlash. Some whites were angry at the idea of saluting blacks wearing the U.S. uniform. There were race riots during the summer of 1919 in several cities as defiant blacks who had served in Europe clashed with segregationist whites. Later accounts referred to this as the "Red Summer," because of the bloodshed and claims that Bolshevik propaganda had prompted blacks to defy the existing racial order. One of the bloodiest of these riots took place just forty miles south of Baltimore, in Washington, D.C. It made a deep impression on young Thurgood.

In early July of 1919, the NAACP's Washington branch sent letters to the editors of the city's four major newspapers, accusing them of "sowing the seeds of a race riot by their inflammatory headlines." The leader in printing such stories was *The Washington Post*. On Saturday morning, July 19, the *Post* ran the headline NEGROES ATTACK GIRL . . . WHITE MEN VAINLY PURSUE. The wife of a navy man had her umbrella grabbed by two black men who made "insulting actions" toward the woman, according to the *Post*. That evening 200 of the husband's fellow white sailors decided to lynch the two men. The white men roamed Southwest Washington, beating any Negroes they found walking the streets.

Two nights of rioting ensued, with knots of black and white men doing battle throughout the city. By Tuesday night hard rain and 2,000 of President Wilson's federal troops had halted the violence.[22]

Word of the riots quickly spread to Baltimore, especially along the railroad with its black workers, including Willie Marshall. Eleven-year-old Thurgood heard dramatic accounts. He later said his light-skinned, blue-eyed father was caught between black and white rioters, fearful that he might be mistaken for the wrong race at the wrong time. "He had a hell of a time," Marshall said. "The Negroes would run one place, the white folks were running the other. So he was running back and forth. Wherever he went, he was wrong. . . . I know that was a tough riot. Nobody will admit it, but the Negroes won that one. They just didn't count the white bodies."

There were no riots in Baltimore, but the D.C. violence sparked Thurgood's imagination and raised his racial consciousness. The idea that black military men would be attacked shocked him. From childhood he had been captivated by stories of his grandfathers' exploits in the Union Navy and the Buffalo Soldiers. And he was thrilled to glimpse his uncles in uniform and hear that they were going to Europe to fight. However, the racist treatment given to returning black soldiers and the Washington riot began to shake Thurgood out of the integrated shelter of his middle-class neighborhood. He understood fully now that black people were treated badly in much of the nation, even if heroes of a victorious war effort.

By 1920 Willie Marshall's savings as a railroad waiter allowed the family to move out of Uncle Fee's house. At first they went ten blocks away, to 2327 McCullough Street. Later they moved to 1838 Druid Hill Avenue, a three-story row house with five bedrooms and the classic white marble steps that could be seen throughout Baltimore. On Saturday mornings Norma and other women washed those marble steps by hand, a Baltimore tradition. The changes in address meant shifts in neighbors. On McCullough the family found themselves in a mostly white area filled with newcomers from Russia and Germany.[23] Druid Hill was mostly black.

As her boys grew, Norma Marshall decided to go back to school. In 1921 she started taking classes at nearby Morgan College.[24] She hoped to get recertified and follow in the footsteps of her mother and sister by getting a full-time job as a kindergarten teacher. But teaching assignments were hard to come by. Black teachers were hired only for the few all-black elementary schools and a single black high school. These were patronage jobs, controlled by the city's Democrats, the segregationists. Few black teachers were getting work. But a persistent Norma Marshall pushed for any substitute teaching assignment she could get for the next few years.

Norma's drive to get a college degree and a teaching job set a strong example for young Thurgood. Her ambition, both for herself and for her sons, put pressure on them to excel. And even though Willie had left school at an early age, he was powerfully intolerant of poor grades from Aubrey or Thurgood, to the point of threatening them if they brought home bad report cards. Willie felt his lack of schooling had prevented him from being more than a sleeping car porter and waiter. And his deep insecurities added to his conviction that the boys should have the very best education.

His parents' constant push for better grades led to a turnaround in Thurgood by seventh grade. He eased up on teasing and whispering to girls long enough to get such high grades that his teachers let him skip to the eighth grade before he had finished the seventh.

*   *   *

Thurgood stepped into a harsher world of segregation as he started high school. In 1921 he began ninth grade at the Colored High and Training School, a two-story, sixteen-room building. The rusted facility had housed Baltimore's German-American Elementary School for several decades. It had become "Colored High" thirty-eight years before Thurgood entered its doors, opening as Baltimore's first public high school for blacks. The school had no library, no cafeteria, and no gym when Thurgood arrived. "This school stands in urgent need of equipment. . . . It is lamentably short of anything like an adequate supply," Principal J.H.N. Waring had written in an annual report to the superintendent of public instruction.[25]

Thurgood was aware that white children had vacated the school; he knew whites had better schools with more books and newer facilities. Additionally, as the only high school for blacks, there was unbearable crowding. The school had almost doubled in size between 1920 and 1922. When Thurgood entered the building, there were bookcases crammed in the corridors. To accommodate all, the principal had to divide the student body and hold half-day sessions.[26]

Thurgood's classmate Essie Hughes recalled that the teachers also divided the students on the basis of test scores. On the first day of school, a large group of ninth graders were seated in several big rooms and tested. Thurgood scored high enough to be put in a class with the best students.[27]

Even as he was doing well at the Colored High School, Thurgood was maintaining his reputation as a cutup and prankster. Charlotte Shervington, one of his classmates, remembered Thurgood acting up one day when the teacher left the classroom. "Thurgood was full of the devil. He threw a piece of chalk and hit me in the eye. He didn't aim to hit me in the eye, he just threw the chalk. He was mischievous."[28]

There was some control on Thurgood's teasing at the Colored High School because his uncle Cyrus Marshall, Willie's younger brother, was a math teacher there. "Anytime that Thurgood would carry on in class, all you had to do was tell Cy Marshall—and Thurgood's father would knock his head off," said Julia Woodhouse Harden.

Thurgood's antics occasionally led to punishment. Once, the principal sent him to the basement with a copy of the U.S. Constitution and told him he had to memorize it before he could leave. "Before I left that school," Marshall said later, "I knew the whole thing by heart."[29]

Thurgood's study of the Constitution gave him an interesting perspective on the conflict between American ideals and the reality of how the law was twisted when it came to black people. Sitting in a second-floor classroom and next to the window, he had a bird's-eye view of the Northwest Baltimore police station. He could see prisoners, mostly black, being brought in by the all-white police. Often he could even hear as black suspects were questioned about crimes and sometimes hit with a club or brass knuckles to loosen up a confession. Essie Hughes remembered Thurgood being so fascinated by the goings-on in the jailhouse that teachers sometimes had to tell him to pull down the window shades.

"We could hear police in there beating the hell out of people, saying, 'Black boy, why don't you just shut your goddamned mouth, you're going to talk yourself into the electric chair,' " Thurgood told friends.

Thurgood's interest in the prisoners, lawyers, and policemen going in and out of the Northwest police station was heightened by stories he heard at home from his father. When Willie Marshall wasn't working on the trains, he was a regular figure in the rear of courtrooms, a hat perched on his lap as he watched trials.[30]

Willie's fascination with the courts made a deep and lasting impression on his younger son. He would use lawyers' tactics on both sons during arguments at the dinner table, demanding that they logically back up any claim they made, while discussing politics or even the weather. "Oh yes, we talked about the law," Marshall later recalled of debating duels with his dad. "We fussed about it and argued and carried on." And he credited his father with forcing him to sharpen his thinking and his arguments, and to be as crafty as a lawyer. "I got the idea of being a lawyer from arguing with my dad. . . . We'd argue about everything." The one issue father and son did not argue about was racial segregation. "We saw eye-to-eye on that."[31]

Even though Thurgood loved to argue with his father, their conversations sometimes crossed the line from boisterousness to hostility, fueled by Willie's drinking. Aubrey and Thurgood had different reactions to their father's verbal bullying. Aubrey shrunk in and kept silent until the first opportunity to leave the house. Thurgood was electrified by his father's bellicose manner and arguments. Consequently Thurgood never turned away from his father; he idolized him and treasured their good moments. He happily credited those shouting arguments as having prepared him to be a star on the Colored High's celebrated debating team.

From his first year of high school, Thurgood was "the main debater" on the team. "We would gather material, but Thurgood would specify certain key points that we would either elaborate on or look up more information on," said his classmate Essie Hughes. The debating team's coach, Gough McDaniels, a black history teacher, loved Thurgood's argumentative style and worked closely with his star. McDaniels picked up where Willie Marshall had left off. He didn't just argue with the loud, cocky boy but made Thurgood do in-depth research on topics for debate. Thurgood took to McDaniels, a college man—he had graduated from Cornell University—who impressed him with his stories about serving in World War I.

In his freshman year Thurgood was elected captain of the varsity debating team. The winning team was so successful in Baltimore that it was invited to compete in nearby Wilmington, Delaware. But during his sophomore year Thurgood had to quit the team to concentrate on his schoolwork. He rejoined the team in his junior year and was immediately reelected captain.

Thurgood's interest in current events and debating did not detract from his interest in teasing girls and playing around with his best friend, Jimmy Carr. His favorite female target was his debate teammate Anita Short. He would pull her hair and call her "piano-legs" or "knock-knees." But he would also eat lunch with her and walk home with her whenever he could.

The girls at the Colored High were taken by Thurgood's lanky walk, the way he swung his long arms and longer legs. In fact, his nickname was Legs. His wavy hair and light skin color added to his appeal in a city where dark skin was often considered lower-class. Thurgood was not much of an athlete. Nevertheless, his success on the debate team made him a well-known figure in school. He won election to the student council and to his class's treasury committee.

One of Thurgood's more adventurous—if not outright crazy—high school friends was Cab Calloway, who later became a famous jazz singer, authoring songs such as "Minnie the Moocher," with the famous refrain "Hi-de-hi-de-hi-de-ho." Calloway was one year behind Marshall at the Colored High School but knew Baltimore's streets as a poor kid. Those streets were different from the ones known by middle-class Thurgood.

By his own admission Calloway was "a hustler" during his high school days. A thin, light-skinned kid who looked not too different from Thurgood, Cab had little use for schoolwork. He preferred "waiting tables, shining shoes, hustling newspapers, walking hots [horses at Pimlico racetrack]."[32] Cab would often skip school to do those jobs and keep money in his pocket. He would return to class with stories—some full of lies—about his exciting life on the streets.

Although he was just a teenager, Cab knew local gamblers, musicians, club owners, and numbers runners because his older sister, Blanche, was a cabaret singer. One of his jobs was to hustle soldiers on leave to come into the nightclub where Blanche was singing.

While Cab was making himself a character in the city's nightlife and clubs, Thurgood was moving in another direction. At his mother's insistence he joined her in becoming a member of St. Katherine's Episcopal Church on Division Street, just a few blocks from Uncle Fearless's house. At age fifteen he was confirmed at St. Katherine's and served as an altar boy.[33]

The next year, 1924, Thurgood had even less time to run around with guys like Cab Calloway because an illness left his father unable to work on the railroad. Aubrey had already left for college, Lincoln University in Oxford, Pennsylvania, but with Willie's illness the Marshalls fell behind on Aubrey's tuition payments. To keep alive her dream of having Aubrey become a doctor, Norma took a job as a playground director while continuing to do substitute teaching.

Jobless, sick, and lacking even a high school education, Willie Marshall was an unhappy man. His only marketable experience came from working in his father's grocery store and his years as a waiter. By all accounts Willie was a complicated man. Fascinated with the law but lacking the education to be a lawyer, he was deeply frustrated, and his drinking problem worsened.

"Yeah, he drank," said Ethel Williams, one of Thurgood's classmates. "He was an alcoholic . . . [but] we always respected him. We always liked him." Another classmate recalled seeing Willie Marshall drunk and falling down on the streets of West Baltimore. Some neighbors remembered that when he was drunk Willie Marshall cursed and threatened people. "He put a lot of fear in you," said Teddy Stewart, who worked with Willie Marshall and lived near him on Druid Hill Avenue. "He was one of the hardest men. He was a mean son of a bitch when he got drunk. But he could work drunk. It didn't affect his work. If you worked around him, you knew he'd been drinking—he would get red."[34]

Willie Marshall's growing drinking problem meant that his conversations with Thurgood increasingly traveled a thin line between shouting and fighting. Aubrey's voice sometimes joined the roar when he came home, but Aubrey would still leave the table while Thurgood and his father continued to one-up each other. "The woman next door," Thurgood said, "would know when we were all home. She'd tell her husband, 'They're all together again.' She could hear it through the walls."

Going away to college brought out more of Aubrey's personality. He had always been the more detached brother, never one for idle chatter or even listening to Thurgood's fabulous stories, much less his arguments. Being a college man gave Aubrey a superior air when he tangled with his father and younger brother. And with the money from his job at school, he bought good clothes that gave him a preppy look. Some neighbors called him classy, others felt he was a snob. In any case, the elder son was living up to his mother's expectations. He was doing well at Lincoln and on a straight path to achieve her dream.

Thurgood, still at home, worked part-time at his father's former job—as a porter on the B & O Railroad. And when Thurgood's relationship with his father hit a bad patch, he turned to Uncle Fee, both for an easier personality and to get a look at the wider world of Baltimore politics and the powerful, white-run corporations that controlled the city.

Fearless Williams treated Thurgood like the son he never had; he would give him a play-by-play on the power games among the corporate bosses as well as gossip about their personal secrets—from booze to gambling. And Uncle Fee would take Thurgood for Sunday car rides to the Eastern Shore. Those trips offered a different kind of education. Uncle Fearless made certain to have extra gasoline in the trunk so the family would never get stuck in some small town with whites who didn't like blacks. Several lynchings had occurred on the Eastern Shore, and Uncle

Fee wanted to be cautious. He also carried extra food because there were no restaurants for blacks outside Baltimore.[35]

With Thurgood's mother a well-known face in the city's few black schools, Thurgood was expected to be a top student. She had prodded and coached Aubrey to top grades and then into pre–medical school studies in college. Now she had plans for Thurgood. Norma didn't think he was as hardworking as Aubrey. He wasn't an A student. But she told relatives she wanted her second son to be a dentist or maybe a lawyer.

Thurgood did have a B average. But with his mother's high expectations and his brother's success, he found it hard to think of himself as a good student. Ultimately, he graduated in the top third of his class. Thurgood's high school transcript shows that he never failed a course, took Latin, history, trigonometry, and physics, as well as machine work and wood trimming. More impressive, in contrast to his pal Cab Calloway and all his talk about being a wild man and a bad student, Thurgood was never late to school and absent just one day.[36]

During their senior year Thurgood's classmate Essie Hughes noticed that he showed signs "of adolescent blossoming as far as girls are concerned. . . . He was muscle-bound and didn't know just what to do with it." A big question was who Thurgood would take to Class Day. His favorite, Anita Short, was not a senior. The answer came when Hughes asked Ivor King, one of her classmates, who her date would be. The surprising reply was Thurgood Marshall. Hughes recalled asking King: "How long has he been going with you?" King replied: "He hasn't been going with me at all, but I've been going with him for four years."

Soon after the dance was graduation day. Even an ill Willie came to see his younger son receive the diploma he never got. The graduation ceremony would stay with people for many years because Cab Calloway sang a powerful version of the popular song "To a Wild Rose."

Because of the family's financial struggles, it was still unclear if Thurgood would go to college. At his mother's direction Thurgood had finished school a semester early and used that time to earn tuition money. But he had the grades and references to get into Lincoln without examination. Colored High Principal Mason Hawkins praised Thurgood in his recommendation as a young man with "very good ability." Thurgood's most telling answer on his college application came in response to the question "What do you plan as your life's work?" The sixteen-year-old wrote simply: "Lawyer."

CHAPTER 4

❧

Waking Up

At age sixteen Thurgood Marshall began a metamorphosis. The teasing, often goofy boy embarked on a journey of experiences that opened his eyes to the painful realities of economic and racial problems crippling most black Americans. With high school behind him he had to find his place in an adult world where legal segregation and poverty plagued black people.

His first revelation came with his struggle to attend college. Despite his mother's protectiveness, it was clear to him that the family could not afford to send him to the school he desperately wanted to attend. Lincoln University was the top choice for the brightest black boys along the East Coast, and Aubrey was still there. Thurgood had been accepted, but the family still owed the school money for Aubrey's junior year. "After consulting with the Treasurer I find that there is a balance of $330.50 [about a year's tuition] on your son Aubrey's account and this raises the question whether it would not be advisable for the younger boy to remain out of school and earn money for a year," a Lincoln University official wrote to Norma in June 1925.[1]

At the request of Norma, W. W. Walker, a minister on McCullough Street and an 1897 graduate of Lincoln, wrote to the president of the university to give personal testimony that Willie Marshall had been ill for a year and that was the only reason for their financial difficulties: "I am well acquainted with the Marshall family. They stand high in the estimation of the people of Baltimore. . . . The mother is very anxious about the entrance of Thurgood into Lincoln U. fearing the faculty will be influenced versus him because of what she owes." Lincoln's president responded that "the case will be considered on its own merits and certainly with a favorable attitude because of your letter and recommendation."[2]

To save money for his college tuition, Thurgood began working full-time as a dining-car waiter on the B & O in February 1925. He had a problem with his uniform, however; it was too small. After he complained to his boss, the chief waiter told Thurgood, "Boy, we can get a man to fit the pants a lot easier than we can get pants to fit the man. Why don't you just kinda scroonch down in 'em a little more?" Marshall later said he had no choice: "I scroonched."[3]

Thurgood's work also taught him a lesson about the control the company held over its black workers. The white engineers, conductors, and mechanics were unionized, but the black waiters were forbidden to organize even though they earned just fifty-five dollars a month and were not given overtime pay. One day while he was working on the train, a group of waiters began talking about the need for a union. When the train arrived back in Baltimore, the white inspector of dining cars boarded and went directly to the waiter who had led the discussion. "He tapped him on the shoulder and said, 'Get your clothes. You're fired,' " recounted Marshall. "Now how did that word get to Baltimore? . . . There was nobody on there but us. It was one of the crew . . . each one looking at the other one like this," he recalled, giving the accusatory glare of a betrayed co-worker.

Thurgood kept his mouth shut and in six months he had saved enough to pay Lincoln's tuition for a year. In September 1925 he packed for the fifty-five-mile car ride up Route One to the small farm town of Oxford, Pennsylvania. Lincoln University, founded by Presbyterians in 1854 (and renamed in honor of President Lincoln after he was assassinated), was known as the Black Princeton, because Presbyterians also ran the famous New Jersey school for young white men and many Princeton graduates taught at Lincoln.

Thurgood traveled to Lincoln with Aubrey, who was then starting his senior year. There were 285 men at Lincoln that year. Aubrey had pledged a fraternity, Alpha Phi Alpha, but he was not well established at the school. According to his first roommate, Franz (Jazz) Byrd, Aubrey was a remote person, "kind of irritable. . . . He just felt that he was superior." Byrd, a star football player, described Aubrey as a very serious person who did not get along with his jocular younger brother. "The dislike between Thurgood and Aubrey was so intense," Byrd recalled. "I've never seen it in any two brothers that I know who came from the same parents, same background and everything else."[4]

Thurgood spent little time with his brother and almost never talked about him. But they did have regular arguments. Much of Thurgood's loud, crude behavior in his early years at Lincoln may have been an effort to set himself apart from the reserved Aubrey.

In Thurgood's first year at Lincoln, Aubrey was on the senior honor roll. Thurgood, by contrast, was having a great time and hardly ever studying. His inventive use of curse words, his love of storytelling, and his joy in card games made him a good fit for the young, all-male social scene.

Thurgood had no problem playing along with the Lincoln custom of freshmen wearing little blue beanies on their heads and short pants with garters to hold up their socks. Upperclassmen called the freshmen dogs and tried to steal their beanies, sometimes starting small fights, known as pushing knuckles. Freshmen were also required to know the names of all the buildings on campus, the history of the university, and the alma mater. And they could only enter buildings through the back door.

In this boys' paradise the only thing that slowed Thurgood was his campus job. He was in charge of baking bread for the school cafeteria. "We would cook it and then put it in a closet and serve it the second day," Marshall recalled. "We'd take a loaf of bread right out of the oven. And slice it open like this and lay a quart of butter right there and griddle it. That's a meal right there, and a good meal, too."

Most of the time Thurgood lived as a boy without a complicated thought in his head. His friends thought he never studied and he became known as a great pinochle player, a fan of cowboy movies, and a connoisseur of comic books. He was always bumming cigarettes. Thurgood roomed with James Murphy, a friend from Baltimore whose family ran the *Afro-American* newspaper. They kept a party going in their room on most nights. On their door was a sign welcoming visitors to the "Land of the Disinherited."[5]

One friend later wrote that during their years at Lincoln, Thurgood was a "harum-scarum youth, the loudest individual in the dormitory and apparently the least likely to succeed."[6]

Norma Marshall, aware that Thurgood was not as studious as Aubrey, urged her younger son to become a dentist despite his ambition to practice law. Black dentists were in demand because many whites refused to work on black patients. Also, black people generally did not trust white dentists, who were known in the South for yanking the teeth out of any black person with a toothache. To please his mother Thurgood took some pre-medical classes. But he had little taste for basic science. Even more of a problem, he had a run-in with a professor who saw him as a less than serious student.

The hardest work he put in was going to the debate team's get-togethers to show off his talent for argument. Thurgood's debating skills got him on Lincoln's varsity team as a freshman. It would be great training for a future lawyer. That year Lincoln's team debated Oxford University at Bethel AME Church in Baltimore before over a thousand people. Thurgood was not one of the four Lincoln men who debated, but he trained for the event and traveled to it with the team, which thrilled black Baltimore by winning. Later in his Lincoln career, Thurgood was one of the principal debaters when the university's team traveled to Boston to debate Harvard and later the British Union team (students from Cambridge, the University of London, and Edinburgh).

After the Harvard debate Thurgood attended a dinner where he was seated next to a white female student. He had dealt with white women while working in Baltimore, but there was always the danger, as the hatbox incident in his youth had demonstrated, of sudden violence when a black man got too close to a white woman socially. To sit next to a white woman of his age in a social setting made him nervous. "I never felt good around them," he said later. "[At the Harvard Club dinner] I was the most uncomfortable son of a bitch in the world. But I managed to just grin and bear it."

Traveling with the debate team wasn't the only occasion for Thurgood to get off campus. On weekends he often went to Philadelphia, about an hour north, or traveled south for an hour and a half to Baltimore. Lincoln men would show off by leaving campus every weekend, claiming to be visiting beautiful women. Thurgood bragged to classmates of being engaged ten times during college. "I went away every weekend—Baltimore, Philadelphia, Wilmington," he recalled. "Wherever there was some pussy to chase, I was there."

His freshman year of college turned out to be a joyride for Thurgood. He had friends all over campus who delighted in the pranks and card games he loved so much. And though he didn't have great grades, he wasn't flunking out. His biggest worry, over money for tuition, had faded. Not only was he working on campus but his father had recovered his health and found a good-paying job as the head steward at the Gibson Island Club. The club, on the Chesapeake Bay, was eighteen miles from Baltimore and a golf and sailing haven for Baltimore's white, upper-class Protestants. Teddy Stewart, who washed dishes there, described it as "one of the best gentile clubs in the state of Maryland if not the best." Sam Daniels, who worked as a busboy on the island, remembered a sign on the causeway that read: "No Niggers and Dogs Allowed."

The light-skinned Willie Marshall was in charge of hiring the all-black dining room staff at the club, and he hired Thurgood as a waiter that summer, after his first year of college.

Working at Gibson Island, Thurgood became a popular figure with the powerful whites who frequented the exclusive watering hole. And Albert Fox, the club's secretary, who was in charge of all the staff and facilities, regarded Thurgood as a son. Fox and Willie Marshall were drinking partners, and Fox delighted in introducing Thurgood to first-rate whiskey, "a forty-year-old hogshead of old Pikesville bourbon."

Thurgood's relationship with Fox gave him protection whenever he had to deal with some of the more racist whites at the club, but he still had to face prejudice. One day Thurgood was waiting on tables when in came a U.S. senator, "a very vulgah individual," according to Marshall. The senator saw Thurgood and shouted, "Hey, nigger."

Marshall, who was taught to fight anyone who called him that, for some reason held his temper and went over to his table.

"Nigger, I want service at this table," the old senator yelled out. The college man decided to play along, not wanting to lose his job. The senator got more and more into showing off for his dinner guests as he hailed Thurgood with shouts of "Nigger" and "Boy." But when dinner was over, he left an astounding twenty-dollar tip. He did the same every day for nearly a week, giving Thurgood the best-paying week of his young life and putting Thurgood a major step closer to paying his tuition for the coming school year.

But one night Willie Marshall overheard the senator's rank language and saw Thurgood running up to the table, bowing and saying "Yes, sir!" His father pulled Thurgood into a corner and told him: "You are fired! You are a disgrace to the colored people!"

Thurgood quickly explained that he was making big money off the senator's obnoxious behavior. In later telling the story, Marshall said he explained to his dad, "Now I figure it's worth about twenty dollars to be called nigger. . . . But the minute you run out of them twenties . . . I'm gonna bust you in the nose!"[7]

This more pragmatic Thurgood was a changed man from the youngster who had dropped the hatboxes and started swinging after being called a name. Having felt his father's money woes, as well as his mother's ambition to get him into a good college, Thurgood was fast learning the importance of playing the game even as he stood up for his principles.

Thurgood had his emerging racial consciousness wrenched on another occasion at Gibson Island. He had a steady friendship with a member of the club who was unfailingly courteous and had been giving him generous tips. One day the man's wife had an accident while driving to the club in her husband's Rolls-Royce. Thurgood made sure she was okay, phoned her husband to let him know about the accident, and even helped repair the car.

Later, the man hired Thurgood to work at a private party at the family's Baltimore home. The woman showed him a room full of toys abandoned by her grown children. Thurgood mentioned that he knew people in Old West Baltimore who worked with handicapped children and that they would love to have the toys. The woman got excited and immediately offered to donate the toys to the children. A moment later, however, she asked Thurgood if the kids were black. "Yes, ma'am," he told her. Her face suddenly red and drawn tight, she responded, "I'm not going to give them anything."

Thurgood finished his work that night with a fascination for what was going on in the mind of that rich, white woman. But he walked away filled with more pity than bitterness.

Despite his hurtful experiences with a few white people at the club, Thurgood never leaped to the conclusion that whites were all racists. He was still close to several white men he considered his mentors, such as the club's secretary, Mr. Fox, and white Jews he knew from the neighborhood, such as Mr. Schoen, the hat store owner. Those positive relationships set a pattern for his life.

His summer of work at Gibson Island left Thurgood free from any fear of not being able to pay his tuition. He went back to school with confidence that he was there to stay and jumped into every activity on campus. He was never on the football team, but during his sophomore year he displayed a talent for talking about the glories of football at the Lincoln team's bonfire rallies. His wild speeches, elegizing the great Lincoln teams of the past as well as commenting on the mothers of the opposing team's players, became legend.

Meanwhile, Aubrey had to take an extra semester to get ready for medical school. Never one for campus life, he spent most of his free time off campus romancing a pretty Baltimore girl, Sadie Prince. And he already had his acceptance to Howard Medical School in hand. In the winter of 1926 he graduated with honors and soon married Sadie.

Thurgood, meanwhile, was at the heart of campus life. He took part in two rituals of young male college society. First, he joined Alpha Phi Alpha, an elite fraternity of mostly light-skinned boys. Although the fraternity was at the top of campus society, its hazing was rough. "We'd get hit in the morning, hit in the middle of the night . . . dousing in cold water and all that kind of crap," recalled Monroe Dowling, who pledged a rival fraternity, Omega Psi Phi. "People came from all over the country to haze you. . . . You'd be beaten, branded, mistreated, and everything. That was Lincoln. The most uncouth place in the world."[8]

The second male ritual Thurgood joined at the start of his sophomore year was to grow a mustache, a small, bushy one right below his nose—the same style his father wore. Marshall would keep a mustache for the rest of his life.

Once he became an Alpha, Thurgood delighted in the nasty tricks fraternity brothers would play on each other and on rival frats. "I can throw water around a curve," he later claimed with pride. "You put the water in a pitcher, and you hold the pitcher straight up . . . then about the third time swirling the water—*whrrrroooo*, throw the water and it will go around the corner."

After one of his friends was doused with water by a competing fraternity while wearing good clothes, Thurgood and his frat brothers decided revenge was in order. "We knew in the Lincoln Hall dormitory for some reason they had little trapdoors on every floor. So if you opened the trapdoors you could go from the fourth floor all the way down. So we decided we'd open them all at one time. We got a big bucket, and everybody on that floor peed in that bucket, and they spit, and some of us were chewing tobacco. And we got a real good bucket of real good stuff in about a week or so. So when the guy is coming in the front door, we dropped the bucket of slop on his head through the trapdoor. Bet it broke him of that habit of throwing water."

Thurgood took to researching the best pranks. In his favorite, fraternity brothers would take the pants off the freshmen pledges and stick pickles between the cheeks of their buttocks before having them hop around the room in a race. After all the pickles had fallen on the floor, the older boys would put them in a punch bowl. While the boys were pulling up their pants, the old bowl would be switched with a bowl of fresh pickles. Then the pledges would be told to take a pickle out of the bowl and eat it. "Everyone would say, 'Can't I get my own pickle?' " Marshall remembered with glee.

Thurgood personally took part in frat pranks such as shaving the heads of other students—against their will. And he used paddles to hit other students, often with too much enthusiasm. The overly aggressive hazing of a younger student got him kicked out of school. "When the blow [the expulsion] descended, Marshall and friends headed for New York to seek jobs on a ship going around the world," a New York reporter later wrote. "They failed to find employment and had no alternative but to head back to Baltimore in disgrace."[9]

The boys were saved when one clever student decided that the administration might have some mercy on the troublemakers if they admitted to their crimes. A confession was drawn up, and the twenty-six sophomores, including Thurgood, signed it and were allowed to return to school. The student who had come up with the bright idea was none other than Langston Hughes.

Hughes, already a well-known poet, was completing his college education at Lincoln. He was twenty-five years old and had lived in Mexico, attended Columbia University, and even worked on the docks in New York. He jumped on one ship that took him to Europe for several months and took another ship for Africa. All the while Hughes's poetry was being published in New York, especially by the NAACP's magazine, *The Crisis*. When he came back to the United States in the early 1920s, Hughes became a celebrated member of the distinctive group of young black artists who were creating the Harlem Renaissance movement. He was circulating in a crowd that included the singer Paul Robeson and the writers Countee Cullen, Zora Neale Hurston, and Jean Toomer. And his first book, *The Weary Blues*, was already attracting critical acclaim.

Hughes was quite the star on the Lincoln campus when he showed up in 1926. He was immediately drawn to the pranks of the all-male campus life and joined the Omegas, the rival fraternity to Thurgood's Alphas. But Hughes had a larger life. He left campus regularly, to attend poetry readings and parties with artists and patrons in Manhattan. He was close to the NAACP's leadership, including the executive director, James Weldon Johnson, and the editor of *The Crisis*, W.E.B. Du Bois.

Thurgood, meanwhile, continued life as the happy-go-lucky college boy. Hughes later described the Thurgood Marshall he knew at Lincoln as "rough and ready, loud and wrong, good natured and uncouth."[10] But Hughes became a friend, largely because he was entertained and sometimes fascinated by Thurgood's free and easy life on campus.

Even on Lincoln's rural campus, however, Thurgood couldn't escape the racial issues that Hughes talked about regularly, much to Thurgood's irritation. In Thurgood's sociology class the students voted on whether Lincoln should integrate its all-white faculty. The majority of students, with Thurgood in the lead, voted to keep the faculty all white.

That vote angered fellow students, such as Hughes, who had long protested the absence of blacks on the faculty. Hughes immediately called for a campuswide referendum on the issue. The final tally showed 81 of 127 students voted as Thurgood had, to keep the faculty all white. On a campus dominated by frat life, the number one reason offered for opposing black professors at Lincoln was "favoritism," which might occur if the professor belonged to one of the competing fraternities. The second reason was "we are doing well as we are." And the third explanation, the most ironic, was that "students would not cooperate with Negroes."[11]

Thurgood's cavalier attitude about race relations went through a pivotal transformation just after the campus vote. He and some college pals, including Monroe Dowling, had gone into the small town of Oxford to watch a Saturday afternoon silent cowboy movie. After they purchased tickets, they were told that they could not sit on the main floor of the theater but had to move to the "colored" balcony. The students became angry and asked for their quarters back. The usher refused to give refunds. "So we had a disturbance . . . pulled down curtains, broke the front door," Dowling said. "I don't know who chased us. They didn't catch anybody." Marshall later said of the incident, "We knew there was only one pot-bellied cop in town and he could not arrest all of us."[12]

The story of the fracas got back to campus as quickly as Thurgood and his friends. Hughes heard about the incident and used it to confront Thurgood about the racial issues he preferred to ignore.

Thurgood, for the first time in his life, began thinking about Jim Crow practices. He had long talks with his favorite instructor, Robert Labaree, a sociology professor who had become close to Thurgood as head of the debate team. And Thurgood now also opened himself to several heart-to-heart conversations with Hughes.

"Langston was really sincere about what he was trying to do," Dowling said. "It was demeaning the way the white folks, the professors and their children, lived on one side of the road and we lived on the other side of the road and never the twain shall meet. They didn't even eat in the same dining room."

Hughes wrote his senior sociology thesis about the referendum: "The mental processes of the hat-in-hand, yes-boss, typical white-worshiping negro is to my mind very strongly shown in the attitude of some of the students there toward an all-white faculty. Sixty-three percent of the members of the upper classes favor for their college a faculty on which there are no negro professors." Hughes went on to note that Fisk and Howard had mixed faculties and these schools produced "graduates no less capable than our own." [13]

W.E.B. Du Bois, writing in the NAACP's magazine, called the vote a "most astonishing blow" to the higher education of Negroes in the United States. He asked readers to imagine the reaction if two-thirds of British students declared "they did not wish to be taught by Englishmen, because they doubted if Englishmen had either the brains or the character to be their teachers." He asked why parents would send children to a school where after four years the young people would "emerge with no faith in their own parents or in themselves." [14]

Hughes's talks and writings in favor of integrating the faculty were powerful and persuasive. After Hughes graduated in 1929, Thurgood took over the campaign. During that fall, with the senior Thurgood in the lead, there was a second referendum. This time the students voted to press the administration to bring in black teachers. The first black professor joined the faculty a year later.

Another factor advancing Thurgood's maturity and willingness to engage serious issues was his health. In the spring semester of 1928, there was an accident as he and some schoolmates were hurrying back from Baltimore. The boys were hitchhiking when the truck they were riding in broke down and they pushed it to a nearby garage in Rising Sun, Maryland. While the mechanic began repairs, a local sheriff came by and saw the six young black men standing around waiting. "How long is it going to take you to fix that truck?" the sheriff asked the mechanic. "You be sure to have it done before five o'clock, because I want these niggers out of here before sundown."

The truck was fixed that afternoon, and the boys—except for Thurgood, who had wandered off—climbed back in. As the truck was pulling away, Thurgood came running, yelling for them to stop. The driver slowed down, but the truck was still moving when Thurgood jumped to get onboard. "In the process of running to catch it, Thurgood got caught on the tailgate [and] injured his testicle," said Dowling. "We stopped . . . and got him back on the truck. . . . The pain was so great. . . . We wanted to take him to the local hospital, but the doctor there said he thought Thurgood's injury was of such a magnitude that we should get him back to Baltimore quickly."

Marshall lost one of his testicles because of the accident and did not get back to Lincoln until the fall semester of 1928, a semester behind his classmates. He was now a member of the class of 1930. And his friends had a nickname for him: One Ball.

His injury and time away from school slowed Thurgood's social life. He began to work harder in the classroom. And his trips off campus became less regular. He was looking to settle down. That year the twenty-year-old Thurgood met Vivian Burey, a seventeen-year-old freshman at the University of Pennsylvania. She had short, wavy hair. Her thin arms and large breasts led boys to call her Buster, and the nickname stuck. She was described as having an outgoing personality, "fair skin and a sparkling smile." [15]

Thurgood said he met Buster in Philadelphia at an ice cream parlor near her parents' church. But Buster told friends that she met her young love much earlier. But he was "so busy arguing and debating with everybody at the table" that he didn't even give her a second glance. [16]

Vivian, born February 11, 1911, came from a middle-class family. Her father was a caterer for hotels in Philadelphia, and during the summers he catered for several country clubs across the Delaware River in southern New Jersey. Vivian was in the school of education at the University of Pennsylvania when Thurgood asked her to marry him.

The wedding, held in 1929 at Philadelphia's First African Baptist Church, known locally as Cherry Memorial, was a society event, followed by a large reception at the bride's home. Thurgood's roommate and friend from college James Murphy served as his best man.

Thurgood returned to Lincoln while his bride lived with his parents in Baltimore. The young man who had been so playful now displayed a serious mind; for the first time friends saw him study. Young Mr. Marshall graduated with honors in January 1930, just months after the stock market crash of 1929.

Thurgood later said the crash had little effect on his family because they had no money to invest and therefore lost nothing. Jobs, however, were harder to find. Thurgood had to work as an insurance agent, an experience he described as "worse than boredom." Another career possibility came when one of his professors, impressed by Thurgood's improved work during his senior year, arranged for a job interview at a bank in New York. Thurgood turned that job down when he was offered just twenty dollars a week; he was making more than that as a waiter at the Gibson Island Club.[17]

The college graduate put on his white waiter's jacket and went back to work at Gibson Island to support his wife and save some money. Marshall now had a clear goal in mind. He told his mother he was on his way to law school.

CHAPTER 5

Turkey

Norma Marshall was not happy that her son, a college graduate, had to wait tables. But the family needed the money badly. They were spending every last dollar to put Aubrey through Howard Medical School. Still, Norma insisted that Thurgood make his job at Gibson Island nothing more than a stop on his way to law school. She told him to save his money and by that fall they would find a way to pay the tuition bill.

Norma's greatest hope was that Thurgood could somehow get into the University of Maryland Law School. It was only a few blocks from Old West Baltimore, and it had low public tuition rates. Thurgood talked to Uncle Fearless about the school and called on several of the black lawyers around town, but the answer was always the same. Only two black students had ever graduated from the law school, and no black student had been admitted since the 1890s.

Until now Jim Crow racism had always been more an inconvenience than an obstacle to Thurgood's success. Suddenly the rules of segregation in Baltimore were like a weight around his neck as he tried to stay above water. In conversations with Uncle Fee and his mother, he railed against the school and insisted that he would get in or find a way to get even. But there was no sign that the school planned to change its policy. And Thurgood did not have the money to pay tuition for any of the northern schools that accepted blacks. He was trapped, and he was bitter about it. He never even bothered to apply to the University of Maryland

Law School.[1] But his bitterness over Maryland's segregationist admissions policy was turning into a hard-edged motivation to get a law school education no matter what stood in his way.

Thurgood's only option was not very appealing. Howard University Law School, in nearby Washington, D.C., was inexpensive and taught the law to black students. But its reputation was mediocre to poor. Thurgood knew of the school's troubles: "Howard Law was known as a 'dummy's retreat' because the only people that went there were those who couldn't get in any other school."

In the fall of 1930, after several months of work, Thurgood was still short of cash for Howard's fall tuition payment. Even though he had been accepted at Howard, he had resigned himself to work another year to save more money. His mother, however, insisted that he go to law school immediately. She even pawned her wedding and engagement rings so Thurgood could matriculate.[2]

Although the tuition was in place, Thurgood still couldn't afford to live in Washington. So every morning at 5:00 he was up and out of the house. With a heavy bag of books under his arms, he took the long walk to the train station and caught the early commuter. Once in Washington he walked from Union Station to his law classes at 420 5th Street, Northwest, a brownstone near the city's courthouse.

On the first day of classes, Thurgood and thirty-five other young black men filed into the school. It was a new day for the students and the school; this was the first year that Howard Law would be solely a day school for full-time students. As Thurgood and the other men walked up the stone steps and into the large first-floor room, they spoke in quiet voices, waiting for the appearance of the dean, Charles Hamilton Houston.

The room fell silent when Houston, an imposing, stiff man in a woolen suit, came in and simply stood looking at the students. He was a tall, brown-skinned man with clipped short hair. The students took their seats, and Houston began to speak. He didn't bother to welcome them. He bluntly announced that Howard was no longer for students who did not want to give their full attention to the study of law. He warned them that their success in college meant nothing to him, and it would give him great pleasure to flunk out Phi Beta Kappas.

His stern lecture ended with a caution: "Each one of you look at the man to your right and then look to the man on your left. Realize that two of you won't be here next year." After Houston left the room there was hushed grumbling. Thurgood thought to himself that he had a lot riding on making the grade. The idea that two of every three students would be gone by next year made him nervous—he was determined to be the one who succeeded.

Houston was the dominant figure among the law school's brand-new eleven-man faculty. It was a thoroughly integrated and first-rate group. There were five white professors, and the six black professors included a young lawyer fresh out of Harvard Law School and a future federal judge, William Hastie. James Cobb, the highly regarded constitutional law scholar, was also on Houston's new faculty.

The students quickly fell into a tightly ordered world, ruled by Dean Houston. The first floor of the school was a large room that could be used for moot court and classes; the second floor was the library, with space for classrooms. On the top floor was the office of the dean. Houston worked at a neat desk with a green visor over his eyes as he read and typed. Students walking by the office would glimpse him typing intensely with two fingers. One student described the dean's rapid, mistake-free typing as "a Gatling gun."[3] Houston's formal manner, his constant focus on work, and his strict regimen for his students led them to call him Old Iron Shoes and Cement Pants.

Despite their carping, the students regarded Houston as a role model. He had been born in Washington, D.C., on September 3, 1895. His father, William Houston, was one of the city's most prominent black lawyers, and his mother was the hairdresser for several wives of white senators. Houston grew up in this middle-class home as an only child. He attended Washington's famous M Street High School (later renamed Dunbar High School) and finished at just fifteen, then went north to the nearly all-white Amherst College. He graduated a top student, Phi Beta Kappa, in 1915. After that he went off to Europe as part of the U.S. Army in World War I, becoming a second lieutenant.

While in the racially segregated Army, Houston acted as a military lawyer for blacks facing charges of misconduct even though he had no formal legal training. He found that black soldiers were often convicted on flimsy charges with no evidence. After he lost several misconduct cases involving black soldiers, he decided to follow his father and become a lawyer.

In 1919, just after the war's end, Houston started at Harvard Law School. He was one of the few blacks at the school and not always welcomed at a time when openly racist behavior was still common, even in

Massachusetts and at Harvard. But Houston worked hard and became the first black student to edit the *Harvard Law Review*. He graduated with honors in 1922 and began working with the law school dean, Roscoe Pound, and Professor Felix Frankfurter, later an associate justice of the Supreme Court, as he pursued a doctorate of law. Harvard gave him a scholarship to study civil law in Spain in 1923. The following year, after earning his doctorate, Houston made his way home to join his father's law firm and start teaching at Howard.

Howard Law was unaccredited and sinking out of business when Houston joined the faculty. To persuade the school's trustees to get rid of the night law school, Houston did studies on black lawyers around the country. He found there were only about a thousand black attorneys in the United States and only a hundred practicing law full-time in the South. By comparison, the nation had nearly 160,000 white lawyers. Houston made these findings the basis of his argument that Howard had to do a better job of training black lawyers. Even while he was sick with TB in 1928, Houston built support among black lawyers and educators in Washington for an overhaul of Howard Law.[4]

When Houston became the school's vice dean in 1929, he began an effort to make Howard a fully accredited day program. He had support from prominent people, including Supreme Court Justice Louis Brandeis. Brandeis confided to Howard's president, Mordecai Johnson, that his colleagues on the high court could tell a black lawyer's brief from a white lawyer's by its lack of research and sloppiness. Houston's effort was to make Howard Law a "West Point of Negro leadership."[5] Thurgood Marshall was in the first class of men Houston wanted to transform into this cadre.

A younger Marshall might not have understood Houston. But Marshall was changing. Now twenty-two years old, he did not mind Houston's high expectations, and by his own account he was scared of what would happen to him if he did not become a lawyer. With the country in the middle of the Great Depression, a wife working to support him, and his mother hocking her valuables to help with his tuition, Marshall was no longer the Lincoln cutup who played pinochle all day and viewed school as a site for fraternity pranks. On his train rides to and from Baltimore, his head was buried in law books. "All of my notes I would take down in the book by hand and that night I would type them up after I rode back to Baltimore," he remembered. "My evidence notebook—got at least half a dozen people by just by reading my notebook."

Marshall's constant hard work paid off. He became the top student in the first-year class. That ranking won him a job as the student assistant in the law library, which helped to pay his tuition and gave him the chance to begin working personally with Houston. "I'd got the horsin' around out of my system and I heard law books were to dig in so I dug deep," according to Thurgood.[6]

Marshall's time in the library was time to do not only his job but also schoolwork and the extra research that set him apart from other students. "You see, as a librarian in the law school for eight hours, I didn't have nothing to do but read law," Marshall remembered. "Sometimes we'd take the rape cases and read all the rape cases. And sometimes we'd get on another kick and we'd read all that." Also in his second year, Marshall's classmates elected him to the Court of Peers, which judged legal arguments presented by students.

By now Houston and Marshall had developed a close personal relationship. Houston admired his willingness to do hard work, and Marshall wanted to be part of the elite fraternity of lawyers, including Hastie and Houston, who were respected, had some money, and seemed to be in control of their destiny.

The library job and Houston's mentoring meant that Marshall did not leave the school until 10:00 P.M. each night. "When I was in law school, in my first year I lost thirty pounds solely from work," he recalled. "Intellectual work, studying. And that's how you get ahead of people."

Even though he was working long hours for the first time in his life, Marshall did not lose his taste for outrageous stories, good liquor, and women. "Thurgood, he walked with a gangling gait, and he always had some new lie to tell you," said Oliver Hill, a classmate and close friend at Howard, recalling that Marshall's strut earned him the nickname "Turkey."[7] Marshall and many of his law school pals ate lunch at a restaurant run by Father Divine, a charismatic black preacher who surrounded himself with young women he called his "angels." Lunchtime was a chance for Marshall to make jokes about Father Divine and ogle the angels.

Marshall's life at Howard also included some fraternity run-ins. Half the class was made up of Alpha Phi Alpha, his fraternity, but the other half included members of Omega Psi Phi and other fraternities. Marshall represented the Alphas as they competed with the Omegas, led by Oliver Hill, to win elections as class officers. "The Alphas thought that they could run the class," Hill recalled. "But the opposition coalesced. We could not or would not agree on who would be the class president, therefore the class was never able to elect an official set of class officers."

Meanwhile the academic pace was severe. Houston began flunking students out. In the first year alone about half were asked to leave. Houston had a standing, icy comment for Marshall and any other student who complained that he was working them too hard: "No tea for the feeble, no crepe for the dead."[8] The high standards did achieve Houston's goal, however. During Marshall's second year the school won its American Bar Association accreditation.

Houston kept the law school jumping for the students who could keep up. He brought in a fabulous cast of visiting professors, including Roscoe Pound from Harvard. Houston also drew world-famous lawyers to lecture, including Clarence Darrow, who was famous for handling the Scopes monkey trial. Another visitor was Arthur Garfield Hays of the ACLU. Being in Washington, Marshall took the initiative to go to the Supreme Court and see some of the best lawyers in action. The most memorable was John W. Davis, a West Virginia native and Democrat who ran for president in 1924. Davis was renowned for his arguments before the high court, and Marshall would skip class to hear the man he regarded as the nation's best attorney. "Every time John Davis argued, I'd ask myself, 'Will I ever, ever . . . ?' and every time I had to answer, 'No never.'"[9]

Houston also kept his students' attention by walking them through the District of Columbia legal system, visiting police precincts, the U.S. Attorney's Office, courts, and jails. Marshall recalled with great pride that he and his classmates discovered that Congress's code of laws for Washington, D.C., included no equal rights protection—a guarantee for all Americans under the Fourteenth Amendment. Houston and the law students brought the omission to the attention of newspapers and Congress. The D.C. code was changed.

By Marshall's final year of law school, Houston began to treat the few remaining students, especially the transformed Marshall, as if they were partners in an elite black law firm. One problem for Houston and the other black lawyers was that no matter how good their school, they could not become members of the segregated American Bar Association. In response to the ABA's whites-only policy, Houston became one of the leaders of the National Bar Association, a black lawyers' group founded in

1925. "I remember in our senior year there was a National Bar Association meeting in Baltimore," Oliver Hill recalled. "Charlie carried Thurgood and me to the convention as his protégés."

Houston also began to give his top students the chance to work on real cases. In 1933, Marshall's senior year, Houston was asked by the NAACP's national office in New York to help with the case of a Virginia black man charged with murdering two white women. The accused, George Crawford, had fled the state for fear of lynch mobs and was arrested in Boston. When Virginia tried to extradite him, the NAACP, which had no legal staff, asked Houston if he could find a way to keep Crawford from being sent back. They feared a return trip to Virginia was a death sentence, since he would have to stand trial before twelve white men in a community itching to see Crawford hang.

Houston took the case but failed to stop the extradition. Afterward he asked Walter White, the flamboyant head of the NAACP, if the civil rights group would hire him to defend Crawford during the trial. The case was an opportunity to take a dignified stand by having black lawyers defend a black man in Virginia, the state that had been the capital of the Confederacy. If black lawyers handled the murder trial, it would "be a turning point in the legal history of the Negro in this country," [10] Houston told White.

White gave Houston permission to use his Howard faculty and students to defend Crawford. Marshall spent countless hours in the library and in Virginia doing research on extradition law. He then joined Houston and Leon Ransom, another law professor, in discussing strategies for defending Crawford. White later wrote: "There was a lanky, brash young senior law student who was always present. . . . [I] was amazed at his assertiveness in challenging positions taken by Charlie and the other lawyers. But I soon learned of his great value. . . . [He did] everything he was asked, from research on obscure legal opinions to foraging for coffee and sandwiches." [11] White's first encounter with Marshall created a lasting impression.

The Howard legal team's first move in the case was to charge that the absence of blacks from the list of prospective jurors was evidence the state was illegally keeping blacks off all juries. The circuit court, however, ruled against the Howard lawyers, and Crawford went to trial in Leesburg. Houston argued the prosecution did not even have the murder weapon or a witness to the crime. Crawford had told police he had tried to rob the women but had not killed them—a friend had done it. Crawford, however, could not produce his friend, and the jury found him guilty. Still, he escaped the death penalty.

Marshall and Houston celebrated as if they had won. "If you get a life term for a Negro charged with killing a white person in Virginia, you've won," Marshall said later. "You've won because normally they were hanging them."

The *Crawford* case was the first time Marshall had seen Houston in action, and it left an impression that would last a lifetime. Marshall felt the preachers, the politicians, the businessmen, and even the civil rights leaders like Walter White could talk and raise money and put stories in the newspapers. But it was up to lawyers, like Houston, to stand up and help a black man with his life on the line. "The lawyer was there to bear the brunt of getting rid of segregation," Marshall said. "And Houston made public statements that black lawyers he trained at Howard would become social engineers rather than lawyers. That was our purpose in life."

The *Crawford* case was the highlight of a senior year that was the best of Marshall's time at Howard. He loved the work, he had a mentor in Houston, and he felt he finally was on the path to achieve his mother's dream that he would be a lawyer. In June of 1933 Marshall graduated from law school first in his class. There were only six people left in what had started out as a class of thirty-six. The men who remained did not bother to take a class photo: "We decided that we'd been rebellious for three years, so why stop now," Marshall explained.

Hill, a classmate known for his humor and love of cigars, fondly remembered that after their last examinations, "Thurgood and I decided that we would have a pregraduation celebration, and in the lingo of that day, we went to a 'nip joint' and 'booted up a few.' "

After law school Marshall went back to Gibson Island for another summer of work, hoping to save money and consider his plans for the future. There were no law firm internships available for Howard's graduates. None of the white Baltimore firms hired black lawyers, and the few black lawyers in town ran one-man shops. With time on his hands, Marshall traveled with Houston to look at black elementary schools in the South. The NAACP had done a study—the Margold report—in 1931 proposing a legal challenge to segregation in the public schools. But the association had not settled on a legal strategy. Houston was asked to take a firsthand look at the quality of schools available to black children in the South.

Marshall and Houston traveled in Houston's car and found abysmal facilities. "Conditions were much worse than we heard they were," Marshall said. They drove all the way to New Orleans, staying in private homes and eating whatever greasy food they could get since they could not go into Jim Crow restaurants. "That's why we carried bags of fruit in the car, most of the time we'd just eat the fruit," said Marshall.

Somewhere in Mississippi Houston stopped one day to look at a dilapidated school building. All around were broken-down wooden shacks that housed black sharecroppers. There was little plumbing, and open drainage ditches, filled with human waste, ran along the roads. The faces of the people showed nothing but defeat. While Houston walked around the drafty old schoolhouse, Marshall began to eat his lunch. A black child saw the young lawyer eating an orange. Marshall thought the child was staring at him or the car; then he realized the boy was fascinated with the fruit. He handed the boy a fresh orange. "The kid did not even take the peeling off. He had never seen an orange before. He just bit right through it and enjoyed it."

Marshall was shocked. Gone was the contented view of a middle-class kid with white neighbors and mentors who easily accepted Jim Crow. Now his eyes were open to racial injustice. And his mind was open to the thought that a lawyer could reshape society. Marshall did not know exactly what a lawyer could do about racists and poor black kids living in such deprived conditions that an orange was an exotic fruit. But for the first time he wanted to do something, and do it soon.

CHAPTER 6

❧

His Own Man

Thurgood Marshall, fresh out of law school in 1933, had a choice to make. He could go to Harvard Law School, on a scholarship offered by Dean Roscoe Pound, for an advanced law degree. Or he could open his own law office in Baltimore. Having lived on the thin edge of every dime he and Buster brought into the house, Marshall had a deep need to show his wife, his family, and himself that he had attained some status in the world. The insult he had felt at the University of Maryland Law School's ban on black students still burned him, and he wanted to show that he was now as good as any white Maryland Law graduate. It was not even a close decision in young Marshall's mind. He wanted to get out of law libraries, deal with real cases, make money, and be his own man.

Marshall's initial challenge out of law school was passing the Maryland bar exam. He did it on his first try, signing an oath in which he promised to act "fairly and honorably" as a lawyer and pledged allegiance to Maryland, the United States, and the U.S. Constitution on October 11, 1933.

He was now on his own, but Marshall's craving for independence had to be balanced with his need to make money. For advice on how to make ends meet, Marshall sought the counsel of the best-known black lawyer in Baltimore, Warner McGuinn.

McGuinn was a small, cocky, Yale Law graduate, who looked close to white and was a former city councilman. Already in his sixties, McGuinn had recently hired one young black lawyer, W.A.C. Hughes, when Marshall came to see him. But McGuinn could not afford another legal associate and did not even listen to Marshall's request for a job. Before Marshall could even begin his pitch, McGuinn interrupted him. "Young man, you save your time, you can save my ears. Forget it, I've known you since you were born, and I have carefully watched your progress in law school. It's unbelievably good. And you want to let me have your beautiful, great brain, and I am not going to accept it. You're going to practice by yourself and get your brains kicked out and then come back to me and we'll talk." The senior lawyer did promise Marshall that he would help him set up his office and get some work.

Marshall was not pleased. "And I can remember now I walked down the hall after him, I said, 'Unreasonable son of a bitch,' " Marshall recalled. "But he was right. I lost more cases, whoo-hoo, but we were always very friendly. He was the only one who helped me."

McGuinn did counsel Marshall on the personalities and politics of judges, prosecutors, and cops. He also encouraged Marshall not to give up, even when money was so short that the novice had to take a part-time job as a clerk in the venereal disease section of the city health clinic.

The Great Depression deepened, and money was tight for whites but almost nonexistent for blacks by 1933. Marshall could afford only a tiny office in downtown Baltimore, on the sixth floor of 4 Redwood Street, the Phoenix Building, which housed most of the city's black lawyers. In addition to Warner McGuinn and Hughes, there were the law offices of Josiah Henry and Robert McGuinn (Warner's nephew). Marshall's office was a single room, dominated by a desk that Warner McGuinn lent him, a black phone, and an old but special rug, donated by his parents from their own living-room floor.

After a few months of sharing a secretary with McGuinn, Marshall got his own assistant, Sue (nicknamed Little Bits) Tilghman. Occasionally McGuinn or one of the older lawyers would hand Marshall a small case. There was not much to share, however. Few black people were willing to trust a black lawyer with their criminal case, divorce, or will. And with the Depression, a paying client was a rarity. Out of his office window Marshall could see bread lines, which had become commonplace in the city. In the fall of 1933 when Marshall opened his office, Baltimore's unemployment rate was over 20 percent, even higher among blacks.[1] He soon began to have regrets about turning down the offer to study at Harvard. In his first year of practice, Marshall lost $3,500. Clients were so scarce that lunch money became a major concern. To alleviate the problem he would bring a lunch of leftovers to the office one day, and his secretary would bring sandwiches the next.

"Once in a while, I got a good fee," Marshall recalled. "Then my secretary would immediately take the check to the bank. She'd call her husband and I'd call Buster, and we'd get the biggest steak in town to celebrate."[2]

It was peanut butter sandwiches more often than steak, however. Marshall hustled for any client he could find, and once in a while the judges at the city court would send black clients to him. But sometimes Marshall did not appreciate the generosity. One day a black woman, with a country accent and a red, tattered skirt, walked into Marshall's office with legal trouble but no money. He asked how she happened to pick him out to handle her case. She said that in her South Carolina hometown, if anyone had a problem they asked a judge what to do. And when she went to see a judge in Baltimore, he sent her to Marshall, telling her, "He's a freebie" lawyer. "So I said, 'I've got to stop that crap right now,' " Marshall recalled with a laugh.

Marshall's lack of work meant he had time to take some more NAACP fact-finding trips with Charles Houston. They toured Virginia, Kentucky, Missouri, Tennessee, the Carolinas, and Mississippi to investigate segregation in schools. Houston often used a movie camera to document the horrid conditions. The schools usually were wooden structures, no more than shacks. They had no insulation, and it was common to be able to see the sky through the many holes in the roofs. The floors were sometimes dirt and ran thick with mud when rain fell.

The two men prepared reports to send back to the NAACP. "Charlie Houston and I used to type sitting in the car with a typewriter in our laps," Marshall recalled. The sight of two black men investigating segregated schools sometimes led to threats from local whites. In Mississippi the concerns were so great that the state NAACP president assigned a funeral hearse, with two riflemen inside, to ride behind Houston and Marshall for protection.

Houston's relationship with Marshall changed during these trips. No longer just Marshall's teacher, he became a senior partner as they looked at how the law could affect race relations. The always serious Houston engaged Marshall in long discussions over the difference racial integration could make in the lives of black people. If blacks and whites went to the same, integrated schools, Houston argued, then smart black children, like smart white children, could become captains of industry. Integration would mean that whites would interact with blacks, and racist stereotypes would melt away. He impressed upon Marshall the idea that integration was the key to equal rights, because it ensured that blacks and whites got the same opportunities.

Marshall returned from his trips to the Deep South more convinced than ever of the need to overthrow the racist laws that kept southern blacks poor and uneducated. His day-to-day life, however, saw him still struggling to make his law firm a success. But the greatest burden on him—a young man desperate to proclaim his independence—was that he was still living with his parents, in a house filled with bickering and tension.

The family house at 1838 Druid Hill Avenue was crowded, with Norma and Willie, as well as Thurgood and his wife, his brother and sister-in-law, and their new infant child, Aubrey Jr. Sadie's mother also came to live in the house, which had five bedrooms and only one cramped bathroom for the eight people.

The rough spots in Marshall's relationship with his father and his brother never did get ironed out; in these conditions they worsened. His father continued to drink heavily, although he still held his job at Gibson Island. The glue that kept the family together was Norma's strong personality. She held sway over her husband and sons and was the final word in any dispute, over money or the rules for taking food out of the refrigerator. In this household the women often eclipsed the men, much as they had when Marshall was a child.

Willie Marshall continued to work during the spring and summer months, but the Depression cut down on the money the rich had to fritter away at the club. Meanwhile, Aubrey Marshall opened his own medical practice on Carey Street as a general practitioner. Business was slow, however. One of his Old West Baltimore friends recalled that most of the black doctors in Baltimore were supported by their wives, who were usually schoolteachers. "Negroes didn't have any money for a doctor," said Pat Patterson, who lived near the Marshalls.[3] As a result, Aubrey was forced to work part-time in the city's health clinic.

Despite the money troubles and tense atmosphere at the house, Thurgood and Buster, by most accounts, were happy together. Their main difficulty was with Buster's attempts to have children. Several of the couple's friends reported that Buster had a miscarriage during these years in Baltimore. The problems with pregnancy caused more than the usual anxiety for Thurgood; since he had only one testicle after his college accident, he feared that he might not ever be able to father children.

Despite the miscarriages, Buster continued to work. She went through a series of jobs to help support the family, including one selling Bond Bread in a Jewish store near their house. She also worked in Sally's Boutique on Druid Hill Avenue, selling women's hats, belts, and shoes.

Even when Buster worked, though, she sometimes had trouble getting paid. Once she went to work for a man writing a catalog of Negro businesses. After two weeks, however, the man stopped paying her. Buster asked Thurgood to sue him, but Thurgood refused, explaining it would be a waste of time because the guy probably did not have the money.

But Buster decided she was going to get her money. She filed a complaint with the local judge, who asked why Thurgood wasn't handling the case. She explained her husband was too busy trying to find paying clients. The judge laughed. But a few days later Buster's nonpaying boss was arrested. She came to court and not only listed the paychecks she had not received but took the time to make an account of all the money the scoundrel owed other people around the city. The judge ruled in her favor and she got her money.

In the meantime, her husband's practice began to pick up. He handled divorces, personal injury, car accidents, murder, and rape cases. Marshall even handled a case for his brother, in which Aubrey was sued for $2,500 and charged by another motorist with "reckless driving." Marshall got the case settled out of court.[4] This was a vintage early case for the young lawyer.

But Marshall would soon find himself with three cases that were critical to his development. The first came in June of 1934. Sitting in his office one afternoon, Marshall got a nervous call from his neighbor Pat Patterson. A young black man had been arrested for murder in southern Maryland, and Patterson had convinced the suspect's parents to hire Marshall to represent their son. Twenty-five-year-old James Gross had been charged with the murder of a man who ran a barbecue stand in nearby Prince Georges County. Local papers ran sensational stories about Gross and his accomplices, dubbing them the Three Black Dillingers, a reference to the gangster John Dillinger.[5]

"I knew the family of the boy," said Patterson, "and they needed a lawyer, so I talked to Thurgood and he was interested. They wanted a black lawyer. There were several black lawyers in Washington that I knew personally, but I didn't think they had a ghost of a chance in Prince Georges County. I wasn't sure that even Marshall would have a chance. But I felt that he probably would have a better chance coming from Maryland."

The trial, in the county seat of Upper Marlboro, lasted only a few days. Marshall argued that his client had just driven the car while the two other men actually shot the store owner. But the jury was not persuaded. The three were convicted of murder in the first degree and sentenced to hang. A few months later one of the men, Donald Parker, had his sentence commuted to life imprisonment. Marshall's client was not so lucky. On April 19, 1935, James Gross was hanged just after midnight at the Maryland Penitentiary.[6]

"The ringleader got off—he had a smarter lawyer than what the other boys had at the time," said Patterson. "Parker's lawyers were white. They had practices in Prince Georges County. And if you could afford to hire either of them or both, you could commit murder and get away with it."

Upon the death of his client, Marshall felt the sting of his own inadequacies as a lawyer. He was enraged by the arbitrary sentencing. The actual murderer was smiling and strolling out of court with a life sentence while the driver of the getaway car was sobbing and babbling for mercy as he walked to the gallows. Marshall had never opposed the death penalty, but now he saw it as a crude instrument, smashing the little guy while missing the bloody murderer.

Another case that deeply affected Marshall came two years later. The Baltimore branch of the NAACP asked him to represent a black suspect, Virtis Lucas, who was accused in the fatal shooting of Hyman Brilliant, a white man. The Baltimore police picked Lucas up and questioned him for three days, severely beating him until he confessed. Marshall, using his brother to help with Lucas's medical condition, went to the city jail and prepared him to stand trial.[7]

In a tense March trial that captivated the city, Marshall stood before an all-white jury and this time pointed the finger of blame at the police. It was an emotional trial for him. He didn't want to lose another client to the death penalty, and he felt the weight of his family's history, recalling the stories of his grandfather's stand against police brutality in the "Cake Walk" homicide.

Marshall began his defense by making sure the jury was aware of just how badly his client had been beaten after the arrest. Then he made his client into a sympathetic figure, a weak-minded boy who had been idly shooting off a gun in an alley a few blocks away around the time of the murder. That youngster, Marshall contended, became an easy target for a murder charge when Baltimore police could not find the real killer.

The all-white jury was swayed by the young lawyer's pleadings. Lucas was found not guilty of murder but guilty of manslaughter and sentenced to just six months in prison.[8] The Baltimore branch of the NAACP was thrilled that Lucas was not sentenced to be hanged. And they were greatly impressed that a black lawyer had been able to defend a black man in Baltimore's white justice system.

Marshall was learning how to work with the white legal system, creating a personal network among lawyers and judges in the city and building a reputation for himself as a criminal lawyer. In the third major case of his young career, he broke ground as the first black lawyer to defend a white lawyer in Maryland. The white lawyer, Bernard Ades, had been defending a black client charged with murder. Ades challenged the conviction on the grounds that his client had not been given a fair trial because of his race.

A radical lawyer best known for his ties to the Communist ILD [International Labor Defense], Ades was not popular with the state's judges. Baltimore judges were openly hostile to unionization of the city's blue-collar workforce. Picketing and strikes intended to shut down factories were often thwarted by court injunctions. Communists were frequently blamed by the city's major employers for union-organizing attempts.

After Ades charged that his client was a victim of the judge's racism, Judge William C. Coleman wanted Ades's right to practice law suspended and started a hearing in state court to take away his license.[9] Ades immediately called Charles Houston, whom he knew from the labor movement. Houston agreed to represent him if he could have Marshall, who knew the Baltimore courts and judges, as his cocounsel. Soon after they took the case, Judge Coleman called the two black attorneys into his chambers. He felt Ades had unfairly damaged his reputation by accusing him of racism. If Marshall and Houston made any similar charges, the judge warned, he would have them jailed for contempt of court.

Marshall and Houston did not know what to do. If they abandoned their arguments, they had no defense for Ades. But if they went into court the next day and contended that racism was at the root of the case, the judge was going to put them in jail. Word of their dilemma spread through Baltimore.

"The judge was about to put me in jail, and this client of mine, John

Murphy [of the *Afro* newspaper], came by," Marshall remembered. "Here, I've got something for you to go to court," Murphy told him. A curious Marshall opened the envelope and found inside five $1,000 bills. His eyes wide with astonishment, he turned to Murphy, who told him, "That's for your bail."

Luckily for Marshall and Houston, Judge Coleman decided to recuse himself from the case, and another judge took his place. The case ended with Ades being given a reprimand, but he was allowed to continue practicing law. Marshall and Houston had won an important case. In local legal circles Marshall's reputation now stood large. He was seen as a good attorney and also the black lawyer who made integrationist history by defending a white lawyer.

Now that he was a courthouse regular, Marshall tried his best to become an insider among the white legal fraternity. He brought a personal yet respectful manner to the legal bar and its white judges. Despite the segregated nature of legal proceedings, he learned to work within the ropes of legal segregation. He only demanded fair treatment.

To bolster his case for racial equality, Marshall took to heart Houston's advice to be twice as good as white lawyers. His briefs were carefully written, and his arguments were well reasoned. "I never filed a paper in any court with an erasure on it. If I changed a word, it had to be typed all over," he said.[10] Marshall's diligence regularly won judges to his side. Once, when an opposing white lawyer asked a white judge for time to check on the legal citations in Marshall's brief, the judge said it was not necessary. Even though the judge had a reputation for giving black lawyers a rough time, he told the white attorney: "You don't have to worry about that—if Mr. Marshall puts his signature on it, you don't have to check."

Marshall's good relationship with white judges, including the bigots, led them to call on him in cases where they wanted a solid black lawyer in the courtroom to protect themselves against charges of racial bias. One night Marshall got a call from the local judge in nearby Frederick, Maryland, alerting him that a lynching was about to happen. Marshall hopped in his rickety, used 1929 Ford, nicknamed Betsy, that he had bought with Uncle Fee's help. When he got to Frederick, Marshall saw a scary, chaotic scene. The police were racing around, some grabbing black men and leading them to the jails. Marshall became worried for his own safety. Working up his courage, he drove his car next to a state trooper and asked for an escort to the judge's house. "You want some protection?" the policeman asked him. Marshall, who by then had sweated through his shirt with worry, replied: "That's what I'm talking about."

When a relieved Marshall arrived at the judge's house, he told him that Geraldine Kreh, the eighteen-year-old daughter of a local bank president, had been beaten up during an attempted rape by a black man. Marshall was called to make sure that all the rules were followed in identifying and charging a suspect.

That night William Carter, a black workman, was identified by Kreh as her assailant. He was charged with assault with intent to rape, a crime punishable by death. The *Afro-American*, the activist Baltimore paper, and the Baltimore NAACP hired Marshall to "observe" the trial and note any evidence of racial bias. With Marshall in the courtroom as a spokesman for the NAACP, the man was convicted but given a life sentence. Marshall later wrote to Charlie Houston, "He is guilty as the devil."[11] Marshall's reputation had now extended outside the halls of Baltimore courts. He had become known to judges around the state as the eyes and ears of Maryland's NAACP.

Marshall's growing profile led local labor leaders to ask him for help in organizing black workers. The young lawyer began to see a role for himself beyond the confines of the court. As Charles Houston had long preached to him, Marshall was using his legal training to become a social activist.

One of the city's biggest employers was Bethlehem Steel. A third of the labor force at its Sparrow's Point plant was black, but they did not trust the all-white leadership of the labor unions. W.E.B. Du Bois, editor of the NAACP's *Crisis* magazine, had come to Baltimore in the early 1930s to give speeches urging black workers to join white workers in unions. In many companies black workers were not even allowed to unionize. And when the companies allowed blacks to join unions, the unions often forced them into segregated units. But high unemployment during the Depression and Roosevelt's New Deal spurred a new wave of labor organizing in the city.[12]

However, the antiunion tenor among Baltimore's white establishment continued to prevail. Eugene O'Dunne, a leading judge in city courts, derided the strikes as evidence of labor radicalism. "A man has a right to work for whom he will and what he will," O'Dunne said during one union-busting trial. He charged that labor groups had no right to set working conditions.[13] Marshall was one of a few activists who challenged this policy.

As a member of the union's organizing committee, Marshall began secret meetings with black workers at Bethlehem Steel. Despite their anxiety about white union leaders, Marshall persuaded the black workers that the best way to protect their rights was to create an integrated union. To reassure black workers of fair treatment, he proposed that they run a candidate for a leadership post in the union. Marshall led a successful campaign to elect a black union treasurer.

Bethlehem Steel was not pleased; they saw a cohesive, racially integrated union as a major threat to their control over workers. The company hired goons, armed with nightsticks, to break up several union meetings where Marshall was advancing the idea of black and white worker cooperation.

One night, Marshall had to run from the company thugs. "It was raining and we started running and two of us saw a church. It had a big hedge around it so we got down in the hedge and these guys were coming by shouting: 'Black son of a bitch' and knocking heads. We lay down in the mud. At first, that mud was cold, but it got real warm. We stayed there until they left, after midnight."

Despite challenging Baltimore's power structure, Marshall was careful to keep good relationships in the city's establishment legal circles. He remained the warm, wisecracking black lawyer with whom white judges felt comfortable dealing. Marshall wanted acceptance from the city's white lawyers; the only sign of defiance came when they would not let him or any other black lawyer in the Baltimore City Bar Association. Marshall became a leader in the Monumental City Bar Association, the black lawyers' alternative bar. Marshall and six other black lawyers incorporated it in April of 1935. That year thirty-two black lawyers were working in the city, an all-time high.[14] The same year Marshall became treasurer of the National Bar Association. Marshall joked that the group had so little money, he could "carry the treasury around in my mouth."

For all his activism Marshall's law practice was still struggling. His biggest client was the Druid Hill Laundry until John H. Murphy, Jr., treasurer of the Afro-American Co., the country's largest black newspaper chain, walked into his office.

John Murphy had had a spat with his longtime lawyer, Warner McGuinn. Marshall had been college roommates with John's nephew, James, who had referred John Murphy to the young lawyer. McGuinn did not object to giving Marshall a little business to keep him afloat. In fact, McGuinn was confident that his disgruntled client would soon return. As Marshall remembered their conversation, McGuinn told him: "Go ahead. You'll fuck it up, and it'll come back to me anyhow."

Marshall's work with John Murphy paid off in more than cash. It brought him closer to the president of the Afro-American Co., John's brother, Carl Murphy. Mister Carl, as he was called in Old West Baltimore, was a tough-minded bantam rooster of a man. He was fluent in German, with a master's degree in the language from Harvard. He came to the paper in 1917 and when his father died five years later took control of the *Afro* at the age of thirty-three.

Mister Carl was an activist editor. He saw no distinction between running the *Afro* and being a key player in the NAACP. A lifelong integrationist, he had been on the board of directors for the national NAACP since 1931, and in 1935 he led the coalition that restarted the Baltimore branch. "I can't remember anytime when I asked Carl for money for legal cases that I didn't get it," Marshall said. "That was when it wasn't so fashionable but Carl always believed."

In 1931 the Baltimore NAACP had only five active members, but the five included Murphy and another dynamic personality, Lillie May Jackson. A driven woman who at a young age had suffered a stroke that paralyzed the right side of her face, Jackson had a shrill voice and no capacity for embarrassment. She regularly harangued city officials, the police, the *Sun*, and the *Afro* about racial discrimination in Baltimore. For years her leading crusade was against the bigoted treatment given black customers in the stores on Pennsylvania Avenue.

Pennsylvania Avenue was the gathering place for Baltimore's black population. Church ladies and teachers as well as gamblers, prostitutes, and bootleggers all watched one another parade along the avenue. The Royal Theater, built in 1921, was a palace of black entertainment. With New York's Apollo and Washington's Howard theaters, the Royal made up the famous black entertainment "Chitlin' Circuit," with regular performances during the 1930s by world-known entertainers such as Fats Waller, Duke Ellington, Count Basie, Louis Armstrong, and the Baltimore native Billie Holiday.

Pennsylvania Avenue, however, also reflected the racial problems of the city. Walter Carr, then a youngster who was a neighbor of the Marshalls in Old West Baltimore, remembered the indignity he felt while on Pennsylvania Avenue: "You were supposed to walk out in the gutter when you saw white folks walking down the street," he said. "My grandmother knocked me in the gutter half a dozen times." [15] The harsh emotional impact of Jim Crow segregation on Pennsylvania Avenue upset Marshall, too: "The only thing different between the South and Baltimore was trolley cars." Many stores on Pennsylvania did not let dark-skinned blacks come in the door; others would sell to blacks but refused to let them try on clothes. Marshall's mother and other blacks had their credit accounts taken away at one point when store owners suddenly insisted that blacks pay up front.

In response to the daily racist practices on Pennsylvania Avenue, Lillie May Jackson, with her daughters, Juanita and Virginia, started a forum to discuss racial and job issues affecting young blacks in Baltimore. It was called the City-Wide Young People's Forum.

One of the biggest complaints at Jackson's forums was that many white store owners in Old West Baltimore refused to hire black workers, but it was not until a religious mystic, Prophet Kiowah Costonie, appeared in Baltimore in June of 1933, that public sentiment was widely stirred to get jobs for black workers in stores patronized by black shoppers.

Costonie was one of many faith healers operating among blacks in big eastern cities during the early thirties. Black people were ripe for any savior. Unemployment and frustration with ongoing oppression in the South resulted in northern neighborhoods crowded with poorly educated blacks. Boston, New York, Philadelphia, and Baltimore all had black cultists promising a better day to people who would attend their meetings.

In Old West Baltimore, Costonie held revivals at which he laid his hands on the sick; newspapers said he supposedly made the deaf hear, the blind see, and cripples walk again. However, Costonie was more than a good tent show revivalist. He began attending the Young People's Forum. With Costonie, often dressed in a turban, drawing the crowds and Lillie Jackson stirring public anger, they began a "Buy Where You Can Work Campaign."[16]

Costonie and Jackson led dozens of people in picketing the stores and had immediate success. Black customers boycotted the stores as Murphy's *Afro* carried headlines that championed the cause. Some white store owners started to lose money and offered to negotiate a settlement.

"The first Saturday that we put the campaign on, we cut their sales off so bad that one store sent a man down from New York to find out what happened," Marshall said later. The NAACP sent Jackson and a young activist named Clarence Mitchell to meet with the man. Marshall went along as the NAACP's lawyer and successfully negotiated a deal in which A & P began training black clerks and store managers.

Not all the stores complied so easily; some owners hired black thugs to beat up the picketers. When Marshall found out that one of the store owners was Jewish, he went to see the man's rabbi. The rabbi promised to speak to the man, but when Marshall returned, the rabbi told him there was nothing he could do. "I'm sorry, I can't do anything. I'm embarrassed. I've never had one of my people in my synagogue talk to me like he did. He told me to go to hell."

The hired toughs attacked some black picketers, including Marshall's wife. He came home one evening to find Buster bruised and crying. She was hurt but announced that she was going to be on the picket line the next day. Marshall sought out one of his clients, Scrappy Brown, and asked him to serve as a bodyguard for Buster and himself. "Scrappy was one of them nice, peaceful guys," Marshall said, laughing. "He carried an ax up the back of his coat."

The campaign ended with mixed results. Some store owners got court injunctions banning picketing in front of the stores. Nevertheless, many businesses on Pennsylvania Avenue began to hire black workers. Murphy, whose *Afro* carried front-page stories about the blacks who were hired, urged Jackson to continue her campaign. He offered financial support and publicity if she could employ her success to revive the city's flagging NAACP branch. With the *Afro* as her booster, Jackson began using the Pennsylvania Avenue boycotts, as well as stories about lynchings on the Eastern Shore of Maryland, to build membership for the local NAACP. In less than a year she enrolled 2,000 members.

Jackson also used Marshall as the local branch's lawyer. She did not pay him but took care to remind Marshall that Mr. Carl might give him more of the *Afro*'s legal work—and fees—if he helped the NAACP. She would call the young lawyer and tell him what she expected and when. At times, Marshall remembered, he would lay the phone down on his desk, continue his other work, and every few minutes shout into the phone: "Yes, Mrs. Jackson. Yes, Mrs. Jackson," as she continued to talk.

But there were times when Jackson and Marshall came close to falling out. "Mrs. Lillie would actually call me up and say, 'I heard a horrible story about my lawyer,'" an exasperated Marshall recalled. "She said that I was drunk at such and such a club. . . . I said, 'I was and I got up there two nights and I got drunk both nights.' She said, 'You're not ashamed of it?' I said, 'Proud of it.'"

Mrs. Jackson also cracked down on Roy Wilkins, Walter White's young assistant from the national office. When Wilkins visited Baltimore he spent time with Marshall drinking at jazz clubs. Jackson complained to Carl Murphy, who sent a letter to New York chastising Wilkins for damaging the organization's image.

Finally Marshall told her his drinking and chain-smoking were none of her business. "Well, look, start paying me some salary and I will think about listening to you. But you don't pay me a goddamn nickel, then you want to run my life. You can't do 'em both."

Despite his bluster Marshall was happiest doing Mrs. Jackson's civil rights work. He was now looking for that one breakthrough case that would make him a leading lawyer. It was coming fast.

CHAPTER 7

❦

Getting Started

Thurgood Marshall decided it was time to take action. He read the *Afro*'s regular stories about the University of Maryland's continuing refusal to take black students with growing disgust. As early as January 1933, the paper reported that blacks were trying to break the Jim Crow admissions policy but had been turned away by white law school officials who declared they were preserving the color line in law school education.

Marshall began to discuss with Charles Houston how to attack the university's ban. At Howard, Marshall had done research for one of his professors, William Hastie, who had tried to get a black student, Thomas Hocutt, admitted into the school of pharmacy at the University of North Carolina. That case failed on a technicality when the black president of North Carolina College, a historically black school, refused to release Hocutt's transcript. The college president said he did not want to integrate the state's university system. Marshall later said Hastie and Houston's theory in the *Hocutt* case was sound; the only reason they lost was because of the school president. "He was a first-class Uncle Tom," Marshall said. Even in defeat Hastie, Houston, and their star pupil were confident that a legal attack against segregation in the graduate schools was the best way to break apart racially separate schools around the country.

In the early 1930s the NAACP had hired Nathan Margold of Harvard, one of Houston's friends, to come up with a legal approach to stop school segregation. Margold wrote that the NAACP should not challenge racial segregation directly but insist that states provide truly equal schools for blacks. His theory was that southern states could not afford to build equal facilities and ultimately would have to admit blacks and whites to the same schools. "I must have read the report at about the time of the *Hocutt* case," Marshall recalled. "It stayed with me. . . . The South would go broke paying for truly equal, dual systems."

With the Margold report in the back of his mind, Marshall now saw his chance to take revenge for the hurt he felt when he discovered his home state law school was closed to him. He had held the anger for years, later saying that the first thing he wanted to do after he got out of Howard was "get even with Maryland for not letting me go to its law school."[1]

When Marshall heard through the Howard grapevine that some lawyers in Washington were thinking about suing the law school, he got upset and wrote to Houston that he wanted to be the first to file suit. He could not bear to allow any other lawyer to take the lead on this case. Working with William Gosnell, another black attorney in Baltimore, Marshall identified a willing plaintiff in December 1934. Donald Gaines Murray was a black student with good grades from a good college. Marshall did not know the twenty-one-year-old Murray, but once he and Gosnell started talking to him, Marshall found out that Murray was related to Uncle Fearless's wife, Aunt Florence. And Murray had attended Lincoln College for two years before transferring to Amherst.

In addition to his good grades from Amherst, Murray had another advantage as a prospective plaintiff. His family was well respected in Baltimore because his grandfather was an African Methodist Episcopal bishop. Murray had been thinking about studying law, and it did not take much for Marshall to convince him to apply to the University of Maryland.

Just as Marshall had anticipated, Maryland turned down Murray's application. University officials suggested he apply to the all-black Princess Anne Academy, part of the state university system. But the academy had no law school. When Murray wrote an angry letter of complaint to the university's board of regents, they replied that he should consider Howard because it was cheaper than Maryland.

Marshall worked long hours on the case with Gosnell and got advice from Houston, who agreed to have the national NAACP finance the suit. Houston later explained that he saw Murray's case as a "springboard for extending the attacks [against racial segregation in the United States] on a larger front."[2] On April 20, 1935, with Marshall acting as his attorney, Murray sued in Baltimore City Court, charging the university with violating the Fourteenth Amendment (giving all Americans equal protection of the laws) by refusing his application.

There was some delay, however, as the state's lawyers tried every trick to keep the case from coming before a judge. Marshall, not wanting to appear combative and keeping with his style of charming the city's white establishment, made no objection to the stalling tactics. Finally, the tough, antiunion judge Eugene O'Dunne confronted Marshall: "Excuse me, Mr. Marshall, do you want to try this case or not?" A stunned Marshall shot up from his seat and said he very much wanted to get going. "Well act like it—say no [to the postponement]!" A newly energized Marshall happily raised his voice to shout out "No," and the judge, now smiling, set the trial date for the next morning.[3]

The case began on June 17, with Marshall and Houston sitting next to Murray in the courtroom. The three black men all wore their best clothes, double-breasted wool suits with handkerchiefs in the breast pockets and stiff white shirts underneath. Marshall had to ask the court to admit Houston to the Maryland Bar [he was a Washington lawyer], and Judge O'Dunne joked that it was funny seeing the student asking that his law school dean be allowed to speak to the court.[4]

As the case started, Maryland's assistant attorney general Charles T. LeViness III declared that the university provided "substantially similar educational facilities for Negroes" at the Princess Anne Academy. LeViness also told the judge that the state provided money to black students who wanted to go to school outside Maryland if there were no state schools open to blacks.

Marshall stood to argue for Murray and cited a 1927 Supreme Court case, *Gong Lum v. Rice*, in which a Chinese girl in Mississippi sued to gain admission to a white school. The Court ruled against her because schools for colored and Chinese children were available in Mississippi. But in Maryland, Marshall argued, there was no state law school for blacks. In addition, Murray could not go to an out-of-state school because no law school in the country could equal the University of Maryland at teaching the laws of Baltimore and Maryland.

The next day, in startling fashion, Judge O'Dunne ruled in Murray's favor. The university appealed but lost. The speed and completeness of the victory surprised Marshall. The young lawyer had expected a longer fight. He had even planned what to do when he lost—he was going to appeal the case to the Supreme Court. "Well, we won," he said, "and in Maryland. And that wasn't easy."

The *Baltimore Evening Sun*'s witty social critic, the columnist H. L. Mencken, wrote that while he did not support mixing black and white children in Baltimore's public schools, he had no problem with Murray studying law with whites as "an Ethiop among the Aryans." Mencken said law students were not children and neither were they "adolescents going through the ordinary college mill and eager only to dance [and] neck." He said they were in school to learn and to join an honorable profession. "To think of [the white students] as crackers hugging idiotically their more fortuitous whiteness is to say at once that they are unfit to be admitted to the bar of any civilized state," he wrote.[5]

The victory made history, and it gave Marshall a rush of pleasure at having defeated the law school that had deemed itself too good for any black, including him. Long after Marshall had beaten his personal dragon, he still crowed about getting "even" with the university.

As the reality of what had happened in the Maryland case took hold and word spread to other cities, the NAACP's national office realized that something special, even magical, had happened in Baltimore. And inevitably they tied the victory to the local branch's young attorney. Marshall was now a rising star to people outside of Maryland.

But Marshall still had to leap two more hurdles to get Murray into the law school. First, Murray could not afford to pay the tuition, and attempts to raise enough money in Baltimore were unsuccessful. At Marshall's insistence Houston wrote to Walter White, the NAACP's executive secretary. Houston said if Murray did not go to the school, the case would "become moot and you can see [what] that would do to our plans and programs."[6] The NAACP's national office and the *Afro*'s Carl Murphy came to the rescue. The NAACP handed tuition money for the first semester to Carl Murphy, figuring that young Donald Murray was more likely to repay Mister Carl, the local legend, than a big organization based in distant New York.

Within a year Carl Murphy began hammering the family to repay the money, asking Murray's sister, Margery Prout, a schoolteacher, to make monthly payments. Prout later said she felt threatened, even "blackmailed" by Murphy's incessant demands for the money and the possibility that he would print critical remarks about her family's debt in the *Afro-American*. Yet, from the NAACP's point of view, the repayment was necessary to allow the group to fund other civil rights activities.[7]

There was still one other hurdle for Marshall to overcome to get Murray into school. When Marshall accompanied Murray to the law school in September, the dean suggested that Murray not sit next to white students. Marshall walked around the campus until he found two white students who agreed to tell the dean they had no problem sitting next to Murray. After Murray's first week of school in October, the *Afro* reported that "classmates were exceedingly cordial and so were professors."[8]

In the summer of 1935, while Marshall was busy protecting Murray, Lillie May Jackson and Carl Murphy began looking for a student to test segregation on the secondary school level. The *Afro* had long written tear-jerking stories about Baltimore County, where there was no high school for blacks. A black child who wanted to go to high school had to travel an average of ten miles to reach Baltimore's segregated Douglass High.

Jackson and Murphy wanted a black high school built in the county. Stirred by their lawyer's unexpected success in the courtroom, they decided to file suit against the county school board. Murphy put up money for Marshall and another young lawyer, Robert McGuinn (Warner McGuinn's nephew), to travel through Baltimore County, charting a map for the NAACP showing the condition of black elementary schools and comparing them with the nearest white schools. Marshall figured that McGuinn could get into the white school buildings because "he look[ed] enough like our white brethren." Carl Murphy's *Afro* published the results of Marshall and McGuinn's trip, reporting that the two found black schools "falling down, [with] tottering roofs, rotten floors."[9]

Houston had taken a leave of absence from Howard Law School to become the NAACP's lawyer at its headquarters. With prompting from Carl Murphy, who was a member of the national NAACP's board, Houston used his new position to get the NAACP to finance a suit against Baltimore County schools. The law school dean successfully argued that the legal work being done in Maryland was a laboratory for developing techniques the NAACP could later use to fight segregation laws across the nation.

In March 1936, Marshall filed a suit that hit Catonsville High School like buckshot. He sued the principal, David W. Zimmerman, and the county superintendent as well as the entire Baltimore County School Board. Even though the suit asked that Margaret Williams, thirteen, be admitted to all-white Catonsville High, the real goal was to get the county to build a high school for black children. By threatening to force black students into the all-white school, Marshall hoped to give the county no choice but to do what Carl Murphy and the NAACP had been pressing for—construction of a separate, equal black high school. Trying to win support from white parents, Houston suggested to Marshall that black parents contact white newspapers to stress that they had no interest in integration but only better schools for black kids.

The case went to trial in September with Marshall as the lead attorney, supported by one of his former law professors, Leon Andrew Ransom. Edward Lovett, a lawyer in Houston's Washington law firm, and Oliver Hill, Marshall's classmate from Howard, rounded out the team.

In court the school board's lawyers treated Marshall with no respect. He wrote to Houston that his adversaries were "exceptionally mean, nasty and arrogant."[10] But Marshall kept to his style of always being the helpful black man in the courtroom, never threatening in his manner to a judge or opposing lawyers. At one critical moment in the trial he stood up to lend a hand to his rude legal opponents: "They did not cite a single case other than the *Gong Lum* case, and we had to tell them the citation of that case."

Even with Marshall helping them, the board's lawyers "injected prejudice" into the case by arguing that admitting a black girl to a white high school would "break down the traits of the state of Maryland."[11] This was the first time Marshall had seen lawyers argue that the essence of southern tradition was to keep blacks on the bottom of the social caste system. He was genuinely hurt. At heart he wanted to be a part of the Maryland establishment. Yet here were educated white people arguing before him in a court of law that all of southern life boiled down to making sure that black people never got above their desperate slave past.

Judge Frank Duncan refused even to consider Marshall's argument that the county's schools were separate but unequal in quality at the elementary level. And he would not consider the absence of a high school for blacks as evidence of racial inequality. The judge limited his rulings to a simple review of whether the plaintiff, Margaret Williams, had passed a qualifying test to get into Douglass High, which she had not. The narrow ruling left little on the record for an appellate court to consider. There was no ruling on the issue of whether schools for black children were inadequate or the wider issue of school segregation. Marshall and Houston decided that an appeal was futile.

Despite the defeat in the Williams case, the NAACP's national office was pleased with Marshall's work. Walter White, the executive director, gained new respect for Marshall and began using him as the NAACP's point man in Washington in a highly publicized crusade to stop lynching. White made passage of federal antilynching legislation the civil rights group's major goal. A 1936 NAACP flyer claimed that 5,105 people were lynched in the United States between 1882 and 1936.

Marshall was well aware of the barbaric act of angry whites lynching blacks, usually in small southern towns. In 1933 Maryland's black activists had been shaken by a notorious lynching in Princess Anne. After a retarded black man had grabbed at a white woman and torn her dress, 5,000 whites had burned the man alive in the courthouse square.

Marshall began to lobby Maryland's senators and representatives. Marshall was ideal for approaching Maryland congressmen. He was a charmer who got along well with whites, and he knew the law. Most important, however, he was persistent. Marshall was already known as a man who would not be brushed aside or intimidated by anyone, including members of Congress.

Marshall wrote a letter to Millard Tydings, a Maryland Democrat, to say NAACP chief Walter White had informed him that the senator had not taken a stand in support of a bill to stop lynchings. "This was indeed as much of a shock to me as I am sure it will be to many of your constituents when they become aware of the fact," he wrote.[12] Senator Tydings replied that he was concerned that states retain the right to handle their own local crimes. It was a transparent political move. Tydings was really worried that whites in Maryland's southern counties would not back him in the next election if he had voted for any bill protecting blacks.

Not wanting to alienate either his liberal or his conservative constituents, Tydings scheduled a long trip to the Virgin Islands to avoid having to take a stand on the antilynching bill. When Marshall found out about the planned trip, he sent an urgent, angry telegram to the senator: "Understand you insist on going to Virgin Islands for last two or three months of Congress despite fact you were absent from early part of session. May we urge you to remain in Washington as our representative until bills of such vital importance as the anti-lynching bill are disposed of?" Tydings gave an angry retort in another telegram: "Please couch your telegrams in the future in more genteel language if you want them answered."[13] Nonetheless, the senator canceled his trip.

White also got Marshall, in his capacity as secretary of the National Bar Association, to write President Roosevelt, urging the White House to flex its muscle in the fight to ban lynchings. Charles Houston, too, wrote the president, asking Roosevelt to speak out against delays in the Senate vote. Roosevelt did nothing.

"We couldn't get a damned thing through Congress," Marshall said later. "You can't name one bill that passed in the Roosevelt administration for Negroes. Nothing. We couldn't even get the anti-lynch bill through. So you had to go to the courts."

While he was increasingly engaged in NAACP work, Marshall's law practice in Baltimore was sinking. He had small cases, but even when he won he had to wait forever to get paid. Although most clients were pleased with the legal work he did, all were not. One black woman filed a complaint with the local bar association charging that Marshall had not earned the twenty-five dollars he charged to represent her in a divorce case. The complaint went before the city's all-white bar, which ruled in Marshall's favor. "The judgment of the committee was that she owed me one hundred more dollars," Marshall said. "And they made her pay it, too."

Marshall's work for the NAACP and his rising profile on the pages of the *Afro* led to a small movement to get him to run for the House of Representatives. Having been on his own for a while now, Marshall was starting to see the advantages of working with other people. When an independent party asked him to consider a run for Congress in 1936, he was flattered and seriously interested. At the time there was only one black in Congress, Arthur Mitchell, an Illinois Democrat.

"The gang that has been trying to get me to run for Congress has just left the office," Marshall wrote to Houston in New York in January 1936. "The fellow whom I thought was a communist has turned out not to be. . . . I am going to talk the matter over with Carl Murphy tomorrow. I have not decided finally as yet and want you to advise me once and for all as to just what you think is best." [14]

Houston advised Marshall in a telegram to accept the nomination and run for Congress but "avoid communism and personal expense." [15] Marshall was not strongly anti-Communist. Living through the Depression led him to be curious about their efforts to build unions in Baltimore, and their outspoken sympathy for the working class, specifically black people. When Marshall had represented Bernard Ades, the Communist

lawyer, he'd never voiced objection to Ade's ideology—just to his courtroom antics.

While Houston gave Marshall the okay on a run for Congress as an
independent, Murphy apparently was not so supportive. A staunch capi-
talist and small businessman, Mr. Carl told Marshall it was a waste of
time to get involved with the left-wing economic crowd when he needed
to build his law practice. Marshall decided against running.

However, he was still in the market for a steady paycheck and looking
to get more work from the NAACP. He was no longer the young maverick, out to prove he could make it on his own. He even asked Leon Ransom, who was teaching at Howard Law, about getting a teaching job at
his alma mater. In April of 1936 Ransom wrote to Marshall, in a letter
warmly addressed "Dear No-Good," that there would be two openings
for the next school year. He offered a recommendation, as did Houston.
But faculty politics, including a faction that resented Houston and saw
Marshall as his protégé, put an end to any chance of Marshall joining the
teaching staff.

By late May 1936 Marshall's law practice was in serious trouble. He
got letters from Prentice-Hall publishing company, complaining that he
was six months late in paying his bill for law books. Sinking in debt, the
persistent Marshall repeatedly tried to convince Houston to hire him.
"The real problem mostly pertains to me," Marshall wrote to Houston in
New York. "As it stands things are getting worse and worse. . . . If there
is a possibility I would appreciate it very much if I could be assured of
enough to tide me over, then in return, I could do more on [NAACP]
cases. For example, to prepare briefs and research, etc. . . . [on] the legal
matters which you would need assistance on." [16]

Marshall was under severe pressure to bring money home. Aubrey
had been unable to work regularly as a doctor for a few months because
of a bad cold. And to make matters worse, Thurgood's father had lost his
job at the Gibson Island Club. Willie's prickly personality had gotten
him into a loud dispute with a white staff person at the club, which ended
with Willie out of work.

"He ran it all until he got in the way of somebody who was white,"
the son recalled later. "I mean after all, a Negro steward is a little high,
you know, for a Negro." Willie Marshall subsequently got a job at the
Afro-American, with Thurgood's help, but that job didn't last long. "He
was on the newspaper a month or so," Marshall said, thinking back to

that time. "I mean he had a low boiling point, man. He'd quit at the drop of a hat for nothing."

Unlike his father, the shrewd young lawyer did not blow his cool over his difficulty with people or jobs. He waited and planned, looking for the right moment to push for a contract with the national NAACP. That effort got a boost in the summer of 1936, when the NAACP held its twenty-seventh annual conference in Baltimore. During the weeklong conference he dined nightly with Houston, Walter White, and Roy Wilkins. Best of all, Carl Murphy arranged for Marshall to give a major speech on disparities between the education of black and white children. White was impressed with Marshall's forceful yet down-home and personal speech. In addition, Marshall benefited from the afterglow of the conference because a record number of new members signed up, and money poured into the NAACP national treasury.

"It was one of the greatest conferences in the history of the association," Wilkins wrote to Marshall just after the convention. "The success of the Baltimore conference was due in no small measure to your assistance on the program." [17]

Houston used the upbeat feelings generated by the conference to press White for help in handling the NAACP's legal affairs; specifically he wanted White to go to the board and ask them to hire Thurgood Marshall. Houston spent most of his time on the road as an "evangelist and stump speaker," raising money for the NAACP. He felt there was a need for someone to take care of the daily legal affairs in the office. White agreed.

"I don't know of anybody I would rather have in the office or anybody who can do a better job of research and preparation of cases," Houston wrote to Marshall. But he insisted that Marshall close his Baltimore law practice. "It simply isn't possible to do two independent jobs to full satisfaction. . . . You would be of more value to the Association at $200 in New York than at $150 in Baltimore." [18]

Marshall did not take long to come to Houston's point of view when he looked at his law practice's lack of profits. And he realized that without Houston's guidance and the NAACP's treasury, he might never get to do the work of breaking down segregation—the work he really wanted to do. In an October 1936 letter agreeing to take a six-month assignment with the NAACP, Marshall wrote to White: "I will be indebted to you and Charlie for a long time to come for many reasons, one of which is that I have an opportunity now to do what I have always dreamed of doing!"[19]

Despite the thrill of getting the big job he coveted, Marshall was torn about leaving Baltimore. The family house on Druid Hill was in turmoil. His mother would never stop him from leaving for the job in New York, but Marshall worried that the family was on the verge of exploding.

CHAPTER 8

Leaving Home

JUST AS BUSTER AND THURGOOD were about to leave Baltimore in
October 1936, all hell broke loose.

Aubrey's lingering cold had gotten worse. Thurgood could hear his
hacking and coughing through the night. His older brother looked frail
and was missing more and more work. His body, as well as his stylish
dress, began to deteriorate. Sadie, his wife, started to shun him, pushing
her husband out of their bed. Aubrey was left to the care of his mother
and father.

Willie Marshall had his own troubles. He was still out of work and
bitter about it. That led to more drinking and more fights with his wife.
And when Sadie and her mother were around, Willie blasted them over
their callous treatment of Aubrey.

Thurgood and Buster tried to support the family as best they could.
But when the job offer came from the NAACP in New York, they did not
know what to do. Norma Marshall, however, did not hesitate. She was
steadfast in her ambition for Thurgood, and told him it was time for him
to go. She even made plans for him and Buster to stay with her sister,
Medi.

Thurgood was still not sure he should go; he felt obligated to his family. Torn between ambition and emotion, he reluctantly decided that
New York wasn't that far away. He began to make plans to close his office
when the family was hit with a jolt. Aubrey's watery eyes and hacking
cough turned out to be tuberculosis.

The once debonair Dr. Aubrey Marshall was totally crushed by the news. As a physician he realized how far developed the potentially fatal disease was in his body and feared he was about to die. The highly contagious nature of the illness forced him to close his medical practice.

Aubrey had no idea where he had contracted TB, but his work had clearly exposed him to a number of people who had it. Both in his office and at the city health clinic in Old West Baltimore, he had tended to patients from areas where the poor were forced to crowd together in alleys littered with open bags of garbage, scrawny stray dogs, and rats. Thirty years earlier the disease had reached epidemic proportions in urban areas throughout the nation. By the mid-1930s it was slowing, but its victims were still a common part of the American scene.

Now that Aubrey was identified as a TB carrier, his wife would not even come close to him. Even worse, Sadie refused to let him within sight of his only child. Norma Marshall and Sadie got into furious arguments over Sadie's unsympathetic attitude. Norma wanted her son at home, with family, where someone would always be with him. But Sadie, fearing for her own well-being, wanted Aubrey out of the house and in a hospital.

"My mother said he had to go because she didn't want him breathing germs around me," Aubrey Jr. said as an adult.[1] The argument between the two women climaxed when Sadie, her mother, and Aubrey Jr. packed their belongings and without a word moved out of the house. Aubrey, already sick and now depressed, was left at home with his mother and father and in need of medical care. The best TB hospitals in Maryland, however, admitted only whites.

Still, Norma Marshall, with tears in her eyes, told Thurgood and Buster that her troubles should not be their troubles. With a plainspoken approach, she said Thurgood's future was in New York and the family owed him as much support as they were giving Aubrey. After she coached Uncle Fearless, Norma brought him in to tell Thurgood that staying in a failing law practice wasn't going to help Aubrey or anyone else.

Thurgood and Buster made the move to New York in October 1936, and began living with the Dodsons (Aunt Medi and Uncle Boots). They were in the same Harlem apartment that Thurgood had lived in as an infant when his father had worked on the New York Central with Boots. The apartment seemed uncrowded and quiet in comparison with the coughing, the fighting, and the crying baby that had filled their home in Baltimore. Thurgood had little memory of his childhood days in

Harlem, but he immediately took to the bustling, big city atmosphere. He had no money and few friends outside the NAACP's offices, but just walking around was a kick for him. He and Buster spent most of their time playing cards with the Dodsons, who were in their late fifties and loved the young couple's energy.

When his mother wrote or on rare occasions called, Thurgood would hear about Aubrey's declining health and the segregated hospitals in Maryland. Norma asked if he could find a good hospital in New York that accepted blacks. "I got him in Bellevue Hospital in New York, where he had an operation to take that lung out," Marshall later recalled. Aubrey also lost half his other lung, leaving him with only half a lung and labored breathing. Aunt Medi, Thurgood, and Buster made frequent visits to the hospital to see him. Thurgood was religious about spending Monday nights visiting his brother.

Aubrey's medical bills, especially for the operation, were a heavy financial burden on Norma. Willie brought money into the house only now and then; his drinking made it difficult for him to find a good-paying job. The family's only steady paycheck these days came from Norma's teaching job. It was the key to what remained of the family's ebbing stability. That job, so crucial to the family, did not come about just because of Norma's intelligence and warmth with children. She had to veil her considerable pride to ask for the job from black Baltimore's political boss, Tom Smith.

A heavyset man who wore only tailored suits and drove a big black car, Smith had earned a small fortune running an illegal numbers game, with backing from white racketeers, out of a small saloon on Jasper Street before he built the grand Smith Hotel in 1912. But he had really made his name in the late 1920s, when he allegedly stole ballot boxes from black precincts that were strongly Republican. With those votes out of the way, Howard Jackson was able to beat his Republican mayoral opponent, and Tom Smith became the king of Baltimore black politics.

And Smith held the key to full-time work in the city's black schools. Essie Hughes, one of Thurgood's classmates, recalled: "Any black person who wanted an outstanding job, even in teaching, had to consult Tom Smith."[2]

"I don't think you will ever see another black with such extensive power in Baltimore," said Teddy Stewart, one of the Marshalls' neighbors. "Yes sir, he was a giant. If you wanted to run an illegal business—liquor, gambling, or prostitution, you had to see Tom Smith. He kept his hotel open during Prohibition. All the whites would come to Smith's Hotel because the policemen were taking money from Smith and they would be standing at the door, nobody bothered, didn't care."[3]

"He controlled everything in the district," said Cab Calloway, who recalled that gambling at Smith's began around 8:00 P.M. and lasted into the early morning, with many patrons dressed in tuxedos. "It was the only spot to be," said Calloway. "It was elite."[4]

To see Tom Smith about a teaching job, Norma Marshall had to go into the Smith Hotel. The short man with the shiny bald head would sit in the lobby on a lounge chair, watching over the characters and businessmen who flowed through the hotel's ornate front doors. Not only did he know everyone in Old West Baltimore, but he made it a point to keep up with neighborhood gossip. So Smith likely knew Norma Marshall the minute she put her head in the hotel. And he no doubt knew about her husband's drinking problems, his difficulty keeping jobs, Thurgood's departure for New York, and the family's money troubles.

Norma Marshall always walked with an erect posture, head held high. One look at her told children and adults that she was a dignified woman with no tolerance for fools, chicanery, or political players. But a humble Norma walked over to Smith and waited until he spoke to her. In the swirl of painted women and cigar smoke, she introduced herself. Smith listened politely as she pleaded with him for a full-time job in the city schools.

Smith liked her daring approach and pride. He took to Norma. He decided he wanted her loyalty and friendship. After all he was a politician, and he understood that the black schools were beloved in Old West Baltimore. If he didn't keep the schools filled with good teachers, it could cause problems for him. Soon after her trip to the hotel, Norma got a call telling her where to go downtown to get a full-time teaching assignment for the coming year.[5]

Even with the job she had long coveted, Norma was still scraping by. She was paying every extra cent she had to the hospitals and doctors who cared for her Aubrey. After a long recuperation from the surgery on his lungs, Aubrey was moved to a sanitarium in Saranac, New York.

Norma's struggle to pay her bills was common for the black middle class in Baltimore. She was lucky to have such a good job, but a black teacher made substantially less than a white teacher, sometimes as much as 40 percent less. Carl Murphy's *Afro-American* had long complained about this disparity. But black teachers were reluctant to risk their jobs by putting their names on a lawsuit challenging racially separate pay scales, especially during the Depression.

Thurgood Marshall knew about the difference between the pay that went to white teachers and the money his mother brought home every week. Just as he had been angered by the segregation at the University of Maryland Law School, he took it personally that his mother's work was valued less than a white teacher's. Even though he had moved to New York, Marshall frequently traveled back to Maryland, seeking black teachers to act as plaintiffs for NAACP suits against school boards to equalize teachers' pay.

The white leaders of the school systems were aware of Marshall's efforts and began taking steps to block a repeat of his victory in the *Murray* case. They intimidated or bought off several black teachers rumored to be involved in NAACP suits.

Marshall could have asked his mother to volunteer to have her name on a pay equity suit. But she worked in Baltimore city schools, which did not have as large a difference in pay as the state's rural counties. In any case, she could not risk losing her job, and her son never put her in the awkward position of having to say yes or no.

He did finally find someone willing to take the gamble. William Gibbs, a principal in Montgomery County, allowed Marshall to use his name. White school officials in Montgomery had not engaged in the tactics used by some of the more southern Maryland counties to scare black teachers. Instead, county officials decided it would be better to avoid a lengthy trial. They had no interest in having Marshall lay out the inequality between school facilities for black and white children as part of his case. Before the July 1937 court date, Marshall won an out-of-court settlement in which Montgomery County agreed to a two-year plan for equalizing the pay between black and white teachers.

"The NAACP won a sudden and sensational victory in its suit to equalize teacher salaries in Montgomery County, Md.," the *Afro-American* reported.[6] The fight was not over quite yet, though.

Several months later, when Marshall traveled from New York to Annapolis, Maryland's state capital, to deal with a similar suit that black school principal Walter Mills had filed against the Anne Arundel County school system, he ran into a fire wall of opposition from the white superintendent, George Fox. In Fox's opinion Montgomery County had caved in, and he decided that he would make a stand. He wanted the case to go to trial and was sure that he could defeat the NAACP and their brash young attorney, Thurgood Marshall.

Superintendent Fox argued in court that "his poorest white teacher was a better teacher than his best colored teacher." An astounded Marshall did not respond to Fox's insult. Instead he adopted a strategy of revealing Fox to be no judge of teaching talent and a simple racist. Marshall asked the superintendent why black teachers, and not white teachers, had to scrub classroom floors. The now indignant Fox testified with a vicious scowl "this had always been blacks' work."[7] Marshall took his seat. It was risky, but Marshall in his charming, deferential way was trying to separate the white judge from the white superintendent by exposing Fox as a hateful buffoon.

The strategy worked. Judge W. Calvin Chesnut ruled for the black teachers. "The crucial question in this case," he wrote in his decision, "is whether the very substantial differential between the salaries of white and colored teachers in Anne Arundel County is due to discrimination on account of race or color. I find as a fact from the testimony that it is."[8]

The governor and the Maryland legislature took grudging note of Marshall's winning streak on the equal pay issue and decided it would cost them money and time to continue this losing fight from county to county. The state passed a law setting a single standard for black and white teachers.

With his victory in Maryland, Marshall began to pursue equal pay cases in other states. He won most. But a few years later he lost a teacher pay case dealing with the Norfolk, Virginia, school system. Nonetheless, a federal appeals court overturned that decision. Norfolk's all-white school board appealed to the Supreme Court. It was the first time a teachers' pay case had risen to that level. The Supreme Court ruled by refusing to hear Norfolk's appeal, effectively handing a golden victory to Marshall and the black teachers. After the Norfolk ruling was let stand, the NAACP used it as a precedent to insist on the ending of two pay scales for black and white teachers around the country.

That victory was a personal one for Marshall. The NAACP trumpeted the high court's ruling as a triumph against racism and an endorsement of the dignity and ability of black teachers. But for the young lawyer behind the lawsuits, it was a victory for his mother and for the regular paycheck his family needed so badly.

With that win behind him, a more secure Marshall began to settle into his work in the national office. The family turmoil that had almost kept him out of New York was now past. His brother was recuperating and was going to live. He and Buster were settled in the city. And the newly confident young lawyer from Baltimore was ready to take on some racial fights that went beyond his mother and Maryland. He was about to redefine America.

CHAPTER 9

✤

69 Fifth Avenue

Right from the start, Marshall was thrilled just to be in NAACP headquarters, at 69 Fifth Avenue in New York. He shared a tiny, second-floor office with Houston, but to Marshall it felt like he was at the center of the world.

He was twenty-eight years old and happy—happy to talk to the janitor, share cigarettes with the secretaries, and let his loud laugh ring through the offices when he told jokes. By the end of most days his shirttail was hanging out and his tie was loose.

He made quite a contrast to the forty-one-year-old Houston. Cement Pants was still the reserved, formal man he had been as a dean at Howard. He came in early, always in freshly pressed suits and heavily starched shirts. He almost never smiled, and when he spoke he addressed everyone as "Mr." or "Mrs." To the secretaries and even the NAACP board members, he was a taskmaster who insisted that every detail, every word, and every letter be perfect.

But Houston and Marshall, an odd couple to everyone who watched them in the office, had become a perfect pair. They had known each other for six years by now, and Houston was constantly impressed with Marshall's ability to handle the most difficult tasks. Houston had even developed a delight in Marshall's antics—his large hands moving as he told stories that usually ended with his big voice booming out in laughter. Marshall, for his part, still had eyes filled with awe for his former dean and saw the opportunity to work with him as the chance to play with the biggest of the big boys. He was eager to learn and willing to live within the small budget Houston had to run the office.

Tearing down the walls of legal segregation was a mountain of a task. There were very few black lawyers in the country, little money to pay them, and in some areas of the South their work on civil rights cases could get them run out of business if not thrown out of town. Given that daunting challenge, Houston had taken the job as the NAACP's lawyer with the idea of enlisting the best and bravest of the black lawyers around the country to form a legal assault team. "This is no star performance," Houston wrote to Marshall and other black lawyers who were working on NAACP cases. "[I want to] make the movement self-perpetuating so that no loss of the head or any set of members will hamper progress."[1]

Houston's plan, based on Margold's blueprint, was to have NAACP lawyers around the country file suits demanding separate and equal facilities for blacks. He expected that whites would not be able to pay to equalize the schools and judges would be forced to end segregation.

When Marshall arrived in October 1936, the NAACP was just blossoming into a major organization. At twenty-six years old, the group had gone through an infancy in which it was nurtured by mostly white social workers and liberal activists to fight lynching. Slowly it had flowered into the premier agency for battling Jim Crow discrimination. And with W.E.B. Du Bois editing *The Crisis*, the NAACP's magazine, the group's name had become a siren call to action for people willing to stand together to fight racism. Just joining the NAACP was an act of defiance for blacks in the South. And among intellectuals and activists in the North, association meetings had become the center for all strategy and organizing discussions about race in America.

Even as it grew, however, the NAACP remained heavily dependent on white philanthropists. The legal department's money came from Charles Garland, a back-to-the-earth advocate who had inherited his fortune and decided to ease the guilt over his good luck by giving most of it away. The legal department's budget during Marshall's first year at the headquarters was only $10,000. Charles Houston was paid $4,000 annually, and after travel and legal expenses there was only $2,400 left for Marshall's salary.

Although he was low on money, Marshall felt rich with the excitement of his new job. Buster, by contrast, not only didn't have any money but she had to get used to a new city and living with a new set of relatives.

A few weeks after their move to New York, Aunt Medi found Buster and Thurgood an inexpensive room on 149th Street. Near their new Harlem apartment Marshall soon ran into an old Lincoln University buddy, Monroe Dowling. The prideful, ambitious Dowling had a reputation for being a great card player because of his ability as a mathematician. When he ran into Marshall he was working as an accountant for New York State after having earned his master's degree in business from Harvard. His wife, Helen, quickly became best friends with Buster, and on most nights the couples ate dinner at the Dowlings' place, played cards, and drank.[2]

Dowling frequently got bootleg liquor from underworld friends. After leaving Harvard, he had become the accountant for one of Harlem's biggest illegal numbers operators. That led to friendships with people who had easy access to whiskey. Marshall and Dowling, both proud and well educated, had a close relationship, although Dowling had little tolerance for Marshall's antics and his grand stories. "Every once in a while he'd say something and we'd disagree about it," Dowling said. "I'd say, 'Thurgood, you know damn good and well that's a lie,' and he'd acknowledge it and say, 'You have to lie sometimes.' "

At the NAACP offices, with Houston often gone on trips, Marshall was left within earshot of Walter White. The ebullient and energetic NAACP leader began enlisting Marshall in a more extensive role in the antilynching campaign. He had him track antilynching legislation and lobby congressmen.

The NAACP was accustomed to a hostile reception in Washington. The capital was a southern town, and the association was viewed as a radical northern group that stirred up trouble. In the 1930s segregationist Democrats in the House had even passed a bill to erect a monument honoring Confederate President Jefferson Davis. It was going to be difficult for a young black lawyer to make much of a difference with legislators in that atmosphere.

In a summary prepared on the status of the antilynching bill in April 1937, Marshall wrote that House Judiciary Committee Chairman Hatton W. Sumners had "boasted for more than four years that he would not report favorably any anti-lynching bill."[3] But Marshall persisted. He began to work around Sumners by lobbying other congressmen for a tough "NAACP" bill to halt lynchings.

Ironically, the lone black member of the House, Rep. Arthur Mitchell, proposed a different bill. His bill was not as strong as the

NAACP's proposal for punishing people who took part in mob action. Charles Houston denounced it as impotent and ineffective. Mitchell dismissed Houston's statements and claimed that the NAACP was "not seeking to aid the race but intend[ing] only to feather the nest of its officials at the expense of the black public." He condemned the NAACP as a dishonest group, which "had deteriorated into a bunch of communists."[4]

Marshall had spent several weeks in Washington working to gain support for the NAACP's bill. Surprisingly, Mitchell's bill was defeated, and thanks to Marshall's diligent work the stronger NAACP proposal passed in the House. But the Senate version of the bill died without a vote. Marshall, Houston, and White were left empty-handed for all their efforts. Still, the NAACP had raised the issue to national prominence and put pressure on federal and state officials to stop lynchings.

In addition to going to Washington, Marshall also started traveling the South for the NAACP. Going to local NAACP chapters, Marshall sought out cases dealing with schools, voting rights, and situations where blacks were unfairly charged with crimes. Marshall's memos to the New York office on his travels were revealing, sometimes even comic. In a memo from South Boston, Virginia, he wrote: "School situation is terrible. Principal of elementary school is gardener and janitor for the county superintendent of schools and is a typical Uncle Tom."[5]

While Marshall took on more responsibility, Houston spent his time on major cases in Tennessee and Missouri. In Tennessee a black student was trying to get into the state's College of Pharmacy. With no pharmacy school for blacks in the state, Houston argued that the white school had to integrate. But the court ruled against him. Tennessee officials claimed a historically black school, Tennessee A & I, was equal to the University of Tennessee and could begin a pharmacy program. "This case means nothing in 1937," Houston told a newspaper reporter. "But in 2000 A.D. somebody will look back on the record and wonder why the South spent so much money in keeping rights from Negroes rather than granting them."[6]

Houston had more success in Missouri. It had no historically black colleges with professional programs to use as a veil. Houston decided that the state was the perfect target for a suit. He got a black college graduate, Lloyd Gaines, to apply to the state law school.

Houston viewed the Missouri suit as key to the NAACP effort to desegregate schools nationwide. He was laying the groundwork for the argument that if no separate but equal schools existed for black students, there was no option but integration. "I firmly believe the Missouri case is going to set the pace for Negro professional and graduate education for the next generation," he wrote in a letter to another lawyer, apparently expecting that this case would end with a victory for integration at the postgraduate level.[7] But the case proved to be more difficult than Houston had anticipated. He lost on the local level and had to go to an appeals court.

The case finally worked its way up to the Supreme Court in December of 1938. In a surprise victory the Court ruled that the University of Missouri had to admit the twenty-eight-year-old Gaines to its law school. Houston had successfully used the *Murray* case in Maryland to persuade the high court that Gaines had a right to attend Missouri's law school. But while the *Murray* case had had impact only in Maryland, the Supreme Court's ruling in the Missouri case was felt nationwide.

"I have been given the right to enter Missouri University in September," the wiry, chain-smoking Gaines said in a speech at a St. Louis YMCA in January of 1939. "And I have every expectation of exercising that privilege."[8]

Missouri did not accept defeat easily. In early 1939 officials built a new, Jim Crow law school at historically black Lincoln University in Jefferson City. The state then claimed that with separate and equal facilities available to Gaines, there was no need to admit him to the University of Missouri. The NAACP lawyers rushed to state court to argue that Gaines should be admitted to the university because the new school was not ready to open. After a lower court disagreed, the Missouri State Supreme Court ruled in favor of the NAACP.

Marshall, celebrating the small victory, wrote to Houston in Washington congratulating him: "I turned the opinion over to leader Wilkins who promised a riproaring press release which can be summed up in the words of the master Joe Louis, 'I glad I winned.' "[9]

Meanwhile, Missouri politicians were still trying to put together a new school for blacks before September. Houston and Marshall got sidetracked, however. Their client, Gaines, wanted the NAACP to treat him like a star. He wanted adulation and stroking from fellow students, from his friends, the press, and anyone else who dared to speak to him. At the same time he complained that he was under pressure from all the attention that came to him because he was the NAACP's client in a case that was attracting national attention.

To quiet his constant carping the NAACP lent Gaines money so he could get a master's degree in economics from the University of Michigan while the Missouri case worked its way through the courts. If Gaines threw in the towel, the association would have to go back to the start with a new plaintiff, spending more time and money on the same case.

While Gaines was throwing tantrums, Houston continued working closely with Marshall on new arguments to thwart Missouri's attempts to circumvent the Supreme Court's ruling. Even if the new black law school were opened in time, the NAACP lawyers planned to contend that it could not be the equal of the ninety-year-old University of Missouri law school.

But no matter what their strategy might be, the NAACP had to have Gaines appear in court. By the first day of school, however, their client was nowhere to be found. The NAACP was unable to proceed with the case. In October newspapers around the country began running headlines about the missing law student. The *Baltimore Afro-American* said Gaines was not missing but had stopped cooperating with the NAACP because they would not give him more money: "The association in refusing [to pay Gaines] said that it was not marrying him but defending him in court," the editorial said. "With Gaines gone, however, it might have proved cheaper for the NAACP to marry him."

An *Afro* columnist, Louis Lautier, suggested Gaines could have been bribed or killed. Walter White agreed with the suggestion of bribery. He heard Gaines had sent a postcard from Mexico to a friend and was having "a jolly time on the $2,000" he had been given to leave the country.[10]

The last undisputed word from Gaines came in a letter to his mother written in March 1939, well before it was known that he was missing. He wrote from Chicago to say that people were glad to pat him on the back and say pleasant things about his contribution to civil rights history but not much more. "Out of the confines of the publicity columns I am just a man—not one who has fought and sacrificed to make the case possible; one who is still fighting and sacrificing—almost the 'supreme sacrifice' to see that it is a complete and lasting success for 13 million Negroes—no!—just another man. Sometimes I wish I were just a plain ordinary man whose name no one recognized. . . . Should I forget to write for a time don't worry about it, I can look after myself."[11]

Gaines was never located, and the NAACP was forced to give up the case. Without Gaines they lost the cutting edge of the fight against school segregation. But in 1940 Lucille Bluford, the editor of a black newspaper, *The Kansas City Call*, agreed to apply for admission to

Missouri's graduate school of journalism. However, the university shut down its white journalism school rather than admit blacks or start a Jim Crow journalism school. The NAACP had lost again.

While the NAACP's legal strategy was going through heart-wrenching setbacks, Houston was going through his own personal difficulties. He left New York to spend a month in Reno, Nevada, where he got a divorce from his wife, Gladys, after thirteen years of marriage. When he got back to Washington, he immediately married his secretary, Henrietta Williams.[12]

Houston's crisis went beyond his love interests. By April 1938 he wrote to his father, William—who had recently been named assistant attorney general of the United States—that he was coming home to run the family law firm. He confided that he was tired of the demands of working for a large organization like the NAACP, especially since he had to report to a sizable board of directors: "I have had the feeling all along that I am much more of an outside man than an inside man; that I usually break down under too much routine."

Another point of irritation for Houston was that he had to take orders from Walter White, a man he viewed as egocentric. White's lust for the high-society scene and having his name in the papers was difficult to swallow for Houston, the disciplined former army officer and law school dean. But Houston had no regrets. Although he had made very little money while working at the NAACP, he said, "I would not give anything for the experience that I have had."[13]

Ironically, just as Houston was reducing his responsibilities at NAACP headquarters, the board of directors, in a December 1937 meeting, said Houston's and Marshall's legal work for the association was critically important and should be continued "at all costs."[14] Nevertheless, Houston left New York in July of 1938. With Houston gone, Marshall was given a raise to $2,600 a year, still far less than the $4,000 that Houston had been paid to run the NAACP's legal office.

"I got a raise after I got up there. I went up there at $2,400, and two years later they raised it to $2,600," Marshall recalled in an interview. "Two hundred dollars a year. My wife said, 'How much is that a week?' " To supplement his small paycheck, Thurgood persuaded Buster to get involved in a co-op market in Harlem. The Marshalls' work with the market was in the tradition of Thurgood's grandparents—all of whom ran markets. The couple even delivered groceries once in a while to earn some money.[15]

Despite the poor pay, Marshall was happy at the NAACP. Unlike Houston, Marshall discovered that he was very comfortable being an inside man and having the support that came from being in a big operation. He was thrilled by the opportunity to travel around the nation and work on the major issues of the law and segregation. Furthermore, he had strong support on the NAACP's board from the *Afro-American*'s editor and NAACP board member Carl Murphy.

Speaking about that time Marshall recalled a man-to-man talk he had with Houston: "We were walking down the street together, and Charlie was saying, 'You know how much money you're making. And you can imagine how much money I make. And I still say you have more goddamn fun than I do." After his high twitter of a laugh, Marshall, who now found himself inheriting his dream job of running the NAACP's legal office, told Houston: "Ain't no question about that."

Five years out of law school, the student who had so much wanted to prove that he could make it—as his own man with a private law practice—now chose to stay within the arguments, the egos, and the bureaucracy of the national office of the NAACP. At age thirty Marshall found he could do more of what he wanted to do—have a free hand to work on civil rights cases around the nation—as an association lawyer than as a starving maverick in Baltimore.

The only problem for Marshall was that having reached a position of power and authority so quickly, he was unsure of himself. He did not know how far he could go without the security of having Houston by his side. In every civil rights case he had handled, from *Murray* to the teachers' pay cases, he had relied heavily on his mentor. And although Marshall had dealt with cases that ended up in the Supreme Court, Houston had always stepped in to argue the NAACP's side before the high court.[16]

But the time was coming for Marshall to step into the leadership role. As Houston had written when Marshall arrived in the national office, "The best administration is self-executing; where all the subordinated have been well trained and . . . any one of them is able to step into the chief's shoes [at] any minute and carry on with no less of a stride."[17]

Now the question was whether Marshall could step into the chief's shoes.

CHAPTER 10

❧

Marshall in Charge

By October 1938 Marshall was in the lead chair at the NAACP's national legal office in New York. The young lawyer did not have to wait long to find a case he could use to establish his name.

In the small office he had once shared with Houston, Marshall kept his desk cluttered with law books and legal files. But always on the top of the pile were newspapers from around the country—especially the black press. Several of the papers ran sensational reports about how George F. Porter, the fifty-five-year-old president of a black college in Texas, had been thrown down the front steps of the Dallas courthouse for insisting on his right to serve on a county jury.

Marshall read that story with a voyeur's fascination in the gory details. He quickly realized that this case could be a national sensation and force a spotlight on the monstrous reality of second-class treatment given black Americans even in a court of law. His exposure to Walter White had opened his eyes to the idea of civil rights as theater and the power of using dramatic situations to the NAACP's advantage. This was a chance to fly the association's flag but also to make his mark in the public mind as the leader of the NAACP's legal office.

The story of how Porter had been thrown down the steps also got Houston's attention in Washington. In the spring of 1938, Houston had won a major victory at the Supreme Court based on the exclusion of blacks from a jury in Kentucky. Joe Hale, a black man, had been convicted of murder by an all-white jury. But Houston had the conviction overturned when he argued that blacks in rural McCracken County had been illegally excluded from juries for decades. The Supreme Court agreed, ruling that "systematic and arbitrary exclusion of Negroes from the jury lists solely because of their race and color constitute[d] a denial of the equal protection [clause] of the . . . 14th Amendment."[1] They sent the *Hale* case back to Kentucky for a new trial.

Marshall rang up Houston to tell him about the Porter case. Houston agreed that Marshall should go to Texas and launch an NAACP investigation that would focus even more attention on the issue of blacks being pushed off juries if not down the courthouse steps. Marshall announced to the press that he was going to Texas. He was all set to go when word got back to him that if Thurgood Marshall, the NAACP lawyer from New York, set foot in the Dallas courthouse, he would be killed.

*   *   *

The story began on September 26, 1938, when George Porter was summoned for jury service with a randomly selected group of Dallas citizens that included several other blacks. As was the segregationist tradition in Dallas, the judge immediately dismissed all black jurors. But Porter knew this dance. He had been summoned to jury duty twice before. Both times white jurors and court officials had threatened to beat him, even lynch him if he persisted in trying to serve. And both times the balding, dark-skinned Porter had left without resistance.

In September 1938, however, Porter made his stand. A deputy sheriff ordered all the blacks in the jury pool to stay behind while the white jurors went to lunch. The deputy sheriff took them into a darkened room, and as the black jurors grew fearful, the deputy told them to go home. Most people quickly headed for the door, but Porter demanded to see the judge, Paine Bush. The deputy stared down at him, not budging until Judge Bush walked into the courtroom. The judge told Porter he could protest the dismissal, but it was too late for him to serve on this jury.

Porter had anticipated the judge's words. He told the surprised judge that he had already filed a protest in advance of being dismissed. The judge was trapped. If he dismissed Porter now it would create a controversy and possibly tar the judge's name. Bush walked away in disgust. He told Porter that he could stay, but at his own risk.

Porter went to lunch, but when he returned a young white man ran into the jury room and threatened to beat him up. Porter ignored the threat, but soon another white man came in. This time there was no warning. The man grabbed the unsuspecting Porter by the collar, dragging him through the halls of the courthouse. When he got him to the front door, with Porter still struggling to regain his balance, he threw the junior-college president out the door and down the front steps.

Looking at the holes in his good suit and wiping his handkerchief over the cuts and bruises on his body, Porter marched back up the steps. At the top, a line of white men stood in front of the door and circled him. Staring past their scowling faces, Porter pushed through and ran back into the courthouse. The white men stopped their pursuit when he ran into Judge Bush's courtroom.

Porter's bravery was not rewarded. The judge filled the grand jury, then dismissed Porter along with sixteen whites.[2]

Just as Marshall was preparing to leave for Dallas, he heard from NAACP officials there that the chief of police was making special plans for his visit. The chief had called his top officers in and told them that a black NAACP lawyer from New York was coming to stir up trouble. And he told them that they were not to allow any acts of intimidation against the lawyer. "Don't lay a hand on him," the chief ordered. "Don't touch Thurgood Marshall. Because I personally will take him and kick the shit out of him. Personally."

Marshall was genuinely worried: "I sort of considered the idea of having a bad cold or something and not going down there," he said. "But I couldn't get a cold."

To ease his mind Marshall decided to find out about the police chief and the rumored threat. He heard that Texas governor James Allred was a fair man and placed a call. Allred said he had heard the rumor too. "Aw no," the governor told Marshall. "I give you my word, if you come down here, you'll not be injured."

"And sure enough," Marshall said, "when I got down there, a Texas Ranger was there." But the ranger assigned to protect him did not seem initially to Marshall's liking. "As he talked he kept saying 'boy.' I said, 'This ain't the man I need.' So I called the governor, and he said, 'He's the best trained I've got. And if I straighten him out, will that be okay?' And I said sure. So I put him on the phone. And, oh, you should have seen his face!"

Luckily for Marshall, the Texas Ranger proved to be the right man for the job. Near the end of his first week in town, after talking with judges, Marshall was leaving the courthouse late one afternoon and walking over to his car, where the ranger was waiting for him. Suddenly Marshall saw the chief of police charging out of the nearby police headquarters, with his gun drawn. Stiff and wide-eyed, Marshall could not move. Running toward him, the chief shouted: "Hi, you black son of a bitch, I've got you now." Those words broke Marshall's trance, and he began to run to the car. The ranger, who had been sitting on the hood of the car, calmly pulled his gun and faced the chief. "Fella, just stay right where you are," he said.

Sweating and huffing, Marshall got in the car and slammed the door as the chief stood there gritting his teeth. The ranger, still holding the gun out, got in the driver's seat, started the car, and drove away.

Despite the investigation Marshall was not able to prosecute anyone in the case. But his trip to Texas put court officials throughout the South on alert. The NAACP, through Marshall's presence, had announced that it had the legal know-how, the political power, and the people to put up a fight for the rights of blacks. By putting pressure on the governor and drawing press attention to rude handling of black jurors in Texas, Marshall got Judge Bush to reverse his position. A few weeks after the trip, Bush allowed a black juror, W. L. Dickson, to remain on a jury. Governor Allred then assigned rangers to protect black jurors in the courthouse. And blacks gradually began to do regular service on juries throughout Texas.

*   *   *

When Marshall got back to New York, he immediately went to work with Walter White and Roy Wilkins on a less dramatic but even more threatening problem. The Internal Revenue Service (IRS) had ruled that money contributed to the NAACP to pay for its high-profile legal cases was not tax deductible because of the group's antilynching lobbying campaign in Congress. Without that tax-exempt status, the legal office would be penniless; it depended totally on donations.

Marshall began negotiations with the IRS and proposed setting up a separate, legal affairs arm of the NAACP that would not be involved in lobbying. The new organization was incorporated on March 20, 1940, and was called the NAACP Legal Defense and Educational Fund, Inc. (LDF). Its first director-counsel was Thurgood Marshall.

There was still a problem, though. The LDF and the NAACP shared board members and often paid each other's employees. The separation was a sham, and Marshall worried that the IRS would see through it. But Arthur Spingarn, president of the NAACP, was a close friend of Treasury

Secretary Henry Morgenthau. "So we didn't have too much trouble," said Marshall, highlighting the NAACP's acceptance and growing political ties to whites in government and legal circles even as the nation's racial problems persisted.[3]

Throughout the late 1930s and early 1940s, an era when the NAACP was closely linked to white, left-wing groups, Marshall's status grew to the point that he was nominated for a seat on the board of the American Civil Liberties Union (ACLU). He accepted in an effusive letter, calling it a "distinct privilege" to be on the board.[4] The National Lawyers Guild, another predominantly white left-wing group, also made him a board member.

Walter White also gave Marshall a personal link to high-society white politicians and corporate lawyers. White moved in upper-class WASP social circles that fascinated Marshall. He would occasionally go to White's Manhattan apartment for dinner with such prominent political figures as the Republican Wendell Willkie, who ran for president in 1940.

Marshall, unlike White, was not a socialite at heart. He was not comfortable with the sensationalism often used by reporters, and he initially resisted being drawn away from legal issues and into highly publicized crusades. For example, White started a media campaign against the continued use of crude, racist stereotypes in popular culture. In magazines, in advertisements, and on the radio, black Americans were commonly referred to as "darkies" and "shines." White had recently fought to get a shrimp company to change the name of one of its brands, Nigger Head Shrimp.

Marshall thought White needed a public relations agent, not a lawyer, for these cultural wars. But as he became closer to White, Marshall saw the potential of such protests. He began by publicizing a letter he wrote challenging the Whitman candy company for selling Pickaninny Peppermints. Whitman's production manager wrote back that the word was not a slur but meant a "cute colored kid." Marshall exchanged letters with Whitman's executives for more than four years. He got Carl Murphy and the *Afro-American* involved. The paper ran a front-page story headlined: IF YOU WANT TO BE CALLED A NAME, BUY WHITMAN'S. Marshall complained to the candy company that Pickaninny was as bad an epithet as "Sheeny, Dago, Kike and Wop."[5] Whitman's eventually relented.

In a second newspaper fight over epithets, Marshall battled with a tobacco company that sold pipe tobacco under the brand name Nigger Hair. A lawyer for the American Tobacco Co., which sold Lucky Strikes, quickly wrote back to the NAACP: "I may inform you that immediately upon the receipt of the communication calling our attention to the . . . use of a certain brand name that was originated back in 1878, [it] was immediately discontinued."[6] In a small way Marshall was making an impact, and he enjoyed reining in the large corporations.

As the NAACP grew as an organization, Marshall had to do more traveling across the South to raise money and meet the local NAACP officials. These frequent trips made him a well-known figure among chapters in the region. He preached that joining the NAACP was the best way for black people to unite. He was steadily becoming the face of the NAACP, the man from New York who was interested in their problems. Back at headquarters, Walter White and Roy Wilkins increasingly relied on him to keep them up-to-date about members and local issues.

Marshall's letters from the road offered a view of local NAACP concerns as well as his humor. He began one by writing that it was another "installment in that stirring saga of unselfish devotion to a great cause, 'Saving the Race,' by Thurgood Marshall."[7]

"Louisville stop was a success," he wrote in another memo in May 1940, after a meeting with local NAACP officials in an effort to build pressure on Kentucky's senators to get their support on antilynching bills. He also complained to White that "it is a crime for the NAACP to take [me] away from Louisville on Derby day." Marshall joked that if he had stayed, "I would have made enough money to pay off the deficit in the legal defense fund."[8]

Marshall traveled through the South by train, and he was welcomed into towns by black people, who would put him up in their homes. There was usually no hotel that would accept a black traveler. Monroe Dowling, Marshall's friend in New York, recalled that even when he stayed overnight in the South, Marshall had to be aware of his enemies. "He never slept in the same place twice," said Dowling. "But he had guts enough to go to Mississippi and walk in the daytime unaccompanied. He was brave."[9]

Marshall was also willing to put up with threats and insults so he could do NAACP business. He was not opposed to saying "yes, sir" and accommodating whites in any way possible, just as long as he could make his case in court.

Once, while changing trains, Marshall came face-to-face with the reality of life for the average southern black man. "I had about a two- or three-hour stopover," he recalled. "And while I was waiting I got hungry, and I saw a restaurant. So I decided that if I got hungry enough I'd go over there and put my civil rights in my back pocket and go to the back door of the kitchen and see if I could buy a sandwich. And while I was kibitzing myself to do that, this white man came up beside me in plain clothes with a great big pistol in a case on his hip and he said, 'Nigger, boy, what are you doing here?' And I said, 'Well I'm waiting.' And he said, 'What did you say?'

"I said, 'Sir, I'm waiting for the train to Louisiana—Shreveport.' And he said, 'Well, there's only one train comes through here and that's the four o'clock. You better be on it, because the sun is never going down on a live nigger in this town.' And you know what? I wasn't hungry anymore. It dawned on me he could just blow my head off and he wouldn't even have to go to court. This was Hernando, Mississippi."

His travels through the South were not all grim conflict with racists and revving up support among poor black people. In New Orleans, Marshall stayed with friends including a local lawyer who was starting to do civil rights work, A. P. Tureaud. He also made friends with Daniel Byrd, a former Harlem Globetrotter, a handsome man who became Marshall's main partner in New Orleans for crawfish and liquor.

"When Thurgood would come down sometimes we would take him out in the state where they were having a rally to raise money," said Byrd's wife, Mildred. "Back then you could lose your job, just for joining the NAACP. All these little one-horse towns we used to take him to. And those people didn't have much to offer. We might have to sit at a table in the kitchen with a lamplight, and those people would be serving their little, meager dishes to us. He would just sit there and eat it like it tastes like turkey. Thurgood, he was humble as a lamb. Because sometimes the gravy looked black as my daughter's hair, but it tasted good and they would just serve what they had."[10]

*   *   *

The travels were also having an impact on Marshall's thinking about how the NAACP could best come to grips with segregation and racism. In rural Louisiana and across the South, blacks lived under the yoke of a white, segregationist political dictatorship. They had no way to break down the leadership of the racist power structure that controlled their lives. Black southerners were not just poor. They lacked political strength because of intimidation or the outright denial of their right to vote. After several months of crisscrossing the South, Marshall wrote to Walter White that winning the right to vote was the key to integrating the South and an issue all blacks could rally around. And he was convinced the case would come from only one place—Texas.

Texas was a completely Democratic state. The Union Army's occupation of Texas after the Civil War led to white resentment that fueled support for the Democratic Party. Blacks were allowed to vote in general elections, but those contests had little meaning because the Democratic nominees always won. And blacks had no power in the selection of Democratic candidates because Texas Democrats did not allow them in the party. At the NAACP's annual conference in Philadelphia during June 1940, Marshall gave a speech asking for financial support for an attack on the white primary system. "I do not believe we will ever be in a better position politically than we are at the present time," he said. "Take Texas, where there are a million Negroes. If we get a million Negroes voting in a bloc we are going to have some fun."[11]

Walter White, too, saw a great political opportunity in attacking discrimination against black voters in Texas. During the 1940 presidential and congressional elections, several powerful Texans in Washington had been blocking the NAACP's effort to get antilynching laws passed in Congress. Sen. Tom Connolly had been involved in the successful filibuster against the antilynching bill. Rep. Martin Dies headed a House committee to investigate Communists and other anti-American subversives, but he refused to investigate the Ku Klux Klan and other racist groups. And Vice President John Garner, a Texan who was less than sympathetic to the NAACP, was a leading contender to run for president if Roosevelt decided against trying for a third term.

Marshall's trip to Texas for the Porter case put him in touch with local black leaders, including the real estate power broker and Texas NAACP leader Maceo Smith. A commanding man who smoked big, pungent cigars, Smith wanted to bring a new lawsuit against the white primary. But the Texas NAACP had already brought three suits against the white system. As early as 1927 the NAACP had gone to court to fight for blacks to be allowed to vote in the primary, but every time the Democrats had found a way to keep the primaries limited to whites. Smith got angry with the association because he was pouring his money and the association's energy into fighting the white primaries and nothing had changed.

Marshall, over drinks and dinners with Smith and his wife, Fannie, persuaded the local leader that now was the time to take one more swing at the white primary system. By January of 1941, with the help of W. J. Durham, a black lawyer from Sherman, Texas, Marshall had brought the fourth NAACP suit in fifteen years against Texas Democrats for not allowing blacks to vote in their primary. He found a plaintiff in Sidney Hasgett, a Houston man who had unsuccessfully tried to vote in the Democrats' August 1940 runoff and was willing to stand up to criticism that he was a pawn for the NAACP and northern agitators.

To get the case into a Houston courtroom, Marshall had to struggle not only with the facts of Texas law but with simply getting the brief typed. "Sometimes he wrote it out in longhand, and then he would get it typed to the best of his ability, by some public stenographer, if she was colored," remembered his friend Monroe Dowling. "He never went to a white public stenographer 'cause they wouldn't write—they were not honest."

Despite the obstacles in his path, Marshall kept pushing and working and winning support from the local NAACP. The case got to federal district court in Houston in April 1941. Marshall and Durham argued that the white primary violated the fifteenth Amendment, which gave all eligible Americans, without regard to race, the right to vote. Lawyers for the Democrats responded that the primary was held by a private club, the Democratic Party, and they were free to select the club's membership.

Unfortunately for Marshall, it turned out that his client had not tried to vote in a primary but only in a runoff election. Marshall had not realized that Hasgett had failed to even try to vote in the primary. The judge swiftly ruled that since Hasgett had not tried to vote in a primary, the suit had no standing and the NAACP had no case.

Maceo Smith and the black civil rights leaders in Texas were devastated. Marshall wanted to appeal immediately, but he was stuck. Even if he won on appeal, the case would have only limited impact because Hasgett had not been denied the right to vote in a normal primary race. However, starting all over again, with a new plaintiff and a new case, would require more money and more political support.

That support was not forthcoming. There was sharp criticism of his handling of the *Hasgett* case in the black press in Texas. Marshall wrote a funny note to NAACP officials in New York about the rising frustration among black Texans: "All agreed that if we did not get another case started all of us would have to leave the U.S. and go live with Hitler or some other peace loving individual who would be less difficult than the Negroes in Texas who had put up the money for the case."[12]

Despite the added pressure, Marshall, with help from Durham and Smith, was finally able to get the NAACP in Texas to put up the money for one more try. Marshall was sure he could win, he told everyone, because of a recent Supreme Court decision, *U.S. v. Classic*. In that case the high court had ruled that fraud in a Louisiana primary election was not a private matter among members of the Democratic Party but a federal offense. Marshall argued that he could use *Classic* to contend that racial discrimination, like fraud, corrupted the entire election system.

With lukewarm support from Texas NAACP leaders, Marshall began traveling to let other people know about his fight against the all-white primary. In speeches in both the North and the South, he wrapped his cause in the American flag. He said the country was preparing to go to war against Hitler and the idea of white racial superiority. Marshall made Hitler the target of his speeches and a friend to racists in Texas as well as Germany. The NAACP lawyer appealed for an America that was fully democratic at home.

In late 1941 Marshall returned to Texas to continue trying to overturn the white primary. He became a whirlwind fund-raiser, giving pep rally speeches before fraternal groups and civil rights organizations, and even from the pulpits of black churches. At a Houston church they passed around a plate until one woman joked that she needed to borrow a quarter if she was going to contribute her last dollar. Those trips into churches introduced Marshall to some memorable characters. One local minister, for example, was not about to turn the other cheek to white lynch mobs. "In the glove compartment of his car, he had two items—a Bible and a .45, and his answer was very simple: 'I'll try the Bible first,'" Marshall gleefully told friends.[13]

When he had raised enough money for his case, Marshall found a plaintiff in Lonnie Smith, a doctor from Houston who had been denied the chance to vote in a straight primary contest. A year after losing the *Hasgett* case, Marshall and Durham started *Smith v. Allwright*. S. E. Allwright was the Houston election judge who had denied Smith the right to vote in the primary.

Marshall's case attracted quite a bit of attention throughout Texas. Even the debonair Duke Ellington, world renowned for his jazz and swing orchestra, got pulled into the drama. "Duke Ellington happened to be in town, and about half a dozen of us played poker and he wanted to know what I was doing down there," Marshall reminisced later. "And I explained the case to him, and he said, 'Man, that's interesting. When is it coming up?' I said tomorrow. He said, 'Well, that'll be no trouble. I'm free until tomorrow night.' So he arranged to go to court the next day, and it was postponed. And it was postponed at least two times, and he kept the whole band waiting, at his expense. You can't imagine what it cost him. But he finally heard that case."

Even with Ellington's magnetic and dapper presence, Marshall and the NAACP lost again. This time, however, Marshall was ready to appeal until the *Smith* case and the issue of the white primary was in front of the Supreme Court. He got the ACLU and the National Lawyers Guild to file amicus briefs with the Supreme Court supporting the NAACP's position. Marshall also asked the Justice Department, which had brought the *Classic* case, to support the NAACP's claim that fraud in the Louisiana primaries amounted to the same result as racial discrimination in the Texas primary.

However, Justice Department officials turned Marshall down, explaining that southerners in the Senate would be angry if Justice entered the fight on the NAACP's side. "When I told Thurgood the answer would be no," said Herbert Wechsler, assistant to the solicitor general, "he said, 'I'm sorry, we'd like to have you with us but we'll just have to go it alone. I see your position.' That was one of his great virtues, seeing things from the other guy's side. He was a good tough advocate who functioned without having to feel that his opponents were either knaves or fools." [14]

In October of 1943 the Supreme Court heard arguments in the white primary case. "OFAY PRIMARY CASE BEFORE SUPREME COURT," read the *Baltimore Afro-American*'s banner front-page headline on October 16. Marshall and Bill Hastie, his former law school professor who was now dean of Howard Law, made the NAACP's case before the high court. Hastie was a crack lawyer, and he was famous for his unflappable manner, even under intense fire.

In April 1944 the Court ruled that white primaries were unconstitutional. If Texas allowed the political parties to limit their nominees and voters to whites, the Court said, "it endorses, adopts and enforces the discrimination against Negroes." [15]

The decision made national headlines. Both the black and the white press put the high court's ruling—and young Mr. Marshall—on their front pages. The *Norfolk Journal and Guide* wrote that with its victory in the white primary case the NAACP had to be given new respect. The association, it wrote, "has often had to bear the wrongfully imposed stigma of 'agitator,' but it has done more to translate the U.S. Constitution and laws of this country in their proper perspective for minorities than any other organization in the field."[16]

Walter White, Charles Houston, and the national membership of the NAACP were thrilled with the Supreme Court ruling. Even at the end of his life, Marshall still bubbled that the victory in the white primary case stood as "the greatest one" of his career.[17]

When news of the high court's ruling on the case reached Marshall in New York, a grand party swept through the NAACP's offices. As the phones rang with calls from lawyers, reporters, and NAACP supporters, Marshall began playing a game in which he had callers passed from one secretary to another while he sat back laughing and drinking. The next day Marshall, still woozy from his partying, got a call from Supreme Court Justice Frank Murphy. The justice said he had called the day before but could not "pierce the wall of secretaries."

"I apologized profusely," Marshall said later, "and Murphy agreed that a guy had the right to get drunk at a time like that. Then he invited me to lunch."[18]

Justice Murphy was not the only one who suddenly wanted to get to know the NAACP lawyer who had made magic and history in Texas. Among black Americans Marshall's name suddenly was celebrated. Everyone wanted him to come to town to speak. Everyone wanted him to handle a case. And Marshall was expected to confront the most racist southern politicians, lawyers, and judges. To prove he was really a legal wizard, Marshall would have to make magic again. This time a dark, politically driven murder case awaited him.

CHAPTER 11

Pan of Bones

THE NAACP WAS GETTING DOZENS OF CALLS and letters from around the country in which black defendants complained that they were being railroaded from jail cell to the electric chair with barely a stop for a trial. In his office in New York, Marshall kept files of letters from local NAACP leaders, news stories, and occasionally long, sad letters in barely legible writing from the jailed men themselves.

Working by himself and with a limited budget, there was no way Marshall could agree to represent suspects in every case. Sometimes he would call the local branch's attorney and discuss the case, offering ideas for building a defense. Just as often he would have to find an attorney in the area who was willing to get involved for a minimal fee from the NAACP. But in some cases Marshall would feel compelled, by an insistent branch leader or by the horror of a case, to get on a train and handle the matter himself.

In the spring of 1940, Marshall began getting alarming letters from one of the most powerful NAACP leaders in the South, Roscoe Dunjee. The fiery Dunjee was the editor of the largest southern black newspaper, Oklahoma City's *Black Dispatch*. Dunjee pleaded with Marshall to help a simpleminded black farmhand who was accused of killing three members of a white family.

On New Year's Eve 1939, Mr. and Mrs. Elmer Rogers and one of their children were shot and their throats were slit in the rural town of Hugo. To destroy evidence of the crime, their house was set on fire. During the barbaric attack, the couple's son, nine-year-old Glen, hid in a closet holding back his screams. Once the murderer left, Glen miraculously escaped the burning house.

Initially two white men were arrested and confessed to the murders. But when it was learned that both men were inmates who had been allowed to leave the nearby state prison for unsupervised visits to bars and whorehouses, newspapers began to criticize the governor and prison warden.

To quiet the public outcry, Governor Leon Chase Phillips sent an aide, Vernon Cheatwood, to Hugo with orders to clean up the mess. Cheatwood was a big, threatening man with stubby fingers and a vicious, sneering smile that showed bad teeth. He carried a gun and brass knuckles under his coat. When he got to town he ordered the release of the two white prisoners even though they had confessed. Cheatwood let them go on the promise they would leave the state and he even arranged to get them into Texas. The governor's office then announced that a search would begin for the real culprit.

A few days later Cheatwood and local police arrested W. D. Lyons. The black sharecropper admitted he had been hunting rabbits near the slain couple's farmhouse but denied that he had anything to do with the murders. The police and the governor's aide called Lyons a liar. Over two days the governor's man beat him repeatedly with a small hardwood nightstick. The handle was wrapped with leather for a tight-fisted grip. Cheatwood told the locals he had made it himself and called it his "niggerbeater."

When they were not beating Lyons, they denied him sleep and food. All the while they demanded that he confess to the crime. Lyons still maintained that he did not do it. Cheatwood and Hugo police then devised a new plan. Well after midnight, with Lyons babbling and disoriented, Cheatwood walked into the cell. A cringing Lyons expected to be beaten again, but Cheatwood had other plans. He pulled out a large, stinking black pan filled with the charred bones of the murder victims and threw them in Lyons's lap. "There's the bones of the baby you burned up," he barked.[1]

Still suffering from his beating, frightened of another attack, and superstitious about human bones, Lyons cracked. He tried to crawl away, but Cheatwood held him, pushing his face toward the pan of bones. Lyons desperately begged Cheatwood to stop. Only a confession would end his misery. A few minutes later Lyons gave police the confession they wanted.

But the police were not satisfied and took Lyons to the nearby state penitentiary, where they showed him the electric chair and got him to sign a second confession, in which he swore he had not been beaten and admitted to killing the Rogers family.

The *Black Dispatch* editor, Dunjee, son of a slave, was incensed by the crooked politics and the governor's calculated appeal to racism. His little paper, some weeks only six or eight pages, played the story in big, angry headlines. And out of his own pocket Dunjee immediately hired a white lawyer from the Oklahoma ACLU, Stanley Beldon, to represent Lyons.

When Beldon reached Hugo a few days later, several of the town's leading white residents pulled him aside in a restaurant to say they did not believe Lyons had committed the crime. The biggest surprise came when another group of whites told him that the murdered woman's father was sure Lyons was innocent and was willing to testify. But the white community's attitude did not make much difference.

After the police announced that Lyons had confessed to the crime, they kept him in jail as the county attorney and the sheriff stalled the trial until after local elections to prevent the scandal from hurting their chances for reelection. Beldon could not break through the stalling tactic, and Lyons was left in jail as outrage over the case grew cold.

Fed up with Beldon's inability to force a trial, Dunjee, also a member of the NAACP's national board, wrote to Walter White. He wanted Marshall to come to Oklahoma and wave the NAACP's name around to make the *Lyons* case a national issue. White and Marshall agreed the case was good material, both to create a cause for the NAACP and to take a stand against forced confession, a tactic often used against black suspects.

Now the pressure was on Marshall. Not only did he have to pay attention to the case but he had to stir up publicity, raise money, and, far from home, maneuver through state politics with the governor wishing him the worst.

Marshall spent three days riding a train to Oklahoma City, then got on a bus for the six-hour trip to Hugo, arriving Sunday, January 26, 1941. As soon as he arrived, a group of black men pushed him into the backseat of a car and quickly hid him away in the small black community. They feared that someone might kill him, so they moved him from place to place every few hours and always had armed guards watching outside. Although white people in Hugo were supportive, the black community did not know what the governor might do to keep his cover-up in place, including having an accident take Marshall out of the picture.

Marshall did not have much time to investigate the case or to worry about threats to his life. Just before his arrival it was announced that the trial was set to start in a few days. The morning after he arrived, the trial began. The courthouse, with its segregated seating, was "jammed," with "at least a thousand white and Negro people." Marshall wrote to Walter White: "Jury is lousy. State investigator and county prosecutor busy around town stirring up prejudice, etc. No chance of winning here. Will keep record straight for appeal."[2] He was convinced the governor had the judge in his pocket and had fixed the trial.

By the second day in court the judge, J. R. Childers, who smoked a large cigar while sitting on the bench, announced to the crowd in his courtroom that it was "a gala day" for the town of Hugo. He was more interested in the large crowd and newspaper reporters than in the case. Marshall felt lost in a political show trial, where his powers of argument and knowledge of the law counted for nothing. The judge's behavior struck him as bizarre, and Marshall wrote him off as a small-time clown in the governor's parade. "Can you imagine a Negro on trial for his life being considered a gala day?" Marshall wrote to White.

But the judge was right to say that people in Hugo were entertained by the trial. The crowd around the courthouse grew as the trial continued. Marshall later explained in letters back home that he became the star attraction as "word went around that a nigger lawyer from New York was on the case—first time they have seen such an animal." Students from local white schools were even allowed to miss class to watch the trial.[3]

Marshall and Beldon sat with Lyons, who stuttered with nervousness the few times they got him to say anything. Marshall's first move in court was to let the judge know that the NAACP had recently won a ruling from the Supreme Court (*Canty v. Alabama* in March 1940) that outlawed forced confessions. In that case, which had been tried by Charles Houston with Marshall's help, the conviction of a black man accused of murder in Alabama had been overturned when the high court ruled that he was beaten and forced to confess.

Norman Horton, the county prosecutor, then called Lyons to take the stand. The trembling defendant testified that Horton had witnessed the police beating him. Horton, however, denied seeing the brutal whipping. But the usually silent Lyons stiffened. Looking Horton in the eye,

he said: "Oh, yes, you were there." Horton's face went white, and pointing a finger he said to Lyons, "Why, I stopped them from whipping you."
The courtroom audience, completely caught up in the drama, erupted in
loud shouting as the judge banged his gavel, trying to restore order.[4]

Once the roar subsided, Marshall had the court take note that Horton had conceded Lyons was beaten by the police. Next Marshall questioned Vernon Cheatwood and got him to admit that he threw the
murder victims' bones on Lyons. "Did you put a pan of bones in his lap?"
Marshall asked. "Yes," said Cheatwood coolly. "I thought it would re-
fresh his mind."[5]

Marshall began to pepper the governor's man with questions about a
wooden and leather weapon, dubbed his "niggerbeater," to get a confession. Cheatwood, becoming flustered, denied he had such a weapon, but
Marshall called a white hotel clerk to the stand who testified that Cheatwood had bragged about how he had used it to beat Lyons for six or
seven hours. As the trial unfolded the sympathy for Lyons among local
whites grew stronger. White residents secretly helped Marshall find a
picture, taken by the police, of Cheatwood and a Hugo policeman standing next to a bloody and beaten Lyons. "Many white people stopped us in
the halls and on the streets to tell us they enjoyed the way the case was
going and they didn't believe Lyons was guilty," Marshall later wrote to
White. "Ninety percent of the white people by this time were with
Lyons."[6]

Cheatwood and the white policemen were not quite so pleased, however. "[Police] became angry at the idea of a Negro pushing them into
tight corners and making their lies so obvious," Marshall wrote to White.
"Boy, did I like that and did the Negroes in the courtroom like that."[7] In
fact, the *Black Dispatch* reported that after Marshall finished questioning
Cheatwood about his "niggerbeater," Cheatwood left the stand "shaking
as though suffering from palsy."[8]

After the police admitted to beating Lyons, Judge Childers threw out
the first confession. But he did allow the second confession. The only
additional evidence the prosecutors had against Lyons was that he admitted to having been hunting rabbits near the murdered family's home.
Glen Rogers, the son of the murdered couple, testified that while hiding
he had not seen the assailant's face. All he caught sight of was a "black
hand."[9]

The case went to an all-white, all-male jury after five days of testimony. With only five and a half hours of deliberation, the jury found

Lyons guilty. To everyone's surprise, however, instead of the death penalty they sentenced him to life in prison.

Marshall sent a letter to Walter White summing up the trial in which he said: "You know that life for such a crime as that—three people killed, shot with a shotgun and cut up with an axe and then burned—shows clearly that the jury believed him innocent. I think we are in perfect position to appeal." Marshall also urged White to use the Lyons case to benefit the NAACP. "We have been needing a good criminal case and we have it." He added, "The beatings plus the use of the bones of dead people will raise money."[10]

The NAACP got an unexpected publicity bonanza from the *Lyons* case when E. O. Colclasure, the father of the murdered woman, went public with his belief that Lyons was framed. The white man even joined the NAACP.

Part of the NAACP publicity drive about the Lyons trial included an educational pamphlet. In it Marshall wrote that police in the South regularly arrested blacks "without warrants, [held] them incommunicado without formal charges or bail, beat 'confessions' out of them."[11]

The case made the front pages of black newspapers nationwide as startling proof of the corruption of the white legal system. Marshall and Lyons were pictured side by side in *The Crisis*, with Marshall portrayed as the hero who had saved Lyons from the death penalty. A year later, in 1942, when Marshall came back to Oklahoma to handle the appeal, he was hailed by Dunjee and the black community as a savior. Dunjee told Marshall he expected that the appeal might be successful because the state judges in Oklahoma City were better trained and not under the governor's thumb. But despite Dunjee's high hopes, the appeals court also ruled that Lyons's second confession was valid.

Marshall was now convinced there was a political cover-up that spread from Hugo to Oklahoma City. An assistant attorney general for the state who befriended Marshall told him there was no way Lyons was going to get out, because "an awful big political power was against letting him out." Lyons, meanwhile, remained in jail until the case was appealed to the U.S. Supreme Court. In a heartbreaking setback for Marshall, the nation's high court sustained the Oklahoma verdict in 1944, concluding Lyons was properly convicted on a valid confession.

Marshall could not believe he had lost. His ego and reputation as the lawyer who worked miracles were deeply invested in the case. More important, he believed that only political pressure from the governor's office had prevented him from winning the case before the appeals court. He was upset, confused, and deeply hurt by the 6–3 defeat at the high court. It was his first loss in a Supreme Court case. In a rare show of public anger against any court, Marshall told reporters that the high court's ruling gave police a license to beat a confession out of a prisoner and "then procure another before the effects of the coercion can fairly be said to have completely worn off."[12]

*   *   *

While Marshall was working on the *Lyons* case, Walter White asked him to handle another sensational criminal case, this time in Connecticut. These cases caught the attention of the papers and stirred rapid increases in black and white membership in the association. And Marshall liked them—they provided a welcome relief from the complex theoretical arguments on how to break down the laws of segregation. There was nothing abstract or dry about murder, brutal police, or, in the Connecticut case, an interracial sexual relationship that went wildly out of control.

The case involved a white Connecticut heiress who charged that her black butler had raped her. The trial began in Greenwich in January 1941. Eleanor Strubing, age thirty-one, a former fashion model, claimed that Joseph Spell, her live-in butler and chauffeur, kidnapped her, raped her four times, and then threw her off a reservoir bridge.

At the trial, Spell said he had not raped Strubing but was caught up in a one-night stand that went bad. Spell testified that he knocked on Strubing's bedroom door one day to ask if he could borrow money. She told him to come in, and he found her dressed only in a skimpy, silky robe.

Spell, represented by Marshall and a Connecticut attorney, Samuel Friedman, told the court that he was excited by the sight of Strubing in her bedclothes and propositioned her: "I told her that I would like to be with her." He said she agreed if he promised to keep their dalliance a secret. But she was afraid of being discovered in the bedroom. Spell suggested that they go down to the garage and have sex in the car. In his deposition Spell said: "Just as I got the head of my penis in her she said that she was still afraid that something might happen. We stopped and I had a discharge in my pocket handkerchief. I suggested we go for a drive. She said that would be all right."[13]

But the car trip was a nightmare. The woman became increasingly paranoid, worried that someone might see them. She ordered the butler to drive across the state line into New York. When they parked near the Kensico Reservoir, however, she ran from the car. Spell tried to go after her, but when he got near her she jumped in the water, then told him to leave her alone and go home.

Strubing told a different story. She claimed Spell had used a knife to kidnap and rape her. She said he forced her to write a ransom note for $5,000 before tying her up with ropes, pushing her into the car, and driving her away from the estate.

At the trial, however, Marshall got the police to concede that they never found a ransom note or any ropes. Mrs. Strubing also failed to show up for court three times, forcing postponements. And the police testified that the doctor who had examined Mrs. Strubing quoted her at the time as saying she pleaded with Spell not to "inseminate her." Marshall and his cocounsel later argued to the jury that since Spell had not ejaculated in her, "there must have been an agreement or arrangement." [14]

The jury of six men and six women, all white, found Spell not guilty. "Yes, the jury turned that man loose," Marshall said later, his voice breaking in high tones with excitement. "But he was supposed to have raped this woman four times in one night. All I got to tell you is when the story got in the newspaper, all the secretaries, all of 'em, came and said, 'Hey, defend that man. We want to see it. Four times! Ha ha. Ha ha. Four times in one night. Yeah, bring him in here, let us see him.' I told 'em get out of my office."

The secretaries' fascination with Marshall's criminal cases was just a sample of the talk going around the nation, especially in the black community. At this point in his career, Marshall was better known to the public for his defense of criminals than for his attacks on Jim Crow. He stood as a living, breathing shield for black people against the lynch mob as well as the judge's death sentence. Marshall, a very good lawyer at this point, was now growing into a mythical figure, a crusader and a savior. And he enjoyed playing the role. He liked people, and he liked to travel. He enjoyed going out drinking in these tiny towns until the small hours of the morning. He could joke with the guys, charm the women, and tease the children.

Marshall would have to call on all those skills and more in the next few years. The nation was beginning a transformation of its own during World War II, fighting overseas in the name of equality and democracy.

On the home front an embarrassed nation would also have to confront its own racism or risk facing the same dark days of trauma that tore apart Europe's soul. In the war against racial hate on its home soil, the United States needed a battle plan. But first the nation and Marshall would have to deal with racism in its own war machine.

CHAPTER 12

❧

The War Years

A MERICA'S WAR EFFORT was aimed overseas, but it would revolutionize race relations at home. As far back as 1937 Charles Houston, who had been an army lieutenant in World War I, had been sending letters to President Roosevelt asking that Negroes be given the right to serve on a nonsegregated basis in the military. But as World War II broke out, the armed forces remained segregated.

Blacks were also trying to break through the Jim Crow line that kept them from good-paying jobs in factories that produced military equipment and weapons. Marshall and the NAACP got involved in two widely publicized cases, one against the Boilermakers Union in Rhode Island and the other against the largest marine shipworkers' union in San Francisco. Both unions segregated their black workers into auxiliary labor groups, which kept the blacks out of any union leadership posts and limited their rights to equal pay and job protection. Just as Marshall had been in the forefront of integrating the steelworkers' union in Baltimore, he wanted to end Jim Crow in these industries.

While Marshall worked in court to break down segregation among boilermakers and shipbuilders, A. Philip Randolph, the president of the Brotherhood of Sleeping Car Porters, the nation's largest black union, took another approach. He applied large-scale political pressure to President Roosevelt. Randolph, a tall, elegant man who had trained to be a Shakespearean actor, spoke in a deep, theatrical voice that mesmerized people. He threatened a march of black workers on Washington if defense industries were not desegregated.

Ironically, though Marshall and Houston were allied with Randolph in the fight to break down segregation in the military and in industry, they differed with him on his plan for a march featuring only black workers. Houston wrote an ideologically revealing letter to Randolph in which he argued for an integrated march: "Fundamentally, I do not believe the Negroes can win the battle for integration and citizenship by themselves. What success Negroes have had in the past has been due in large part to their ability to interest and enlist other persons in their cause." [1]

Randolph was not convinced by Houston's letter, but the split among the civil rights leaders didn't matter. President Roosevelt, hoping to avoid a racially explosive march as the nation prepared for war, negotiated a settlement. He established the Fair Employment Practices Committee [FEPC] and desegregated some munitions factories.

Houston's focus on integration and using political ties with whites to advance the black cause was exactly in line with the views of Walter White, Thurgood Marshall, and other leaders of the NAACP. There was intense concern at the association over whether blacks would be given the chance to serve in integrated military units and become officers. Marshall and others even held discussions about whether Marshall or one of the other leaders of the NAACP should enlist and force the all-white military hierarchy to promote him to a high-ranking officer. But White did not want to lose Marshall or the momentum the NAACP had going in its legal campaign to end segregation.

In fact, Marshall, then in his mid-thirties, held lengthy conversations with officials of the New York draft board to avoid being drafted. "The director of selective service thought I was more valuable in than out," Marshall said. "He thought that the Negro soldiers needed me to handle their courts-martial and stuff like that. Which I did." Marshall added that he also had friends at the draft board in New York who told him not to worry about being drafted because they wanted him at the NAACP and had the situation "under control."

As the war progressed, however, Walter White worried that Marshall still might be drafted. White appealed to Bill Hastie to speak to military officials in Washington about allowing Marshall to stay at the NAACP.[2] Hastie had been a civilian aide to the secretary of war but had resigned in protest over the continued segregation of blacks in the military. He was happy to help. He wrote a strong letter to the draft board, asking them to consider the damage that would be done to the NAACP and the nation's race relations if Marshall were drafted.[3] The appeal succeeded. Marshall never served in the military.

While White was trying to keep Marshall out of the military, he was also trying to keep the Justice Department from recruiting Marshall, who had gained a good reputation in Washington for his legal work. Several lawyers in the ACLU recommended Marshall for a post at Justice.

"Sometime ago I suggested to Justice that Thurgood Marshall ought to be put on the staff—I understand that you are blocking this brilliant move on my part," Morris Ernst, a prominent white lawyer and board member of the legal committee of the NAACP wrote to White. "For God's sake, lay hands off. You can pick up a dozen Thurgoods and you can tell him so, but Justice cannot get a guy as good as Thurgood."[4]

White replied in blunt language: "I don't want to lose him, but I told [a Justice Department official] that I would not stand in the way of any member of the NAACP staff doing a necessary job or advancing himself. Now that that's off my chest I'd be ever so grateful to you if you would let me know the place where I 'can pick up a dozen Thurgoods!' "[5]

Marshall's high profile as an NAACP leader also meant he was a target for the association's enemies. The FBI, which investigated subversive and anti-American groups during the war, kept watch on Marshall beginning in 1938, when he traveled to Dallas to argue that blacks had a right to serve on juries. But the bureau's surveillance of Marshall increased during the war, as the agency began to aggressively patrol the activities of all left-wing organizations, including the NAACP. The FBI was probing for Communists who might be using liberal groups as fronts for their operations inside the United States.

An FBI report on a 1943 speech Marshall gave in Florence, South Carolina, said: "Informants state the meetings dealt principally with general betterment of conditions for Negroes, but all were urged to be Americans first and look for racial advancement secondly." Marshall was described by one of several FBI informants as a "loyal American who will go far as he can to further the aims [of the NAACP] . . . but will not permit anything radical to be done to accomplish desired ends."

The FBI informants also noted that Marshall praised the Army's treatment of blacks. One informant wrote: "Marshall said the war was being fought for the benefit of all and that colored people had more to gain than white persons—for white persons already had all rights that could be desired, whereas victory could also open the door for the black man. He said colored persons also had more to lose, for they would be punished more, should Axis nations be victorious."[6]

Marshall's positive comments about the military may have been made partly out of concern that he was being watched. Overly critical remarks could have undermined his relationships with federal officials in Washington at a time when he was making appeals for black soldiers. The NAACP was getting hundreds of complaints from black soldiers about unfair assignments, phony charges that led to dishonorable discharges, and top officers' failure to give medals and honors to black soldiers. The wave of such complaints led the biggest black newspaper, the *Pittsburgh Courier*, to start a "Double-V" campaign, for victory over racism both abroad and at home. More and more black soldiers and black workers in the United States were becoming vocal in their demands for equal treatment.

The volume of complaints from soldiers in 1943 led Marshall to hire two new lawyers for the LDF, Milton Konvitz and Edward Dudley. Marshall's work on the soldiers' cases also brought more contributions into the NAACP, allowing him to expand his budget and staff. The next year he hired an Army Air Force veteran and Howard law graduate, Robert Carter, to strengthen his staff.

Dudley, in an interview, recalled that when he first came to the LDF's office, "Thurgood was a one-man band." Carter gave much the same description of the LDF: "There was no law library and few books in the office and for a long time I did my research at Columbia University. . . . It is only in retrospect that I am amazed at how much Thurgood had been able to accomplish."[7]

With the LDF busy with military discrimination, Marshall now found his life picking up to an even faster pace. Between traveling, giving speeches, and staying abreast of politics in Washington, he had to keep track of the cases being handled by his new assistants in New York. Time with his wife was rare. When a reporter from the *Baltimore Afro-American* came to visit Marshall at the LDF's offices in 1944, their interview was interrupted by a phone call from Buster. Marshall barely spoke during the conversation. He simply said, "Yes, baby . . . yes, dear . . . right away, darling."

"That's my wife," Marshall said to the reporter after hanging up the phone. "I'm henpecked. My wife is jealous of every minute I have to spend here. Most of the time I'm on the road."[8]

Marshall was traveling over 30,000 miles a year and was away from home for the better part of any month. When he was in New York he and Buster would spend time cooking and entertaining. The Marshalls' favorite pastime was still playing cards with Thurgood's old college buddy, Monroe Dowling, and his wife, Helen. They dealt games like bid whisk, tonk, and Pokeno. And Dowling said the two couples would "drink and eat until three in the morning."

Dowling noticed some tension between Buster and Thurgood because of Thurgood's frequent absences from home. While Thurgood was away Buster spent her time with her uncles, who lived in New York. She also belonged to the Urban League and organized events for a black women's social club, The Girlfriends. She would go to dances and social affairs with the Dowlings and other friends.

The couple remained childless as Buster had another miscarriage. Doctors had prescribed bed rest, but she nonetheless lost the fetus. The miscarriages added pressure to a relationship that already had its problems. Thurgood very much wanted to have a child. While he gave Buster comfort, she felt her husband's regret to the point of becoming melancholy. And Thurgood resented that. "They wanted children so bad it was pathetic," said Dowling. "I had a son, a baby boy. And everybody that Thurgood knew had something, even Aubrey."

Marshall's difficult life at home made the rush and whirl of his work for the NAACP all the more attractive. Racial flare-ups increased in the big northern cities during the war, as blacks migrated north and clashed with working-class whites over housing and jobs. Marshall became the NAACP's voice on race riots, one of the most difficult domestic situations during the war years.

Marshall had been in Detroit, home of the association's largest chapter, to deliver a controversial speech, "Securing Democracy at Home," at the NAACP Emergency War Conference. The June 1943 speech highlighted racial discrimination in the United States even as black Americans fought against fascism in Europe. Black soldiers and workers faced continuing bias in hiring for jobs, as well as in schools, in housing, and in transportation. The conference was blasted from the start by the *Detroit Daily News* and other critics who charged the NAACP with hurting the war effort when the country needed a united front against its foreign enemies.

Despite efforts by white political leaders to downplay racial problems, signs of simmering racial tensions existed all around. Two weeks after the NAACP conference, on Sunday night, June 20, rioting broke out around Detroit, involving more than 100,000 people. The trouble started at Belle Island, a city-owned park, when blacks and whites began fighting.

Rioting spread as rumors flew downtown about what was happening at Belle Island. One rumor heard among whites was that a black man had raped a white girl. Among blacks a rumor spread that a white sailor had thrown a Negro woman and her baby into the lake at the park. Neither report was true. But all night and continuing until Tuesday morning, there were outbreaks of violence. Shots were fired throughout the city, people ran from place to place, and houses were firebombed from moving cars. The rioting stopped only after President Roosevelt authorized 2,500 federal soldiers to take control of the city.

Marshall and Walter White flew into Detroit on Thursday, as the city remained tense with soldiers and a curfew in place. The NAACP leaders took rooms at the YMCA and began to investigate the riot, which the *Detroit Daily News* blamed on the association's conference. That meeting "sowed seeds of violence in the hearts of youths both colored and white," wrote A. M. Smith in a *Daily News* article. "To contend that a strictly militant convention which ended with a mass meeting of 20,000 colored people had no influence on the fighting spirit of younger, irresponsible colored people is a denial of the laws of psychology."[9] Marshall responded that right-wingers who talked up segregation, not the NAACP, were responsible for dividing the races and creating the tense atmosphere in Detroit.

Michigan's governor, eager to proclaim that he was fair to both races, agreed to support Marshall's NAACP investigation into the cause of the riots. But even while working with the governor, Marshall was threatened by whites in Detroit who hired some black thugs to work him over. The governor provided a bodyguard with a "good-sized .38," but Marshall still had violent run-ins with angry whites.

"I was going up one of the main Negro streets—this was about a day or so after [another outbreak of violence] happened, and a guy drove by, a white fellow," Marshall said in an interview. "He said something. I said something back to him. And he pulled out a great big shotgun, and I was so glad there was a trooper standing there with a machine gun. And the cop said, 'Now who is going to drop what?' So this guy drops his shotgun."[10]

In his report on the riot, which was circulated nationwide as an NAACP pamphlet, Marshall pointed at the police for sparking the vio-

lence: "The trouble reached riot proportions because the police of Detroit once again enforced the law under an unequal hand," he wrote.
"They used 'persuasion' rather than firm action with white rioters while
against Negroes they used the ultimate in force. . . . 25 of the 34 persons
killed were Negroes. Of the 25 Negroes killed, 17 were killed by police.
. . . 85 percent of persons arrested were Negroes."[11]

*   *   *

Meanwhile, the nation's military leaders paid little attention to the riots.
They were too busy winning a war against Hitler. But that wall began to
break down as black soldiers continued to bombard Marshall's office with
thousands of letters detailing daily insults and second-class treatment.
The NAACP became the ideal tool for black soldiers who wanted to put
pressure on white military commanders.

One of the early military cases Marshall handled involved three black
soldiers from Camp Claiborne who were charged with raping a white
woman. Although they were in the Army, the men were tried not in a
military court but in a federal court in Louisiana. The case revolved
around a strange story. A black sergeant and two black privates said the
woman was a prostitute and they had paid her two dollars to have sex.
But Alexandria, Louisiana, police later said the three black soldiers gave
them signed confessions of rape.[12]

The soldiers were convicted and asked Marshall and the NAACP for
help. They said the confessions were signed only because the police beat
them and threatened to let white mobs lynch them. Marshall agreed to
appeal the case after he became convinced that they were wrongly
charged. More important, he found that they had been improperly tried
in a federal district court when they should have been tried in either a
military or a state court.

The U.S. Circuit Court of Appeals for the Fifth Circuit agreed with
Marshall's appeal. The Supreme Court then confirmed the Fifth Circuit's
ruling and sent the case back to military court for retrial, at Camp Maxey,
Texas. The men were again convicted and sentenced to be hanged. But
further appeals saw the sentences reduced. The men were paroled after
serving five years.[13]

Marshall quickly became involved in another military justice case in
1944, when fifty black sailors at Yerba Buena Island, near San Francisco,
were charged with mutiny because they refused to load ammunition during time of war. The mutiny occurred just a few weeks after an explosion

at Port Chicago, a nearby naval depot. Over 300 men, mostly blacks, were killed when white officers began playing a deadly game. The officers placed bets on which group of black sailors was fastest at loading ammunition. They shouted and bullied the sailors to hurry, even instructing them to throw boxes of ammunition so they could win the bet. One case fell, triggering the deadly series of explosions. Reports about what happened spread quickly among black sailors, especially to Yerba Buena, where some of the survivors from Port Chicago were transferred.

Marshall lost his usually cool demeanor in this case. He was incensed that black soldiers were treated like animals for the pleasure of their officers. He flew out to California to begin work. "It was arranged for me to attend the trial on Saturday," Marshall wrote to Walter White in New York. "Defense counsel are good and know what they are doing. Prosecutor is vicious and dumb. . . . Most of the accused testified that they told the lieutenant that they were willing to obey orders but that they were afraid of loading ammunition after the Port Chicago incident. . . . There is no evidence of mutiny and we should be able to beat this in the reviewing board."[14]

Despite Marshall's presence and a good team of defense lawyers, the men were found guilty of mutiny. Marshall could not believe it. He appealed and personally handled the case in Washington, D.C., before the Navy's judge advocate general [JAG]. Standing in front of a formal military court, with all white officers in their dress uniforms, Marshall appealed for justice. "They obeyed all other orders and did everything they were requested to do," he said in his oral presentation. "And the attitude was altogether perfect with the one exception of loading ammunition. . . . At best, it is refusal to obey an order."[15]

The case gained attention all over the country. Even the White House got involved. First Lady Eleanor Roosevelt, who was alerted to the matter by Walter White, wrote to Navy Secretary James Forrestal asking that the black sailors be treated with compassion given that racism may have played a role in the incident. Forrestal, well aware of the First Lady's power in the Roosevelt administration, cautiously said he would consider the matter.[16]

Two months later, in July 1945, the judge advocate general upheld the guilty verdict against the fifty men. A spokesman for the secretary of the Navy said: "The trials were conducted fairly and impartially. . . . Racial discrimination was guarded against." Marshall immediately insisted on a meeting with the secretary of the Navy to argue that racial discrimination was a factor. Forrestal refused to see him but allowed Marshall to "submit to me any memoranda in this matter which you may desire."[17]

A subsequent Navy review of the trial found problems with "hearsay" evidence and suggested a retrial. Forrestal, however, was not interested in a second trial that would attract more publicity. And he didn't want to deal with more political pressure from the likes of the First Lady. He handled the matter quietly and to Marshall's satisfaction. "The conclusion of that case was extremely interesting, because there was no official notice of what happened," Marshall said later. "The records of the final disposition were never entered, but I happen to know, from Secretary Forrestal himself, that all of the men were released, and put back onto active duty in the Pacific. But there's no record in the Navy Department about it."[18]

Thurgood Marshall was now the man people called when they needed legal help with racial issues. He was celebrated by blacks as their top criminal defense lawyer and a civil rights leader. The attorney general and politicians in Washington turned to him with civil rights questions. But he was not yet forty years old. As black war veterans came back to the United States with new energy, the nation was poised for the next stage in the civil rights struggle. The question for the NAACP was whether their young chief counsel had the ability to channel the growing momentum into a national legal fight against segregation in the postwar era. Could Thurgood Marshall, using his legal blueprint, construct an America that did not tolerate racism?

CHAPTER 13

Lynch Mob for a Lawyer

ON THE NIGHT OF NOVEMBER 18, 1946, Marshall was in a black sedan, driving out of the small farm town of Columbia, Tennessee. He had just finished representing two black men charged with rioting and attempted murder. This was the start of the forty-five-mile ride he and his fellow NAACP lawyers took back to Nashville every night because they feared they would be killed if they lay down to sleep in Columbia.

On that final trip from Columbia, at about 7:30 P.M., Marshall drove two lawyers, Z. Alexander Looby, Nashville's most prominent black lawyer; Maurice Weaver, a white labor lawyer from Chattanooga; and a reporter for the Communist Party's *Daily Worker* newspaper, over the bridge leading out of town. The sun had just gone down, and there were no streetlights. As Marshall drove his headlights picked up a gray car blocking his lane. On the shoulder of the road there was also a police car. Marshall pulled around them and picked up speed. In a few seconds, however, the police car came after him with its siren in full blast. Then another car, with men in civilian clothing, pulled in front of him, forcing Marshall to stop. The men, carrying blinding flashlights, told Marshall and his colleagues to get out of the car. They announced they had a warrant to search for illegal whiskey.

Marshall walked alongside the policemen as they searched to be sure they did not plant evidence. Ironically, the lawyers had tried to buy liquor from a bootlegger on their way through town, but the bootlegger had been sold out. "I just sold the last two bottles to the judge," he had told Marshall.

Unable to find any liquor in the car, the police had no reason to detain Marshall. But when they started to drive away, the cops began screaming and waving their arms, ordering Marshall to stop again. Marshall was getting angry, but he knew this was not the time to mouth off. This time the policemen ordered Marshall out and pushed him into their police car. They told him he was under arrest for drunken driving. The lawyer protested that he hadn't had a drink in several days. The police told him to shut up, then ordered Looby and the others to drive away.

In the backseat of the police car, Marshall was squeezed between two deputies holding guns. They started back to town but then suddenly turned down a small dirt road that led to the secluded Duck River. Marshall, surrounded by four strange, armed, and unsmiling men, was grim and silent as the car drove into the dark woods. As sweat poured off him, he wondered how he had gotten into this situation, and how he was going to get out of it alive.

*　　*　　*

Marshall had come to Columbia because the small Tennessee town was the scene of the first southern race riot after World War II. Dozens of people, black and white, exchanged gunfire in Columbia on the night of February 26, 1946, after a white store owner slapped the mother of a nineteen-year-old black navy veteran. James Stephenson, a tall, athletic boy, and his mother, Gladys, had gone into the Caster-Knott electrical appliance store at about ten o'clock that morning. The Stephensons were upset because the store's repair shop had not fixed their radio—even though they had paid to have it repaired. The repairman, Billy Fleming, age twenty-eight, said that he had fixed it but that Gladys Stephenson had broken it again. When the woman argued that she had done nothing to the radio, Fleming slapped her and pushed her out of the store. The woman's son became enraged and punched Fleming, knocking him through the store's plate-glass window.[1]

When the police arrived they immediately sided with Fleming, who was bleeding badly. While the store manager was taken to the hospital, Stephenson and his mother were handcuffed and brought to the police station in the middle of the town square. News of the fight, the blood, and the arrests raced through town, and by early afternoon the black community was full of fear of a white lynch mob. In fact, by 6:00 P.M.

seventy-five white men—many drunk—had gathered on the town square, looking to get their hands on the Stephensons.

Columbia, with its 8,000 white and 3,000 black residents, had a history of racial problems. It was near Pulaski, Tennessee, the birthplace of the Ku Klux Klan. And everyone in town still talked about the 1933 lynching when a mob in Columbia had brutally beaten and then hanged and burned a black teenager who had been accused, but acquitted, of raping a white girl.[2]

J. J. Underwood, the town's sheriff, was a good man with no taste for mob violence. He watched the mob grow from his office window. He put several deputies in front of the police station, then called the two leading members of the black community, Sol Blair, a barbershop owner, and James Morton, an undertaker. Underwood proposed that Blair and Morton meet him at the back door of the police station and secretly drive the mother and son out of town.

Jack Lovett, who was deputized by the sheriff that night, recalled that by late afternoon the square in front of the police station was so crowded he could not walk. "It was pretty rough around here," he said, explaining that he had just returned to Columbia after serving in the Army in the South Pacific. On that night, Lovett found the small town as dangerous as any war zone in the jungle.[3]

After the Stephensons, with blankets over their heads, were rushed out the back door and smuggled out of town, police blocked roads leading into Columbia in an attempt to control the still-growing mob. Meanwhile, black residents armed themselves and gathered in stores and homes along Eighth Street in the black business district, known as Mink Slide. They were worried that the white men might start shooting people or setting fires. The tense atmosphere led black residents to shoot out the streetlights and put armed men at every window.

When reports of shooting in Mink Slide reached the police, the sheriff drove a squad car out. As he entered Mink Slide at around 8:00 P.M., the black residents, thinking the police had given their cars to the crazed mob, shot at the car from windows and doorways throughout the area. Threats were also shouted. The black residents, many of whom were returning war veterans, made it clear they were ready to fight before allowing another lynching in Columbia. As he was racing away from the gunfire, the sheriff heard one black man's voice shout, "We fought for freedom overseas and we'll fight for it here."[4]

Sheriff Underwood decided the best thing to do was to keep the scared blacks and the angry whites apart. He set up his men to prevent the whites already in town from going into Mink Slide. His strategy worked until about 10:00 P.M., when two police cars decided to check on Mink Slide. The officers, without the chief's permission, turned their engines off, put the car in neutral, and rolled through the darkened neighborhood. To the surprise of the police, a watchman shouted, "Here they come." Buckshot rained onto the cars. At the sound of the gunfire, some of the mob from the town square came running, as did other policemen.

Raymond Lockridge, a black carpenter who was in Mink Slide that night, remembered that as the policemen and white members of the mob came running, they were also greeted with gunfire. There was "blood running in the gutters," Lockridge remembered. He swore that four or five white people were killed but that the local authorities would not admit to it. "They'd say instead, 'He took a trip out of town,' " Lockridge recalled.[5]

The *Afro-American* later reported on this supposed cover-up, writing, "Whites whose obituaries stated [they] died suddenly of heart failure may also have suffered slight cases of Mink Slide bullet poisoning." The paper said that white members of a potential lynch mob "can't admit even to this day that it took a beating when colored [people] decided to protect themselves and prevent one of the most dastardly crimes known to mankind."[6]

That night's shooting prompted the mayor to ask the governor to send state troopers and the National Guard to Columbia. State Safety Director Lynn Bomar, a former All-American football player, was sent to Columbia to coordinate the antiriot efforts of 500 National Guardsmen and 100 state troopers.

Early the next morning, Tuesday, the police force, troopers, and guardsmen began an assault against the poorly armed residents of Mink Slide. They chopped down the doors with axes and broke shop windows. And once inside businesses and homes, they tore apart furniture and stripped rugs from the floors. They claimed they were looking for weapons, ammunition, and hidden teams of gunmen. "The streets were soon littered with furniture hurled out of windows," an NAACP study later reported. The greatest destruction was visited on James Morton's funeral home, the most ornate and beautifully furnished place in the black community. The state troopers trashed everything in sight: "The hate-ridden orgy was topped off with a huge KKK scrawled in white chalk across one of the caskets."[7]

The large and angry force of police and state troopers ordered blacks out of their houses, confiscating guns and in some cases jewelry and cash before marching them to jail. That night and into the next morning, seventy black people were brought to jail and twelve were charged with murder. Police continued to make arrests through the week. A total of 101 blacks were arrested; only two whites were arrested, for drunkenness.

"We urge the white citizens of the city and county to keep calm, cool and collected," the *Columbia Daily Herald* wrote in a Tuesday afternoon editorial. "The situation is in the hands of the state troops and state police. They will round up those responsible for last night's attack and clean up the city . . . there is no use in arguing the matter. The white people of the South . . . will not tolerate any racial disturbances without resenting it, which means bloodshed. The Negro has not a chance of gaining supremacy over a sovereign people and the sooner the better element of the Negro race realize this, the better off the race will be."[8]

The violence continued later that week while police were questioning two black suspects. The police said while they interrogated the two at the station house, one of the black men grabbed a weapon that had been confiscated from the rioters and tried to escape. Both men were shot and killed as police returned the gunfire.

But while police said they shot in self-defense, Wallace Gordon, the brother of one of the suspects, blamed the police. Gordon claimed that the guns confiscated from blacks in Columbia had no ammunition. But the deaths of William Gordon and James Johnson were later ruled by the courts to be justifiable homicides.[9]

Columbia's black community, now sensing it was under siege, called the national office of the NAACP for help. Thurgood Marshall immediately understood the importance of this case. So did Walter White. They quickly phoned Maurice Weaver and asked him to help. But Weaver, who was ridiculed as a left-wing kook by many of the state's segregationist politicians, had difficulty even getting into the jail to see any of the prisoners. With Weaver unable to help, Marshall got Z. Alexander Looby, who spoke with the West Indian accent of his native Jamaica, to rush to Columbia a day later.

Working together, Looby and Weaver obtained cooperation from Sheriff Underwood and succeeded in getting most of the black prisoners out of jail within the next two weeks. Walter White, reading the sensational press coverage of the rioting and shooting, got Attorney General Tom Clark to begin an FBI investigation. A grand jury was convened to see if federal civil rights statutes were violated.

Meanwhile, the *Nashville Banner* and other papers in the state began to report that several long-distance phone calls had been placed from Columbia on the night of the rioting. The papers speculated that Communists and black militants had been responsible for the riot.[10] The state's leading politicians were pushing reporters to write that black folks in Columbia would never have fought like that without "outside agitation."

After centuries of bowing and scraping, there was a new attitude growing among black Americans, and it was coming from the black veterans. They had gained more self-respect while fighting in the military and now demanded respect from whites. So Marshall understood the resentment that took shape that night in Columbia as black people fought against a white lynch mob. He felt that this resentment could be used to support an emerging civil rights movement and a growing NAACP. This was the reason he decided to personally defend the twenty-five blacks charged with inciting to riot and attempted murder.

*   *   *

When he arrived in Columbia on May 30, 1946, three months after that night of violence, Marshall found the town still tense. He and his defense team wanted to use that to their advantage. They attacked the all-white power structure in Columbia as vicious and discriminatory. Marshall's main plan was to get all the indictments thrown out because no blacks had served on the grand jury that had handed them down. Paul Bumpus, the tall, smooth-talking Maury County district attorney, responded that while it was true that blacks had not been invited to serve on juries, it was also true that many prominent whites had not served either. Marshall responded, "The fact that one or any number of white people have never been called for jury service has no bearing whatsoever on this case. Our pleas in abatement are directed at the contention that no Negroes have *ever* served on the jury and that no Negroes have been called for jury service."[11]

The judge ruled that the absence of blacks on the grand jury was not sufficient reason to throw out the indictments, but he agreed to move the trial to nearby Lawrence County to avoid having Maury County's excited racial atmosphere taint the trial.

The trial was set to start in August of 1946, but Marshall got seriously ill in late June with pneumonia. Even as he got sick, Marshall traveled to Columbia to prepare the case. But he became so ill that he had to go back to New York, and the trial began without him. A chain-smoker and a steady drinker, Marshall never exercised. His long work days, bad diet, and constant travel had begun to wear him down. Friends started to notice that he looked weak and they missed his normally loud, boisterous laugh.

Marshall became so seriously ill that he went into Ward 2D at Harlem Hospital and special intensive-care nurses were assigned to keep constant watch over him. After visiting Marshall, Walter White wrote to the NAACP's board to ask that they allocate $500 to pay his medical bills. "Mr. Marshall's present condition is in a large measure due to the physical and mental strain of the Columbia, Tennessee trials, the last three days [of which] he continued going with a temperature of 103 degrees." But by mid-July Marshall was looking better and his spirits were rising. "Give [the staff] the bad news that I'll live," he joked with White.[12]

His clients in Columbia did not forget Marshall. He later told an oral history interviewer that he got a big package while in the hospital with a note attached: " 'Dear Lawyer . . . we decided to get you something. . . . The wives all wanted to send you flowers. But we knew what you'd rather have.' They sent a twenty-pound ham."[13]

Marshall's condition improved—he was soon able to walk across the room without losing his breath. But he was still too sick to go back to work. He and Buster took an extended leave—to the Virgin Islands, where Bill Hastie had been appointed governor by President Truman. "Mr. Marshall's condition is due solely to the fact that he has worked himself almost to death without any thought of self," White wrote the NAACP board, requesting approval for Marshall's leave. Marshall and his wife also traveled to Jamaica, Haiti, and Cuba.[14]

While Marshall was recuperating, the Columbia riot trial was handled by Looby, Weaver, and the high-energy Howard law professor, Leon Ransom. They gave Marshall regular telephone reports, and he offered pointers for their use. The lawyers on the scene needed more than legal advice, however. They were under pressure inside and outside the courtroom. The black lawyers, for example, had no bathroom or water fountain available to them in the entire courthouse. And the courtroom crowd was hostile. One local paper said the trial was packed with spectators who came to town to see "those niggers up there wearing coats and ties and talking back to the judge just like they were white men." The large group of black defendants were fenced off from the rest of the court by wooden pickets, and a reporter said that one white "oldtimer" sat nearby "spitting tobacco on each picket."[15]

Weaver, the lone white defense lawyer, was a special target for abuse by police and prosecutors. At one point in the middle of the trial, the district attorney asked him to come outside for a fistfight. The burly state safety director, Lynn Bomar, became infuriated with Weaver during one round of cross-examination. Bomar had a yardstick in his hand to point out landmarks on a map of the city. "For a split second newsmen and spectators held their breath while Bomar reddened and had to restrain an obvious desire to crack the young lawyer with the yardstick," one paper reported.[16]

In court the judge repeatedly ruled against the defense lawyers. Vincent Tubbs, a reporter for the *Baltimore Afro* who covered the trial, wrote: "During the past week no less than four major infractions of decency and due processes of law have been enacted in the dirty little county courthouse here." One prosecutor referred to a black witness for the defense as "a nigger woman" before the judge told him to stop. The lead prosecutor called Ransom a "son-of-a-bitch" and later threatened to "wrap a chair around his God-Damn head."[17]

October 4, the final day of the trial, was tense. The jury returned quickly, and newspapers later wrote that the judge was in disbelief as he announced the verdict. The all-male, white jury acquitted twenty-three of the twenty-five black men charged in the riot; only two were found guilty of attempted murder for shooting a policeman, and the jury recommended a sentence of three years for each man.

Paul Bumpus, the lead prosecutor, said the jury never seriously considered the case. He said the people in Lawrence County "felt Maury County had dumped its dirty laundry on them." To get rid of the case, he said, the jury had convicted only two. "And those were the two weakest cases," Bumpus said. "I didn't think it was fair so I got up and asked the court to dismiss those two defendants."[18]

The *Afro-American*, reflecting the nationwide euphoria among black Americans, wrote in an editorial that the all-white jury's verdict stood "in legal significance" alongside the infamous *Dred Scott* decision as one of American history's landmark legal rulings. Walter White was quoted as saying: "American justice has triumphed over the Klan" and congratulated Looby, Ransom, and Weaver by describing them as lawyers who had "under the most trying conditions fought courageously to ensure the defendants a fair trial."[19]

*   *   *

Despite the acquittals two other men still had to be tried on attempted murder charges that stemmed from the riot. William "Rooster Bill" Pillow and Lloyd "Papa Lloyd" Kennedy were charged with firing shots at Tennessee highway patrolmen. The other twenty-five defendants had been charged only with firing at Columbia police. The judge refused a change of venue for this case; the trial was held in Columbia. Marshall, now over his pneumonia, came back to town to handle the case on November 16, 1946.

He tried to argue that the absence of blacks in the jury pool meant there would not be a fair trial, but the judge again dismissed his objections. Marshall was left with trying to convince the jury that the defendants had not fired the shots but were caught in the middle of a community simply trying to defend itself from a lynch mob. Marshall told the all-white jury that he was a fellow southerner from Baltimore, and he would not have traveled to Columbia to handle the case unless he sincerely believed these men were innocent.

District Attorney Bumpus, always the quintessential southern gentleman, nonetheless belittled Marshall. "I wonder why he wanted you to believe that he wasn't from New York," Bumpus said to the jury. He quipped that if Marshall only represented innocent people, as he had claimed to the jury, "he belongs on Ripley's radio program [*Believe-It-Or-Not*] as the greatest curiosity in the nation."[20]

The four-day trial ended with a "not guilty" verdict for Rooster Bill Pillow, but Papa Lloyd Kennedy was found guilty. "They were guilty and they weren't guilty. They were defending themselves," Marshall said in an interview. "The mob came down there, and the police were in front of the mob when they shot."

The trial ended at about 7:00 P.M. on November 18. Marshall, with Looby, Weaver, and Harry Raymond, the reporter for the *Daily Worker,* got into Looby's car to go back to Nashville, celebrate their victory, and plan an appeal for Kennedy. It was then that state highway patrolmen and Columbia police stopped them and Marshall was pushed into the backseat of the unmarked police car.

The police did not want any eyewitnesses. One of the plainclothesmen got out and told Looby he was to drive away immediately. Looby pulled off slowly, but when he saw the police car head in the other direction, he turned around and sped after it. He watched with growing horror as the car turned off the highway and headed down a dirt road toward the river. Undaunted by their threats, Looby followed the police car. Pulling over, one policeman got out shouting, his face red in anger, and ordered Looby to get back on the highway and drive to Nashville. Speaking slowly out of fear, Looby said he wasn't leaving until he saw Marshall.

Looby stood there, waiting to be arrested. But to his surprise the policeman stomped away to talk with the others in the car. The police were worried that even if Looby were to leave then, there would be witnesses to the fact that Marshall had not been driven back to town. There was also worry that if word of these events got back to Mink Slide, there might be another riot by blacks who now felt empowered after their court victories.

The policeman got back in the car. To turn around they had to drive closer to the river, and that was when Marshall, from his uncomfortable perch in the backseat, saw an angry group of men waiting by the water. But the police car did not stop. It simply made a loop and headed back to the highway.

With Looby still driving his car behind them, the police drove back to town. When they got to the square, they ordered Marshall out of the car and told him to go to the judge's chamber on the second floor of the courthouse by himself. Marshall told them he would walk over, but only with them. "You ain't gonna shoot me in the back. We'll go together," he said.

Across the dusty and strangely empty street that separated the police station from the courthouse, Marshall and the officers walked side by side. Marshall kept turning his head, looking for trouble. Looby and the others had followed and stood outside their car watching. Inside the turn-of-the-century courthouse, Marshall was taken before an elderly judge, just over five feet tall and completely bald. The policemen told the judge: "We got this nigger for drunken driving." The little judge looked up at the six-foot-one-inch Marshall and said: "Boy, you wanna take my test? I never had a drink in my life, and I can smell a drink a mile off. You want to take a chance?"

All of Marshall's legal training went out of his mind. He decided he had a better chance with this offbeat judge than he had an hour ago with the white mob at the river. So he blew into the judge's face so hard that the judge rocked back. "That man hadn't had a drink in twenty-four hours, what the hell are you talking about," the judge declared. And in an instant the policemen left Marshall and walked out the door. "I turned around to look and they were gone," he said.

Marshall walked outside, and to his surprise Looby wasn't there. Taking quick action, Marshall ran down to Mink Slide and found Looby and the other lawyers in a barbershop with several of Columbia's leading black citizens. They hurriedly took Marshall into a back room to make sure he was okay. Then they made plans to leave town, this time in different cars. A decoy driver took Looby's car in one direction while the lawyers went the other way. "And sure enough, the mob was coming around the corner when we left," Marshall recalled. "So they followed Looby's car, which we'd hoped they'd do. And incidentally, when they found out that I wasn't in it, they beat the driver bad enough that he was in the hospital for a week."

The mob never caught up with Marshall. He made it back to Nashville, where he immediately called the U.S. attorney general, Tom Clark, Marshall recalled: "When I told him I was arrested for drunk driving, Tom said, 'Well, were you drunk?' I said, 'No, but five minutes after I talk to you . . .'"

In a 1993 interview Flo Fleming, the older brother of Billy Fleming, the radio repairman who was pushed through the window, setting off the events that led to the Columbia riot, said he was one of the men who arrested Marshall for drunk driving. "They were drunk, but the magistrate turned them loose," said Fleming.[21] Jack Lovett, who was a deputized member of the Columbia police force at the time of the riot, however, described Marshall's drunk driving arrest as "a cock-and-bull story." Lovett said, "They just wanted to harass him, that's all. They had nothing to pick him up for."

The FBI, which was asked by the Justice Department to do an investigation, issued a report in which Flo Fleming was identified as the person responsible for stopping Marshall's car. In the FBI report, one source claimed that "Fleming wanted to get a 'last crack' at Weaver, Looby and Marshall."[22]

The FBI never brought any federal charges in the case. And Papa Lloyd Kennedy, who was initially given a five-year sentence as the only person convicted in the Columbia riot, had his sentence reduced and served only ten months. Gladys and James Stephenson, the mother and son involved in the fight with Billy Fleming, were never charged with any crime.

Three weeks after his near escape from Columbia, Marshall gave a speech to a youth conference in New Orleans. His usual confident and cocky personality was now muted. He had a newly found fear of white mobs and violent policemen.

Asked if he supported the idea of nonviolent protest as exemplified by Mahatma Gandhi's civil disobedience campaign against the British in India, Marshall said nonviolent protest movements did not interest him. He said he wanted the right to defend himself against lynch parties. And as for nonviolent protests against segregation in the United States, Marshall said they would "result in wholesale slaughter with no good achieved."[23]

Thurgood Marshall had defined himself as not wanting to lead protests, but the massive publicity given to the Columbia riot and trials made his name and face synonymous with the growing civil rights movement. Personally and professionally, Marshall found he was achieving a long-held ambition. He was now in the lead of the burgeoning social revolution to end racial segregation.

CHAPTER 14

✦

Jim Crow Buster

M ARSHALL'S SUCCESS IN COLUMBIA, TENNESSEE, and his victories in defending black soldiers made him a regular face in newspapers both black and white. And in 1946 he was selected as the winner of the NAACP's top award, the Spingarn Medal. Walter White, whose ego needs rarely allowed him to profusely praise others involved with civil rights, was the first person to tell Marshall that he had won the award. Afterward White dropped Marshall a note to say, "No more suitable choice could possibly have been made."[1]

Marshall was thirty-seven when he won the medal in May of 1946, making him the second youngest person to receive the prestigious award; only Richard Wright, the author of *Native Son*, had won it at a younger age, thirty-one. The award had previously been given to such people as the author W.E.B. Du Bois and Paul Robeson, the human rights activist, actor, and singer.

Marshall stood to receive the award at the NAACP convention in Cincinnati. Robert W. Kenny, the attorney general of California, handed him the honor after introducing him as an American hero: "The very immensity of the task [of ending racial discrimination] is one of the things which makes the work of Thurgood Marshall more significant. . . . His efforts have reached into the lives of many, many thousands—hundreds of thousands—of Americans and throughout the history of the United States."[2]

In the heart of his acceptance speech Marshall proudly declared his integrationist ideal once again: "A Negro sharecropper's baby born in the most miserable shack of Mississippi," he said, should have the same rights as the richest white child born in a mansion. But Marshall added that such equality had yet to be achieved. Reaching back to the Civil War period, Marshall said that after "the shooting war was won," the northern states had enacted civil rights amendments to the Constitution but did not have the courage to enforce "the principles for which the war was fought." [3] So, Marshall concluded, the South continued to treat blacks as people without rights—slavery by another name.

Marshall got a standing ovation, and he was genuinely thrilled. Part of the kick for him was that he was being honored by some of America's most celebrated figures. At that dinner he was sitting next to Joe Louis, the heavyweight boxing champ, yet he was the one getting the applause.

Marshall and Louis were quite a contrast. The lawyer was not much of an athlete. "I couldn't hit the side of a barn with a paddle or catch a cold in a rainstorm," he told a reporter for the *New York Post*.[4] But Marshall liked sports, especially boxing. He attended several of Louis's fights, including the boxer's famous victory in New York over Max Schmeling, the German fighter who had been cited as a living example of white racial superiority by Adolf Hitler. "I knew Joe very well, a marvelous guy but just not too intelligent," Marshall remembered. "The only trouble with Joe was, you know, wine, women, and song, the bad features that kill off all men. He didn't drink wine and he didn't play any music. The only thing left was women."

Marshall's Spingarn award speech was excerpted in the *Baltimore Afro-American* and the *Pittsburgh Courier*. It was reprinted in its entirety in the *NAACP Bulletin*. The *Afro* also wrote a long feature story on Marshall's parents, who still lived in Baltimore. The story was almost a psychoanalysis of young Marshall. Its headline read: MOTHER CONSIDERED POWER BEHIND SPINGARN MEDALIST.

"Throughout his mother's role has been that of providing the type of constant and dynamic support and encouragement on which both Thurgood and his older brother, Aubrey, a doctor, have leaned heavily," said the story. It portrayed Mrs. Marshall as a ranking member of black society because of her son's success. The paper said she had recently switched churches, from St. Katherine's, where Thurgood had been baptized, to the black bourgeois pews of St. James Episcopal Church.[5]

The *Afro* story barely mentioned Willie Marshall, except as Norma Marshall's husband of forty-two years and a former headwaiter at the

Gibson Island Club. Now sixty-four years old, Willie had been working as a janitor at an FBI training academy in Baltimore for several years and was fast approaching retirement. After his unhappy departure from the Gibson Island Club, he had continued to drink heavily. His communication with Aubrey and Thurgood had been cut to a minimum. Willie on rare occasions visited Thurgood in New York, but Norma would regularly come North to see her son and spend time with Buster and Aunt Medi. "Thurgood and his mother were very close," Alice Stovall, Marshall's secretary at the NAACP, recalled in an interview. "She and his Aunt Medi were the two main people in his life."[6]

After the whirlwind of the Spingarn Award, Marshall settled back into the demanding reality of the NAACP's overwhelmed legal department. He was now juggling two key cases that would end up in the Supreme Court.

In the first case, *Morgan v. Virginia*, Marshall asked the high court to ban segregated seating on buses that traveled between states, no matter what local segregation laws might be in place. Irene Morgan, a black woman from Baltimore, had taken a Greyhound bus from a town in Gloucester County, Virginia, to Baltimore in July 1944. But when the bus reached Saluda, Virginia, and more whites got on, the driver, citing Jim Crow laws, asked her to take a seat in the back with other blacks. She said no and was arrested and fined ten dollars.[7]

Morgan appealed the fine with the help of Howard Law School Professor Spottswood Robinson, a rail-thin, brilliant black lawyer who went nowhere without his pipe. When she lost, Robinson took her case to the Supreme Court of Virginia. She lost again, but Robinson, working with Marshall and the NAACP, took the case to the U.S. Supreme Court.

A lanky Marshall, in his best double-breasted dark suit, stood before the nine justices of the high court with just a slight case of nerves. It was only his fourth Supreme Court appearance, but his easy, polite manner— stripped of heavy academic language and flowery rhetoric—and his light humor made the young black lawyer a fast favorite among the older white justices. Marshall always took a moment to thank the justices, whisper some confidence, and make each of them feel as if he were relying on their superior knowledge to help him through the maze of laws.

In the *Morgan* case, heard in March 1946, Marshall elaborated on the expertly crafted argument Spottswood Robinson had made in Virginia. For seventy years, Marshall explained, showing his reverence for the court, the justices had "consistently condemned" state laws that tried to require segregation of interstate commerce. He added that these Jim Crow laws were "invasions of an area where national power under the commerce clause is exclusive."

Marshall reached back to 1878 to cite *Hall v. DeCuir,* a Louisiana case decided while the Civil War was still fresh in the Supreme Court's mind. "Even then," he told the justices, "this court was quite sure that the nation, to the exclusion of the states, must have control of this aspect of interstate travel." In fact, the federal government wanted total control of interstate travel to give businesses the greatest possible protection. The rights of black passengers were secondary but still a concern. Even in the 1896 *Plessy v. Ferguson* decision, the Supreme Court had ruled that Louisiana laws compelling segregation of rail passengers was valid only if the train did not cross into another state.

"Today we are just emerging from a war in which all of the people of the United States were united in a death struggle against the apostles of racism," Marshall told the justices. "How much clearer must it be today than it was in 1877 that the national business of interstate commerce is not to be disfigured by disruptive local practices bred of racial notions alien to our national ideals."[8]

Marshall's presentation to the high court was widely praised, especially by Walter White, who now found it useful to be Marshall's top booster inside the NAACP. White even used NAACP funds to pay for Buster Marshall to travel to Washington to hear Thurgood argue the Morgan case. It was the first time she had seen him argue at the Supreme Court.[9]

Two and a half months later, in early June 1946, the Supreme Court gave a near-unanimous victory to Marshall. In a 7–1 ruling [Justice Jackson was at the Nuremberg war crimes trials], the court said Irene Morgan had been wrongly forced to give up her seat. The opinion concluded that state segregation placed an "unfair burden" on interstate commerce.

*   *   *

The Morgan victory got attention in the black press, but the nationwide reaction was muted because hard-line segregation on buses was generally limited to a few states in the South. Emotionally, however, the case was a big confidence booster for Marshall, who was at the time feeling overwhelmed by an endless stream of criminal cases bubbling up from NAACP branches. The constant phone calls about black people doing hard time on phony charges and death sentences for black defendants stretched the legal office's resources and Marshall to near the breaking point.

He had to turn away far more of these cases than he could accept. His favorite strategy was to argue that indictments and convictions of black defendants were illegal when blacks were intentionally excluded from trial juries. He had first seen this strategy used by Charles Houston in the George Crawford murder case during law school. Marshall had subsequently used it in several cases, although it almost always failed.

The strategy finally worked for him in two cases in 1947 and 1949. In *Patton v. Mississippi*, Eddie "Buster" Patton was given the death penalty after being charged with killing a white man. The Supreme Court overturned the conviction and ruled unanimously that any practice of excluding citizens on the basis of race from jury duty resulted in unconstitutional indictments and verdicts.

In the other case, *Watts v. Indiana*, Robert Watts, a black man, was charged with murdering a white man in Indiana. In a letter to the NAACP written in barely legible script, he complained that he was framed: "They questioned me for six days and nights standing up. . . . I just couldn't take it any longer and they forced me to sign about ten confessions to every unsolved crime in Indianapolis." [10] Again the Supreme Court ruled in Marshall's favor. The Court found that the confessions were invalid because they were coerced and that the state had intentionally kept blacks off the jury.

But Marshall did not have a perfect record on high-profile criminal cases. In one surprising defeat the Supreme Court ruled against Samuel Taylor, an illiterate teenager who was convicted in Alabama of raping a fourteen-year-old white girl. Marshall challenged the conviction, claiming that police beat Taylor to force him to confess. The Court ruled Marshall's appeal was unfounded. It was Marshall's second defeat at the Supreme Court, and, as in the first (the *Lyons* case from Oklahoma), he had failed to persuade the justices that a defendant was beaten or scared into confessing a crime he did not commit.

Marshall's work on criminal cases sometimes took him to unexpected places. On one occasion, to stop an execution he had to find U.S. Supreme Court Chief Justice Fred Vinson. It was already late when he realized that Vinson was his only hope and that the chief justice was neither at home nor at his usual club. Marshall called other justices as well as Vinson's friends, but no one knew where he was. Finally, he started asking around among the black janitors, maids, and chauffeurs at the

Supreme Court. He quickly got the word that he should try the Statler-Hilton Hotel.

There he found Vinson in an elegant suite, complete with grand piano and plush purple carpeting, playing cards with President Truman. "How did you find me?" Vinson asked. "I can't tell you," Marshall said. He then handed Vinson his brief. The always cold, skeptical Vinson looked it over with a scowl on his face. "Can you vouch for this being true?" Vinson demanded, waving the brief in the air as the president looked on. "Yes sir, I wrote it." Vinson held his breath for a second, looked at Truman and then back to Marshall. "I'll tell you one thing, if you've got guts enough to break in on this, I've got guts enough to sign it," said the chief justice.

Despite Vinson's willingness to sign the stay of execution, Marshall never developed any admiration for the chief justice. "No, no," said Marshall. "Vinson was awful. I think he was one of the worst people." Marshall liked Vinson's predecessor, Harlan Fiske Stone, whom he saw as a kindly grandfather of a judge. But Vinson was different. "He'd put your ass in jail," said Marshall.

The criminal cases took up a lot of Marshall's time. They led him into some tricky situations, and ultimately they were unsatisfying to him. He was looking for cases that would have nationwide and lasting impact on legal segregation.

He found one such case in complaints from NAACP branches about restrictive covenants in property contracts that banned blacks and Jews from buying houses in select neighborhoods. Getting decent housing had been a particularly large problem for black veterans returning from the war. While black soldiers qualified for housing loans, they often could not buy the houses they wanted because of these covenants. The Federal Housing Administration added to the NAACP's alarm over the issue because they permitted blacks and whites to be segregated in federally subsidized housing.

Marshall was familiar with restrictive covenants because they were first devised in his hometown, Baltimore. When well-to-do black businessmen began moving into white neighborhoods in the early 1900s, segregationists on the Baltimore city council passed laws restricting the sale of property in mostly white neighborhoods. Cities across the South followed suit.

In 1917 the Supreme Court ruled that citywide residential segregation laws were unconstitutional. Baltimore's advocates of whites-only neighborhoods reacted to the ruling by creating an ingenious new instrument of segregation—restrictive covenants. The covenants were clauses in the deeds of houses that prohibited their sale to people stereotyped as undesirables, such as blacks, Jews, or other ethnic and racial minorities.[11] This new technique of keeping blacks out of white neighborhoods proved very popular, not only in the South but throughout big cities in the North.

In July 1945, as the war was coming to an end, Marshall held an NAACP conference for lawyers to look for new approaches to attack housing discrimination. "Restrictive covenants are increasing in number and we are constantly being requested to work out some procedure for invalidating them," he wrote in a letter asking lawyers as well as housing experts, politicians, and top social scientists to attend the gathering.[12] At that meeting Robert C. Weaver, a leading authority on housing in big cities, pinpointed residential segregation as a major source of racial hostility in the nation as well as a negative factor in health and crime statistics.

Walter White, Bill Hastie, and the NAACP's chairman, Charles Toney, attended Marshall's Chicago conference, making it a major event. Marshall positioned himself as an able shepherd for this flock of black intelligentsia. He was a charmer who defused all the big egos by blowing everybody else's horn, making them all heroes. He would tell jokes about himself, usually about how scared he was in some small southern town. He kept everybody laughing with his larger-than-life tales, accentuated with his big hands, and his impersonations of stupid, bullying sheriffs. Even after long days Marshall was in the blues clubs with the scholars and policy makers until late. But he was up early for every meeting so that nothing got away from him. The conference heightened Marshall's status because it showed him to be without a doubt the leader of the NAACP's effort to defeat restrictive covenants. This was Marshall in full flower, for the first time acknowledged by senior black leaders as one of their own.

After the conference Marshall began tracking dozens of housing bias cases. Four of those reached the Supreme Court, headed by the St. Louis case *Shelley v. Kraemer.* Marshall made the fight a constitutional issue by having his lawyers focus on the idea that racial covenants violated the Fourteenth Amendment, which gave equal protection to all Americans. Charles Houston, who represented clients challenging restrictive covenant laws in Washington, D.C., was one of a team of lawyers in court with Marshall. Walter White and the editors of several black newspapers, including the influential Louis Martin from Detroit and Carl Murphy from Baltimore, went to the Supreme Court for the argument.

Marshall picked up on Bob Weaver's contention that ghettos created crime and endangered public health. It was the first time Marshall had used sociological evidence in making a presentation to the Supreme Court. The case generated headlines when three of the nine justices had to remove themselves because of a conflict of interest—they owned properties with deeds that included restrictive covenants. "It shows how deep the case cuts," Charles Houston told news reporters, "when one-third of the nation's highest court disqualifies itself." [13]

The heart of the NAACP's challenge to the covenants came when Marshall, on January 22, 1948, told the justices that restrictive covenants worked only because the states acknowledged them as legal. The Constitution guaranteed that government cannot sanction a racially discriminatory contract, Marshall told them. In his low-key way he argued that a state court was "not a mere arbiter in a private contractual dispute" but "the arm of the state," which enforced discrimination. [14]

Justice Felix Frankfurter, one of Houston's old Harvard professors, expressed doubts about the relevance of the NAACP's sociological evidence to an argument over the constitutionality of the law. Marshall responded that the sociological material was presented only to display the damage a bad law can have on the nation's crime rate, health care, and schools. [15]

The justices peppered Marshall with questions about the right of individuals to sell to whomever they pleased. The questions came with particular force because the lawyer who had preceded him had made a bad, even comic, presentation that did not address the obvious question of the sellers' right to do business with whomever they chose.

"I mean he was a blunderbuss," Marshall said, describing George Vaughn, the NAACP lawyer who handled the St. Louis restrictive covenant case. "And we'd all worried about this guy. So we tried to tell him what to argue and he would not listen. He wanted to argue the Thirteenth Amendment [which freed the slaves]."

"Vaughn didn't get a question from any of the justices," Marshall said. "And at the end of his argument he stood up in that damned courtroom, filled to the gills with people, and he said in a loud booming voice that you could hear out in the streets: 'And Moses looked across the River Jordan and looked across the Mississippi River and said, let my people

G-o-o-o-o-o-o.' And we were all sitting like this," Marshall said, his eyes wide and mouth hanging open.

"Then he got through and sat down, right in the front row, and promptly went to sleep. The guard got up and walked over toward him. I got up and said to him, 'Are you goddamned dead?' "

When Marshall was sure that Vaughn was still breathing, he began his argument. But the justices interrupted him almost immediately. They were loaded with questions that they had been unable to ask Vaughn. "I got a thousand questions all the justices were scared to ask him."

Marshall's approach—to say the covenants violated the right to equal protection under the law—found surprising support from Attorney General Tom Clark and Solicitor General Philip Perlman. Perlman, a Jewish lawyer from Baltimore, gave a powerful hour-long presentation. He told the justices that white Americans were "under a heavy debt to colored Americans. We brought them here as slaves," Perlman said. "Yet after three-quarters of a century, attempts are made by such devices as restrictive covenants to hold them in bondage, to segregate them, to hem them in so that they cannot escape from the evil conditions under which so many of them are compelled to live." [16]

Philip Elman, an assistant solicitor general who was working behind the scenes on Perlman's brief, later said Perlman's "Fourth of July speech" to the Supreme Court was a politically calculated presentation, aimed at helping President Truman's sagging popularity with white liberals. [17]

On Monday May 3, 1948, the Supreme Court announced a 6–0 vote to end the use of restrictive covenants. Marshall was elated. [18] This victory got the nation's attention because it reached into every city and every neighborhood. Marshall's name appeared in the headlines of white as well as black newspapers. Black America, which sat by radios to hear every move of Joe Louis's championship fights, now began hailing Marshall as the Joe Louis of the courtroom. And when he gave speeches around the country, NAACP leaflets heralded him as the "Jim Crow Buster." Marshall was making his distinctive mark on American law, literally changing where and how the races interacted. But his success was also stirring segregationist passions. Old Jim Crow was not ready to throw in the towel.

CHAPTER 15

Groveland

T HE FOUR BLACK MEN could not run faster. They kept their legs
churning through the cypress, moss, and mud of the steamy groves
and swamps as the sounds of the lynch mob and their hunting dogs grew
closer. The black men used the velvety dark of night in rural central
Florida to hide where possible. But the angry flares of the mob's torches
cast long shadows. And when they ran from their hiding places, the tree
roots tripped them up. In the distance they could hear the cries from
Groveland, where four hundred black people's homes were set afire and
white-hooded night riders terrorized their neighborhoods. It would be
many hours before the state militia moved in to protect the blacks in
what remained of Groveland.[1]

Hyperventilating with fear and fatigue and imagining their own
deaths by lynching, the men began to fall behind. The frenzied mob
grabbed and beat each one, sending sickening shrieks into the air. They
killed the first one they caught and beat the three others long after they
had lost consciousness.

The three men were dragged into jail, strung up from iron pipes in
the boiler room, and given more bloody beatings. As they faded in and
out of consciousness, the men could hear their jailers demanding that
they confess to raping a lovely, wild-eyed seventeen-year-old white
housewife. They wanted them to admit they had been on the highway
where the blonde said her clothes were ripped by black men who had
kidnapped and violated her.

The men didn't know enough to answer. One of them was so severely beaten that his testicles remained swollen for days. Another was injured so badly that his pants were still caked with dry blood days later when NAACP lawyers came to question him.[2]

In his New York offices Thurgood Marshall got barely coherent phone calls from NAACP officials in Florida. They told about the black neighborhood being burned and about the men being beaten. Marshall heard that the mob violence had spilled over from that ghastly night. The next day the families of the young men had been threatened, then forced to go into hiding for fear that they would be lynched.

Although police claimed the three survivors had confessed, NAACP officials told Marshall none had signed any written confession. Marshall decided to send Franklin Williams, one of his deputies, to Groveland to figure out what was going on and mount a legal defense. Williams called back within hours of arriving to tell Marshall that what had happened made no sense and that the black community was so dazed with fright they had barely managed to hold a public funeral for the suspect who had been killed by the mob.

On Marshall's orders Williams stayed and defended the three men. The trial began with temperatures reaching 105 degrees. And Williams faced a hostile white jury. But he thought he had a strong case. Despite the beatings, there were no confessions from these men. He also argued that the state had not even presented evidence that the woman had been raped. But the jury still convicted the three. Samuel Shepherd and Walter Lee Irvin were sentenced to death in the electric chair; Charles Greenlee, sixteen, was given life because of his age. The NAACP lawyer was chased by a jeering group of white toughs as he left town. He had to speed down the highway to get away, all the time recalling what had happened to Marshall in Columbia, Tennessee.

The NAACP appealed the case to the U.S. Supreme Court, which overturned the Shepherd and Irvin convictions. Greenlee, fearing he might get a death sentence if there was a new trial, chose not to appeal. Justice Robert Jackson said the convictions did not "meet any civilized conception of due process of law." The high court ordered a new trial. But just when the case seemed back on track, it took another bizarre turn.

While Shepherd and Irvin were being transferred to another jail, Sheriff Willis B. McCall shot both men. The two were handcuffed together, but McCall claimed they were trying to escape. Shepherd was killed, but Irvin, who was shot three times—in the shoulder, chest, and neck—survived by lying facedown in the mud and playing dead.[3]

Sheriff McCall's brutal actions caused an uproar. Newspapers from around the world sent reporters to cover the incident and the upcoming new trial. The expanded attention to the case caused trouble among Marshall's legal team in New York. Franklin Williams wanted to continue as lead counsel. But with the Supreme Court having ordered a new trial and press all over the story, Marshall decided to take charge. "He thought he was great, and I did too, [but] I didn't think he was as great as he thought he was," Marshall later said about Williams.

The angry Williams told Marshall it was unfair for him to take over the now prominent case. Williams went to Walter White to complain, and finally White promised him that he "didn't have to worry about Thurgood Marshall." White told Williams that he would have a job "as long as he was secretary." When Marshall heard about White's promised protection for Williams, he fired him.[4]

"[Franklin Williams] had a big fight with Thurgood, around the time I was [first] there [at the NAACP]," Jack Greenberg, a young staff lawyer, later said. "There was a lot of yelling and screaming and carrying on, that sort of thing. . . . He and Thurgood clashed constantly."[5] In the battle of egos Marshall had defeated Williams. No doubt he was a more experienced lawyer, but Marshall was also drawn to the spotlight now focused on Groveland, and he was not going to play second fiddle to his junior. Marshall's actions damaged his relationship with White, who was forced to send Williams to California as the staff director for the NAACP's West Coast office.

With Williams gone, Marshall personally led the NAACP legal team to defend the accused Irvin at the second trial, which was moved to nearby Marion County. And right from the start, they faced troubles. In the December 1951 proceedings, Judge Truman Futch ruled that Marshall and Jack Greenberg were not allowed to represent their clients because the NAACP, according to the judge, was a group of agitators who had "stirred up trouble in the community."[6]

But Marshall would not back down. A few days later, speaking before an electrified Mount Zion Baptist Church in Miami, he stood to full height and defied the white powers of Florida to stop him from defending his client: "They can keep me from the courts of Florida but there is no man alive or to be born who can prevent me from arguing the Groveland Case before the U.S. Supreme Court."[7] Armed men were positioned around the building where he spoke as bomb threats were promised against Marshall's life. Guards were even posted around the pulpit as Marshall addressed the biracial crowd. A few days later, on Christmas night, the home of the NAACP's state coordinator, Harry T. Moore, was bombed, killing Moore. It was the first murder of an NAACP official.[8]

Under threat of further appeals, Marshall finally forced Judge Futch to allow him back into the case. When he walked into the small southern courtroom with its whirring overhead fans and segregated seating, Marshall became the first black lawyer to argue a case in Marion County, Florida. During the trial Judge Futch showed his disdain for Marshall and the defense by taking out a knife and whittling whenever they stood to speak.

"When I went down for the Irvin trial," Marshall recalled in a quiet, conspiratorial voice, "a white man met me in the hallway, and it was real tense. And he showed me his credentials from the governor's staff. He said, 'They're trying to get you.' And I said, 'Who, Sheriff Willis Mc-Call?' And he said, 'No, the deputy is going to get you.' I said, 'Well, thank you, I appreciate that.'" The threats caused Marshall to walk everywhere, even to the toilet, with two bodyguards. He began shifting houses from night to night and even eating at different homes so no one could predict his movements.

In addition to physical threats Marshall had to cope with a good-old-boy justice system. The governor had phoned the judge, who agreed to give Irvin a life sentence if Irvin pleaded guilty. The judge sent word to Marshall to have his client accept the deal immediately or go to trial and take his chances with the death penalty.

In his client's jail cell Marshall described the judge's offer. Irvin asked what he would have to do to accept the plea bargain. "Just stand up there and when they say are you guilty or not guilty, you say: I'm guilty," Marshall explained. Irvin, a dark-skinned man with a long face and sad eyes, looked dead into Marshall's eyes. He asked if admitting guilt meant he had raped the woman. Yes, replied Marshall. Irvin spat on the floor in disgust. "That I raped that whore? I didn't and I'm not going to say so." Marshall said in that moment he became convinced that while Irvin may have had sex with the woman, he had not raped her. "I knew damn well that man was innocent."

But persuading an all-white, male jury that Irvin was innocent of raping a young white woman was a mountain of a challenge. Marshall began by eliciting testimony from a white soldier who found the girl wandering on a highway the morning after the crime. The soldier testified that the woman never told him she had been raped, only that she had been kidnapped. He added that she said she could not identify the men who grabbed her because it was too dark. Marshall also got sheriff's deputies to concede that they had no medical evidence the woman had been raped.

He next tried to undermine the sheriff's effort to put Irvin at the scene. The sheriff claimed prints in the mud matched Irvin's shoes. However, under questioning from Marshall, a criminologist testified that while the shoe prints matched Irvin's, the prints had been made when the shoes were empty.

Marshall began his closing argument by reminding the jury that there was no evidence any rape had occurred. He closed with a patriotic appeal. "There's nobody who believes in the democratic principles of government more than my people," he said. "Cases like this are cases that try men's souls."[9]

As he was talking to the jurors, Marshall noticed that every one of the men had on a Shriner's pin. After the jury went out, Marshall went to Judge Futch's chamber and asked if he had seen the state's attorney motion to the jury, three times, using a secret Masonic distress signal. "Yeah, as a matter of fact, it was four," Futch told Marshall with a laugh. Marshall said, "I'm going to make an objection." Futch told him he would be overruled. "There's nothing racial about that," Judge Futch told Marshall. "He does it *all* the time, whether you're white, black, or green. He gives the distress signal all the time."

The jury came back within ninety minutes. One court observer later told Marshall they only took that long because the men wanted to smoke their cigars.

The verdict was guilty. Irvin was sentenced to death in the electric chair. For the first time in his legal career, Marshall had to fight back tears. He immediately rushed over to Irvin's mother to reassure her that the NAACP would appeal again. "Irvin's mother had me awake all night, every night," Marshall said. "She had the most impressive face I've ever seen on a woman, real high cheekbones and a whole lot of red in that black, a lot of Indian. And she just had these piercing eyes, and she told me not once but four times, 'Don't you let my son die.' I'm going to be stuck with that for life."

The emotions in the *Irvin* case resonated with Marshall's still unsettled emotions about the "Black Dillingers" case in Prince Georges County, Maryland. He had lost that client to a death sentence by hanging, and that time he'd blamed his inexperience. Now a more experienced Marshall decided he would do anything to stop Irvin from being executed.

Marshall appealed the case at every level until the Supreme Court refused to review it. But the lengthy appeals delayed the execution and gave Marshall time to work on other options to keep Irvin alive. Using political and NAACP contacts, he put public pressure on the governor and generated loud headlines, week after week, about various details in the case. The black press as well as international newspapers made the Florida case almost a running feature. The state legislature, the U.S. Congress, and the Justice Department were all well aware of the negative fallout from the *Irvin* case. With the pressure building from all sides, Gov. LeRoy Collins, three years after Irvin had been assigned to death row, changed the sentence to life in prison. Several years later, Irvin was finally released.[10]

The governor's decision was pure politics. And it was a win for Marshall, who had been able to apply just the right political pressure to get the governor to act. The *Irvin* case had shown Marshall to be a wily political player, both inside the NAACP and even in an unsympathetic southern state. But Marshall's political skills were about to face an even tougher test, on the national stage, from FBI director J. Edgar Hoover.

CHAPTER 16

❧

Lessons in Politics

J. EDGAR HOOVER TOOK A STRONG, IMMEDIATE DISLIKE to Thurgood Marshall. Hoover's boss, Attorney General Tom Clark, kept getting complaints from the NAACP lawyer about the behavior of Hoover's FBI agents in the South. Marshall regularly charged that the FBI was not investigating hate crimes committed by white racists—even lynch mobs—against black people. Marshall said Hoover's agents were spending their time covering up for their friends in southern sheriffs' departments, who were often sympathetic to the mobs.

The NAACP lawyer was particularly incensed over the FBI's failure to properly investigate the notorious 1946 beating of Isaac Woodard. The day of his discharge from the army, after fifteen months of jungle fighting in the Philippines, Woodard was on his way to visit his mother. At one stop he delayed the bus driver while using the bathroom. At the next stop, in Aiken, South Carolina, the driver asked him to step off the bus for a moment. Two policemen were there to greet him. The driver shouted that Woodard was drunk and creating "a disturbance" on the bus.

When Woodard protested that he had done nothing wrong, the policemen clubbed him and put him in their car. Once they got Woodard to the jail, they beat him with a blackjack and nightstick. At one point, as Woodard was on the ground and helpless, the policeman purposely shoved the end of his nightstick at both of Woodard's eyes, completely blinding him.

News of the attack rang like an alarm through much of the nation.

The horrific beating drew attention from people who had previously ignored claims that southern police regularly beat blacks for no reason. When the prosecutors failed to convict the policemen who beat Woodard, explaining that the FBI's investigation of the incident had turned up little evidence, Marshall became angry and sent another fiery letter to Attorney General Clark. In the December 1946 letter Marshall charged that the bureau was suspiciously incompetent when it came to protecting the rights of black people: "[The FBI's] great record extends from the prosecution of vicious spies and saboteurs . . . to nondescript hoodlums who steal cheap automobiles. . . . On the other hand, the FBI has been unable to identify or bring to trial persons charged with violations of federal statutes where Negroes are the victims."[1]

Despite the sharp twang of his Texas accent, Clark was well known for liberal tendencies on civil rights. He sent a copy of Marshall's stinging letter to Hoover and demanded a response. Hoover wrote a four-page retort that dripped with deep, personal anger at the NAACP attorney. He said he did not think Marshall would accept a "factual explanation" of the bureau's investigations: "I have found from previous dealings with [Marshall] that he is most careless as to the truth and facts in the charges which he makes against the FBI." The FBI chief argued that the bureau's problem with race crimes was that civil rights laws required a high level of evidence, and it was difficult to find evidence or witnesses willing to talk about these crimes. "I believe that Mr. Marshall's obvious hostility to the Bureau dominates the thinking of his associates in the legal operation of the National Association for the Advancement of Colored People," he concluded in his January 1947 response.[2]

Hoover didn't let the issue drop there. He decided to call Marshall's bluff and embarrass him in front of the attorney general. Hoover dared Marshall to give him the names of people who claimed to be victims of FBI wrongdoing in the South. Marshall was trapped. He didn't want to appear to have made up the complaints, but he was more concerned that if he gave Hoover the names of the people, FBI agents and local authorities would go after them. Marshall decided not to release the names, and a newly defiant Hoover held fast to denials that his agents had looked away from criminal actions by white police.

Hoover had headed the FBI since 1924 and was deeply entrenched at the bureau and in political Washington. Clark was Hoover's boss, but he understood that by 1946 Hoover had seen attorneys general come and go. He also had to face the fact that Hoover was right—the laws were weak and difficult to prosecute. In January, Clark wrote to Marshall that after his review he felt it was not fair to blame Hoover's agents for the continuing problems facing black people in the South.

Marshall was irate that Hoover had outmaneuvered him. But worst of all, Marshall was in a weaker position than when he started. The FBI and Hoover now considered him an opponent and were less likely to take strong action against race crimes in the South. Marshall decided his only choice was to travel to Washington and speak with the attorney general himself.

Marshall had no assurances that Clark would make the time to see him. But Clark was sensitive to President Truman's need to hold together a Democratic Party that was splintering after the death of Roosevelt. He recognized the NAACP's growing political clout, not only with blacks but with moderate and liberal whites. When Clark decided to meet one on one with Marshall, it was a sign not only of the NAACP's power but also of Marshall's growing status as the nation's best-known civil rights attorney.

In the meeting Clark caught Marshall off guard by agreeing that the government had to do more to end attacks on black people. And the bow-tied Texan said he wanted tougher antilynching laws. Just when Marshall felt he had Clark totally on his side, the attorney general engaged the young lawyer in a long conversation about the need to keep an open line to Hoover and the FBI. The bureau, Clark insisted, was the only federal agency in position to keep watch over the bigots in southern police departments. He persuaded Marshall to tone down his criticism or risk alienating a potentially powerful ally in Hoover and the bureau.

When Hoover found out about Marshall's visit with Clark, the FBI director sent a sharp letter to Walter White, whom he had known for some time, complaining that Marshall was hurting the NAACP's reputation and relationship with the FBI. "I wanted to bring to your attention a situation which is causing me increasing concern," he wrote. The hostile lawyer, he charged, had repeatedly tried "to embarrass" the FBI and to discredit the bureau's investigations, "particularly of cases involving civil rights of Negroes."

Hoover charged Marshall with being dishonest. "I, of course, recognize the right of Mr. Marshall to have a personal opinion. . . . I do not think, however, that when Mr. Marshall in his official capacity, addresses a letter to the Attorney General of the United States relating to the work of the Federal Bureau of Investigations [*sic*] he might reasonably be expected to be truthful as to the facts in the situation about which he complains."[3]

White didn't fall for the bait. In a show of support for Marshall, he simply wrote a letter asking the FBI director to talk face-to-face with Marshall. Stubbornly, Hoover refused. "I note that you suggest that much good might come if Mr. Marshall and I . . . talked frankly with each other," he responded. "I think that this would have indeed been the proper procedure . . . before Mr. Marshall resorted to gross misstatement and unfounded accusations against the Federal Bureau of Investigation and my administration of it."

Despite his support of Marshall, White was very sensitive to the possible political fallout from a battle with Hoover. White continued to court the bureau's leader because he knew the NAACP could not afford to be on Hoover's hit list. In April, White even asked Hoover and Tom Clark to write messages of support for the NAACP. The letters were for a publicity drive to proclaim the group's patriotism and allay charges that they held Communist and antigovernment sympathies. Both men responded with kind words. Hoover wrote: "Equality, freedom and tolerance are essential in a democratic government. The NAACP has done so much to preserve these principles and to perpetuate the desires of our founding fathers."[4]

Hoover's good feelings with White continued through the summer of 1947 and hit a high point when he finally agreed to a private talk with Marshall in October. Hoover decided this was a good chance to size up the civil rights attorney, whom he had never met. Marshall had to go onto Hoover's turf for the meeting, but he, too, wanted the chance to size up his opponent. The encounter was initially very polite, with coffee for Marshall and introductions to some of Hoover's top aides, who sat in on the meeting. Through all the niceties, Hoover made it clear to Marshall that no sane person would want the FBI as an enemy. And he said the bureau would be glad to have Marshall as a friend.

Marshall had come to the meeting with instructions from White to go slow and not upset the NAACP's tenuous peace with Hoover. When the director held out the prospect of an ongoing and personal relationship, it appealed to Marshall's desire for respect and power. Marshall, in turn, won Hoover over with his charming, good-ol'-boy, "I'm a little ol' Baltimore lawyer" persona, which worked so well with southern sheriffs and politicians. As Hoover opened up to Marshall, the NAACP lawyer suggested that the FBI could use the NAACP as an ally against charges that the FBI was racist. But the FBI, he said, had to do a better job investigating racial attacks on black people. The meeting ended with smiles, handshakes, and promises to stay in touch.

The new relationship was evident a few months later when Hoover made handwritten notes on FBI case files involving a black man who had been badly beaten by whites in Washington, D. C. Marshall had written him about the incident, and Hoover wrote on the file that he wanted "very special attention paid to this case." Hoover and Marshall seemed to have achieved a truce, if not peace, in their personal war.[5]

A few months later, however, in July of 1948, D. M. Ladd, one of Hoover's top aides, wrote the director that an angry Marshall had called a New York FBI agent to report finding a listening device in his office wall. Ladd told Hoover, "It should be noted that the Bureau does not have and has not had a microphone installed on the NAACP." Hoover was immediately concerned with the potential for public relations damage. He knew that Marshall would be able to get lots of publicity if he claimed the FBI was bugging him.

As a result of his relationship with Hoover, Marshall's complaint about eavesdropping was immediately given serious attention. Hoover personally instructed his staff to handle the story carefully: "In accordance with your instructions," Ladd wrote to Hoover, "I told [the New York FBI agent] to call Mr. Thurgood Marshall, to be very courteous to him, and to suggest to him that he endeavor to determine the make and serial number of the microphone from the instrument itself and thereafter, through the manufacturer, endeavor to determine to whom it had been sold."[6]

Marshall described the device to the New York agent. The FBI man denied that the bureau used that kind of bug but told Marshall he would make calls to check on who might be interested in putting the NAACP under surveillance. Marshall was still suspicious and asked a private investigator, Buck Owens, to take a look at the situation. But Owens told Marshall he could not trace the bug unless he tore out the walls of the whole building.

The mystery appealed to Marshall's mind. He wanted to know who had the power, the money, and the need to know about the NAACP's affairs. He called in secretaries, the night watchmen, and the building superintendent to question them about the bug. To Marshall's surprise the building superintendent came back a week later with the answer. "Hey, Mr. Marshall, I've found out about your bug," the elderly man called out as he walked into Marshall's office. "Calvert Whiskey owned that building before we bought it, and the vice president in charge of personnel bugged every room."

Marshall was almost disappointed by the news. He thought he might have attracted the attention of some powerful segregationist. In fact, Marshall was gaining a higher national profile. His travels to deal with cases around the South, his many trips to Washington, both to the Supreme Court and to talk with members of Congress, made him an important voice on race relations. One measure of his new status was his meetings with Clark and Hoover; he also received his first honorary degree in 1947, from his alma mater, Lincoln University.

Marshall's easygoing manner and lanky good looks also made him popular with average folks. "Thurgood Marshall is the amazing type of man who is liked by other men and probably adored by women," wrote Michael Carter, an *Afro-American* columnist in a feature article on Marshall during this period. "He carries himself with an inoffensive confidence and seems to like the life he lives."[7]

On the road Marshall's casual approach to life, the law, and people meant he got along well with blacks and whites, even white racists. "I ride in the for-colored-only cabs and in the back end of streetcars—quiet as a mouse," Marshall later said. "I eat in Negro cafes and don't challenge the customs personally, because I figure I'm down here representing a client—the NAACP —and not myself."[8]

As skillfully as he managed his public life, however, his family life continued to be a trouble spot. On March 3, 1947, Thurgood's father died at home on Druid Hill Avenue of a heart attack. He was sixty-five. Willie had not been well for over a year, and he had worked only sporadically. But between his income and the money sixty-two-year-old Norma Marshall earned as a kindergarten teacher, they took care of themselves. The large funeral was a homecoming for a Marshall family that had grown apart. Willie Marshall's brothers and sister, as well as his children, buried him at Arbutus Cemetery in Baltimore.

Thurgood also struggled with his own home life. His NAACP work pulled him out of town three weeks during most months. And when he was at home he and Buster had to deal with constant frustration and the grief that hung over their inability to have a child. "Buster had a weak uterus," said Alice Stovall, Marshall's secretary at the NAACP. "And Buster became pregnant quite a few times because she said she knew how much Thurgood wanted children."

Bob Carter, Marshall's top aide in the NAACP's legal office, often kept Buster company. "Buster liked to play cards, and I'd sometimes come over and play cards with her and a friend," Carter said. "And Thurgood might be away. He was away a lot."

And on the rare days when he was home, the couple loved to entertain their friends. Buster was especially proud of a new apartment she found for them, a two-bedroom at 409 Edgecomb Avenue in Harlem. Alice Stovall recalled that Buster began to call her to occasionally come over to the new place for "Thurgood's famous crab soup."

As a well-known black American, Marshall also got invitations to meet several of the stars who were then breaking the racial barrier in professional sports. After Jackie Robinson, the first black baseball player in the major leagues, began to make some money, he had every charity sticking its hands in his pockets and could not manage his money. Branch Rickey, the Brooklyn Dodgers' general manager, decided it would be best if another black person helped Robinson with his financial problems. Marshall was not a tax lawyer and on his NAACP salary had little experience in saving and investing large sums of money. But as the best-known black lawyer in New York and the nation, he was the man Rickey called. Marshall was thrilled to be asked and held two meetings with Robinson to work out a financial plan.

Marshall's interest in sports was literally colored by his professional work on civil rights. He rooted for the Dodgers and Robinson but also for the Cleveland Indians, who had the first black player in the American League, Larry Doby. In football he liked the Cleveland Browns, again because they had black stars, Marion Mottley and Buddy Young. Marshall, however, denied to a *New York Post* writer that he was prejudiced in favor of black athletes: "Why I just love to see Spec Sanders lug that ball for the football Yankees and Spec is a white man from Texas."[9]

Other than sports Marshall enjoyed playing cards. He did not have time or money for big-money games but was known to win or lose a few hundred dollars while traveling or at all-night games among lawyers, doctors, and businessmen in Harlem. In the late 1940s his annual income was about $10,000. But his constant travels meant he lived on his expense account most of the time; his NAACP paycheck went to Buster.

With the success of the NAACP's legal work, Marshall's reputation grew. His regular appearances before the Supreme Court also boosted his standing among lawyers. As a result of his high profile, Marshall's name regularly came up when federal judgeships began opening to blacks in the late 1940s. In political circles, speculation about Marshall becoming a judge peaked in 1949, when Congress created four new judgeships for the southern district of New York. The press wrote that President Truman was seriously considering naming a black lawyer to one of the positions.

There were only a half dozen black men in the nation, including Marshall and Bill Hastie, who were considered qualified for the federal bench. The only sitting black judges were in low-level courts, such as the U.S. Customs Court or municipal court judges in Chicago and New York. They had been given their jobs as patronage appointments by their cities' political machines.

As talk of an appointment intensified, the president of the NAACP, Arthur Spingarn, sent a letter to his nephew, Stephen Spingarn, who was an aide in the White House. Spingarn encouraged the administration to appoint Marshall: "Personally I feel that there could be no better choice for this [job] than Thurgood Marshall," he wrote. He noted that Marshall had given political support to Truman when a black "left-wing group" condemned the president for not pressing for passage of civil rights bills. *The New York Times,* Spingarn noted, had recently quoted Marshall as standing up for Truman before black critics, saying the president had "done more . . . for civil rights than all other Presidents put together."

Spingarn specifically asked that no "political hack" be given the new judgeship. It should be reserved for "a really good lawyer," he wrote. "With the possible exception of Governor Hastie of the Virgin Islands and Charlie Houston, of Washington, Marshall is by far the best and most favorably known lawyer among the Negro public. . . . I think that Thurgood Marshall would be an outstanding choice." [10]

Spingarn's effort seemed to have paid off a few days later when the *New York Post* reported that President Truman would nominate Marshall for the federal judgeship. Similar news stories in Washington and Baltimore cited White House aides as saying Truman wanted to give him the job.

Marshall got further support from one of the country's most preeminent figures, the former First Lady, Eleanor Roosevelt. Mrs. Roosevelt, who remained close to Walter White, had come to know Marshall while she was on the NAACP's board. Marshall's secretary, Alice Stovall, remembered meeting Mrs. Roosevelt at the NAACP's offices. "She stopped [in], and she said, 'And who do you work for?' And I said, 'I work with Mr. Marshall.' And she said, 'Oh, young lady, you are so lucky. I said, 'Yes we are.' "

In August of 1949, Mrs. Roosevelt wrote to Paul Fitzpatrick, head of the New York State Democratic Committee, to urge Marshall's appointment as a federal judge: "I understand that Thurgood Marshall's name is being presented to the president for one of the new judgeships which has been ear-marked for a Negro. I do not think that there is anyone I know who would do a better service to New York State if he should get the judgeship. You and all of the others could be proud of him."

Mrs. Roosevelt urged local Democrats to see Marshall's value despite his lack of any ties to the political machine. "He has been so completely out of politics that I fear he will not know anyone to back him unless you know how good a person he is," she wrote.[11]

While Spingarn, Truman, and Mrs. Roosevelt wanted to give Marshall the judgeship, black Democrats in New York City did not support him. They wanted someone who was part of the Tammany political machine. A comment about Marshall appeared in a *New York Post* political column around that time in which an unnamed "local Negro Democratic politician" complained that Marshall had "never done any doorbell ringing for the organization." Later stories in the *Post* said a black assemblyman, Harold Stevens, was New York's black political bosses' choice for the judgeship.

Eventually Paul Fitzpatrick decided that it was better not to appoint any black candidate than to defy Harlem's political leaders. He sent word to the White House that he preferred not to fight with Harlem Democrats or the black lawyers and simply would not accept any black candidate for the judgeship. Marshall was out, and he was sorely disappointed. He saw the judgeship as a step up, in both pay and status.

The defeat left Marshall suffering internal doubts. He didn't know where he was going next in his career. He wanted to move up, but given the segregation of the nation's top law firms, the best hope for him seemed to be starting his own practice. However, his early failure as a private lawyer in Baltimore made him afraid to give up the guaranteed pay and the NAACP's national platform. To keep a wider and wider sea of personal doubt at bay, he lived his day-to-day life on an island of frantic activity. And increasingly he spent his time battling with Communists inside his own organization.

CHAPTER 17

On the Front Line

MARSHALL WAS DEEPLY WORRIED that his critics would tar him as a Communist. Since the 1930s the NAACP's opponents had derided it as anti-American for focusing on racial problems while the nation was trying to stand united through the Great Depression and World War II.

The NAACP, with Walter White taking the lead, made every effort to knock down charges that it was linked with any Communist group. But W.E.B. Du Bois, the famous founding editor of the association's magazine, *The Crisis,* had recently returned to New York from sabbatical and become openly involved in left-wing activities.

Marshall's office was next door to that of the short, elegantly attired Du Bois, and initially Marshall was excited to have Du Bois so close. He greatly admired the old man, having read *The Crisis* since high school. And he was fascinated by the scholar's every move—his stylish goatee as well as his status as Harvard's first black Ph.D. The professorial Du Bois, however, rarely spoke to the younger lawyer. "His whole office was fenced in with books that ran all around the room, and we were always impressed by it," Marshall said later. One day Marshall decided that he would try to break through his colleague's aloof demeanor. He stopped Du Bois one morning and said: "Look, Doc, your office and mine are side by side and you come in here every morning and you just walk right by." Without stopping, or even glancing up as he walked into his office, Du Bois mumbled, "Yeah, that's one of my bad habits." Then he shut the door.

Du Bois's relationship with Marshall never had a chance to improve. During the 1948 presidential campaign, the magazine editor began working with Henry Wallace, the Progressive Party's candidate for president. Wallace was challenging the incumbent Harry Truman, a close friend of Walter White. White responded by telling Du Bois to stop making comments about politics because his public support for Wallace amounted to a political endorsement, which could endanger the NAACP's status as a tax-exempt, nonpartisan group.

Despite the warning, Du Bois continued to support Wallace and was highly critical of Truman and his policies in the Third World. Writing to the NAACP's board, Du Bois said Truman had opposed black liberation efforts to end white colonial rule in Africa. Du Bois's battle with White became personal when Du Bois opposed the NAACP chief's plan to take a leave of absence to become a member of the U.S. delegation to the United Nations.

Finally the board stepped in, forcing Du Bois out of the organization he had helped to found. He tried to rally allies among the membership for his right, as an individual, to support Wallace. But Marshall took an active part in killing any budding support for Du Bois. "I have been running around from post to pillar trying to hold things in line and I am convinced that the campaign against the Board for its action involving Du Bois is falling flat on its face," Marshall wrote in a letter to White, who was by then at the U.N. "In other words, I think we have it under control and you need not worry about it until you get back."[1]

Du Bois's dismissal, however, had little to do with his support for Wallace, and everything to do with the fact that he was a Communist. In the midst of a nationwide anti-Communist frenzy, the NAACP was acting to protect itself from allegations that it sympathized with Communism. But Du Bois remained defiant. He told the NAACP board that he advocated many so-called Communist plans: "If you call that following the Communist line, I did it, I did follow the Communist line."

Marshall had no second thoughts about having helped to push Du Bois out. With Du Bois gone and White on leave, Marshall and Roy Wilkins took charge. Wilkins became acting director of the association, and Marshall was his second in command for all affairs, allowing him to range far beyond legal issues. With control over every decision, Marshall and Wilkins decided to make the fight against Communist influences in the NAACP their hallmark.

Marshall went to great lengths to distance himself personally from

Communists. In 1949 he quit the National Lawyers Guild, where he had served on the board. Robert Silberstein, the group's executive secretary, had been critical of a federal judge for putting several lawyers in jail for their aggressive defense of eleven Communist Party leaders in New York.

Marshall wrote to Silberstein that because the guild's board had not been consulted before his protest letter was sent to the judge, he would quit the organization. With an eye on the fast winds of political attacks on Communists, Marshall wrote: "I cannot allow myself to be placed in such a position in the future and therefore I hereby tender my resignation as a member of the board of directors." [2]

Marshall's paranoia was not baseless. While he was divorcing himself from the guild and any other Communists, the FBI was increasing its spying on Marshall and the NAACP. The surveillance was conducted out of concern that the group could become an easy point of entry for Communists into the American political mainstream. The primary focus was on Communists who tried to gain influence by joining local branches, notably in Los Angeles, Philadelphia, and New Orleans. Dan Byrd, the NAACP's regional coordinator in the South, wrote in 1949 that left-wing activists were taking over some branches in his area. "It is of the utmost importance for appropriate action to be taken . . . to weed [Communists] out of our Jefferson Parish [La.] branch," Byrd wrote. "I am convinced that the infiltration is almost complete." [3]

At the NAACP's next convention, held in Boston in 1950, Marshall and Wilkins spearheaded a resolution giving the national board authority to root out and "eradicate [Communist] infiltration" in the membership and leadership of local branches. The *Afro-American*'s front-page stories on the convention ran under the banner headline NAACP BOOTS REDS. Walter White, recently back from his leave of absence, issued a statement to reporters: "The communists brought it on themselves. We have always kept the door open. But they alienated and infuriated the members by their clumsy efforts to take over the NAACP." [4]

*   *   *

On the last day of the convention, fighting began between the United States and Communists in North Korea. Soon after, the NAACP started getting letters from American soldiers filled with bitter complaints about continuing discrimination and unfair treatment in the military. President Truman had issued an executive order desegregating the military in 1948. Under Truman's new rules, black and white servicemen were to be fully integrated. But the Army's hierarchy was particularly slow to begin implementation.

Marshall began to notice a large number of reports that black soldiers were being charged with cowardice and failure to obey orders on the battlefield. With black soldiers being disproportionately singled out, it became clear to him that something was not right. Thirty-six black soldiers who were convicted of various charges asked the NAACP to represent them at hearings to be held in Washington. As Marshall's concern over the racial problem in Korea was growing, James Hicks, the *Afro-American*'s correspondent there, sent back firsthand accounts of black soldiers being wrongly accused and convicted on sham charges.

"Jimmy Hicks told me about these Negro prisoners, shackled, being brought into the railroad station in Tokyo, how horrible it was," Marshall said later. "So I went to Walter and I told him about it. Walter then decided I could take it." Marshall would later describe this investigation as "the most important mission of my career."[5]

The first case that came to Marshall's attention involved Lt. Leon A. Gilbert of the Twenty-fourth Infantry. Gilbert, a thirty-one-year-old veteran with ten years experience, was charged with disobeying an order to lead his men into battle just a month after the war started. Gilbert later called the order "sure death" because his unit was heavily outnumbered. Gilbert pleaded his innocence due to "lack of mental responsibility." But he was found guilty and sentenced to die.

By November of 1950 Marshall had put his office in gear to handle the cases of black GIs such as Gilbert. Although Gilbert was convicted by a military court in Korea, his appeal was sent to a military court in Washington and Marshall acted as his legal counsel on the appeal. The sentence was reduced from death to twenty years upon the review board's recommendation to President Truman. Marshall's success generated headlines and more requests for help from black soldiers. Finally, he decided to go personally to the military's Far East headquarters, to review more cases of court-martialed black soldiers.

On December 1, 1950, he applied for a passport to travel to the military command headquarters in Japan. He first phoned J. Edgar Hoover, with whom he maintained a fragile but still effective relationship. He hoped that the FBI director would want to help him get the military clearance, since Marshall had been at the forefront of efforts to stifle Communist activities in the NAACP. Hoover was out of the office, but Gen. Douglas MacArthur, the commander of U.S. troops in Korea, had already been on the phone to the FBI. MacArthur had requested incriminating information on Marshall's background, to give him a reason to deny Marshall permission to come to the Far East.

While Marshall was left waiting, FBI agents immediately responded to MacArthur. Their records from 1950 indicated that the forty-two-year-old attorney was a member of two groups cited as Communist fronts by the House Committee on Un-American Activities—the National Lawyers' Guild and the International Juridical Association. The FBI report also noted that he "appeared on the same speakers' platform with the Ohio State Chairman of the communist party."[6]

This was just the ammunition that MacArthur needed. After receiving the FBI report, a military official in Washington called Marshall to say that MacArthur had refused permission for him to come to Tokyo. Walter White, meanwhile, began making frantic phone calls and sending telegrams, appealing the decision. White, Wilkins, and Marshall even appealed directly to the Truman White House. They struck gold. As Marshall recalled in a later interview: "The president said the hell with [MacArthur's refusal]. Who's running this damned show?" Under White House pressure, MacArthur relented and wired White that Marshall had his permission to come.

After several weeks in Tokyo, Marshall had interviewed thirty-four prisoners. He later wrote that he visited the imprisoned Lieutenant Gilbert half a dozen times. In his diary of the trip, Marshall said he regularly dined at the Press Club, listened to a "good" orchestra at the "Rainbow Room," played the slots, and slowly made charts on all the cases, allowing him to see patterns of bias in how the trials were handled.[7]

Marshall did finally get a chance to meet with General MacArthur in Tokyo. Maj. Gen. George Hickman, on MacArthur's staff, was in the meeting and recalled that MacArthur said he wanted all records and prisoners to be made available so that Marshall could be convinced that "there are not two systems of justice going on in the Far East Command." After MacArthur and Marshall finished their talk, Hickman said, "it was suggested that he go to the Twenty-fourth, to the front lines. Mr. Marshall turned a little bit whiter than he was, but he said 'Okay.' "[8]

The lawyer traveled to Seoul, Taegu, and Pusan—three large cities—before going to the battlefront. As he rode in a jeep to the front with his escort, Col. D. D. Martin, enemy shells began exploding around them. "All of a sudden they shot, *wwwhhhhhhsshh*, like that," Marshall said. "And everybody ducked." Colonel Martin, who was responsible for

Marshall's safety, found himself lying in a ditch with Marshall nowhere in sight. Martin began screaming to his men, "Where is he? Where is he? Where's Thurgood?" A loud voice bellowed out: "Underneath you! Goddammit, I don't need no instructions on how to run!"

After several conversations with both blacks and whites on the front, Marshall found that black soldiers were in fact being disproportionately charged with violating orders. On the single charge of showing cowardice and disobeying orders in front of the enemy, for example, Marshall found thirty-two black soldiers but only two white soldiers had been sentenced for misbehavior in combat. Thirty of the thirty-two blacks got ten years or more in jail, while the two white soldiers were given sentences of five years or less.[9]

Marshall prepared a statistical report on the disparate treatment of black soldiers. He returned to Tokyo and presented the report to MacArthur, who was not impressed by the findings. While speaking to the general, Marshall mentioned that he had heard from Japanese officials that there was not a single black military man on the entire headquarters staff or MacArthur's personal guard. The general responded that no blacks were qualified by battlefield performance to be in his personal guard. A stunned Marshall said, "Well, I just talked to a Negro yesterday, a sergeant who has killed more people with a rifle than anybody in history, and he's not qualified?" MacArthur said no and expected that Marshall would back down.

But Marshall had taken a dislike to MacArthur. In that moment Marshall saw him as nothing more than a racist. Pointing toward the parade ground, Marshall said, "Now, General, remember yesterday you had that big beautiful band playing at the ceremony over there." MacArthur, thinking the conversation had shifted, smiled, saying, "Yes, wasn't that wonderful?"

Marshall's eyes brightened as MacArthur fell into his trap. Marshall noted that there was not one black soldier in that band. "Now, General, just between you and me, goddammit, don't you tell me that there is no Negro that can play a horn." MacArthur's face reddened, and he turned away before announcing that it was time for Marshall to leave. The NAACP lawyer later said MacArthur was as "biased as any person I've run across."

When the attorney returned from his monthlong investigation, Walter White immediately sent him out on a speaking tour. White wanted to raise NAACP funds on the basis of the nationwide black outrage over the indignities black soldiers were suffering in Korea. In gritty detail Marshall told about how Lieutenant Gilbert and others were being given "hasty" trials, which offered "the letter but not the substance of the law." [10]

An editorial in the *Pittsburgh Courier* praised Marshall. "Being one of the ablest lawyers in the land, there was confidence that Attorney Marshall could help these men if anybody could," the *Courier* wrote. "Mr. Marshall has become, in a way, the leader and symbol of this legal success which has had such a revolutionary impact on American life." [11]

Two months after Marshall returned to the United States, MacArthur and Truman got in a row over U.S. military strategy, and the president fired him. Shortly after MacArthur's departure the Army began to comply with Truman's executive order to desegregate its personnel.

Marshall continued to work on one case from his Korea trip for several years. After he returned from the Far East, he wrote to President Truman asking that Lieutenant Gilbert's sentence be reduced from twenty years to time already served. In 1955 Gilbert was released with a dishonorable discharge. He had served only five years of a sentence that originally called for his death.

CHAPTER 18

Direct Attack

M ARSHALL WAS STUCK. Since 1938, when Charles Houston had left the NAACP's national office, Marshall had put the problem of segregated schools on the back burner. He was preoccupied with race riots, highly publicized criminal cases, and suits challenging segregation in housing and transportation. But when Houston got Marshall on the phone or came through New York, he continued to complain that his former student was not doing enough to crush the heart of racial separation.

Marshall did see schools as the key to ending segregation in the country. If children could sit in classes together not only would all children get to know people of other races at an early age but they would have the benefit of a first-rate education. Until now Marshall had been content to work through the strategy set forth in the 1930s Margold plan, which called for going to court to insist on equalizing separate black and white facilities. The plan was to get the school districts to concede that they didn't have the money to equalize and thus force them to consolidate and integrate their students.

Houston and Marshall had started the process on the law school level. But it had proved time consuming and expensive—and it hadn't led to widespread desegregation of law schools. To break the logjam and put some new energy into NAACP legal action, Marshall called an April 1946 meeting in Atlanta with lawyers from the South who had worked on local NAACP cases. The men, including A. P. Tureaud from New Orleans and Arthur Shores from Birmingham, all had private practices but were loyal to Marshall. He held a similar brainstorming meeting in New York with nationally known law professors.

Marshall later told *Time* magazine that these get-togethers stirred a new sense of conviction that schools could be integrated: "Somebody at the [lawyers'] meeting said, while it was true that a lot of us might die without ever seeing the goal realized, we were going to have to change directions if our children weren't going to die as black bastards too," Marshall said. "So we decided to make segregation itself our target."[1]

Marshall and the lawyers agreed to bombard eleven southern states and the District of Columbia with simultaneous lawsuits demanding equal educational facilities for existing Jim Crow schools. In addition to opening fire on several fronts, for the first time Marshall's legal team agreed to take on cases where black students demanded integration. The new idea was to go for "the whole hog," by arguing that segregated schools were illegal even if they were equal.

However, the basis from which Marshall's team would challenge segregated schools remained the *Gaines* case. The Supreme Court had ruled that since Missouri did not have a law school for blacks, it could not equalize its facilities and had to admit Gaines to the all-white state law school. To make use of that precedent, Marshall planned to present similar cases and then ask for integration. Now it was only a matter of finding plaintiffs who were willing to sue and, unlike Gaines, willing to stay around and take the flak.

Lulu White, the high-energy Houston-based director of Texas NAACP branches, wrote to her top local lawyer, W. J. Durham, that she had found a plaintiff willing to challenge the University of Texas's whites-only admission policy. In the midst of a stirring sermon, White had pleaded for someone to stand up and challenge segregation at the state-funded law school. A balding, thirty-three-year-old postman and war veteran, Heman Marion Sweatt, stood before the Houston congregation and in a trembling voice said he was willing to go through with it.

Sweatt was a graduate of Wiley College in Marshall, Texas, and he had done a year of graduate work at the University of Michigan. During his time at Michigan he had become friendly with the infamous Lloyd Gaines, who had been studying there while waiting for the Supreme Court to rule on his right to attend the University of Missouri Law School.[2]

Sweatt later wrote to Walter White that, unlike Gaines, he felt no pressure from having his name on a lawsuit challenging segregation.

Sweatt proudly declared he wouldn't break under the scrutiny and frustration that came with a major lawsuit because he did not suffer from Gaines's "egoistic inflation" and "personality weaknesses." The postal worker said he was also aware that the NAACP's struggle had implications for future generations of black students: "I am seriously interested in contributing to the earliest possible ending of the system [of school segregation]."[3]

Walter White was happy that this plaintiff seemed so mature. But White still had problems with the Texan. Sweatt had also sent him a rambling five-page letter in which he declared that he was a Communist sympathizer. Alarmed, White talked with Marshall. But they decided that despite his Communist inclinations, the NAACP needed Sweatt if the case were to go forward.[4]

To get the case going, Marshall had Sweatt apply to the University of Texas Law School. University authorities acknowledged that Sweatt was qualified to earn admission except for one thing—he was black. Sweatt immediately filed suit. Marshall, who still had strong support in Texas after his victory in the white primary case, used his relationships to develop financial and emotional support for the case. Maceo Smith, the influential head of the Texas NAACP, helped to raise money for the case and build statewide support among black Texans. Smith later said Marshall "practically made his home in Texas by that time because they had such fertile ground here and [so many] people to work with."[5]

After an initial finding that the University of Texas Law School would have to be integrated because there was no law school for blacks, the courts gave Texas officials six months to begin a Jim Crow law school. Marshall had no choice but to wait things out. But in that time he went to neighboring Oklahoma and began work on a case in which the state law school had similarly refused to admit a black woman.

*   *   *

Marshall got involved in the Oklahoma case after another excited phone call from the NAACP board member Roscoe Dunjee, the editor of the *Oklahoma Black Dispatch*, who had brought Marshall into the *Lyons* murder case a few years earlier. This time Dunjee had directed a young woman, Ada Lois Sipuel, to apply to the all-white University of Oklahoma Law School. He wanted to force a confrontation that he hoped would generate headlines and break open the university's doors to black students.

The NAACP hired Amos T. Hall as their local counsel and filed suit against the university. But the district court threw out the case. Under the separate-but-equal law, the judge said Sipuel would be entitled to a good law school but not admission to the all-white University of Oklahoma. Hall consulted with Marshall before filing an appeal to Oklahoma's highest court.

In April 1947, Marshall argued Sipuel's appeal before the Oklahoma Supreme Court. He lost. The next step was to appeal to the U.S. Supreme Court, which ruled in January 1948 in favor of Sipuel. Dunjee printed screaming headlines in his paper and published stories that said the Supreme Court's decision was the final victory. Marshall and Dunjee expected Sipuel to be admitted to the law school in the spring of 1948.

Oklahoma state officials, however, responded with a surprise. The State Board of Regents created a new school—Langston Law School—in the state capitol building. They appointed three law professors and sent a letter instructing Sipuel to apply to the new Jim Crow school. She called Marshall, who told her, "Forget it, Ada Lois, don't even show up in the same block of that law school."

Marshall immediately petitioned the Supreme Court to order the University of Oklahoma to admit Sipuel. But in a 7–2 decision the high court ruled that since Oklahoma now had a separate law school there were new issues and the case had to be heard again in the lower courts. Marshall was deflated by the ruling; he told Sipuel and others that the justices had chickened out. Now the NAACP would have to sue to prove the obvious—that the newly created Langston School of Law was inferior to the state law school.

Marshall went back to Oklahoma accompanied by several black lawyers from around the country, including James Nabrit and Robert Ming, as well as his New York secretary, Alice Stovall. No hotel in Norman, Oklahoma, the site of the trial, accepted black guests. So Marshall's gang stayed in the homes of black NAACP members in Oklahoma City, some forty miles away.

Despite working long hours preparing for the trial, Marshall found time to party. Liquor was not sold in the state, but friends pulled strings to keep him supplied. "We had a good rapport with the police department," said Jimmy Stewart, the president of the Oklahoma City branch of the NAACP. "We'd just call up there and tell them, 'Our NAACP lawyer is in town.' Next thing we saw coming through the door was the guys with whole cases of liquor from the bootleggers."[6]

Joining Marshall in his late-night strategy sessions were some of the top legal experts in the nation, including Erwin Griswold, the dean of Harvard Law School, as well as the deans of Pennsylvania, Columbia, and Yale law schools. They would debate the law over bottomless glasses of whiskey before taking off at dawn for the trial in Norman. Constance Baker Motley, who was on the NAACP legal staff, said Marshall was able to draw these high-powered legal minds at no charge because of his magnetic personality. "They knew they were gonna be in a relaxed atmosphere with somebody that was congenial, full of stories. It was an optimistic sort of thing," Motley said.[7]

At the trial the law school deans unanimously described the new school as a fraud. Walter Gellhorn, of Columbia Law School, one of the expert witnesses supporting the NAACP, saw the argument Marshall presented in the Oklahoma case as the breakthrough in the association's challenge to school segregation. "The first time I heard of the possibility of making an argument against separation as such . . . [was] in the case of *Sipuel*."

The Jim Crow school actually had a better library than the university's law school; it was the law library for the state supreme court. Overall, the quality of Langston's facilities were never in doubt. As a result, Marshall had to focus his argument on the disadvantage to black people that came from being educated apart from the others who were to be in their profession.[8]

For that opening day in court, Marshall had planned for every contingency except one. There was no restaurant in Norman that served lunch to black people and no time to drive anywhere during the noon recess. So Marshall had to organize a strategy for feeding his legal team. In the hall he saw a penny peanut machine. He rushed back into the courtroom and got all the hungry faces to empty the change in their pockets. A few minutes later he came back with two fists full of peanuts and began portioning out the nuts to quiet growling stomachs. When everyone had something to eat, he turned to Sipuel and gave her marching orders. "I'm going to put you in charge of baloney sandwiches; don't you let this happen no more," he told her. A few days later Dunjee arranged for a downtown restaurant to open a segregated section.[9]

The highlight of the trial came when Marshall cross-examined the dean of the Jim Crow school. The NAACP lawyer loudly dragged his chair next to the witness's chair. Leaning forward and holding a copy of the new school's catalog, Marshall began a series of rapid-fire questions.

"What kind of bulletin does your Langston Law School publish?" The dean, looking embarrassed, said the school didn't have a bulletin. Waving the catalog in the air, Marshall said, "The catalog says you have one. What did you do, lie?" Finally, after forty minutes of browbeating, Marshall's cocounsel Jim Nabrit called out, "Turn him loose, Thurgood, let him go." The tense courtroom erupted in laughter.

Before the trial ended the judge called Marshall into his chambers and made an unusual confession. He said the expert testimony and Marshall's revealing questioning had "opened [his] eyes," to the wrong of school segregation. Then the judge went out, got back on the bench, and ruled against Sipuel and Marshall.

But before Marshall could appeal to Oklahoma's high court, the university decided to short-circuit the legal process. They admitted Sipuel, as well as several other black graduate students who had been pressing for admission. The sympathetic university president had convinced the state attorney general to let Sipuel in, but she had to sit in the back of the classroom. Not wanting to risk having higher courts rule that the law school be completely integrated, the attorney general agreed.

Sipuel was warmly greeted by the people in the law school, although she started classes two weeks late. "I wouldn't have made it without the white students," she said. "The fellows in the law school came over and said, 'Ada, we're so glad you finally got in, we know you're behind, but we're going to help you. We're going to loan you our books, we're going to loan you our notes, we're going to tutor you until you can catch up with us,' and they did that and that was the only way I made it." However, she was still not treated as an equal by school officials. She had to sit four rows behind the rest of the class, with a big sign overhead that read COLORED. But by Sipuel's second semester all the "colored" signs in the law school were taken down. "I just moved down to the first row," she said.

*   *   *

At the end of his legal work in Oklahoma, Marshall became distressed over reports from the New York office that the NAACP had emptied its treasury to litigate the desegregation cases. To refill the coffers Dunjee arranged some speeches for Marshall. Amos T. Hall, the NAACP lawyer from Tulsa, came up with another idea to raise money. Hall was more famous for being the head of the local Prince Hall Masons than for being a lawyer. The Prince Hall Masons were an all-black group founded in

Boston in 1784 by a former slave named Prince Hall. Operating separately from white Masonry, the black Masons spread around the nation after the Civil War as a select fraternity for newly freed black men.

"Amos told Thurgood and me that if we joined the lodge he could get some money for us. And we dearly needed money at that time," Oklahoma City branch president James Stewart said. "So I joined the lodge, and so did Thurgood. From then on we got a substantial contribution from the Masons."

Marshall had enough money to turn his attention back to the University of Texas Law School case. Even after the six-month grace period given by the courts, Texas officials had not built their Jim Crow law school, and Heman Sweatt's suit had new life.

As he had done in the *Sipuel* case, Marshall brought in law professors and deans from around the country to testify the Jim Crow school had not even a semblance of the quality of the University of Texas. And to show that law school integration would not cause riots, Marshall had Donald Murray come from Maryland to testify about his experiences breaking the racial barrier there. But Marshall never had much of a chance with Judge Roy Archer on the bench. "Judge Archer was not insensitive to politics," said Joe Greenhill, the deputy attorney general who defended Texas in the case. At one point the judge told Greenhill, "Sweatt's got two chances, slim and none."[10]

The climactic moment came when Sweatt testified he would never go to a segregated law school, even at a newly proposed $3 million Jim Crow facility. Sweatt told the judge that any segregated school was inherently unequal. Under intense cross-examination from the Texas lawyers, the NAACP plaintiff was unflappable. Greenhill, who later became chief judge of Texas's state supreme court, walked over to Marshall during a break to compliment him on his preparation of Sweatt. In his typical style Marshall had befriended the opposing counsel.

"I thought it was a masterful job," Greenhill told him. "Well, you know we woodshed our witnesses pretty well," Marshall responded. "Matter of fact, I expected him to do well. We went out early this morning and filled him full of gin."

The courtroom also became a theater of race relations as white law students from the University of Texas crowded in to hear the arguments. Black Texans, many of them from the local NAACP, were in court, too. When bailiffs told one Texas law student not to sit in the black seating section, the student refused to move unless a black person told him to get out. Soon blacks and whites were seated together all over the courtroom. The drama took another turn when white students began booing as their own dean testified that segregation was necessary to ensure a quality education for white students.

Despite the NAACP rooting section, Archer again ruled against Sweatt. Marshall had expected to lose, but to hear Archer's ruling nonetheless hurt. He always held hope that judges, even southern judges, would rise above the pressure and the racism and rule fairly. Just after the decision, Marshall confided to his fellow lawyer Jim Nabrit that he was going to curse out the judge. "I told him to take it easy," Nabrit later said. Marshall said nothing.

As the NAACP legal team walked out of the court, their faces looking long with disappointment, Nabrit saw Marshall lingering behind, standing over in a corner and mumbling. Out of concern he called to him and Marshall slowly walked over. Nabrit asked him if he was okay. "I told you I was gonna tell that judge what I thought of him, and I just did," said Marshall.[11]

The NAACP appealed Judge Archer's ruling in February 1948 and again lost. The state court said that the separate-but-equal standard was satisfied by the Jim Crow law school for black students.

Marshall's battles in the Lone Star State, however, were not limited to the courts. Carter Wesley, publisher of the *Houston Informer*, the leading black newspaper in Houston, began regularly attacking the New York lawyer in his columns. In his frenzy for integration, Wesley said, Marshall was undermining black schools and especially black colleges.

Wesley's argument reflected a major divide among black Americans over whether school integration or equal funding for black schools should be the NAACP's priority. Marshall and Charles Houston had pushed a pro-integration resolution through the 1947 NAACP convention in Washington in an attempt to shut off people like Wesley. The landmark resolution mandated that NAACP lawyers bring only suits that asked for full integration: "The NAACP cannot take part in any legal proceeding which condones segregation in public schools or which admits the validity of segregation statutes."[12]

But several local black leaders, including Wesley, objected. These NAACP members feared that demands for integration might anger white state officials and lead them to cut back already meager funding for existing black schools. If that happened black students would be hurt by the NAACP's risky strategy.[13]

"Is it the NAACP's position that it will take no action to better the educational lot of Texas Negroes except [to] fight for admission of Negroes to non-segregated schools?" Wesley asked in one heated column. He also suggested that there were "communists" in the NAACP and called the civil rights group "cuckoo" for its lack of interest in getting more financial support for segregated, all-black schools.

Marshall responded with increasingly personal anger. In a speech at the Texas state conference of NAACP branches in 1947, he publicly belittled Wesley. Marshall said one *Informer* column "obviously written by editor Carter Wesley" supported a "return to the days of Booker T. Washington" and separate, all-black schools.

"It no longer takes courage to fight for mere equality in a separate school system," Marshall told the large crowd gathered on a humid Friday night in Denison, Texas. "I think everyone knew that when the state legislature in Texas agreed to advance more than $3 million for a Jim Crow University there would be Negroes who would be willing to sell the race down the river in order to either get jobs in the school, or to determine who should build the school, or to determine where the school should be built, or any other method whereby the individual could get personal gain."

A sweat-drenched Marshall told the crowd the NAACP was not going to stop demanding integration because of Carter Wesley. "When you realize that Negroes have been fighting for equality in separate schools for more than eighty years and have not obtained a semblance of equality," he said, it made no sense to ask for more segregation. He concluded that Wesley was just looking for "the easy way out" by asking whites for "Jim Crow Deluxe."

Marshall ended the speech with a fist-pounding statement: "We are convinced that it is impossible to have equality in a segregated system, no matter how elaborate we build the Jim Crow citadel and no matter whether we label it the 'Black University of Texas,' 'The Negro University of Texas,' 'Prairie View Institute,' or a more fitting title, 'An Apology to Negroes for Denying Them Their Constitutional Rights to Attend the University of Texas.' "[14]

Marshall returned to New York, where his legal team got busy preparing to argue the *Sweatt* case before the Supreme Court. Charles Houston gave his advice and even sent a catalog from the new Jim Crow law school. Houston wrote, "This may be introduced as evidence of equality of opportunity. . . . It would appear as if we had a new Columbia

University in Houston, but my Atlanta friend tells me that this is all a paper set up of fairy tales in place of actual offering." [15]

Houston also pulled strings to get the Justice Department to file a brief with the Supreme Court supporting Sweatt. The administration's brief said Sweatt's case was significant because it tested "the vitality and strength of the democratic ideals to which the United States is dedicated." Most important, the brief also argued that segregated state law schools were part of a pattern that harmed black citizens and asked that the separate-but-equal doctrine be overturned. [16]

Hundreds of people stood in line for hours outside the Supreme Court hoping to get a seat to hear the case argued in April of 1950. Those who were lucky enough to get in saw Marshall make an emotional argument, asserting that Sweatt had a right to attend the state law school without regard to how white segregationists might feel or objections from blacks. "The rights of Sweatt to attend the University of Texas cannot be conditioned upon the wishes of any group of citizens," Marshall told the justices. "It matters not to me whether every single Negro in this country wants segregated schools. It makes no difference whether every white person wants segregated schools. If Sweatt wants to assert his individual, constitutional right, it cannot be conditioned upon the wishes of every other citizen."

Price Daniel, the attorney general of Texas, responded by quoting Abraham Lincoln as saying that blacks and whites should be free but live separately. As a practical matter, Daniel told the justices, if Sweatt were admitted to the law school, then blacks would have to be admitted to swimming pools, grammar schools, and hospitals. "All we ask in the south," he said, "is the opportunity to take care of this matter and work it out [ourselves]." [17]

While waiting for a ruling in the *Sweatt* case, Marshall was hit with a shock. Charles Houston died of heart failure in Washington. They no longer spoke every day, but his impact on Marshall was still great. Their relationship had evolved from that of mentor and student to professional confidants, but Marshall remained heavily dependent on the fifty-five-year-old Houston, both as a legal mind and as a friend. "Thurgood . . . didn't make any moves without [either] Houston [or] Hastie," remembered Constance Baker Motley, who had joined the NAACP Legal Defense Fund's staff in 1945. [18]

Houston had encouraged the direct attack approach Marshall had employed in the *Sweatt* case. He wrote to Bob Carter, the number-two man in the NAACP's legal office, that he was pleased to see an aggressive Marshall arguing that segregation was wrong even if the state said they could build separate and "equal" schools for blacks. "These education cases are now sufficiently tight so that anyone familiar with the course of the decisions should be able to guide the cases through," Houston wrote, reaffirming his support for abandoning the Margold plan's strategy. "You and Thurgood can proceed without any fear of crossing any plans I have." [19] But before Houston could see if the direct attack plan would work in the *Sweatt* case, he died at Freedman's Hospital, a few blocks from Howard University's main campus.

At the funeral William Hastie, governor of the U.S. Virgin Islands and Truman's nominee for the U.S. Third Circuit Court of Appeals, stood in the pulpit of Rankin Chapel on the Howard campus looking over a distinguished group of mourners. There in the pews on Wednesday, April 26, 1950, were Thurgood Marshall, Walter White and Roy Wilkins, cabinet officials, and two Supreme Court justices—Hugo Black and Tom Clark. "He guided us through the legal wilderness of second-class citizenship," said Hastie in a tear-filled eulogy for Houston. "He was truly the Moses of that journey. He lived to see us close to the promised land." [20]

Houston had laid the groundwork for the NAACP's legal fight for integration. It was Marshall's turn to take the crusade to the next level. Marshall had lost his greatest mentor, the man who had for twenty years nurtured him and guided his development as the nation's top civil rights lawyer. "Whatever credit is given him is not enough," Marshall told reporters. [21]

Houston's advice to Marshall had paid off. The bold new strategy that he had encouraged resulted in the Supreme Court's stunning unanimous decision in June 1950 in favor of Sweatt. Chief Justice Fred Vinson, a hard-nosed Truman Democrat, wrote the opinion: "We cannot find substantial equality in the educational opportunities offered white and Negro law students by the state. . . . The University of Texas Law School is far superior. . . . A law school, the proving ground for legal learning and practice, cannot be effective in isolation. . . . Anyone who has practiced law, would not choose to study in an academic vacuum, removed from the play of ideas and the exchange of views with which the law is concerned." [22]

Vinson's decision included an idea that caught the attention of NAACP lawyers. He said that a school's alumni, its prestige and influence, and its history were all to be considered when comparing it with any other school. By that standard, no makeshift Jim Crow school could ever be presented as a facility "equal" to a long-standing state school.

The ruling meant that for the first time in American history an all-white school was being compelled to admit a black student *despite* the separate-but-equal laws. The lawyers at the NAACP saw the decision as a sea change in the high court's thinking on school segregation. Marshall called Sweatt to tell him the good news. "We won the big one," he said. In the future, Marshall told him, Texas was going to have to "age law schools like good whiskey."²³

News of the *Sweatt* victory sent the NAACP office into full-throttle celebration. "Thurgood, he's a party man," Constance Baker Motley later said. "You would not have to have much of an excuse for him to throw a party. I mean, that's the kind of person he was. So anytime we won a case, people came by because they knew there was a party going on there, no question about it."

Sweatt started law school in the fall of 1950 and ran into a string of racist incidents and tough breaks. When he first applied to the school, Sweatt had had to deal with suggestions that the real reason he wanted to go there was to meet white women. In *The Texas Ranger,* the University of Texas student magazine, Sweatt wrote: "I want to get a legal education at the university, not a wife," noting he was already married.²⁴ After he began attending the university, a cross was burned next to his car and his tires were slashed. During the same time he broke up with his wife and became ill. By the end of his second year, Sweatt had flunked out. He later got a degree in social work and remained in Texas.

But Sweatt's personal struggles had little importance to Marshall. His fight remained over the legal ground for segregation, and in truth he did not always focus on individual soldiers in the battle. After his victory in the *Sweatt* case, Marshall gave a speech at Fisk University's Institute of Race Relations in which he summed up the significance of the ruling and suggested that it was a foreshadowing of even more important changes in race relations. "Despite the fact that the 'Separate-But-Equal' doctrine was not technically overruled by these decisions," he said, "the force and significance of the language certainly robs the doctrine of most of its validity. . . . We now have the tools to destroy all governmentally imposed racial segregation. It will take time. It will take courage and determination."

At age forty-two Marshall would try to replace Houston, the veritable Moses of the struggle for equal rights. Would Marshall, by himself, be able to finish leading the NAACP on the trek through the desert of laws that separated black and white Americans? He would first have to find out if he had the courage and determination to lead this fight.

CHAPTER 19

∽❀∼

Number One Negro
of All Time

WITH HIS BREAKTHROUGH VICTORY in the *Sweatt* case, Marshall became a celebrity. He was the most requested speaker for NAACP events. With ten victories before the Supreme Court by 1950, black and white lawyers, including top politicians, saw him as the leading civil rights expert in the nation. His reputation was golden.

The black press had Marshall's picture on the front page almost every week, and he was quoted on any civil rights controversy. He was a burgeoning legend; he was trumpeted as the one man able to defend black Americans against the Klan, racist judges, and bigoted small-town cops. "Thurgood's coming" became shorthand among blacks in the South for the day when the sword of justice would strike out against white oppressors. This esteem was reflected in one poignant letter, filled with misspellings and bad grammar. It opened: "Mr. Turgood—I see by the Courer [*Pittsburgh Courier*] that you ar the No. 1 negro of all Time, so I take my pen in han as you must be the man I have been lookin for all these yers.

". . . . I hop' you will come quick because these white folks down hear dont ack like they heard of Supreme court or any court or anything. They is runnin wild and we shure could use the No. 1 negro of all time or somebody to stop them from mistreatin' us."

The letter, from Charles Jones who lived in a small town in Georgia, was signed with a big "X" and was written by Jones's wife, Essie Mae. She added in a postscript that "Charlie, he cant read or rite but he got real good sense."[1]

Marshall was now eclipsing Walter White, the NAACP's ego-driven executive secretary. White had been a mentor to Marshall, but his pride in his young associate was wearing thin as he got more and more attention. Even White's socialite friends were talking up Marshall.

White's relationship with the lawyer had been on rocky ground since 1948, when the NAACP's national office found itself caught up in gossip and scandal involving its executive secretary. White, who to all appearances was white, had divorced his wife, Gladys, a black woman, that year. He quickly married Poppy Cannon, a wealthy South African socialite. Black NAACP members, still trying to quiet the ruckus that had ensued after White's ouster of W.E.B. Du Bois, were outraged that White would divorce his wife of twenty-seven years to marry a white woman who had three children, all by different men.

Carl Murphy, publisher of the *Afro-American*, was so upset he wrote to Eleanor Roosevelt, a fellow NAACP board member, to complain that white board members did not understand that Mr. White was damaging the NAACP's name. "His sudden divorce and marriage to Mrs. Cannon has so weakened his usefulness that the association will assume a grave risk in attempting to keep him in office. You and I . . . may marry whom we please without involving the association in a controversy. . . . But not the chief executive. . . . My own belief is that Walter White and Mrs. Cannon have a right to marry if they love each other. But, hundreds of colored people in our area do not agree."[2]

White took a leave of absence from the NAACP, but the controversy he had created did not die down. A new round of alarms sounded when he wrote an article for *Look* magazine in which he extolled the benefits of having blacks take a chemical treatment that would turn their skin white. "Consider what would happen if a means of racial transformation is made available at reasonable costs," he wrote. "The racial, social, economic and political consequences would be tremendous." He quoted Lena Horne as saying that the availability of the chemical was "wonderful" and the "greatest thing for world peace." White also announced that science had now perfected a treatment that would make blacks' hair "permanently straight." And he suggested plastic surgery to make Negroid features appear more like Caucasian noses and lips.[3]

The reaction was overwhelmingly negative. Thurgood Marshall was highly critical in private, but he had no public comment. However, others didn't hold back. William L. Patterson, executive secretary of the Civil Rights Congress, said White's proposed use of chemicals on black Americans "would be laughable were it not such a grievous insult." Patterson added that White was asking black Americans to "suffer in silence" until "the coming of an insulting and degrading chemical messiah."[4]

While Marshall and Roy Wilkins refused to throw any more fuel on the fire, it was now clear that White's days at the NAACP were all but over. He had used his connections with white politicians and corporate leaders as the basis for his power inside the organization. But now his base in the black leadership was shaken. And his infamous article cut him off from a broad range of the NAACP's membership. Still, with Eleanor Roosevelt leading his defense, the board voted 16–10 to let him keep the title of executive secretary, if nothing else. White returned to work with no authority; Wilkins and Marshall now had day-to-day control of the NAACP.

As Wilkins's and Marshall's roles grew, so did their resentment and jealousy of White. "Roy did the work," Marshall later said. "If it wasn't for Roy that thing would have fallen apart every day, every hour on the hour."

Marshall, even more than Wilkins, had serious problems with White, because the executive secretary would sometimes try to meddle in the legal affairs of the association.

White was drawn to the high-profile drama of Supreme Court cases involving the NAACP. He would regularly go to Washington for Marshall's arguments and sit in the section reserved for lawyers. Marshall let it go on for several years, but as their relationship turned icy, he came to resent this behavior. "Now look, you're not supposed to be in there, and they know you're connected with me, and one of these days they're going to find out that you're not a lawyer," Marshall told White. "And I'm going to get blamed for it. And it's going to affect my standing. And I don't believe in letting anything affect my standing in the Supreme Court. So I'm telling you, don't let me catch you sitting there again. If you do, I'm going to tell the guard."

White said: "You wouldn't." Marshall replied, "Try me," and walked away.

A few months later Marshall was back at the Supreme Court. White was not in his usual seat, and Marshall thought he had prevailed. Then came a surprise. White was in the judges' box, where friends of the justices were seated. He had gone over Marshall's head and asked Justice Hugo Black for the special seat.[5]

Marshall had no such tensions with Roy Wilkins. Their common distaste for White had led them to become fast friends. Both were in their forties, and they shared power in the NAACP's New York headquarters. They also lived in the same Harlem apartment building, and they often traveled to and from work together. "In New York, Roy Wilkins and I would get on the subway," Marshall said, smiling at the thought. "And we would get a *Daily Worker* [published by the Communist Party] and *The Wall Street Journal*. How're you going to know what they're doing if you don't read their paper?"

Marshall and Wilkins first teamed up against White when he announced to the press that the NAACP was bringing a suit for Josephine Baker, the flamboyant black nightclub entertainer. She wanted to sue Walter Winchell, the nationally syndicated gossip columnist, because Winchell had written that Baker had supported European fascists before World War II. Marshall was angry that White had put the NAACP in the middle of a high-society pissing match. Eventually Baker backed out of the suit, but the episode left White and Marshall barely speaking. "Thurgood was quite furious. He felt, and I think quite correctly, that that was sort of an inappropriate use of the energies and resources of the Legal Defense Fund," remembered Jack Greenberg, a young white lawyer who had come onto Marshall's staff.[6]

The political warfare also split co-workers inside the NAACP office. "I think it's fair enough to say that there was a conspiracy to get rid of White," said Henry Lee Moon, the NAACP's director of public relations, who was a friend to the executive secretary. "I think the way [Roy and Thurgood] treated Walter was unworthy." But others in the office saw White's troubles as his own creation. "Walter thought of himself as the ambassador to the white world," said Herbert Hill, a white staff member who headed the NAACP's labor relations department. "Walter was obsessed with important white people."[7]

While White struggled to stay afloat, Marshall began to strut about. He became more of a party-going, drinking man, who wore his courtroom success and increased power on his sleeve. "Thurgood loved to pat women's asses, drink, and be hearty company," Hill said in a later interview. "Marshall would parody Uncle Toms [by using a deep southern accent and making his eyes big]. His zest for how he lived—drinking, fucking, arguing—made him a near legendary figure."[8]

Marshall's reputation for the wild side of life certainly did grow during this period. One letter from a friend ended, "Hoping that you have recovered from your cold and your one night stands." William Coleman, a Harvard law graduate and the first black Supreme Court clerk, got to know Marshall during this time period. He recalled in an interview that Marshall was a well-regarded Romeo: "He was an exciting and powerful person around women. I don't think Thurgood would sleep with everybody, but there were some very attractive women who also had status . . . [who] Thurgood was very close to."[9]

By this time Thurgood's relationship with his wife, Buster, had become distant and lifeless. His heart was in his highly publicized lawsuits and the people who cheered his words every time he spoke at NAACP rallies. The reality of a childless marriage and a husband who spent more time with fawning female fans was tearing at Buster.

Buster's nephew, Claude Conner, said that "she knew" Thurgood was having a good time with women on the road, although no single affair caused a particularly loud explosion between the two of them. "I don't think that she made a big fuss about it," he added. Penny Monteiro, who was related to Marshall by marriage to one of his cousins, said, "I am pretty sure she did [know about his women]." But Buster felt Thurgood's life was often in danger on the road and he was often lonely. As a woman of that generation, she decided to close her eyes to his extramarital dalliances.

While Thurgood was having his fun, he was not above becoming jealous. Buster was regularly seen at Harlem social events dancing with Charlie Bease, a mailman who was in many of Buster's social clubs. "It was gossip," said Conner, "because Buster was always with Charlie and his wife, Helen, at the dances. Thurgood wasn't in a position to say a whole lot because there were all sorts of rumors about who he was sleeping with all over the country."[10]

In addition to his sexual adventures, Marshall enjoyed the New York party scene. Evelyn Cunningham, a columnist with the *Pittsburgh Courier*, recounted in an interview how she and Marshall were once caught by police in a bust of an illegal after-hours club in Manhattan. "The place didn't open until three A.M.," she said. When they walked in it was darkly lit, noisy, smoky, and crowded. "There was a lot of music, a lot of interesting people, some not particularly savory, and he immediately loved the atmosphere and got a little loud," Cunningham said.

About an hour after they had settled into the fun, blue-uniformed policemen came crashing in the front and back doors. "I was scared to death," Cunningham recalled. "People started running out, and I saw one young cop that I knew. I said to this cop, 'You can't arrest this man. He is very, very important, he's with the NAACP, you've got to let him go.' "

The cop recognized Marshall and led them to a side door, where Cunningham and Marshall escaped into the night. But Marshall was reluctant to walk away. With a few drinks bolstering his ego, he looked back at the scene of policemen handcuffing the partygoers and taking them off to jail. He turned to Cunningham and in a loud voice said: "I would like to defend these guys—these cops got no right doing this." Cunningham grabbed his coat sleeve and pulled him away, telling him it was time to go home. "I swear to God he was ready to mess up the whole deal," she recalled with a laugh. "He was a bit high." [11]

Marshall's prominence made him a name even in white America. *Collier's*, then one of the nation's top white magazines, identified him as "Our Greatest Civil Liberties Lawyer." In a nod to his busy social life, the magazine noted: "He's equally at home on a dance floor or before the U.S. Supreme Court."

The magazine featured Marshall's successful challenges to segregation in graduate schools but went a step further by portraying him as a hero to the common black man because of his ability to break racism's grip. As an example, *Collier's* told of Marshall being called late one night while he was playing poker in a Washington, D.C., hotel. Over the phone he heard that a lynching was about to take place in the South. Marshall called the FBI and the White House but was told they could not get help to the man before the next day.

"He then performed an instantaneous, cerebral tour-de-force," the magazine wrote. "He put through a long-distance call to an influential southern lawyer representing strong anti-Negro factions. When he had the man on the phone he said, 'Look, just two sets of people can't afford a lynching at this time—us Negroes and you people. You are right in the midst of a Dixiecrat political campaign and a lynching is going to make your people look awful bad.' The man's answer was 'Check. Give me the details and get off the phone so I can get moving. Call you back in half an hour.' In twenty minutes, Marshall's telephone rang and he was told, 'The state troopers made it in time—call this number in a few minutes and your man will be there unharmed.' And he was, although he was still too shaken to talk."

The article celebrated Marshall as a "tall, burly, gregarious man, light-skinned and light-hearted. . . . He has consciously chosen to follow a hedonistic, non-worrying philosophy." Marshall offered his motto for life in the story: "I intend to wear life like a very loose garment, and never worry about nothin'."

Aunt Medi was featured as the special woman in Marshall's life, the one who told funny stories about his long nights playing cards and his inability to carry a tune. Buster was quoted just once. At the very end of the article, she said he worked constantly. "He's aged so in the past five years," she said. "His disposition has changed. He is nervous where he used to be calm. This work is taking its toll on him. You know, it's a discouraging job he's set [for] himself." [12]

Despite his hectic life on the road and his troubles at home, his celebrity created new opportunities for Marshall. His private ambition had long been to become a judge, and by the early 1950s newspaper stories floated Marshall's name again as a candidate for a federal judgeship. *Collier's* magazine made public for the first time his effort to land a federal judgeship a few years earlier. The magazine's sources said Marshall didn't get the job because he would not join hands with politically influential blacks in Tammany Hall.

Marshall told the magazine that the anonymous source was right. He had refused even to meet with Tammany Hall's black regulars because, he said, "in my book a federal judge is a different animal—he shouldn't have to play patty-cake with the club house boys." [13] Marshall wanted to be a judge but only on his terms. The willful lawyer was not above using the magazine to remind people that he was qualified to be a judge and didn't have any political dirt on his hands.

He succeeded in getting his message out. The *Collier's* article stirred a new round of talk, as well as several more newspaper stories, connecting Marshall to the possibility of a federal judgeship. There were two vacant seats, in Philadelphia and New York. Marshall offered no comment to reporters about the judgeships except to say, "I'll cross that bridge when I come to it." [14]

Even with support from the press, Marshall still did not have the blessings of local black political powers in New York. The open judgeships went to white lawyers.

But even as half of his soul was pulling him toward the federal bench, the other half of Marshall saw his most important work as the unfinished business of ending school segregation. It was the work that Charles Houston had told him from his first day in law school would revolutionize American race relations. The question now was whether Thurgood Marshall could find a winning way to lead a twentieth-century American revolution.

CHAPTER 20

⚜

Planning a Revolt

END OF JIM CROW IN SIGHT screamed the *Afro-American*'s banner headline announcing the Supreme Court's June 1950 decision in *Sweatt*. Thurgood Marshall triumphantly predicted: "The complete destruction of *all* enforced segregation is now in sight. . . . Segregation no longer has the stamp of legality in any public education."[1]

Marshall was full of excitement and anticipation when he called a conference of attorneys from across the country to meet in New York. He was looking for a way to make the leap from desegregating graduate-level schools to integrating all public schools. The meeting attracted wide attention. Black newspapers covered it, and so did *The New York Times*. Jimmy Hicks of the *Afro-American* quoted Marshall as saying that the lawyers had mapped out plans to "wipe out . . . all phases of segregation in education from professional school to kindergarten." Hicks also reported a new defiant tone to the lawyers' discussion.

The militant attitude in public statements from Marshall and the lawyers, however, was quite different from their private discussions. Marshall was still deeply concerned that a direct attack on all school segregation could be time-consuming and, even worse, ultimately lead to defeat. Integrating law schools, professional schools, and even colleges with adult students might not have been hard. But racial integration of boys and girls in grade schools, Marshall suspected, was going to provoke the strongest possible backlash.

At the New York meeting the voice most strongly pressing for the direct attack belonged to Spottswood Robinson. The Richmond lawyer, revered for his photographic memory and precise legal writing, wanted the NAACP to be more aggressive. When they sat down at the meeting, Marshall began by expressing doubts about a strategy of asking the courts to rule that segregation was unconstitutional. This eventually goaded the gentlemanly Robinson into forcefully making the case for a direct attack. It also gave Marshall a chance to listen to the best arguments Robinson and the other lawyers could make for a court to disregard the *Plessy* decision and declare school segregation unconstitutional.

"I did not mention this to Thurgood, the plan for a direct attack before the meeting," Robinson said many years later in an interview, calmly smoking a pipe. "I didn't want any roadblocks. Thurgood was always cautious in the beginning of any of these cases, no matter how good they might look. We finally recommended that the NAACP go after segregation directly. Well, that was a bombshell, and it set up all kinds of commotion."[2]

Other than smoking his cigarette and sometimes smiling, Marshall kept quiet as Robinson led the discussion of the new strategy. It was typical Marshall to let the arguments rage while he soaked in all sides to the debate. He would glare at times, sometimes throw in a biting comment or shout out "bullshit." But slowly Marshall became more animated. He began smiling and nodding along with the talk of a direct challenge.

Robinson's argument for a strong attack got its most vigorous support from Marshall's deputy, Robert Carter. Known for his attention to detail and for keeping his bow tie knotted tight even while spending late hours at the office, Carter brought up a case from California, *Mendez v. Westminster School District*.

It was "sort of a dry run" for the theory of challenging segregation directly. The case involved segregation of Mexican children "on the theory that they couldn't speak the language." Carter noted the NAACP had prepared an amicus, or friend of the court, brief in that case, which argued for the first time that segregation for any reason was wrong.[3]

The NAACP position won out when the federal courts ruled in 1946 that, under the equal protection clause of the Fourteenth Amendment, California schools "must be open to all children by unified school association regardless of lineage." NAACP lawyers were particularly struck by the idea that the judges had noted they were not ruling that school facilities for the Spanish-speaking children were unequal. Instead the judges ordered school integration because segregation created "antagonisms [among] the children and sugges[ted] inferiority among them where none exist[ed].' "[4]

Carter told the lawyers at the meeting that the *Mendez* ruling had great significance in the aftermath of *Sweatt*, which had nailed down the idea that no Jim Crow school could ever equal the prestige and social status of a long-standing state school. *Mendez* had bolstered the argument that school segregation always increased racial tensions and problems for minorities. The NAACP lawyers now saw the outline of their argument and a strategy to challenge all school segregation.

Then Carter made a more radical suggestion. He recommended that the lawyers begin to use a controversial sociological method to show the damage segregation did to black Americans. "Bob gets all the credit for it," Marshall later told an oral history interviewer about the proposal to use Kenneth Clark, a black psychologist from City College of New York, as an expert.[5] Clark and his wife, Mamie, had conducted tests on black children using black and white dolls. The results were powerfully emotional. When black children were presented with black and white dolls, they almost always said the white dolls were prettier, smarter, and better at everything they did.

"I remember one young man," Clark recounted. "I've never forgotten him, in Arkansas, when I asked [which doll he liked], he pointed to the white doll. And I asked him which one don't you like, and he pointed to the brown-skinned doll. He was brown-skinned. And he said, 'That's a nigger, I'm a nigger,' and he laughed. I don't know what the laughter meant."

In the northern states Clark similarly found that black children had negative views of themselves. "I remember one young girl, about six or seven, who cried," he recalled. When the girl realized that she preferred white dolls, "she sort of walked out of the testing room because she did not like the fact that she was rejecting herself."[6]

When Carter presented the idea of using Clark's research to the lawyers at the NAACP, there was little support. Spott Robinson, for example, thought it was crazy and insulting to try to persuade a court of law with examples of crying children and their dolls. But Marshall, in a surprise to his colleagues, sided with Carter. He stood up and said if the time was coming for a direct challenge to segregation, then there was no reason not to use sociology, psychology, or anything else if it might help to win the case.

*   *   *

The first hurdle for the NAACP remained finding a plaintiff. Black parents nationwide, but especially in the Deep South, were understandably reluctant to get involved in segregation suits. They expected a white backlash would get everyone involved fired from their jobs. Their children might be attacked by white bullies on the streets. A. P. Tureaud, the NAACP's lawyer in New Orleans, explained in a 1950 letter that his efforts to get a suit started against all-white public schools in Louisiana failed because he could not find one parent willing to challenge local segregation laws.[7]

While most black parents were fearful, a few in Kansas contacted the national NAACP office in the late forties to say they would be willing to put their names on a suit challenging the constitutionality of Jim Crow schools. Isabel Lurie, of the Topeka NAACP, told the New York office that black schools in Topeka were just about equal to the white schools. But she wanted black children to be able to attend the nearest school on an integrated basis.[8] Similar requests were coming in from other Kansas towns, such as Wichita and Merriam. And in Virginia and the Carolinas there had been NAACP chapters willing to begin work on desegregation suits.

Before the *Sweatt* decision Marshall had considered it a waste of time and money to attack segregation in elementary and secondary schools. But now, after the Supreme Court ruling in *Sweatt* and with the NAACP lawyers anxious to test a direct-attack strategy, he was aggressively looking for the right place to take the big gamble. As luck would have it, he found a school segregation case in South Carolina, where he personally had a long history with the federal judges and good support from the local NAACP.

Marshall first came to the state in the early 1940s. He had won an equal pay case for black teachers in the state in 1944. He had also come there in 1947, in the aftermath of his victory ending the Texas white primary system, to argue successfully for an end to a similar all-white primary system in South Carolina. And in 1949 Marshall had visited the state capital to discuss with local NAACP officials a possible suit to integrate South Carolina's elementary schools.

The South Carolina NAACP had recently lost a case in which they asked for new buses for black students. That setback prompted Harold Boulware, the local attorney working on the case, to call Marshall. Boulware promised that if the national office would lend its support, the local NAACP would find Marshall plaintiffs willing to stand up for complete school integration.

It took eight months, but the South Carolina NAACP produced twenty parents willing to have their childrens' names attached to a suit. "I was dispatched to go to South Carolina, and I met with all the plaintiffs," said Robert Carter. "I went down to be certain that the people in Clarendon County understood precisely what we were talking about. Because at that point people were being threatened. They had to realize that there was a possibility of them losing jobs, even threats of physical violence." But only one parent decided to back away after Carter's presentation.[9]

The NAACP filed suit, and the trial was set to begin in May 1951 in Charleston, South Carolina. Marshall and Carter arrived by train from New York with Ken Clark. On the train Clark and Marshall had their first long conversation about school segregation. Marshall was initially his usual glib self, telling Clark vivid stories filled with colorful characters about his trips to southern courtrooms. However, as they traveled deeper into the South and day turned to night, Clark remembered watching Marshall become quieter, spending most of his time staring out the window. "What's the matter?" Clark asked him. Looking up, Marshall said, "I'm tired, tired of trying to save the white man's soul."[10]

Once they arrived in South Carolina, Marshall showed no sign of the burden he had displayed to Clark. A determined Marshall began preparing the NAACP brief with Carter, Boulware, Spot Robinson, and a Birmingham lawyer, Arthur Shores. Clark meanwhile started conducting psychological testing with his dolls on black children attending Clarendon County's segregated schools. Marshall had little time to pay attention to Clark's work, but he had grown fond of the man. The lawyer was worried that Clark might be attacked by white thugs who didn't like seeing a black university professor in a suit. However, Marshall was not willing to have one of his lawyers stop working on the case to accompany the young psychologist. To ease his mind, Marshall gave Clark a fifty-dollar bill. He told Clark that if any white men bothered him, to hold out the money.[11] He also got the local NAACP to assign some men to accompany Clark.

Clark never had to use the fifty-dollar bill, but a white local school superintendent tried to stop his testing. When he first saw the psychologist, the white superintendent told the local NAACP official with Clark, "You fuck, I told you I didn't want you to come back here to create trouble. I don't want to have to harm you."

The threats did not stop Clark, however. He tested sixteen black children between the ages of five and nine and, by using black and white dolls, asked them to give their views of black and white people. The only difference between the dolls was their skin color. Ten of the sixteen children said they preferred the white doll. Eleven of the children referred to the black doll as "bad," while nine said the white doll was "nice." Seven of the children pointed to the white doll when they were asked to choose the doll most like themselves.

Marshall and the lawyers, meanwhile, were busy collecting information on the disparities between the state's white schools and its threadbare black schools. Their initial brief was based solely on the existing inequality between the schools.

In both the teachers' salary case and the white primary case it was Judge J. Waties Waring who had ruled in Marshall's favor. In fact, Waring had for years been privately urging Marshall to directly challenge the constitutionality of school segregation. "The NAACP legal staff apparently was quite hesitant about bringing a formal attack on legal segregation in schools," Waring recalled later. The judge had no such fears. While Marshall was working on the brief, Waring invited Marshall to dinner at his house—at a time when "decent" white people never invited Negroes into their homes as social equals—and told him it was time to make law by making history.

But Marshall was still hesitant. The judge insisted that Marshall rewrite his suit, bringing an even stronger, more direct challenge to school segregation. "He looked rather astonished, but said, 'Yes,' " Waring recounted later.[12]

Marshall had to rewrite the brief twice before Waring was satisfied that the NAACP was truly challenging the constitutionality of segregation. The trial began on May 28, 1951, before a three-judge federal panel. Waring was joined on the bench by George Timmerman and Federal Circuit Court Judge John Parker, the senior judge for the Fourth Circuit, who presided.

When the trial opened, over five hundred people tried to crowd into the federal courthouse in Charleston, which could seat only seventy-five. News reports said two women fainted in the ninety-degree heat while trying to get into the court. "The plaintiffs and all the spectators in that South Carolina case were rural people," recalled Alice Stovall, Marshall's secretary. She had gone to South Carolina to help the lawyers prepare for court and found herself caught up in an exhibition of excitement and passion she had not expected.

"They came in their jalopy cars and their overalls, and they had this little section of the court where they could go," Stovall said. "All they wanted to do—if they could—just touch him, just touch him, *Lawyer Marshall*, as if he were a god. These were poor people who had come miles to be there."

Marshall and Bob Carter were awed too. "If anyone ever tells you that colored people want segregation, remind him of these people," they wrote a few days later in a letter to the *Afro-American*.[13]

At the start of the case, South Carolina's lawyer, Robert McC. Figg, a tall, studious man in a white suit, gave the judges and the NAACP a surprise by conceding that schools for black children in South Carolina were not equal to those for white children. Figg said the state was prepared to upgrade the black schools. He asked the court to give South Carolina a "reasonable period of time" to make the changes before considering the NAACP's case.

Judge Waring immediately saw that Marshall was unprepared for Figg's admission of guilt. Marshall had prepared a great number of witnesses and evidence to prove the state had inadequate facilities. Now that evidence was irrelevant.[14]

The three judges accepted the state's concession that schools for black children were inadequate. The chief judge was about to bring the session to a close without protest from Marshall when Waring spoke up. He said there was still a major issue in Marshall's brief for the court to consider—the newly inserted question of whether segregation of schoolchildren was unconstitutional. Judge Waring, speaking without any hint of his private talks with Marshall, added: "This court has got to face the issue of segregation, per se."[15]

Buoyed by Waring's remarks, Marshall began a parade of expert witnesses, including social scientists and educators—college professors from Columbia and Harvard—who testified about the effects of segregation on black children. "Legal segregation hampers the mental, emotional, physical and financial development of colored children and aggravates the very prejudices from which it arises," said Dr. David Krech, a social psychologist from Harvard. "Damage if continued for ten or twelve years will be permanent."[16]

As Marshall and his witnesses tried to make their case, their voices were often drowned out by the sound of jackhammers. State workers were repairing a street outside the courthouse. Whenever Marshall got to his feet the jackhammers "coincidentally" began to pound into rock and concrete. Eventually Judge Waring asked Judge Parker to order the workers to halt: "The administration of justice is more important than the paving of a street." Parker had the workers quit.[17]

Marshall's star witness was Ken Clark, the mild-mannered psychology professor. In two days of studying black schoolchildren in South Carolina, Clark told the court, he "found that the majority of black children tended to reject themselves and their color and accept whites as desirable. . . . "[18]

Clark testified that school segregation was distorting the minds of black youngsters to the point of making them self-hating. "The conclusion which I was forced to reach was that these children in Clarendon County, like other human beings who are subjected to an obviously inferior status in the society in which they live, have been definitely harmed in the development of their personalities; that the signs of instability in their personalities are clear, and I think that every psychologist would accept and interpret these signs as such." Clark concluded that the damage was "likely to endure as long as the conditions of segregation exist."[19]

The state's attorney responded to Clark's testimony with the smug comment that schools were responsible for education, not personality development. The real issue, Figg told the judges, was that South Carolina was willing to equalize spending. If the state was forced to integrate its schools, violence was certain to break out and South Carolina would be forced to stop offering public education.

A month after the trial, the judges ruled with Figg and against the NAACP. Chief Judge Parker and Judge Timmerman said the 1896 *Plessy* decision established the idea of separate but equal as a legal, constitutional concept, and the state was within its right to separate black and white children. Parker and Timmerman disregarded Clark's testimony. In their written opinion they said judges had no "right to read their ideas of sociology into the constitution."[20]

Judge Waring, however, cast a dissenting vote. He said the concept of separate but equal violated the Constitution. "And no excuse can be made to deny [black children] these rights which are theirs under the constitution." He stated that "beyond a doubt the evils of segregation and color prejudice come from early training." And he added that being separated from other young Americans because of skin color had "an evil and ineradicable effect upon the mental processes of our young." [21]

Despite Waring's dissent the court gave the state six months to equalize the black schools. In March of 1952 the panel reconvened. Judge Waring had retired, and this new court was unanimous in finding that the state had met its pledge. At the end of the proceedings, above the noise of the crowd leaving the courtroom, one of the state's lawyers shouted at Marshall, "If you ever show your black ass in Clarendon County again you'll be dead." [22]

Marshall, walking with Carter and his colleagues, glared at the man but did not respond. It was not his way. His mind was already set on sending an appeal to the Supreme Court. Judge Waring offered to help with the appeal, but he was also busy stabbing Marshall in the back. Waring was a close friend of Walter White, and he sent letters to White and NAACP board members in which he criticized Marshall's legal staff as "not sufficiently equipped" to handle the appeal.

Waring proposed that the NAACP hire a special counsel to present the case before the Supreme Court. In a letter to Judge Hubert Delaney, a leader of the NAACP board, Waring criticized Marshall as too cautious. The South Carolina case, Waring wrote, "has got to be won by a determined fight by determined lawyers calling for a reversal [of *Plessy*] and not apologizing for appealing." [23] All the while, Marshall was unaware that Waring had little respect for his legal ability.

Criticisms of Marshall weren't just coming from those who wanted a more forceful attack on segregation.

Marjorie McKenzie, a *Pittsburgh Courier* columnist, wrote after the South Carolina decision that Marshall was leading the NAACP over the edge of a high cliff with his strategy. She said the association's victories in *Sipuel* and *Sweatt* had put black Americans on a sure path to getting better schools by forcing states to equalize facilities. By abandoning that approach, Marshall was risking what had been won in those fights. [24]

McKenzie's criticism opened the door for others who wanted to take shots at the NAACP's special counsel. No one went public, but she got calls and letters from people who supported her, especially black lawyers. "He was not eager for the little lawyers around the country who brought these cases in to follow through in front of the Supreme Court," she later told an interviewer. "A lot of black lawyers around the country came to feel that Thurgood Marshall was stealing the show." [25]

Marshall did keep a tight grip on other lawyers working on NAACP cases. He wanted to coordinate any legal arguments made under the NAACP name. His goal was to avoid segregationist victories that could be cited in later cases to upset NAACP attempts to uproot the separate-but-equal doctrine.

*   *   *

As Waring and McKenzie were sparring with Marshall, the NAACP legal fight against segregated schools continued. Just two days after the federal appeals court in South Carolina had ruled against the NAACP, a second major school segregation case began in Topeka, Kansas. Marshall sent the scholarly Bob Carter and an eager young white assistant, Jack Greenberg, to try the case. The local attorneys were Elisha Scott and his two sons, John and Charles, longtime lawyers for the Topeka NAACP.

The Topeka case fit with Marshall's grand design. He picked it out of the several potential school segregation cases which NAACP branches had sent to his New York office. Topeka was a uniquely good fit. "The schools in Topeka are physically substantially equal and in some cases the Negro schools are even better than the white schools," an NAACP official wrote in a memo to NAACP headquarters.[26] Unlike in other states, where the inferior facilities in the black schools might become the main issue and allow the court to order equalization, the case in Kansas would force the court to confront the state's policy of segregating black students.

The case opened before a three-judge panel on June 25, 1951, with Carter and Greenberg sitting with local NAACP lawyers at the plaintiffs' table. There was no crowd in this courtroom; the case did not generate the passion of school segregation suits in the South.

Black parents gave simple, compelling testimony about how their children had to take long trips to segregated schools because they could not go to nearby all-white schools. One parent testified that Topeka's black teachers and black schools were good but "my children are craving light. . . . The entire colored race is craving light and the only way to reach the light is to start our children [black and white] together in their infancy and they come up together."[27]

Under Marshall's instructions Greenberg brought in expert witnesses to testify that segregation always meant inequality. Hugh Speer, a professor of education at the University of Kansas City, said there were significant differences in the curricula at Topeka's black and white schools, even if the facilities were comparable. The personalities of black children, their social interests, and their friends were all hurt by segregated schools. "If the colored children are denied the experience in school of associating with white children . . . then the colored child's curriculum is being greatly curtailed."[28]

Lester Goodell, the school board's attorney, responded that racial segregation in schools was within the law under separate but equal. He dismissed Speer's testimony about the psychological impact of segregation on the young as not relevant.

The three-judge panel issued a strong opinion that at first glance seemed to support the NAACP: "Segregation of white and colored children in public schools has a detrimental effect upon the colored children," the judges wrote. "The impact is greater when it has the sanction of the law. . . . Segregation has a tendency to retard the educational and mental development of Negro children and to deprive them of some of the benefits they would receive in a racially integrated school system."

But despite that position the judges somehow ruled unanimously against the NAACP. They said they had no choice since the law of the land, as set by the Supreme Court in *Plessy*, called only for equal schools for black and white children, not for integrated schools.[29]

After the Topeka case ended, Carter wrote an upbeat memo to Marshall saying the trial had gone well and there was a good basis for a Supreme Court appeal. The "record in this case is actually better than the one in South Carolina," he wrote, adding that he expected the two cases to reach the high court at the same time and possibly be consolidated.[30]

Meanwhile, Marshall was keeping tabs on several other cases with the potential to join the South Carolina and Kansas cases before the Supreme Court. Spott Robinson and Oliver Hill, two Howard Law School graduates who formed a Richmond law firm, remained close friends with Marshall. Both men had attended the NAACP lawyers' meetings to discuss new strategies for dealing with school segregation, and Robinson had been with Marshall at the South Carolina case. With Marshall's encouragement Hill and Robinson were on the lookout for a good case from Virginia, capital of the Confederacy, and they traveled from one local NAACP meeting to another to discuss the fight against school segregation.

While Hill and Robinson were trying to select a county for a case that fit with Marshall's efforts, a sixteen-year-old girl from Farmville, Virginia, called them to say she had started a black student walkout to protest segregated schools.

The two lanky black lawyers from Richmond made the short car ride south to Prince Edward County. At the First Baptist Church, they met with Barbara Johns and a group of black students who took part in her walkout. "The students in Farmville had already gone on strike," Robinson recalled. "They got 456 students involved in this, and they organized it, got everything ready. And didn't tell their parents or anybody."

The high school students made a deep impression on Hill. "The kids were so well disciplined and had such high morale and expressed themselves so well. We didn't have the nerve to break their hearts," he said. "We didn't pick the Prince Edward County case, it just developed, and we just went to their rescue."

But just as judges had ruled against the NAACP in South Carolina and Kansas, the federal judges in the Virginia case said the law allowed the state to keep separate schools for black and white children. Although the schools were unequal, the judges said in their written opinion, they found "no harm or injury to either race—This ends our inquiry."[31]

*   *   *

While the Virginia case was being argued, Marshall was distracted and upset. June Shagaloff, a pretty twenty-three-year-old Jewish woman who had come to work as an assistant to Marshall, had been arrested and jailed. She had gone to Cairo, Illinois, at Marshall's direction to help the local NAACP branch negotiate a voluntary plan for school integration with the all-white school board. The idea was to see if Shagaloff could help the board and the NAACP avoid a time-consuming, expensive legal fight.

Illinois, unlike its neighbors to the south, did not have state laws requiring school segregation. But schools in the southern part of Illinois were segregated as a matter of local custom, and they were as hard-line as anywhere in the South. Shagaloff quickly found Cairo a "very hostile" place. Marshall had arranged for his assistant to stay in the home of an elderly black woman and for two black men to take turns guarding her.

But constant threats led Shagaloff to fear for her safety, and her guards taught her how to shoot a gun. Just as Shagaloff began to make headway with the school board, the home of a prominent NAACP member was bombed. In a strange turn of events a few days later, seven local NAACP officials, as well as Shagaloff, were arrested on charges of conspiracy to harm children by creating a volatile situation in the schools.

The black NAACP members were set free on $1,000 bond shortly after their arrest, but Shagaloff remained in jail since she had no local property to offer. Although the black residents of Cairo volunteered their homes as bond for her, the police chief refused. Association leaders in Cairo were hysterical with fear over what might happen to her in jail, and they made frantic long-distance phone calls to Marshall. After telephoning the FBI and demanding protection for Shagaloff, Marshall immediately flew to Cairo.

A day and one terrifying night after her arrest, a downcast and scared Shagaloff brightened when she saw Marshall stride into the jail. "The police chief had his feet up on the desk," she recalled. "He had a triple belly over his belt—a fat, slobby, uneducated man with this big, stubby cigar. He looked like a caricature from a Grade C movie. Mr. Marshall took a straight chair and straddled it, had his arms wrapped around the back, and just chewed the fat with this police chief. You would think they were old buddies. And that went on for half an hour, forty-five minutes. And finally Mr. Marshall said, 'How about that man's bond that he put up for her, pretty good isn't it?' And the police chief said, 'I guess so.' " A few minutes later the chief got up and unlocked the cell door, releasing Shagaloff. The charges were later dropped.

Shagaloff's efforts eventually paid off. "We got the schools desegregated in Cairo, in Carbondale—a radius of about thirty miles." She recalled.[32]

Even as Marshall had to put out fires around the country, his strategy for school desegregation was beginning to bear fruit. The Supreme Court agreed to review Marshall's appeals in the South Carolina and Kansas cases. When the court opened its new session in the fall of 1952, the appeal of the Virginia case was added to its docket. Marshall was thrilled; they would be heard together, and the constitutionality of segregation would have to be addressed directly. With cases coming from different parts of the country, and with a variety of scenarios—some where schools for black and white children were already equal and some where they were grossly unequal—the court's ruling would apply nationwide.

The addition of the Virginia case, however, led the high court to delay the arguments, until December 1952, which caused another surprise development. The court asked for two more cases—one from Washington, D.C., and another from Delaware—to be presented at the same time.

The District of Columbia case was atypical. The nation's capital was not a state, and the Fourteenth Amendment requiring the states to grant equal rights to all citizens did not apply. Washington's school board had to be challenged to integrate schools under the Fifth Amendment's due process clause. The D.C. case had started back in 1948 under Charles Houston, but when he fell ill, the Howard law professor James Nabrit agreed to pick it up. The case was waiting to be heard by an appellate court when the Supreme Court asked that it be added to its docket.

The high court soon became interested in a fifth case from Wilmington, Delaware. It was being handled by a local NAACP lawyer, Louis Redding, with the assistance of Jack Greenberg. What was odd about the Delaware case was that the NAACP had not appealed it to the Supreme Court. The state of Delaware was appealing a lower court order that black students be integrated into previously all-white schools.

Associate Justice Tom Clark later said the decision to bring together all five cases—and to seek out the Delaware and District of Columbia cases—was done out of concern for the court's image. "We felt it was much better to have representative cases from different parts of the country," he said in an interview after leaving the Court. "If we got a number of states involved, especially some of them that were historically more liberal towards blacks, it would help [in not making it an antisouthern case]. . . . It would give us broader coverage."[33]

The cases were ready. The Court was ready to hear the argument. After more than a hundred years of protests and meetings and plans, the NAACP had the pieces in place. Now Thurgood Marshall had to prepare his legal team to argue the biggest case of their lives, one that could revolutionize the heart of twentieth-century race relations.

CHAPTER 21

❧

Case of the Century

The year leading up to the oral arguments before the Supreme Court on school segregation took a heavy toll on forty-four-year-old Thurgood Marshall. His eyes became puffy from lack of sleep and too many cigarettes. He put on weight. And he was grumpier than ever—now snapping at secretaries who were used to his good humor. Marshall fixated on the school segregation case, and everything else, including his wife, took a backseat.

No one had to tell him this was the biggest case of his career. This case could change the face of American society. Marshall began calling conferences of the brightest minds from around the nation to discuss every angle of the case. Lawyers, law professors, sociologists, anthropologists, and even psychologists, notably Ken Clark, all came to Marshall's office to discuss how to convince the Court that separate but equal was a devastating burden to black people, nothing more than racism.

Although everyone was united on the idea of directly challenging segregation, the NAACP team split over whether to use social science data to make the case before the high court. Spott Robinson and a young, Harvard-educated Philadelphia lawyer, Bill Coleman, led the fight against anything but a serious, strictly legal approach. "We'll absolutely lose. It's weak, it's a weak legal decision, the justices won't buy it, they won't go for it," said one of the lawyers, pounding the wooden table in the conference room.

Marshall had to act as a peacemaker when the lawyers and the social scientists began sniping. But even as he tried to smooth out the tensions, some of the lawyers got mad at Marshall for giving any credence to the work of the social theorists. Finally, Marshall had to lay down the law. He had become a fan of Ken Clark's studies—the psychologists, the historians, and the political scientists were going to stay.

Charles Black, then a Columbia law professor and adviser to the NAACP, described Marshall's manner as direct but never heavy-handed: "You had to be impressed most by the firmness with which he was in charge. He could be the next thing to autocratic, but he did it always in a nice way." [1]

Marshall's resolve to use sociological studies in the schools cases was rooted in his life experience—as the son of a bright man who never got an education and never became more than a waiter. Marshall saw the same trap still catching many young black people. They were defeated at a young age by limits they accepted about their talents and their right to an education.

When Marshall spoke to NAACP youth groups and asked the youngsters what they were going to do when they grew up, the kids answered: "I'm going to be a good butler" or "I hope I might be able to get in the post office." He thought to himself, That was it for them. He understood he was watching their lives get shut down before they were even grown up. He wanted to unravel this rope that was choking so many. [2]

Marshall saw the crippling insecurity among those black children as a legal issue. The government, by its endorsement of segregation, was promoting self-hate in black children. [3] He wanted to force the government to confront its own action against America's black citizens, and the schools cases were the perfect vehicle for putting the issue in court.

As the time approached for him to argue the cases, Marshall brought in more professors and lawyers to go over every possible angle and throw around ideas. "It was an amazing feat to bring in black lawyers from the South and white lawyers and historians from the law schools," said Jack Weinstein, another Columbia law professor who was helping with the case. "It almost became a national enterprise."

Conference rooms in the LDF's offices were crammed, often with sixty or more people standing and shouting. It was smoky, with Spott Robinson's pipe sending aromatic puffs into the air, followed by steady streams from Marshall's cigarettes and several cigars. Law books were strewn everywhere, and some people had to sit on the edges of tables because there weren't enough chairs. In this atmosphere tempers occasionally flared, and Marshall had to diffuse the tensions. Sometimes he would tell a joke or use his "Uncle Tom" voice to get everyone laughing and back to work.

Despite the arguments and egos, Marshall, like the spirited conductor of a swing band, orchestrated lively meetings of legal talent. The meetings became renowned as great fun even though they involved hard work and little or no pay. At one session a mischievous Marshall turned to Charles Black. He asked the southern white lawyer why he was joining forces with the dreaded NAACP to work for integration.

"Well, I'll tell you, Mr. Marshall," Black replied. "I come from deep, deep in Texas . . . [and I] heard of this really terrible organization way up north called the N-A-A-C-P. It was an awful place, with great big offices all the way up there in New York, they said. And the worst thing of all about it was that right in that big office there was this room, this special secret room. A room with no windows and no doors and walls about a foot thick—the only way that you could get in was with a combination to this huge lock. And inside that room, they said, there was nothing but hooks on the walls—hundreds and hundreds of hooks—and do you know what was hanging on each and every one of those hooks? Why, they said that on each of those hooks was a key to the bedroom of a southern white woman. And so I figured that's an organization I wanna get involved in!"[4]

"Thurgood had an incredible gift," said June Shagaloff. "He'd have his feet up on the table, with all these learned minds around him, in awe of him. He'd make them feel at home. He would pull out from other people their thinking, and he synthesized it and made it his."

The laughs and backslapping helped, but they were also motivated by the realization that history was on the line. Those gathered would work on drafts of the brief well past midnight. The exacting Spott Robinson would go over each line of each page of each draft. Every few hours he would come out with more changes for Alice Stovall, Marshall's secretary, or one of her assistants to type into a new draft. "If I have to do this one more time—" a frustrated Stovall finally shouted to one of the other secretaries. The older woman looked at Stovall and said: "But, Alice, I don't know whether you know it, but you're helping make history here tonight. If Mr. Robinson tells you to do that fifty times, you type it!" Every person in the NAACP's office was overworked but energized by the prospect of the big case. Walter White, Roy Wilkins, the board

members, and activists down to the branches across the country were focused on Marshall's preparations to take the big gamble.

*   *   *

Marshall still had to travel to make speeches and to raise money for the
historic cases. Even on the road he would call into the office several times
every day to instruct Bob Carter or one of the other lawyers about what
to do next. "Thurgood Marshall kept a hectic pace," said Ken Clark, recalling the months before Marshall went before the Supreme Court.
"You could really see the toll that the pace was taking on him."[5]

In a magazine interview, Marshall joked: "Isn't it nice—no one cares
which twenty-three hours a day I work?" The magazine went on to say
that Marshall had two temporary fillings placed in his teeth and had been
unable to find the time to get back to the dentist during the last seven
years.

The weekends were especially busy, with out-of-town lawyers and
academics rushing in to give help. On Friday evening Marshall's office
would be crowded with people, and as the night wore on he would pull
out the bottle of bourbon he kept in his desk drawer.

Most nights Marshall would go over to the Blue Ribbon, a German
restaurant on Forty-third Street, and have several drinks while eating a
variety of bizarre food meant to impress his dining companions. One of
his famed meals was fried roast beef bones. It was nothing out of the ordinary to see Marshall smoking cigarettes and drinking martinis while
dining on steak tartare, with a raw egg in the middle of the raw chopped
steak surrounded by onions and capers.

Meanwhile, Thurgood's relationship with Buster was failing. He was
preoccupied with work and was not putting much energy into saving the
marriage. Buster, too, had a life apart. She spent her time in social clubs
and as a leader of the Democrat Adlai Stevenson's presidential campaign
in Harlem. She became an active member of the black Democratic club
in the neighborhood and spent time with her uncle in Brooklyn.

At age forty-one Buster still dearly wanted to try one more time to
have a child with Thurgood. But the last miscarriage left her bedridden
for a time. Her several miscarriages—some friends say as many as five—
left her deeply disappointed, even morose. She felt she had failed herself
and Thurgood. One Christmas, Buster gave Thurgood a gift he had always wanted but had been waiting to share with his firstborn son—an
electric train set. He also got an engineer's cap, and when the Marshalls

had friends over for the holidays, the most memorable event would be seeing Thurgood, in the cap, running his trains.

The train set was a charming reminder to Thurgood of the big trains he saw as a boy in Baltimore and a stirring connection to the memory of his father's work on the B & O. But the gift was also a painful reminder that he and Buster still had no children. And as the schools cases drew closer and excitement mounted, Marshall spent almost all his time at work.

Often, especially in the last days before the NAACP brief was sent to Washington, the lawyers and staff would still be at the Forty-third Street office at sunrise. "When we were preparing for the *Brown* decision, sometimes we slept there," said June Shagaloff. "The proofs would be taken to the printer at 1:00 in the morning and come back at 4:30 or 5:30."

Marshall edited the briefs several times himself to remove little "snide cracks" about the opposing white lawyers arguing for segregation.[6] It was typical of Marshall to keep the fight on the most professional level, even to make his adversaries comfortable, so they would accept him as a part of the legal fraternity.

When the briefs were finally submitted, Chief Justice Vinson scheduled the oral arguments for Tuesday, December 9, 1952. Thurgood Marshall, Bob Carter, and the rest of the NAACP team spent a week in Washington going through last-minute debate and holding mock arguments at Howard University Law School, with students and professors throwing questions at the lawyers. Marshall sat through the practice sessions, listening and working over the smallest details and difficulties. The pressure was showing. He was irritable, regularly appearing with his tie twisted to one side and never without a Winston cigarette burning between his fingers.

Marshall's tension apparently was not relieved when Justice Department officials called him to say they had filed a friend-of-the-court brief supporting the NAACP's claim that school segregation was unconstitutional. "The failure of a state to provide equal educational facilities to some of its citizens solely because of their race or color is . . . a violation of the 14th Amendment," Justice Department officials wrote to the Supreme Court.[7] But to Marshall's great disappointment the department's brief did not call for the immediate dismantling of segregated schools. It only asked the Supreme Court to set a timetable for school districts to comply with integration.

"When we filed our brief I went on the NAACP shit list as a gradual-ist," said Philip Elman, then assistant solicitor general. "[I felt] Thurgood Marshall . . . made every conceivable error. It was too early to go for overruling segregation with Vinson as chief justice."[8]

Elman thought that the Justice Department had created a framework to allow the Supreme Court to outlaw school segregation without creat-ing social chaos. In his mind the government's brief was a formula to solve the problem—schools would slowly be desegregated, with lower courts handling the day-to-day oversight. But Marshall didn't agree. He felt Elman and his colleagues had made a halfhearted gesture when he needed their complete support. Ever a pragmatist, though, he decided he would live with the equivocal support of the Justice Department and hope for better in the future. So while he complained bitterly to Elman, Marshall praised the brief to reporters.

In the middle of the hectic preparations for the court argument, Mar-shall made time to have lunch with John W. Davis, the man who would oppose him in the South Carolina case. As a law student Marshall had admired Davis, skipping classes to hear him make arguments at the Supreme Court. Even toward the end of his life, he retained awe for Davis's ability as a lawyer and called him "unbelievable." Marshall added, "I learned most of my stuff from him."

When Marshall the law school student had listened to Davis, he had fantasized about the day he would stand to argue against the dean of American lawyers. By the 1950s Davis had argued more cases before the Supreme Court than any American except the legendary Daniel Webster. Now, days before they would meet as opponents, Marshall, age forty-four, had lunch with the seventy-nine-year-old.

The lunch went well. The impeccably dressed, white-haired Davis was a courteous and kind southern gentleman. And Marshall, accus-tomed to southern gents from his days at the Gibson Island Club, was thrilled to be treated as a peer by a man so well respected in the most ex-clusive, and all-white, circles of American law. Davis was a former con-gressman from West Virginia, a former U.S. solicitor general (in the Wilson administration), and he had served as U.S. ambassador to En-gland. In 1924 he was nominated as the Democratic candidate for presi-dent but lost to Calvin Coolidge. By 1952 Davis, who had also served as the president of the American Bar Association, was prospering in private law practice with a big New York firm. Only a personal request from his good friend South Carolina governor James Byrnes persuaded him to argue one last case before the Supreme Court. This would be his one hundred and fortieth at the high court's bar. As a member of the South's upper class he had a sense of social obligation, and as a segregationist Davis agreed to make the presentation at no charge to the state.

The lunch with Davis caused widespread puzzlement at the NAACP. Everyone knew Marshall happily played the role of the good ol' boy with southern sheriffs. It was no secret that he was also willing to eat in the back and sit in the "Negro" section of southern streetcars without a thought. But why, some asked, was he going out of his way to sit down and break bread with an old segregationist like Davis?

"John Davis was the enemy," said Shagaloff. "He was everything that we were fighting. How could Mr. Marshall go to lunch with him?" When Shagaloff and some other NAACP staffers confronted him about it, Marshall explained, "We're both attorneys, we're both civil. It's very important to have a civil relationship with your opponent."

Although Davis had a good relationship with Marshall, several people, including Davis's law partners, suggested that by taking on this case Davis risked being painted as an Old South racist. His daughter, Julia, openly urged her father not to take the case. She tried to convince him that he "wouldn't win it," because segregation was contrary to the integrationist "spirit of the times." But Julia Davis recalled that her dad responded that the law was on his side, with *Plessy* as a precedent, and the southern way of life was at stake. He told his family that he had no problem with educating black people but that school integration would cause bad feelings between blacks and whites and lead to more racial polarization.[9]

Davis instructed his top assistant to write a brief that would make the case for segregated schools but not contain any negative words about blacks or integration. "I worked with him very closely on [the brief] for several weeks and [the goal] was to put the case before the court in a non-inflammatory manner based on the law and not try to beat the drum about race or anything like that at all," said Taggart Whipple. "He honestly believed that the lawyer's duty was to represent a people or cause no matter how unpopular their cause may be."[10]

Although Buster had been feeling ill for some time, she drove down to Washington with Ken Clark to see Thurgood make the most important argument of his career. "She had tremendous respect for Thurgood, and I think vice versa," Clark later recalled.

On December 9, 1952, a line of over two hundred people stretched beyond the cold, white marble steps leading into the Supreme Court.

Many of the people had been there overnight, hoping to get a seat to hear the celebrated case. Every seat in the august chamber was filled, and the anxious crowd just about leaped to attention when the nine justices walked in and took their seats behind the high, polished wooden bench.

The crowd was hushed as Bob Carter rose to make the first NAACP presentation. He did not waver. He said black students in Topeka who attended segregated schools, even equally good facilities, were being denied equal educational opportunity. "The Constitution does not stop with the fact that you have equal facilities, but it covers the whole educational process," Carter said.

Paul E. Wilson, an assistant attorney general for Kansas, really didn't want to argue against Carter. He had even tried to refuse to come to Washington. It was only after the Supreme Court found out that Topeka was willing to let the NAACP's case go unchallenged that the high court insisted he come. Wilson based his defense on the 1896 *Plessy* decision. "It is our theory that this case resolves itself simply to this: whether the separate but equal doctrine is still the law." Wilson's argument put the issue squarely on the Supreme Court. The state of Kansas, he argued, was happy to do whatever the Court decided, and the Court had never overturned the law of separate but equal.

But after lunch the real drama began as Marshall rose to make his oral presentation on the South Carolina case. The *Afro-American* reported that "all of the Supreme Court justices came to attention" when Marshall stood to speak.[11] Even without microphones his voice boomed all around the crowded room and its high ceiling.

"We are saying that there is a denial of equal protection of the law," Marshall told the packed chamber. Inferior schools and resources were not the issue, it was segregation itself. Racial separation hurt the "development of the personalities of [black] children" and "deprived them of equal status in the school community . . . destroying their self-respect." He concluded that the "humiliation" black children went through was "not theoretical injury" but "actual injury."

Marshall pointed out that not a single lawyer for any of the states with segregated schools had refuted any of his sociological evidence of the damage done to black children. And since there was nothing to refute this point, he said, the state had an obligation to integrate its schools. All black parents wanted, Marshall said, was for state segregation laws to be ruled unconstitutional.

Associate Justice Felix Frankfurter, who had been an adviser to the

NAACP when he was teaching law at Harvard, stopped Marshall's presentation and asked if school integration might not lead to white neighborhoods "gerrymandering," or limiting their school boundaries, to keep black students out. A confident Marshall shot back: "I think that nothing would be worse than for this court . . . to make an abstract declaration that segregation is bad and then have it evaded by tricks." His solution was to give local districts the opportunity to create their own plans and allow lower courts to review them. "It might take six months to [desegregate] in one place and two months to do it in another place," Marshall told the justices.

Frankfurter continued to pepper Marshall with questions, asking if South Carolina had the right to make any classification based on differences among children. For example, could a state separate smart students from dumb students? What if there was a good reason for having separate schools for blue-eyed children? Would Marshall object to a plan to have "all blue-eyed children . . . go to separate schools"? Decisively, Marshall answered: "No, sir, because the blue-eyed people in the United States never had the badge of slavery which was perpetuated in the [segregation] statutes."

Despite Marshall's cool demeanor at the time, this questioning got under his skin. He had expected Frankfurter to be an NAACP ally and, as a Jew, sensitive to the minority perspective. Instead Frankfurter seemed intent on posing theoretical questions that Marshall felt were taking the case off track.

"Frankfurter was a smart aleck, you know," Marshall said later with a glare. "I was going to hurt him in the school case, but I didn't have time. But if he'd have pushed me one more time, I was going to say, 'May it please the Court, I wish to mention the fact that we have not come as far as some people think. For example, if this involved Jewish kids, I don't think we'd have this problem.' "

After Marshall's presentations, John W. Davis stood to make the case for South Carolina's segregated schools. The elderly Davis spoke in softer tones, and the justices asked him only a few questions. Davis's point was that if racial segregation were outlawed, so would other kinds of classifications be illegal.

Davis went on to read from the writings of the former NAACP activist W.E.B. Du Bois to bolster his proposition that segregation was actually beneficial. "We shall get a finer, better balance of spirit, an infinitely more capable and rounded personality, by putting children where they are wanted and where they are happy and inspired, than in thrusting them into the hells where they are ridiculed and hated." Davis added, "There is no reason assigned here why this court or any other should reverse the findings of ninety years."

He downplayed the Supreme Court's earlier rulings, in the *Sweatt* and *Gaines* cases. He strongly made the point that in both cases the high court had refused to declare that separate but equal was unconstitutional. Davis emphasized that states had the right under current law to continue to segregate. So why, he asked, was the Court now willing to reverse years of precedent?

Marshall was quick to rebut. He argued that the issue was not whether states had the right to segregate but whether individual rights were being violated by racial segregation. The Fourteenth Amendment guaranteed every American equal protection. And he stressed that history made segregation by race very different from other state-imposed distinctions. Only blacks had been "taken out of the mainstream of American life," Marshall told the justices. "I know in the South, where I spend most of my time, you will see white and colored kids going down the road together to school. They separate and go to different schools, and they come out and they play together. I do not see why there would necessarily be any trouble if they went to school together." [12]

Over the next two days the Virginia, Delaware, and D.C. cases were argued with Spottswood Robinson, Louis Redding, and Jack Greenberg repeating the earlier arguments. By Thursday, three days after it started, all five cases had been heard and an exhausted Marshall went home to New York for Christmas.

*   *   *

In the first week of January 1953, the *Afro-American* published its man-of-the-year selection. Only Adlai Stevenson, the Democratic nominee who had lost the presidency to Eisenhower, got more votes than Marshall. Later in February Marshall was the guest of honor at a testimonial dinner in Baltimore, with his mother and wife. Also on the guest list were Joe Louis, Jackie Robinson, Ralph Bunche, Roy Wilkins, and Bill Hastie. Before those celebrities and an audience of six hundred people, Baltimore's black bar, the Monumental City Bar Association, feted Marshall as "an archangel of God's own freedom" and a man who "has sowed his life in the ground like a wheat seed that has come up bearing the fruit of liberty." [13]

Despite the growing mythology surrounding his power in the courtroom, Marshall was anxious about what the Court was going to do with the cases. By April he was hearing gossip about splits among the justices. He privately told NAACP leaders that he expected to win three of the five cases—South Carolina, Virginia, and Delaware—with the Court ruling that school facilities must be exactly equal. The two cases where he expected defeat were Kansas and Washington, D.C. In Kansas schools already had comparable facilities, and D.C. was a federal territory.[14]

Newspaper columnists speculated about the vote, as did the justices themselves. Justice William O. Douglas later wrote that after the justices met in secret conference to discuss the cases he concluded there were five votes in place to defeat the NAACP on all the cases.[15]

William Rehnquist, who later became chief justice, was a clerk to Justice Robert Jackson in 1952. He prepared a memo for Jackson that laid out the argument for keeping schools segregated. "To the argument made by Thurgood not John Marshall [a shot at Marshall by referencing the great legal thinker and first chief justice of the Supreme Court] that a majority may not deprive a minority of its constitutional rights . . . , while this is sound in theory, in the long run it is the majority who will determine what the constitutional rights of the minority are. . . . I realize that it is an unpopular and unhumanitarian position, for which I have been excoriated by 'liberal' colleagues, but I think *Plessy v. Ferguson* was right and should be re-affirmed."[16]

With arguments pro and con still percolating, the justices were deadlocked. Then on June 8, 1953, the Supreme Court surprised Marshall and the nation. The Court issued five questions to the lawyers on either side of the cases. The questions were mostly historical. For example, did the framers of the Fourteenth Amendment intend to end school segregation? Did the Supreme Court have the power to abolish school segregation? And how would school integration be managed if the court voted to mix black and white schoolchildren?

The questions were a legal puzzle but, more important, a delaying tactic. The 1952 election had brought a new president to office, the Republican Dwight D. Eisenhower, and some members of the Court felt that the Eisenhower administration needed time to deal with a decision certain to stir the nation—one way or the other. "I've always thought that one of the reasons that they [listed the five questions]—and it's been confirmed by other people— . . . was that a new administration was coming in," said Warren Burger, later chief justice, but then an assistant attorney general. "They wanted to get them in the act. So they had them reargue it, and then the [new] government was to file a brief as a friend of the court."[17]

The court scheduled the reargument for October 1953, ten months after the first argument in the case. Marshall telephoned historians around the country and asked them to research what state legislatures had said and written when they ratified the Fourteenth Amendment. He also called on historians familiar with the U.S. Congress to fill him in on the history of the amendment and what, if anything, the Congress had thought about integrated schools.

The NAACP lawyers who had battled over allowing psychologists like Ken Clark into the original case now had to cope with historians and their interpretations of evidence being thrust to the forefront. John Hope Franklin, a black Howard University historian, was in charge of research on how the Fourteenth Amendment had been put in practice after ratification in 1868. Alfred Kelly, a white historian at Wayne University in Detroit, was in charge of research on the original congressional debates on the amendment.

The combination of straitlaced lawyers who looked down their noses at everyone and Marshall's freewheeling style, including dirty jokes and liquor bottles in his desk, sometimes made Kelly uncomfortable. And he recalled that Marshall's moods could swing from pleasant to quite bitter and savage. Kelly recalled seeing Marshall turn fierce on one occasion when a secretary failed to bring some documents to him immediately. When the woman finally walked into Marshall's office, he told her, "I hope you isn't forgettin' who the H.N. is around here." Once the secretary had left, Kelly turned to Marshall and asked, "What's an H.N.?" According to Kelly, Marshall "just sat back and laughed and then he said, 'That's the Head Nigger.' "

Once, when Kelly and Marshall were at work on the brief, their debate became heated and Marshall gave Kelly a nasty look. "Alfred," he said, "you are one of us here and I like you, but I want you to understand that when us colored folks takes over, every time a white man draws a breath he'll have to pay a fine."

Kelly also recalled seeing Marshall read an old newspaper story headlined NIGGER IN A PIT, about a black railroad worker who had fallen off a train and into a pit. "Thurgood read it to us," Kelly later said, "and kept saying the headline over and over—'Nigger in a Pit—Nigger in a Pit—Nigger in a Pit,' just savoring it, rolling it over and over on his tongue.

. . . It seemed to epitomize the whole tragedy of the black man's situation."[18]

Although Kelly was overwhelmed by Marshall's personality, he and Franklin happily spent hours working with aides to review old historical documents and search for any hint of approval of integrated schools. To their disappointment, most of the research indicated that the congressmen who wrote the Fourteenth Amendment, and the state legislators who ratified it, had no intention of integrating schools.

Kelly, however, concluded they could make an argument that segregated schools violated the Fourteenth Amendment "even though very little, or nothing, was said specifically about segregated schools as such."[19] He focused his argument on the words of liberal congressmen like Thaddeus Stevens, a Republican from Pennsylvania. After the Civil War, Stevens argued that Congress always had the right to stop the states from making distinctions in law between people.

Franklin meanwhile researched the discussions among state legislators during the debates on ratification of the Fourteenth Amendment. He too was disappointed with what he found. For the most part the states had not considered ratification to be a vote for ending school segregation.

"I suppose I was afraid that we wouldn't win," Franklin said in an interview. "Not only was the historical evidence stacked against [us] . . . but it was not possible for me to conceive of a society [where] little white kids, 5, 10 years old could go to school with blacks. I just didn't believe it."[20]

While Marshall was trying to synthesize a legal argument out of the historical research, the Supreme Court was suddenly transformed. Chief Justice Vinson died of a heart attack in September 1953, just a month before the reargument was scheduled. Marshall had never thought of Vinson as a supporter, although the chief justice had ruled for the NAACP in the *Sweatt* and *Sipuel* cases. "We knew he was against us, but we managed to get it reargued," Marshall said later. "And then he died. The Lord was on my side!"

However, Marshall's concern grew when President Eisenhower nominated California governor Earl Warren to be chief justice. Warren, after all, had been in charge of California's program to put Japanese citizens in internment camps during World War II. "When Earl Warren was appointed by the president, I had the job of finding out what the hell he was all about," Marshall said. "And I went out to California, and I checked with the conservatives and the liberals, and all of them said the same thing. That the man was simply great. Great! And two judges whom I spoke with on the California Supreme Court said, 'If he doesn't do right, call us up and we'll come and kick his ass.' "

When Marshall got back he told his legal team that he now calculated they had five sure votes on the Court to end school segregation: "You damn right, that was the first time we thought that we had a five-to-four."

In November, five months after the Court had posed the five questions to the lawyers, the NAACP responded with a 256-page brief that Marshall estimated cost them $40,000 for research, travel, and printing. The heart of the answer was that the Court had previously ruled discrimination was not constitutional: "Time and again," the brief read, the Supreme Court had ruled that if a state had "deprive[d] a Negro [of] the right which he would have freely enjoyed if he had been white, then that state's action violated the 14th Amendment."

On the basis of the research, Marshall made highly selective use of history. Despite inconclusive supporting evidence, the NAACP made a strong argument that when Congress passed the Fourteenth Amendment, "the framers intended that the Amendment would deprive the states of power to make any racial distinction in the enjoyment of civil rights."

In its most powerful language, the NAACP's brief said the only way the Court could allow blacks to be segregated in public schools was if it concluded that blacks were inferior to whites. Marshall argued school segregation could not be upheld on any other grounds.[21] John W. Davis, meanwhile, filed a brief that indicated, with far greater support from historical evidence, that Congress and the states that ratified the Fourteenth Amendment did not want to abolish school segregation.

The Supreme Court then asked the Justice Department to file a friend-of-the-court brief on the five questions. The high court even delayed oral arguments, from October to December 1953, to allow the department extra time to prepare the brief. Marshall confided to friends that he doubted President Eisenhower's Justice Department would ever write a brief favorable to the NAACP.

When Justice did submit its answers, it responded that Congress was inconclusive about whether it intended to outlaw segregated schools. Despite its lack of clarity on the history, the brief stressed that the current "compulsory segregation" of schoolchildren was a violation of the Fourteenth Amendment's guarantee of equal rights.[22]

Just after Thanksgiving, Marshall and his best lawyers went to Washington for a second time to prepare oral arguments. This time Marshall was less tense. He stayed up late most nights, drinking and entertaining fellow lawyers and famous visitors. "I always used to thank God that the Court didn't start until [after] 12:00, because during the *Brown* argument, Thurgood was out until around 4:00 in the morning," said Bill Coleman, one of the young lawyers advising Marshall.[23]

Marshall also went back to Howard University's law school for another round of practice arguments. Lou Pollack, a respected New York lawyer who was advising the NAACP, recalled that while the "mock" arguments were intense and rigorous, they could also be filled with laughter. During one session, a faculty member asked if the court had the power to end school segregation unilaterally. "Thurgood fell on one knee, Al Jolson–like, and said, supplicant-like: 'Power? Power? White boss, you got the power to do anything you want!' "[24]

While in Washington, Marshall and his staff became accustomed to a nightly knock at the door. When they answered, a black man dressed in a butler's uniform offered a freshly baked cake, then walked away. Marshall had no idea who the man was but decided he would offer him one of the NAACP's tickets to get into the Court on the day of the argument. The kindly butler told Marshall not to worry about it and left as mysteriously as he appeared.

On Monday, December 7, 1953, the Supreme Court opened its session to hear responses to the five questions. As Marshall was settling into his seat, he saw a surprising face. There, seated among the wives of the justices, was the butler who had been bringing him cakes at the hotel. Marshall made a quick connection between the man and Nina Warren, the wife of the chief justice, who lived near where Marshall had been staying. It was the Warrens' butler who had been providing the NAACP lawyers with their nightly dessert.[25]

Marshall, with Spott Robinson, began the presentation by arguing that Congress intended the Fourteenth Amendment to end school segregation. He focused on the Supreme Court's history of rulings that protected individual rights over any claim of states' rights. But the justices found the arguments weak; they openly showed a lack of interest and left Marshall fumbling before he finally stopped. He later told Jack Greenberg that he sent a Masonic hand signal—indicating distress—to Justice Jackson, a fellow Mason.

After his subpar performance, Marshall was deeply worried that the experienced and venerated John W. Davis might take advantage to score heavily with the Court. Marshall watched closely as the silver-haired Davis stood and with confident ease announced that there was no doubt that Congress had intended to keep schools segregated. He noted that the schools had remained segregated after ratification of the Fourteenth Amendment and Congress had never even prohibited school segregation in the capital. This was evidence, Davis continued, of the true intent of the men who wrote the amendment. And he said the Supreme Court had ruled several times that the practice of segregation was legal.

"I am reminded," Davis concluded, "of Aesop's fable of the dog and the meat: The dog, with a fine piece of meat in his mouth, crossed a bridge and saw the shadow in the stream and plunged for it and lost both substance and shadow. Here is equal education, not promised, not prophesied, but present. Shall it be thrown away on some fancied question of racial prestige? . . . I entreat [my opponent] to remember the age-old motto that the best is often the enemy of the good."

For all his years of admiration for Davis, Marshall was not impressed with his opponent's argument. He felt Davis had not capitalized on the weakness in the NAACP's position. In Marshall's opinion Davis had looked like a struggling old man. "Well, he was down, he was over the hill," said Marshall. "He was old. And he cried. Real tears, while he was arguing. He was telling the story about the dog with the bone in his mouth. When he told that story he had tears in his eyes. He sure did."

In his rebuttal the next day, Marshall showed no signs of the fumbling that had bedeviled him the first day. He began with a razor-sharp swipe by reminding the justices that Davis had said blacks were seeking "racial prestige" and social status by going to schools with whites. "Exactly correct," said Marshall. "Ever since the Emancipation Proclamation, the Negro has been trying to get . . . the same status as anybody else regardless of race." In an impassioned conclusion, Marshall told the Court that the only justification for continued school segregation was the desire to keep "the people who were formerly in slavery . . . as near that stage as is possible."

His second-day argument drew a strong, positive response. "This time he took a different, more effective approach—he came on like a locomotive," Paul Wilson, the lawyer for Kansas, later wrote. Bill Coleman, the young Harvard Law graduate who had been a clerk to Justice Frankfurter, sent Marshall a letter two days later that read: "I must say that your rebuttal was the most appropriate and the most forceful argument I have ever heard in any appellate court. . . . While you were making it I could not help but watch the smile of understanding on Mr. Justice Frankfurter's face."[26]

With the final arguments done, Marshall was left in limbo. The Court's ruling was not due until the spring. Marshall's legal team, however, had run up huge bills. So despite the upcoming holidays, he went on the road to give speeches at NAACP fund-raisers. One of the biggest was in New York just before Christmas. Calvert Whiskey sponsored a $15,000 testimonial at the Hotel Astor that attracted more than a thousand people. At the dinner Marshall thanked the corporation as well as the Masons, who contributed $24,000 a year to the NAACP's legal fund, and the local branches. In January, Marshall went to a national meeting of black publishers, who had raised almost $18,000 with special ads calling for contributions to the NAACP. The special counsel, speaking to the publishers in Tuskegee, predicted that the Supreme Court would end school segregation. He said he expected full integration to take place in four to five years, with the worst trouble in "some sections of the black belt, some of them right here in Alabama, where the Supreme Court decision . . . would have no effect for 30 years."[27]

Marshall was on the road again in March 1954, when he told an audience in Charlottesville, Virginia, that "come Hell or high water, we are going to be free by '63." Asking them to remember the promise of the emancipation of the slaves by President Lincoln on January 1, 1863, Marshall made a prediction. "On freedom's 100th anniversary we will be free as we should have been in 1863. . . . The soul of the white man is in the hands of the Negro, because we are the only ones who—with blood, sweat and tears—got the money to go to court to get the rights others enjoy as a matter of course."[28]

By early May the Supreme Court still had not ruled, and Marshall was beginning to wonder if the ruling might be delayed until the next term. He was in Mobile, Alabama, where he had spoken on Sunday, May 16. He was scheduled to speak in Los Angeles the next day when he received a phone call—he never said from whom—telling him that he might want to be at the Supreme Court instead. Marshall caught the next flight to Washington.

At 12:52 P.M. Chief Justice Warren, with all the associate justices in attendance, started reading the Court's decision in the schools cases. As Warren began to read, Marshall was not certain which way he was going. Warren said: "In approaching this problem we cannot turn the clock back to 1868 when the [Fourteenth] Amendment was adopted or even to

1895 when *Plessy v. Ferguson* was written. We must consider public education in the light of its [current role] in American life."

Marshall, seated in the lawyers' section, focused a glare at Justice Stanley Reed. Marshall thought Reed, a Kentucky native, was the most likely leader of a bloc of votes to keep school segregation in place. Marshall heard that Reed had prepared a dissent, with the help of a privately hired law clerk. He wanted to watch Reed's face as a clue to what was going to happen. Reed only stared back at him, wide-eyed.

While Marshall and Reed were staring each other down, Warren continued: "In these days, it is doubtful that any child may reasonably be expected to succeed in life if he is denied the opportunity of an education . . . a right which must be made available to all on equal terms. . . . To separate [black children] from others of similar age and qualifications solely because of their race generates a feeling of inferiority as to their status in the community."

Then in dramatic style Warren made a historic pronouncement: "We conclude that in the field of public education the doctrine of 'separate but equal' has no place. Separate educational facilities are inherently unequal." Marshall later recalled that when he heard those words, "I was so happy I was numb."[29]

"When Warren read the opinion," Marshall recalled, "Reed looked me right straight in the face the whole time because he wanted to see what happened when I realized that he didn't write that dissent and I was looking right straight at him. I'm sure Reed laughed at that."

In fact, one of Reed's clerks, John Fassett, had done research on arguments to support a possible dissent. Reed, however, decided to vote with the majority. The ruling was unanimous. "Earl Warren," said E. Barrett Prettyman, Jr., a clerk to Justice Jackson, another possible dissenter, "worked very hard, to his credit, to convince people and particularly the last one or two holdouts that it would not be in the interest of the court or the country to have divergent views on this vital subject."[30]

After the justices stood and filed out, Marshall was quickly surrounded by reporters. But first he turned to James Nabrit II and George Hayes, the two lawyers who had argued the Washington, D.C., case, and said, "We hit the jackpot."[31] Marshall was filled with brash confidence and told the press that he did not think southern states would "buck the Supreme Court."

The *Afro*'s next edition read: SEGREGATION ILLEGAL NOW. The story quoted Marshall as saying: "It is the greatest victory we ever had . . . the thing that is gratifying to me is that it was unanimous and on our side." [32]

One of the few children in the courtroom that day was the son of Joe Greenhill. An assistant attorney general in Texas, Greenhill had argued against Marshall in the *Sweatt* case. He was on vacation and just happened to be visiting the Court that day with his family. After talking with reporters, Marshall, bursting with happiness, picked up Greenhill's kid. The large brown man began running through the grand marble halls with the small white child. "He picked up our son Bill and put him on his shoulders and ran down the corridor of the Supreme Court," said Greenhill. "He was having a good time, we were having a good time, and to hell with dignity. He just won a biggie." [33]

CHAPTER 22

No Radical

Shouting into a pay phone in a hallway at the Supreme Court, Thurgood Marshall announced the big victory to NAACP officials in New York. He had grabbed the golden ring, the prize that had been sought so long by Nathan Margold, by Charles Houston, by the people contributing their coins in the branches all over the country, and here it was—the end of school segregation. Elated by the unanimous ruling, he stopped only to allow reporters to snap pictures of him on the steps of the Court before hopping on the next flight to New York, racing the news that was spreading around the country like electricity. "We were ecstatic," remembered Bob Carter. "It was a very heady day."

At the NAACP's office Marshall walked into a crowded press conference being held by Walter White. The NAACP executive secretary, prancing like a rooster, told the reporters that his next plan was to attack segregation in housing and transportation. Marshall shifted from elation to anger as he watched White taking all the credit for the Supreme Court's ruling. He was literally being pushed to the rear as White stood up front to make pronouncements about the NAACP's great victory over segregation. Toward the end of the press conference, in an uncharacteristic outburst, Marshall shouted, "What law school did you graduate from, Mr. White?" Despite the tension, everyone laughed it off as a joke.

"Walter was carrying on as if this was his achievement, this was his victory, as if he prepared the case, got the plaintiffs, wrote the briefs, even went to court," recalled Herbert Hill. "I watched Thurgood, and I said to myself, 'How much longer is Thurgood going to take this stuff?' I knew he was going to start to blow up."[1]

Despite that ego battle, the sounds of popping champagne corks and loud laughter filled the rooms. Roy Wilkins, Marshall, and the entire staff, from the receptionists to the board members, were celebrating the decision with reporters and friends.

"We'd always had parties, drunken parties, after winning, but that was the best," Marshall said later, a smile on his face. "Yeah, I thought I was going to win but not unanimously." John W. Davis was the first to get through on the telephone. He congratulated Marshall on the victory but threw in a word of caution: "I hope you realize that the only way you can win a case is somebody has to lose." When Marshall got off the phone, several people pulled into a circle around him to find out what Davis had said.

As was typical, Marshall was empathetic with Davis. Sounding almost apologetic about Davis's defeat, Marshall shook his head, a look of condolence washing over him, and said, "I did, I beat him, but you can't name many people who did."

As the party spun into the night, Marshall and several of the NAACP staff went to his favorite restaurant, the Blue Ribbon, for food and drinks. Ken Clark was in the group, and Marshall stopped the festivities at one point, less to honor Clark than to tease Clark's critics. "Thurgood was his usual ebullient self," Clark recalled. After toasting the psychologist's work on the case, Marshall looked across the table at some of the lawyers who had fought his use of the social science data. "Now, apologize," he told them,[2] as the table broke into laughter.

People at the party began saying the NAACP's work was done and it was just a matter of time before all the nation's schools were integrated. Marshall, who shifted into a more pensive mood as the clock passed midnight, made a prophetic remark: "I don't want any of you to fool yourselves, it's just begun, the fight has just begun."[3]

The party continued until after 1:00 A.M. Buster was not in the group; she had been ill for months now, sometimes bedridden. She had visited doctors and been diagnosed with colds, flu, and even pleurisy, an inflammation of the lining of the lungs. In her absence Marshall had begun to hang around with one of the NAACP's secretaries, Cecelia [Cissy] Suyat, born in Hawaii of Filipino parents. It was at this dinner at the Blue Ribbon that many of his colleagues first noticed what appeared to be a special relationship between the pair.

"Thurgood was very discreet about his affairs," said John A. Davis, a Lincoln professor who had advised the NAACP on the school segregation suit. "There was never an example of it except at the victory celebration. He was leaving with Cissy. . . . That was the first time I'd ever seen any indication that she wasn't just another worker there."[4]

The next morning's newspapers were filled with stories on the Supreme Court's ruling. Marshall was on the front page of *The New York Times*, standing on the steps of the Supreme Court, shaking hands with his fellow lawyers George Hayes and James Nabrit. The *Times* noted that the decision amounted to a death knell for separate but equal. But the court had delayed until the next term arguments on how to begin integrating the schools. In a second article on the front page, the *Times* wrote that southern leaders were incensed by the ruling, and their outrage was "tempered" only by the Court's decision not to set forth "the time and terms for ending segregation in the schools."[5]

Southern politicians uniformly blasted the Court's decision. "The South will not abide by or obey this legislative decision by a political court," said Sen. James Eastland, a Democrat from Mississippi. Sen. Richard Russell of Georgia said the ruling "strikes down the rights of the states, as guaranteed by the constitution, to direct their most vital local affairs." Georgia's governor, Herman Talmadge, said, "There will never be mixed schools while I am governor." He said if school integration became a reality, it would be "a step toward national suicide."[6]

The backlash from the South intrigued Marshall. He did not think the southern politicians could stop school integration, but he was surprised by the psychological distress being expressed by some whites over the notion of racial equality.

He came into the office one day and told NAACP staffers that he had heard a revealing story: Three southern white guys got together, Marshall said, and began discussing the *Brown* decision. Two of them were upset over the call for school integration. But the third man said he didn't agree. In a booming, theatrical voice, Marshall mimicked the shock of the two segregationists: "You mean you are for integration?" The lone dissenter shook his head and said no. "I'm not for integration— I'm for slavery." Marshall looked around the room, an intense expression on his face, and said the story was a warning about what was to come. "There's a whole lot to that story," Marshall said. "A whole lot."

But in black America there was little of Marshall's foreboding of a coming backlash. Harlem's *Amsterdam News* wrote, "The Supreme Court decision is the greatest victory for the Negro people since the Emancipation Proclamation." The ruling was far bigger than a decision about schools, the paper wrote, it was the end of all segregation. The day after the Supreme Court ruled, the *Chicago Defender* wrote that "neither the atomic bomb nor the hydrogen bomb will ever be as meaningful to our democracy."[7]

President Eisenhower, meanwhile, had little to say publicly about the ruling other than he expected all states to comply. Privately, however, he was fuming. "I personally think that the decision was wrong," Eisenhower told a staffer a few weeks later.[8]

The president also told Herbert Brownell, his attorney general, that he strongly disagreed with the decision. At one point a temperamental Eisenhower told Brownell that since Chief Justice Warren and the Supreme Court had made the ruling, "let them enforce it." Brownell sympathized with his president's position. Eisenhower was caught between a decision he had not made and a public uproar that created political problems nationwide. "Any president would have the same reaction when they had a hot potato handed them by the judiciary," Brownell later said. Nonetheless he pointedly told Eisenhower that it was his duty to uphold the decisions of the Supreme Court.[9]

Marshall, however, had no idea about the president's private expressions. And despite angry statements from southern politicians who pledged to resist integration, he pressed ahead. By the Saturday following the Court's Monday decision, he was meeting with his team of lawyers in Atlanta. At the end of the two-day conference, they issued instructions for black parents to petition local school boards for integration "without delay." Marshall pledged the national NAACP's help to battle recalcitrant school boards. "We know there has to be a reasonable time to adjust and the question is the definition of what constitutes reasonable time," Marshall said to reporters. "Our people are ready to take part in conferences, but we are determined to attain this goal without compromise of principles."[10]

Marshall continued celebrating the decision in speeches and appearances around the country. In one of the many laudatory profiles of Marshall after the May 17 ruling, the *Pittsburgh Courier* portrayed him as a man flying high above any complaints or criticism: "I'm in a hurry," Marshall told the *Courier*. "I want to put myself out of business. I want to get things to a point where there won't be an NAACP—just a National Association for the Advancement of People." [11]

Marshall also began to talk openly about his willingness to sacrifice the jobs black teachers had in segregated schools as well as the future of historically black colleges for his integrationist ideal. "What's going to happen to the 'Negro College'?" he asked in one of his many speeches around this time. "I'll tell you what's going to happen. It's going to cheerfully drop the word 'Negro.'" But Marshall cautioned that if these schools did not quickly measure up to the white schools, they could die off. The impact of the *Brown* ruling, he told audiences, would be to force black people to compete with white schools and white students. "And you are going to have to measure up." Black colleges and the United Negro College Fund, which raised money in the name of helping black students, "will have to find another sales talk." [12]

Marshall's unyielding integrationist worldview had few critics in the NAACP or the black press. At this point there were no Carter Wesleys or Marjorie McKenzies launching attacks at him for sacrificing black institutions for the promise of integration. He was universally celebrated by black Americans. At Howard University, Mordecai Johnson, the school's president, called him the "greatest constitutional lawyer in history" and gave him an honorary degree. At the NAACP's forty-fifth annual convention in June, he was honored before a jubilant crowd of 700. As he entered to speak, the *Afro-American* reported, "to add dignity to the occasion, the little people abandoned their comfortable shirt sleeves and . . . put on their coats" on a heavily humid Texas summer day.

Marshall electrified the crowd as he again outlined his view of a color-blind, fully integrated America. Every American should be judged on "individual merit rather than to be limited by such irrelevant considerations as race and color," he said. And he optimistically added that schools should be desegregated "in no event, later than September of 1955." [13]

*   *   *

By the fall of 1954, having articulated his dream of complete racial integration in the United States, Marshall was back in his New York office working on a brief for the Supreme Court on a timetable for beginning desegregation in the five cases under *Brown*. Normally, after establishing that a person's rights were being violated, the Court would immediately order that the violation be stopped. In the schools cases that would have meant immediate school integration. But the high court decided to allow local school districts to end segregation gradually.

Marshall was caught between his respect for the Court and his disagreement with its failure to order immediate desegregation. Bill Coleman, who had advised him during the first part of the case, sent him a letter suggesting that he not demand immediate integration. Instead, Coleman's idea was to have Marshall propose to the high court that the school boards be allowed only a year to submit plans that "would permit the gradual effective transition" to integration.[14] With that letter in the forefront of his thinking, Marshall made a strategic decision to go along with the gradualist approach. The NAACP's brief, submitted in November 1954, asked only that integration plans go into effect by 1955—with complete school integration to be fully achieved no later than the fall of 1956.

The southern states, meanwhile, responded with briefs asking the Court to avoid *any* deadline. Their argument contended it was best to leave the process up to local school districts. The Eisenhower administration submitted a friend-of-the-court brief that proposed no delay be tolerated, but also asked that no firm date be set for integration. President Eisenhower personally read the brief and, treating it as a political document, took the unusual step of rewriting portions to reflect his go-slow approach.[15]

Even though Eisenhower failed to endorse the NAACP's proposal for a strict deadline, Marshall made no objection. He did not want to risk publicly criticizing the president or the brief. But in a telephone conversation with *Afro* publisher Carl Murphy, Marshall said, "Between you and me, it stinks." But Marshall told Murphy a fight between the NAACP and the Eisenhower administration would delight segregationists: "That's just what the other boys would love." Marshall's solution was to "find and pick out a couple of paragraphs and say I agree with them."[16]

Meanwhile, resistance to school integration was building among southern politicians to the point of petty vindictiveness. When Marshall appeared that fall as the featured guest on the NBC series *Youth Wants to Know*, the show was blacked out in Georgia; the NBC affiliate substituted a taped speech by the state's segregationist governor, Herman Talmadge.

The fast pace of Marshall's life, the speeches and planning for more arguments before the Supreme Court, hid the troubles in his private life. Buster was now constantly ill, but Thurgood was not in a position to stay home and comfort her. In fact, he was often out of touch with what she was going through. By November, she was hospitalized. Her illness had now dragged on for over a year. She looked painfully thin and was weak. Buster's mother, Maude Jones, came from Steelton, Pennsylvania, and moved into the apartment. Her sister and father also were regularly there, leaving Thurgood to feel more and more distant from his wife.

Just before Thanksgiving, Buster told Thurgood she had cancer. He had to go from frustration with his crumbling marriage to the reality that his wife was dying. His reaction was to embrace Buster and try to find the best doctors. Marshall could not understand why no one, especially Buster, had told him about the cancer. On her insistence even the doctors had kept the illness a secret from him until she was so sick that they had no choice but to tell him.

Despite his infidelities and constantly being away from home, Thurgood loved Buster. She had been the most constant figure in his life since he came to New York. And he felt responsible for the chill that had come between them. The fact that he was among the last to know she was dying was a reminder of how little intimacy remained between the college sweethearts. But the full emotional force of her impending death hit him when Buster asked to spend her last weeks at home.

"He took her illness and her death very, very hard," said Alice Stovall, Marshall's secretary at the NAACP. "She was in the [Fifth Avenue Flower] hospital—I guess it was around Thanksgiving time—and she wanted to come home. Monroe Dowling—his wife, Helen, was a nurse. And Helen more or less lived in the apartment day and night."

That Christmas was bittersweet for Marshall. The readers of the *Afro-American* voted him "Man of the Year." At home, however, Buster continued to deteriorate. There were other problems, too. He had never had a strong relationship with Buster's mother. Now, with the illness at a critical stage, Maude Jones became the dominant player in his house. Friends said the mother-in-law "shunned" Marshall, leaving him emotionally racked.[17]

After the holidays Thurgood stopped working to be with Buster during her last days. "He stayed by her bedside constantly," said Mildred Byrd, the wife of Thurgood's close friend Dan Byrd. "Thurgood said, when he realized she was dying, he just came off like 'Our Father who art in heaven.' He was praying while she was dying."[18]

Thurgood's caring for Buster took a heavy toll on him. He had never been one to visit sick people, much less change bedpans and kiss cheeks hollowed from disease. "My first wife, who died of cancer, I watched her for three months. That took three months out of me," he later said.[19]

Vivien "Buster" Marshall died on her birthday, February 11. She was forty-four years old and had been married to Thurgood for twenty-five years. Buster's death threw Thurgood into an emotional plunge that got worse as he tried to deal with her family over funeral preparations. First, Buster's mother brought in friends, who took clothes, silverware, blankets, and even wedding presents out of the apartment, claiming that they belonged to Buster and that the family wanted them. Monroe Dowling watched as one of the family's friends "scurried to hide jewelry so I wouldn't see it." Dowling said when Marshall went to the bank to begin funeral preparations, he found that Buster's mother had taken most of the money out of the account.

"After she died there were a lot of disagreements about who got the fur coat and who got the jewelry," said Claude Connor, Buster's nephew. "Almost immediately after the funeral, Thurgood gave back jewelry, rings, and things that were heirlooms. He also gave my mother Buster's mink stole, for example. Now my grandmother, on the other hand, was a matriarch and a bitch too. She was very, very upset because Thurgood gave his mother Buster's beaver coat."[20]

The funeral service was held at St. Philip's Episcopal Church in Harlem, the place of worship for the city's black bourgeois. William Hastie, Channing Tobias, and Manhattan borough president Hulan Jack came. Father Shelton Hale Bishop and others credited Buster as "the other half of Thurgood Marshall." Papers quoted her as once telling reporters: "If I had my life to live over again, I wouldn't change any part of it. I have wanted most, all these years, to help him make good."[21]

Monroe Dowling arranged for the casket and family to occupy several cars of a train to Philadelphia, where Buster was to be buried. On the train Thurgood and Maude got into a loud argument over a set of pearls Thurgood had brought Buster from his trip to Japan. Maude had taken the pearls. The two would never speak again. After the casket was put in the ground, Thurgood literally turned his back on Buster's family. He rode home to New York alone; in Harlem he found the apartment stripped of furniture. The sink was filled with dirty dishes Buster's family had left behind.

"He was in a condition of very considerable depression," Jack Greenberg later told an interviewer. "He was morose and unhappy for a long time after that. . . . He lost a lot of weight, in fact so much that he looked like a skeleton, and he was really in very bad shape. So he really didn't function for a period of maybe several years in his job."[22]

Marshall took a long vacation for the first time. He went to Mexico for a few weeks. While he was there Roy Wilkins sent him a telegram informing him that Walter White had died. Marshall's name immediately surfaced as a candidate to replace White. "There are many who would like to see attorney Marshall in the number one spot," reported the *Pittsburgh Courier*.[23] But Marshall, still depressed, had little desire for fundraising and other bureaucratic tasks. And he trusted Roy Wilkins. He was confident that Wilkins, unlike White, would leave all legal issues in his hands. Consequently, Marshall did nothing to encourage people who wanted him to run the NAACP. Wilkins got the job.

There had been so many changes—Buster's death, White's death, and Wilkins's promotion. And in the last few years, most of Marshall's male mentors had gone, too. Uncle Fearless, Charles Houston, and Marshall's father had all died in recent years. He was now struggling for balance. "He needed somebody definitely, because between Buster's many miscarriages and losing Buster, he was just no good," said Mildred Byrd.

He found solid footing by going back to work. Fortunately, there was a lot to do. Only two months after Buster's death, on April 12, 1955, Marshall stood before the Supreme Court and accepted the gradualist approach. He offered local school districts up to two years to fully integrate.

The scene in the courtroom was also different. John W. Davis, who had argued against Marshall in the South Carolina case, had died a few weeks earlier. The new attorneys for South Carolina and the other southern states argued that school integration could not be done under deadline pressure. They contended that "there are forces at play in this situation over which the [school officials] have no control," specifically the possibility of a violent white backlash.

Lindsay Almond, the attorney general of Virginia, rose to say that while Marshall had praised the people of the South as "law-abiding," the NAACP lawyer had asked the Court to "press this crown of thorns upon our brow and hold the hemlock up to our lips." Southern lawyers also cited the Prohibition era, when the government had unsuccessfully tried to ban liquor, as evidence of the federal government's inability to force people to accept unpopular laws.

Marshall began his rebuttal with an emotional outburst: "I am shocked that anyone would put the right of Negroes to equal participation in our system of education on a par with the right to take a drink of whiskey." He continued, in high thunder, to rebuke southern lawyers for always speaking to the Court about the damage school integration would do to southern traditions. "You have heard references to one state's 'greatest and most cherished heritage,' and when you look for it, you find that greatest and most cherished heritage is to segregate colored people."

In defiant tones Marshall said that he was only asking for equality. Black children would be expected to compete with white children with no special consideration. Teachers would be free to put "dumb colored children with dumb white children and smart colored children with smart white children." Marshall finished by challenging the Court to set a deadline of September 1956 for complete school integration.[24]

* * *

Behind the scenes there were stories circulating that Chief Justice Earl Warren was under pressure from the White House to give the southern schools all the time they wanted for desegregation. Eisenhower was up for reelection in 1956 and trying to avoid any crisis that could damage his political future. Marshall began hearing that Eisenhower was leaning on Warren. Ralph Bunche, the U.S. envoy to the United Nations and a black man, told Marshall that at a White House dinner he had seen Eisenhower corner Warren and begin an intense discussion. Bunche said he overheard Eisenhower use the words "school cases" and "segregated schools." At that point the stout, gray-haired Warren pulled off his wire-rimmed glasses and stared at the president. "I thought I would never have to say this to you, but now I find it necessary to say to you specifically—you mind your own business and I'll mind mine."

Marshall was incensed when he heard the story. He nursed his anger for years and later told an interviewer that he considered Eisenhower's effort to lobby Warren "the most despicable job that any president has done."[25]

However, less than two months after the oral arguments, the Supreme Court unanimously ruled against setting any deadline for school boards to desegregate. The Court said local federal judges would hold school districts only to the requirement that they desegregate "with all deliberate speed." The ruling was right in line with Eisenhower's proposal. Marshall suspected that the power of the presidency had unfairly prevailed.

Marshall was at the Court when the ruling was announced, and he immediately flew back to New York to attend a press conference with Roy Wilkins. His disappointment was evident in his long, tired face. The somber atmosphere in the NAACP's office was a stark contrast to the laughter and joyful noise that had followed the 1954 decision. Marshall tried to make the best of the ruling. He emphasized that the Court remained committed to ending school segregation. There had been no change of mind or heart, he said. And the justices had made it clear that indefinite delays would not be tolerated. Finally, he said he personally would fight any school district that intentionally stalled: "It will not take a hundred years, that I can guarantee," Marshall said.

At the news conference only one NAACP board member, Judge Hubert Delaney, openly expressed disappointment with the ruling. He made critical remarks about the decision, albeit mildly, but Wilkins quickly stepped in to tell reporters that the Court's failure to set a deadline was offset by the justices' unbending support for school integration.

Even as Wilkins put on a good face, the NAACP legal staff was in the background grousing. They had wanted a clear-cut victory of the sort they had won in 1954. "I think we had the view that by winning *Brown* we were going to end the whole era of discrimination," Bob Carter later remembered. "We thought that the law would be obeyed and blacks would count." [26]

When the reporters left, Marshall, Wilkins, and Delaney went into the privacy of Marshall's office and let off steam. Marshall disparaged the phrase "deliberate speed." He found it a dangerous euphemism, a nice name for delaying justice until it was convenient and comfortable for whites to accommodate the rights of black citizens. Some of the staff lawyers came in and began to discuss where that phrase had originated and what it meant. Finally, one of the secretaries brought in a dictionary. "I am looking at *Webster's*," she said, "and I'm looking at *deliberate*, and the first word of similarity for *deliberate* is *slow*. Which means 'slow speed.' " The lawyers in the office nodded their heads, but hearing those words triggered something in Marshall's mind—the phrase could have come from only one source—Justice Felix Frankfurter.

During the first round of arguments on school desegregation, Frankfurter had been one of Marshall's toughest critics from the bench. He had grilled him on whether schools had the right to separate students, such as his hypothetical case of blue-eyed students and brown-eyed stu-

Left: Norma Marshall (location and date of picture unknown). Thurgood's mother was an ambitious, driving personality who made her sons into a doctor and a lawyer. It was an extraordinary achievement for a mother of two black boys born at the turn of the century. She died in 1961. *Courtesy of Aubrey Marshall, Jr.*

Right: Aubrey Marshall standing at the entrance to Lincoln University in Oxford, Pennsylvania, around 1925, Thurgood's first year at Lincoln. Aubrey was a junior, in pre-med. *Courtesy of Aubrey Marshall, Jr.*

Above: The young men pledging Alpha Phi Alpha fraternity, including Thurgood Marshall (second row, second from the right), during Marshall's freshman year, 1926, at Lincoln University. *Courtesy of Langston Hughes Memorial Library, Lincoln University.*

Right: Thurgood Marshall's high school graduation picture at age seventeen. *Courtesy of Supreme Court Historical Society.*

Thurgood Marshall (center) with his mentor and law school dean
Charles Houston (at his right) and fellow lawyer Edward Lovett
shortly after his 1933 graduation from Howard Law School.
Copyright © Afro-American Newspapers.

Left to right: Thurgood Marshall, Donald Gaines Murray, and Charles Houston
at the plaintiff's table in a Baltimore courtroom during Murray's suit against
the University of Maryland, June 1935. *Library of Congress.*

Flier for a speech by
Thurgood Marshall in
Baltimore, 1950.
Courtesy of the NAACP.

HEAR.....
"**Mr. Civil Rights**"
BALTIMORE'S OWN
THURGOOD MARSHALL
Chief Council NAACP
New York City
The man who fights your battles in the
Supreme Court of the United States.
"**Democracy Now Or Never**"
Sun. March 27th - 3 P.M.
Douglas Mem. Church
Madison and Lafayette Avenues
NAACP Mass Meeting
ADMISSION FREE
GOOD MUSIC, SENIOR CHOIR
MRS. EVANGELINE MITCHELL, Dir.   MRS. LILLIE M. JACKSON, Pres.
WILBUR STEWART, Treas.   REV. JENTRY McDONALD, Membership Chm.

Left to right: Paul C. Perkins, a local NAACP lawyer in Florida; Jack Greenberg,
one of Marshall's assistants from the New York office of the NAACP Legal
Defense Fund; Walter Lee Irvin, who was charged with rape; and Marshall.
They are at the defense table at Irvin's trial in Ocala, Florida,
on February 17, 1952. Irvin was found guilty and sentenced to die
in the electric chair. *UPI/Corbis-Bettmann.*

Marshall and a young neighbor playing with Marshall's new train set, a 1950 gift from his first wife, Buster. Marshall desperately wanted a son of his own. *Photo by Cecil Layne.*

Left: Marshall with John W. Davis in 1952, before they argued opposite sides of the school desegregation case before the Supreme Court. Davis, a segregationist, was nonetheless Marshall's role model because of his legal prowess. *UPI/Corbis-Bettmann. Right:* NAACP board member and former First Lady Eleanor Roosevelt at a meeting in the late forties at NAACP headquarters in New York. She is with (*left to right*) Dr. James J. McClendon, who served on the national board with Mrs. Roosevelt and was president of the Detroit branch of the NAACP; Walter White; Roy Wilkins; and Marshall. *Library of Congress.*

Marshall meets with his legal team in New York after writing the briefs for the *Brown* case. *Left to right:* Oliver Hill and Spottswood Robinson, who argued the Virginia case; Robert Carter, who argued the Topeka, Kansas, case; Jack Greenberg, who argued the Delaware case; Marshall, who argued the South Carolina case; and George E. C. Hayes and James Nabrit, Jr., who argued the Washington, D.C., case. *Photo by Cecil Layne.*

Baltimore Afro-American editorial page cartoon, November 28, 1953. At that time Marshall was arguing the school desegregation case, *Brown v. Board of Education*. Baltimore Afro-American *Archives.*

Marshall with George E. C. Hayes (at his right) and James Nabrit, Jr., on the steps of the Supreme Court on May 17, 1954, after hearing the Court's unanimous verdict in the *Brown* case. *UPI/Corbis-Bettmann.*

Baltimore Afro-American editorial page cartoon, July 2, 1955. The Supreme Court had ruled the month before that desegregation could proceed "with all deliberate speed." Marshall and his legal team felt they had been defeated; they wanted an order requiring immediate compliance, not gradual acceptance. But *Afro-American* publisher Carl Murphy felt the ruling was a win for Marshall, since the Court adhered to its plan to end school segregation in the United States. Baltimore Afro-American *Archives.*

Above: A happy, whistling Marshall takes a cigarette break during the NAACP's forty-sixth annual convention in Atlantic City, New Jersey, in 1955. He was the star of the convention for his victory in the school desegregation case.
Photo by Fred Hess & Son Photo. Hollie I. West Collection, Moorland-Spingarn Research Center, Howard University. *Below:* Marshall with his top aide, Robert Carter, at an NAACP regional meeting in Atlanta, Georgia, on June 4, 1955. Roy Wilkins and South Carolina NAACP chapter president James M. Hinton are at Marshall's right. *UPI/Corbis-Bettmann.*

President Dwight D. Eisenhower receiving the annual *Chicago Defender* Award on May 6, 1955, at the White House for his efforts to desegregate the federal government. The award was given to the president on the *Defender*'s fiftieth anniversary. John H. Sengstacke, publisher of the *Defender,* is handing the award to Eisenhower. Marshall, standing between the president and Sengstacke, was furious with Eisenhower for failing to offer strong leadership in support of school integration. *Courtesy of Dwight D. Eisenhower Library.*

Time magazine cover, September 19, 1955, featuring an oil portrait of Marshall.
Copyright © 1955 Time Inc.

Marshall leading Autherine Lucy and several of her supporters from the federal courthouse in Birmingham, Alabama, on February 29, 1956. *Left to right:* Lucy, Marshall, and Birmingham attorney Arthur Shores. *Library of Congress.*

The christening of Thurgood Marshall, Jr., at St. Philip's Episcopal church in Harlem in August 1956. *Left to right:* Cissy Marshall; Judge William Hastie; Daisy Lampkin, a renowned NAACP activist, holding baby "Goody"; Helen Dowling, the wife of Marshall's college buddy Monroe Dowling; Roy Wilkins, then head of the NAACP; and Marshall. *Photo by Cecil Layne.*

Several of the black high school students who Marshall represented before the Supreme Court during their effort to desegregate Little Rock's Central High. The picture was taken on the steps of the high court in Washington, D.C., in September 1958. The youngsters had attended the school the previous year, but now the school board wanted them out. Marshall was arguing against the school board's effort, and the students came to watch. *Left to right:* Melva Patillo; Jefferson Thomas; Gloria Ray; Daisy Bates, head of the NAACP chapter in Little Rock; Marshall; Carlotta Walls; Minnie Jean Brown; and Elizabeth Eckford. *UPI/Corbis-Bettmann.*

Marshall with Martin Luther King, Jr., and Roy Wilkins at the NAACP convention, 1959. Marshall saw King as a glib newcomer to the movement and doubted mass protest would advance civil rights. In public, however, they presented a united front. *Photo by Cecil Layne.*

Left: Jomo Kenyatta with Marshall in Nairobi, Kenya, on July 14, 1963. Marshall had helped Kenyatta write the newly decolonized nation's constitution three years earlier. *Library of Congress. Right:* Marshall holding his sons, Goody and John, in his family's New York apartment in the late fifties. Thurgood's Aunt Medi is seated in the background. *Courtesy of the Moorland-Spingarn Research Center, Howard University.*

Marshall huddles with Senator Jacob Javits, Republican from New York, and Senator Robert Kennedy during the July 1965 confirmation hearings on Marshall's nomination to be solicitor general. Marshall was suspicious of Kennedy's motives in any fight. He felt Kennedy was solely concerned with gaining political advantage and not committed to civil rights. *AP/World Wide Photos.*

Marshall being sworn in as solicitor general at the White House, August 24, 1965.
Left to right: Marshall's sons, Goody and John; Cissy Marshall; President Johnson;
Marshall; Justice Hugo Black, a former member of the Ku Klux Klan; Attorney
General Nicholas Katzenbach; and Justice Tom Clark (behind Katzenbach).
UPI/Corbis-Bettmann.

Marshall, President Johnson, presidential assistant Clifford Alexander, and
Louis Martin, vice chair of the Democratic National Committee on June 13, 1967,
moments after Johnson told Marshall that he was going to nominate him to the
Supreme Court. *Photo by Yoichi R. Okamoto. LBJ Library Collection.*

Marshall with President Johnson in the Oval Office on June 13, 1967, the day Johnson announced that he was nominating Marshall to the Supreme Court. Johnson is reaching for the phone because he wants to be the first to tell Cissy Marshall the news. *Photo by Yoichi R. Okamoto. LBJ Library Collection.*

'Should Be a Good Fit . . . It Took Us 177 Years to Make.

THURGOOD MARSHALL

FIRST NEGRO ON THE SUPREME COURT

Washington Daily News cartoon, June 14, 1967. *Copyright* © The Washington Post; *reprinted by permission of the Washingtoniana Division, D.C. Public Library.*

President Johnson addressed members of the National Council on Crime and Delinquency at the White House on June 26, 1967. The White House put Marshall on the panel in an effort to separate Marshall from black rioters and strengthen his image as an advocate of law and order. *Left to right:* FBI director J. Edgar Hoover; Supreme Court nominee Marshall; and Attorney General Ramsey Clark. *UPI/Corbis-Bettmann.*

Marshall during tense Senate hearings on his Supreme Court nomination, July 21, 1967. *Photo by McNamee. Copyright © 1967 The Washington Post.*

'Let's come to order!'

Washington Star cartoon, May 6, 1969, after Marshall gave a widely covered speech denouncing black militants. *Copyright © 1969 The Washington Post; reprinted by permission of the Washingtoniana Division, D.C. Public Library.*

Marshall in his Supreme Court chambers, August 27, 1976. In the far right corner of his desk is a small bust of Frederick Douglass. *Photo by Gerald Martineau. Copyright © 1976* The Washington Post.

Marshall jokes with his liberal ally and best friend on the high court, Justice William Brennan, during a public appearance in 1985. *Photo by Ray Lustig. Copyright © 1985* The Washington Post.

Marshall in front of his home in Falls Church, Virginia, with his grandson, Thurgood William Marshall, June 28, 1991. The picture was taken the day Marshall announced his retirement from the Supreme Court.
AP/Wide World Photos.

Former clerks Kevin Baine and Karen Hastie Williams stand by Marshall's casket, January 27, 1993. Marshall's official portrait is at the head of the casket.
Photo by Franz Jantzen. Collection of the Supreme Court of the United States.

dents, when teachers felt separation was appropriate. Now Marshall's intuition told him that it was Frankfurter, again, who was undermining his argument.

He called Paul Freund, a former Frankfurter student who was still very close to the justice. "He knew it—he said right away that it was Felix," Marshall later recounted with a laugh. Then Marshall added: "Integration hasn't happened yet, that's how slow 'deliberate speed' is."

After two days of privately griping about the decision, Marshall began to accept the setback. In a telephone conversation with Carl Murphy, he said on second thought maybe the decision wasn't so bad: "You can say what you want," he bellowed over the phone, "but those white crackers are going to get tired of having Negro lawyers beating 'em every day in court. They're going to get tired of it." [27]

To get the staff—and himself—out of a funk, Marshall began work on pressuring school boards throughout the South to desegregate. When any board dragged its feet, the NAACP was ready to take them to federal court and even back to the Supreme Court. "If there is a difficult situation," Marshall told *Time* magazine, "and a school board says, 'This will take us six years,' we may well say, alright let's take six years. But if the board says, 'We'll never sit down and talk our problems over with Nigras,' then we'll say, let's go to court as soon as we can." [28]

The public's reaction to part two of the school desegregation decision was not nearly as lukewarm as Marshall's. It was as if the Court had handed him another complete victory. He was widely praised now, by both the black and white press, as the reasoned, smart leader of the nation's efforts to defeat racism. The Jewish community in particular praised Marshall as the hero of all minorities. The Junior Page of the *Afro* magazine even ran a children's song, set to the tune of "The Ballad of Davy Crockett," titled, "Thurgood Marshall, Mr. Civil Rights."

> *Thurgood . . . Thurgood Marshall, Mr. Civil Rights.*
> *Born in Maryland, the state of the free,*
> *Went to Howard for his law degree,*
> *Took his training at Charlie's knee,*
> *Said, "It isn't so free, as you can see."*
> *Thurgood . . . Thurgood Marshall, Mr. Civil Rights.*
>
> *Fought for the teachers, fought for the schools,*
> *Went down south where they broke all the rules,*

Now he's working on the swimming pools,
Justice and right are his fighting tools.

Thurgood . . . Thurgood Marshall, Mr. Civil Rights.[29]

The celebration of Marshall extended to the white press. A flattering oil portrait of him appeared on the cover of *Time* that fall. The story said that Marshall's name was "indelibly stamped" on the Supreme Court's historic desegregation rulings. *Time* credited Marshall with starting a "vast and complex social revolution." The magazine also anointed him as the American who would shoulder the burden of shaping the future of race relations. "What he decides to do about a thousand practical legal questions will . . . determine the pace, the style and the success of an effort to remove from U.S. life . . . the ugliest blot upon its good name in the world," *Time* wrote.

The magazine judged Marshall a "sound" and "imaginative legal scholar, although by no means the best of his day." When it came to explaining the underpinnings of Marshall's thinking on race relations, the magazine said he was both an idealist and a pragmatist. He preached the ideal of integration but when faced with resistance he would accept halting steps, such as the deliberate speed ruling, toward that ideal. *Time* described the split within Marshall as "a delicate balance of turmoils."[30]

The seemingly adulatory story got a surprising response from Carl Murphy's *Afro*. The paper blasted *Time* for running a profile that was "counterfeit and . . . falsely drawn." And *Time*'s suggestion that Marshall was willing to bargain to get whatever he could from the court was also wrong. "Neither Marshall nor the NAACP in this crusade against racial bigotry can accept anything less than total victory," the paper wrote. "To settle for less would be to destroy themselves."[31]

The split between the *Afro* and *Time* magazine reflected a genuine split in Marshall. On the one hand, *Time* was right. Marshall was an accommodationist—he had accepted the Supreme Court and its "all deliberate speed" ruling, even though he personally disagreed with it. He even defended the ruling in speeches, while more militant blacks were condemning the Court for failing to defend the rights of black children. On the other hand, the *Afro* was right that Marshall was disappointed, even angry, that no deadline was set for school integration. Marshall was privately telling friends he was worried that southern politicians and weak-kneed lower courts would conspire to delay integration.

By late fall Marshall's divided mind on race relations was put on full view before a crowded church on a Friday night in Brooklyn, New York. He was invited to speak as the hero of black America, the man who had battled white segregationists and defeated them in court. But Marshall's speech was a rebuke of his black audience for giving in to calls from black militants for racial solidarity. "Let's stop drawing the line [between] colored and white," he told the audience. "Let's draw the line on who wants democracy for all Americans."

Marshall also criticized the attention that many black Americans were giving to the murder of Emmett Till, a fourteen-year-old black boy who was killed by two white men in Mississippi for whistling at a white woman.

Marshall told the audience that the South had bigger problems than Till's murder. Black people were being lynched every day in the South, he said. And marching to protest racism in Mississippi was not a good idea. It created a situation where angry segregationist mobs would attack marchers, who would then fight back, and "violence has never been an answer to violence." He also condemned boycotts as a "double-edged" sword—not a good tool to protest segregation—because segregationists could also boycott black businesses.

* * *

While he was chiding blacks in New York for becoming too militant, some federal and southern state officials were worried that Marshall was becoming too powerful and was too close to Communists. The attorney general of Georgia made speeches in which he pointed out that Marshall once was an official of the National Lawyers' Guild, a "Communist front."

Roy Wilkins defended Marshall and the NAACP by circulating copies of the letter J. Edgar Hoover had once written to Walter White saying, "The NAACP has done much to preserve these principles [of equality, freedom, and tolerance] and to perpetuate the desires of our founding fathers." When Hoover learned that Wilkins was using the letter to shield the NAACP from attacks, he got mad. The political climate in Washington was strongly anti-Communist in the aftermath of Sen. Joseph McCarthy's hearings. And with the Cold War escalating, Hoover did not want to be tied to the NAACP by comments he'd made nine years ago, "when the NAACP, under Walter White, was a well-disciplined group." Now that Hoover did not want to be associated with them any longer, he had his agents target the NAACP for investigation.[32]

Those probes may have included phone taps on Marshall and other NAACP officials. In October 1955, Marshall told a group of delegates to the New York NAACP state conference that both long-distance and local calls going out of the national offices were being "listened in on." Marshall said he was certain, from "unimpeachable sources" that the phones were tapped.[33]

Records of the FBI from that period were subsequently censored, possibly to remove evidence of the wiretaps. But bureau officials concluded that while Communists had gained access to local NAACP branches, they had been unable "to dominate the organization of the national level." However, the FBI continued to investigate the NAACP, giving special attention to Marshall and building up a large file on him.[34]

In the fall of 1955, Marshall was hardly ever in New York. His celebrity made him a big draw at NAACP fund-raisers in the South. He left Bob Carter to monitor school desegregation efforts while he traveled. When Marshall came back to New York, he had curious news for his friends. Just ten months after Buster's death, he was getting married. The bride was one of the NAACP's secretaries, Cecelia Suyat, the woman he had been seen celebrating with at the Blue Ribbon the night of the 1954 decision.

Suyat was a cute, short woman with a formal, polite manner. Hidden behind her demure smile was a steely young woman with strong opinions and a determined personality. She had essentially raised herself since her mother's death in 1936, when she was nine. Her father, Juan Suyat, a print shop worker, was overwhelmed with the task of caring for seven children on his own. Cissy pushed herself through high school and into business college before shocking her father by announcing she was going to New York. He let her go only when she promised to return home after school. The twenty-year-old arrived in Manhattan and enrolled to study stenography at Columbia University. But to her father's disappointment she stayed in New York, and a few months later an employment agency sent her to a secretarial job at the NAACP.

"Cissy was my secretary for eight years," said Gloster Current, the national office's director of NAACP branches. "I was surprised because I really didn't know they were courting. She was a lovely person, very charming and a good cook and convivial. Everybody loved Cissy."[35]

While Current was in the dark about the relationship, others close to Marshall had long been aware that he had been seeing Cissy. William Coleman, the lawyer who became Marshall's close friend, described the decision to marry as the outgrowth of an extended relationship: "They were together, you know, even before his first wife died," Coleman later said.

Monroe Dowling, another of Marshall's good friends, remembered meeting Suyat in August 1955 at the Red Rooster restaurant in Manhattan. When Marshall had walked away for a moment, Dowling directly asked her, "Are you Thurgood's girl?" Suyat said, "Yes." At the time Dowling wondered if the relationship was serious and how it might affect Marshall's public image. He distinctly recalled the negative reaction to Walter White's marriage to a white woman. How would black America react, with Buster not yet dead a year, if Thurgood married an Asian-American woman? Would the gossip tear Marshall up? Dowling asked Suyat, "Are you going to marry him?" She replied, "If he asks me."

Marshall said he had asked Suyat to marry him "several times" before she agreed. She, too, was concerned that his marriage to a woman who was not black might hurt him. And she had her own worries about how her family would react to a Negro son-in-law. But her family was far away; NAACP members were close enough to voice their criticisms. "They called me a foreigner," Suyat said, recalling that period. "Not at the office—at the office people knew me—but the outside forces."[36]

But there was one important factor that may have overwhelmed the tittering criticism and convinced Thurgood to marry Cissy: the possibility that she had become pregnant. "He would not, probably, have gotten married before the end of the year if she had not been pregnant," said Claude Connor, Buster's nephew. Cissy and Thurgood's first son, Thurgood Jr., would be born eight months after their wedding.

"Thurgood was the kind of man who, first of all having wanted children for so long, if he knew this woman was pregnant, he would move heaven and earth to legitimize that child," said Connor.

Given the potential controversy about the interracial marriage and the pregnancy, Marshall talked it over with Wilkins and other NAACP officials. They decided that Marshall could marry Suyat without too much damage to his public image if it was handled properly. The key,

Wilkins concluded, was to have the marriage first, on December 17, 1955, then hold a press conference at which association officials would endorse Suyat as a member of the NAACP family and describe her as "just about black."

The wedding took place at St. Philip's Episcopal Church, where Buster's funeral had been held. Wilkins gave the bride away, and Thurgood's mother and Aunt Medi were there as well.

Then came a press conference at the Red Rooster restaurant. None of the reporters asked about Marshall's decision to marry a Filipina. Arnold DeMille, the NAACP's public relations director, was relieved, but he noticed that the reporters were talking about the issue among themselves. "It wasn't a secret," DeMille later said, but the strategy was to wait until after the wedding to put it in the papers.[37]

The top of the *Afro*'s next front page announced in bold letters, THURGOOD LOSES HEART. The *Afro* took care to say that Marshall had been "devoted" to his first wife, who died of cancer. The paper's usual nose for scandal was not in evidence.[38]

The lone editorial attack on the interracial marriage came from a white newspaper in Jackson, Mississippi. The paper reported that Marshall, like Walter White, "has broken down and admitted his racial prejudice by marrying a white woman," Marshall later recalled. "And I wrote a letter back to them and I said, not that I object to it, but I just think you ought to be accurate. . . . I've had two wives and both of 'em are colored."

The couple went to the Caribbean for a two-week honeymoon. Left behind was all the backbiting over interracial relationships, school integration, and the FBI's phone taps. Marshall had a clear vision of an integrated America, with blacks and whites in schools, on buses, and everywhere else. He was now a living model of the integrationist life. As he went off to blue skies and emerald seas with his Asian beauty, he had no idea of the turbulent fights yet to come.

CHAPTER 23

❧

Martin Luther King, Jr.

A FEW DAYS BEFORE HE GOT MARRIED, Marshall received a phone call from E. D. Nixon, the former president of the NAACP's branch in Montgomery, Alabama. Nixon asked him to represent a group that was planning to boycott the city's segregated buses. Marshall was interested in helping only because he was pals with Nixon. Like Marshall's dad, Nixon was a train porter who had a deep southern accent and loved to tell a joke. As a favor to Nixon, Marshall directed Robert Carter to handle this minor affair while he and Cissy went off to the Caribbean.

But when Marshall returned to New York in January, he was stunned to find that the Montgomery bus boycott was national news. Nixon had initially hoped for a one-day boycott, in which blacks would stay off the buses, walking or taking taxicabs to work. But with the support of a black women's group and black ministers, the boycott had caught fire, and by the time Marshall got back to the office it was in its second month.

"We were advising them of the legal steps to be made," Marshall recalled in an interview. "We were proceeding when all of a sudden this preacher started jumping out of there. We'd never heard of him before. I knew his father before in Atlanta, but I'd never heard of him until then."[1]

The "preacher" was twenty-seven-year-old Martin Luther King, Jr. King had been in Montgomery just over a year. A graduate of Morehouse College and Crozer Seminary, the five-foot-seven-inch minister was a dapper dresser even as a college student. He was also the son of a well-known Atlanta minister, Martin Luther "Daddy" King, of the large Ebenezer Baptist Church.

Young King had been finishing his Ph.D. at Boston University when the most prominent black church in Montgomery made the surprising decision to hire him. King had visited and delivered a stirring sermon in his gripping bass voice. The vestry decided to take a gamble on the up-start, and he arrived in the fall of 1954, still working to finish his doctor-ate in theology.

Even before King arrived in Montgomery, a small group of civil rights activists had been petitioning to stop rude treatment of blacks on the city's buses. The effort had barely made a ripple until a well-respected forty-three-year-old black woman was arrested for refusing to give up her seat to a white passenger. Rosa Parks's arrest led the local NAACP and the Women's Political Council to activate plans for a bus boycott campaign. E. D. Nixon phoned several local black ministers, in-cluding King, to ask for their support. King was initially hesitant, but after much urging, he agreed to attend an organizing meeting at his church. At that meeting King was convinced to take a leading role in the growing mass movement.

"We are tired—tired of being segregated and humiliated, tired of being kicked around by the brutal feet of oppression," a fiery King told a loud meeting on a Monday night. "If [we] will protest courageously and yet with dignity and Christian love, when the history books are written in future generations the historians will pause and say, 'There lived a great people—a black people—who injected new meaning and dignity into the veins of civilization.'"[2] King's riveting speech focused heavily on nonvio-lence, a concept he had learned at Crozer while studying the Indian leader Mahatma Gandhi's nonviolent opposition to British colonial rule in the 1940s.

At the NAACP's offices in New York, Wilkins and Marshall found themselves reacting to this homegrown movement, which they did not start and over which they had little control. Ironically, critics in Al-abama and around the nation were blaming the NAACP for fomenting the bus boycott and the lawsuit against segregation on the buses. In a *New Yorker* article Marshall, the man identified as the NAACP ring-leader, conceded that he often did not feel in control of the fast-changing movement: "[I'm] supposed to be masterminding this whole campaign. . . . That's funny because our people in the south are actually way ahead of us on this thing."[3]

Nixon's request for legal help had been granted almost as a casual favor, and now the New York office found itself running to catch up with a train that had left the station. In the aftermath of the *Brown* decision, NAACP officials faced growing impatience among black people for an end to segregation everywhere.

While Marshall made supportive comments about the boycott, he had deep reservations. In his heart he viewed the bus boycott and King's speeches as street theater that did not come close to equaling the main event—the NAACP's effort to get the courts to end legal segregation. Marshall's negative view of King's rhetoric and mass protests came out of his experiences investigating riots. He had seen black communities in Columbia, Tennessee, Harlem, and Detroit torn apart by white mobs. That experience led him to fear that organized resistance by black activists inevitably would lead to a white backlash, and "wholesale slaughter with no good achieved."

Even before King began his advocacy of nonviolent protest, Marshall had been approached by students who wanted him to shift from law books and move toward street demonstrations. At Howard Law School, Harris Wofford (a white student who later became a U.S. senator) gave Marshall a paper on Gandhi's nonviolent strategies and urged him to get the NAACP to use the same approach against segregationists.

A few weeks later Marshall sent a handwritten letter to Wofford telling him that Gandhi's ideas were a bad fit for an American civil rights movement. Marshall wrote that he "couldn't imagine a worse prescription," and that it "would devastate and undermine the progress that had been made," Wofford remembered. Marshall told him he was trying to get people to obey the laws and the courts, even if they disliked them. "For American Negroes or American Civil Rights people, black or white, to start disobeying laws on grounds that it was against their conscience would set it all back," Marshall wrote, according to Wofford.[4]

Despite Marshall's private misgivings, he acted as if he were in full support of King's protest. He had already assigned Carter to help King with legal advice. The lone objection Marshall voiced openly to the King-led boycott was that King was only asking for polite treatment of blacks on segregated buses and not demanding an end to the Jim Crow practice. The LDF had filed a transportation suit demanding full integration on buses in Columbia, South Carolina, and it would be damaging, Marshall said, for the NAACP to endorse a suit in Alabama that stepped back from that demand.

Marshall pressured Fred Gray, the attorney for the Montgomery bus boycott, to file a suit on the exact lines the NAACP was pursuing in South Carolina. Gray worried that Marshall might simply shut off legal support if he did not go along with demands that their suit insist on integrated seating. Gray also realized that the suit was going to have to be appealed all the way to the Supreme Court, and he needed Marshall's expertise to win. When in April 1956 the Supreme Court ruled in Marshall's favor in the South Carolina bus case, Gray knew that he had made the right decision.

While Marshall was able to control Gray and the legal maneuvering in Montgomery, he grew irritated at the front-page attention being showered on King. Having won the *Brown* decision only two years earlier, Marshall saw King as a man who had yet to make a significant mark on American life. Despite his misgivings, Marshall knew it would be damaging to reveal a split among black leaders in the civil rights movement. On the national TV program *Youth Wants to Know* that spring, Marshall praised King for his refusal to use violence in the bus boycott. King's house had been bombed, and Marshall said King and the NAACP were in agreement that there should be no violent response to such segregationist attacks.

*   *   *

While King kept the bus boycott going and raised money nationwide, segregationists started their backlash. In March 1956 a hundred members of Congress signed a "Southern Manifesto" written by South Carolina senator Strom Thurmond, denouncing any attempt to force integration on the South. The manifesto stirred Confederate pride. The manifesto had little real impact on the NAACP, but other battles in the State of Alabama were of genuine concern to Marshall.

When the twenty-six-year-old Autherine Lucy had tried to integrate the University of Alabama, she was trapped in a classroom building by a violent mob until the state police rescued her. Marshall had won a Supreme Court case in 1955 giving Lucy the right to study at the university, but the mob made his legal victory meaningless by throwing rocks and eggs, and menacing her. The university suspended her, claiming that the threat of violence was too great for the school to handle.

Marshall and one of the leading figures on his New York staff, Constance Baker Mottley, quickly traveled to Alabama to argue before federal judges that Lucy was not the source of the problem and should be readmitted. Local black leaders surrounded Motley and Marshall with armed bodyguards out of fear that the famous lawyers would be attacked. Marshall worked and slept in the home of Arthur Shores, the NAACP's lawyer in Birmingham; outside guards armed with machine guns patrolled the sidewalk. The fear in Montgomery's black community was particularly high because a few weeks earlier, King's house had been fire-bombed.

Despite the precautions an attempt was made on Marshall's life. He and a group of lawyers were at Shores's house when a car careened onto the sidewalk, with smoke from a lit bomb pouring out of one window. A man tried to throw the explosive, but it went off in his hand, blowing off part of his arm. The car drove away, leaving the injured man behind. Marshall and the lawyers rushed out as the guards stood over the scream-ing man. Towels and bandages were applied, even while some cursed the bomber. An ambulance eventually took the man away.[5]

Back in court, the federal judge ruled that the university had to end Lucy's suspension. But in a surprise move the university trustees voted to expel her. They charged that Lucy's criticism of the school amounted to defamation and merited her expulsion. Lucy had said in court that there was a conspiracy to keep her out of the all-white school.

Marshall finally decided that he could not win the case. The board was within its rights to expel her, he concluded, even if the heart of the matter had nothing to do with defamation and everything to do with keeping the university's student body completely white. Marshall was convinced any suit against the school would end up costing the NAACP a lot of money and put the traumatized Lucy under tremendous stress for a weak case that would ultimately fail.[6]

The pressure was building on Marshall. As far back as the Supreme Court's ruling allowing schools to desegregate with "all deliberate speed," he was being torn between the racist backlash among segre-gationists and the increasing militance among black Americans. Even in 1955 the forces pushing and pulling on Marshall prompted a friend to tell *Life* magazine that the usually easygoing lawyer was becoming up-tight and was like "a tea kettle about to explode." He told friends he could no longer sit in any meeting where he could not chain-smoke and revealed that he stopped drinking during Lent "to prove to myself that I don't need liquor."[7] Marshall was also still grappling with grief over Buster's death. Jack Greenberg, one of his assistants, later said he felt Marshall continued to suffer through a depression.

The ray of sunshine Marshall found during this turbulent time was his relationship with his new wife. He and Cissy still lived in the apartment Thurgood had shared with Buster, but the place had been revamped with new furnishings and Thurgood was home more than he had been in the past. Cissy had shown no signs of possible miscarriage, and they were more and more excited at the prospect of having a baby. By March, Thurgood and Cissy made it public. The *Afro-American* reported on the front page that "the Thurgood Marshalls are expecting."[8]

Marshall initially told reporters the baby was not expected until October. He was still leery of negative public reaction to his interracial marriage, although there had been a minimum of unfavorable gossip so far. But if anyone counted the months between the marriage and the baby's birth, Marshall feared, a new round of gossip might ensue. But he scaled back his estimate when he told the *Pittsburgh Courier* that the baby was expected in September.[9]

The boy was born August 12 at 12:23 A.M. Monroe Dowling remembered that the night Thurgood Marshall, Jr., was born, he and Marshall "pitched a drunk" in the Marshalls' home to celebrate.

Thurgood Jr. was christened at St. Philip's, and the godparents included Helen Dowling, Monroe's wife; Judge William Hastie; and Roy Wilkins. Thurgood's lifelong desire for a child, and a male child, had finally been fulfilled. His deep insecurity over whether the loss of one of his testicles had somehow led to Buster's many miscarriages was now put to rest.

The new mother also had to deal with her Filipino family, who were still concerned over her marriage to a black man. Now twenty-nine years old and having worked for the NAACP for many years, Cissy did not see Thurgood as another black man. He was a star to her, the man who had made her life. But her father, Juan Suyat, was concerned that the baby's skin not be too dark. "Her family was not particularly fond of blacks," said Monroe Dowling, who with his wife was helping the Marshalls with the baby. "Cissy was very independent—she didn't give a damn."

With a newborn baby and pressure coming down on him at the office, Marshall was glad to have his mother living in New York. She had initially moved from Baltimore to help take care of her sister Medi, who was living alone and suffering from diabetes. Marshall would sometimes go to visit his mother and aunt, and they would often come to see the baby and cook dinner. It was the first time in many years that Marshall had an extended family near him.

*　　*　　*

At the office Marshall's troubles showed no signs of letting up. The Montgomery bus boycott was a half year old, and Marshall's legal team was still fighting the issue in the courts. To make matters worse, King was now being sued by the city for promoting the boycott. The NAACP was representing him at no cost, but there were growing strains in the group's relationship with him.

At the NAACP's annual convention in San Francisco that summer, King had been invited to speak and was treated as a celebrity. When he was asked by reporters if his nonviolent method could be used to desegregate schools, he said yes. Marshall considered the comment disrespectful of his legal efforts. He barely kept his emotions in check when he told reporters that King was over his head when it came to school desegregation, and they wrote that Marshall viewed King as a "boy on a man's errand." [10]

Marshall, however, did not enter into public jousting with King. During his own speech to the convention, Marshall praised the bus boycott and the "unblemished forthright Christian leadership of men like Rev. M. L. King, Rev. Abernathy and E. D. Nixon." Even as he dismissed King's protest tactics in private, Marshall told the delegates that the NAACP had to evaluate King's nonviolent technique to see "to what extent it can be used in addition to our other means of protest." [11]

Behind the scenes, however, the NAACP leadership had more serious problems with King. One official, Herbert Hill, remembered that Marshall and Wilkins saw King as taking money away from the NAACP. "The major resentment, and on this point I heard Roy many times, was that King would raise vast sums of money, and that there was never any accounting," said Hill. When Wilkins asked King to account for his spending, King reacted as if he was being pestered about trivia. "Roy would be furious," Hill said. "We heard about a meeting in Los Angeles where they collected something like $20,000. It was put in a suitcase. King leaves with a suitcase full of money. Never accounted for, never reported."

While the NAACP was critical of King, his supporters were often highly critical of the NAACP. They called it an old, stuck-in-the-mud group for its ponderous, legal approach to every issue and its failure to embrace the spirit of mass movement that was electrifying the nation. But King still asked the NAACP for legal advice, bail money, and funding. "While King's people were shitting on the NAACP," said Hill, "Roy and Thurgood took a very principled position—the struggle always came first." [12]

So, despite the bad feelings, Marshall continued to handle the lawsuit demanding integration on Montgomery's bus lines. He and Bob Carter wrote the petition to the Supreme Court asking that a lower court's ruling striking down bus segregation be allowed to stand. The city's appeal to the Supreme Court was based on a states' rights argument; it was a matter of local custom for blacks and whites to sit separately.

On November 13, 1956, the Supreme Court rejected Alabama's appeal and ruled in favor of the NAACP and King's bus boycott. The court wrote no opinion in the case [*Gayle v. Browder*] but simply affirmed a lower court's ruling in supporting King. In Montgomery, King told reporters: "The universe is on the side of justice." [13] The boycott's goals had been achieved through the courts, although national attention had been focused on King and the people who stayed off the buses.

King became the first passenger to ride an integrated city bus in Montgomery, Alabama. The 382-day boycott was over, and King was the hero in the press. But Marshall felt that King had stolen his glory because the preacher would still have been marching and boycotting if not for Marshall's victory in the high court.

Marshall's troubles with King symbolized the growing distance between the NAACP lawyer and a burgeoning, activist, civil rights movement often focused on the energy of young people. This increasing alienation from the movement brought Marshall closer to his former nemesis, FBI Director J. Edgar Hoover.

CHAPTER 24

❧

Machiavellian Marshall

At age forty-eight Thurgood Marshall had become a pure political player. His idealism had shrunk as he took steps to protect his turf and power within the NAACP as well as to nurture relationships that offered him entrée into mainstream politics and power. By 1956 he was juggling three potentially explosive political balls—his ties to the FBI, his fierce distaste for Communists, and battles within the NAACP, especially with his top assistant, Bob Carter.

The first intrigue began in early 1956. J. Edgar Hoover was growing increasingly worried that race relations in the United States were about to erupt in violence. In January, when Marshall became involved with Martin Luther King's bus boycott, Hoover had sent a memo to President Eisenhower's special assistant, Dillon Anderson, expressing concern over a possible war between the races. The FBI director told the White House official that his field agents were reporting dangerously high levels of friction between the NAACP and its opponents in the aftermath of the Supreme Court's school desegregation ruling and the start of the bus boycott.

"Tension is mounting to the point where the two forces may clash," he wrote. "The potential for violence not only is present but is daily increasing in intensity." Hoover specifically pointed to the growing number of White Citizens Councils, groups of segregationists who organized to use economic and political pressure against the NAACP's drive for school integration. And on the other side, Hoover noted, there was a strong black "cult" in Elijah Muhammad's Nation of Islam—"a violently anti-white, anti–United States government group . . . [which has] embarked on a tour of the south to spread their teaching."

The Communists were taking advantage of this racial strife, Hoover reported, to "propagandize" its efforts and advance its own cause. "The communist party has seized upon every possible incident," he explained. "In addition the party has increased efforts to infiltrate and influence the NAACP." He said the Communists had tried to exploit the Emmitt Till murder case to open doors with the Chicago branch of the NAACP and had held a secret conference in New York with unnamed "NAACP leaders."[1]

Inside the national office Marshall was in fact worried that militants and Communists were making inroads into the branches and contributing to growing criticism of him. The Montgomery bus boycott caught Marshall off guard and increased his discomfort with the rising power of independent black activists. But he was also worried that the growing infatuation with mass movements among black Americans would open the door to more Communist activity. He had no doubt that was a deadly trap for Americans trying to gain their rights in the rabidly anti-Communist politics of the mid-1950s.

During this time Marshall began an intense, unpublicized political dance with the director of the FBI. The first short, awkward steps in the minuet occurred when Dr. T.R.M. Howard, a fearless black voice demanding equal rights in Mississippi, gave a spit and fury speech to an NAACP meeting at the Sharp Street Methodist Church in Baltimore. Howard harshly criticized J. Edgar Hoover and the FBI: "It's getting to be a strange thing that the FBI can never seem to work out who is responsible for killings of Negroes in the south. . . . " FBI agents in Baltimore sent reports on the speech to Hoover, who wrote a long letter of complaint to Marshall—not the association's head, Roy Wilkins.[2]

Almost from his first days at the NAACP, Marshall had been vocal about the FBI's failure to protect black people in the South. In 1946 Marshall had taken his concerns to the Justice Department, writing to the attorney general that Hoover's FBI was too cozy with white southern sheriffs. After Walter White's death, however, Marshall became the NAACP official whom Hoover knew best. So when Dr. Howard criticized the FBI, Hoover chose to complain to Marshall. Since Howard had used the NAACP as "a forum" to criticize the bureau, Hoover said he was taking "the liberty of writing you to set the record straight."[3]

Given the sometimes barbed comments that had passed between them, Hoover was pleased by Marshall's response. The NAACP attorney wrote back that Howard had wrongly criticized the FBI with "misstatements of facts." And in a real stunner Marshall said he knew the FBI had done a "thorough and complete job" in three recent cases where blacks were murdered in Mississippi. "We do feel a responsibility . . . during these very tense times . . . to try and keep the record straight," he said.[4]

Marshall's alliance with the FBI was as strategic as any of his courtroom maneuvers. He had disdain for the Communists, the radicals, even Martin Luther King, Jr., and his nonviolent tactics. Marshall viewed the Communists as a particularly strong threat to the NAACP, a harmful extension of the militants and loudmouths who were coming to the forefront of the movement. Marshall was also concerned that the FBI might mix him up with the radicals and make him a target for their wiretaps and investigations. His new alliance with Hoover was protection, Marshall hoped, against FBI interference with his ongoing legal work to defeat segregation.

The strategy worked. Hoover was so pleased that in a follow-up note he told Marshall to let him know whenever the NAACP had concerns about "improper actions" of FBI agents in the South. Marshall could be assured that such charges would "receive my urgent and vigorous personal attention."[5] Hoover also had an agenda. He desperately wanted inside information from the NAACP, and Marshall was now the key to Hoover's access to the top ranks of the civil rights movement.

Marshall and Hoover continued to correspond. Meanwhile, Dr. Howard continued to charge the FBI with racist behavior. In January 1956 Marshall wrote, almost apologetically, to Hoover that the black Mississippi physician was a "rugged individualist" who could not be controlled by the NAACP. He emphasized that Dr. Howard had no official connection with the association.[6]

Two weeks later Marshall took advantage of his newly cooperative relationship with Hoover to gain unprecedented access to the FBI. Marshall had conversations with Lou Nichols, the assistant director of the bureau. Marshall said he wanted to meet with Hoover to find out which civil rights groups were Communist fronts. That information, he explained, could be used to keep communists out of an upcoming civil rights conference. Nichols later wrote in a memo to another FBI official that the NAACP lawyer confided to him that "the communist party's effort to get in the NAACP was the single most worrisome issue."[7] While

Marshall was gravely concerned about the Communist influence on the civil rights group, he was also playing a role to put himself in the FBI's confidence.

Hoover personally signed off on the meeting. Nichols was instructed to give Marshall information on Communist activities inside civil rights groups, but only from "public source material." Marshall met with Nichols, with Hoover sticking his head in the door for a brief hello. Nichols gave Marshall the information he wanted, and the two talked generally about Howard and other agitators in the NAACP.

Afterward Marshall went to lunch at the Palace restaurant in downtown Washington and ran into an FBI agent and a Justice Department lawyer. He warned them to be prepared for a resolution at the upcoming conference that would criticize the FBI for failing to jail violent white racists. Marshall, according to an FBI memo on the lunch, said he was "not sympathetic" to people like Dr. Howard who were making such attacks.[8]

Marshall continued to use similar tactics to distance himself from NAACP members he viewed as radicals. In the spring of 1956, he placed another telephone call to ask Hoover about the latest FBI reports of Communist infiltration.

Lou Nichols wrote in a memo that Marshall wanted information he could use to disparage Communist sympathizers during his keynote speech to the NAACP's 1956 convention. This was the same convention at which Marshall had aimed barbs at Martin Luther King after he claimed nonviolent protests and boycotts could have desegregated schools. "He stated that no one would know where he got the information and he wondered if I could be of any help to him," Nichols wrote after his conversation with Marshall. "I think that it might be to our advantage to give him a little guidance if we can on the basis of public source and well-documented material."[9]

Marshall recalled the meeting vividly years later: "I remember one time I had a conversation with Lou Nichols about something very important," he said, still refusing to divulge exactly what they talked about. "In the FBI office, in some of these secure offices, I met him," Marshall said. "I sat down. He tossed a yellow pad over to me. I said, 'You must be kidding. I know you guys don't allow copying.' He said, 'These are instructions from the boss. Make your copies and use 'em.' And I did. But I still ain't gonna tell ya what it was. We were helping each other. It was something he wanted and there was something I wanted."

Marshall's notes on the FBI's yellow pad apparently focused on new tactics being used by Communists to infiltrate the NAACP. Those tactics included creating fronts—labor organizations that then approached the NAACP and its branches for help with fighting discrimination. On the basis of the notes he took at FBI headquarters, Marshall sounded the alarm at the 1956 convention:

"[Communists] are all sweetness and light these days, trying to persuade us to join their front organizations, the names of which are constantly changing," he told the crowd at San Francisco. "For example, the National Negro Labor Council, which we exposed and condemned last year, has been disbanded and now they are working up other organizations such as the National Association of Trade Unionists. Whatever the name, whatever the avowed purpose, we know them for what they are. We know their master plan for Negroes is 'self-determination,' which simply means that all Negroes are to be set aside in a separate 49th state. . . . At this convention we must continue to keep our membership abreast of new tactics of infiltration. We must continue to make it clear that there is no place in this organization for communists or those who follow the communist line."

It was a deeply ironic speech for the middle-aged Marshall. As a young lawyer he had worked with left-wing labor groups. Socialists had even asked him to run for Congress. But now Marshall was aggressively separating himself from any radicals and militants.

In fact, Marshall lumped the segregationists with the Communists as having similarly negative impacts on black people. In several speeches he said oppression by racists on the right was pushing black Americans into the Communist camp because they pretended to be defenders of black people. In one speech he specifically condemned Georgia's Attorney General, Eugene Cook, for playing into the hands of Communists by failing to protect the rights of blacks. "The wave of anti-Negro terror in the Deep South [has] given new weapons to the communists for their propaganda," Marshall said.[10]

In an interview later Marshall showed no regret for his willingness to go after Communists and get them out of the NAACP: "I did more than anybody else did and if you don't believe me ask. . . . I didn't like 'em and I didn't like what they were doing."

Similarly, Marshall had no regrets about working with the FBI: "I let Hoover know that I wanted the communists out. He didn't help us." Marshall did not consider Hoover's decision to let him see FBI files as an effort to make him a tool of the FBI. He viewed Hoover's decision as an act of generosity, the sharing of information between like minds. He felt he had manipulated Hoover—Hoover had not manipulated him.

"We did it on our own," Marshall insisted. "We got rid of them [Communists]. They'd either go against religion or something like that and that's how you could tell they were communists."

*   *   *

After his Hoover-aided attack during the June 1956 convention, Marshall found himself caught up in another controversy. Many NAACP convention delegates felt he needed to be as aggressive, even militant in his tone and action with white segregationists as he was fighting Communists.

Since the *Brown* decision there had been growing demands from NAACP branch leaders for Marshall to file more lawsuits, specifically against housing discrimination. Marshall had ignored the pressure. He did not want to detract from his ongoing work to integrate schools. But the dispute boiled over at the convention. Under pressure from delegates, Roy Wilkins had become more insistent with his friend that the rank-and-file NAACP members wanted to see a more activist legal department. It prompted an argument in which the lawyer angrily told Wilkins that the convention delegates were not going to set the agenda for his department.

That led to speculation that Marshall might leave the NAACP for a high-paying job in Hawaii. Even before the convention there had been news reports that Marshall "has reached the point where he is ready to stay in one spot—he's tired of hopping around the country and will [leave the NAACP to] accept the first federal judgeship that comes his way."[11]

The disagreement at the convention took on an especially sharp edge because of ongoing concern over the battle to open NAACP membership lists. As Marshall had been working on the bus boycott, the state of Alabama tried to outlaw the NAACP. Southern states like Virginia, Louisiana, and Texas joined the effort. They charged that the organization was violating its status as a nonprofit group by engaging in political activities, including promoting lawsuits and creating public protests. Alabama's attorney general, John Patterson, joined the attack, claiming that the NAACP was behind King's "illegal" boycott.

In June 1956, Patterson won a lower court ruling banning NAACP activities in the state on the grounds that the organization had engaged in a conspiracy to promote the bus boycott. The judge demanded that the membership list for Alabama be released. When the NAACP refused, they were fined $100,000 and held in contempt of court. Their only choice was to appeal and close down their operations in the state.

Alabama's growing success in fighting the NAACP put Marshall in a bind. He was loyal to the NAACP, but having had so much success in the courts, he was now incapable of ignoring a judge's order. Marshall made it clear to NAACP officials that he would ultimately have to honor demands for membership lists if appeals to the Supreme Court were unsuccessful.

In Marshall's mind the NAACP's concern with racial equality was one part of a larger effort to promote individual rights under the Constitution: "The core of his concern was not the Negro but the individual human being," a magazine reporter wrote after interviewing Marshall. "Other people were engaged in efforts to improve the . . . status of Negroes as a race," the article said. But Marshall's cause was to make a reality of individual rights for all.[12]

But NAACP officials, including some members of the legal staff, wanted no part of Marshall's high-minded, philosophical approach if it meant turning over the names of their rank-and-file members. Inside his office Marshall was being isolated as an accommodationist whose affection for the courts, no matter how biased and crooked, was allowing the civil rights organization to be crippled. One of the leading challengers to Marshall's decision to abide by a possible Supreme Court order to release membership rolls was Bob Carter, his second in command.

Roy Wilkins polled the NAACP's national board and found that most supported Carter's view. "We cannot in good conscience risk exposing our loyal members to economic pressure, personal threats, and acts of violence for no cause other than their membership in the NAACP," Wilkins told reporters. The only common ground between Marshall and other NAACP leaders was that no final decision had to be made on releasing the lists until the Supreme Court ruled.[13]

There was even more to the story of the split between Marshall and NAACP leaders than was publicly known. In the months before the convention Marshall had been engaged in a high-stakes game of office politics. He was trying to pull the legal office away from the NAACP and make himself free from all meddling by Wilkins, Carter, the NAACP board, and the rank and file.

Marshall's strategy centered on the tax-exempt status of the Legal Defense Fund. Technically, the legal department of the NAACP had been separate as far back as 1940. The groups were made into distinct entities to allow tax-exempt contributions to flow into the LDF. The

NAACP, which was openly political and lobbied Congress, was not tax exempt. Despite those separate roles the NAACP and the LDF continued to share staff members, board members, and finances, and to work as one. As part of the backlash against the *Brown* decision, southern senators had petitioned the Internal Revenue Service to investigate whether the LDF should lose its tax-exempt status for working too closely with the NAACP.

With Wilkins and the association trying to exert control over the legal department, Marshall began to use the technical separation of the LDF and NAACP to his advantage. He insisted that he alone had day-to-day authority to decide what the LDF would do. And Marshall conveniently started to repeat the southern senators' complaints about the close relationship between the LDF and the NAACP.

Citing tax reasons, Marshall persuaded Wilkins to have Bob Carter assigned to the NAACP as its in-house lawyer. That meant Carter had to give up his post as Marshall's assistant and the number two lawyer at the LDF. Marshall then resigned his job as special counsel to the NAACP. He had staged a one-man coup.

"[Bob Carter's new job] leaked out to the press and elsewhere as this big promotion. 'He's now the lawyer of the NAACP' and so forth," said Jack Greenberg. "But he had no budget and no staff and he didn't even have a law library. He was allowed to stay on our premises and use our facilities as a courtesy." [14]

"The LDF breakup didn't have a damn thing to do with taxes," recalled Ed Dudley, a lawyer on Marshall's staff. "The reason was that Thurgood was getting too big. Thurgood had gotten to the point where he wanted to make his own decisions." [15]

To many people who were watching this drama, the NAACP-LDF split had really been an ego battle between Marshall and Carter. Marshall saw Carter as a first-rate legal mind who handled the office's affairs expertly. But Marshall also saw that Carter had come to resent him. Carter complained to board members that Marshall often behaved like a prima donna. He wanted all the public attention, he made all the speeches, and he got all the credit, while day-to-day issues and concerns fell on Carter's desk.

"In the period of about 1956, my relationship with Marshall deteriorated . . . ," Carter remembered in an interview decades later. "As time went on, I began to gain my confidence. Marshall had given me my head and I was sort of point guard in the office . . . I began to give him ideas that I was some kind of threat . . . at that point Buster died. And she, I think, recognized that I had a value to Thurgood because my willingness . . . to do the research and the necessary work to keep the office running. And when she died, a bad relationship developed between us."

Although Carter saw Marshall as the Machiavellian hand who pushed him out of the Legal Defense Fund, others in the office saw Carter as a man who had also played office politics and come up short against Marshall. "[Thurgood] claimed . . . that Carter was traveling around the country to NAACP branches and others saying that 'Marshall isn't doing his job' . . . and Marshall was drinking a lot and so forth, and essentially Carter was trying to undermine his position," said Jack Greenberg.[16]

Similarly, Gloria Branker, a secretary at the LDF, recalled that Carter was going "behind Thurgood's back" to tell NAACP board members about his boss's personal and professional problems. The stories reached Bill Hastie, and Hastie called Marshall.[17] "[Thurgood] was distrustful of Bob," said Henry Lee Moon, the NAACP's director of public relations. "Roy mentioned this many times to me." Moon added that "Roy did not come to [Carter's] rescue" when Marshall forced Carter to resign from the LDF.[18]

By May 1957, Marshall had solidified his control of the LDF with a two-step maneuver that put the board of directors firmly in his hands. First, he got them to agree that no one should serve on both the LDF and NAACP boards. Then he asked for the resignations of LDF board members who were not in his pocket, such as former First Lady Eleanor Roosevelt and former New York governor Herbert Lehman.

The new board became Marshall's board. There was no longer any question who was in charge and no possibility of pressure from the NAACP's staff or its members. Decades later Marshall's perspective on the board he created was simple and to the point: "My board backed me up. I had fights [with Wilkins, the previous board, and Bob Carter], but I won 'em. If I didn't win, I'd quit. Course I would, I'd quit and go someplace else. It ain't worth talking about the fights, I don't think. Dirty linen should be kept in the closet. Well, that's what I'd consider it, dirty linen." While he had no interest in talking about it, Marshall had proved to be a skilled political manipulator in his battles with Hoover, Communists, and inside the NAACP.

But Marshall still felt under assault from some NAACP members, who were beginning to question the value of the celebrated *Brown* decision. After the initial rush there was an obvious decline in efforts to integrate schools. Marshall's critics charged that the legal struggle to desegregate the schools had changed little or nothing. Marshall took the criticism as a personal rebuke, and by the summer of 1957 Marshall felt the need to answer it. At the NAACP's forty-eighth annual convention, in Detroit, he charged that the failure to integrate schools and neighborhoods was the result of the "inaction" of black people. "The responsibility . . . rests on the shoulders of Negroes who for one reason or another are unwilling to make an effort," to buy homes in white areas or to enroll their children in white schools, Marshall told the audience.[19]

Despite his increasing fights with black critics, including his longtime support base inside the NAACP, Marshall kept up an optimistic pose. In a long interview with *Newsweek*, he said the NAACP and the LDF were happily working together and in full agreement on negotiating with white school boards to slowly integrate schools. But wasn't it true, the reporter asked, that going slowly about school integration was "gradualism," and that word had a "nasty" connotation for many black activists?

"I'm the original gradualist," Marshall shot back. "But let's make sure what we're talking about. If by gradualism you mean a policy of doing nothing, letting things drift and hoping for the best, I'm dead set against it. . . . Say we take a case into court. It may take two or three years before we get a final decision. Isn't that gradualism? We intend to work this out in an orderly fashion. . . . We are making progress. . . . In general we are completely optimistic."[20]

But to vindicate that optimism, Marshall would have to put himself on the line against white mobs whipped into a racial frenzy as they fought the desegregation of schools. Thurgood Marshall had cunningly played off diverse factions, ranging from J. Edgar Hoover through the NAACP's Bob Carter to the Communists. Now he would face a nasty street fight, in Little Rock, Arkansas.

CHAPTER 25

The Second Civil War

B<small>Y THE TIME</small> M<small>ARSHALL</small> <small>ARRIVED</small> in Little Rock, the violence
had already started. Daisy Bates awoke to find a cross flaming
in front of her house even before schools opened in the fall of 1957.
Mrs. Bates, a tall, attractive woman with curly hair, was the NAACP
chapter president and with her husband published the *Arkansas State
Press*, the state's major black paper. Daisy Bates had been threatened before, but as the opening day for school approached, the segregationists
became more violent. First, the cross was burned. Then a rock shattered
her front window, showering her with sharp-edged glass. Bates picked up
the heavy rock and found a note attached: "Stone this time. Dynamite
next."

It had been over a month since Bates had arranged for nine black students to integrate Central High School. Now every night Bates was
awakened by honking horns and bright lights as people screamed,
"Daisy, Daisy, did you hear the news? The coons won't be going to Central." Arkansas governor Orval Faubus went on television to announce
that he was putting the state's National Guard around the school to keep
out the black students. If any attempt at school integration succeeded, he
warned, "blood will run in the streets."

When Central High opened on September 4, 250 armed National
Guardsmen surrounded the school. Fearful black parents sent their children to Bates's house so they could travel to school together and with
adult protection. But one child, Elizabeth Eckford, took the bus to

school by herself and was surrounded by the mob. When the sixteen-year-old tried to get into the building, the soldiers lowered their bayonets at her and ordered her away. As she walked back to the bus stop, a mob gathered and began to shout, "Lynch her! Lynch her!" Grace Lorch, a white woman, finally stepped in and shielded her until she could flee. The other children, who were driven by Bates to Central High, were also turned away.[1]

The crisis in Little Rock became national news. Governor Faubus sent a telegram to President Eisenhower warning him that despite the Supreme Court's 1954 decision and subsequent court orders "it is impossible to integrate some of our schools at this time without violence."[2] Faubus asked Eisenhower not to intervene even though the court's order was being defied. Marshall got a call from Wiley Branton, the NAACP's attorney in Little Rock, saying that the school board, under pressure from the governor, was trying to get the court to delay the integration of Central. Marshall took the next flight to Little Rock, where armed men escorted him to the Bateses'.

The atmosphere was tense; guards in front of the Bates home stared at every passing car to see if anyone was about to throw a rock or a bomb. Somehow Marshall—with his confident manner and comic storytelling—reassured the city's black leaders that everything was going to be all right. Branton escorted him into the guest room, where they would be staying. Branton had his suitcase on the bed farthest from the window—and a safe distance from any rock that marauding segregationists might heave. Marshall joked with the nervous people in the house that he planned to sneak back when Branton was not paying attention and move his roommate's gear to the bed near the window.

Three years after the *Brown* decision, the intensity of the violence and anger that confronted school integration in Little Rock caught the nation and Marshall by surprise. Events in Little Rock put the slow progress of school desegregation squarely in front of the president, the courts, the press, and the American people.

"I had thought, we'd all thought, that once we got the Brown case, the thing was going to be over," Marshall said later, looking back on the events leading up to Little Rock with regret over his failure to anticipate what was coming.

"You see, we were always looking for that one case to end all of it. . . . Well [Brown] did not [solve all our problems], because we all shouted and sat down. . . . We should have sat down and planned. . . . The other side did," Marshall said. "The other side planned all the delaying tactics they could think of."[3]

After the Supreme Court's 1955 ruling that school boards around the nation could act in "all deliberate speed" to integrate, most school districts did drag their feet, with bogus claims that their elaborate integration plans needed more review. Little Rock, however, had been one of the cities most open to beginning integration.

In the summer of 1954, the school superintendent, Virgil Blossom, had drafted a plan. He wanted to start integration with two new high schools, then come down to the junior highs before integrating the elementary schools. The black community in Little Rock wanted speedier action but was willing to live with the superintendent's plan. Unexpectedly, however, the school board rejected Blossom's approach. Instead they approved a slower, smaller effort to integrate one school, Central High, in the fall of 1957.

Even after he had forced acceptance of the slower plan, Gov. Faubus saw the chance to score political points. A combative little man with a strong desire to be liked, Faubus saw himself becoming a hero throughout the South, the champion of frustrated segregationists. He claimed to reporters that he had received confidential reports indicating mobs of segregationists from all over the South were converging on Little Rock. He predicted violence and a "blood bath" if he did not halt school integration.[4]

Branton, a light-skinned country lawyer with a broad, handsome face, lived just outside Little Rock in Pine Bluff. Marshall liked Branton but was worried that the whirlwind approaching the state might be too much for the friendly, mild-mannered fellow. "I just figured he was a normal, local lawyer," Marshall said, looking back on Little Rock. "And I would say to my surprise he was one of the most competent guys I ever ran across. They had crosses burning on his lawn and everything. But he was a really tough guy. Any kind of jam you got in, you'd call Wiley."

On Saturday, September 7, 1957, the day after he arrived, Marshall was in federal district court with Branton. Under pressure from Faubus the school board had requested that Judge Ronald Davies halt the integration plan because of possible violence disrupting Central's classes. "The threat of tension and the emotional agitation referred to in the petition [from the school board] has no bearing on this [effort to integrate the schools]," Branton told the judge. Judge Davies agreed. Later that day he ruled that the school integration plan was to go forward. With

Marshall and Branton present, the judge told a courtroom packed with the governor's political supporters: "It must never be forgotten that I have a constitutional duty and obligation from which I shall not shrink."[5]

But on Monday, September 9, the governor had the Arkansas National Guard back in place, blocking the black students from entering Central. Marshall, who had been focused on the courts, now realized that this was a political fight and President Eisenhower would have to get involved. Trying to use public opinion as leverage, Marshall had the NAACP issue a press release calling for the president to federalize the National Guard and take command away from Faubus.

Eisenhower, however, was reluctant to take action. He did not want to be labeled as the president who used troops against American citizens. He felt there was no political capital to be gained on either side of the dispute. He had confided to his secretary that the Supreme Court's ruling in *Brown* had created "the most important problem facing the government, domestically, today."[6] But Eisenhower's only immediate action was to have the Justice Department go to court seeking an injunction to force Faubus to pull the National Guard away from the school.

Faubus, meanwhile, was growing paranoid. He had already wired the president, expressing alarm that his phone lines were tapped and that he was about to be arrested by federal agents. Eisenhower had reassured the governor that there was no plan to arrest him, but Faubus was not convinced. He asked to meet with the president in person. On Saturday, September 14, Faubus traveled to Newport, Rhode Island, the president's summer home, to have a private talk.

Governor Faubus pleaded with Eisenhower to defy the Court and support his call for a one-year delay in the school board plan to integrate Central. The governor promised that with extra time he could calm the angry white community. Eisenhower said no. The Supreme Court's ruling, he said flatly, had the force of law. Faubus nodded and seemed to understand. The meeting ended with handshakes and smiles. But Eisenhower, according to his secretary's notes, was not pleased. "I got the impression," she wrote, "that the meeting had not gone as well as had been hoped, that the Federal government would have to be as tough as possible in the situation. . . . The consensus is that it will backfire badly for the Governor."[7]

Marshall watched Eisenhower's polite exchange with Faubus with growing disgust. He could not believe that the president was allowing this Jim Crow politician, this yokel, to defy the federal courts. Marshall got even more angry when Faubus continued to keep the National Guard in front of Central. Marshall could not understand why the president let Faubus run over him. Then came news reports that Eisenhower was planning a meeting on the Arkansas crisis with black political leaders, such as New York congressman Adam Clayton Powell. No one representing the children or the NAACP was asked to attend, and Marshall was incensed.

"As representative [of the] Negro pupils directly involved in litigation being discussed," he said in a telegram to Eisenhower, "[I] would suggest you discuss matter with either parents or children involved or their lawyer before discussing matter with sundry people not directly connected with litigation involved."[8]

Eisenhower did not respond. Marshall felt personally slighted. "If President Eisenhower had used his good offices to say that this is the law and it should be obeyed, that would have accomplished much," Marshall said years later. "We hoped for it. And we found out too late that indeed, President Eisenhower was opposed to it and was working against it. . . . I think [Little Rock was] a black mark on President Eisenhower, and there's nothing in his record that would correct it, in my book."[9]

With Eisenhower ignoring him, Marshall went back to federal district court to ask that an injunction be issued to stop Faubus from interfering. A week later the judge directly ordered that the National Guard was not to be used to stop black children from going to Central High.

Pressure was building on Faubus, and this time he obeyed the court order. But angry mobs of Faubus's supporters, white segregationists, remained around the school. City police could not control the crowds. On September 23 the nine black students were rushed into the building by a police escort and attended school for half a day. While the students were inside, rioting broke out, and the mob grew to more than a thousand. They began screaming, "Oh, my God, they're in the school." The white mob started attacking reporters and black passersby. The police chief decided he could not control the situation and ordered the black students to be packed in cars and secretly driven away.[10]

Little Rock's mayor, Woodrow Mann, sent a telegram to the president explaining that Faubus was behind the violence: "The mob that gathered was no spontaneous assembly," Mann said. "It was agitated, aroused, and assembled by a concerted plan of action."[11]

Daisy Bates, meanwhile, telephoned the NAACP's national office to report that the teachers and white students inside Central were "very nice" to the black students. But Bates was worried that the mob on the street was growing and becoming more violent. "They are imported from the rural areas—real rednecks, " she said, announcing that she did not plan to take the children back to the school the next day. "I am afraid the children may be killed. . . . It is vicious down here. You just don't know."

A day later Bates was back on the phone to New York after a group of segregationists, carrying dynamite, was stopped a block from her house. The mob at the school, she reported, continued to beat up anyone black they could get their hands on, and "if the mob can't find a Negro to jump and beat up, they beat up all the New York reporters." At night black neighborhoods in Little Rock went completely dark so as not to provide targets for drive-by shooters and arsonists.[12]

With the situation growing more violent, Mayor Mann wired the president again. In this telegram he begged for federal troops to take control of the high school: "I am pleading to you . . . in the interest of humanity, law and order and . . . democracy worldwide to provide the necessary federal troops within several hours."[13]

This time the president acted. He ordered the 101st Airborne from Fort Campbell in Kentucky to go to Little Rock. And he traveled from his summer home to the White House to give a nationally televised speech. "I could have spoken from Rhode Island," Eisenhower began, "but I felt that in speaking from the House of Lincoln, of Jackson, and of Wilson, my words would more clearly convey both the sadness I feel in the action I was compelled today to take and the firmness with which I intend to pursue this course."[14]

Bates, Branton, and Marshall were elated. At the same time there was wide concern that sending armed federal troops into an American city might mark the beginning of a second Civil War. "In fact, I'll confess to you," Branton later said, "when Eisenhower federalized the Arkansas National Guard and I looked up and I saw the 101st Airborne and all those damn Army troops, . . . I said, 'My God, what have I brought on?' "[15]

Several prominent southern politicians attacked the president for using federal troops in the South. Sen. James Eastland, a Mississippi Democrat, referred to Eisenhower's action as an attempt "to destroy the social order of the South." And Texas senator Lyndon Johnson said, "No troops from either side [should be] patrolling our school campuses."[16]

The next morning federal troops arrived at Daisy Bates's house to drive the black children to school. The Airborne also circled the school and escorted the black children in the hallways. Integration had come to Central.

In newspapers across the country, Thurgood Marshall was defiant. "Little Rock is not an occupied town," he told the newsman Mike Wallace. "Troops are there for one purpose only—to see that those children are able to go to school. I hope it's gotten over to the Southern people that if they allow their governors to defy the Federal Government this is inevitable." When Wallace asked if he and the NAACP had started a second Civil War, Marshall replied: "If you mean by Civil War that there is continuing effort to emancipate Negroes, towards accomplishing what the Civil War was intended to accomplish—yes." [17]

Marshall's triumph lasted only until the end of the school year. The following summer, after Central had graduated its first black student, the Little Rock school board went to court to ask that desegregation be stopped because of threats of more violence. Marshall, with Branton at his side again, argued that the court should not give in.

Federal District Judge Harry Lemley did not agree. He stunned Marshall and Branton by accepting the school board's plan to delay integration for another two years. Marshall was angry, but even in his anger he worried about the threatening atmosphere he was in, especially when he looked around the courtroom. Among the spectators, he later recalled, were "the most horrible looking women, with Confederate flags and all that—boy, they were tough looking." [18]

The extent of the power of white anger went beyond keeping children out of white schools for an additional two years. It damaged the self-image and confidence of black people in the state. Marshall saw this firsthand when he went drinking with Branton in a local pool hall.

A young black man, smoking a cigarette and carrying a pool cue, walked over to Marshall and said, "Hey, lawyer—you know anything about this thing—where you come back after you die?" Marshall asked the pool player if he was talking about reincarnation. The guy nodded, and a laughing Marshall said he knew more about law than about spirituality. But the young man looked straight at him and said, "Well, if you find anybody that has anything to do with it, tell 'em when I come back I don't care what it is, whether it's a man or a woman, a horse, a cow, a dog, a cat, whatever it is, let it be white."

Though weary, Marshall found the Little Rock crisis spurring him to fight back. It triggered his old spirit of determination. To counter

Lemley's ruling Marshall immediately appealed to the federal circuit court and boldly told the *Afro-American*: "We are going to drop all other cases and the full legal staff will concentrate on the Little Rock case. The pupils will be back in school in September." [19]

Marshall's appeal went to the Eighth Circuit Court in early August 1958. The appeals court called a special session in St. Louis, with all seven judges sitting. The courtroom was packed with more than 150 people, including many blacks who came up from Arkansas. Marshall said that Judge Lemley's decision sent a message—"that if you merely dislike integration and speak against it, you won't be successful, but if you throw rocks or commit acts of arson, bombing or other violence then you will be successful." [20]

Two weeks later the Eighth Circuit ordered that Central High was to continue desegregating that fall. But Marshall's victory had little effect. The Little Rock School Board appealed the ruling to the Supreme Court.

In an extraordinary summer session, all nine justices of the high court gathered in Washington to hear the case. Marshall argued that no society should sacrifice the rule of law to appease violent agitators. He demanded that the Court not "surrender to obstructionists and mob action." He told the justices that when banks were robbed, "you don't close the banks—you put the bank robbers in jail." [21]

Richard Butler, the attorney for the Little Rock School Board, responded that integration would "destroy the public school system of Little Rock" because of the threat of more violence. Butler's view was shared by the state's top politicians, including Sen. William Fulbright, who sent a supporting brief. Butler also told the Court that "the people of Arkansas had not accepted the court's desegregation decision and . . . Gov. Faubus [has said] that the ruling is not the law of the land."

Chief Justice Warren was aghast: "I have never heard such an argument made in a court of justice before. . . . I never heard a lawyer say that the statement of a governor . . . should control the action of any court."

But Butler's argument seemed to have support from Eisenhower. Just the day before the president had issued a statement that said he preferred a slow pace of integration. Marshall began to lose his usual cool. He was angry at being painted as a crazy radical for simply asking that the Supreme Court's decision be enforced.

"Thurgood Marshall, attorney for the NAACP, who had made the opening argument for the Little Rock Negro students, listened to Mr. Rankin [the solicitor general] with a hint of a scowl on his face, looking like Othello in a tan business suit," *The New York Times* wrote.[22]

It came as a surprise to Marshall, however, when Solicitor General Lee Rankin, in contradiction to Eisenhower, told the Court: "We are now at a crossroads—the people of this country are entitled to a definitive statement from the court as to whether force and violence will prevail."

Two weeks after the final argument, the Supreme Court issued a short, decisive ruling in *Cooper v. Aaron:* "Law and order are not here to be preserved by depriving Negro children of their Constitutional rights. . . . The enunciation by this court in the Brown case is the supreme law of the land." Marshall had won his nineteenth case before the Court. The *Pittsburgh Courier* reported in joyous tones that he had "pleaded his second straight 9–0 shutout" in the Supreme Court.[23]

After the Supreme Court ruled in September 1958, Governor Faubus ordered a citywide referendum on whether to keep Little Rock's public schools open. Shutting down the schools was the overwhelming choice [19,000 to 7,500], and the city immediately set up private, segregated schools. Marshall and Branton had to go back to the Supreme Court to win confirmation that closing the public schools was illegal. It was not until the fall of 1959 that Little Rock's public schools were reopened and Central and other high schools allowed black students to study with white students.[24]

*   *   *

When Marshall returned to New York, he was greeted as a conquering general. He was on radio and TV, and reporters were literally lined up to interview him at the NAACP offices. But while he was celebrated as a civil rights hero in public, the story was different inside the office.

While Marshall was preoccupied with Little Rock, he had turned down a request from the NAACP chapter in rural Dollarway, Arkansas, demanding that Marshall file a suit for immediate school integration there. Marshall had explained that he wanted to get control of the crisis in Little Rock before taking on another fight in Arkansas. But on his return to New York, he found that a suit had been filed in Dollarway against his orders. And an Arkansas judge had issued a terrible ruling, which allowed the local school board to slow its integration to a near stop and left little room for appeal. There were almost no school integration cases in the nation not being directed by the Legal Defense Fund. Marshall asked his staff if they knew about the case, *Dove v. Parham.*

"There was this mysterious case," Jack Greenberg said in a interview much later, "[and] a number of us in the office—Jim Nabrit, Thurgood Marshall, and I—were looking at this thing and wondering what in the world this case was, because we didn't know anything about it."

Marshall went to Bob Carter, who was now technically separate from the LDF and acting as counsel to the NAACP, and asked about the case. As Greenberg recalls, Carter denied knowing about it.[25] Several days later, however, as the LDF got hold of the court records, they found that Carter's name was indeed on the case. "It turned out it was actually his case and he was handling it, and that totally infuriated Marshall," said Greenberg.[26]

Soon thereafter Marshall banned Carter from using the LDF's offices or law library. Just as he had used concern over the LDF's tax status to separate himself from Wilkins and the NAACP board, Marshall now cited the IRS problem to totally isolate Carter from the LDF.

Although he and Marshall were fighting, Carter had done first-rate legal work for the NAACP. While Marshall and the LDF had been preoccupied with the Little Rock case, it was Carter who had taken the lead on protecting NAACP membership lists. Attorneys general from southern states had continued trying to force the organization to release its members' names. Carter's defense was extremely popular with the rank-and-file. He won a Supreme Court case in 1958 protecting the association's right to keep its membership confidential.

Despite the personal feud and the behind-the-scenes legal dramas, by 1959 Marshall was internationally known as Mr. Civil Rights. And in polls among black Americans, he either beat or tied Martin Luther King, Jr., for the title "Most Important Black Leader."

He was also finding comfort with a growing family. Cissy had a second boy, John, in July 1958. Just before John Marshall was born, Thurgood and Cissy found an apartment on the seventeenth floor of a brand-new Harlem development, Morningside Gardens. Among Thurgood's favorite pastimes was running his toy trains with two-year-old Goody and doting over little John.

Marshall was on the road far less these days. At age fifty he was also no longer working day and night when he was in New York. Unlike during the turbulent final years with Buster, he was happy to go home. The office had changed too; the staff was bigger and less intimate. Also, success had brought the LDF more money. There was less need for Marshall to be on the phone or out giving speeches to raise a few dollars.

Once in a while the Marshalls would throw parties, and Thurgood might cook some crab soup or appear wearing an apron and promising a "mystery stew." Cissy would cook the main course in case Thurgood's culinary experiments proved unpalatable. "We'd go up there, especially on New Year's Eve," remembered Marietta Dochery, a friend and neighbor. "We had a Fourth of July party here, and Thurgood and Cissy had over Alex Haley and Daisy Bates and Lena Horne. People liked to be around Thurgood, he had lots of friends. Cissy would cook her soul food—pigs' feet, greens, spare ribs, black-eyed peas. Sometimes Thurgood would sing. Maybe he had a couple of drinks or something, and he would sing 'Happy Am I.' "[27]

By now Marshall was also becoming more involved in the political life of New York City and Harlem. After his victory in Little Rock, there were regular rumors that he was up for political posts and judgeships. Times had changed since the late 1940s, when black Tammany Hall leaders had blocked the efforts of the Truman administration to put Marshall on the bench. Now his name was put up for a seat on the New York State Board of Regents, which oversaw education in the state. He would have been the first black person to serve on the powerful board, but the Republican-run state legislature killed the appointment.[28]

His popularity made even national political office a serious possibility. In 1958 Harlem's congressman, the flamboyant Adam Clayton Powell, found himself under indictment for tax evasion. Prominent politicians, including Gov. Averell Harriman, pushed Marshall to take the seat. He was also the leading choice of Democratic bosses in Tammany Hall. "Tammany leader Carmine De Sapio was credited by the leaders with proposing Marshall," wrote the *New York Post*, which noted that New York's Liberal Party was also trying to get Marshall to run for Congress.[29]

Marshall did not seriously consider going after Powell's seat, however. He did not want to join hands with Tammany Hall, and he did not have the appetite for raising money and campaigning. Marshall also didn't want to be labeled as the man who ended Powell's career. "If Carmine De Sapio or anyone else is putting out a trial horse, they should at least have discussed it with the horse," he told the *New York Post*.[30]

Congressman Powell responded to Marshall's decision not to run by inviting him to speak at the next Sunday's eleven o'clock service at

Harlem's famous Abyssinian Baptist Church, which had been founded by Powell's father. The church was packed as usual, and from the high, white pulpit, Marshall made a passionate speech that drew Amens from the congregation. When he finished, Powell walked to the pulpit to hug and praise him. "And he came up and made a little talk, saying that I was the greatest this and the greatest that. When Powell spoke, he told the congregation: 'The one man that I will let succeed me in Congress—the only one—is Thurgood Marshall.' " As Marshall and Powell walked out, arm in arm, the lawyer exclaimed: "Adam, what the hell you tell that goddamn lie for?" Powell, pulling his cigar out of his mouth to laugh, said, "Didn't it sound good!"

A few weeks later the *Amsterdam News* wrote that Powell was quitting Congress. A reporter asked him to give names of people he would accept as his replacement. Powell named a dozen people. "My name wasn't on the list," remembered Marshall. "He forgot about me five minutes after he said it." Powell, hungry for the spotlight despite the threat of scandal, eventually changed his mind and won reelection.

By the late 1950s Marshall had passed on several opportunities to leave the LDF—he had said no to running for Congress and to a federal district court job. His position at the LDF remained secure, and he was more popular than ever. Even so, he knew his time at the NAACP and the LDF was coming to an end. He had a family now and wanted more money; and he wanted the prestige he felt he deserved after his years of sacrifice and many victories for the NAACP. A middle-aged Marshall could also see that the civil rights movement was being transformed. Student sit-ins and mass protests had stirred a storm far outside the courtrooms he dominated. Times were changing for the nation and the question for Thurgood Marshall was whether the times had passed him by.

CHAPTER 26

❧

Marshall and the Militants

IT HAD BEEN MORE THAN TWO DECADES since Thurgood Marshall had arrived in New York, and life on Harlem's streets had taken on a new color. The jazz, the sparkling late-night clubs, and the loud, funny newcomers from the Old South were being replaced by the angry faces of a new generation. On the street corners in 1959, he could hear spokesmen for the Nation of Islam cursing the white man. In the barbershops there were mouths full of rhetoric, the troubled voices of young blacks frustrated with poor jobs, forced to make a buck in the spreading drug trade if not strung out themselves and contributing to the city's rising crime rate.

Despite his shining civil rights credentials, Marshall knew the anger of the streets was also aimed at him as a middle-class lawyer with strong ties to the black elite and the white establishment. On several Saturday nights he had made brief talks between acts at the world-famous Apollo Theater. The place was packed for rock-and-roll shows with young, often more militant black people looking for a good time, full of laughter and drink. If a performer was boring or hit an off note, the Apollo crowd was infamous for loudly booing the offending act off the stage.

Marshall's optimistic, flag-waving, up-by-the-bootstraps rhetoric did not always go over well there. Several times the crowd booed, and threatened him by throwing bottles. The trouble at the Apollo followed him home, taking on a more harsh, threatening tone. Some nights, while in his apartment, he could hear Black Muslims denounce him as a "half-white nigger" and a tool of the Man, working "hand in glove with the white folks." Marshall ignored them for the most part, although the police would sometimes send him transcripts of speeches in which especially vicious language was used to attack him by name.

Listening to the Black Muslims' intimidating words reminded him of his youthful encounters with Marcus Garvey's followers. When he had visited Aunt Medi's apartment in Harlem as a teenager, he had been pushed and shoved, as well as called half-white, by Garveyites who crowded Seventh Avenue for their Back-to-Africa parades. The experience left him with a bitter distaste for black radicals.

One street-corner voice Marshall easily identified from his apartment belonged to the famed Malcolm X. Now in his mid-thirties, the six-foot-three-inch Black Muslim minister, with reddish brown hair and a goatee, had been born to a poor Baptist preacher in Omaha. Malcolm Little's father was killed by Klansmen, leading Malcolm to drop out of school and become a small-time hustler—pimping women, selling drugs, and running numbers.

During a prison stint he got his first exposure to the teachings of Elijah Muhammad and the Nation of Islam, a black cult that said white people were the devil's children sent to oppress black and brown people. Working with black prisoners, the Nation of Islam encouraged education, black unity, and respect for family while condemning the use of tobacco, alcohol, and drugs. Black people were viewed as Allah's chosen. When he left prison in 1952, after a six-year stint, Malcolm X became a minister of the Nation and by the late 1950s was renowned in Harlem for the power of his cutting oratorical attacks on white America. He was equally hard on token blacks working in the white establishment, such as Thurgood Marshall.

Marshall was aware that Malcolm X regularly lampooned him as a "fool." The Black Muslims advocated separatism, including having the government give blacks reparations for slavery and a separate state so they could govern themselves. Marshall let most of the Nation of Islam's barbs and epithets, including Malcolm X's name-calling, roll off him. But he could not ignore the threats when they were made to his face.

One evening as Marshall got off the subway, two men wearing bow ties, pressed white shirts, and long black coats approached him. When he tried to walk past them, they blocked his way. "Excuse me," Marshall said. The men, glaring at him, replied: "Excuse me, you half-white son of a bitch. We ought to kick your ass."

Marshall was tensed for trouble when a police car screeched to the curb and two white policemen got out. They had apparently been keeping an eye on the Black Muslims. One policeman asked the lawyer if he was having any trouble. "Not now," said Marshall. With the two white detectives now shoulder to shoulder with the Black Muslims, Marshall quickly walked away.

Under pressure from the Black Muslims, including several other occasions where they jostled him in the street, Marshall found himself developing a closer relationship with New York's police department and its commissioner, Stephen Kennedy. The two met when Kennedy sought Marshall's advice on how to handle racial flare-ups between the mostly white police department and the city's growing black population. Marshall, who took great pride in having done NAACP investigations into race riots in big northern cities such as Detroit, was pleased that the New York police commissioner would acknowledge his expertise.

Kennedy particularly needed Marshall on the night of July 15, 1959, after rumors spread that a white cop had brutally beaten a black woman. Malcolm X led a march of Black Muslims, who loudly condemned the police and talked up the beating. As it got late more and more bottles were thrown at police cars by crowds hanging out on hot, summertime streets. Commissioner Kennedy got the baseball players Jackie Robinson and Willie Mays to urge people to calm down, go home, and wait until all the facts were out.

Then Kennedy called Marshall and asked him to go to the hospital and interview the cop and the woman. "Number one, she wasn't black," Marshall later recalled. "She was a Puerto Rican, spoke practically no English, and was drunk as anybody you'd ever run across."[1] Shaking his head, Marshall later added, "Then we went up to Harlem Hospital to see Police Officer Gleason. He was white. He kept on telling us what she had done. Both of his legs, when he took the bandage off, there was no skin. She'd kicked all of it off his shins. I said, 'I think the police are right.' She should be arrested. Incidentally, they didn't hit the woman, she didn't have no bruises on her. . . . I sided with the policemen."

Marshall was quoted in the newspapers as supporting the police and endorsing Commissioner Kennedy's decision to send extra officers into black neighborhoods on the night of the incident. Several NAACP members openly questioned his embrace of the police. Nonetheless, Marshall stood by the law enforcement officials, claiming "they are crucifying that man [Commissioner Kennedy]."[2] The Black Muslims were outraged.

The next night Commissioner Kennedy showed up at Marshall's apartment with a small package. When he handed it to Marshall, the lawyer asked, "What's this?" Kennedy smiled while Marshall unwrapped it and found a snub-nosed gun, complete with a permit. Cissy had been watching and immediately grabbed the gun from her husband. "Uhn-uhn, don't put your damn hands on it," she said, worried about the possibility of the boys handling the weapon. Kennedy reluctantly took the gun back, but he put an officer outside Marshall's apartment to keep an eye on him as he went around town.

Despite the criticism and threats he received from the Nation of Islam, Marshall did not back down. In October he made a speech at Princeton University in which he labeled the Nation a "bunch of thugs organized from prisons and jails." Elijah Muhammad responded in a newspaper column titled: "Muhammud [sic] Hits Thurgood Marshall."

"The Negro leadership is in love with the Negroes' enemies," Muhammad began. "One would think that Mr. Marshall would be in sympathy with freedom, justice and equality for the so-called Negroes. . . . But the weight of his . . . false charges made indirectly against me and my followers proved otherwise. . . . We have not been opposed to the NAACP's cause," Muhammad continued, "only we feel . . . that they should not at this late date seek integration of the Negroes and the Whites, but rather separation. . . . Seeking closer relationship between the slaves and their masters only will provide total destruction of the Negroes by the wise, old slavemaster's children. . . . Thurgood Marshall does not care for the recognition of his kind or for the Black Nation. He is in love with the white race. He hates the preaching of the uplifting of the Black Nation unless it is approved by the white race."[3]

Muhammad's criticism, like Malcolm X's street-corner jeremiad, had little impact on Marshall, who viewed Muhammad's appeal for a separate black nation as lunacy. "I don't know of any better way to sink the ship than that way," Marshall said, scowling, when asked about the Black Muslim ideology. Muhammad's ideas were a thorough repudiation of what Marshall stood for in arguing that the Constitution protected American citizens equally, without regard to race. And Muhammad's talk of Black Nationalism was the exact opposite of Marshall's lifelong advocacy of racial integration that required whites to accept blacks as equals.

While Muhammad and his followers continued to attack him in their speeches, an unbowed Marshall was drawing even closer to J. Edgar Hoover and the FBI. Hoover had been keeping tabs on Malcolm X and the Nation for several years and was aware that Marshall was the target of Black Muslim fury. The bureau was also a target of criticism from Malcolm X and the Nation for its failure to go after the KKK and other white racists. In fact, the Black Muslim critique was very similar to the criticism that had come from Marshall and the NAACP more than ten years earlier, specifically that the FBI was cozy with white hate groups that violated the rights of black people.

In March 1959, Hoover had authorized an FBI visit to Malcolm's mosque in New York. The agent reported that during a speech, Malcolm asked if there were any policemen in the room. When one stood, Malcolm said he wished more law enforcement agents would visit the mosque. The FBI agent later reported, "Malcolm also stated that the officer should report that they [members of the Nation] are law-abiding people [but] they do not teach their people to love 'white folks.' Malcolm further stated: 'Man, you should arrest them [whites]. We were kidnapped. We were not brought here on the *Queen Mary* or the *Mayflower.*' "[4]

Hoover and Marshall now had a common enemy. Although Marshall had cooperated previously with the bureau, he was now totally free to work with Hoover. With funding from large foundations, he no longer needed the NAACP's money. And since his takeover of the LDF, he didn't have to respond to Roy Wilkins and the NAACP branches.

While the FBI continued to monitor Malcolm X's speeches and travels closely, blacks in the South continued to complain about the FBI's failure to investigate race crimes. When a *New York Post* reporter telephoned Marshall for a story on FBI misconduct, the lawyer got angry and immediately contacted the bureau. He spoke with one of Hoover's top aides. According to an FBI memo on the telephone call: "[Marshall] wanted the Director to know that he planned to tell the reporter to either 'put up or shut up' and he would demand to know specific cases and not generalities if they wanted his opinion on things. He stated he had learned this from the Director many years ago and he thought this was the best way to handle the *New York Post.*"[5]

Marshall did not want Hoover to think that he was feeding information to the reporter. He was acting to prevent a repeat of the events that had led to Hoover's charge years before that the NAACP and Marshall were making unfounded complaints about racist FBI activity.

After Marshall did the interview with the *Post*, he called the FBI again, this time speaking with the New York office. In a 1959 memo titled "Smear Campaign," an agent wrote that Marshall said the reporter wanted his opinion of the FBI's record in the South. Marshall said he was "satisfied" with the FBI's investigations.

According to the agent's memo, Marshall's biggest concern was that the reporter would next visit NAACP branches in the South and hear rumors about FBI misconduct. Marshall told the agent that if he had evidence with "teeth" of FBI wrongdoing, he would contact the bureau. And Marshall confided to the agent that he did not like the newspaper's attempt at muckraking and damaging the FBI.[6]

*   *   *

A month later, in June 1959, Marshall was in touch with the FBI again about the black militant Robert Williams. As the NAACP branch president in Union County, North Carolina, Williams had been quoted in papers across the country urging blacks to "meet violence with violence." Wilkins and the NAACP immediately suspended Williams for contradicting their stand against racial violence by whites or blacks. The suspension made national headlines, and Williams was portrayed as being disgraced. Days later, however, a Communist-backed group formed the Robert Williams Defense Committee to offer him legal and financial support. Their work was not widely publicized, but it came to Marshall's attention, and he wanted to make sure the FBI knew about it.

Marshall, concerned by this mixture of black militants and Communists, asked for a face-to-face meeting with the FBI's agent in charge of the New York office to discuss how the NAACP was responding to Williams's call to arms. He also wanted the bureau to know that neither he nor the NAACP had anything to do with the Communist-led defense committee. At the start of the meeting, Marshall gave the agents three documents that linked the defense committee with Communists. But his greatest alarm was over Williams's defiant call for self-defense.

The agents later wrote in a memo to Hoover, "Mr. Marshall mentioned that his purpose in furnishing the information was due to the fact that he believed [Robert Williams] will seek to arouse the people in the North Carolina area to take action which could become violent and cause racial unrest and tension. . . . He is afraid of people agitating on such matters in the South, since race tensions can be easily aroused, especially during the summer months."

At the end of the memo the agents noted that Marshall told them,

"No one else in the NAACP was aware of the fact that he had furnished the above information." More and more, Marshall was acting on his own and at a distance from the organization. He promised to keep the FBI updated on the case, a few days later sending the New York FBI office an advertisement he had found in Detroit for a meeting of the "Friday Night Socialist Forum" held in support of Williams.[7]

Robert Williams's ties to Communists had started a year earlier, when two black boys, ages nine and seven, were arrested and charged with rape after they were found playing a kissing game with a seven-year-old white girl. Williams, as the head of the local NAACP branch, tried to get the national office to defend the boys. But Williams said Marshall and the NAACP told him they did not want "anything to do with the case because it was a 'sex case.' " A frustrated Williams turned to a New York civil rights attorney with Communist ties, Conrad Lynn. Despite Lynn's efforts the boys were found guilty and sentenced to fourteen-year terms in a state reform school.

Williams remained a loyal member of the NAACP. But just a few months later he butted heads with the national office. In the spring of 1959, a Union County white man was charged with attempting to rape a black woman who was eight months pregnant. The man was acquitted by an all-white jury after the defense concluded its argument by saying, "This man is not guilty of any crime—he was just drinking and having a little fun." Following the acquittal Williams told reporters: "This demonstration today shows that the Negro in the south cannot expect justice in the courts. He must convict his attackers on the spot. He must meet violence with violence, lynching with lynching."[8]

It was this call for violence that prompted Roy Wilkins to suspend Williams and led to Marshall's secret meeting with the FBI. But the case was not over. Wilkins and Marshall feared that the suspension would lead to heated debates at the NAACP's fiftieth annual convention, set for New York in July. The leaders were specifically worried that the Black Muslims might try to exploit the controversy to disturb the convention.

"We went to see Malcolm to make sure that we could have our convention without any disruption, and Malcolm said he wouldn't disrupt it," said Gloster Current, the NAACP's director of branches.

But Marshall and Wilkins could not stop Williams and his supporters from launching floor fights and holding large street demonstrations outside the convention. Inside, Williams justified himself by telling the delegates that when Klansmen and Nightriders attacked, "we must defend ourselves." A good number of the delegates applauded. "This is all I advocated. If I advocated it then, I advocate it now," he said.

Wilkins and Marshall argued that Williams was undermining the NAACP's tradition of achieving change through peaceful protest and appeals to the law. They led the convention to vote in support of Williams's six-month suspension. "We abhor violence," the NAACP said in a statement. "We reject violence in any way to achieve any of [our] objectives."

However, there were enough pro-Williams voices to force the addition of a statement supporting black people who defended themselves. Delegates said blacks facing violent racists need not be compliant sheep going to slaughter: "We do not deny, but reaffirm the right of individual and collective self-defense against unlawful assaults."[9]

Williams later was reelected president of the Union County NAACP and in 1960 traveled to Communist-led Cuba. He also went to China and other Communist countries. His travels seemed to validate Marshall's tips to the FBI. But the Union County NAACP's vote to reelect Williams indicated their comfort with his militancy and cemented the distance between Marshall and elements of the NAACP rank and file.

Marshall's alienation from radicals such as Malcolm X and Robert Williams was based on his judgment that they did little to make life better for black Americans. The radicals may have touched a nerve and given release to pent-up anger among black people. But Marshall accurately concluded that compared with his efforts to end legal segregation and win voting rights for all Americans, there was nothing the radicals had to show as evidence of how they improved black life in America.

Hurt by what he perceived as a lack of appreciation for his efforts to create real change in race relations, Marshall became emotionally distant from much of the burgeoning activism in the civil rights movement by the end of the 1950s. He didn't see the nonviolent strategies of Martin Luther King, Jr., as effective, and he viewed Malcolm X's talk about separatism and violence as destructive. Marshall thought Robert Williams's infatuation with Communists was just plain stupid. In an era when government leaders were paranoid about Soviet expansion, Marshall was right to conclude that there was no advantage for already maligned black people to gain by signing up with Communists.

Marshall's decision to provide information to Hoover's FBI could have cost him his credibility among civil rights activists had it become known. But the relationship was kept secret. And Marshall did succeed in keeping the FBI from mistakenly attacking the NAACP and the LDF as Communist fronts or bases for militant violence. In his heart Marshall wanted to protect mainstream civil rights groups from becoming easy targets for attacks that could set back the fight to defeat segregation and win equal rights for all.

Marshall's secret ties to the FBI and the information he gave the bureau were justified by the arc of the African-American struggle, dating back to antislavery efforts, to end government-sanctioned racism in America. But once he had made his pact with Hoover and set himself apart from the likes of Malcolm X, not to mention much of the NAACP, Marshall had all but ended his time as the much-honored legal leader of the movement.

CHAPTER 27

Exit Time

MARSHALL FELT TRAPPED. He was tired of the young militants who criticized him. And he had grown discouraged with fighting segregationists over issues he thought he had won long ago. His frustration peaked when he lost a Supreme Court case in which the state of Virginia accused the NAACP of instigating frivolous lawsuits against segregation. The Supreme Court ruled on a technicality; the state court had not reviewed the case.

Marshall was upset that the high court would give credence to such a case by allowing it to continue. It just added to the foot-dragging by segregationists. The decision came down in June, and Marshall spent the summer restless and distracted, unable to focus his mind or his legal strategy. His efforts had hit a brick wall—less than 6 percent of black children in the South attended integrated schools despite the *Brown* decision. In the fall he surprised his staff by announcing that he was taking a two-month leave of absence to travel overseas.

The trip came as an invitation from Tom Mboya, the leader of black Kenyans involved in the movement to gain independence from Britain. Mboya had come to the United States early in 1959 and while in New York met black American leaders, including Marshall. Mboya told New York papers that he found "the American Negro community incredibly impressive."[1] He was particularly struck by Marshall's success as a lawyer. Mboya asked if he would come to Africa and assist in drafting a constitution for Kenya's independence.

It was the perfect reason to take a break from the U.S. civil rights struggle. Before leaving in January 1960, Marshall did extensive research. "When I did the constitution for Kenya, I looked over just about every constitution in the world just to see what was good," Marshall said, pounding his fist on the desk to drive home the point. "And there's nothing that comes close to comparing with this one in the U.S. This one is the best I've ever seen."

But when he arrived in Kenya, not everyone welcomed him. As he tried to go into the constitutional conference in Nairobi, he was barred by police because he and Mboya were seen as supporters of the radical Jomo Kenyatta. Kenyatta had been convicted and was in jail for leading the Mau Mau rebellion, which had resulted in the widespread murder of white settlers in the early 1950s. Marshall, barred from the meeting, started to argue and push by a white policeman, but he stopped when he realized a police search could land him in jail since he had anti-British pamphlets in his pocket.

Marshall backed away from the confrontation but asked if he could say a few words to the large crowd of black Kenyans waiting outside the negotiations room. The police refused, but Marshall said he would not give a speech, simply offer "one word of greeting." The policeman, seeing that the light-skinned foreigner with his lawyer's satchel had attracted attention from the locals, agreed.

Marshall pulled his six-foot-two, 220-pound frame on the top of an old station wagon and waved his arms to quiet the crowd. Then, in his booming voice, he shouted, 'Uhuru,' and pandemonium broke out. The policeman was stunned. The one word Marshall had shouted was political dynamite. It meant "freedom now." [2]

Marshall was never allowed into the talks in Nairobi. But when meetings resumed in England a week later, the Kenyan delegation asked him to fly with them to London, where he was welcomed by the British.

The black Kenyan nationalists wanted democratic elections in which natives would be given the right to vote. But hard-line white settlers were fearful that majority rule would mean a black-run government that would confiscate their land and property. Marshall told reporters that without a constitution allowing for black rule, there would be an uprising "that nobody can control—any more than they could control the Mau Maus." [3] He was not, however, without concern for the whites. Just as he had made a career of asserting black minority rights in the United

States, Marshall was anxious to protect the white minority in Kenya. "Well, I said that I was going to give the white Kenyan the same protection I would give a Negro in Mississippi. That's what I did," he later recalled.

Marshall's key contribution to the Kenyan constitution was to make it illegal for the government to claim land belonging to white settlers without paying for it. "Kenya only has one asset and that's land," he explained. "So I provided in my constitution that they could take the lands but they had to pay you. And if they don't give you the price you like, you can file an action in the highest court—I'm damn proud of the constitution I wrote."

Not everyone was pleased to see Marshall in London exercising his influence. Writing from Nairobi, Robert Ruark of the *New York World Telegram and Sun* said Marshall should have stayed home. Under the headline AFRICA ISN'T MARSHALL'S BUSINESS, he wrote: "The intrusion of Thurgood Marshall . . . into the muddled mess between Great Britain and its colony seems to me to be meddling of the highest order. . . . He is not an African. He is an American and a mostly white one at that. If he knows anything about Africa or Africans, he read it somewhere."[4]

But Marshall's work on the Kenyan constitution was celebrated in black American newspapers, which focused on kinship ties between black Africans and black Americans. The *Afro-American* quoted Marshall as saying the efforts to integrate schools in America and the fight for independence of the colonies in Africa were part of the same "emergent struggle for freedom all over the world."[5]

Not all of Marshall's time was spent reading legal documents. While in London, he met Prince Philip. The prince teased him by asking, "Do you care to hear my opinion of lawyers?" Marshall, with a playful grin, shot back, "Only if you care to hear my opinion of princes."

*　*　*

There were some final details still to be cleared up on the constitution, but Marshall was being swamped with telegrams and calls from New York about a new wave of mass protests in the United States. Student sit-ins at segregated restaurants in the South were spreading quickly after their start at a Woolworth's lunch counter in Greensboro, North Carolina. The sit-in tactic, supported by Martin Luther King, Jr.'s Southern Christian Leadership Conference, produced big headlines around the country as southern sheriffs began arresting hundreds of young people on charges of trespassing. The students' parents asked the LDF to get their children out of those dangerous southern jails.

Marshall came home in late February to deal with the crisis. As lead lawyer for the LDF, he became a singular voice of caution. He challenged his staff to tell him why the LDF should do anything for the students. "Thurgood stormed around the room proclaiming in a voice that could be heard across Columbus Circle that he did not care what anyone said, he was not going to represent a bunch of crazy colored students who violated the sacred property rights of white folks by going in their stores or lunch counters and refusing to leave when ordered to do so," wrote Derrick Bell, a young lawyer who had just joined the staff. Bell recalled that Marshall told the LDF staff it was futile to go before any judge and talk about a sit-in when the law was clear that the students were trespassing on private property. Almost as if he was defying the popularity of the cause, Marshall told his lawyers the only way he would take the cases was if they could find some new, convincing arguments. But he added, "I know you can't, because they don't exist."[6]

The LDF prepared several memos on possible legal strategies for getting the students out of jail, but none made the grade with Marshall. However, an outpouring of telephone calls from NAACP members, as well as pressure from black newspapers and offers of money from churches and foundations, persuaded him that the LDF had no choice but to act as the students' legal representatives. Money was pouring in, even from conservative, older southern blacks who felt sympathetic to the young demonstrators.

Looking for strategies for defending the students, Marshall called a conference of civil rights lawyers at Howard University on March 18. Most of the lawyers, like Marshall, were skeptical of finding any legal basis for defense. The courts had long held that store owners had the right to refuse to do business with anyone they chose not to serve.

Marshall's young, activist staff, however, put forward the idea that a restaurant had to deal with anyone who walked in the door, regardless of race, under the equal protection clause of the Fourteenth Amendment. And Marshall became a convert when he began to consider that if racial prejudice were enforced by the state's police and courts, then it was unconstitutional. By the end of the three-day conference, Marshall had set aside $40,000 to defend sit-in protesters. "Once a store is opened to the public it means it is open to everybody—without discrimination," he told the *Washington Star* after the conference. "If it sells pins and needles to a

Negro at one counter, it can't keep him from buying hamburgers [at another counter]."[7]

The legal strategy was in place, but there was another battle to be fought. While Marshall wanted to be totally in charge of the legal representation of the students, Roy Wilkins and Bob Carter wanted to limit the LDF to the role of advisers. Marshall won out by agreeing to let Wilkins deal with local NAACP leaders while he, using his ties with civil rights lawyers around the country, retained control of how the cases were argued in various state courts.

The response from segregationists to Marshall's support for the students was sharp. Georgia's senator Richard Russell told reporters that sit-ins were an attempt to "invade and impair the right of private property in this free America." He concluded that if Marshall and the sit-in students won the Supreme Court's support, the Constitution would be "distorted" and no one could "feel secure in his property rights."[8]

While Marshall was staving off Senator Russell's attacks, he found himself the target of barbs from black students who were leery of him. They did not want Marshall, one of the older black leaders—people they saw as too conservative—taking charge of their budding movement and the energy, publicity, and money it was attracting. In fact, the LDF was raising substantial sums of money because of the sit-ins. They brought in more than $500,000 in 1960, about one and a half times what they had raised the year before.

While Marshall remained dubious that the sit-ins would do any good, he nevertheless made fund-raising speeches around the nation, praising the students' activism and asking for donations to help with their legal bills. The students were "furnishing a lesson for all of us," Marshall told an AME Zion convention in Buffalo. "What they are doing is telling us that we are too slow," he said to one audience. "I am telling you they are right."[9]

Marshall filed several suits in support of students demanding food service at Jim Crow lunch counters. In one case, Bruce Boynton, a Howard Law student, had been arrested for insisting that a Trailways bus station lunch counter in Richmond serve him. Just before Marshall was to argue the case in the Supreme Court (it was to be his last NAACP oral argument before the court), the third-year student appeared at the door of Marshall's hotel room to tell him how to do it. Boynton's arrogance prompted the LDF lawyers in the room to break into laughter the minute he left. Their laughter was a double-edged sword, a sign of the growing distance between Marshall and the young people now in the vanguard of the civil rights movement. The case ended successfully when the court ruled in Marshall's favor, voting 7–2 that the bus station's refusal to serve a black patron was a violation of the Interstate Commerce Act.

The dramatic confrontations at lunch counters continued, however. By the end of 1960 some 1,700 students had been arrested throughout the South for disturbing the peace by demanding to be served in segregated restaurants. In 1961 Marshall filed a brief in the Supreme Court (*Garner v. Louisiana*) that argued that the Fourteenth Amendment gave the students the right to be served in a public restaurant and made the point that the well-dressed, polite young people had never disrupted the peace. The Supreme Court unanimously ruled at the end of the year in a sweeping decision in favor of Marshall and the students. The sit-ins had succeeded.

*   *   *

This new civil rights crisis brought on by the sit-in movement and marches was a major concern for candidates in the 1960 presidential election. The issue was particularly difficult for the Democrats, since southern segregationists were an important constituency for their party. Sen. John Kennedy of Massachusetts, the leading Democratic candidate during the primaries, called Marshall for advice. At a two-hour lunch in Kennedy's office, he asked Marshall if a northern Catholic could win in the nation's racially charged atmosphere.

"He told me that he was thinking about running for president and what did I think about it?" Marshall said, describing the conversation. "And I told him, 'No way.' I remembered Al Smith [1928 Democratic candidate for president who was Catholic]. The Masons killed Al Smith, and the Masons would kill him off. And he said he didn't think so. I said, 'Well, you asked for my opinion, and that's my opinion.' "

Kennedy ran, captured the Democratic nomination, and was in a very close general election against the sitting vice president, Richard Nixon. The Republican had substantial black support thanks to his association with the popular Eisenhower and a fairly good civil rights record. In October, however, the black vote took a decisive turn. Martin Luther King was arrested in Georgia for taking part in a student sit-in protest at Rich's department store. Most of the protesters were released within a week when Marshall and the LDF put up bail money and went to court to defend them. But King was denied bail because of an earlier arrest for driving without a Georgia license. He was sent to a rural penitentiary infamous for its cruelties to prisoners. The LDF continued to argue in court for his release as King began a four-month sentence.

Candidate Nixon asked the Justice Department to check on King's rights and make sure that he was being properly treated. Candidate Kennedy, however, made a call to King's wife, Coretta, and promised to do what he could to get King out of jail. Robert Kennedy, the candidate's younger brother, also called an Atlanta federal judge about King's detention. A day later King was set free.

After King was released the Kennedy campaign printed pamphlets for black churches telling the story of how Kennedy had worked to get King out of jail. The strategy paid off; Kennedy won 68 percent of the black vote in an election decided by less than 1 percent of the vote. But Marshall was filled with resentment. NAACP attorneys had been working around the clock and he felt upstaged. Right after King's release he phoned Donald Hollowell, the NAACP attorney in Atlanta who was handling the case. After congratulating Hollowell, Marshall let out a snicker and said: "You know they tell me everybody in the world got Martin Luther King, Jr., out but the lawyer." Both Hollowell and Marshall burst out laughing.[10]

After the election black voters, politicians, and newspaper publishers had high expectations for Kennedy. They were counting on him to enact new civil rights laws and appoint blacks to high-level federal jobs. Attention quickly turned to several vacant federal judgeships, with Marshall as the most prominent candidate. Just before the election Marshall, age fifty-two, was described in a newspaper interview as "getting to the age when elevation to the bench becomes an increasingly attractive goal."[11]

Just two months into the new administration, the *Afro* ran an editorial titled "Thurgood Marshall Next?" In it Carl Murphy named several black Democrats who had been given jobs in the new administration, then said, "We boldly submit that President Kennedy will find also a wise and able federal judge in Thurgood Marshall."[12]

But Marshall's relationship with the administration hit a rough patch. First, he was asked to come to Washington to talk with the new attorney general, Robert Kennedy, under the guise of discussing civil rights. The two really wanted to size each other up. It was a disaster. "I had a very unsatisfactory conference with Bobby about the civil rights movement shortly after they took over," Marshall remembered. "He spent all this time telling me what we should do."

By late March, Marshall was among the first to accuse the administration of forgetting black voters. He criticized President Kennedy for failing to include any civil rights legislation among the bills he sent to Congress in the first 100 days.

Despite the tensions between Marshall and the Kennedys, the new administration surprised the lawyer with an invitation to represent the president at a celebration of the independence of Sierra Leone, which had been under British colonial rule. In an apparent effort to stroke Marshall and tone down the criticism, he was not only asked to attend the celebration but given the rank of "special ambassador." He took an ambulance, a "mobile x-ray and medical center," as a gift from the United States to the people of the new black nation.

By the time Marshall returned to the United States, the good publicity generated by his trip had the White House again looking at him as a possible nominee for a judgeship. Frank Reeves, who had worked for Marshall at the NAACP, was now a special assistant to the president. Reeves got a letter from William Coleman, then the most prominent young black lawyer working at one of the nation's major white law firms, which were still highly segregated. Coleman urged Reeves to get the president to appoint Marshall to the federal bench. He went so far as to suggest that some southerners might be angry, but Kennedy could assure Dixiecrats that Marshall would be in a New York court and would "handle no matter which would adversely affect the interests of the south."[13]

By late May the House Judiciary Committee sent a list of black nominees to Attorney General Kennedy for openings on the federal bench in New York. Marshall's name was on the list, and so was that of Robert Carter, Marshall's former top aide who he had come to view as his private antagonist. The memo indicated that President Kennedy was "strongly of the opinion" that one—but only one—judgeship in New York go to a black person. The contest was quickly shaping up as Carter versus Marshall. Carter, although he was not as well known as "Mr. Civil Rights," was far more acceptable to white southern congressmen, who would have to vote on the nomination.

"Thurgood Marshall is a Democrat," the House Judiciary Committee wrote to the attorney general. "He is an excellent lawyer. Of course, we recognize that he is a controversial figure and we may have difficulty in getting him confirmed. As you know, he is a man of very positive and forceful convictions, perhaps a little too rigid in his views, yet, probably, the best qualified of all Negro applicants." [14]

Despite the problems a Marshall nomination might cause, it had its strong points. Robert Kennedy did see the political advantage in making the best-known civil rights lawyer in the country a Kennedy appointee. However, the younger Kennedy was only willing to put Marshall on the district court bench, not on the higher appeals court. That created a problem because Marshall refused to have his name put in for the lower court. He wanted an appeals court job, which would put him on the same level as his old Howard law professor Bill Hastie, who, as a member of the Third Circuit Court of Appeals, was the highest-ranking black judge in the country.

Marshall felt his lifelong accomplishments were being overlooked because the attorney general was making a purely political judgment about the cost of putting a civil rights lawyer on the appeals court. He viewed Attorney General Kennedy as "awfully ruthless," but he agreed to another meeting

"I told Bobby Kennedy that I was not district judge material, because my fuse was too short," Marshall subsequently told an interviewer. "I lose my temper. And that wasn't good. But I would like to be on the Court of Appeals."

Kennedy gave Marshall a take-it-or-leave-it offer for the district court. "It's that or nothing," Kennedy told him.

An indignant Marshall looked the attorney general dead in the face as he stood to leave. His eyes narrowed, and his voice dropped: "Well, I've been dealing with nothing all my life, there's nothing new on that." [15]

With Marshall locked in an emotional, political, and ego-driven fight with Kennedy, Bob Carter became the front-runner. One newspaper profiled him as the likely winner among contenders for the district court judgeship, which Carter was willing to accept. But Carter's nomination was unexpectedly pushed off track after he interviewed with the judicial committee of the bar association. What happened during the interview was not revealed. But Jack Greenberg, who had replaced Carter as Marshall's top assistant at the LDF, later said that Marshall told him Carter was undone by "his arrogance."

Some of Carter's friends thought Marshall had used his influence among the liberal, all-white bar to damage Carter. "Now what role Marshall played in that or any of Marshall's friends can't be said," Greenberg later told an interviewer. "Some of Carter's friends at least thought there was some such role." [16]

The bar association's failure to give Carter unqualified support left the administration in a jam. They still needed a black nominee to fill one of the vacant court seats in New York, and Thurgood Marshall's name again floated to the top of the list. It was then that Marshall had a serendipitous meeting with Louis Martin, the lanky, honey brown newspaper publisher who was now the leading black politico at the Democratic National Committee. Martin and Marshall had long been friendly and often crossed paths on the political circuit.

"I saw Thurgood in the La Guardia Airport at a hot dog stand," Martin recalled years later. In the hubbub of the busy airport, Martin said, "You know, we're trying to get the president to appoint you to a judgeship, and we have to have you because you're Mr. Civil Rights." Marshall held the line he had set with Robert Kennedy; he would not accept a district court appointment. Martin now understood that Marshall was not bluffing.

"When I got back to Washington I talked to Bobby," Martin recalled. "At first Bobby said, 'How in the hell are we going to make an NAACP guy an appeals court judge?' And I said, 'I don't give a damn how you could do it, you've just got to do it. That's Mr. Civil Rights. We've got a lock on the civil rights thing if we get him.'"

Martin began an intensive campaign to persuade Bobby Kennedy to name Marshall. First he got several prominent white lawyers to speak highly of Marshall's legal skills to the young Kennedy. Then Martin spoke with Assistant Attorney General Ramsey Clark, who wrote a memo to Kennedy's deputy, Byron White. Clark characterized Marshall as "a symbol throughout the nation. He stands for peaceful efforts of a race to secure equal justice under law. [The] appointment of Marshall to the second highest court in the nation should be a wonderfully meaningful thing to millions of people and the culmination of a brave fight." Martin's efforts got a surprise boost when J. Edgar Hoover sent over a memo that while occasionally critical of Marshall, generally praised the civil rights attorney. A week later Bobby Kennedy called Martin and relented: "I think we might be able to do something for Thurgood." [17]

Ironically, while Marshall was waiting to hear from Washington, he was stopped on the street by a New York policeman who accused him of following a pretty woman. Marshall came back to the office fearing that if newspapers heard about the incident and ran a story, his nomination would be dead. According to Greenberg, Marshall decided not to do anything until the story hit the papers. Luckily, it never did.[18]

The next time Marshall's name appeared in the paper was when news of his appointment to the appeals court leaked. Meanwhile, the reports that Carter was being considered for a lower court judgeship quickly faded. Marshall was to be the only black lawyer from New York nominated by the Kennedys.

The nomination was carefully timed. The Kennedy brothers, anticipating opposition, nominated Marshall a week before the Senate Judiciary Committee was to go out of session for the rest of the year, not leaving the committee time to act. Thus the president was able to give Marshall a recess appointment, allowing the new judge to be in place until Congress could reconvene. That meant Marshall would be on the bench and acting as a judge before segregationist opposition to his appointment could take shape.

Marshall got word that the Kennedys were going to nominate him in mid-August. By the time the news arrived, it was wrapped in bittersweet overtones. Earlier in the month Thurgood's mother, age seventy-four, had died. She had moved to New York to take care of Thurgood's ailing Aunt Medi and to be closer to her son. But Norma Marshall grew ill herself. Aunt Medi and Thurgood helped to take care of her for nearly a year. The funeral was held at St. Philip's in Harlem; Aubrey came up for the simple affair.

*   *   *

The good news of his nomination was also tempered by Marshall's ongoing wrangle with Carter. Marshall did not want Carter to succeed him at the LDF, and he was busy behind the scenes trying to defeat him. Marshall called Jack Greenberg into his office one afternoon. He told the white Jewish lawyer that he was the best person to become the next head of the LDF. "I was astonished," Greenberg later wrote.[19] Marshall told Greenberg he was already working to get the board to select him.

Although Bob Carter had left the LDF and been assigned to the NAACP in 1956, there was still a widespread sense that he was second in command when it came to legal matters. Carter was bright and a hard worker who was well known in civil rights circles. He was expected by most casual observers to be Marshall's successor. But the degree of rancor between Marshall and Carter was not widely known.

"He felt a responsibility to replace [himself] from within the staff, and the two options were Connie Motley and me," Greenberg later said in an interview. "Obviously Carter was out of the question because of their relationship. . . . Thurgood spoke to the board of directors, and said I was eminently qualified, and of course, to quote Thurgood, 'It would be better if he was a nigger, but nevertheless. . . .' "[20]

Carter learned of Marshall's efforts to bypass him, but there was not much he could do. The current LDF board was loyal to Marshall. There was some grumbling from Carter's supporters on the NAACP side of the fence, but Marshall ignored it. John Hope Franklin, the historian, later said Carter was "bitter" and "felt he had been done in" by Marshall.[21]

Years later, Marshall tried to play down the politics and egos involved in the battle of succession: "I did make Greenberg my replacement because he had six months of seniority over Motley. Why would I have to appoint someone black? Should I just pick a man out of the street, get a damn street-cleaning black and appoint him? I mean, black isn't it. Black isn't it."

Carter, in an interview years later, said it had long been clear to him that Marshall was doing all he could to prevent the LDF from ever having him as its director: "I knew damn well that [Thurgood made] the decision that I wasn't going to replace him," he said. "I felt very, very strongly that blacks up to this point had carried the load and been the intellectual force in civil rights. And I felt that it was not good to have a white man running that. I felt that from now on, history was going to be rewritten, and it was going to be the whites who had done all the work, which was not true. Jack and I got to have a very antagonistic personal relationship."

Carter also felt that Marshall may have had ulterior political motives in selecting a white person to succeed him. "It could have been that by picking Jack he was therefore pulling the fangs out of those people who felt that he was a racist in reverse," said Carter. "He felt that this would ease congressional opposition to him getting a judgeship."[22]

Marshall certainly wanted a smooth transition as he went from the mostly black NAACP family, which had raised him to prominence, to the white world of federal courts and high-stakes politics. For all his success and status as "*the* Black Lawyer" in America, he was still worried about making it outside the NAACP. Marshall had no idea how difficult that transition would be.

CHAPTER 28

᪐

Black Robes

Thurgood Marshall had realized a dream. Thirty years earlier, when starting his law practice on a shoestring, he'd fantasized about one day becoming just a local judge: "People call me a liar when I tell them that when I was a young lawyer in Baltimore, my highest aim was to be a magistrate—man, there were only two Negro magistrates in the country then."[1]

Now at age fifty-three, Marshall's reality turned out to be better than his boyish daydream. On October 23, 1961, he was sworn in as a federal judge and the first black American to serve on the U.S. Second Circuit Court of Appeals. More than 200 people gathered for the ceremony, held at the courthouse on Foley Square, on the lower end of Manhattan. Cissy and the boys joined a proud Thurgood along with Bill Hastie, the only other black federal appeals court judge. New York senator Jacob Javits, Labor Secretary Arthur Goldberg, and Roy Wilkins were also there.

J. Edward Lumbard, the chief judge of the Second Circuit, swore Marshall in and then told the large audience: "During the past twenty years few—if any—members of the American bar have had so varied an experience." Lumbard said the late John W. Davis, Marshall's opponent in the *Brown* cases, once predicted, "This fellow is going places." Lumbard concluded, "All I need to say, is: Here he is."[2]

A smiling Marshall thanked his wife and President Kennedy. He promised to do his best. There were no hints that getting the Senate to confirm this nomination was going to be a grueling ordeal.

Behind the scenes, however, support for Marshall was fractured. Supreme Court Justice Felix Frankfurter had supported Bob Carter for a district court judgeship and was telling friends that Marshall was not qualified for the appeals court. Bill Coleman, Marshall's friend and Frankfurter's former clerk, got word of the negative comments. Full of concern, Coleman sent the justice a letter praising Marshall and asking him to hold off his criticism. Frankfurter responded, "I have said nothing to anyone that I did not say to you, and what I did say was merely to negative the perfectly absurd hallelujahs with which his nomination was greeted, as though a great lawyer had been elevated to the judiciary." Frankfurter went on to express admiration for Bob Carter and noted that Carter had made "a deep impression" on several other Supreme Court justices, a compliment he did not extend to Marshall.[3]

Coleman wrote back, pleading with Frankfurter not to make his criticisms public. Coleman wrote that while he liked Marshall, he had "never stated that a great lawyer had been elevated to the judiciary."[4]

Frankfurter ceased his public critique of Marshall, but similar comments were making the rounds in legal circles and on Capitol Hill. Marshall's nomination remained in limbo until the Senate Judiciary Committee, chaired by the segregationist James Eastland of Mississippi, scheduled hearings. While waiting for the committee to act, Marshall began working as a federal judge. "I talked to him about writing opinions. This was something new to him," Judge Lumbard said in an interview. "Well, I helped him with some opinions [because] he wanted to quote a lot of stuff, verbatim. He was a good beginner, he wanted to do things right. He was very cooperative and carried his share of the burden."

Many of Marshall's critics complained that he was expert in only one area of the law, civil rights. Lumbard said that was not a crippling problem. "We knew damn well he couldn't have known much about corporate law, that was taken for granted, that was true of most of us," he said. "He was diligent, he had good law clerks to help him. . . . It was a good thing to have somebody like Thurgood to be the first [black] man on the court. He was not abrasive, he didn't have a chip on his shoulder. We all respected him."[5]

Even with the chief judge's respect, Marshall was not given his own office in the courthouse. Since he was not confirmed, Lumbard made no permanent arrangements to house him. Marshall and his staff had to find new office space every few days. "We had a pretty lousy set of spaces," recalled Ralph Winter, a Yale law student and Marshall's first clerk, who later became a federal judge. "They weren't judicial chambers, they were some bureaucratic offices. When another judge would go on vacation, we'd move down there."[6]

As the low man on the circuit court, Marshall had to deal with the least interesting cases—taxes, corporate law, even the "Doctrine of Unseaworthiness in Admiralty." He also did a lot of Wall Street securities cases because the other judges would recuse themselves when their stock ownership put them in a potential conflict of interest. Marshall joked with his friends that since he was a poor black man and had never owned any stocks, the other judges automatically assumed that he could hear all those cases.

A judge's life was very different from the daily routine Marshall knew at the LDF. There were no wild characters coming in and out of his office. Marshall's phones hardly rang, and there was almost no talk of the latest racial crisis. And while he got a raise (up $7,000 to $25,000 a year), he missed the sudden requests to jump on the next plane and walk into hostile courtrooms.

To remind himself of the old excitement, Marshall would occasionally take a twenty-minute subway ride uptown to the LDF's offices to say hello. But those visits became fewer and fewer. As a judge he had to distance himself from the LDF's legal cases and his successor. And in a painful act he had to pull away from his old friend Roy Wilkins. "He and Roy were so close," recalled Cissy Marshall in an interview. "They were like brothers. He was closer to Roy than to his own brother. And then we had to cut all that out, cut it off."

Marshall may have lost some friends, but he was an oddity who attracted attention in the staid corridors of the federal courthouse. Several of the secretaries would come by to see Marshall and even to get a glimpse of Alice Stovall, the first black secretary on the circuit. The new judge was extremely popular among law clerks. Every morning clerks from other judges' chambers would come by to have coffee and listen to Thurgood Marshall stories. "He had a remarkable ability to take a situation fraught with violence and other terrible things and have a humorous end to them," said Winter. "He could talk about things they never imagined," added Stovall.

In January of 1962, three months after Marshall had been sworn in, the White House resubmitted his nomination to the Senate. Chairman Eastland handpicked three senators to handle the nomination. The subcommittee included two segregationist Democrats from the South [John

McClellan, an Arkansas Democrat, and Olin Johnston, a South Carolina Democrat] and Roman Hruska, a Nebraska Republican who was described by one newspaper as "at best, lukewarm," when it came to civil rights.[7]

The Kennedy brothers were rumored to have made a deal with Eastland to ensure that Marshall would get a fair hearing. Eastland supposedly demanded that the White House nominate W. Harold Cox, his college roommate and a segregationist, for a federal judgeship before he would send Marshall's name to the Senate. "Tell your brother that if he will give me Harold Cox, I will give him the nigger," Eastland reportedly said to Bobby Kennedy.[8] The story may be more apocryphal than true; Cox had been confirmed for a federal judgeship before the Kennedys agreed to nominate Marshall to the bench.

Whether any deal had been struck or not, Senator Johnston, the chair of the subcommittee, showed no interest in holding quick hearings on Marshall's nomination. Johnston was in a dogfight of a campaign against his state's segregationist governor, Ernest Hollings. He could not afford to have Marshall confirmed because Hollings was sure to use the confirmation as a platform for racist demagoguery. Johnston twice scheduled hearings and even had Marshall come to Washington. Both times he canceled the hearings.

By April, six months after Marshall had been sworn in, there still had not been a hearing on his nomination, and stories began to appear criticizing the Senate for its stalling. Reporters pointed out that two judges, both ardent segregationists, had been confirmed just days after they had been nominated. W. Harold Cox had been confirmed in one week, and J. Robert Elliott had been confirmed in only two.

As Marshall's nomination lingered, the Second Circuit's chief judge wrote to Senator Eastland. Judge Lumbard complained that the court could not make decisions on critical cases if one of its judges was in danger of not being confirmed. Even though Lumbard had an uneasy relationship with Marshall—he was angry that Lumbard refused to give him permanent chambers—the chief judge wrote to Eastland that the Kennedy appointee had done "diligent and cooperative work." Lumbard, clearly upset, added, "I have heard no complaint concerning him and I know of no reason why action upon his nomination should be delayed."[9]

Similarly, Sen. Kenneth B. Keating, a New York Republican, publicly criticized Eastland for allowing the Marshall nomination to be put in "a committee pigeonhole." Keating also revealed that Eastland had ordered

Senate staffers to dig up scandals that could smear Marshall. He said such a witch-hunt was unprecedented in Senate history: "Quietly and deliberately a distinguished American jurist is being victimized."[10]

With pressure building Senator Johnston agreed to have one day of hearings in May, a month before his primary contest. But Johnston did not show up, and neither did Senator McClellan. Nebraska's Senator Hruska sat uncomfortably by himself as the two senators from New York, Keating and Jacob Javits, testified in praise of Marshall's ability. Marshall also made a brief, nervous statement. He tried a preemptive strike by admitting he had been a member of the National Lawyers Guild but explained he had quit in protest when he realized Communists were running the organization. Meanwhile, Senator Keating charged that Marshall was being given a rough time simply because he was a symbol of the civil rights movement: "The controversy about Judge Marshall centers not about the man, but the results he has achieved. . . . If others do not share [Marshall's] view, their arguments should be with the courts which have upheld his contentions, not with his persuasiveness as an advocate."[11]

There were to be no more hearings on Marshall for another two months. The delay left Marshall frustrated and nervous. He and his clerk, Ralph Winter, feared that if they made a mistake on any case, it would be used by Marshall's detractors to stop his confirmation.

While Marshall worried about every step he made as a judge, President Kennedy did little to press the Senate for speedy action on the nomination. The president invited Marshall to a White House dinner, and the nominee complained to Kennedy that the lengthy wait was wearing on his nerves and his family. The president dismissed Marshall's worry. "Forget about it—it takes time," he said.[12]

The hearings resumed in July, a month after Johnston won his primary. McClellan of Arkansas still refused to attend. With two of the three senators looking on, the subcommittee's lawyer hurled desperate accusations at Marshall. He charged that Marshall had violated canons of legal ethics by encouraging blacks in Texas to participate in lawsuits. Marshall was supposedly guilty of stirring up trouble where none had existed and hurting race relations. Senator Hruska tried to defend him, weakly noting that the NAACP, not Thurgood Marshall the man, had tried to get people to fight segregation. He urged the committee to focus on Marshall's credentials, but to no avail.

As the hearing was ending, Marshall tried to get the panel to set a date for the next hearing, even asking if they could resume the next day. A surly Johnston fired back: "Not tomorrow, I can tell you that right now." No date was set, and the next hearings were not held until August.[13]

Ten months had now passed since Marshall was nominated by the White House. Under federal law his paycheck would stop in another two months if he were not confirmed. A worried Marshall called the White House. The president told him, "It's been taken care of." Marshall later explained, "I gathered . . . that maybe his father or somebody [would have paid me]."[14]

Aside from the salary issue, Marshall's supporters were getting indignant about the delay. Jackie Robinson wrote in his newspaper column that Marshall was being punished because of his skin color, "the accident of birth."[15] Eleanor Roosevelt wrote about the delay, calling it a worldwide embarrassment to a nation that professed equality among its citizens.[16] Senator Keating appeared at the third hearing on Marshall, held in early August, and pointedly noted there had been no probes into the activities of the newly appointed judges Elliott and Cox or their law firms. But Marshall was being burdened with responsibility, Keating said, for every action ever taken by any member of the NAACP.

The committee, responding to the growing political pressure, scheduled a fourth hearing for a week later. At that session his critics let loose their full barrage. He was attacked for his association with left-wing legal groups, such as the International Juridical Association and the National Lawyers Guild. His opponents were trying to smear him by painting Marshall as a Communist sympathizer.

Later, one senator pressed Marshall to explain why he once told a Memphis audience that the NAACP had "the law, religion and God" on its side. In the same speech he was quoted as having blasted the NAACP's white opponents as people who put all their "faith and hope in the devil." Marshall denied ever making the remark but conceded that he had spoken about "opponents," which he said were "groups like the KKK and the groups that defy God, law and everybody else." Marshall had finally had enough. He threw a challenge back at his Senate inquisitors: "Anybody who takes a man out and lynches him, I believe is working with the devil."[17]

Three days later, at yet another Senate hearing, Marshall was peppered with questions about whether he was a racist. The questions grew out of an essay written by Alfred Kelly, the historian who had helped the NAACP do research for the second *Brown* case. Kelly described Marshall as a man who made racially charged jokes such as: "When us colored folk take over, every time a white man draws a breath he'll have to pay a fine."

Marshall told the subcommittee that Kelly had misquoted him. Senator Johnston pointed out that Marshall had now charged that reporters in Memphis as well as a respected historian were guilty of misquoting him on explosive racial comments. He said further hearings were necessary. Sen. Philip Hart, from Michigan, came to the front of the room and complained that the hearings were being needlessly diverted into issues that did not matter. "Judge Marshall doesn't have a thing to worry about," Hart told the subcommittee. "His reputation in American jurisprudence is established. We will indict ourselves if we fail to acknowledge it."[18]

The subcommittee, however, insisted on having Kelly, a Wayne State University professor, come to Washington to testify. A week later, at a remarkable sixth hearing, Kelly was the panel's first witness. He began to do damage control by praising Marshall as a man with a "remarkable personality and vast abilities." As for Marshall's comment about charging white people for breathing, Kelly said, "The remark was mordant humor, given exclamation by a man possessed of a powerful sense of humor. . . . To lift the remark out of context and treat it as a threat or even a philosophical observation is absurd, even grotesque in its bizarre distortion of reality."

The next witness was the reporter from the *Memphis Commercial Appeal* who had quoted Marshall as saying that the NAACP's opponents were working with the devil. Paul Molloy said the quotation was accurate but conceded that another reporter, from the *Memphis Press-Scimitar,* had quoted Marshall's words differently and with less controversial impact.[19]

After a parade of witnesses offering unsubstantiated accusations, the hearings abruptly ended. A week later the *Washington Star* reported that the subcommittee had privately voted 2–1 to reject Marshall's nomination.[20] The Kennedy brothers grew concerned that the nomination was now on its way to defeat. After the subcommittee's vote the attorney general took Marshall to meet with several senators in an attempt to pick up support for the nomination. Marshall was not impressed with the younger Kennedy's political gamesmanship. "Bobby was like his father," he later said. "He was a cold, calculating character."

Kennedy insisted that Marshall visit Senator Eastland, "to pay our respects." Marshall balked at going into the segregationist's office. "What do you want me to do?" he asked. "I'm not going to go in there and genuflect to that man." Kennedy, growing irritated, said flatly: "Well, you ought to." Marshall walked off.[21]

Despite Marshall's refusal to meet with Eastland and the negative subcommittee vote, the full Judiciary Committee voted on his nomination on September 7. The tally was 11–4 to confirm, with four southern senators—Eastland of Mississippi, McClellan of Arkansas, Johnston of South Carolina, and Sam Ervin of North Carolina going against him. The powerful segregationists had delayed as long as they could. Four days later the full Senate confirmed Marshall, 54–16, with only southern Democrats voting against.

* * *

The newly confirmed judge was in New York when he got the good news. In a statement to the press he thanked the president and the Senate and said: "I will do my level best to live up to their expectations." The journalist Eric Sevareid did a series of articles on Marshall that celebrated the man who "carried Negro Americans considerably closer to the citadel of full citizenship." Sevareid concluded by saying Marshall remained "a whole man in a society half sick from racial prejudice . . . and a human being of the first rank."[22]

Marshall's new status changed his image with some of his long-standing detractors, specifically the Black Muslims. Malcolm X, the leader of the Nation of Islam in New York, saw Marshall's prestige around the country as a potential plus for a Black Nationalist movement.

During the summer of 1962, Malcolm wrote to invite Marshall to join other prominent blacks and "speak to the Black Masses of Harlem" at a rally at 125th Street and Seventh Avenue. Writing on stationery from Muhammad's Mosque No. 7, he said, "Conditions in Harlem have deteriorated," and black "leaders must now take an intelligent and unselfish stand." He predicted summer riots: "The fuse has already been lit, the crisis has been reached, and if something is not done immediately there will be an explosive situation in the Negro community, more dangerous and destructive than a hundred megaton bombs."[23]

Marshall wasn't persuaded by the letter. He wrote on it, "File, No Reply," and did not attend the rally. But the judge did meet Malcolm X one day on the streets of Harlem. "Hell yes, I met him," Marshall recalled. "I think we called each other sons of bitches and that was all there was. We met on Seventh Avenue."

At the heart of Marshall's dislike for Malcolm X were two key issues:

First, Marshall was an integrationist who had never related to Malcolm's hatred of whites; second, Malcolm, unlike Marshall, believed that violence was a useful tool for dealing with white racism.

"Malcolm X and I never got along because I just don't believe that everything that's black is right, and everything that's white is wrong," Marshall said in an interview years later.

After Malcolm X had left the Nation of Islam and traveled to Mecca, where he began to reconsider his black separatist beliefs, he again phoned Marshall and asked for a meeting. "In the end, he kept wanting to talk to me and I kept telling him to go to hell. He changed. When he went over there to Mecca . . . he really changed. . . . I don't know why he wanted to meet with me. I think he was trying to convince me or something."

While he gave Malcolm X credit for breaking out of the grip of Elijah Muhammad and the Nation of Islam's ideology, Marshall never could see why Malcolm was held in such regard: "I still see no reason to say he is a great person, a great Negro," he told one interviewer. "And I just ask a simple question: What did he ever do? Name me one concrete thing he ever did."[24] Years later Marshall's judgment was that for all the books, movies, and fascination with the man, Malcolm X was "a bum, hell, he was a damned pimp—a convicted pimp, about as lowlife as you can get." Asked why Malcolm X had folk hero status, Marshall smirked and shook his head before answering: "White people."

Meanwhile, at the Second Circuit, Marshall's confirmation was cheered by Chief Judge Lumbard, who used the occasion to arrange a group photo of the circuit's nine judges. The photographer took some test shots before the judges arrived and blew a fuse. A secretary called for an electrician. Marshall arrived a few minutes later. Seeing a black man walk in, the secretary instinctively said, "Oh, you're the electrician?" Judge Marshall let it go with a laugh. And the secretary, recognizing her mistake, apologized. When Marshall got back to his chambers, he told his clerk what had happened, with less bitterness than irony: "Boy, that woman must be crazy if she thinks [a black man] could become an electrician in New York City."[25]

Even though he had been there for a year, Marshall's career as a judge was still skating dangerously close to the edge of his ability because he was dealing primarily with big business. He heard cases involving the Securities and Exchange Commission, the National Labor Relations Board, and corporations that were suing each other. For advice when he was

over his head, he walked over to the chambers of J. Henry Friendly, a politically conservative judge who became Marshall's mentor.

He also relied heavily on his clerks, often learning the law with them.
His first two clerks came from Yale Law School at the recommendation
of a Yale professor, Louis Pollack, who was on the LDF's board. Two
later clerks were from Harvard. Marshall felt he had to have the very best
law students to compensate for his lack of experience. One consequence
of Marshall's insecurity over his legal skills was that he selected no clerks
from less prestigious law schools, such as his own alma mater, Howard.
And with virtually no blacks at the Ivy League schools, none of Marshall's
clerks were black.

"When I worked for him, I did a lot of the writing, but I always knew
exactly what to say," Ralph Winter, Marshall's first clerk, said in an interview. "I was not out there composing my own stuff. There is no question
who was making the decisions, absolutely no question about that."

Marshall developed an intimate relationship with his clerks as he
spent less time with old friends at the LDF. "He never drank in the office, ever, but when we went to his home in the evening—going to his
home for dinner was quite an experience," recalled Marshall's second
clerk, James O. Freedman. "Cissy would make dinner, and then all of a
sudden all of these people would start wandering in. And these were his
buddies, his card-playing buddies. Marshall was in his shirtsleeves and his
suspenders and people started playing cards and the bourbon came
out."²⁶

With his new paycheck Marshall bought a big white Cadillac and had
vanity tags put on it, USJ for United States Judge. Marshall delighted in
driving the car around Harlem, Freedman recalled, and gave off a sense
of "I come from here and these people worship me."

However, being a federal judge also meant that Marshall was no
longer in the limelight, and he hated that. He missed reading about himself in the New York papers and told Freedman he could not understand
why Edward Bennett Williams, then a young hotshot lawyer defending
several Mafia dons, won headlines as a legal wizard. When Williams
came to the Second Circuit to argue a case, clerks as well as reporters got
into a frenzy, and Marshall grew irritated. He took quiet pleasure in the
court's later ruling against Williams's client.

Being hidden away as a judge also meant fewer people recognized
Marshall. He told his friend Bill Coleman that his lower profile came in

handy one day. "When he was on the Second Circuit," Coleman recalled, "this lady who lived on Park Avenue used to call him and ask him to come over, and he said, 'Oh I can't do that, I'm a judge now.' And he finally said he worked it out to come over . . . around lunchtime, but he stayed until about [midnight], because he just assumed that the same guy wouldn't be on the elevator. So he comes over, goes up, and at midnight, the same guy's on the elevator, and the guy says, 'Gee, you must have had a good time with Mrs. So-and-so.' When he gets down to the bottom, the guy says to him, 'Gee, Congressman [Adam Clayton] Powell, I still want you to give those white folks hell in Washington.' And Thurgood said, 'I certainly will.'"[27]

During his first few years as a judge, Marshall became taken with the high-society party scene in New York, according to his good buddy Monroe Dowling. "There was a hell of a party in one of the Waldorf Towers, and I took Thurgood with me," Dowling said in an interview. "In fact, every time I went somewhere I took Thurgood. He was good company, and he always had something to say in groups. He'd tell jokes, be loud and crazy."

At the Waldorf party Dowling and Marshall were the only two black faces in the room. The liquor was flowing, the music was pumping, and then the host brought in three white prostitutes. Marshall, feeling good after a few drinks, tried to talk Dowling into staying and playing with the girls. "Yeah, we ought to stay, but I haven't got the nerve enough," Dowling told him before dragging Marshall out.[28]

Aside from partying Marshall had little to stir his mind or soul. His big challenge was coping with the tedium of being hidden among law books and untangling the minutiae of tax laws. "My sense was that during those years he was very unhappy, that he was bored," said Freedman. "He found it very hard to be alone. . . . He would spend a lot of time standing at the window looking out. They were doing some construction and he would watch this great big construction ball."

One of his few thrills came in the fall of 1962, when Marshall found himself back in the newspapers after he was invited to be the lone black speaker at a Lincoln Memorial ceremony commemorating the approaching hundredth anniversary of the Emancipation Proclamation. The last-minute invitation came after the Kennedy White House sparked an uproar by not asking any black people to speak at the event. To mollify black leaders who were planning a boycott, the administration announced that Marshall would join the former presidential candidate

Adlai Stevenson, New York's governor, Nelson Rockefeller, and others for the ceremony.

About the same time the administration found itself thinking it might want to nominate a black person for the Supreme Court seat left vacant by Felix Frankfurter's retirement. Marshall's name did not come up, though. The Kennedy brothers fixed their sights on the more experienced William Hastie, age fifty-eight. However, Bobby Kennedy thought Hastie's nomination would hurt the president politically. Also, the attorney general worried that Hastie was too conservative. The job went to Kennedy's labor secretary, Arthur Goldberg.

Although Marshall had not been considered for the Supreme Court seat and had prickly feelings about Bobby Kennedy, he stayed in touch with the attorney general on civil rights issues. "Marshall knew every Alabama judge," recalled James Freedman. He not only knew which judges played straight on race but had an in-depth understanding of civil rights laws. Marshall's expertise helped the Kennedys during integration crises at such universities as Alabama and Mississippi. Justice Department officials also consulted Marshall in June 1963, when Medgar Evers, the NAACP's field secretary in Mississippi, was assassinated. Marshall had befriended Evers and greatly admired his low-key, effective style, and he advised the Kennedys on how to deal with the NAACP as well as local officials after the murder.

The State Department then asked Marshall to travel to Africa as the president's representative on a goodwill tour. Berl Bernhard, director of the U.S. Civil Rights Commission and a prominent white lawyer, accompanied Marshall on a trip designed to help newly independent nations in East Africa deal with civil rights and economic development.

In July of 1963 Marshall met Bernhard in Rome, and together they flew to Nairobi, where three years earlier Marshall had been involved in writing the Kenyan constitution. "All the way down on the plane I was hearing from Thurgood, 'Everybody's going to be at the airport when I get there,' " Bernhard recalled in an interview. "Thurgood, we're getting there at three-thirty, quarter to four in the morning, nobody is going to be there." Marshall insisted there would be a red carpet lined with the president's cabinet. As they approached Nairobi's airport, Bernhard looked out the window and saw an empty tarmac. He teased his companion that there was no welcoming party.

"So we land," Bernhard continued, "and son of a bitch, if it isn't— these people come running out and pull a red carpet out." As the door

opened Marshall quickly elbowed his way in front of Bernhard: "Get behind me, they don't want to see no Europeans down here. This is for
Thurgood." Bernhard protested that they both represented the U.S.
government. "You are a white representative of the government," said
Marshall. "They want to see Thurgood."

In Kenya, Marshall met with many of the friends he had made while
working on the constitution. Whenever he introduced Bernhard, he
joked that his companion was the "mouthpiece from the Kennedy administration." Bernhard laughed with Marshall, but he understood that
beneath the laughter Marshall did not like Bobby Kennedy and considered both Kennedys lacking genuine commitment to civil rights at home
or in Africa.

At one point Marshall asked Kenya's secretary of the interior to get
him a leopard skin because he'd promised to bring one home to Cissy.
But the secretary told him that leopards were out of season. "I don't want
to listen to that, I promised Cissy a leopard skin," Marshall replied. "I'm
not going home without one, she'll just whip the shit out of me."

Marshall took his request to the top, Jomo Kenyatta. With his arms
waving and his deep voice booming, Marshall told the president that he
had to have a leopard skin for Cissy. Bernhard watched in amazement: "I
think he called him Jomo, for God's sake. Kenyatta was very deliberate,
very dignified, you know. So he just listened to Thurgood and he said,
'Which leopard?' "

Kenyatta and Marshall also had long, sometimes heated, talks about
how the Indian minority was being treated. The Indians, whose land and
property were being confiscated by the government, complained that the
nation's bill of rights, written by Marshall, was not protecting them.
Kenyatta told Marshall that during the ongoing transition from colonial
rule to independence, which did not officially start until December, the
guarantees of rights and protections were not yet in place. But Marshall
challenged him: "I don't care about listening to that, that's why we have
the Bill of Rights." [29]

Years later in an interview, Marshall recalled his talks with the
Kenyan president and said he viewed Kenyatta as one of the world's true
leaders: "I think he was one of the greatest individuals in history. One of
the strongest willed, effective people I know of. And slightly rough.
When violence was necessary he was with it."

Kenya's president had good feelings about Marshall, too. "Kenyatta
obviously adored Thurgood," Bernhard recalled. "Thurgood was a god,

there was no question about it. At one point I told Thurgood that he should not be telling Kenyatta how he should be running the government. I said, 'You're behaving like the Emperor Jones.' " Marshall responded: " 'White boy, when we're in East Africa, I am the Emperor Jones!' "

The trip was a success in strengthening ties between the United States and East Africa. But when Marshall returned to the United States, the nation was caught up in several heated battles over civil rights issues. The most explosive was an effort by A. Philip Randolph, the seventy-four-year-old black labor leader, to have a massive march on Washington. Randolph and several other civil rights leaders wanted to take a stand against the violent attacks that Birmingham sheriff "Bull" Connor had used to put down black demonstrators, including Martin Luther King, Jr.

The Kennedy brothers, as well as most of the Congress, were afraid the march would incite race riots. President Kennedy met with the leaders and asked them not to march. He told them that a large number of blacks marching through the capital not only was dangerous but would endanger passage of a civil rights bill.

Marshall shared many of the president's concerns. He did not see the point in marching and making speeches and did not go to Washington. Marshall acknowledged that he watched it on TV, but he refused to say what he thought of it. "No comment."

By late 1963 Marshall was trying to focus on his work at the Second Circuit when he—and the nation—was devastated by President Kennedy's assassination. "I think Jack was terrific," Marshall recalled. "I said I was going to stop reading newspapers when I picked up the paper about Kennedy. Nothing but bad news. That was awful."

Digging into his work in the difficult time after the assassination, Marshall began to find his voice as a judge. He did not often dissent, but in early 1964 he dissented in a major case, *Angelet v. Fay*, which involved a drug bust. The defendant claimed that after his conviction federal law had changed and that the evidence used against him would now be inadmissible. A majority of the judges on the Second Circuit ruled that the new, stricter laws on search and seizure could not be applied to past cases. But Marshall objected, arguing that protections against illegal searches should be retroactive.

His voice in dissent was also heard during the May 1964 celebration of the tenth anniversary of the *Brown* decision. At a news conference commemorating the event, he said, "Desegregation obviously has not proceeded as fast as we would have liked." Unlike his 1954 prediction of rapid school integration—"come hell or high water we'll be free by '63"—ten years later he said it would take "at least a generation to bring about any social change" in the nation's still heavily segregated schools. When asked about his decision to send his own children to a private academy, the elite Dalton School, instead of the mostly black and Puerto Rican public schools near his apartment in Harlem, Marshall replied: "I think they should have the best education I can afford."[30]

Judge Marshall's contrary voice grew sharper in the fall, when he traveled to St. Louis as the first "Negro delegate" from New York City to represent the Episcopal Church at its triannual convention. When southern laymen led the convention in a vote to condemn civil rights activists for disobeying the laws of segregation, Marshall stormed out, leaving behind nationwide headlines. Marshall was angry over the defeat of a resolution that would have "recognized the right of any person, for reasons of conscience, to disobey laws or social customs in conflict with the law of God so long as such person is willing to carry out his protest in a non-violent manner."[31]

The walkout illuminated the tension between Marshall's strong belief in the law and his opposition to segregation, even if it were legal. A few weeks later at a panel discussion, Marshall was asked how he could have supported the idea of protesters disobeying the law. "The [resolution] didn't advocate disobedience," he argued. "[It] gave everyone the right . . . to disobey a law which they considered against their conscience. . . . I seem to remember some place in the Bible where Jesus grabbed some money-changers and kicked the living daylights out of them, which I assume was against the law."[32]

By late 1964 Marshall's dissident voice was creating enemies. He became worried that his telephone might be bugged and got Buck Owens, the private detective who had found a bug for him at the NAACP, to take a look around his apartment. Owens found one, but while Marshall suspected the FBI was shadowing him, Owens could not prove the bureau had placed it.

Shortly after Owens found the bug, he told the judge that Martin Luther King, Jr., was also being bugged. According to Marshall, Owens said an FBI agent confided in him that King was being targeted by the agency. "It was personal between King and Hoover," Marshall said years later. "He bugged everything King had. Everything." An FBI agent phoned Owens and admitted to being part of the team assigned to bug King. The agent asked Owens to have Marshall tell King that he was surrounded by listening devices, in his bedroom and even his bathroom. Marshall agreed to let King know what was going on. But when an alarmed Marshall got him on the phone, King was unconcerned. "Oh forget it, nothing to it," he responded. Marshall later said, "It just didn't interest him. I've never been able to understand that. Maybe he felt that he wasn't doing anything wrong."

The FBI's surveillance led the bureau to circulate stories about King's indiscriminate philandering. Marshall heard the stories, but he did not give them a lot of credence. His critical view of the civil rights leader had softened after King won the Nobel Peace Prize. But the sex stories continued to flow, presenting Marshall with a puzzle. "I don't know if a man can humanly do all the things that he was supposed to be doing," Marshall said. "Five and six times a night with five and six different women. We added it all up, I mean, he just couldn't be all them places at the same time. I don't believe in it personally. That's between him and Hoover. I don't know whether he was right or Hoover was right, but I never found Mr. Hoover to have lied once, not once."

King's troubles, as well as the explosive events of the civil rights movement during the early 1960s, were like news from a distant shore to Marshall. These days he generally learned about the movement's crises in the morning papers. At lunch with Ralph Winter one day, he remarked that he was amazed that civil rights had finally become "a front-page issue" in major papers.

Marshall continued grappling with the law, doing diligent, if not brilliant work. "When he was on the Court of Appeals in the Second Circuit here in New York, I think he was regarded as tolerable but not in any sense as a strong addition to the bench," said Walter Gellhorn, then a Columbia law professor who had worked with Marshall at the LDF.[33] By mid-1965 Marshall had written ninety-nine majority opinions, eight concurring opinions, and only twelve dissents. His dissents showed an inclination to embrace a wider interpretation of constitutional protections than the other judges.

In his most celebrated dissent on the Second Circuit, People of New York v. Galamison (1965), Marshall sided with civil rights protesters who were blocking access to a main road leading to the New York World's Fair. The demonstrators were angry over poor-quality housing and a lack of jobs for blacks in New York. He argued that the demonstrators had guarantees of free speech—even if they were violating traffic laws. When asked about the rights of people who wanted to go to the World's Fair without interference from demonstrators, Marshall replied that fair-goers' rights were not compromised by the protest. "They'll go around to another entrance," he said.

In another example of his central belief in individual rights, Marshall wrote the majority opinion for a three-judge panel that found a murder suspect could not be tried twice for the same crime by a Monroe County, New York, court. The opinion, *Hetenyi v. Wilkins* (1965), was the first time that federal law prohibiting double jeopardy was extended to local courts.

Although his work on the court did not make national news, Marshall had adjusted to life on the federal bench after four years. He was respected by his fellow judges, he had lifetime tenure in a good-paying job, and he had a happy life in New York. His sons were in good schools, and he had a steady routine with his wife and friends. Then, in July 1965, he got a phone call.

As he was eating in the judges' dining room, a bailiff came running over to his table. Panting and red-faced, the bailiff could barely speak once he got Marshall's attention. Concerned, Marshall said, "Fred, what in the world is wrong?"

"The president wants to speak to you," the bailiff sputtered. "He's on the phone!" Marshall gave him a bewildered look and asked: "The president of what?"

"The president of the United States!"[34]

CHAPTER 29

Johnson's Man

IN JULY 1965, when President Johnson called Thurgood Marshall, the civil rights movement had taken to the streets with marches, protests, and even riots. With TV news cameras rolling, state troopers in Selma, Alabama, had beaten people demanding their voting rights. Malcolm X had been assassinated and become a martyr. Black militancy was on the rise, and whites were fleeing the cities. In the middle of all this turmoil, Marshall had unique status. He was a respected black leader, a living symbol of America's ability to achieve peaceful racial progress, and an advocate of law and order.

As he went to get Johnson's call, Marshall was puzzled. Why would the president be calling him? He had met Johnson in Texas during the 1940s. At that time Marshall was fighting the all-white primary system. Later the NAACP had supported Johnson in his race for the U.S. Senate. He had bumped into him a few times in Washington when Johnson had been Senate majority leader. Johnson had even invited him to a White House Fellows ceremony a few days earlier. But that had been their only recent contact.

When he got to his chambers, Marshall was surprised to find it really was the president of the United States on the phone. They talked for two or three minutes before Johnson, in his abrupt way, said: "I want you to be my solicitor general." The job offer hit Marshall like a lightning bolt. It was a godsend for a man who was trudging along—if not bored—as an appeals court judge. But he immediately realized that he couldn't leap at the job. He had deep concerns about leaving a lifetime appointment with a guaranteed pension. And the annual salary of the solicitor general was $4,500 less than his current salary.

"Well, Mr. President, I'll have to think it over," he responded. The president told him to take as much time as he wanted. A flattered, excited Marshall went home to tell Cissy about the offer and the prospect of a high-pressure job in the vicious political hothouse that was Washington, D.C.

As soon as Marshall arrived at the office the next morning, the phone rang and his secretary announced that the president was on the line again. The judge was surprised to hear from him so quickly: "Well, Mr. President, you said I had all the time I needed." Johnson replied, "You've had it." In an instant Marshall had to make a decision that would affect the rest of his life. Marshall decided to grab the moment and the excitement. His voice breaking with emotion, he told the president he would be glad to be the nation's first black solicitor general.

The next day, July 9, 1965, Marshall flew to Washington to see Johnson in the Oval Office. He was excited but played coy by complaining about the loss of salary he faced if he took the job. Johnson was not sympathetic: "You don't have to tell me. I can tell you everything about your situation, including what you've got in your bank account. I'm still asking you to make the sacrifice."

As the two large, strong-minded men sat in the quiet of the Oval Office, the blustery and charming Johnson made two points to Marshall.

First, he complimented Marshall's ability as a lawyer and said he needed an outstanding legal mind to represent him before the Supreme Court. The compliment was not made casually. Marshall would be replacing Archibald Cox, who had stayed on as solicitor general after Kennedy's assassination. The Harvard professor was widely respected for his hard work and knowledge of the smallest detail of the law. Cox had not wanted to leave, but when he sent a note to the president asking for a vote of confidence, Johnson used it as an opportunity to move him out. Given the ruffled feathers in legal circles, there were sure to be questions about whether Marshall was up to the task of replacing the esteemed Cox.

Johnson's second point had to do with the color of Marshall's skin. The president told him that he wanted people, young people of both races, to come into the Supreme Court and ask who was that "Negro" up there arguing? And somebody would say, "He's the solicitor general of the United States."

Johnson did his usual masterful job of persuasion. But nothing the president said was as large in Marshall's mind as his unspoken desire to be on the Supreme Court. However, the president refused to make any promises about future appointments. "You know, this has nothing to do with any Supreme Court appointment," the president said. "I want that distinctly understood—there's no quid pro quo here at all. You do your job. If you don't do it, you go out. If you do it, you stay here. And that's all there is to it."[1]

Contrary to what Johnson may have told Marshall, the president had given thought to putting him on the Supreme Court. Johnson viewed the solicitor general's job as a tryout for the possible first black associate justice of the Court. Ramsey Clark, then a deputy attorney general and a fellow Texan, had mentioned Marshall's name to the president a few weeks earlier while sailing, and the president had seemed excited.

"I saw Marshall give a speech at a luncheon in '65," Clark said in a later interview. Shortly after that speech the president asked Clark and his wife, Georgia, to come on a boat trip with him and Lady Bird Johnson. Johnson and Clark had gone belowdecks to talk about appointments. The president lay down on a bunk as the conversation droned on. Finally the two came to the opening for solicitor general.

"When I mentioned Marshall's name, Johnson sat bolt upright," Clark recalled. "He nearly bumped his head on the low ceiling. I don't think he ever thought of anybody else; he wanted Thurgood Marshall to be his solicitor general." Clark recalled that the first words out of Johnson's mouth were, 'Ah ha, he's going on the Supreme Court.'"[2]

Johnson later confirmed that he intended to put Marshall on the high court the minute he appointed him as solicitor general. "I did not tell Marshall of my intentions at this time," Johnson said in an interview. "But I fully intended to eventually appoint him to the Court. I believed that a black man had to be appointed to that body. . . . I wanted him to serve as Solicitor General as an advocate to prove to everyone, including the President, what he could do."[3]

Johnson also told his wife, who wrote the pledge in her diary: "Lyndon admires Judge Thurgood Marshall and spoke of the possibility of asking him to be Solicitor General, and then if he proved himself outstanding, perhaps when a vacancy on the Supreme Court opened up, he might nominate him as a justice—the first of his race," Lady Bird wrote two weeks before Marshall's selection as solicitor general was announced.[4]

When Johnson called his attorney general, Nicholas Katzenbach, to tell him about Marshall's appointment, Katzenbach warned the president that if Marshall did not eventually get a seat on the Supreme Court, it could cause problems: "If you do that, you are making an implied promise." Katzenbach was concerned that if a vacancy opened and Johnson failed to put Marshall on the Court, the president would have to deal with the political fallout, from both liberals and blacks. "All of Johnson's record on civil rights, and it was a hell of a record, would go down the drain," said Katzenbach.[5]

On Tuesday, July 13, Marshall and Johnson walked into the White House press room to announce that Marshall would become solicitor general. The moment the two appeared, Marshall could hear whispers as reporters began asking each other, "Who's resigning from the Supreme Court?" Once they quieted down, Johnson formally introduced Marshall, calling his nominee one of the country's most distinguished advocates.

There was immediate concern that segregationists would fight Marshall's confirmation, much as they had tried to kill his nomination to the Second Circuit. However, Johnson privately assured him that he could "take care of the confirmation." Putting an arm around his new nominee, the president told him, "If you can stand the gaff, I can."[6]

Johnson held a strong hand in dealing with Marshall's potential opponents in the Senate. As the former majority leader, he knew a lot of secrets about the senators. And he had nominated former Mississippi governor James P. Coleman, a renowned segregationist, for a federal judgeship. The nomination had its critics, but the president had firmly supported Coleman. Johnson let segregationists know that if Marshall's nomination faltered, his support for Coleman would disappear.[7]

Two weeks later Sen. Robert Kennedy, the former attorney general and Marshall's old foe, introduced Marshall to a Senate Judiciary subcommittee. "I think that he has big shoes [to fill] with his predecessor Mr. Archie Cox," said Kennedy. "But I know of the talents Thurgood Marshall has. . . . He will make one of the great solicitor generals in the history of this country."

The hearing opened with Sen. Jacob Javits asking the nominee if he could represent the government in civil rights cases since he had been the NAACP's chief counsel. Marshall replied, "I am an advocate and I represent the U.S. government and I will do the best I can." He said "personal emotions" did not matter. Marshall added, as proof of his legal skills, that none of his more than 100 rulings on the Second Circuit had been overturned by the Supreme Court.

Javits, exploring whether Marshall was being primed for a high court appointment, also asked him why he was giving up a fully tenured judgeship for a temporary political appointment. Marshall dodged the question with a patriotic response. "The president of the United States told me that he thought I was the best person at the time to represent the United States," he replied.[8] In marked contrast to his second circuit nomination only one fifteen-minute meeting was held and the subcommittee voted 5–0 to recommend Marshall's nomination to the full Senate. On August 11, 1965, less than a month after he was nominated, the full Senate confirmed Marshall, without debate, to be solicitor general.

Between the time Marshall was confirmed by the Senate and when he was sworn in as solicitor general, the nation was shaken by rioting in the Watts section of Los Angeles. More and more Marshall became the federal government's walking symbol for a responsible, peaceful civil rights movement. The president had him in a front-row seat at the Capitol for the signing of the Voting Rights Act. And Johnson appointed him to lead a delegation to Sweden for a UN conference on crime. At that conference Marshall was in charge of a group of Americans that included his former nemesis from the NAACP, Bob Carter.

He was back in Washington by August 24 and was sworn in by Associate Justice Hugo Black in the White House Cabinet Room. President Johnson spoke to a large group, including Supreme Court Justice Tom Clark (Ramsey Clark's father) and FBI Director J. Edgar Hoover. Also in attendance were more than two dozen of Marshall's family members from Baltimore. His brother, Aubrey, who was working as a doctor in Delaware, led the family delegation.

"Thurgood Marshall symbolizes what is best about our American society: the belief that human rights must be satisfied through the orderly process of law," President Johnson said in remarks that had particularly strong resonance in the week after the Watts riots. At one point Johnson slipped up and referred to his new appointee as "Justice Marshall." He quickly corrected himself, but everyone in the room took note.[9]

While Johnson did not say it, Marshall now ranked as the top black official ever to serve in the U.S. government. He outranked Robert Weaver, the head of the housing department, which was not yet a cabinet-level post.

During the swearing-in ceremony, Johnson whispered to Marshall that he had heard his family was remaining in New York. The new solicitor general tried to change the subject. The president, however, was genuinely upset. "What the hell is this about you commuting?" he said, pushing his face next to Marshall's ear. "But—" Marshall stammered. Johnson, now standing face-to-face with Marshall, planted a stiff finger in Marshall's chest and said, "But nothing! Move down!" [10]

Three weeks later Marshall sent the president a note: "I took your gentle hint, which you gave me at the swearing-in ceremony, and am moving the family to Washington. Cissy and the boys will be down early next week. The boys will be going to Georgetown Day School, and I have rented a small house at 64-A 'G' St, SW." The president wrote back that he was "delighted." [11]

The idea of a black solicitor general did cause some concern at the Justice Department. Ralph Spritzer, the chief assistant solicitor, recalled in an interview that even before Marshall arrived there was particular nervousness from one secretary from South Carolina. The woman told Spritzer that she had never worked for a black man and said, "I don't know if I'd be comfortable." At the time there was only one other black person in the office, Grafton Gaines, a courier. Gaines was very aware that whites were uptight about the arrival of a black boss. But to his surprise the trepidation soon melted away. "When Marshall walked in, he had his hand a going and said 'Good morning, how you doing.' He walked in there and acted so relaxed, and you could see them relaxing. And it was just like he had been there all his life," said Gaines. [12]

Marshall made a special point of being friendly to the white secretary from South Carolina. After a week she not only had decided to stay but was telling co-workers that she loved her job. [13]

But for the all-white legal staff the concern was not only about race. The lawyers didn't know whether Marshall could handle the work when it went beyond civil rights cases. "There was such apprehension," recalled Louis Claiborne, another attorney working in the office. "People were pleasantly surprised to see that Marshall was much more up to it than they had imagined." [14]

*   *   *

Within his first two months in Washington, Marshall was busy with the transition in his office as well as at home. In addition to getting Cissy and the boys settled, he had to prepare to make his initial appearance before the Supreme Court. Like any other solicitor general, he had the option of sending one of his assistants to argue cases. But Marshall, who had not argued before the Court since 1960, when he was still with the LDF, felt the need to make a statement.

His first case involved a Texas woman, Ethel Mae Yazell, who claimed the government was wrongly trying to get her to repay a government small business loan. Her lawyers argued that her husband had taken the loan, and under Texas law they could not hold her responsible for his default. Marshall, wearing the traditional tuxedolike jacket with a long tail and striped dark pants, argued the Texas law was "archaic." His presentation took only eighteen minutes.

Not only was Marshall's presentation brief but he was sufficiently at ease to joke afterward with reporters. The fifty-seven-year-old lawyer told them he was not nervous. One newsman described Marshall's performance this way: " 'Hell,' says the 33rd solicitor general of the United States, putting on a cotton-field Negro dialect, 'I ain't had de jitter in de Supreme Court since de day I was admitted to practice nearly 30 years ago. But dat day, oh boy. You couldda heard mah knees knockin' way down in de hall.' " [15]

Despite his grand entrance the Court later ruled against Marshall and for Mrs. Yazell. But that small case was quickly forgotten as he presented the government's arguments in a series of high-profile cases, particularly a sensational case involving the murders of three young civil rights workers.

Michael Schwerner, Andrew Goodman, and James Chaney, ages twenty-four, twenty, and twenty-one, were traveling through the small town of Philadelphia, Mississippi, on their way to investigate the burning of a nearby black church. They were arrested for allegedly speeding, put in jail, and then released. As they left the jail, some of the deputies followed them. It was unclear what happened next, but their bodies were found a month and a half later, buried in an earthen dam. The three had been shot with .38-caliber bullets, and Chaney, the lone black worker, had been brutally beaten. Twenty-one white men from Philadelphia, including the deputy sheriff, were charged with murder, but charges were later dropped in Mississippi state court. The federal government then brought federal civil rights charges against eighteen of the men.

In November 1965, Marshall appeared before the Supreme Court to defend the federal government's authority in bringing the charges. He cited an 1870 federal statute outlawing "conspiracies" intended to intimidate blacks and deny them their constitutional rights. Lawyers for the accused argued that any charge of murder was the legal responsibility of the state, not the federal government. In a unanimous decision the Supreme Court ruled in Marshall's favor (*U.S. v. Price*). Six of the men were later tried for conspiracy and found guilty.

Marshall soon had two other major victories. First, in January 1966, he argued that Virginia was violating the Twenty-fourth Amendment—which outlawed poll taxes—by requiring its residents to pay a tax to vote in state and local elections. Marshall argued that poll taxes in any election were illegal and had the effect of putting a coin-operated "turnstile" in front of the voting booth. The Court, in a 6–3 decision, ruled in Marshall's favor (*Harper v. Virginia Board of Elections*).

A few months later the solicitor general broke new ground before the Court by claiming that New York State was violating the Voting Rights Act. The state had prohibited American citizens born in the U.S. territory of Puerto Rico who were literate but spoke only Spanish from voting. The new solicitor general said the government had no problem with requiring that voters be literate; it was opposed to the English-only restriction. The Court ruled 7–2 in favor of Marshall (*Katzenbach v. Morgan*).

While Marshall argued a fair number of cases, he did not spend as much time in court as had Archibald Cox. His predecessor had sometimes argued three or four cases a week, and his style was formal and academic, as if he were lecturing the justices. By contrast, Marshall's style was fairly casual. He was conversational with the justices and deferential to their points. Nonetheless, Marshall was seen as an effective advocate, and fears about his ability to handle anything but civil rights cases faded, even if they did not go away.

As he took control of his new post, Marshall became a well-known figure in the administration. During 1966 he was in and out of the White House, for meetings with the president as well as for state dinners and ceremonies. Marshall and the president frequently talked about civil rights, but their discussions ranged through American policy and history. "I know that when he was solicitor, President Johnson called upon him for advice in many things having nothing to do with civil rights," said Bill Coleman, lawyer and close friend to Marshall. "He and Johnson really got along, they both had that hearty laugh, they were both gutsy, and could tell stories. They were awfully good friends."

"We talked about a lot of things that I ain't gonna talk about," Marshall said later. "Johnson's ambition was, 'That history must show that compared to me, Lincoln was a piker.' He wanted to outdo him. Takes a hell of a lot of doing. But that man, I loved that man."

As Marshall was getting to know Johnson, the president was preoccupied with the military buildup in Vietnam. The war was quickly becoming unpopular, damaging Johnson's public standing day by day. Marshall defended him as a victim of bad advice. "That was the military's fault," he said. "The military got McNamara in a box, and the generals fed this stuff to him, and McNamara parroted it to Johnson. Not once did I go to the White House that McNamara wasn't either going in or going out. He must have gone over there two or three times a day."

Black Nationalists were some of the most vocal critics of Johnson's policy in Vietnam. They pointed out that 20 percent of U.S. troops in Vietnam were black and called it a "race war" run by white politicians who were using blacks to kill Asians. In March 1966, Marshall made a point of hitting at these opponents. He said black soldiers were patriotic, willing to die for their country, and neither black nor white military people should be criticized for fighting Communism. "If our country needs fighting men we are always there," Marshall told a crowd at Bethel Methodist Church in Baltimore.[16]

Marshall's frequent visits to the White House were not limited to serious policy matters. Over glasses of bourbon and Dr Pepper, Johnson and Marshall would also trade gossip. One of their targets was the new senator from New York, the former attorney general, Robert Kennedy. Marshall still remembered Bobby Kennedy's reluctance to nominate him for the Second Circuit, and Johnson viewed the younger brother of the assassinated president as a possible foe in the 1968 Democratic primaries. Johnson regularly dumped on Bobby in his talks with Marshall.

"Whooooo! That started with Bobby," Marshall said in an interview. "They had a big conference in the Kennedy White House on some big deal. And sure enough Johnson heard about it. So he called and wanted to know about the meeting. An aide announced: 'The vice president's on the phone and he wants to know whether he's to come over or not?' And without even covering up the phone, Bobby said, 'We don't need that stupid son of a bitch for nothing. Tell him to go to hell!' "

Marshall said Johnson held a grudge from that point on. When Johnson became president and Bobby Kennedy asked him to support his campaign for the Senate, Johnson quipped: "Remember what you said about me before. That goes for you now!"

Away from Washington's political wars, Marshall led a cloistered life.

The family lived in a small town house, hidden in a new development not far from his downtown office. He had some small dinner parties, where guests recalled that he liked to carve roasts with a new invention, the electric knife. Generally, Marshall spent little time on the social scene or hanging out with friends.

"When he moved down to D.C., from that point on they took Thurgood out of circulation, told him he couldn't move around, talking, catting around, and all that kind of stuff," said his friend Monroe Dowling. "And he started getting disagreeable. You know, he couldn't play around with women, or even come out and play poker with the boys and things like that." The new solicitor general, who by now had to wear bifocals everywhere, also began to put on weight in his new sedentary life. A *New York Times Magazine* piece on Marshall claimed that he now weighed far more than two hundred pounds: "While not exactly fat, Marshall is comfortably thick, with a double chin that hangs like a testament to a man whose idea of physical exercise is to avoid all thoughts of it."[17]

To blow off steam while under the strict demands of a bureaucratic job, Marshall began to drink more. His colleagues in the Solicitor General's Office were impressed with a man who could have three martinis at lunch. He smoked cigarettes constantly. And there were stories about the boss being free with his hands around women at dinners and social parties.

"He did have a tendency to let his hands stray," said Louis Claiborne. "I don't know to what extent that occurred. I know that it was said that he had touched—I mean, in these days it would have been called sexual harassment, I'm sure. I don't know that he ever forced himself on anybody. I think probably his manner of being affectionate was less than entirely subtle." *Ebony* magazine quoted a "friend" of Marshall's as referring to the same problem: "His human frailties are the same as every male," the source said. In the same article Marshall's appetite for a good drink was touched on delicately by a person who said, "He never lets a highball get in the way of a case."[18]

His personal flaws, however, never created a scandal. Instead, his shortcomings led friends to feel that they had to look out for the first black solicitor general and a man who was in a position to rise even further. Despite all his disavowals there was persistent talk that Marshall was on track for the Supreme Court. Ted Poston of the *New York Post*, an old friend of Marshall's, frequently reminded his readers that Justices Reed and Jackson had both occupied the solicitor general's job before being elevated to the high court. And when *The New York Times* sent a reporter to interview Marshall for a magazine article, Marshall had to knock down several questions about whether he was being prepped for the high court.[19]

At the Solicitor General's Office, Marshall was busy. As the government's lawyer, he sometimes had to handle cases in which he was forced to go against his lifelong tendency to side with the little guy. In one case a defendant claimed that his confession was illegal because federal agents had not informed him of his right to remain silent and have a lawyer while being questioned. Marshall responded that having federal agents take the time to spell out constitutional rights to every defendant interfered with their ability to get to the bottom of the case quickly.

"We start from the premise that it is essential to the protection of society that law enforcement officers be permitted to interrogate an arrested person," Marshall told the Court. "An inflexible Constitutional rule turning on the presence or absence of council or on the recitation or omission of a warning may be easier to apply, but we believe that it will, more often than not, cast out the baby with the bath water."

The high court disagreed. Ruling on Marshall's case and others, grouped under the title *Miranda v. Arizona*, the justices said that under the Fifth Amendment every defendant had a right to avoid self-incrimination. Confessions were invalid, the Court said, unless the suspects were first informed that they could remain silent and ask for a lawyer.

The 5–4 ruling was a landmark for the Supreme Court in setting out the rights of any suspect. *The New York Times*, in a front-page article, described the ruling as imposing "sweeping limitations on the power of the police to question suspects in their custody." *The Washington Post* later described Marshall's loss on the *Miranda* ruling as "his most notable defeat as Solicitor General."[20] The *Miranda* case also established that Thurgood Marshall had completed the transition from the NAACP lawyer who was frequently at odds with the FBI to the government lawyer who was able comfortably to represent a federal agent's point of view before the Supreme Court.

* * *

Marshall also demonstrated his ability to play hardball Washington politics when he found himself caught in a nasty cross fire between President Johnson, FBI Director Hoover, and Sen. Robert Kennedy. The case involved Fred Black, a prominent Washington lobbyist who was under FBI investigation for alleged ties to the Mafia. Black was never charged with working for organized crime, but a Justice Department investigation led to charges of tax evasion, and Black was found guilty. The conviction was appealed to the Supreme Court, but they refused to review the case.

As the Justice Department had prepared to deal with Black's appeal, they uncovered the fact that the FBI had placed electronic eavesdropping devices in Black's hotel suites in Washington and Las Vegas. Some of the taped conversations included talks between Black and his lawyer, which as privileged lawyer-client exchanges were considered confidential by law. Alarmed at the potential damage to their case, department lawyers began pressing Marshall to inform the Supreme Court about the bugging. The lawyers hoped the high court would not throw out the case if the government admitted its error.

When Hoover found out that the Justice Department wanted to tell the Court of the buggings, he exploded, fearing that he would be the fall guy if Black's conviction were overturned. And he argued there was no reason for the department to inform the Court about the taps because those conversations had not been used to convict Black on the tax evasion charges.

Attorney General Nicholas Katzenbach and Marshall decided that despite Hoover's objections, they were obligated to tell the justices about the buggings. Hoover then demanded that Marshall tell the Court that former Attorney General Robert Kennedy had authorized the tap. He claimed Kennedy had intimate knowledge of the FBI buggings and had even listened to taped conversations. Kennedy, however, denied that he had listened to any such tapes and claimed never to have authorized Black's bugging.

When on May 24 Marshall sent a letter to the Court revealing the illegal electronic surveillance, he sided with Kennedy and Katzenbach. He made no mention of any Justice Department authorization for the FBI's bugging. Hoover and the FBI were left exposed, and a furious Hoover came out swinging. He threatened to issue a press release saying that Kennedy had signed those authorizations. Hoover also insisted on a meeting with the president's top aides to complain. On May 27, 1966, Hoover first wrote to Marvin Watson, one of Johnson's assistants, that Robert Kennedy "was either lying or had a very convenient lack of memory."[21] Watson let the president know that political warfare had broken out between Hoover, Katzenbach, and Kennedy—with Marshall caught somewhere in between. Johnson called his solicitor general in for a half-hour meeting in the Oval Office the next day.

In a later interview Marshall said Johnson expressed a strong distaste for bugging. Marshall asked, "Hey, you know about this bugging business?" Johnson said he did. He wanted Marshall to tell the Court that Bobby Kennedy had dirty hands in the *Black* case. He felt it should be known that Kennedy had at least given Hoover a general authorization for secret surveillance of organized crime. And, most important, the president wanted Marshall to confirm Hoover's claim that Kennedy was fully aware that Black's rooms were tapped.

The FBI knew Johnson was on Hoover's side. One of Hoover's top aides, Cartha DeLoach, wrote in a memo that Johnson's personal secretary at the White House "told me in strict confidence on Saturday, June 4, 1966, that the President . . . is chiefly concerned over the fact that the Attorney General [Katzenbach] appears to be 'fronting' for others, namely Bobby Kennedy." [22]

Marshall was trapped. He was caught in Johnson's fight with Kennedy as well as in Katzenbach's feud with Hoover. While he tried to figure out how to shelter himself in the political storm, a new player entered the game. Associate Justice Abe Fortas, who had been appointed to the Supreme Court by Johnson in 1965, began meeting with the FBI about the case. "Justice Fortas stated that the entire matter boiled down to a continuing fight [between Johnson and Kennedy] for the Presidency," DeLoach wrote in a memo. "If the facts, as possessed by the FBI, concerning Kennedy's approval of wiretapping were made known to the general public then it would serve to completely destroy Kennedy [with liberal voters]."

Fortas convinced his colleagues on the Court to request that Marshall provide more information on the extent of the FBI's bugging and the contents of the tapes. He was looking to embarrass Kennedy and help Johnson. Fortas also took the opportunity to deride Marshall. He played heavily on Hoover's fear that Marshall was willing to let the FBI director take the blame. Fortas told FBI Agent DeLoach that Marshall had "ineptly and inadequately presented the matter of electronic devices to the Supreme Court." Fortas added that in his opinion Marshall had also given a "stupid presentation to the Supreme Court" on how the FBI handled confessions a few months earlier during arguments over *Miranda* warnings. Hoover later wrote in a personal memo that he had heard from a Supreme Court justice, undoubtably Fortas, that Marshall was just a "dumb Negro." Justice Fortas kept the president informed about what was going on, even bragging to DeLoach that he was going to "slip in the back door and see the president" about the matter.[23]

Despite all the behind-the-scenes maneuvering, the Supreme Court's request for more information had still not been answered. After two more weeks of heated meetings and phone calls, Marshall responded to the high court with a letter that walked a high wire over the chasm between Kennedy and Hoover. Without naming Kennedy, Marshall wrote that past attorneys general had allowed the FBI to use electronic bugging in cases involving "the interest of internal security or national safety." With that general authorization, Marshall told the Court, the FBI did place electronic bugs on Black.

Marshall's letter pleased all sides. Kennedy continued to deny that he had knowledge of any specific illegal surveillance of Black. Hoover was satisfied that the Justice Department had acknowledged authorization for the surveillance. And in deference to President Johnson, Marshall's letter painted the current administration as the good guys who had stopped illegal bugging practices permitted under previous administrations. Marshall wrote: "Present department practice, adopted July 1965, in conformity with the policies declared by the president on June 30, 1965 . . . prohibits the use of such listening devices."[24]

The letter also worked for Black. The Supreme Court ordered a review of his conviction. He was retried and this time acquitted of tax evasion. For his part Marshall had the fortunate look of a man who had survived a political war. Katzenbach recalled how delicately Marshall handled the situation: "Whatever Thurgood's feelings about [Kennedy or Hoover] were, he was very helpful to me in working that out, because it protected Bobby and it protected Hoover."

Shortly after Marshall had sent his memo on the *Black* case to the Supreme Court, he got a surprise invitation to the White House for a party celebrating Hoover's fiftieth year at the Justice Department. "Johnson said, 'The director told me to invite you,' " Marshall recalled with great pride many years later.

*   *   *

While Marshall was finding his way through Washington's political thicket, he continued to play a key role as the top black figure in the U.S. government. For the second straight year several big cities were dealing with summer riots. To calm the racial storm the administration invited civil rights leaders to Washington for a conference called "To Fulfill These Rights." Johnson wanted the nation to see federal policy makers and black leaders working together to provide more jobs and better education for blacks. But the conference itself was in danger of collapsing. The president's approval ratings had fallen sharply as black militants, riots, and nationwide anger over the escalating Vietnam War had the administration on the defensive.

"There was a very high degree of nervous anxiety over the conference, a lot of worry that it would be a disaster," said Harry McPherson, the White House counsel, who had to get on the phone with the president several times to reassure him that it was wise to go ahead with his appearance at the conference. But the situation outside the conference, at the Sheraton Park Hotel in Washington, was growing worse. "We had pickets, we had all kinds of stuff. There were a lot of guys in blue overalls with kerchiefs around their heads and sullen looks on their faces," McPherson recalled.

To calm things down, McPherson thought about posting policemen or plainclothes FBI agents inside the conference. But the sight of lawmen might offend black leaders. Louis Martin, the black vice chair of the Democratic National Committee, came up with a better idea. He got sexy co-eds from Howard University, dressed in evening gowns, to act as hostesses for the event. The young women transformed the evening, defusing the mood of militancy. There was still concern, however, that when the president stood to speak, he might be shouted down.

Surprisingly, the president was greeted like a hero. "LBJ got to this huge hall, and the crowd was terrific. They were standing and cheering, 'L-B-J, L-B-J,' " McPherson recalled in an interview. "And Johnson made an altogether full-throated speech of warmth and appreciation and praise. And then he said, 'It gives me the greatest pleasure to introduce your main speaker for this evening. A man that I am proud to say is my friend and that I am proud to say I have helped to put in a position to serve America—Thurgood Marshall.' Well, Thurgood had tears in his eyes, and he was shaking hands with Johnson—and I'll never forget—the applause went on and on."

When the applause quieted down, Marshall said, "Thirty years ago, when I began in this business, you wouldn't have heard a president of the United States saying something like that about somebody like me." McPherson remembered a spontaneous ovation: "Boy, the place—people stood up and yelled. Everybody understood Thurgood—there was no one like him."[25]

Thurgood Marshall's elevation to a national symbol of racial peace was confirmed a month later when President Truman, retired and living in Missouri, asked him to be his stand-in at ceremonies honoring the former president in Israel. The Israelis had put Truman's name on a center for peace studies at Hebrew University as a tribute to his role in establishing the Jewish state. Marshall was pictured in newspapers worldwide as representing America.

When Marshall returned from Israel, fallout from the Black case was still in the air. Attorney General Katzenbach apparently had shown too much concern for Bobby Kennedy's reputation in President Johnson's eyes. He was out. Johnson decided he wanted someone totally loyal to him in charge of the Justice Department. His acting replacement, Ramsey Clark, was a fellow Texan and a personal friend to the president. Clark was a tall, quiet man with wavy dark hair and a slow drawl, a graduate of the University of Chicago Law School. He was more liberal than most of Johnson's Texas cronies, better educated and younger, without any of the racial hang-ups of the older crowd.

The change in leadership at the Justice Department gave Marshall more prominence. As the acting attorney general, Clark relied on the older Marshall's advice, as well as Marshall's independent relationship with the president. In fact, Marshall's name was briefly floated as a possible candidate for permanent attorney general. But most prominently, his name was being mentioned as the person for Johnson to nominate to the Supreme Court whenever a seat opened. "A negro on the U.S. Supreme Court bench by 1968—the year of the next presidential election—is the goal of the Lyndon Johnson Administration in Washington," *Jet* magazine wrote in its December 1, 1966, edition. Marshall was the most likely candidate to get the job.[26]

Jet's report was right. In private conversations Johnson still said he wanted to name a black person to the Supreme Court. But in January 1967, Johnson began to have doubts about moving Marshall to the bench. The president told the acting attorney general that he was displeased over Marshall's failure to point a finger at Kennedy for authorizing wiretaps and electronic bugging. Johnson said it was "disgusting" that Marshall had "humiliated" himself in front of the Supreme Court by defending the use of eavesdropping devices. He added, "I didn't think he was of very strong character" to have done it.[27]

Johnson was also concerned that Marshall was too liberal at a time when the country was going through riots and crime waves and a substantial right-wing backlash was under way. Law-and-order voters would not see Marshall as anything but soft on crime. "The votes they [liberals] wanted, he'd give them," Johnson told Clark, later adding that putting Marshall on the Court might mean that his hopes for reelection in 1968 were "long gone."

The president's discussions with Clark had the sharp edge of political maneuvering. Johnson knew that Clark was close to the solicitor general and wanted him to have a seat on the Court. The president, in turn, was using Clark to force open that seat. Johnson told him that he could not become the permanent attorney general unless his father, Tom Clark, resigned from the Supreme Court. Ramsey Clark was reluctant to see his father leave, but Johnson persisted. He told the younger Clark that if he became attorney general while his father remained on the Court, then "every taxidriver in the country" would assume there was favoritism at work.[28]

In February, President Johnson announced that he was nominating Ramsey Clark to become the permanent attorney general. The same day Tom Clark announced that he was stepping down from the Supreme Court at the end of the term. The timing of the announcements seemed to indicate that a deal had been cut. But the younger Clark said in an interview thirty years later that if there was a deal between his dad and the president, he was not in on it.

There were, however, many people in Washington who thought the president had cleverly manipulated father and son to open a Supreme Court seat. "Johnson said, I can get rid of Tom Clark by putting Ramsey in as attorney general. That's the way LBJ's mind worked," said Katzenbach in an interview. "What I think LBJ did was tell Tom Clark, I'm going to make Ramsey attorney general, and I'm sorry that's going to raise a problem for you, Tom, and I'm not going to do it if you don't want to resign."

Justice Clark's decision to quit the Supreme Court at the end of the term, June 1967, meant the president had four months to name his replacement. New candidates for the seat began popping up, including Rep. Wilbur Mills, Sen. Abraham Ribicoff, and Labor Secretary Willard Wirtz.

Growing concerned, Louis Martin began lobbying the president to select Marshall, who now seemed to have fallen from favor. The president gave Martin some strongly negative comments about Marshall, telling him that Marshall "wasn't worth a damn" as an administrator and he didn't "pay any attention to half the cases; he just gets those he likes."

Katzenbach, who was now at the State Department, was hearing similar critiques from the president. "I think probably he heard stories about Thurgood being lazy—he didn't work all that hard—he'd leave at four, four-thirty," said Katzenbach. "I expect Thurgood always had a little bit of a drinking problem, but it never interfered with his work."

Johnson's doubts about Marshall led him to ask Katzenbach about other black lawyers who were qualified to be on the Court. Katzenbach warned the president that in the black public's mind, there was only one renowned black lawyer, Thurgood Marshall. "I think [Johnson] was seriously thinking about Hastie," Katzenbach recalled in an interview. "He would have been fine, as a member of the Court, nothing wrong with Bill Hastie. It was just that the first black on the Supreme Court in that time, in my view had to be Thurgood."

Marshall's supporters had several points in their favor. One, the president genuinely liked Marshall and continued to see him regularly, both for business and to drink and tell stories. Two, Johnson considered Marshall a man in his own image, a person who had worked his way up from the bottom, not a person born to wealth. "He and Marshall could talk the same language," recalled Jack Valenti, who was one of the president's top aides. "The chemistry, I'll tell you, is so important." [29]

Maybe most important, Johnson wanted his name in the history books as the first president to appoint a black person to the Supreme Court. "Johnson believed in civil rights. He thought we ought to do it," said Harry McPherson, the White House legal counsel. "He said he wanted to change Texas, he wanted to change the South. And now he wanted to say, 'I did it, I've integrated the Supreme Court.' "

On the last day of the court's term, June 12, 1967, Associate Justice Tom Clark's resignation took effect. Clark told reporters that his replacement would more than fill his shoes, heightening rumors about who would be Johnson's choice. That night Thurgood and Cissy Marshall went to a party in Clark's honor. The president, full of energy and charm, was there. But to Marshall's dismay Johnson pulled him aside at one point and told him not to expect the job.

On Tuesday morning, however, Marshall was told to stop by the Oval Office. After waiting for several minutes in a room outside the door, Marshall walked in and chatted casually with the president. Suddenly,

Johnson said, "You know something, Thurgood? . . . I'm going to put you on the Supreme Court." Before Marshall walked out of the White House that day, the president, changing from his smiling face to a serious expression, told him: "Well, I guess our friendship is about busted up now." Marshall recalled that Tom Clark had been very good friends with President Truman but had voted against the president's wishes in a major case. "Tom Clark really socked it to Truman—his very best friend." Even at this moment, Marshall showed his strong independent streak and told Johnson, "I would have no hesitancy in socking it to you. Do we understand each other?" Smiling, Johnson told him he was certain he had made the right choice and said, "I'm glad we understand each other."

For all their brave talk, from that moment on Marshall and Johnson were inextricably linked. Johnson's political fortunes for reelection were on the line with a Supreme Court nominee who was no cinch to be confirmed. This was not going to be the easy trick that Johnson had managed when he got Marshall confirmed as solicitor general. Hearings on Marshall's nomination to the Supreme Court were sure to become a stage for all sides in the nation's racial turmoil.

Johnson needed a happy, quick confirmation for Marshall. And Marshall needed Johnson's skills and support as a master politician to get him through potentially treacherous hearings. Marshall did not want to be just the first black man ever nominated to the high court. He wanted to be the first black Supreme Court justice.

CHAPTER 30

✣

Justice Marshall

Now Marshall was nervous. The three most recent Supreme Court nominees (Byron White, Arthur Goldberg, and Abe Fortas) had gone from nomination to confirmation and a seat on the Court in under two weeks. But the Judiciary Committee delayed the start of hearings on Marshall for a month. They wanted time to go over every inch of his background.

Sen. Robert Byrd of West Virginia wrote to J. Edgar Hoover to ask for FBI checks on Marshall's alleged ties to Communists. Sen. Strom Thurmond of South Carolina had his staff prepare obscure questions on the Constitution to test Marshall's knowledge of the law. Senators Sam Ervin and John McClellan had their staffs comb Marshall's opinions from his time on the Second Circuit as well as read over the briefs he filed as solicitor general. Marshall's opponents were loading up to attack him as a weak lawyer and a judicial activist who was soft on crime. One congressman, Rep. John Rarick of Louisiana, did not bother with research. He immediately put a statement in the *Congressional Record* that described Marshall as a "scamp" and a "cheat."

The FBI had no official comment on Marshall's nomination. The help he had given the bureau over the years apparently neutralized the anger Hoover normally felt toward civil rights activists. Hoover even sent a personal note to Marshall congratulating him. But at the bottom of the director's file copy of the letter, he wrote that in the past Marshall had been "critical of the FBI." The note added that Marshall "had alleged in his criticism that the FBI's record in cases involving Negroes was notably one-sided. . . . On one occasion when he charged misconduct on the part of special agents in the FBI while serving as a judge, he was requested to supply details . . . and never answered the request." The note also mentioned that Marshall, as solicitor general, had been involved with disclosing FBI wiretaps to the Supreme Court.[1]

Despite these privately held reservations, Hoover gave Marshall his public support. There was no indication that he leaked any damaging material to segregationist senators on the Judiciary Committee. Marshall had caged a raging lion that could have destroyed his career.

Still, the delayed start of the hearings gave the segregationist press time to take shots at him. The *Lynchburg News* began its editorial by supposedly quoting a Marshall speech to black leaders at Howard University in 1961: "Wait and see what I do when I get on the Supreme Court—I will send every whitey to jail I can." The paper added that Marshall belonged to Communist groups and that he would fall in with a "clique of soul brothers" on the high court, namely Earl Warren, Abe Fortas, William O. Douglas, and William Brennan. "The opinions of these five liberals will continue to distort the shape of American society, institution and culture for years to come."[2]

James J. Kilpatrick, a popular segregationist columnist and genuine student of the Court, similarly wrote that Marshall was a liberal addition to an already left-leaning court. The appointment, Kilpatrick wrote, was "a great tribute to Marshall's own skill and industry. . . . No critic would wish to take away from the heart-warming success story that came to its climax." But he concluded: "All the same, in any conservative view of the workings of the court, the nomination is . . . bad news—and we shall be living with it for the next ten years at least."[3]

While the right wing fired away, liberal and moderate writers praised the nominee as a wonderful American who easily stood astride the nation's racial divide. "He is one of the special ones—a great rumpled bear of a man. . . . Irrepressibly nonchalant, . . . [who] smokes almost compulsively and confronts life with a gargantuan verve that etches him indelibly in the memory of anyone he meets," wrote *Newsweek*. The magazine, describing Marshall as a "black Horatio Alger," added that "America may romanticize its radicals but it more often rewards its reformers. And Marshall is a reformer in the best tradition of the rule of law." Martin Luther King, Jr., was quoted as saying the Marshall nomination was a "momentous step toward a color-blind society."[4]

At the White House there was concern that the delay was giving momentum to senators opposed to the nomination. The president began to discuss with his aides how to keep the nomination afloat. "We had many discussions—his confirmation was a major struggle," Clark recalled in an interview.

The White House decided that one way to build public support for Marshall was to put him on a national commission to study crime and violence in American cities. The idea was to keep Marshall's name in the news as a sober, rational voice able to respond to black militants. He was the only black commissioner. He joined former Supreme Court Associate Justice Arthur Goldberg, then the U.S. ambassador to the United Nations, and Associate Justice John Marshall Harlan on the panel. The White House had put Marshall in the protective company of respected legal minds.

In another strategic move, the president had Marshall speak with the NAACP's Roy Wilkins to ask that civil rights leaders not launch any protests. Johnson felt Marshall stood a better chance of confirmation if the racial tension in the country subsided, at least temporarily. Wilkins told Marshall he was happy to help. "Roy was extremely protective of Thurgood," recalled Herbert Hill, who then was heading the NAACP's labor relations.

The White House was thrilled when the American Bar Association rated Marshall "highly acceptable" as a nominee. James Eastland, chairman of the Senate Judiciary Committee, after prodding from the president, began the hearings on July 13, exactly one month after Johnson had named Marshall as the nominee.

The opening day of the hearings was highlighted by Senator McClellan's questioning. The Arkansan, whose thick, black-framed glasses stood out against his weathered white face, began the hearings by expressing alarm at the nationwide outbreak of riots. Making a statement for more law and order in the streets, McClellan asked Marshall if he would allow police to use wiretaps. And would he try to overturn the *Miranda* decision and permit the police to operate more freely.

Calmly, Marshall said he could not answer because the issues were still being settled in the courts. He repeated the answer several times, but the senator grew irritated and persisted by asking Marshall if he were a judicial activist. Should a judge go beyond the Constitution in making a ruling? "The Constitution is what is written," Marshall said flatly, leaving the senator staring at him. As he had been coached by White House advisers, Marshall said nothing more.

McClellan, in disgust, finally stopped asking questions. "I will not pursue it any further at the moment but I must say to you that this leaves me without the necessary information I need . . . to consent to your appointment," McClellan said. Marshall had lost his vote.

The hearings resumed the next day. North Carolina's senator Sam Ervin, a large man with heavy jowls who was a Harvard-trained lawyer and an ardent segregationist, took the lead by peppering Marshall with questions about how judges should interpret the Constitution. In the aftermath of the *Brown* case, Ervin and other southern politicians had become bitterly opposed to judges who asserted individual and minority rights over states' rights. When Ervin asked Marshall if judges should stick to what was written in the Constitution, a states' rights argument, Marshall replied, "Yes, Senator, with the understanding that the Constitution is meant to be a living document." Senator Ervin scolded Marshall for talking about a living Constitution: "That statement does not mean to me that the Constitution is a living document; it means that the Constitution is dead and we are ruled by the personal notions of the temporary occupants of the Supreme Court."

Ervin also turned to the *Miranda* ruling and asked Marshall if the courts should accept voluntary confessions when the suspects had no lawyers and had not been told of their right to remain silent. Marshall, speaking slowly, as if considering his response, said: "Well, Senator, the word *voluntary* gets me in trouble. . . . I tried a case in Oklahoma where the man 'voluntarily confessed' after he was beaten up for six days." The hearing room erupted with laughter.

Ervin and Marshall continued to spar, with Ervin trying to get Marshall to disavow the *Miranda* rules and Marshall repeatedly explaining that he could not talk in specifics. Ervin finally replied, "If you have no opinions on what the Constitution means at this time you ought not to be confirmed." The hearings were going badly for the nominee, and the Johnson White House was distressed.

On July 20, Chairman Eastland, apparently convinced that he and his fellow southerners had Marshall on the ropes, dropped the veil of questions and went to the heart of their fears about putting a black man on the Supreme Court. "Are you prejudiced against white people in the South?" he asked. Lifting his eyeglasses off in a studied manner, Marshall replied: "Not at all. I was brought up, what I would say, 'way up south' in Baltimore, Maryland. And I worked for white people all of my life until I got in college. And from there most of my practice of course was in the South and I don't know, with the possible exception of one person that I was against in the South, that I have any feelings about them."

The response was good but not good enough. Senator Strom Thurmond felt free to launch his own attack, asking Marshall detailed questions about the history of the Thirteenth and Fourteenth Amendments. At one point the senator's questioning became absurdly arcane: "What constitutional difficulties did Rep. John Bingham of Ohio see—or what difficulties do you see—in congressional enforcement of the privileges and immunities clause, article IV, section 2, through the necessary and proper clause of article I, section 8?"

The room fell silent as Thurmond, the former Dixiecrat presidential candidate, then in his sixties, finished a speedy, barely understandable reading of the question in his South Carolina accent. Newly elected Sen. Ted Kennedy, the younger brother of Sen. Robert Kennedy and the assassinated president, looked befuddled. He asked Thurmond for "further clarification" of the question. When Thurmond repeated the same question twice, Kennedy asked if the senator could get out the point of the question in some other way.

"I don't think I can make it any plainer," Thurmond said with a huff and continued to talk about sections and clauses in the Constitution, reaching new heights of obscure reference that lost most listeners.

"That's the answer, I see," said a flabbergasted Senator Kennedy as howls of laughter broke out in the hearing room.

Chairman Eastland called the room back to order and promptly began another volley of fire by asking Marshall if he was aware that the author of a book cited in one of his Second Circuit opinions was a Communist. "I positively did not know that," Marshall replied, adding he would not have cited the book if he had known the author was a Communist.

The question was a bald setup. To bolster charges that Marshall was a Communist, the committee allowed the general counsel for Liberty Lobby, a right-wing political group, to testify. Michael D. Jaffe listed Marshall's association with groups such as the International Juridical Association and the National Lawyers Guild. Jaffe added that Marshall had "a record of duplicity and arrogance unparalleled by that of any nominee to high judicial office in recent times."

Marshall, sticking with the White House game plan, sat calmly and made no reply, giving no credibility to the attack. His body language seemed to say the accusations were beneath his dignity.

The committee recessed for the weekend, and beginning that Friday night President Johnson began nonstop lobbying that carried into Sunday. On Monday, the final day in the two-week hearings, the negative tone had shifted. Several senators voiced kind words for the nominee. Only Senator McClellan took one last shot. He equated the riots in black ghettos around the nation with Marshall's efforts to overturn laws of segregation. "A sentiment has been built up over the country to the point where some people feel that if you don't like the law, violate it," said McClellan, angrily slamming his fist on the dais. "And the Supreme Court takes the position that at its whim it can reverse decisions. . . . No wonder the fellow out in the street thinks—'why can't I do as I please.' "[5]

The hearings ended on July 24, and despite an eleven-day delay orchestrated by Chairman Eastland, President Johnson's power to persuade carried the day. The committee voted on August 3, by 11 to 5, to recommend Marshall be confirmed. But the final vote of the entire Senate was held off until the end of the month. By that time it would be more than two and a half months since Marshall had been nominated. The tension was getting to him and to his family. Marshall's supporters tried to buck him up, but the nominee told friends and his White House helpers that he was concerned. Johnson's staff assured him they had enough votes to seal his confirmation, but Marshall wondered if they were keeping him in the dark.

A few days later Senators Ervin, Thurmond, Eastland, and McClellan engaged in what newspapers called a six-hour mini-filibuster against Marshall's confirmation. Thurmond returned to Marshall's lack of knowledge about the history of the Fourteenth Amendment. The senator derided Marshall as a man who did not even know the names of the people who had drafted the Fourteenth Amendment—which Marshall was supposed to be an expert on. Senator Kennedy interrupted to ask Thurmond if he knew who the members of that committee were. Thurmond turned red and finally said he would let Kennedy know later. "He didn't know himself," said Marshall.

When the filibuster ended, the Senate voted 69–11 to approve Marshall for the high court. Southern senators were almost uniformly opposed to Marshall. But Johnson had succeeded in persuading twenty senators to simply not vote. That was a safety-valve strategy for southerners who were up for reelection. They couldn't afford to be on the record supporting Marshall, but they could live with having missed the vote. And without those votes, the margin of victory was that much greater for Marshall and Johnson.

After the victory the new justice got a call from President Johnson. He congratulated Marshall and immediately added, "But the hell you caused me, goddammit, I never went through so much hell." Marshall, never at a loss for a comeback, said, "It was your idea, it wasn't mine." Johnson cracked a laugh and said, "I guess that's right."

*   *   *

On September 1, 1967, Marshall privately took the judicial oath in the chambers of Justice Hugo Black, a former Ku Klux Klansman from Alabama. Black, a leathery, hunched man at seventy-nine, was the senior member of the Court, having served since 1937. Black's tenure made him the dean of Supreme Court justices, and he volunteered to administer the oath as an act of friendship. He and Marshall had known each other for thirty years, since Marshall and the NAACP had supported Black's nomination to the high court despite criticism from many in the liberal fold.

The new job, in addition to its prestige, came with a $10,000 raise, taking Marshall's salary to $39,500. On one of his first days at the Court, he called a former aide in the Solicitor General's Office, Louis Claiborne, and took him to lunch. "We went to Mr. Henry's on Capitol Hill and had our three martinis," Claiborne said. "He picked me up, and here he was in this cream-colored, gaudy, twenty-foot Cadillac. And he says to me, 'See this, I haven't gotten me my first paycheck yet, but that's the nigger in me. I went out and bought one of these for me and one for Cissy.' "

On Monday, October 2, Marshall was publicly given the constitutional oath at the U.S. Supreme Court, making him the ninety-sixth justice. President Johnson, former justice Tom Clark, Attorney General Ramsey Clark, and several of Marshall's family and friends were there for the ceremony. "People were everywhere when he took his seat," recalled Grafton Gaines, Marshall's courier from the Solicitor General's Office. "You know, that was a big thing. Even the ones that hated blacks came to the Court."[6]

Although he was the first black person in the tight-knit fraternity of justices, the so-called Brethren, Marshall immediately fit in well. He had been before the Court enough times as solicitor general—and as the NAACP's lawyer—that he was greeted as a friend. Justice Byron White, in an interview years later, noted that Marshall had been expected to get a Supreme Court seat for several years. And Justice William Brennan immediately befriended Marshall. "When he came on the Court there were many others delighted, too," Brennan said in an interview later, "but none was so much as I."[7]

Marshall did ruffle a few feathers in his first days, however. He began asking the three justices who had been on the Court in 1954 (Chief Justice Warren, Hugo Black, and William O. Douglas) about an unpublished opinion, written by Justice Stanley Reed, dissenting against the school desegregation ruling. Warren had persuaded Reed to vote with the majority so the *Brown* ruling would be unanimous. Now, thirteen years later, Marshall wanted to see the stillborn dissent.

"I just asked," he said in an interview later. "And nobody knew at all. They all took the Fifth Amendment!" When Marshall persisted over several weeks, unable to get anything from men he called "the great liberals," he went to see his friend Earl Warren. When he asked about the *Brown* case all conversation ceased and the chief justice gave him a chilly stare. At that moment Marshall thought to himself that even though he was now in "the club," he was "still a nigger."

Making one last try, Marshall asked Tom Clark, now in retirement, about *Brown*. The conservative Texan surprised Marshall. He told him about the dissent and said there were no major surprises in it—just an argument in favor of separate but equal as the law. Even after Clark came clean with him, Marshall nursed resentment that his fellow liberal justices had not been direct with him.[8]

But Marshall quickly settled into the routine of a Supreme Court justice. In November, just a month after he joined the Court, Marshall wrote his first opinion in a unanimous decision granting defendants the right to an attorney at every stage of the criminal process. In *Mempa v. Rhay*, a case where a poor teenager was convicted of stealing a car but given no legal counsel at his probation hearing, Marshall wrote: "All we decide here is that a lawyer must be afforded [to the defendant] at this proceeding whether it be labeled a revocation of probation or a deferred sentencing."

Justice Black had been prepared to vote against the defendant, but when he read Marshall's draft of the opinion, he decided to make the ruling unanimous. "Although I voted the other way [in conference among the justices] on the assumption that probation here was separate and apart from sentencing, I am now persuaded by your analysis that the so-called probation was in reality a deferred sentence," Black wrote to Marshall, adding that "your first opinion for the Court [was] written with brevity, clarity and force."⁹

The new justice did not isolate himself from Washington politics as he went about learning the job. President Johnson stayed in touch with him, sending the justice to Africa with Vice President Humphrey as co-leader of the U.S. delegation to Liberian president William Tubman's inaugural. Johnson also invited Marshall to prayer breakfasts, White House luncheons, and some off-the-record meetings. Johnson's presidency was going through a dizzying roller-coaster ride; the war in Vietnam was getting worse, and there were more antiwar protests and race riots at home. Johnson was also facing challengers for the 1968 Democratic nomination, with the biggest name on the horizon belonging to Bobby Kennedy.

A discouraged president sometimes turned to Marshall for private chats. His influence with the civil rights community and Johnson's need to nail down the black vote in the primary in the face of a possible Kennedy candidacy, were key areas where Marshall could provide help. But with crisis aflame on every front, Johnson saw his campaign for a second term as futile. Despite Marshall's support and promises of more help in the future, the president announced his decision not to seek reelection.

The political scene was thrown into chaos. Senators Robert Kennedy and Eugene McCarthy were mounting serious challenges to Johnson's chosen successor, Vice President Humphrey. The sense of turmoil reached a new high on April 4, 1968, when Martin Luther King, Jr., was assassinated in Memphis, Tennessee. Marshall was at the Court when he heard about the shooting and the immediate explosion of riots across the nation.

He phoned the White House and the Justice Department to see what he could do. In the crisis atmosphere, however, there was no clear role for him to play. "The night Dr. King was murdered we were having a staff meeting," Ramsey Clark recalled in an interview. "I went down to Memphis that night, and when I came back, Washington was on fire. When you flew in, you could see flames and smoke going all the way down the Potomac, ten miles or so.

"Thurgood was profoundly affected," Clark continued. "Thurgood came and sat in—almost like a witness, he sat out in the front office. I said, 'What are you doing?' He said, 'I just wanted to be here in case there is anything I could do.' "¹⁰

All Marshall could later recall about the time he spent sitting at the

Justice Department was that it was "a rough night." The morning after the assassination Marshall attended a meeting in the White House Cabinet Room with the president, congressional leaders, and civil rights leaders, including Roy Wilkins of the NAACP and Whitney Young of the National Urban League. The president was worried about urban violence and began the meeting by reading a wire service story quoting Stokely Carmichael, the militant leader of the Student Non-Violent Coordinating Committee, as calling for black people to strike back at white America. After Defense Secretary Clark Clifford said he hoped he would not have to send troops into American cities, the president called on Marshall to speak.

According to Johnson's notes, Marshall's emphasis was on finding a way to end demonstrations because they could lead to more violence: "The important thing is to keep people out of the streets and change the mood in the country." [11] After the meeting, Marshall joined Johnson for a memorial service for King at the White House, followed by an Oval Office meeting with Johnson and Chief Justice Earl Warren.

Marshall's relationship with King created emotional difficulty for him. He particularly disliked King's criticism of President Johnson's policies on the Vietnam War. And he had never been a fan of the marches and boycotts King used to protest segregation. Marshall had once mocked street protest by saying he was "a lawyer, not a missionary." [12]

"I used to have a lot of fights with Martin about his theory about disobeying the law," Marshall said in an interview years later. "I didn't believe in that. I thought you did have a right to disobey the law, and you also had a right to go to jail for it, and he kept talking about Henry David Thoreau, and I told him that Thoreau wrote his book ["Civil Disobedience"] in jail. If you want to write a book, you go to jail and write it."

But Marshall conceded that King had tremendous influence. "He came at the right time," said Marshall. "It's very interesting how people pop up at the right time. . . . I think he was great, as a leader. As an organizer he wasn't worth shit. . . . He was a great speaker . . . but as for getting the work done, he was not too good at that. . . . All he did was to dump all his legal work on us [the NAACP], including the bills. And that was all right with him, so long as he didn't have to pay the bills." [13]

King's death did not change Marshall's attitude toward the activists in the streets. When Marshall went back to work at the Supreme Court after the April riots, a group of demonstrators from Resurrection City, a tent community near the Capitol, tried to march into the Supreme Court building. Marshall was not sympathetic to their demonstration or their claim to be operating in King's spirit. When they asked Marshall to come out and speak to them, he replied, "I have talked to people before they broke the law, and I've talked to people after they've broken the law, but I've never talked to people while they were breaking it."

The activity in the streets and in national politics continued to overshadow Marshall's profile as the first black justice on the nation's high court. Segregationist George Wallace, the governor of Alabama, entered the 1968 presidential race as a favorite son of the Old South, further inflaming racial tensions. In June, Sen. Robert Kennedy, who had just won the California primary and appeared to be on his way to claim the Democratic nomination, was assassinated in Los Angeles.

And bringing the turmoil close to home, Chief Justice Earl Warren decided to resign at the end of June. His departure gave President Johnson the chance to appoint the next chief justice before the fall election. Johnson nominated his old pal Justice Abe Fortas for the top job, but Fortas was quickly attacked by conservatives. It was discovered that his former law partners had solicited money to fund a lecture series the justice had given at American University. The fact that Fortas was a Jew also complicated his nomination. Senator Eastland was overheard saying at a party: "After [Thurgood] Marshall, I couldn't go back to Mississippi if a Jewish chief justice swore in the next president." [14]

Marshall was supportive of Fortas as a fellow justice and fellow Johnson appointee. He sent him a note telling him to hang on despite the scandals and barbs. Marshall had never learned of the contempt with which Fortas had spoken about his intellect while Marshall was solicitor general. Fortas had also made derogatory comments about Marshall to other justices after Marshall had joined the Court. But Marshall had no idea that Fortas despised him.

As the scandals mounted, however, Marshall's support for Fortas made no difference. Fortas was compelled to withdraw his nomination, and Warren continued to serve as the chief. The defeat of the Fortas nomination was a serious setback for Johnson's already crumbling presidency.

Meanwhile, riots continued to break out in the big cities, and there was more and more talk of "Black Power." It became the hip slogan for the militant black youth who viewed Marshall as an establishment voice. Justice Marshall's uneasy relationship with black militants reached a boiling point when he spoke at the University of Wisconsin in late September 1968. A disruptive group of Black Panthers and antiwar protesters threatened him, and Marshall became fearful. When he got back to Washington, he phoned the FBI. "[Justice Marshall] stated he was somewhat of a 'practicing coward' and that he had been deliberately harassed at the University of Wisconsin while attempting to make an appearance there," a senior FBI agent, Cartha DeLoach, wrote to the assistant FBI director, Clyde Tolson. "They were vociferous and very active in their harassment. He indicated he became somewhat afraid for his safety." [15]

Three days later Marshall had a six-minute off-the-record meeting with the president in the Oval Office, possibly to discuss the growing influence of black militants as well as what was going on at the Court with the failed Fortas nomination. The brevity of the talk between the normally chatty pair may have been caused by the many pressures on Johnson. Vice President Humphrey was in the middle of a desperate campaign for president against the Republican Richard Nixon. A little over a month later Nixon defeated Humphrey.

Marshall was upset by Johnson's departure and Humphrey's defeat. At a farewell party for Johnson sponsored by his black appointees, Marshall gave the president a desk set and thanked him profusely for taking the lead on getting the Civil Rights Act and Voting Rights Act passed. He also expressed gratitude to Johnson for appointing black people to government jobs previously reserved for whites. "The people in this room have just one purpose, to say thank you, Mr. President," Marshall said. "You didn't wait. You took the bull by the horns. You didn't wait for the times, you made them." [16] Johnson responded to the affection from his middle-aged, middle-class black appointees by calling them "the vanguard" of the movement. [17]

A few months later, after Nixon had been sworn in as president, Marshall gave a widely covered speech in which he made it clear that, like President Johnson, he regarded the black adults who had been fighting segregation for decades—and not militant black college students—as the true leaders of the civil rights movement. "Why demonstrate if you don't know what you're demonstrating for?" he asked in the May 1969 speech at Dillard University in New Orleans. He derided most demonstrations as achieving little other than "getting onto television." As for the militants' call for Black Power and even an all-black state, Marshall scoffed: "Black separatism will breed nothing. . . . I know of a group of people that said we should have rigid separation, from cradle to grave. And do you know who that group was? The Ku Klux Klan."

Throughout the speech Marshall criticized black people who used race "as an excuse" for not taking care of their property or educating their children. And he hit hardest at militants who paraded around with guns and called violence as American as apple pie. He said rocks and fire-bombs would settle nothing because the nation would fall apart if the law did not punish people who used guns and rocks to take over. "I am a man of law, and in my book anarchy is anarchy is anarchy," Marshall said. "It makes no difference who practices anarchy. It's bad, and punishable and should be punished."

Marshall told the students that well-educated black people were the key to future racial integration and equal rights. He said he had no objection to black studies programs and African culture courses, but he warned: "You're not going to compete in the world with African culture alone. You're going to compete in this world [only] when [your education] is a little better."

His voice loud with passion, Marshall concluded by saying: "It takes no courage to get in the back of a crowd and throw a rock. Rather, it takes courage to stand up on your two feet and look anyone straight in the eye and say, 'I will not be beaten.' "[18]

The speech hit a national nerve. Editorials and articles lauded Marshall for standing up to the militants and advocates of violence. The *Washington Star* ran a lead editorial, "Anarchy Is Anarchy," which praised Marshall for speaking out and challenged other black leaders to follow his example. The paper also ran a political cartoon that depicted Marshall, in black robes, leaning down from his judge's bench to hit a gun-toting "black separatist" on the head with his gavel. "Let's come to order," read the caption.[19]

*　　*　　*

While the world of politics and civil rights continued to thunder outside the Supreme Court, Marshall was making a relatively easy transition into the closed world of the Court. In his first years on the Court, Marshall signed very few dissents. Generally, he was voting with the liberal majority. Chief Justice Warren often had Marshall write the opinions in key cases. In *Stanley v. Georgia*, for example, Marshall wrote for a unanimous Court that police were wrong to prosecute a man for owning a porno-graphic film. He wrote that under the Constitution, the government could not prevent a citizen from privately watching or reading any material, including adult movies.

"[The defendant] is asserting the right to read or observe what he pleases—the right to satisfy his intellectual and emotional needs in the privacy of his own home," Marshall wrote. "If the First Amendment means anything, it means that a State has no business telling a man, sitting alone in his own house, what books he may read or what films he may watch. Our whole constitutional heritage rebels at the thought of giving government the power to control men's minds." [20]

"I think grown people are entitled to do what they damn please," Marshall said later, defending his position. "Ain't nobody makes you look at it. Nobody takes a gun and says you've got to. Of course it hurts children, but keep it away from them. Liquor hurts children too, keep it away from them. Drugs hurt children, keep it away from them."

In June 1969, at the end of his second year on the Court, Marshall wrote an important 7–2 ruling in *Benton v. Maryland*, which gave defendants protection against double jeopardy in state courts. The case was similar to *Hetenyi v. Wilkins*, the 1964 Second Circuit case in which Marshall had ruled that a murder suspect could not be prosecuted twice on the same charges. Now as a Supreme Court justice, Marshall's ruling extended double jeopardy protection to every court in the nation.

Marshall's ideological comfort on the Warren Court was reflected in the easy social life he led with the other justices. Once a week Marshall joined Brennan, an impish and liberal Irishman from New Jersey, and two federal judges, David Bazelon and J. Skelly Wright, for lunch at a warehouse that belonged to the liquor distributor Milton S. Kronheim. *The New York Times* described the lunches as casual affairs, at which politics were rarely discussed. Kronheim said the judges liked eating at his warehouse because they could relax without fear of eavesdroppers or reporters.

While Thurgood settled into life at the Court, Cissy was busy at home. She drove the boys to school and kept house and a social calendar for her husband. She also disciplined the boys, went to their ball games, and kept watch over their friends. Her husband was preoccupied with the Court, and she did not expect him to be actively involved with the children. "When the boys came along, he said, 'I am not ever going to punish them for something that I did in my lifetime,' " Cissy Marshall said in an interview. "So he never punished them because he had done everything." [21]

Another issue was Justice Marshall's drinking. Since his arrival in the fishbowl of official Washington, Thurgood had fewer card-playing buddies and nightclubs to frequent. He had taken to drinking more, at lunch and after work, and Cissy increasingly had to act as her husband's proctor, monitoring his drinking and his sometimes abrupt, rude behavior.

Monroe Dowling, Marshall's longtime friend, said the justice's behavior hit a crisis point when he had several drinks one night and went for a walk in his Southwest Washington neighborhood. "See, he would get drunk and get out of the house and get out on to the street," Dowling said in an interview. "And in his drunkenness, he would accost women, any woman. He had no choice about that women business. One of these days, we thought, he was going to grab some woman and her husband was going to kill him." Dowling recalled one episode in which Cissy and a friend had to drag Marshall into the house after he grabbed a woman. "With whiskey he could not discriminate," Dowling recalled.[22]

By November 1968, Cissy Marshall decided there was less chance for nosy neighbors to gossip about Thurgood's behavior if they moved to the suburbs. She also wanted more green space for Goody and John, now twelve and ten. With help from Georgia Clark, the wife of Attorney General Ramsey Clark, Cissy found a house near the Clarks in Fairfax County, Virginia. The Clarks, as well as Warren Christopher, the deputy attorney general, and several other Johnson aides, lived on scenic Lake Barcroft, about an hour from downtown.

The Marshalls' move to Lake Barcroft was complicated by two factors. First, Marshall needed a mortgage to buy the property. Second, the 1,000-family community was all white. The Clarks helped to find a bank willing to make the $52,000 mortgage loan on the five-bedroom ranch house. The racial integration of Lake Barcroft was another matter. The *Washington Star* reported that a neighbor did a poll of area residents to see how they felt about having a black family move there. "One resident of Lakeside Drive commented, 'I am not happy about it at all because this might be encouragement for more of the same,' " the *Star* reported.[23]

"But we didn't think of it as integrating," said Ramsey Clark in an interview years later. "I mean, we knew it was virtually lily-white out there, but the suburbs were all white all over the country. And we wanted to do something about that, but this wasn't an integration effort, it was a desire to have a friend out there and his desire to get the boys out of the city."

The move away from Washington came at a pivotal moment. President Johnson was going back to his native Texas. And Chief Justice Warren finally quit in June 1969. Nixon replaced him with the Minnesotan Warren Burger, a D.C. federal appeals court judge known for his conservative opinions. Burger consistently voted in support of police and prose-cutors, placing limits on constitutional protections for criminal defen-dants.

Warren's departure signaled a change in the Court's political balance. Just as important to Marshall, he no longer had an ally and friend at the helm. "They clearly adored each other," said Tyrone Brown, who was Warren's clerk during Marshall's first year on the Court.[24]

Just a month before Warren left the Court, another liberal, Justice Fortas, was forced to resign. He was waylaid by another scandal, this one over evidence that he took money from a former client, a convict, to run a charity. For the next year the Court would be down to eight members. Further damaging the Supreme Court's image, it got caught up in tawdry dramas as two of Nixon's conservative nominees were rejected by the Senate.

The president's first unsuccessful nominee, Clement Haynsworth, a Fourth Circuit judge, was found to have voted on cases despite holding stocks in companies affected by his rulings. Nixon's second failed candi-date was G. Harrold Carswell, a Fifth Circuit judge who critics charged was a racist. One newspaper column reported that Marshall told friends, "Carswell's record on the federal bench is markedly more hostile to civil rights than was Haynsworth's."[25]

Nixon then nominated Harry Blackmun, another Minnesota conser-vative, to take Fortas's seat. Blackmun, an intense man with a high fore-head and a penetrating stare, was not nationally known. But his reputation as a stalwart conservative immediately earned him the nick-name Minnesota Twin, pairing him with Chief Justice Burger. He joined the high court in June 1970.

While the Court was going through these wringing transitions, Mar-shall became ill. On May 15 he was hospitalized with a bad case of pneu-monia. When he did not respond to antibiotics, there was widespread alarm. Dr. Walter Tkach, in a May 19 memo to the president, wrote that "this is not an ordinary pneumonia." Nixon began to pay close attention to Marshall's condition, thinking he might have a chance to appoint a third right-wing justice in less than two years. A week after Marshall was hospitalized, Chief Justice Burger called Dwight Chapin, one of Nixon's top aides, to advise him that "Marshall is much sicker than anyone presently realizes."[26]

Marshall recalled that he was in the hospital for thirty days and it was "touch and go." But as he was getting better and about to leave, the head of the hospital came into his room and said: "Mr. Justice, we've got a request for a report on your stay—and I wouldn't think of releasing it without your permission." Marshall, still coughing, asked who wanted to see his chart. The doctor said President Nixon. Marshall, knowing Nixon was not wishing him well, said: "Fine, you can release it, but providing you put the following note on the bottom of it. *Not yet!*"

Marshall's recovery proceeded slowly. In June of 1971 he was back at Bethesda Naval Hospital. He underwent tests and returned home still "not feeling well." Eventually he had an appendectomy. Marshall's constant smoking, drinking, and lack of exercise—he claimed his walk from his car into the Supreme Court was enough—began to show as he put on weight and his face grew heavy.[27]

Then in July 1972 Marshall was driving his sixteen-year-old son, Goody, in the Virgin Islands when his Jeep ran up on a curb, slammed into a stone wall, and threw the justice out. The Jeep rolled over, pinning the elder Marshall under it. "Doctors say the sixty-four-year-old suffered a fractured ankle, a damaged finger, and bruises, but described his overall condition as 'excellent,' " wrote the *Baltimore Sun*. The *Sun*, apparently aware of Marshall's drinking, took care to note that the accident was caused when Marshall's "foot [was] caught on the throttle and he lost control of the vehicle."[28] When President Nixon learned of Marshall's accident, he showed great interest in the justice's condition and sent an Air Force plane to bring him back to Washington.

With his shaky health, Marshall was now even more confined and grumpy. There was widespread speculation that he was about to leave the Court. *Jet* magazine, which regularly celebrated Marshall as a black hero, wrote in November 1972 that "several of the Supreme Court justices, including Thurgood Marshall, are expected to resign during the next term." *Jet* said Marshall's rival from his LDF days, Bob Carter, and the Republican Samuel Pierce were the leading black lawyers under consideration to replace him.

Marshall was angry. He quickly shot off a letter to *Jet*'s Washington editor, Simeon Booker. "Where in the world did you get the idea that Thurgood Marshall is 'expected to resign during the next term'?" he wrote. "Certainly it gives little comfort to people in the United States to believe that the only Negro in the Supreme Court expects to resign." He added that he had been writing as many opinions as ever and chastened Booker for not checking the story out before running it. "If this is too much to ask, forget about it," he wrote.[29]

But the talk about his health continued, and in late November of 1972 his office was forced to issue a statement that said the judge was "in fine health."[30]

The mention of Carter as his possible replacement particularly rankled Marshall. Just a few years earlier, in 1968, one of Carter's lawyers at the NAACP had written an article criticizing the Supreme Court for failing to do enough to support racial integration. Marshall took it as a personal slap. Roy Wilkins fired the author from the NAACP, over Carter's objections. Then Carter resigned in anger.

Amid all the turmoil in Washington and New York, Aubrey Marshall, age sixty-seven, died in Delaware on October 8, 1972. Thurgood had had little contact with his brother since the early 1950s, when Aubrey's drinking had led to troubles on his job and arguments with his brother. But since his battles with TB and then nearly losing his job, Aubrey had built a solid medical career at Bissell Hospital, a sanitorium, and become medical director in 1971. Still, Aubrey had a difficult time playing second fiddle to his little brother, according to his relatives and friends. When Aubrey's son from his first marriage, Aubrey Jr., was looking for a job and asked his father if he should ask his famous Uncle Thurgood for help, the father reacted strongly. "He told me to stay away from him," Aubrey Jr. recalled in an interview.[31]

Despite his chilly relationship with his brother, there had been occasional visits, and Aubrey had come to Thurgood's swearing-in, both as solicitor general and for the Supreme Court. But the visits were the doing of Aubrey's second wife, Helen, who made a point of staying in touch with Thurgood and Cissy. Helen enjoyed the status that came from being related to a Supreme Court justice, a point of pleasure that did not sit well with Aubrey.

Thurgood attended his brother's funeral in Wilmington. But the justice's health problems and busy schedule made the trip into more of an obligatory gesture than an expression of his grief.

Despite Aubrey's death and his own health problems and rumors about having to step down, Marshall kept up his work on the Court, especially when school desegregation cases began to pick up pace. Justice Brennan had several conversations about the subject with Marshall, who was still viewed as its foremost authority. The lone black justice consistently expressed his frustration to the Brethren about the slow pace of desegregation. In 1968 Brennan wrote an opinion that concluded, "The time for mere deliberate speed has run out" (*Green v. New Kent County*).

By 1970, however, with the conservative Warren Burger leading the Court, there was growing pressure, on both the Court and politicians, to stop school desegregation. An angry white backlash began to take shape. Marshall nonetheless persuaded his colleagues in *Swann v. Charlotte-Mecklenburg* to unanimously confirm that there was nothing wrong with using busing to integrate public schools. Burger and the other conservative justices were generally supportive of busing from the start, given the Court's stand in the *Green* case. But Marshall withheld his full support of the majority opinion while pushing Burger for several small changes. Marshall wanted to give federal courts as much leeway to get black and white students into school together, and his posturing forced the Chief Justice to make the strongest possible ruling. "The objective today remains to eliminate from the public schools all vestiges of state-imposed segregation," Burger wrote. Heeding Marshall's advice, the Chief Justice concluded that "desegregation plans cannot be limited to the walk-in schools," and busing was an appropriate way to create racially mixed schools.[32]

School desegregation was not the only issue on Marshall's mind. In 1972, while Justice Brennan was ill, Marshall became a leader of the justices opposed to capital punishment. In *Furman v. Georgia*, he succeeded as part of a coalition that won a difficult 5–4 vote outlawing the death penalty. The majority insisted that strict guidelines be put in place to prevent its consistent use by different juries and judges. Of particular concern to Marshall was the high incidence of poor people and blacks getting the death penalty for crimes that were punished with lesser sentences for rich whites. Stephen Saltzburg, one of Marshall's clerks that year, recalled the unusual sight of an energetic, passionate Marshall going to see each of the other justices, trying to win converts.[33]

"In striking down capital punishment, the court does not malign" legislatures who approved of the death penalty and judges and juries who sentence criminals to death, Marshall wrote in his opinion. "On the contrary, it pays homage to [our system of government]. Only in a free society could right triumph in difficult times and could civilization record its magnificent advancement. In recognizing the humanity of our fellow human beings, we pay ourselves the highest tribute. We achieve 'a major milestone in the long road up from barbarism' and join the approximately 70 other jurisdictions in the world which celebrate their regard for civilization and for humanity by shunning capital punishment."[34]

Conservatives accused Marshall and his four colleagues of going easy on criminals at a time when the crime rate was rising. Marshall had been moving toward opposition to the death penalty for years. Going back to his days in private practice, when one of his first clients was put to death, and later when as a lawyer for the NAACP he saw white prosecutors railroad black defendants before all-white juries, he had come to believe that the death penalty was not administered fairly.

But philosophically Marshall had not been opposed to putting people to death. Just ten years earlier, as a Second Circuit judge, he had been willing to vote for a death sentence. "He was not against the death penalty when I worked for him," said Ralph Winter, who was Marshall's clerk during the 1961 term on the Second Circuit Court of Appeals. "We had a case [*U.S. v. Denno*] and I said this guy has got to get a new trial. Ultimately I wrote him a memo and persuaded him, but he was not anti–death penalty."[35]

But by the late 1960s, with a voice on the Supreme Court, Marshall became absolutely opposed to the death penalty. Justice Brennan, a longtime opponent of capital punishment, had several animated conversations with Marshall about the issue. Brennan convinced Marshall they had a unique responsibility because the Supreme Court was the final place of appeal.

"No way, José. How are you going to not kill a person after he has been executed if you find out he is innocent?" said Marshall. "I mean, you can't un-ring a bell. When you kill him, he's gone."

Marshall's 1970s legal battles sometimes spilled out of the courts. He was among the justices who took the lead in opposing President Nixon's attempt to stop *The New York Times* and *The Washington Post* from publishing portions of a military report on U.S. involvement in Vietnam. The "Pentagon Papers" were viewed by the Nixon White House as national security documents, and Nixon's lawyers asked the high court to stop newspapers from publishing them. The *Times* was given a restraining order after printing some of the material, but the *Post* published other documents before the Court could act.

The Court voted 6–3 against the president. In his concurring opinion Marshall said Congress had not given Nixon the power to stop newspapers from publishing material even if the president labeled it SECRET. The ruling kicked up another political storm, and conservatives again identified Marshall as one of the high court "liberals" allowing the country to go haywire.

Nixon's loss in court did not hurt him politically. He trounced the

Democrat George McGovern in 1972, proclaiming himself the spokesman for a "Silent Majority" that wanted tougher sentences for criminals and support for the U.S. military in Vietnam. Marshall was clearly on the other side of popular opinion and beginning to feel that the Court was turning more conservative too. His sense of becoming politically isolated was manifested when he gave away his tickets to Nixon's inaugural and stayed home. The sixty-four-year-old's alienation only increased when, two days later, Lyndon Johnson died.

"He thought that moving me up there was what killed him off [politically]. They used the Vietnam War as an excuse," Marshall said in an interview after Johnson's death. "He told me that as late as a week before he died." Marshall asked the former president if he had changed his mind about Marshall's Supreme Court nomination costing him the presidency. "Nope. More and more, I'm sure I'm right," Johnson responded.[36]

Johnson, a savvy political operator, may have been appealing to Marshall's ego and even trying to persuade him to stay on the Court and justify the sacrifices made to get the seat for him. Marshall was now the only Johnson appointee left on the high court. Whatever Johnson's motives, Marshall took his words to heart. In the coming years he struggled to stay on the Supreme Court. As if carrying his dead leader's shield into battle, he crossed swords with an increasingly conservative court and fought politicians, including Democrats, who tried to force him off.

CHAPTER 31

Backlash on the Court

By 1973 Marshall found himself working hard to keep his balance on a high court shifting fast to the right. There were two longtime liberals still in place, William Brennan and William O. Douglas; they usually sided with Marshall's opinions. But now a conservative majority was taking shape. William Rehnquist, a tall, learned Arizonian who had clerked on the high court during the *Brown* case, joined the Court in 1972. Also that year Lewis Powell, a stately Virginia gentleman and former president of the American Bar Association, came on the Court joining Potter Stewart and Warren Burger. A new era of conservatism dawned on the Court. Those four were often joined in decisions by two moderates, Byron White and Harry Blackmun. That new voting bloc pushed Marshall into the far left corner of dissent, an unfamiliar place for the sixty-five-year-old.

Marshall was not initially put off by the changes on the Court. He told friends he still felt like "family" up there, and he was an active voice in the justices' arguments over cases. Once, when a complex corporate tax case was being argued, Justice Powell recalled that Marshall leaned over and whispered: "Lewis, I'll trade you my vote in this case for a future draft choice."

While he still enjoyed working with his colleagues, Marshall's image to the world outside was changing. After struggling through pneumonia, appendicitis, and the car crash, he made fewer public appearances. It was rare for him even to venture out with his boys, who were now sixteen and fourteen. Marshall sent his court courier, Grafton Gaines, and Cissy to most of their games and school programs. He saved his energy for the Court.

Marshall was intellectually energized when two explosive cases, *Roe v. Wade* and *Doe v. Bolton*, hit the docket. The cases revolved around Texas and Georgia statutes restricting abortions. Norma McCorvey (identified as Jane Roe to protect her identity during the case) was a single woman in Texas who said she had been raped. She demanded a legal abortion under her constitutional right to privacy.[1] Mary Doe, an unidentified Georgia woman, was not pregnant but had a neural-chemical disorder. Her doctor said a pregnancy could threaten her life. Doe wanted to be able to get an abortion if she became pregnant.

The cases were argued in December 1971 and reargued in October 1972. The high court was immediately buffeted by a storm of public argument, with feminist groups asserting that the decision to have an abortion was a private issue for a woman. Marshall was sympathetic to this perspective from his experience as an advocate for poor blacks. Going back to his days in Baltimore and Harlem, he had heard stories about penniless black women who suffered or died at the hands of any hack willing to perform an illegal abortion. In the justices' conferences Marshall asserted that poor women needed to be able to have legal abortions since rich women could get around state laws by going to private clinics or leaving the country. He took an active role in arguing that abortion should be viewed as a constitutional right.

The conservative wing was divided over the issue, with Rehnquist and White firmly opposed to making abortion a constitutional right. However, Chief Justice Burger and Justices Powell and Stewart signed on with Marshall and the three other liberal justices. The writing of the historic decision was assigned to Harry Blackmun.

Marshall was openly aggressive in trying to shape Blackmun's opinion. The initial draft limited abortions to the first three months of a pregnancy. Justice Brennan, however, proposed that the three-month limit be replaced with a new standard—when a fetus was "viable" outside the mother's body. At the urging of his clerks, Marshall sent a memo to Blackmun in support of Brennan's idea. "Given the difficulties which many women may have in believing that they are pregnant and in deciding to seek an abortion, I fear that the earlier date may not in practice serve the interests of those women," Marshall wrote. He argued that it made no sense to outlaw an abortion if the baby could not live on its own outside the womb.[2]

Marshall's letter, in combination with Brennan's arguments, persuaded Blackmun. The controversial ruling allowed abortion until the fetus had "viability" outside the mother's body. Also, any pregnancy that threatened the "life and health of the mother" could be ended in a legal abortion.

The success Marshall was having with major issues—busing, pornography, the death penalty, and now abortion—made him a happy member of the Court despite its more conservative membership. But as the activists of the old Warren Court eked out a few major victories, they attracted political fire from the White House. In 1973 President Nixon privately derided Marshall to his staff as "a boob." Nixon also put down the Court's two other liberals: Justice Brennan was in the "boob" category, and Justice Douglas was not even worthy of "mention." The president's conversation would not become public until tapes revealed it years later, but Nixon's assessment was an indirect acknowledgment of the impact Marshall and the liberals were having on the Court.

Ironically, Nixon would soon be glad that the old "Boob"—Marshall—had enough influence on the Court to help protect the president's power. In July 1973, Rep. Elizabeth Holtzman of New York filed suit in U.S. District Court seeking an injunction to end Nixon's bombing of Cambodia. Nixon's attack on the Southeast Asian nation was an attempt to cut off supply routes to the North Vietnamese and end the Vietnam War. But Cambodia was not involved in the war, and Holtzman asked the court to block the assault on a neutral country. The lower court ordered the bombing stopped. But the Second Circuit Court of Appeals, Marshall's former court, overruled the decision. Holtzman appealed to the Supreme Court, which was recessed for the summer. She then had to take the appeal directly to the justice in charge of the Second Circuit— Thurgood Marshall.

Marshall listened to the argument but promptly ruled against Holtzman, allowing Nixon to continue the bombing. Infuriated, Holtzman turned to William O. Douglas and asked him to overrule Marshall. Douglas, who was vacationing in Washington state, agreed and issued an order for a stay of the bombings.

Marshall felt that Douglas had slapped him in the face. He immediately telephoned the remaining justices and got them all to agree that Douglas was acting improperly. Then, writing on behalf of the Court,

Marshall overturned Douglas's decision. Without speaking to Douglas, a champion to the antiwar movement, Marshall wrote that no one judge had the right to act alone and reverse a ruling. The Cambodia bombing campaign, Marshall wrote, "may ultimately be adjudged to have not only been unwise but also unlawful [however] the proper response to an arguably illegal action is not lawlessness by judges charged with interpreting and enforcing the laws. Down that road lies tyranny and repression." *Holtzman v. Schlesinger* (1973).

Douglas, age seventy-five and the senior member of the Court, was stung. He felt Marshall had conspired with his colleagues to overrule him. Douglas immediately wrote a dissent in which he complained that the Court could act to reverse him only if six of the nine were together.

The dispute had become personal. Despite their common standing as heroes to liberals, Douglas and Marshall entered a nasty enmity that would last the rest of their lives. Years later Marshall said: "Douglas was no friend of mine. We overruled him. And he never did forgive me for that. I don't think he was [truly a liberal]. I think he went along."

Douglas was similarly angry and disdainful of Marshall. In an autobiography published a few years after the high court's battle over Cambodia, he wrote that the only reason President Johnson put Marshall on the Court was "simply because he was black, and in the 1960's that was reason enough." Douglas explained: "The public needed a competent black on the court for symbolic reasons. . . . A black reaching the top was likely to be anxious to prove to society that he was safe and conservative and reliable."[3]

Douglas, because of bad relations with the other justices and deteriorating health, was isolated and largely ineffective during his remaining three years on the Court. Marshall, in contrast, continued to be a force. When the Court ruled that it was a violation of the First Amendment to censor or withhold mail from prisoners, Marshall wrote a concurring opinion that was widely quoted and praised for its humanity: "Whether an O. Henry authoring his short stories in jail or a frightened young inmate writing his family, a prisoner needs a medium of self-expression."[4]

While the two titans of the left did battle, the nation was generally going through a conservative period, including a backlash against much of the Court's effort to break down school segregation with busing. By 1973 the increasing flight of middle-class families out of the big cities and their schools led the Supreme Court to hear two cases that reinterpreted its support for racial integration. First, the Court agreed to hear a case in which Hispanic parents sued the San Antonio school district because affluent districts spent more money per pupil. That inequity, the parents contended, amounted to discrimination against the minority children concentrated in poorer residential areas of the state.

In a 5–4 decision that found Marshall on the losing end of a major case, the Court ruled for the school district. Poor children were guaranteed some minimal level of spending but not equal spending, the Court said. Affluent school districts had the right to spend added money if they so chose. Marshall dissented by arguing that a disparity in spending amounted to a "denial of equal protection of the laws."[5]

Marshall was hailed by many in the press and legal circles for his dissent. Even inside the Court, one of Justice Burger's clerks, John Oakley, sent a note to Marshall, congratulating him for taking a stand: "I believe your opinion will in time be acknowledged as one of the great dissents in the history of the court, not only because its erudition is inspired by humanism, but also because it must eventually become the law of the land."[6]

The next year, 1974, another critical school case came to the Court. As white middle-class families fled Detroit, they had created an overwhelmingly black school district in the city. Any attempt to bus students within Detroit's city limits to integrate schools was doomed because of the shortage of white students. Lawyers for Detroit's black parents wanted the courts to approve a plan to merge the mostly black urban and the mostly white suburban school districts to allow for integration. The state resisted, and the black parents sued. After the parents won in the lower court and appeals court, the Supreme Court reversed the rulings. It decided that federal courts were wrong to violate school district boundaries and hold suburban areas responsible for segregation in the city.

Marshall took the unusual step of reading a part of his dissent from the bench. Sitting in front of the red velour curtains that lent a hush to the chamber, he spoke with the singular voice of the NAACP lawyer who had ended legal segregation in American schools in 1954: "In *Brown v. Board of Education*, this court held that segregation of children in public schools on the basis of race deprives Negro children of equal educational opportunities and therefore denies them the equal protection of the laws. . . . After twenty years of small, often difficult steps toward that great end [of school integration], the court today takes a giant step backwards."

Marshall added that the state of Michigan had a duty to eliminate, "root and branch," every aspect of racism. Arguing that integration was difficult given the nation's history of segregation, he said it would be easy to carve the nation's cities into two, with whites on one side and blacks on the other. "But it is a course, I predict, our people will ultimately regret," he concluded. "I dissent."[7]

Although Marshall was on the losing side of 5–4 votes in both these cases, he did not feel defeated so much as engaged in a fight. While he was emotionally and intellectually caught up with this battle, there were heated fights outside the Supreme Court too. The nation was in a frenzy over a growing scandal threatening the Nixon presidency.

The story began in 1972, when the Nixon White House approved a break-in of Democratic campaign headquarters in the Watergate office complex in Washington. When some of the burglars were arrested, the administration tried to distance itself from the crime, but several of the president's aides were implicated and convicted. An independent prose-cutor subpoenaed tapes of Nixon's conversations about the matter, but the president refused to release them. He claimed "executive privilege" until federal courts ruled against him. The president appealed to the Supreme Court.

The high court ruled unanimously against Nixon, ordering him to release the tapes. Marshall, given his ties to President Johnson, had never been a Nixon fan. And in his conversations with other justices, he was es-pecially angry at Nixon's claim that only the president could determine if it were in the national interest to release the tapes. When the first draft of the Court's opinion was circulated among the justices, Marshall wrote a tough-minded note to its author, Chief Justice Burger, a Nixon ap-pointee. Marshall wanted the Court to hammer home the point that Nixon's claims about acting in the national interest were egotistical blather. The Court did take a hard stand. A month later, Nixon resigned.

*　　*　　*

As the 1970s wore on, Marshall's health continued to deteriorate. Early in 1975 Marshall was in Las Vegas when he came down with a bad fever and severe respiratory infection. Still smoking two packs of cigarettes a day, Marshall saw his infection quickly develop into pneumonia. He flew to Washington and went directly to a room at Bethesda Naval Hospital. Justice Douglas had suffered a stroke and was also off the bench. With Marshall hospitalized the Court was down to seven justices, and both of the ailing justices were among the liberal minority. Marshall would miss a month on the bench. Doctors warned him to quit smoking and lose weight (he was now way over 230 pounds), but he could do neither.

In June 1975 Marshall was well enough to travel to Baltimore for one of the few speeches he was willing to give in an increasingly cloistered life. The occasion was the fiftieth anniversary of his graduation from Douglass High School, and Marshall was the commencement speaker. Standing before 450 mostly black students, he blasted away at contemporary black youth culture, with its heavy focus on black pride and talk about black power. "I don't care how many Afros you wear or how many dashikis you carry on your shoulders, you will never get anything unless you are able to compete with everybody else at the same level and be superior," Marshall said. As for Washington affairs, he urged the students not to be cynical about politics because of Watergate. "We've got to get involved in the machinery of this country because if we will not, somebody else will be running it."[8]

Over the next year Marshall's work on the Court centered on one issue: the death penalty. He had helped to engineer the 5–4 ruling in the 1972 *Furman* case, which outlawed capital punishment because of arbitrary sentencing. Now the Florida, Georgia, and Texas legislatures had put in place guidelines for sentencing criminals to death in an attempt to make executions more consistent and end any racial bias in sentencing.

In the 1972 case Marshall had been absolutely opposed to the death penalty. He viewed it as cruel and unusual punishment and therefore unconstitutional. But that argument had persuaded only his fellow liberal justices, Brennan and Douglas. To get the votes of Justices White and Stewart, Marshall had argued that the death penalty was being applied inconsistently in different courtrooms and to different defendants.

Now, in *Gregg v. Georgia*, that argument no longer held water because of the new state statutes. Also, Justice Douglas had been replaced by the quiet, bow-tie-clad John Paul Stevens, a moderate from Chicago who was appointed by President Gerald Ford. To gain the five votes he needed, Marshall recounted stories in the judges' conferences about his own experiences defending poor black men in front of all-white juries. He talked about being the only one of the justices ever to have defended a client in a death penalty case and how he considered it a victory to see innocent clients sentenced to only life in prison because it meant they had escaped the electric chair.

This time his stories and arguments failed to sway the Court's moderates. Justices White and Stewart voted against him, as did Justice Stevens. They joined Justices Rehnquist, Powell, and Blackmun, and Chief Justice Burger in a 7–2 vote to reinstate the death penalty. Marshall's only supporter in dissent was his good friend William Brennan.

In a frustrated voice, Marshall read his dissent from the bench on his sixty-eighth birthday. He maintained his hard line and concluded that there was no case in which the death penalty could be viewed as anything but "unconstitutional because it is excessive."[9]

The decision was more than a defeat. It signaled a new isolation for Marshall. He and Brennan were now removed from the mainstream; they were off on the Court's left wing, and their arguments were becoming distant voices as the conservative majority charged right. The days of Marshall as an active force in the Court's thinking seemed to be slipping away, and he was deeply troubled by his loss of standing among his new peers. But for Marshall as well as Brennan, there was little room for accommodating the right wing on issues such as the death penalty.

"We seemed quite often, as we do to this day, to be the lone dissenters in many cases," Brennan said later in an interview. "I mean if you're against the death penalty there's no possible way you can accommodate. You can't." Brennan said it was not a matter of being stubborn, but expressing heartfelt positions which is "a responsibility expected of a justice."[10]

Many years later Marshall, too, saw the *Gregg* case as the instant he lost touch with the Court. He still had no idea how seven justices could have voted to allow the death penalty to be imposed on convicts. "My colleagues?" Marshall said in exasperation during an interview. "I don't know why they vote for the death penalty. I've told them about a thousand times." During the interview Marshall was asked if he would reject the death penalty even if a person killed his mother or someone in his family. Without hesitation he replied: "That's right."

After reading his dissent on a Friday morning, Marshall went home but continued to stew over his loss. That Sunday he woke up with chest pains at 4:00 A.M. and started walking around his home. By 7:00, Marshall later said, he "started to get worried" and called a doctor, who told him to go to a hospital. When he got to Bethesda, he asked the doctor, "Is this it?" The doctor replied, "It sure is." He had suffered a heart attack. Over the next three days he had two milder attacks.[11]

During the following two months, Marshall was either in the hospital or lying on his back at home. Doctors pleaded with him to quit cigarettes and prescribed a forty-pound weight loss, but he could not. The heart attacks spurred a new round of reports that Marshall was going to retire. The question around the Court was whether President Ford could successfully nominate someone for the seat before the fall election.

Lyle Denniston, the Supreme Court reporter for the *Washington Star,* forecast that Ford would have to name "a black with a national reputation" and suggested that person might be William Coleman, Ford's transportation secretary. Marshall again told reporters he had no intention of leaving the Court, even if his friend Bill Coleman was set to replace him.[12]

In the fall of 1976, the former Georgia governor Jimmy Carter defeated Ford, and the Democrats gained control of both the White House and the Congress. That combination created new pressure for Marshall to retire. He could be assured that Democrats would have the opportunity to name his replacement. But Marshall told friends that he and Cissy had a deal. "When I start to get senile she's going to tell me, then I'll retire."

It was a rough time for a sick man to be on the Court. The 1976 term put Marshall under tremendous pressure as a new debate erupted over abortion. These cases, under the heading *Maher v. Roe,* centered on instances in which healthy but poor women with normal fetuses wanted abortions and asked state governments to fund them through Medicaid. The issue went to the heart of Marshall's logic on why abortion should be legal. He felt a poor woman—just as a rich woman—should be given the best possible care when she made the difficult choice to abort a pregnancy.

As he had failed to persuade his colleagues in the latest death penalty cases, Marshall failed to get any justices to join Brennan and Blackmun (the author of the *Roe* decision) in supporting government-funded abortions for healthy women. This was not the active Marshall filled with stories, making arguments, and walking around to lobby his colleagues. This was a less engaged man, lacking the energy or the inclination to argue with people who disagreed with him.

In his dissent, however, Marshall was in full throat, condemning his colleagues for turning their backs on the poor: "The [state laws restricting abortions] challenged here brutally coerce poor women to bear children whom society will scorn for every day of their lives. Many thousands of unwanted minority and mixed race children now spend blighted lives in foster homes, orphanages and 'reform' schools. . . . The effect will be to relegate millions of people to lives of poverty and despair."[13] Marshall's comments were extreme, even offensive to some of his fellow justices. He wrote as if lecturing people who were beneath him. His rhetoric about the lives of poor children and minority children also seemed dark and tortured. This was an unhappy and angry man.

By now Justice Marshall rarely got outside the Court or his suburban home. His poor health gave him an easy excuse for turning down any invitation. He was also exiled from the nation's legal establishment. White lawyers in the top firms and law schools had never been convinced that he was a strong legal mind, and their snide private digs at him began getting into the public debate. Archibald Cox, whom Marshall had replaced at the Solicitor General's Office, told a reporter: "Marshall may not be very bright or hard-working but he deserves credit for picking the best law clerks in town."[14]

All the while Marshall continued to hear that the Carter White House was looking at people they could name to the Court once he announced his retirement. Now the most often named candidate was the nation's second black solicitor general, Wade McCree. McCree had not only followed in Marshall's footsteps by becoming solicitor general but had also served as a federal appeals court judge.

Griffin Bell, Carter's attorney general, acknowledged in a later interview that he had advised the president that Marshall should step down and McCree be nominated as his replacement. "I told President Carter that [Justice Marshall] ought to leave," Bell said, explaining that his age and health were limiting his effectiveness on the Court. "The president was going to appoint Judge McCree."[15]

Some of Bell's aides spread word of the attorney general's conversations with Carter. Bell said he soon heard from several of his assistants that Marshall's response was that McCree was never going to take his seat. Bell's aides were upset at what they took to be Marshall's low personal assessment of McCree. "What Marshall was saying was that he didn't want *anybody* replacing him," Bell recalled. "He wanted to stay as long as he could function. Some people thought that was a bad sign."

Marshall was in fact hearing from Carter officials that it would be smart for him to cooperate with the president's plan. Although the president never personally called, Marshall said, he took the messages to be coming straight from the Oval Office. According to Marshall, some Carter emissaries, whom he would not name, came to his chambers. "He sent people to me to ask me to resign. I told them my usual. The expression is one I love, *Fuck yourself!*"

The tension between Marshall and McCree exploded into a public spectacle during May 1978. A banquet was held in the main hall of the Supreme Court building, with beautifully decorated tables placed among the large marble columns. The honoree was Dan Friedman, an assistant solicitor general who had recently been named chief judge of the U.S. Court of Claims. Several Supreme Court justices were there, including Marshall. Solicitor General McCree was the master of ceremonies for the black-tie affair.

At one point McCree began to list the former solicitors general. He called out the name of Marshall's predecessor and the name of Marshall's successor. He had skipped Marshall's name entirely. "He had not yet mentioned Thurgood Marshall," said Dores McCree, Wade McCree's wife, in an interview, "when all of a sudden, we heard this rustling of noise. We heard someone jump up and say, 'I'm here, I'm here, I'm a judge too, you know.'

"And Marshall got up and stalked out of the room," she continued. "And the shock of everybody, you could not ignore it, you could not overlook it." According to Mrs. McCree, her husband planned to save Marshall's introduction for last because Marshall had served as a judge, as solicitor general, and finally as a Supreme Court justice. "He was to be the crowning glory, he was to be the pièce de résistance, he was the person Wade wanted to emphasize the most," she said. "But Thurgood couldn't wait; he thought he'd been bypassed and overlooked. He just stalked out in this big huff, and everybody said, 'Oh, he's been drinking again.' "16

The guest of honor, Dan Friedman, who had worked with Marshall at the Solicitor General's Office, went rushing after the justice. "I went down to his chamber to ask him to come back. He refused," Friedman recalled in an interview. Marshall told him, "I'm not putting up with this." In his rage Thurgood had left Cissy behind. She made desperate apologies for her husband's behavior before hurriedly exiting.17

A few weeks later Dores McCree and Cissy Marshall met at a luncheon of the Supreme Court justices' wives. Justice Stewart's wife had invited Mrs. McCree to the lunch, and Mrs. McCree took the opportunity to apologize to Mrs. Marshall. Afterward, the two women walked up to Justice Marshall's chambers. When they walked into the office, Mrs. McCree began to apologize. "It was as if I had never spoken," she said. "He didn't respond, didn't say a word, not one word."

A month later there was a party for Marshall's seventieth birthday. The event was held at the Washington home of Wiley Branton, who had been Marshall's cocounsel in the Little Rock Central High School case. Invitations had long ago been sent to the justices. Also invited were McCree and Marshall's former colleagues at the NAACP as well as good friends such as federal judge Damon Keith. McCree showed up with a gift for Marshall and the hope that he could repair the relationship and possibly get Marshall's blessing to be his successor. He carefully approached the justice, but Marshall quickly turned away and set the gift aside.

"Marshall had not quite rejected it but had snubbed his present," recalled Louis Claiborne, Marshall's former colleague in the Solicitor General's Office who was now working for McCree. Turning to Claiborne out of frustration, McCree said, "Why is that man so angry with me? I haven't done anything." Claiborne, with a lawyer's detachment, replied, "Well, surely you've figured out that he thinks you're just waiting for him to die or resign so you can succeed him." [18]

*   *   *

Marshall's feeling that he was being disrespected came at the same time that he was under assault inside the Court. Since October 1977 the Court had been preoccupied with a critical case that touched directly on Marshall's lifelong effort to bring more black students into the nation's professional schools. The case involved a young white man, Allan Bakke, who sued the University of California at Davis because minority students with lower grades had been admitted to the medical school, while Bakke had been denied admission. The school had set aside sixteen slots solely for students from "economically or educationally disadvantaged" backgrounds, most often black students. Bakke complained that the policy amounted to a quota for minorities and discriminated against him, violating his Fourteenth Amendment right to equal protection.

The case drew front-page attention the moment Bakke filed suit. His argument crystallized the national divide over affirmative action plans. Polls showed there was a widespread backlash against giving preference to blacks in hiring or education, with some saying the preference would reward unqualified applicants. A California state court ruled in Bakke's favor and ordered him admitted to the medical school, but that order was overturned by the state supreme court. Finally Bakke appealed to the U.S. Supreme Court.

The case energized Marshall. He was back at center stage after a string of defeats at the hands of the conservative majority. The nation's obligation to make up for its racist, exclusionary history was the heart of his career. Marshall expected to take the lead on this case and believed his colleagues, even the conservatives, would defer to him.

In conference there was no clear majority. Marshall made three arguments to his colleagues. First, he said the nation's legacy of slavery was still being felt and blacks had not yet "arrived." Second, he noted that the Constitution had never been color blind. He pointed out that in *Plessy v. Ferguson*, the landmark 1896 case, the Court had set forth a separate-but-equal doctrine, branding blacks as second-class citizens. Third, Marshall said the Court should not view the university as trying to exclude Bakke. Instead, he argued that affirmative action was intended to include black people who had suffered from the nation's history of state-sanctioned racial discrimination.

By the end of the conference, Marshall wrote on his yellow legal pad that he needed just one vote to win a 5–4 victory on the *Bakke* case. He wrote the initials of three justices as sharing his opinion—Brennan, Stewart, and Powell. The swing vote, Marshall concluded, belonged to Justice White, who had voted with Marshall on several earlier desegregation cases. "We heard that after the first conference, it wasn't entirely clear how it was going to come out," recalled Phillip Spector, one of Marshall's clerks that term.[19]

Marshall began a full-court press to win White's vote. White was a fascinating character. His broad shoulders and huge hands hinted that he was not another bookish lawyer. He had been an All-American football star at the University of Colorado before playing professionally for the Pittsburgh Steelers. In his first year as a pro, he led the league in rushing and quit only because he had a Rhodes scholarship. He later graduated with honors from Yale Law School before clerking for Chief Justice Vinson. White was also a judicial moderate who was sensitive to racial issues. Marshall began lobbying for his vote on *Bakke* using emotional arguments about the continued damage done to black people by racism.

"I guess I listened to him pretty carefully on race matters because I had known about Marshall before he became a judge and I knew his work on the Second Circuit and as S.G., but I really wasn't prepared for the impact he would make," said White in an interview years later. "He spoke with such conviction. It was conviction that came out of experience. He could embellish his points with examples that would scare you to death, experiences he had trying cases in the South."[20]

White agreed to vote with him, so Marshall thought he had the fifth vote necessary to form a majority approving of the university's affirmative action plan. But while Marshall had been engaged with White, Justice Powell had decided to switch his vote. Chief Justice Burger had personally appealed to him to vote against quotas and for Bakke.

Justice Powell's switch was based on his discomfort with the idea that sixteen seats in the medical school had been set aside on the grounds that they went to those with "disadvantage." He agreed with Marshall that racial discrimination had severely damaged the nation's black citizens and that there was no ignoring race. But Powell, responding to Burger's appeal, also agreed that quotas were unacceptable. After the initial conference, in which he agreed with most of what Marshall argued, Powell concluded that a vote for the university would be a vote to legalize the use of racial quotas. Nothing Marshall could argue about the history of racism in the United States was sufficient to get over Powell's objections to quotas. Meanwhile, Burger acted to make sure Powell would remain part of the 5–4 majority voting against the university. He assigned Powell to write the opinion.

Marshall, sensing he was beaten on this key case, fired off an angry memo to the other justices:

> I repeat, for the next to last time: the decision in this case depends on whether you consider the action of the Regents as admitting certain students or as excluding certain other students. . . . As a result of our last discussion on this case, I wish also to address the question of whether Negroes have "arrived." Just a few examples illustrate that Negroes most certainly have not. . . . This week's U.S. News and World Report has a story about "Who Runs America." They list some 83 persons—not one Negro, even as a would-be runner-up. . . . It would be the cruelest irony for this court to adopt the dissent in Plessy now and hold that the university must use color-blind admissions.[21]

Justice Powell, unlike Justice White, was not convinced. But he understood the importance of his black colleague's argument and took it into account in writing the majority opinion. Powell emphasized in his draft that he had no problem with the university's decision to take race into account. But after reading Powell's draft, a bitter Marshall wrote back that he would dissent "in toto."

However, Marshall did not completely dissent from Powell's final draft. Realizing that he needed to confirm Powell's judgment that race could be a factor in considering an applicant, Marshall voted with him on that one, key, point. But Marshall strongly dissented from the rest of Powell's majority opinion, which ruled that the sixteen seats set aside amounted to an unconstitutional use of a racial quota.

In his emotional dissent, Marshall wrote:

> It must be remembered that during most of the past 200 years, the Constitution as interpreted by this court did not prohibit the most ingenious and pervasive forms of discrimination against the Negro. Now, when a state acts to remedy the effects of that legacy of discrimination, I cannot believe that this same Constitution stands as a barrier. . . .
>
> Three hundred and fifty years ago, the Negro was dragged to this country in chains to be sold into slavery. Uprooted from his homeland and thrust into bondage for forced labor, the slave was deprived of all legal rights. It was unlawful to teach him to read; he could be sold away from his family and friends at the whim of the master; and killing or maiming him was not a crime. . . . The position of the Negro today in America is the tragic but inevitable consequence of centuries of unequal treatment. . . . The dream of America as the great melting pot has not been realized for the Negro; because of his skin color he never even made it into the pot.[22]

Marshall didn't say it in his dissent, but compounding his frustration was the fact that Jewish leaders, his former allies at the NAACP, had used their political strength to support Bakke. Quotas had been used for much of American history to limit the number of Jews at schools and in top jobs. That ugly history led Jewish groups to oppose the use of all quotas, even though the U.C. Davis plan did not limit slots for Jews or anyone else. Marshall felt this division in the liberal coalition gave Bakke his victory.

"Well, the trouble with Bakke to my mind was that the Jewish people backed it," Justice Marshall said in an interview over a decade after the decision. "And that gave me great problems. I wanted to win it. And there were times when I almost won it. They were playing with the word 'quota.' Worried about the word as if they can't handle the words. We can all handle words."

Particularly galling to Marshall was the suggestion made by some of his fellow justices during the arguments over *Bakke* that poor whites as well as blacks should benefit from any program intended to help the disadvantaged. "There's not a white man in this country who can say he never benefited by being white," Marshall said with certainty.

*　　*　　*

The *Bakke* defeat left a deep scar on the seventy-year-old Marshall. He took it as a personal affront, a signal that he, the only black justice, no longer had a major influence on the nation's legal approach to race relations. Marshall's isolation, combined with his recent illnesses, his sense of being threatened by the Carter people, and his drinking, began to bring out a grumpy, gruff, even rude and imperious side to his character. Friends, people who worked with him, and his fellow justices reported at about this time that Marshall seemed depressed.

The public saw his pained personality, too. As the highest ranking black man in American government, Marshall had made a rule of lambasting black militants for their failure to obey laws and work hard. Now he changed his tune. Marshall made one of his rare public appearances at Howard University Law School. He agreed to attend only because his good friend Wiley Branton was being installed as dean of his alma mater. For the first time he did not focus on opportunities for well-prepared black students. Instead he spoke about the continuing presence of racists who were still ready to defeat any black person.

Marshall warned against the "myth" that blacks were doing better economically and socially. Race relations were not getting better, he said. He pointed to the resurgence of the KKK—"The Klan never dies"—and said black students needed to outperform whites in law, politics, or business if they hoped to succeed because whites would never treat blacks as equals. The raging justice went so far as to say it was ridiculous for him to try to act as a role model for young black people, even though he was on the Supreme Court: "For what? These Negro kids are not fools. They know that if someone says they have a chance to be the only Negro on the Supreme Court, the odds are against them."[23]

His relationship with his colleagues soured further when Marshall was on the losing end of a 6–3 decision in *Herbert v. Lando*. The Court ruled that a person suing for libel, publication of a "damaging falsehood," had the right to probe the thinking of newspaper editors—or TV and radio producers—for evidence of bias or intent to do harm to the person's good name. The ruling struck Marshall as a clear violation of the First Amendment protections for a free, aggressive press.

In his dissent Marshall said journalists should be able to argue about stories without fear of later having those discussions used against them. It was an angry dissent, but the real expression of his anger came out when he spoke to the annual conference of the Second Circuit Court of Appeals. "My personal view on editorial autonomy can be succinctly stated: It must be afforded the utmost protection to ensure that the public is exposed to the widest possible range of information and insights," Marshall said. "Ill-conceived reversals [by the conservative majority on the Supreme Court] should be considered as no more than temporary interruptions." [24]

While Marshall was now freely firing off public criticism of the Court, there was even greater return fire. In 1979 Bob Woodward, the *Washington Post* reporter who had done groundbreaking work on the Watergate scandal, coauthored *The Brethren*, in which Marshall was depicted as failing to pay attention to cases, not doing his work, and being criticized by his fellow justices. To a public wondering what the now reclusive justice was like behind the marble walls of the Court, the authors told stories of Marshall regularly watching TV at work and leaving in the middle of the day. When he was around, the authors wrote, Marshall was less than serious, greeting Chief Justice Burger by saying, "What's shakin,' chiefy baby!" They also reported that Marshall was more admired for cracking dirty jokes during obscenity cases than for his legal skills.

Woodward and his coauthor, Scott Armstrong, also wrote that Marshall's fellow justices told each other stories about his "laziness and inattention." They reported that several justices had concluded that Marshall was overly dependent on his clerks in preparing for cases and writing opinions. The book told the story of the day Justice Stevens visited Marshall to ask a question about a case. "He asked Marshall about one opinion that Marshall was writing and he concluded that Marshall did not really understand the issues in it," they wrote. "Stevens was sure that Marshall was capable of being a good lawyer, but he had not done his homework and was relying entirely on a clerk." [25]

The book enraged Marshall, already feeling unappreciated and disrespected by the Court's new majority. Now his public reputation was being slurred, and he suspected that other justices, whom he considered family, had talked to the authors. There was also the worry that the book would give a new burst of energy to efforts to force him to retire.

Marshall remained angry about the book for years. His face became red at the mention of its title. "I would say ninety-nine and forty-four one-hundredths of the words in *The Brethren* are goddamn lies," he bellowed in a later interview. "When *The Brethren* came out I didn't even have a radio, much less a TV. Ask the guy who wrote it. He has never talked to me in his life. If he says so, he's a liar."

The deep hurt was evident to the people closest to Marshall—his wife and clerks. They had always been careful to protect the only black Supreme Court justice, but now they grew even more fierce in guarding his reputation. Karen Hastie Williams, Marshall's goddaughter and the daughter of his friend William Hastie, who clerked for Marshall in the 1974 term, said the book's damaging description of Marshall was offensive and not true. "The clerks in his chamber, as well as in a number of other chambers, usually wrote a first draft of the opinions," said Hastie Williams. "But then T.M. would go over it, and would talk with the clerks about it. He would talk about the draft opinions, what he liked, what he didn't like, he'd make editorial comments. He was very hardworking and very devoted to his work at the Court and took it very seriously." [26]

"I think *The Brethren* was really unfair," said Phillip Spector, who clerked for Marshall in the 1977 term. "I think, first of all, if he wants to spend his lunch hour watching TV instead of socializing, that again is his privilege." As for writing his opinions, Spector recalled that "all of the justices depend heavily on their clerks." He noted that Marshall was one of three justices who took the time to have their clerks, and sometimes themselves, read every petition, often from prisoners, requesting the high court to hear appeals of lower court rulings. [27]

But Susan Bloch, who clerked for Marshall in the 1976 term, saw the justice primarily focused on areas of law that interested him: "He cared mainly about civil rights, death penalty cases, abortion, people kind of cases. He cared less about corporate kinds of cases." [28]

Marshall's fellow justices gave ambivalent views of his work on the high court. Chief Justice Burger, in a cagey response to questions about Marshall's reputation said no member of the Court ever told him "directly or indirectly" that Marshall was not competent and worthy of "complete respect." [29]

And while Justice Powell dismissed *The Brethren* as having "a good deal of fiction in it," he added, in only circumspect praise: "I don't think there's ever been any lack of respect for Thurgood Marshall on this court."[30]

Justice Brennan, Marshall's closest colleague on the Court and fellow liberal, was one of the few justices to strongly dispute the image of Marshall as little more than an empty head on top of a black robe. "If it appears in history books that Justice Marshall never did his own work, that would just be false," said Brennan in an interview. "That just isn't true. The truth is that Thurgood Marshall is one of the ablest—and he's been one of the ablest on the Court since its origin. There's no doubt about it."

The Brethren's release caught Marshall at a low point. He had been ill, and his defeats on key cases had drained much of his interest in the work of the Court. Despite his health problems Marshall had braved discomfort to do the work he considered important, defending minorities and the poor. The book was not inaccurate in its reporting, but it was limited. The more aggressive and engaged Marshall of his early tenure on the Court was not on view. Although he did often use his clerks to keep the wheels turning in his office, he had maintained control of the decision-making in his chambers. And Marshall's playful behavior with his fellow justices could easily have been interpreted as the actions of a man who worked at happy relationships with justices, even when he disagreed with them. But out of that context, the book's judgment of Marshall hit the public as condemning.

Marshall felt under siege and was less trusting and more cantankerous than ever. It was becoming more difficult for old friends and the clerks to get through his gruff exterior. And in October 1979 Marshall's health took another blow when he fell down the Capitol's steps. He broke both arms and cut his forehead. He was at home for two weeks and seemed to become even more withdrawn—to the point of rudeness. "I went over, my wife had baked some cookies for him, and I took them over to his house," Justice Rehnquist recalled in an interview. "And you know, he was quite cordial, but he never turned off the television set the entire time I was there. He would just watch television part of the time and then talk to me part of the time."[31]

Marshall continued to distance himself from people in 1980, when the University of Maryland named its new law library in his honor. He refused to go to the dedication and cursed the law school dean, Michael Kelly, when Kelly called to plead with him to come. The justice told Kelly that since there had been no place for young Thurgood Marshall at the school, he would not have anything to do with it now. When school officials invited other members of the Court to attend the ceremonies, Marshall wrote a memo to the justices urging them not to go. "I will not be there and I have made this clear to them from the beginning," Marshall wrote. "I am very certain that Maryland is trying to salve its conscience for excluding the Negroes from the University of Maryland for such a long period of time." [32]

Justice Brennan traveled to Baltimore for the ceremony and acted as a stand-in for his good friend. "They named it the Thurgood Marshall Library and they have a beautiful bust of him as you come in the door and a portrait as well . . . " Justice Brennan recalled in an interview. "Thurgood refused to go. I was very, very happy to do it. He never thanked me. Never said a word to me about it. That's Thurgood."

Marshall could not, however, turn down one offer. Baltimore officials asked him to sit for a sculptor so a statue could be made of him and placed in front of a new federal building in downtown Baltimore. The *Baltimore Sun* ran a story on Marshall's three visits to the studio of the artist, Reuben Kramer. Marshall brought his sons, Goody, twenty-one, and John, nineteen, along and even tried to show the boys the house where he was born on McMechen Street, but there was only a vacant lot left. When the statue was dedicated in 1980, Justices Blackmun, Brennan, Powell, Stevens, and White all trekked up to Baltimore to join Marshall for the ceremony.

The Marshall statue was a tribute, but it also reflected the growing sense that even though he was very much alive, he belonged to the past. The Carter administration, desperately trying to hold on for a second term, wanted Marshall to retire. Marshall's refusal became more important when the conservative Republican Ronald Reagan defeated Carter in November 1980. Even after the defeat, administration people pressed Marshall, hoping that Carter would be able to name a nominee before the right wing took control of the White House.

Since Marshall had rejected all direct appeals to retire, Carter officials began urging reporters to speak with him. The story being circulated was that Carter, even as a defeated president, would get the Democrat-controlled Congress to confirm his nominee. Hints of a breaking story sent reporters to the phones, calling Marshall and his friends to see if and when the big announcement would be made. Some reporters even called the Marshalls at home, forcing Cissy constantly to deny that he was soon quitting.

The phone calls and rumors became so intense that Warren Burger heard a report that Marshall was dead. The chief justice immediately had his secretary call the Marshall home to offer condolences to Mrs. Marshall. Burger's secretary said, "Excuse me, Mrs. Marshall, please remain calm. I just got a call from the chief justice. He just heard over the radio that Justice Marshall had died." Cissy Marshall was first more amused than shocked. "I'm very calm because he's there in the living room having his dinner!" she said.[33]

The phone calls and stories about Marshall's imminent retirement continued until Reagan was inaugurated. That week *The Washington Post* quoted Marshall as calling any report he was leaving a "bald-faced lie." The justice told the paper: "I'm serving out my term. . . . And it's a life term."[34]

CHAPTER 32

Hangin' On

W ITH RONALD REAGAN IN THE WHITE HOUSE, Marshall
was now one of the unfashionable left-wingers in Washington.
No conservative president was going to celebrate an old civil rights activist. And Marshall would be out of tune with the president's policies
and any new appointees to the Supreme Court.

Martha Minow, one of Marshall's clerks in 1981, recalled that the full
shock of the Reagan landslide hit Marshall the day the Republican-
controlled Senate began new committee appointments. The former segregationist Strom Thurmond—Marshall's old adversary—was named
chair of the powerful Judiciary Committee.

Hearing the news, Justice Brennan walked over to Marshall's nearby
chambers to commiserate. Afterward they walked out of the office, sadness hanging over them. Brennan, short and thin, ambled slowly arm in
arm with the tall, thick Marshall. The sight struck an emotional chord
with Minow, who stood in the hallway to watch the old men walk away.
"You could just see there was a sense of everything they had worked for
being turned around," she recalled.[1]

The political temperature inside the Court was changing, too. Chief
Justice Burger, long a law-and-order advocate, stepped up his hard-nosed
speeches on crime. He complained that the courts offered little protection to Americans victimized by vicious crimes but gave every protection
to criminals.

An outraged Marshall was reluctant to duel with the chief justice in public. He was still intensely loyal to the Court. But his resentment continued to build, and finally he spoke out against the climate. He told a judicial conference that no judge had any business promoting safeguards for victims of crime or helping police and prosecutors win convictions if it meant taking away protections for people accused of crimes. "[There are those who claim] that the judiciary has not taken an active enough role in combating crime," Marshall said without naming Burger. "The suggestion that we take sides frightens me. . . . Our central function is to act as neutral arbiters of disputes that arise under the law. . . . I therefore urge that you politely disregard any suggestion that you give up the robe for the sword." [2]

Burger did not directly respond to Marshall, but relations between the two became distant. Chief Justice Warren had frequently visited with Marshall and made sure that he wrote a fair share of the high-profile opinions. Burger, by contrast, almost never spoke to the justice and gave him the most tedious writing assignments. "Until Burger, the low man on the totem pole got all the income tax cases, because those are the driest things," Marshall said. "They give them all to me and Blackmun" as liberal members of the Court. Justice Brennan, another liberal, was spared because he was the senior justice.

Despite his bumpy relationship with Burger, Marshall did not dislike him. He considered Burger a "mystery," a Nixon-appointed chief justice, though not in hock to conservatives. "I can tell you this," Marshall said. "There were enough votes here to get rid of the *Miranda* rules [requiring police to inform suspects of their rights to have a lawyer and to be silent]. And Burger wouldn't let it go through. He just hung it up."

Marshall's favorite conservative justice was Sandra Day O'Connor. An Arizona Republican, O'Connor was Reagan's first nominee and the first woman on the Supreme Court. She was a tall, athletic-looking woman with a deep concern for issues of discrimination and a strong appreciation of Marshall's role in history. From her first day on the Court she treated Marshall as her personal hero. Seeing another pioneer breaking into the highest ranks of the legal fraternity, he became fond of O'Connor despite her views.

Aside from O'Connor, however, Marshall began taking more public slaps at some of his right-wing brethren. At a 1982 oral argument during a death penalty case, Justice Rehnquist asked a prosecuting attorney if it would not be cheaper to execute a young convict than to pay to feed and jail him for a lifetime. An angry Marshall interjected, "Well, it would have been cheaper just to shoot him right after he was arrested, wouldn't it?"[3] The comment made headlines around the country. But Marshall had no regrets and did not think it hurt his relationship with the other justices, including Rehnquist. "I thought it should be said," he replied years later in an interview.

Occasionally Marshall's critical attitude came out in edgy racial humor, such as addressing other members of the Court as "Massa" in a deep slave dialect. Especially in the justices' conferences when the case being discussed involved racial issues, Marshall used his humor to belittle justices who disagreed with him. "In conference there's no question about where Thurgood stood," Brennan recalled. "No matter how uneasy it made any of us. That's the way he felt about it, and he expressed it that way. I got worried about whether he carried that too far."[4]

While he felt free to take shots at his fellow justices, Marshall was extremely sensitive when critics made fun of him. In February 1982, *National Lampoon* published a satirical article under Marshall's byline. It detailed how he had become a connoisseur of dirty movies while setting the Court's standards for obscenity. In the parody Marshall complained that too much pornography was badly written. To remedy the problem he offered guidelines to help writers produce better-quality obscene material.

"To write dirty well, pick topics your audience will be interested in, like fellatio, blow jobs and white women. Especially white women. They're my favorite. Oh, yeah." The article then offered an example of good porn: "Handsome Thurgood X. was sitting in his chambers one day. . . . Suddenly he was interrupted by Sandra Day O., a distinguished white woman. 'You certainly look foxy in your big, black robes,' Sandra purred. 'I've got something even bigger and blacker underneath,' replied Thurgood. Thurgood had always had a way with women—you could say he was a sort of Afro-disiac."[5]

Marshall was not amused by the attempt at humor. A few days after he saw a copy of the article, he wrote to FBI Director William Webster that it was "scandalous" and asked if the bureau could start a criminal investigation. Webster wrote back that there was no basis for them to get involved and that FBI lawyers had concluded the article was written "to produce humor" and was "patently absurd."[6] Marshall, still stinging, decided to drop the issue.

Although he was becoming more thin-skinned and had testy relationships on the Court, Marshall's arguments in conference proved persuasive on the first major race relations case of the 1980s, *Fullilove v. Klutznick.* The case dealt with the constitutionality of a federal government plan to set aside 10 percent of its contracts for minority businesses. Some white contractors complained that the set-asides were discriminatory. But the Court voted 6–3 that given the history of government-approved discrimination, Congress had the power to employ a contract set-aside plan. In his concurring opinion Marshall focused on the history of racial discrimination and the need for the government to remedy the damage it had created. "Such classifications may disadvantage some whites, but [not] whites as a class. . . . Today, by upholding this race-conscious remedy, the court accords Congress the authority necessary to undertake the task of moving our society toward a state of meaningful equality." [7]

Marshall's stand in the *Fullilove* case did not, however, fit with his own record on hiring clerks. His clerks on the Second Circuit were all white, and the ones he hired on the Supreme Court were overwhelmingly white. Out of the twenty-eight clerks he hired in his first ten years on the high court, only one, Karen Hastie Williams, his goddaughter, was black. In 1980, the year of the *Fullilove* case, Marshall apparently became newly sensitive to appearances. He saw to it that two of the four clerks he hired were black. The two, Stephen Carter, a Yale Law School graduate, and Adebayo Ogunlesi, a Harvard Law graduate, were more than qualified. But Marshall, concerned about his own performance on the Court, had not instituted an affirmative action plan of the kind he was advocating in his Supreme Court opinions. Marshall's hiring rate for black clerks was about 15 percent through the rest of the 1980s, although he never hired any clerks from his alma mater, Howard University, or from any other predominantly black law school. He did better with females; almost a third of his clerks were women.

Despite his limited hiring of black clerks, Marshall remained a revered figure among civil rights activists. In fact, it was Marshall who was unhappy about the direction of the civil rights movement. Roy Wilkins, his longtime friend and head of the NAACP, had suffered a serious stroke in 1977 and died in 1981. In an interview after Wilkins's retirement, Marshall expressed his displeasure with the state of the NAACP. He said the group's current leaders were not worthy heirs to the scrappy, inspired group he had worked with. He complained that the group was paying too many people big salaries: "They've got six million here and three million there—maybe they've got too much money, I don't know."[8]

Marshall was similarly disdainful of Jesse Jackson, a former aide to Martin Luther King, Jr., who had become the leading civil rights figure in the nation during the 1980s. Marshall found Jackson's rhyming speeches, hunger for TV appearances, and regular threats of boycotts unappealing. The justice saw Jackson as a self-promoter, and when Jackson tried to make appointments to see Marshall, the justice said no.

While he felt the civil rights movement lacked direction and leadership, Marshall began to assert a new definition of civil rights in his Supreme Court opinions. He argued that constitutional protections should be extended to the homeless, to the poor, and to convicts.

In *Clark v. CCNV,* a 1984 case, Marshall challenged both the federal government's lawyer and his fellow justices on the right of homeless people to sleep in Lafayette Park, across from the White House. They claimed to be there to protest poverty and homelessness in America.

Chief Justice Burger dismissed the argument as "frivolous" and an attempt to "trivialize" the Constitution. And Paul M. Bator, attorney for the government, said the homeless had a right to protest in Lafayette Park but not to sleep there. Marshall interrupted Bator during oral arguments to ask: "Did you ever sleep on a grate?" When Bator replied, "No sir," Marshall nodded as if to say Bator had no idea what the poor had to go through to survive. "Well, these people want you and others to understand what that's like," he said. He went on to draw parallels between blacks who engaged in lunch counter sit-ins at segregated restaurants during the 1960s and the protests by the homeless. "These demonstrators want to get over the message there are many people who have no place to sleep. How can you get over that message without being allowed to go to sleep?"

Despite his passionate arguments, Marshall did not win the support of his brethren. In a 7–2 decision they ruled against the protesters. Marshall's only support came from his liberal ally Justice Brennan. The case was typical of the Court's actions in the early 1980s, with Marshall reduced to writing strongly worded dissents while the majority went off in the other direction.

Although he was clearly isolated on the Court, Marshall had some surprising victories, in which he championed a more expansive view of civil rights. For example, he successfully made himself into an advocate for prisoners and inmates with mental problems.

One of his major victories came in *Ake v. Oklahoma* (1984). A convicted murderer, Glen Ake, appealed to the Supreme Court arguing that his sentence should be overturned because the state had refused to pay for a psychiatrist to evaluate him. Ake claimed that he needed the exam to prove he was insane when he committed the crime and should not be given the death penalty because of his mental problems. Marshall persuaded the other justices to vote with him on the theory that the state had an obligation to make certain that every suspect got the fullest possible defense.

Two years later Marshall continued the same line of argument. He contended that a murderer who was found to be insane could not be sent to the electric chair. In *Ford v. Wainwright*, Marshall got a majority of his colleagues to agree. He argued it was unconstitutional under the Eighth Amendment's ban on cruel and unusual punishment. But these wins were exceptional, and every win came only after great struggle.

*   *   *

Marshall's health continued to be a problem. In February of 1984 the seventy-five-year-old was hospitalized with viral bronchitis for a number of days. By now the justice looked like an old, sick man. His eyes teared up uncontrollably from glaucoma, and he had difficulty reading. His hearing was so bad that he had to wear hearing aids in both ears. And on occasion he had to go to the hospital for anticoagulants because of blood clots that doctors feared might cause another heart attack. Reporters regularly called the Supreme Court to ask about Marshall's health. But the justice refused to make any comment. He scribbled on the margin of one inquiry from the Court's press secretary, Toni House: "I'm not hanging on for life." [9]

Marshall's chronic health problems led *The New York Times* to write: "He is enormously overweight, tipping the scales, he says, at 250 pounds. . . . He gave up smoking years ago but his occasional wheezing and gasping as he moves about the court have frequently alarmed his admirers." [10]

The age and poor health of Marshall and his lone liberal colleague, eighty-year-old Justice Brennan, were highlighted as the Court's conservatives took more power. In 1986 Chief Justice Burger resigned. President Reagan named a relatively young Antonin Scalia, fifty, to the Court and nominated William Rehnquist to be chief justice. With younger, more active conservatives now leading the Court, the aging liberals were having a difficult time making any impact. The best the liberal wing could do was hold on. *Life* magazine wrote that "neither man [Brennan or Marshall] has any intention of retiring while Reagan—whom Brennan refers to as 'That Man'—is in office to appoint their successors." [11]

While he was widely assumed to be near resignation if not death, Marshall continued to focus on cases that meant a great deal to him. He not only wrote dissents in every death penalty case, but also maintained his lifelong crusade against laws that allowed prosecutors to use race as a basis for keeping blacks off juries. Throughout the 1980s Marshall had been systematically filing dissents in any case where black defendants charged that blacks had been forced off juries with peremptory challenges. His regular dissents on the issue caught the attention of his colleagues on the high court as well as federal appeals court judges around the country. When a black man appealed his conviction on burglary charges because prosecutors had excluded blacks from the jury, the Supreme Court agreed to review the case.

In a 1986 ruling (*Batson v. Kentucky*), the justices held 7–2 that in criminal cases black jurors could not be excluded simply because they were the same race as the defendant. It overturned a two-decades-old precedent. Marshall had won a surprising and deeply satisfying victory; the high court had finally limited the use of race as a basis for disqualifying jurors.

But Marshall pushed the issue even further. He wanted to get completely rid of the use of peremptory challenges. Ironically, that effort split the two-man liberal wing of the Court. Justice Brennan was not willing to do away with the long-standing right of lawyers to strike jurors whom they suspected might not be fair to their case.

Brennan, wanting to sign on to Marshall's concurring opinion, finally wrote to ask him if he could accommodate his concern that lawyers not be unfairly hamstrung in jury selection. But Marshall refused his friend's invitation to soften his stand. "I continue to believe that [allowing the use of peremptory strikes] will by its nature be ineffective in ending racial discrimination. . . . I see no reason to be gentle in pointing that out and I doubt that pulling my punches would make the situation any better." [12]

Marshall's unyielding position was similar to the stance he almost always took with his fellow justices in the 1980s. During that period, he spent as little time as he could at the Court, coming in around 10:00 A.M.

and sometimes leaving by 3:00 P.M. He was less interested in engaging the other justices in conversation or even argument than in writing eye-catching dissents and occasionally making angry public comments about the direction of the Court. His detachment and anger deepened after he lost two key cases dealing with race, *Wygant v. Jackson Board of Education* and *McCleskey v. Kemp.*

In *Wygant*, a 1986 case, the Court ruled 5–4 that when teachers were being laid off, the board of education could not use race as a consideration to keep black teachers on the job while firing more senior white teachers. In the 1987 *McCleskey* case, the Court ruled against Warren McCleskey, who had appealed his death sentence on the ground that capital punishment was given to blacks more often than to whites. McCleskey's case was the first to challenge the death penalty in the Supreme Court on purely racial grounds. Justice Marshall argued that since blacks were more likely to get the death sentence, they were being given "cruel and unusual punishment," in violation of the Eighth Amendment and their rights to equal protection. Again he lost 5–4. In both cases Marshall proved unable to persuade the swing vote, which belonged to Justice Powell.

In an interview Powell acknowledged that Marshall talked with him about the cases. And Powell conceded that Marshall sometimes became angry at his colleagues when they voted against him: "I think Thurgood was perhaps more demonstrative than the rest of us," said Powell politely.[13]

Justice White, in a separate interview, said because of these setbacks Marshall became resentful of his colleagues in the mid-1980s. With a solid conservative majority in place, White said, Marshall "was not averse to writing strong dissents and speaking out that way in conference—I don't blame him."[14]

Marshall confided to his longtime friend Monroe Dowling, who was now living in Washington, that he was furious with the conservatives and was using the justices' conferences to raise hell. "Thurgood would say how mean and unpleasant they could be. If it hadn't been for Brennan, I guess they would have put him in jail. Thurgood called them everything but the son of God in conference."[15] Marshall began to make his unhappiness public in more speeches and interviews during the late 1980s. He had previously made some critical comments to fellow judges at Second Circuit conferences, but now he made speeches before wider audiences that featured harsher tones.

The first major outburst came in a speech commemorating the two hundredth anniversary of the Constitution. Former Chief Justice Burger was the head of the bicentennial celebration, and no one expected Marshall to do anything but join his former colleague in the spirit of an all-American celebration. But Marshall's attitude toward the bicentennial became apparent when he turned down Burger's invitation to Philadelphia to take part in a proposed reenactment of the signing of the Constitution, with the justices playing the founding fathers. "If you are going to do what you did two hundred years ago," he said, "somebody is going to have to give me short pants and a tray so I can serve coffee."

He stepped on toes again at a convention of patent and trademark lawyers in Hawaii. Marshall said the original, unamended Constitution was "defective from the start" because it allowed slavery and denied women the right to vote.

In a defiant speech on what had seemed to be a motherhood-and-apple-pie subject, the justice said it took a "bloody Civil War" to abolish slavery and the nation was still struggling with the consequences of having been born with a Constitution that treated some citizens as less than human. He added that only the post–Civil War amendments guaranteeing equal rights and due process had saved the country. The authors of the Constitution "could not have imagined nor would they have accepted that the document they were drafting would one day be construed by a Supreme Court to which had been appointed a woman and a descendant of an African slave," Marshall said.[16]

While he was in Hawaii, Marshall ran into his old NAACP colleague Bob Carter. The two had rarely spoken since they began feuding in the late 1950s. Now, with Cissy Marshall leading the way, they agreed to have dinner. Carter was a federal district judge in New York, a widely respected man and a veteran of the civil rights movement. Late in life the two had more in common than they would have guessed thirty years earlier.

Carter later said the Hawaii dinner was not a big deal even as it signaled that the two had come together again. "We were just pleasant with one another—there wasn't any feeling in mind—it just was Thurgood and I were free. I don't hold grudges long." Similarly, Marshall found himself even wishing his former nemesis had been named to a higher court. After the dinner he felt that Carter "should at least have been on the Court of Appeals."

When Marshall got home from Hawaii, his critical remarks about the Constitution were still in the news. And a few weeks later he broke with Supreme Court decorum by making personal comments about current

politics and personalities, including some on the Court, in an unprecedented televised interview with the columnist Carl Rowan. "Well, a couple of more decisions like that Georgia sodomy case and we won't have
any privacy left, but I'm going to raise my voice against it as long as I got
breath," he said, criticizing the ruling in *Bowers v. Hardwick*, a 1986 case
in which the Court upheld a Georgia law making sodomy criminal.

Marshall was also extremely critical of Attorney General Edwin
Meese's Justice Department for trying to "undermine the Supreme
Court itself." He told Rowan that he no longer read legal briefs from the
Justice Department because "they write political speeches and put the
word 'brief' on them." He offered a particularly venomous assessment of
the current solicitor general, Charles Fried. Marshall said Fried represented only "the president and not the rest of the government."

These comments sparked a lot of grumbling inside the Supreme
Court and in legal circles. But around the nation they got less attention
than Marshall's uncensored judgments about American presidents. He
said Roosevelt did not "do much for the Negro," but Truman "did everything he could." Marshall said Eisenhower did nothing but "try to undermine the [1954] school decision." He reserved judgment of President
Kennedy except to say that he "was held back by the Attorney General,
his brother."

Marshall's highest praise went to President Johnson. He told Rowan
that Johnson's plans "were just unbelievable, the things he was going to
do—but he was too far for Negroes and civil rights." However, he had
less kind words for Jimmy Carter, saying "his heart [was] in the right
place . . . [but] he's going to be a non-entity anyhow."

Marshall's worst rating for any president went to Ronald Reagan:
"The bottom. . . . I think he's down with [Herbert] Hoover and that
group and [Woodrow] Wilson, when we didn't have a chance." When
Rowan reminded the justice that Reagan was an extremely popular president, he responded: "Is he more popular than the average movie star?"[17]

The *Baltimore Sun*, Marshall's hometown paper, expressed surprise at
his lack of propriety. The *Sun* noted that the last Supreme Court justice
to make such harsh comments about a sitting president was impeached
and urged Marshall to practice "judicial lockjaw."[18]

Reporters asked President Reagan about Marshall's low assessment of
his civil rights record during a state dinner at the White House. The
president responded that as a child he was taught that "the greatest sin
was prejudice," and as governor of California and president he had

fought for civil rights. "I am just sorry that he is not aware of that," Reagan said coldly.[19] The president's response apparently did not change Marshall's mind. In an interview a few years later he continued to express contempt for Reagan: "I wouldn't do the job of dogcatcher for Ronald Reagan." The justice said Reagan's administration had "started the downhill slide which is proceeding as planned in civil rights. You just get the feeling that it's hopeless."

In conversations with his best friend on the court, Justice Brennan, Marshall also said that during the Reagan years, he felt the court's right-wing majority was guilty of casting votes that were racist. "It's a fact," Brennan said in an interview, that Reagan's appointees to the court took a regressive stand on civil rights cases. "The principles that we had thought were settled are now upset. See, Thurgood, as I suggest, thinks that this shows innocently or otherwise that there's still a streak of racism. I agree that there is. There's no question. But I will not accept his feeling that that may also be true of our colleagues, that they are personally racist or that their votes reflect any racism."

As Marshall got more crotchety and indifferent to arguments about ending affirmative action, he became a favorite target for conservatives. When the *National Review* magazine ran an article on how the Court had become home to older liberal justices who relied heavily on their clerks, they put a picture of a sleeping Marshall on the cover. "Is the fellow in the black robes, second from the left, actually listening?" the conservative author Terry Eastland asked. "Or has his mind drifted elsewhere, perhaps to what *TV Guide* offers that afternoon? And of the 15 or so opinions of the court assigned to him during the term, how many does he—not his clerks—actually write?"[20]

The article outraged Marshall's supporters. "It's utterly untrue, utterly, utterly, utterly untrue!" said Justice Brennan in an interview. "Thurgood would say, if he'd say anything, he would say I'm sure that it's simply another illustration of the survival of racism."

Marshall confided his hurt feelings about the article to Brennan, but in an interview he claimed never to have seen it. "I'll bet you they never sent me a copy of it," he railed. "If they still got their teeth they didn't send it."

By the late 1980s Marshall's brusque manner was on display wherever he went. His friends and clerks treated him as a grand, frumpy old lion, a sage emperor who had earned the right to be gruff and indifferent to critics as well as friends. His family, clerks, and secretaries made excuses for his behavior but privately worried about him. "Once in a while he'll explode," Cissy Marshall said in an interview when asked about her husband's frustration with the conservative court and what remained of the civil rights movement. "I wish he would explode more and get it out of his system. But he keeps a lot in."

Marshall's pal Monroe Dowling said Cissy Marshall worked endlessly to keep her husband out of situations where he might embarrass himself in public or bring shame on the Court. Dowling recalled, "I think drinking diverted his attention sufficiently. Cissy worked her heart out, and she did the best she could to make him a great man."

In September 1988, Marshall was honored in celebration of his eightieth birthday by the Congressional Black Caucus with a dinner at the Washington Hilton. Colin Powell, then the national security adviser; the former National Urban League Secretary Vernon Jordan; the former attorney general Ramsey Clark; and the newly appointed Supreme Court justice Anthony Kennedy were in the audience. Despite the outright adulation, Marshall was still in a difficult mood. When he stood up to speak, he pointed to a large, flattering photo of himself: "What worried me about this thing . . . doesn't it look like a memorial? If I can put it in the best English available, *I ain't dead yet!*" After a short speech he quickly left.[21]

* * *

To counter negative publicity about him, Marshall's friends and family began urging him to write about his life. Marshall had stayed away from reporters until he sat down for the TV interview with Rowan in 1986. He had turned down interview requests from the networks, newspapers, and magazines, even his former law clerks. But after publication of *The Brethren*, he encouraged Stephen Carter, one of his former clerks, to write favorable pieces about him. "He felt that maybe it was time to have some people do some talking who were going to say good things about him," said Carter.

After the headlines he created with the TV interview and the growing pressure for him to create a first-person record of his life, Marshall agreed to write his life's story jointly with Rowan. The justice signed the contract and got a check for $100,000 from the publisher, Little, Brown. The two began to sit down for interviews but soon found themselves divided over the project. Rowan, having heard about Marshall's tirades in the Supreme Court case conferences, wanted to focus on the confidential conversations. And in recounting Marshall's career as a lawyer, he wanted to focus on a case Marshall had lost, the Lyons murder case. Marshall was outraged. He told Rowan to leave him alone and sent the money back to the publisher.

"Well, he was very angry at Rowan for asking him to reveal conference secrets, and he said to me, 'I can't believe it, I could just see the *Washington Post* headlines: "First Nigger on the Court Opens up the Conference," ' " said Susan Bloch, one of Marshall's former clerks.[22]

By July the *Legal Times* newspaper reported that Marshall told friends the book deal was dead. "All I can tell you is that I decided that the first-class materials for a book were not available," Rowan told the paper. Marshall refused to explain why the deal was off, but the paper said his friends still hoped he would do the book with another writer.[23]

Marshall subsequently responded to a letter I wrote him requesting an interview with *The Washington Post Magazine*. In more than a dozen interviews over a six-month period in 1989, Marshall spoke about everything from his childhood to the *Brown* decision. The interviews took place in his office, where he had a small bust of Frederick Douglass on his desk along with pictures of his grandchildren. On the walls were animal skins and spears from his trips to Africa. On the shelf behind his desk was a small TV that he would turn on and watch while eating Campbell's soup for lunch. His secretary, Jane McHale, would come in with messages, and if he wanted some hot tea, he would call for his assistant, Grafton Gaines.

By this time in his life, Marshall walked with the help of a cane. He wore white support socks because of circulatory problems. He was gruff but wonderfully full of opinions, attitudes, and a strong sense of irony about the ways of the world. At one point I asked him whether he had a problem with liquor. Without missing a beat he shouted: "Hell yes. Not enough! Not enough to go around." Then his face turned serious, and he added, "It runs in my family." When I asked why he often happily told stories about drinking too much, the justice confided that it was a strategy. "It keeps people off of you," he said. "I figure if I can tell it, it ain't nothing new."

One day, after a clerk had come into the office to drop off a document, Marshall shook his head. "These guys, my law clerks," he said laughing, "they get from $100,000 to $120,000 when they leave here." Marshall clearly regretted that he had never made big money as a lawyer and his jibe had the edge of envy to it. But he said he had never given any thought to leaving the Court and entering a lucrative private practice. "I've said it three or four times—I took the job for a tenure of life, I took it for life so I'm going to stay for life," he added. On another day he described his tenacious effort to stay on the Court in this way: "I expect to die at the age of a hundred and ten, shot by a jealous husband."

In 1989, after two terms of Reagan and the election of the Republican George Bush, Marshall's politics were way out of touch with the American public. The divide was particularly evident in his views on crime. While much of the debate in Congress was about stiffer, mandatory sentences and applying the death penalty to more crimes, Marshall insisted that the rights of suspects and even convicted criminals needed strong protection.

One area in which Marshall was willing to limit individual rights was gun control. "Oh, I'm for complete gun control," he said. "I don't believe you have any right to carry a gun, except for policemen and law enforcement officers. But I don't see why anybody else needs a gun. If he does, let him have it licensed."

During another visit Marshall spoke of his disappointment with the current civil rights movement. He was particularly concerned that the nation's commitment to the ideal of integration was no longer in evidence. Television and magazines were filled with young black people who were far more excited by talk of Malcolm X–style black nationalism than Thurgood Marshall's lifelong work to bring about equality of the races and integration under law. "Oh hell yes, we've made progress since the 1950s," Marshall said. "In my mind, no question. But since the 1970s you haven't made as much as you should have made."

One of the difficulties some younger, more race-conscious black Americans had with Marshall was that he was married to a woman of Filipino ancestry and his two sons had married white women. His grandchildren looked white. In an era of strong emphasis on blacks taking pride in being black, Marshall and his focus on integration was out of sync.

The *Washington Post Magazine* article brought a new round of attention to him and pleased Marshall. He spent the next several weeks autographing copies of his cover photo for colleagues, his staff, and Court personnel.

More media attention came to Marshall when he began using the term *Afro-American* in his legal opinions. In October 1989, Marshall filed a dissent in a death penalty case and for the first time used the expression. He told reporters that he chose not to use *African-American* because it was not in the dictionary—*Afro-American* was.

He had never used the term *black*, which had become a common label in the 1960s with the "Black Power" movement. He preferred the word *Negro* with a capital *N*, or on occasion *colored*. He said he was uncomfortable using the term because he remembered a time when calling someone "Black" would start a fight. Marshall said, "I don't think you get pride by calling yourself this or that. . . . I think you get pride by studying your background . . . and finding that you have nothing to be ashamed of."[24]

Just as Marshall was doing the interviews with the *Post*, he was caught up in his last major battle in defense of affirmative action programs. He filed strong dissents in two 1989 cases, *Ward's Cove Packing Co. v. Atonio* and *Richmond v. J. A. Croson Co.*

In the first case the conservative majority ruled that people who claimed discrimination had to prove they were being treated in a biased manner. The Court declared that there was no convincing evidence of discrimination if one racial group disproportionately outnumbered another in management or any other area of a company's operations. The majority opinion said such differences could be attributed to the level of education and training of the people in one group.

In the second case the majority ruled 6–3 that the city of Richmond could not have a 30 percent set-aside for black-owned companies in its municipal contracts. The conservatives argued that individual contractors, be they black or even Alaskan Aleuts, must first show that they had personally suffered discrimination in contracting before they could benefit from any set-aside.

Marshall, noting that Richmond had been the capital of the Confederacy and renowned for strict segregation, could not believe that his colleagues would doubt that blacks continued to suffer discrimination in the city. "[A] majority of this court signals that it regards racial discrimination as largely a phenomenon of the past. . . . I, however, do not believe this nation is anywhere close to eradicating racial discrimination or its vestiges. In constitutionalizing its wishful thinking, the majority today does a grave disservice . . . "

Although Marshall lost both cases and did little personally to try to win votes from the conservatives, he was still having an impact on his colleagues, according to one of the Court's conservative newcomers, Antonin Scalia. "Marshall could be a persuasive force by just sitting there," Scalia said in an interview. "He was always in the conference a visible representation of a past that we wanted to get away from, and you knew that as a private lawyer he had done so much to undo racism or at least its manifestation in and through government. Anyone who spoke in conference on one of these race issues had to be looking at Thurgood when you're speaking. You know you're talking in the presence of someone who devoted his life to that matter. Therefore, you'd better be doggoned sure about it. . . . He wouldn't have had to open his mouth to affect the nature of the conference and how seriously the conference would take matters of race."[25]

In Marshall's mind the key to the Court's future action on cases dealing with race was the Fourteenth Amendment, requiring equal protection and due process. He wanted the Court to "stop looking around for excuses not to enforce it." By his own account during this period, Marshall failed to change votes on affirmative action and contract set-aside cases. In one interview a dejected Marshall conceded: "I haven't done as much as I could—I don't know why."

The problem with the high court's understanding of race, Marshall later added, was that few of the justices knew much about the lives of black Americans. "What do they know about Negroes?" he asked. "You can't name one member of this Court who knows anything about Negroes before he came to this Court. Name me one. Sure, they went to school with one Negro in the class. Name me one who lives in a neighborhood with Negroes. They've got to get over that problem. What you have to do—white or black—you have to recognize that you have certain feelings about the other race, good or bad. And then get rid of 'em. But you can't get rid of them until you recognize them."

In 1990, Justice Brennan, who was still more willing to engage his colleagues than Marshall, led a fight to get a majority to support federal government set-asides for minorities on broadcasting licenses. Marshall was resigned to writing his dissent by this point, but Brennan won a majority by visiting with other justices and arguing that Congress had the power to improve the nation's quality of life by having radio and TV stations in the hands of racially diverse owners.

A month after the ruling, in July 1990, Brennan, age eighty-four, suffered a minor stroke. That same month he retired. President Bush appointed a federal appellate and former New Hampshire state supreme court justice, David Souter, to replace him. Souter had a moderate to conservative record far different from Brennan's. Justice Marshall, age eighty-two, was alone holding down the Court's left wing.

After Souter's nomination Marshall, in an unusual step, agreed to tape an interview with one of his favorite Washington TV correspondents, Sam Donaldson of ABC's newsmagazine show *PrimeTime Live*. Marshall, looking disheveled and speaking in short, mumbled sentences, was clearly upset about Brennan's departure, telling Donaldson that Brennan "cannot be replaced." Marshall specifically explained that there was now no one on the Court to engage the right wing because "no one here can persuade the way Brennan can persuade."

When Donaldson mentioned Souter, Marshall turned sour and said: "When his name came down I listened to television and the first thing I called my wife and asked, 'Have I ever heard of this man?' She said no. . . . So I promptly called Brennan because it's his circuit. And his wife answered the phone . . . she said he's never heard of him either."

Donaldson then asked the justice about President Bush. Marshall became even more dour. "It's said that if you can't say something good about a dead person don't say it," said Marshall. "Well, I consider him dead."[26]

The interview stirred a Washington storm. Attorney General Richard Thornburgh said Marshall's comments "saddened him." Thornburgh said it was "the first time any Supreme Court justice has ever criticized, in our history, an appointment and indeed the president who made the appointment." Senate Minority Leader Robert Dole told reporters that Marshall's comments amounted to "cheap shots . . . [that were] partisan and demeaning." *Newsweek* magazine later reported that many of Marshall's friends found the justice's performance on TV "embarrassing."[27]

Souter was easily confirmed (90–9), but the damage to Marshall was considerable. Questions about his physical health now extended to questions about his mental health. His public attack of a fellow justice created tensions inside the Court, even among justices who had always supported him.

A few days after the television interview, Marshall was in Chicago to give a speech at the American Bar Association when his cane got caught in a floor sign and he suffered a serious fall on his left shoulder. He did not break any bones but was sufficiently shaken and bruised that he canceled the speech and went back to Washington to see his doctor.

The next several months saw Marshall's health continue to worsen. He walked with a pained, slow motion. His eyes teared almost constantly, and it was hard for him to read. His circulatory problems worsened, and his heart was weak. Meanwhile, President Bush's popularity climbed to record-breaking heights after the U.S. military successfully pushed Iraq out of Kuwait. Bush looked to be a shoo-in for another four years as president. The justice told friends he no longer thought he could stay on the Court until Democrats regained control of the White House.

Emotionally and physically on the decline, Marshall paid attention only to cases that had to do with the death penalty. Now that Brennan was gone, Marshall was the lone voice objecting to capital punishment. In a 1990 case he took a stand against victim impact statements—allowing crime victims to offer emotional testimony intended to encourage a jury to hand out death sentences. But it was another futile fight. Marshall lost when the conservative majority ruled 6–3, in *Payne v. Tennessee*, that victims should be able to testify.

At the last conference for the term in June 1991, Marshall privately told his colleagues that he was going to retire. He said he had already called Justice Brennan. There was silence as the other justices took in the meaning of their colleague's words. Chief Justice Rehnquist got up and uncharacteristically hugged Marshall. Justice O'Connor cried. Other justices came up and held his hands.

The people in Marshall's chambers were just as shocked and surprised. Scott Brewer, one of his clerks that term, said he never gave them any sign he was about to retire. As word spread among his clerks and assistants, the office filled with crying and hugs.

But the very next day, Marshall's dissent in the Payne case came out, revealing the distance between Marshall and his colleagues. "Power not reason, is the new currency of this court's decision making . . . " Marshall wrote.

That day Marshall sent President Bush an official letter announcing his retirement, a week short of his eighty-third birthday. He had been on the court for twenty-four years. In a final gesture he also walked down from his seat on the bench, removed his black robes, and stood in the lawyers' well, the same place he had stood to argue *Brown*. With his son Thurgood Jr. and his daughter-in-law, Colleen Mahoney, behind him, the retiring justice vouched for their qualifications as lawyers and asked that they be admitted to the Supreme Court bar.

News of his retirement stirred memories and emotions nationwide. It was the end of an era. Marshall's reclusive behavior, bad health, and rough manner had taken him out of the mainstream of popular culture for more than a decade. But his retirement gave new life to Marshall's status as a national icon, a symbol of this century's civil rights struggle. A large group of reporters—far bigger than the Supreme Court press corps—jammed into the Court's East Conference Room. Marshall came in leaning heavily on his cane. His collar was unbuttoned, and his tie was off to one side as he sat down heavily in a grand old mahogany chair.

"How do you feel, Justice?" a reporter shouted. The ornery side of Marshall came right out. "With my hands," he replied, ending with a harrumph. His wife, his oldest son, his daughter-in-law, and grandchild (Thurgood William Marshall, whose middle name was a tribute to Justice William Brennan) stood in the shadows, joined by Marshall's friend and former cabinet secretary William Coleman.

When reporters asked if President Bush should name a black person to succeed him, Marshall said that Bush should not use race as a "ploy" to allow the "wrong Negro" to get the job. "I think the important factor is to pick the person for the job not on the basis of race one way or the other." Marshall quoted his father as once telling him that there was no difference between a white and black snake—"they both bite."

One reporter asked about Martin Luther King, Jr.'s mountaintop vision of a day when black Americans were free at last. Had black America achieved the dream? Marshall said, "I'm not free. All I know is years ago when I was a youngster, a Pullman porter told me that he had been in every city in this country. . . . And he never had been in any city in the United States where he had to put his hand up in front of his face to find out he was a Negro."

And how did he wanted to be remembered? Marshall quipped: "He did what he could with what he had."[28]

Within weeks of his departure, Marshall's complaints about light-headedness led his doctors to hospitalize him. His doctors implanted a pacemaker and told reporters that he should soon be able to resume a normal life.

While Marshall struggled with failing health, he was still technically a member of the Court. He had resigned pending the confirmation of his successor and even wrote one pro forma dissent in a death penalty case. But he was concerned that he might have to stay on the Court for several more months because of a storm swirling around the man nominated to replace him, Clarence Thomas.

Thomas, age forty-three, had been on the U.S. Court of Appeals for the District of Columbia for only sixteen months. He had served as President Reagan's appointee to chair the Equal Employment Opportunity Commission for eight years before President Bush put him on the D.C. circuit. The stocky, cigar-smoking Thomas was a strong opponent of affirmative action. He once wrote to *The Wall Street Journal* that the Constitution should always be applied in a "colorblind fashion." He had moved the EEOC away from class-action suits against big companies. Under Thomas the agency emphasized cases where people could prove that they, personally, had been the victim of discrimination.

Thomas was also more of a black nationalist than a Marshall-style integrationist. He was an admirer of Malcolm X, a man who had openly cursed Marshall. Thomas had even criticized the *Brown* decision as based on sociology, not law, and asked why black children had to sit next to white children to get a good education. He supported the death penalty, and he was opposed to abortion rights. But none of those positions proved sufficiently controversial to stop overwhelming support for a poor black boy, raised by his hardworking grandfather, who had gone to Yale Law School and then made his way to become a Supreme Court nominee.

Thomas seemed set for certain confirmation until a former employee, Anita Hill, testified before the Senate Judiciary Committee that he had made crude sexual comments to her. The hearings became a national sensation, with TV networks broadcasting her testimony and then his denial, claiming he was the victim of a "high-tech lynching." People across the nation began impassioned conversations about sexual harassment and racial politics. Feminist groups, already opposed to him because of his stand on abortion, bombarded both Thomas and the all-male panel of senators as members of an old boys' club that just did not "get it." The NAACP, which had not opposed Thomas, now came under pressure to stop his confirmation.

In his chambers Marshall watched the tawdry TV drama unfold with pain. He did not much care about Hill's charges but felt the Court was being damaged by TV's crass and steamy coverage of the serious business of a Supreme Court nominee's confirmation. If his own hearings had been televised, with charges of Communist association, hatred of whites, and incompetence flying around, Marshall was sure he would not have been confirmed. Stephen Carter, one of his former clerks who spoke with him at the time, said Marshall "thought TV coverage was a very poisonous thing."

Also, the aged justice saw the selection of a young black conservative with views contrary to his own as a slap in the face from President Bush—whom Marshall had excoriated on national TV only a year before.

"It hurt Thurgood deeply," said Monroe Dowling. "He said, 'Think of them comparing him with me.' He just cussed—'They think he's as good as I am'—and to him the comparison was odious."

Bill Coleman watched some of the hearings with Marshall. "If you want to suffer through the most miserable time, sit in Justice Marshall's chambers with the television on during the time of the Thomas hearings," he said. "I think that if he'd ever felt that the guy to replace him was going to be Thomas, he would have stayed on. . . . He just thought it was terrible that a person with that small ability and with that lack of commitment, would be on the Court at all, much less to take the seat that he had vacated."

Despite the hearings, Thomas was confirmed in a close vote, 52–48. When Thomas joined the Court he did the usual round of courtesy calls for brief conversations with the other justices. But his introduction to Marshall was most memorable. The meeting with Marshall lasted more than two hours, with Marshall doing all the talking, telling stories about his days as a civil rights lawyer as well as his time on the Court. Marshall also offered a tip to the newcomer: treat the other justices like a family, where ideological differences do not amount to personal differences.

"It could not have been a pleasant experience for him to see his seat filled by someone who did not have his view on the matters that were the closest to his heart," said Justice Scalia, who is closely allied with Thomas. "But Marshall handled it with dignity and with class, as he did everything else."

As a retired justice Marshall kept an office on an upper floor of the Supreme Court with one clerk and his longtime secretary, Jane McHale. The key issue he faced was what to do with his papers. He had long boasted that he planned to burn them because he did not want anyone poking around in them. The Library of Congress had approached him as early as 1965 to ask for them. Marshall had always turned them away. But the passing years and persistent requests that he tell his story had appealed to his ego and softened his position. He was particularly touched by the attention the newspapers and networks had given his retirement. Without explanation he called James Billington, the Librarian of Congress, and invited him over. Marshall announced he had decided to leave the papers to the library on the condition that they be made public only after he died.

His heart trouble soon put him in a wheelchair. It was a struggle to get around, but in January 1992 he was able to spend a week as a visiting judge on the Second Circuit Court of Appeals. In August the American Bar Association gave him its highest award.

Marshall, still in a wheelchair, made brief remarks in a raspy voice. He finished by reading from a poem by his college classmate Langston Hughes.

> *O, let America be America again—*
> *The land that never has been yet—*
> *And yet must be—the land where every man is free.*
> *The land that's mine—the poor man's, Indian's, Negro's, ME—*
> *Who made America,*
> *Whose sweat and blood, whose faith and pain,*
> *Whose hand at the foundry, whose flow in the rain,*
> *Must bring back our mighty dream again. . . .*
> *O, yes,*
> *I say it plain,*
> *America never was America to me,*
> *And yet, I swear this oath—*
> *America will be!*

At the end of the poem Marshall added his own signature, offering a churchlike "Amen!" Jack Valenti, who had worked as an aide to President Johnson, saw Marshall at around that time and was shocked by his friend's appearance. "He looked so tired, and so worn and so sick," said Valenti. "I felt this terrible sadness, because I really—I don't think anyone is irreplaceable, but some people leave a larger gap in the society than others. And I thought, My God, he's mortal, and he's going to die. It's just a question of when."[29]

By the late fall of 1992 Marshall was rarely leaving his house as his medical problems worsened. Ralph Winter, who stayed in close touch, recalled that Marshall was now unhappy because he was living in pain. "I think cancer was discovered at the end," said Winter. "He was very uncomfortable." In the November election President Bush was upset by the governor of Arkansas, William Clinton, giving the Democrats control of the White House for the first time in twelve years. It was a year too late for Marshall. Al Gore, Clinton's running mate, asked Marshall to swear him in, and Marshall agreed. But by January, the justice had deteriorated further and did not have the energy to do it.

Gloria Branker, one of Marshall's former secretaries, went to visit him at his home in late January. He was in bed. "Do you want to sit up?" she asked him. No, he replied. Then she asked, "Don't you want to try?" No, he said again. A grim look crossed her face, and she said, "It would be good, Thurgood." He said, "Why?"

Branker spoke to him for a few more minutes without any reply. Then he puckered his lips as if to give her a kiss. "I knew that was the signal for me to leave," she said, "and I knew that was the last time I would see him. He had given up."[30]

The next day, January 21, Marshall was taken to Bethesda. Three days later, at 2:00 P.M. on a cold Sunday afternoon, the eighty-four-year-old died.

CHAPTER 33

❧

Resurrection

A LINE OF MOURNERS stretched down the white marble steps of the Supreme Court, onto the street, and around the corner. It was cold, below twenty degrees, and getting colder as the late January sun went down, but the mourners kept coming. They formed a thin, shivering line, every breath visible by the freezing dark of sunset. But still they came. Eventually, the chief justice ordered that the building be kept open late into the night so that people could continue to file by Thurgood Marshall's flag-draped casket as it lay in state in the Court's Great Hall.

The simple pine casket, set on a bier that had once held President Lincoln's body, had been carried into the Court that morning as all the living justices stood on the marble steps to form an honor guard. Justice Souter had to help his predecessor, Justice Brennan, who had difficulty walking since suffering his stroke. The casket was set next to an oil painting of Marshall. His former clerks flew in from around the country and took turns standing guard by the casket. Eighteen thousand people walked by that day, some stopping to weep. Others left roses, and even an original copy of Marshall's brief in the *Brown* case.

The next morning the National Cathedral overflowed with more than 4,000 people, including the president and vice president. Justice Marshall's funeral service was televised live and nationwide by several networks. Chief Justice Rehnquist spoke first and noted that the words above the entrance to the Supreme Court read "Equal Justice Under

Law." In slow, deep tones, the chief justice said: "Surely no one individual did more to make these words a reality than Thurgood Marshall."

Vernon Jordan, the powerful Washington lawyer, stirred the large crowd when he rose to speak. With his velvety baritone booming through the high-vaulted main chapel, Jordan's words brought tears to the eyes of the mourners: "We thank you, Thurgood . . . your voice is stilled but your message lives. Indeed, you have altered America irrevocably and forever." [1]

After the services a private burial was held at Arlington National Cemetery. Rev. William Pregnell, who had been Marshall's minister at St. Augustine's Episcopal church in Washington, presided over a service limited to family, clerks, and a few friends. [2]

In the week following his death, newspapers, TV news shows, and magazines were filled with tributes to Marshall. For several days in a row the front pages of *The New York Times*, *The Washington Post*, and *USA Today* carried story after story about him. In a cynical era it was an unusually passionate outpouring of love for a public figure.

"It brought tears to my eyes to see people lined around the block, waiting to come into this building to walk up to where his casket lay, just to peek," said Justice O'Connor. "Every sort of person came through that day. I was so moved by what I saw." O'Connor paused as emotion welled up in her. Her voice quivered and cracked as she said that at the end of his life Marshall had no idea that people would go out of their way to remember him. [3]

This affection shown Marshall upon his death stood in sharp contrast to the indifferent public reception he had received for most of his time on the high court. He felt undervalued because he thought the white legal community did not appreciate his legal skills. And he felt dismissed by younger, more militant blacks. To top it off, Marshall's signature battle, the push to integrate black people into white America, had also come under attack.

In the thirty-nine years between his triumph in the *Brown* case and his death, Marshall saw the nation go from complete segregation through halting attempts at integration to occasional resegregation. When he first joined the high court in the late 1960s, almost two thirds of black students were in integrated schools. When he died, however, two thirds of black students were back in mostly segregated schools.

The rise of conservative, white Republican politics under President Reagan in the 1980s had pushed black Americans to the left, where they were isolated and became disillusioned about the promise of integration. Voluntary resegregation among black Americans, middle class as well as poor, came into vogue. Enrollment rose in historically black schools. Blacks of all classes created new black suburban and urban neighborhoods instead of attempting to integrate white areas. Even among students at elite colleges and universities, there was a rush toward segregation, with some creating separate housing and dining facilities for different ethnic and racial groups. In that framework Marshall had become an anachronistic figure, not in touch with the raw emotional power of popular black leaders such as Jesse Jackson. And Marshall was far from the anger and defiance of polarizing Black Muslim Louis Farrakhan, who openly espoused a completely segregated black nation.

Ironically, though, by the time Marshall died, several powerful forces, many produced by his lifelong work promoting equal rights, conspired to resurrect him as a national hero. First, as a lawyer Marshall had forced colleges and graduate schools to open their doors, producing more black professionals. As a federal judge he had become a champion of programs to expand business contracts and wealth for that black middle class. This rise in education and affluence among black Americans led to an unparalleled peak of black political power. At the time of his death, the number of blacks in Congress had reached record heights, forty in the House and one in the Senate.

This new, politically powerful black middle class was large enough to demand respect for the death of a major black figure. These younger black people were not Marshall's generation, and because of his reclusiveness, they did not know him well as a popular figure. But it was in their political self-interest in a conservative era to use his death to generate support for policies—such as affirmative action—that Marshall had championed as the highest-ranking black American ever to serve in the national government. Liberal and moderate white Americans also wanted to celebrate him. For them Marshall was a positive black figure, a law-abiding, educated man, a strong counter to the hateful black perspective of a Farrakhan.

But even among those celebrating Marshall's life for their own reasons, it went largely unremarked that Marshall had provided the grand design, a vision that led to a new structure of race relations in the United States. His demands for integration and his legal strategies were at the heart of the twentieth century's battle to end legal segregation. As a child of turn-of-the-century Baltimore, he grew up in a Jim Crow world of strict segregation in stores, restaurants, and water fountains. But he was also heir to a Baltimore community where free black people actively asserted their rights to live with whites as equals.

The young Thurgood Marshall's experiences in this unique city were the foundation for his advocacy of equal treatment. It led him to realize that the law was the only tool for resolving the damning racial problems confronting America in the aftermath of legal slavery. Marshall eventually took those ideas into the courts, creating new laws, ending Jim Crow segregation, and reshaping American race relations. His legal work in the *Brown* decision is now heralded by both conservatives and liberals. In the words of Duke law professor and former solicitor general Walter Dellinger, *Brown* stands as "the most important legal, political, social and moral event in twentieth-century American domestic history."

"When I think of great American lawyers, I think of Thurgood Marshall, Abe Lincoln, and Daniel Webster," said Thomas Krattenmaker, a professor at Georgetown University Law Center. "He is certainly the most important lawyer of the twentieth century."[4]

"He, in my opinion, did more to establish equal justice under the law than Martin Luther King or any other single individual," said the former associate justice Lewis Powell. "No American did more to lead our country out of the wilderness of segregation than Thurgood Marshall."[5]

The scope of Marshall's achievement in American law, however, was wider than the black American civil rights movement. His every argument spoke to individual rights for all. Protections for black Americans or any other minority, in Marshall's vision, were a function of the inviolable constitutional principle of individuals. When Marshall spoke about the nation's future, he projected that when the law put blacks and whites on equal footing, racial discrimination would be submerged in a greater sea of protections for individuals. As Marshall once said, black Americans are not members of the Negro race but individuals in the human race.

As Marshall won case after case advancing the rights of black Americans, he left behind him case law protecting the rights of *all* citizens to vote in primaries, to protest, to live in any neighborhood, go into any park, get on any bus.

And once he was on the Supreme Court, Marshall's rulings, both majority opinions and dissents, reflected an expansive view of the Constitution as essentially a manifesto of individual liberty. He was a guardian of free speech, even obscenity, for individuals and the press. He argued that a woman's right to have an abortion was protected as a matter of privacy under the Constitution. He supported prisoners' rights to have unlimited appeals of rulings and unfailingly opposed the power of the state to impose the death penalty on anyone.

On cases dealing with school desegregation and affirmative action, Justice Marshall also cast his opinions as statements of individual rights, not simply as a class action for all black people. For example, his support of busing to integrate schools, even across jurisdictional boundaries, was based on the need to protect the rights of individual children who were being denied access to the best schools. And he viewed affirmative action as a matter of individual rights for black Americans, victims of discrimination who needed remedial action to be made whole.

"Thurgood Marshall stood for the broadest interpretation of almost all the provisions of the Constitution," said Chief Justice William Rehnquist. "He was a very stout champion of individual rights. And he was an equally stout champion of minority rights."[6]

His critics, however, argued that Marshall was to blame for an America that had become a battleground for lawyerly arguments over competing special interests and increased racial and ethnic divisions. Critics, for example, saw affirmative action as a contest of rights. They insisted that any preference based on race was a violation of every citizen's right, regardless of race, to be treated equally.

Critics also argued that integration was not a cure for all that ailed black America. They contended that quality education, not integration, should have been the goal of *Brown*. Marshall had held that integration assured black children access to equal resources. Integration, by itself, however, had not improved the education of black children. Poor black children, for example, were often left behind in run-down schools as whites and even the black middle class fled to the suburbs to escape forced integration plans. Also, tracking children according to test scores had led to separation of black and white children even in nominally integrated schools. The black children, who generally scored lower on placement tests, were put into classes for lower achievers, while white children were generally taught in classes for top learners. This was a new version of separate but equal.

Marshall's response to the critics had never been to back away from the promise of the *Brown* decision. Instead he called for even greater efforts at integration, such as busing children across city and suburban boundaries and government equalization of funding among the checkerboard of affluent and poor school districts.

Critics said Justice Marshall's prescriptions for dealing with continued racial inequities simply added to racial polarization in the nation. They denounced his regular votes on the high court for any plan to advance the interests of black Americans and said he failed to engage in arguments over how blacks and whites could promote their unity. "I think he [will] be thought of as a great legal advocate, but I don't think he would have been thought of as a great legal thinker," said Chief Justice Rehnquist. "If you are a legal thinker, more or less, you can't just champion the cause of a particular litigant. You have to deal with broader rules of conduct and rules that govern society and figure out how they would affect everybody."

"Justice Thurgood Marshall will be lucky to rank somewhere in the middle of the 105 Supreme Court justices who have served the United States," said the conservative legal writer Terry Eastland in a *Baltimore Sun* column. Eastland said that Marshall voted with Justice Brennan 94 percent of the time and that he "wrote few opinions of major significance, either for the Supreme Court or in dissent. He was not an intellectual force."[7]

Even critics who questioned Marshall's work on the Court, however, did not doubt his pathbreaking work as a lawyer and that he had shattered the ramparts of Jim Crow segregation. That was the real story—how Marshall built the infrastructure of American race relations in the twentieth century. He did not set out to do it; he was relatively indifferent to racial issues as a comfortable child of the black middle class. Even after his racial consciousness was raised in law school, he was content to make money instead of making history.

Once he found his true work with the NAACP, however, Marshall became a genuine American revolutionary. He could lay claim to the rare mantle of Americans who literally transformed their nation and defined not only their era but what would come after them.

Where Marshall's grand construct of American race relations most strongly comes into question is in affirmative action. On the Supreme Court, Marshall nurtured the activist proposition that the law could be extended to offer preferences and other remedies to certain classes of Americans who had been victimized by bigotry in the past. However, as rapidly rising rates of immigration bring ever higher numbers of racial and ethnic mixtures to the United States, the conversation over race is no longer just between a once enslaved black minority and a white majority. Hispanics and Asians now share a larger percentage of the population than blacks. This is a different America than Thurgood Marshall imagined. Even a rising rate of racial intermarriage has added substantial new numbers of people who spill out of the Census Bureau's standard boxes of black, white, and other.

But despite the growing distance between his experience of race in America and the current reality, the nation still relies heavily on the protections and individual rights Thurgood Marshall put in place to maintain successful race relations.

As I am writing this in 1998 there is an unparalleled rush of immigrants entering the United States. As a result there is a growing nativist backlash based on the new arrivals' reluctance to fully assimilate into American culture. That has led to calls to make English the nation's official language and sparked complaints that immigrants are taking jobs and seats in the universities, while also occupying a larger percentage of welfare rolls.

It is true that this generation of immigrants is not leaping aboard the bandwagon of assimilation; they want to live with people from their native land and often want to build schools and churches that will allow them to retain their ethnic and racial identities despite the heat of the great American melting pot. But even as the immigrants celebrate their heritage, they nevertheless insist on their individual rights and protections as Americans. They have often come to America for the same reason that previous generations of immigrants came here. They want to escape political and social oppression, they want more opportunity for their children, and they expect that the law will give them the right to be treated as equals in the political and business world.

What allows immigrants to thrive in America, despite continuing racism, anti-immigrant politics, and their own tendency to segregate themselves, is the bedrock of individual rights and freedoms developed by Thurgood Marshall's legal work.

Due to Thurgood Marshall's lifework, those rights are not going to be diluted even though the nation is experiencing rising rates of segregation in neighborhoods and schools. The cutting issue today is whether different levels of wealth and opportunity will attach themselves to different classes, limiting economic mobility.

Immigrants with money are able to move into the best neighborhoods regardless of who else lives there. However, both immigrants and native-born Americans who lack education and skills increasingly find they have little hope of moving up in society. This new divide in America still falls heavily on blacks and other people of color who are disproportionately poorer than whites. But this division is not based solely on race or immigrant status: The dividing line now is access to education and professional opportunities.

This new version of separate but equal creates dilemmas that, ironically, will also have to be resolved within the legal framework of individual rights set in place by Thurgood Marshall. His expansive view of the law as a tool of social engineering to help the disenfranchised requires that the government take steps to bridge the inequalities among its citizens. Insuring adequate funding for schools, expanding basic health care to include all Americans, and protecting the hungry and the homeless are issues that need to be addressed before America breaks down into a savage society with only rich and poor. Adequate protection for the poor has to come from extending the idea of individual rights to soften the harsh realities of economic inequity.

That framework of rights is Marshall's legacy. He saw integration as the only possible way to ensure equality: It protected minorities and the poor from being isolated and left behind. Integration of racial groups and economic classes guarantees that everyone has an investment in the common good and a mutual concern about the nation's future.

Segregation leads to an erosion of individual rights. Whether the segregation is done under Jim Crow laws or because people say they prefer to be with their own, it exacerbates inequities and creates a society where some people's rights are more important than others (usually the poor and people of color). Protection of individual rights in an integrated society is the crux of Marshall's legal design and is key to any blueprint for the future.

Marshall was right that full integration is a necessary precondition for assuring equal rights. How those rights are protected will be the civil rights story of the next century. It is evidence of his tremendous impact on America that the nation will be testing its most important principles against a standard he set in place.

If history is biography, then Marshall's story is that of the architect of American race relations for the twentieth century. He was a revolutionary of grand vision who laid the foundation stone for race relations in his time and for generations beyond.

AFTERWORD

BIOGRAPHY, BY ITS NATURE, focuses on a single life, but is worthless unless the story of that single life reflects the stories of many others. Thurgood Marshall, the black lawyer who stood before the Supreme Court to argue for racial equality in America, never stood alone. As special counsel for the NAACP Legal Defense Fund, he represented millions of people who faced the personal pain of living in a nation where the law and the government supported racism. In the five years since this book was published the phone still rings several times a month with these very people on the other end of the line, people who want to go back to 1954. They want to talk about the *Brown* decision.

All these years later, many of the people are quite elderly. Some cry as they remember people who fought alongside them but are no longer alive. Before the entire generation is gone, these people want to personally share their role in the great drama of the *Brown* case. As the watershed decision rendered in *Brown v. Board of Education of Topeka* reaches its 50th anniversary they also have stories to tell, stories they want in the history books.

Their stories vary in the details, but they all circle that one critical moment in American history like planets orbiting the sun—the momentous ruling in *Brown*. It was *Brown* that raised the possibility of integration becoming a reality in their minds, whether they were for it or against it; it was *Brown*, in a single ruling, that put the power of the federal government's judges, FBI agents, and even the US military's force on the side of equal rights for all; it was *Brown* that made segregation not only immoral, but a crime.

In Prince Edward County, Virginia, the people who went to school with sixteen-year-old Barbara Johns want the world to know that she lit the fuse on the only student-led fight against school segregation that became part of the *Brown* case. The Virginians also speak with awe of Spottswood Robinson and Oliver Hill, the lawyers who helped Barbara Johns stand up against the fearsome power of segregation in a small, rural town.

The letters and phone calls from South Carolina speak to the pressure on black farmers, laborers, and preachers who dared to sign a petition in support of the lawsuit to end segregated schools. Black families working as sharecroppers on white-owned farms were thrown off the land they had worked for generations because they supported Lawyer Marshall and the NAACP case. But the farmers and preaches held together to challenge the system.

Callers from Kansas are sometimes moved to tears of the power of Rev. Oliver Brown's dedication to school integration. Others want to be sure that history does not forget the surprising support of many white Kansans for opening school doors—including lawyers representing the state who are proud to have fought for integration. And the emotional testimonials from Kansas extend to NAACP lawyers Robert Carter and Jack Greenberg who came west to represent "Little Linda" Brown, the reverend's daughter who wanted to go to the whites-only school near her house.

Time and again these testimonials come back to a man the old folks call Lawyer Marshall. Sometimes the boisterous big man stayed in their homes while working on a case. Once in a while the people calling about Marshall are the lawyers who worked with him or even against him on a case. A surprising number of people mention the sacrifice they made to get into a court to see him at work. Some still have receipts from the money they sent to the NAACP to support his work.

All of these personal acts of sacrifice and inspiration built to a crescendo with the May 17, 1954 decision. When Thurgood Marshall was at his best in a courtroom, he made his clients into real people suffering real damage from the laws of segregation. He told their stories—both as a legal argument for equal rights and as an appeal to the ideals and conscience of white Americans. At the time, some people condemned Marshall for using personal anecdotes and sociological evidence. The same critics condemned the high court for citing such evidence when they ruled in Marshall's favor in *Brown*. But while the facts, the law, and basic fairness were on Marshall's side, it may have been the power of those individual narratives that ultimately tipped the balance in the Supreme Court and the court of public opinion. Those stories were not just ornamentation, but gave the legal arguments the ineffable force of human justice.

* * *

Fifty years later a complex set of fresh challenges confronts us, and a new river of powerful and personal stories flows.

In 2003, minority students at the University of Michigan Law School had their own stories to tell the Supreme Court as they successfully fought to preserve the idea that race should be a legitimate factor when students are chosen for the nation's most selective schools. White students who have filed suits against affirmative action programs at the University of Michigan and University of Texas law schools also had stories to tell. Their stories are about the frustration of achieving the grades necessary to get into colleges or graduate schools only to be rejected in favor of minorities with lower test scores. In a way, their plight was also heard when the same Supreme Court struck down numerically based racial preferences in college admissions at the University of Michigan's undergraduate school.

Then there are the angst-filled stories from the generation who fought academic integration but now see top universities allowing blacks, Hispanics, whites, and Asians to live in separate housing, dine separately, and even hold university-sponsored graduation ceremonies that are racially exclusive. The rationale of students and administration is that minority students at these white schools need the emotional support that comes with strong racial cohesion. But to the outside world it appears these schools are teaching students lessons on the value of separatism. In the Michigan cases of 2003, Justice Clarence Thomas, a polarizing figure on the Court when it comes to matters of race, harshly criticized affirmative action for generating just this kind of "aesthetic" diversity at elite institutions. It is a deeply ironic story that this voluntary separatism is a fact of life at institutions that advertise themselves as enlightened examples of racial diversity.

These modern-day stories seem to collide with the stories told by Marshall's generation, stories focused on the battle to improve education through integration. This new generation doesn't deny the validity of the stories told by Marshall and his peers. Instead they argue the relevance of those stories in light of the bitter reality they face fifty years after the *Brown* case: that America's schools are still very segregated and the remedies devised in the past—including affirmative action—seem to have failed.

The impression of renewed segregation is borne out by statistics: A 2003 study by the Civil Rights Project of Harvard University found that the nation's largest twenty-seven school districts are "overwhelmingly" black and Latino and are segregated from white private and public schools—the study labeled them Apartheid Schools. And the trend is getting worse. As a result of a reversal that began in 1988, the percentage of white students attending public schools with black and Hispanic students "is lower in 2000 than it was in 1970 before busing for racial balance began." As a consequence, according to the report, "at the beginning of the twenty-first century, American public schools are now twelve years into the process of continuous resegregation."

Several key trends have contributed to the new segregation. First, a continuation of "white flight" to the suburbs and a series of setbacks on the Supreme Court during the 1970s have stopped efforts to fully achieve desegregation. For example, *San Antonio Independent School District v. Rodriguez* (1973) denied efforts to equalize spending between rich and poor school districts. And *Milliken v. Bradley* (1973) prevented busing between suburban and urban school districts in Detroit to achieve integration. Together these decisions effectively brought the era of active integration to a halt. In his dissent in the Detroit case, Marshall said that the ruling would allow the nation's cities to be divided into black and white enclaves, and as a result, the schools themselves would be segregated. "It is a course, I predict, our people will ultimately regret," he concluded in his dissent.

The problems he predicted have arrived. According to a 2001 study from the National Center of Education Statistics, 70% of black students attend schools that have minority enrollment of more than 50%. Meanwhile white students are attending schools where, on average, 80% of their fellow students are also white. Latinos were described in the study as the "most segregated minority group."

A second key trend that has shifted the dynamics of race in America is immigration. Five years after the publication of this book, one thing stands clear—demographic changes have forever altered this new generation's stories about race in American society. The influx of immigrants from Mexico and Latin America, as well as Asia, the Caribbean, Africa, and Eastern Europe, has reached unprecedented heights in this nation of immigrants. The Hispanic population grew notably during the 1990s and with over 37 million Hispanics residing in the United States, this ethnic group now surpasses African Americans. For the first time in U.S. history, black people, whose numbers stand slightly more than 36 million, are not the biggest minority group. Though they do not yet have the political or economic clout that African Americans continue to exercise, these new voices are telling different stories about race relations and creating a new American reality of race.

In America's highly diverse population, the race question has transformed; it is no longer simply a matter of blacks making demands of the white establishment by pointing to the history of slavery, legal discrimination, and cultural bigotry. The new immigrant's story, whose starting point is usually a heroic effort to get to America, seen as a land of economic and political opportunity, stands in sharp contrast to traditional black narrative of slavery and racism. In this new America, where more than a third of the population belongs to a minority group and nearly half of all public school students are minorities, school integration is not universally viewed as key to equalizing educational opportunities.

These new trends have created a new reality in which many judges, school boards, and parents have tired of race occupying the primary position in the discussion of school reform. Their refrain is that race is too divisive and legal segregation is not the issue. Thurgood Marshall's critics have long contended that equality education, not integration, should have been the goal of *Brown*, and must now be the goal of American leaders. The black middle class fled to suburban enclaves and poor black children were left behind in failing neighborhoods and schools. Black children across the country continue to score lower as a whole on achievement tests. Hispanics remain at much greater rates of poverty, with higher dropout rates, and higher segregation rates. Both groups remain far behind their Anglo and Asian-American counterparts on test scores. These facts, say Marshall's critics, must be addressed with better schools—not with more theoretical worries over integration. Are Marshall's remedies, particularly affirmative action, even relevant anymore?

From its inception, affirmative action has been under fire by critics who claim it unjustly rewarded lesser-qualified individuals, and did nothing to address long-term problems of discrimination. But since Marshall left the court in 1991, the slow whittling away at affirmative action programs across the nation has continued unabated. Circuit courts held, in cases such as *Hopwood v. State of Texas* (1996), that schools might be limited in their use of race to determine admissions. In a case that affected African Americans and Hispanics equally, the Fifth Circuit determined that the University of Texas had not given enough evidence that the Fourteenth Amendment permitted them to use race as a factor to benefit African Americans and Hispanics.

The high court also took a more direct control of affirmative action programs. In *Adarand Constructor's v. Pena* (1995), the court held that when it came to set asides, affirmative action programs must meet strict scrutiny standards. This meant that the governmental program must meet "compelling" national interests and be narrowly tailored. This had the effect of greatly limiting many affirmative action programs.

In many ways the most visible opponent to Marshall has been his replacement on the Supreme Court, Justice Clarence Thomas. Previewing the turn away from race in a 1987 Howard University Law Review article, Thomas wrote: "*Brown* was missed opportunity as was all of its progeny, whether they involve busing, affirmative action, or redistricting." Thomas concluded that the Warren Court made a mistake by basing its 1954 decision on stories about the damage that school segregation did to hearts and minds of black children. He wrote that by making "sensitivity the paramount issue," the court lost sight of the Constitution and the Declaration of Independence, which call for liberty and equality for all citizens. Americans should be free, Thomas wrote, to rise above "petty squabbling over 'quotas,' 'affirmative action,' and 'race conscious remedies for social ills.'"

Thomas's stand is in keeping with his judicial philosophy as a strict constructionist and his laissez-faire justice when it comes to government intervention about race. He would have no problem with allowing the "market" to determine whether and how people segregate.

In other words, the future Justice Thomas was one of the first to make a case that is widely accepted today—that Americans should be free to create public schools with students of any color as long as they are good schools. In that way of thinking, all-black schools can be just as good as all-white schools. And schools made up of poor children can be just as good as schools made up of rich children.

While Thomas's approach is strong in the American tradition that embraces individual rights, it could lead to rigid re-segregation and catastrophe without some governmental oversight. And the truth is, despite all of these trends, the Marshall affirmative action view may be heavy-handed and clumsy at times in its efforts to overcome discrimination. But like the "trust-busters" of the last century, it recognizes the role that government must play to ensure that racial majorities—even if they are not racist but simply looking out for their best interest—do not impose a disadvantage on minorities. People can be free to associate, but they must not exclude. And the fact is that segregation has not gone away. While political leaders may not want to talk about race, American's neighborhoods are becoming more segregated, there is a greater divide between blacks and whites on standardized tests, and the upper echelons of corporate life remain exceedingly white for such a diverse nation. As the stories in the quivering voices of those that lived through Jim Crow can attest to, segregation does nothing to positively affirm a person's sense of liberty, freedom, or racial pride.

*　　*　　*

All of these judicial actions and ongoing debates point to just how important Marshall's ideas and presence remain. The arguments in the 2003 Supreme Court case over the University of Michigan revolve around Marshall. Marshall's work in the 1978 *Bakke* decision to get Justice Powell to agree to consider race as a factor in admissions is the central issue at stake in the current affirmative action debate—it was Justice Powell's discussion of race in *Bakke* that was ambiguously confirmed in the Court's latest confrontation of the issue. Regardless of whether Thurgood Marshall's views have always won the day, one thing is very clear after a quick look at the nature of discussions taking place in contemporary life: one would have to say that Marshall remains very relevant.

Looking back at Marshall's work, one can take a different view of him in today's light. Previously he had been seen as a plodding legal mind, slowly working to overturn the Jim Crow system of segregation. He refused to make direct attacks on segregation as unconstitutional until after he had won some significant court decisions that he would use as a basis for the final blow. Even after his 1950 victory in *Sweatt v. Painter* desegregating the University of Texas Law School, he had to be pressed to abandon the legal strategy of insisting on equalizing separate facilities for blacks. Only after being repeatedly pushed did he use the direct attack—and argue that the very idea of school segregation was unconstitutional because it violated the idea of equal rights for all Americans.

This path was successful for him and his cause. But even more than a methodical strategist, Marshall can really be seen as a visionary. His creative mind was molded by crucial experiences—his years of growing up in segregated, but racially mixed Baltimore; early brushes with great thinkers such as Langston Hughes and Charles Houston; an uncompromising view that segregation must be overturned. All of these factors led him to develop the notion that integration, and only integration, was the remedy that cured what ailed society. His notion that no legal barrier to interaction should exist between different racial groups was (and is) a powerful demonstration of an ideal. And despite growing rates of segregation, despite setbacks, Marshall as the visionary and the architect of race relations is indubitable.

Though the ongoing debate flourishes about affirmative action and the consequences of desegregation decisions, it is clear that *Brown* still ranks as one of the most significant legal decisions in U.S. history. Since the Supreme Court ruled, "separate facilities are inherently unequal," life for black Americans and other minority groups has improved by every measure—graduation rates, income, and home ownership to name just a few.

The importance of *Brown* is that it finally led to the complete dismantling of Jim Crow segregation throughout the country, and slowly but surely the nation has changed. Fifty years later, no state is permitted to enforce segregated schools. A once enslaved and isolated class of citizens has seen the political, economic, and social power rising over the past five decades.

History celebrates Marshall as a Supreme Court justice and as an attorney for the NAACP. But in fact it was his creativity and ideals that set him apart. This persistent vision—the promise of America as an open, full democratic nation—could only become a greater reality with the possibility of a more integrated society. This was Marshall's goal in *Brown*, his life work and his legacy.

Fifty years after the *Brown* decision, Thurgood Marshall's role as its architect remains at the core of the never-ending, great debate about race in America. And in this debate, amid the millions of individual stories that harmonize and diverge, Marshall's voice still echoes loudest of all.

—Juan Williams and Christopher Teal

ACKNOWLEDGMENTS

FIRST WORDS OF THANKS go to Christopher L. Teal, my research assistant. His energy, commitment, and passion for this biography were a constant source of encouragement. His talent and hard work made a valuable contribution to this book. His keen criticism, good sense, and friendship kept the writing on track. My hope is that he will go on to enjoy a career as a writer.

Special thanks to the Ford Foundation, the Marjorie Kovler Foundation, the Woodrow Wilson International Center for Scholars, the Brookings Institution, American University, Eastern Illinois University, and Georgetown University; to researcher Jane McWilliams, a guiding light through Maryland history; to Jonathan Karp, an insightful mind and terrific editor; to Peter Bernstein and Carie Freimuth, the strong, supportive publishing team at Times Books; to Sybil Pincus, production editor; to Mary Beth Roche, director of publicity, and Kate Larkin; and to Amy K. Sutton, marketing manager for Random House.

My personal thanks to Russell Adams; Mufutau Adeleke; Roger Ailes; Jodie Allen; Ben Amini; Esme Bahn; Robert Barnett; Sue Bennett; Cherea Bishop; Lucille Blair; John Blassingame; Charles Blitzer; Rick Blondo; David Bogen; H. B. Bouma; Peter Braestrup; Taylor Branch; Gloria Branker; Philip Brown; John Buckstead; Patricia Camp; Nixon Camper; Adrienne Cannon; Clay Carson; Reese Cleeghorn; Lovida Coleman; Chet Collier; Lindsey Collins; Cary Beth Cryor; Rick Davis; Charles Debnam; Marvin Delany; Herbert Denton; Lucille Denton;

Joseph Duffy; Frank Ferraccio; Charles Firestone; Gail Galloway; David Garrow; Cheryl Gibert; Donald Graham; Ron Greile; Gina Wishnick Grossman; Joe Haas; Deborah Newman Ham; Louis Harlan; Kathleen A. Hauke; Michael Hicks; Doug Hock; Natalie Hohn; James Hudson; Britt Hume; Dennis J. Hutchinson; William Hyde; Donna and Marshall Jackson; Dante James; Pheobe Jacobson; Beat, Elena, Jonathan, and Alexandra Jenny; Jeanne Jordan; Tom Johnson; Raymond Jones; Michael Kelly; Damon Keith; Randall Kennedy; Ethel Kennedy; Linda Kloss; Whitman Knapp; Peter Kovler; Ken Kraven; Kim Lays; Theresa Layne; Michael Lacy; Rilda Lemons; Byron Lewis; Byron Lewis, Jr.; David L. Lewis; William and Cynthianna Lightfoot; James Loadholt; Norman Lockman; Dee Lyon; Ginger Macomber; Khalil Mahmud; Tom Mann; Ligia and Jonathan Mason; Wayland McClelland; Deborah McDowell; Jane McHale; Nancie McPhail; Ghebre Mehreteab; Courtland Milloy; Frances Murphy; Jocheol Nam; Barrett and Judy Nnoka; Prentice Nolan, Robert Novak; Susan Nugent; Gina Oglesby; Peter Osnos; Lesley Oelsner; Gayle Potter; Charlynn Spencer Pyne; Miriam Raymond; John David Reed; Olaf Reistrup; Chuck Richardson; Dr. Harry Robinson, Jr.; Marty Ryan; John Roper; Ann Sheffield; Tony Snow; Mrs. Stewart Symington; Fannie Smith; J. Clay Smith; Rod Smollah; Michael Sosler; Niara Sudarkasa; John Sununu; Brook Teal; Brook Thomas; Mark Tushnet; Vernon Thompson; Diane Thomson; Roberto Waithe; Lynn Walker; Joseph Walkes; Steve Wasserman; Dr. Arthur M. West; Dr. Arthur N., Chip, Marisa, and Arleathia West; Minna West; David Wigdor; Armstrong Williams; Roger, Chris, and Ashley Williams; John Wolter; Janet Sims-Wood; Robert Zangrando; and Li Zhao.

NOTES

1. *Right Time, Right Man?*

1. Author's interview with Louis Martin.
2. Author's interview with Nicholas Katzenbach.
3. Author's interview with Clifford Alexander.
4. *Baltimore Sun*, June 13, 1967.
5. *Baltimore Sun*, June 14, 1967.
6. Thurgood Marshall interview with the Columbia Oral History Project.
7. Ibid.
8. Diary backup, June 13, 1967, LBJ Library.
9. Thurgood Marshall interview with the Columbia Oral History Project.
10. *Newsweek*, June 26, 1967.
11. A. E. Cahlan, *Las Vegas Sun*, July 18, 1967.
12. *Chicago Sun-Times*, June 16, 1967.
13. Joseph Kraft in syndicated column, June 15, 1967.

2. *A Fighting Family*

1. Isaiah O. B. Williams's U.S. Navy pension records claim 28357; widow's pension claim 14302.
2. 1860 Maryland Census, Baltimore Census, Ward 11, p. 649.
3. Death certificate, Feb. 6, 1948, Baltimore City Health Department, no. G59968.
4. 1860 Maryland Census, Baltimore City, Ward 3, p. 790.

5. Frederick Douglass, *Life and Times of Frederick Douglass* (New York: Collier Books, 1962).

6. *Time*, Sept. 19, 1955. Note that in discussion with reporters, Marshall referred to this character as his great-grandfather. That story does not fit with documentation of the Marshall family and indeed seems closer to fable than to fact.

7. 1880 Maryland Census, M4741, p. 13, indicates that recently emigrated German families were among those that made up the neighborhood around Isaiah's home.

8. *Time*, Sept. 19, 1955, p. 24.

9. Logbook of the USS *Powhatan*, Aug. 20, 1867, National Archives.

10. 1870 Maryland Census, HR M7241, p. 199, Isaiah Williams was listed as a baker. His 1872 marriage certificate, State of Maryland, National Archives, listed his occupation as grocer.

11. Catherine Reef, *Buffalo Soldiers* (New York: Twenty-first Century Books, 1993), p. 27.

12. Joseph C. Sides, *Fort Brown Historical* (San Antonio: Naylor Co., 1942), p. 141.

13. Army of the United States Certificate of Disability for Discharge for Thorney G. Marshall, pension claim 368747.

14. Records of Post Hospital, Fort Brown, Tex., Jan. 11, 1887, pension claim 368747.

15. Certificate of Disability for Discharge for Thorney G. Marshall.

16. Record of Marriage, Baltimore City Court of Common Pleas, liber AD 17, folio 116, Maryland State Archives CR 10, 288-2.

17. Board of Health, Baltimore City, Office of Registrar of Vital Statistics, A14968.

18. Margaret Callcott, *The Negro in Maryland Politics: 1870–1912* (Baltimore: Johns Hopkins Univ. Press, 1969), p. 95.

19. Ibid., pp. 134–36.

20. Foreword, *Blackletter Journal* (Harvard Univ.), Spring 1989, p. 3.

21. Robert Jack, *History of the National Association for the Advancement of Colored People* (Boston: Meador Publishing, 1943), p. 6.

22. Roderick Ryon, "Old West Baltimore," *Maryland Historical Magazine*, vol. 77, no. 1 (Spring 1982), p. 59.

3. *Educating Thurgood*

1. Ponchitta Pierce, "The Solicitor General," *Ebony*, vol. 21, 1965, p. 68.

2. Ibid., p. 67.

3. According to the family friend Archer B. Owens, from ibid., p. 67.

4. Arnold DeMille, "Thurgood Marshall," *Chicago Defender,* May 8, 1954.

5. Richard Kluger interview with Thurgood Marshall, Dec. 28, 1973, Brown Collection, Yale Univ.

6. Board of Health, Baltimore City, Office of Registrar of Vital Statistics, A39924.

7. Health Department, City of Baltimore, Certificate of Death, registered no. C81814. Note that his death certificate lists Thorney's age as sixty-five, but other records indicate he was sixty-six years old.

8. Ryon, "Old West Baltimore," pp. 59–60.

9. As cited in Garrett Powers, "Apartheid Baltimore Style: The Residential Segregation Ordinances of 1910–1913," *Maryland Law Review,* vol. 42, no. 2 (1993), p. 295.

10. David Bogen, "Race and the Law in Maryland," p. 188.

11. An amendment to the ordinance issued on Nov. 21, 1910, Baltimore City Council, 1st Branch Journal, 1910–11, pp. 397–401.

12. "Fearless Williams in the News," *B & O Magazine,* Sept. 1951, p. 39.

13. Author's interview with Douglas Turnbull, Jr.

14. Ryon, "Old West Baltimore," p. 57.

15. Author's interview with Enolia McMillan.

16. Author's interview with Agnes Patterson.

17. Author's interview with Julia Woodhouse Harden.

18. Author's interview with Carrie Jackson; DeMille, "Thurgood Marshall."

19. Author's interviews with Ethel Williams, Pat Patterson, and Elizabeth [Penny] Monteiro.

20. "Colored People's Mass Meeting," *Baltimore Sun,* Aug. 6, 1875, p. 1; "The Colored People's Meeting . . . ," *Baltimore Sun,* Aug. 7, 1875, p. 2.

21. "The Cake Walk Homicide," *Baltimore Sun,* Nov. 25, 1875, p. 4.

22. Accounts of this incident come from Arthur Waskow, *From Race Riot to Sit-In, 1919 and the 1960s* (Garden City, N.Y.: Doubleday, 1966), pp. 21–27.

23. 1920 Maryland Census, Enumerated District 240, sheet 4.

24. Register of Baltimore, School Records of Norma A. Marshall.

25. Mason A. Hawkins, "Frederick Douglass High School: A Seventeen Year Period Survey" (thesis, Univ. of Pennsylvania, 1933).

26. Randolph C. Hinton to Thurgood Marshall, May 13, 1962, NAACP Files, Library of Congress.

27. Author's interview with Essie Hughes.

28. Author's interview with Charlotte Shervington.

29. "The Law: The Tension of Change," *Time,* Sept. 19, 1955, p. 26.

30. It has been reported that Willie Marshall may have been one of the first blacks in Baltimore to serve on a jury. But court records offer no evidence that he did so. When asked if his father was ever a juror, Thurgood Marshall

later said: "Not that I know of. As we say down South, I 'disremember'—I'm sure it's not true."

31. *Washington Star,* Aug. 28, 1958; *Newsweek,* June 26, 1967, p. 35.
32. Author's interview with Cab Calloway.
33. Record of St. Katherine's Episcopal Church, p. 152.
34. Author's interview with Teddy Stewart.
35. Author's interview with Elizabeth [Penny] Monteiro.
36. Certificate of Recommendation, Frederick Douglass High School, Baltimore, Md., and Permanent Record Card, Colored High School, Baltimore, Md., for Marshall, Thurgood.

4. *Waking Up*

1. Lincoln University to Norma Marshall, June 24, 1925, Archives of Lincoln Univ.
2. Rev. W. W. Walker to William H. Johnson, June 13, 1925; William H. Johnson to Rev. W. W. Walker, June 17, 1925, Archives of Lincoln Univ.
3. *Time,* Sept. 19, 1955, p. 24.
4. Author's interview with Franz Byrd.
5. Ponchitta Pierce, "The Solicitor General," *Ebony,* vol. 21, 1965, p. 69.
6. Quotation from Arna Bontemps, as cited in Pierce, p. 67.
7. Richard Kluger interview with Alfred Kelly, Dec. 28, 1971, Brown Collection, Yale Univ.
8. Author's interview with Monroe Dowling.
9. Irwin Ross, in *Baltimore Afro-American Magazine,* Aug. 13, 1960, p. 1.
10. Hughes as quoted in Pierce, p. 67.
11. Langston Hughes, "Three Students Look at Lincoln," Mar. 1929, Archives of Lincoln Univ., p. B.
12. Irvin Ross, *Baltimore Afro-American,* Aug. 13, 1960, p. 4.
13. Hughes, "Three Students Look," p. 2.
14. W.E.B. Du Bois, in *The Crisis,* 1929.
15. *Afro-American Magazine,* Jan. 31, 1948, p. M-7.
16. Ted Poston, "On Appeal to the Supreme Court," *The Survey,* Jan. 1949.
17. Pierce, "Solicitor General," pp. 67–68; Arnold DeMille, "Thurgood Marshall," *Chicago Defender,* May 8, 1954.

5. *Turkey*

1. "No, I never applied there," Marshall told the author Richard Kluger in 1973, Brown Collection, Yale Univ. He reiterated it during my 1989 interview.

2. Susanna McBee, "Advocate for U.S.," *Life*, Nov. 12, 1965, pp. 57–60.

3. Author's interview with William Bryant.

4. Charles Houston, "The Need for Negro Lawyers," *Journal of Negro Education*, Jan. 1935.

5. Oliver Allen, "Chief Counsel for Equality," *Life*, June 13, 1955, p. 141.

6. James Poling, "Thurgood Marshall and the Fourteenth Amendment," *Collier's*, Feb. 23, 1952.

7. Author's interview with Oliver Hill.

8. Allen, "Chief Counsel," p. 141.

9. *Time*, Dec. 21, 1953, p. 19.

10. Charles Houston to Walter White, Oct. 16, 1933, NAACP Papers, Library of Congress.

11. Walter White, *A Man Called White* (Bloomington: Indiana Univ. Press, 1948), p. 154.

6. *His Own Man*

1. Jo Ann E. Argersinger, *Toward a New Deal in Baltimore* (Chapel Hill: Univ. of North Carolina Press, 1988), p. 30.

2. Irwin Ross, "Thurgood Marshall," *Afro-American Magazine*, Aug. 20, 1960, p. 5.

3. Author's interview with Pat Patterson.

4. Baltimore City Court, 1936, *Harvey Moses v. Doctor W. Aubrey Marshall.*

5. *Annapolis Evening Capitol*, July 13, 1934, p. 1.

6. "Negroes Executed," *Baltimore Sun*, Apr. 19, 1935.

7. Thurgood Marshall to Lillie M. Jackson, Mar. 4, 1936, NAACP Papers, Library of Congress.

8. Baltimore Criminal Court Docket, 1936, *State of Maryland v. Virtis Lucas.*

9. Andor Skotnes, "The Black Freedom Movement and the Workers' Movement in Baltimore, 1930–1939" (Ph.D. diss., Rutgers Univ., 1991), p. 325.

10. Thurgood Marshall interview with the Columbia Oral History Project.

11. *Baltimore Afro-American*, n.d., NAACP Papers, LC; Thurgood Marshall to Charles Houston, Dec. 18, 1934, NAACP Papers, LC.

12. Linda Zeidman, "Sparrow's Point, Dundalk, Highlandtown, Old West Baltimore: Home of Gold Dust and the Union Card," *The Baltimore Book* (Philadelphia: Temple Univ. Press, 1991), pp. 187–90.

13. Jo Ann E. Argersinger, *Toward a New Deal in Baltimore* (Chapel Hill: Univ. of North Carolina Press, 1988), p. 156.

14. David Bogen, "Black Lawyers in Maryland in the Forgotten Era," p. 14.

15. Author's interview with Walter Carr.

16. Skotnes, "Black Freedom Movement," pp. 211–37.

7. *Getting Started*

1. Thurgood Marshall's interview with the Columbia Oral History Project.
2. As cited in Genna Rae McNeil, *Groundwork* (Philadelphia: Univ. of Pennsylvania Press, 1983), p. 138.
3. Ken Gormley, "Justice Thurgood Marshall," *ABA Journal*, June 1992, p. 64.
4. Richard Kluger interview with Thurgood Marshall, Dec. 28, 1973, Brown Collection, Yale Univ.
5. H. L. Mencken, "The Murray Case," *Baltimore Evening Sun*, Sept. 23, 1935.
6. Charles Houston to Walter White, Sept. 19, 1935, NAACP Papers, Library of Congress.
7. Author's interview with Margery Prout.
8. *Baltimore Afro-American*, Oct. 5, 1935, p. 1.
9. Thurgood Marshall to Charles Houston, Feb. 10, 1936, NAACP Papers, LC; *Baltimore Afro-American*, Feb. 22, 1936.
10. Thurgood Marshall to Charles Houston, Apr. 7, 1936, NAACP Papers, LC.
11. Thurgood Marshall to Charles Houston, July 13, 1936, NAACP Papers, LC.
12. Thurgood Marshall to Milford [*sic*] Tydings, Jan. 29, 1935, NAACP Papers, LC.
13. Thurgood Marshall to Millard Tydings, Apr. 10, 1935; Millard Tydings to Thurgood Marshall, Apr. 12, 1935, NAACP Papers, LC.
14. Thurgood Marshall to Charles Houston, Jan. 21, 1936, NAACP Papers, LC.
15. Charles Houston to Thurgood Marshall, Jan. 23, 1936, NAACP Papers, LC.
16. Thurgood Marshall to Charles Houston, May 25, 1936, NAACP Papers, LC.
17. Roy Wilkins to Thurgood Marshall, July 8, 1936, NAACP Papers, LC.
18. Charles Houston to Thurgood Marshall, Sept. 17, 1936, NAACP Papers, LC.
19. Thurgood Marshall to Walter White, Oct. 6, 1936, NAACP Papers, LC.

8. *Leaving Home*

1. Author's interview with Aubrey Marshall, Jr.
2. Author's interview with Essie Hughes.
3. Author's interview with Teddy Stewart.
4. Author's interview with Cab Calloway.
5. School records of Norma A. Marshall, Register of Baltimore. By the time of Aubrey's illness she had been a full-time teacher for ten years. She began in 1927, earning $1,300 annually.
6. *Baltimore Afro-American*, July 31, 1937.
7. Philip Brown, *A Century of "Separate but Equal" Education in Anne Arundel*

County (New York: Vantage Press, 1988), p. 81; Letter to the Editor from Rose Wiseman, *The Capitol*, Jan. 30, 1993.
8. *Mills v. Board of Education of Anne Arundel County*, Opinion of Judge Chesnut, 1939.

9. *69 Fifth Avenue*

1. Charles Houston to Thurgood Marshall, Sept. 17, 1936, NAACP Papers, Library of Congress.
2. Author's interview with Monroe Dowling.
3. Memo from Thurgood Marshall, Apr. 3, 1937, NAACP Papers, LC.
4. *Baltimore Afro-American*, Oct. 5, 1935.
5. Thurgood Marshall to NAACP, Oct. 17, 1937, Yale Univ. Archives.
6. *Buffalo Courier Express*, Mar. 23, 1937, Papers of Charles Houston, Moreland-Spingarn Research Center, Howard Univ.
7. Charles Houston to Sidney Redmond, Sept. 24, 1936, NAACP Papers, LC.
8. Edward Clayton, "The Strange Disappearance of Lloyd . . . ," *Ebony*, vol. 7, no. 7, p. 32.
9. Thurgood Marshall to Charles Houston, Aug. 4, 1939, NAACP Papers, LC.
10. *Baltimore Afro-American*, Oct. 28, 1938; Walter White to Sidney Redmond, Jan. 23, 1940, NAACP Papers, LC. The NAACP never did locate Gaines, and subsequent inquiries by newspapers and magazines similarly found nothing. In 1995 Gaines's remaining relatives said they still had not heard from him; the Social Security Administration said that year there was no record of Gaines's death.
11. As cited in Clayton, "Strange Disappearance," p. 30.
12. Genna Rae McNeil, *Groundwork* (Philadelphia: Univ. of Pennsylvania Press, 1983), pp. 146–47.
13. Charles Houston to William Houston, Apr. 14, 1938, NAACP Papers, LC.
14. As cited in McNeil, *Groundwork*, p. 149.
15. Unnamed source, interview with the FBI, Sept. 13, 1961, FBI file 77-26395.
16. Richard Kluger's interview with Thurgood Marshall.
17. Charles Houston to Thurgood Marshall, Sept. 17, 1936, NAACP Papers, LC.

10. *Marshall in Charge*

1. *Hale v. Kentucky* (1938).
2. Asst. Attorney General Brien McMahon to J. E. Hoover, Dec. 27, 1938, FBI file 44 227-1.
3. Thurgood Marshall interview with the Columbia Oral History Project.

4. Thurgood Marshall to ACLU Board, Apr. 26, 1939, NAACP Papers, Library of Congress.
5. *Baltimore Afro-American*, Nov. 22, 1941, p. 1.
6. *Baltimore Afro-American*, Dec. 19, 1942, p. 24.
7. Thurgood Marshall to NAACP, Nov. 25, 1941, NAACP Papers, LC.
8. Thurgood Marshall to Walter White, May 5, 1940, NAACP Papers, LC.
9. Author's interview with Monroe Dowling.
10. Author's interview with Mildred Byrd.
11. Thurgood Marshall to 31st NAACP Convention, June 20, 1940, NAACP Papers, LC.
12. Thurgood Marshall to Office, Nov. 17, 1941, NAACP Papers, LC.
13. Thurgood Marshall interview with the Columbia Oral History Project.
14. Richard Kluger interview with Herbert Wechsler, Nov. 21, 1973, Brown Collection, Yale Univ.
15. *Smith v. Allwright* (1944).
16. *Norfolk Journal and Guide*, Apr. 15, 1944.
17. Thurgood Marshall interview with the Columbia Oral History Project.
18. Irwin Ross, *Baltimore Afro-American*, Aug. 6, 1960.

11. *Pan of Bones*

1. Sheriff Roy Harmon quoted in *Oklahoma Black Dispatch*, Feb. 8, 1941, p. 5.
2. Thurgood Marshall to Walter White, Jan. 29, 1941, NAACP Papers, Library of Congress.
3. Thurgood Marshall to Walter White, Feb. 2, 1941, NAACP Papers, LC.
4. *Oklahoma Black Dispatch*, Feb. 8, 1941, p. 5.
5. Ibid.
6. Thurgood Marshall to Walter White, Feb. 2, 1941, NAACP Papers, LC.
7. Ibid.
8. *Oklahoma Black Dispatch*, Feb. 8, 1941, p. 5.
9. *Oklahoma Black Dispatch*, Feb. 1, 1941, p. 2.
10. Thurgood Marshall to Walter White, Feb. 2, 1941, NAACP Papers, LC.
11. Undated pamphlet on legal defense, NAACP Papers, LC.
12. *Baltimore Afro-American*, June 10, 1944, p. 3.
13. Statement by Joseph Spell to his attorneys, Dec. 14, 1940, NAACP Papers, LC.
14. *Baltimore Afro-American*, Feb. 8, 1941, p. 1.

12. *The War Years*

1. Charles Houston to A. Philip Randolph, May 20, 1941, Houston Papers, Moreland-Spingarn Research Center, Howard Univ.

2. Walter White to William Hastie, May 4, 1943, NAACP Papers, Library of Congress.

3. William Hastie to Walter White, May 4, 1943, NAACP Papers, LC.

4. Morris Ernst to Walter White, Oct. 29, 1942, NAACP Papers, LC.

5. Walter White to Morris Ernst, Oct. 31, 1942, NAACP Papers, LC.

6. FBI Report, Dec. 17, 1943, FBI file 100-3050.

7. Author's interview with Edward Dudley; George Stevens interview with Robert Carter, American Film Institute, Kennedy Center.

8. Michael Carter, *Baltimore Afro-American*, June 3, 1944.

9. As cited in *Baltimore Afro-American*, July 17, 1943.

10. Thurgood Marshall interview with the Columbia Oral History Project.

11. Thurgood Marshall, "Gestapo in Detroit," *The Crisis*, Aug. 1943.

12. *Baltimore Afro-American*, Aug. 14, 1943.

13. Mark Tushnet, *Making Civil Rights Law* (New York: Oxford Univ. Press, 1994), p. 66.

14. Thurgood Marshall to Office, Oct. 8, 1944, NAACP Papers, LC.

15. Thurgood Marshall before Judge Advocate General, Apr. 3, 1945, NAACP Papers, LC.

16. Eleanor Roosevelt to James Forrestal, Apr. 8, 1945, National Archives.

17. NAACP Press Release, July 13, 1945, NAACP Papers, LC; Secretary of the Navy to Thurgood Marshall, undated, National Archives.

18. Thurgood Marshall interview with the Columbia Oral History Project.

13. *Lynch Mob for a Lawyer*

1. "Four Police, Two Civilians Shot . . . ," *Nashville Tennesean*, Feb. 26, 1946, p. 1.

2. "Terror in Tennessee," NAACP pamphlet, 1946, NAACP Papers, Library of Congress.

3. Author's interview with Jack Lovett.

4. Report on Investigation made on Feb. 27–28, 1946.

5. Author's interview with Raymond Lockridge.

6. Vincent Tubbs, *Afro-American*, Oct. 10, 1946, p. 3.

7. "Terror in Tennessee."

8. "We Urge Calm," *Daily Herald*, Feb. 26, 1946, p. 2.

9. Leslie Hart, "Long Distance Calls . . . ," *Nashville Banner*, Mar. 2, 1946, p. 2.

10. Ibid.

11. Danny Bingham, "Maury Hearing Resumed . . . ," *Nashville Banner*, June 14, 1946, p. 8.

12. Walter White to the Committee on Administration, July 12, 1946, NAACP Papers, LC; Memo from Walter White to Staff, July 12, 1946, NAACP Papers, LC.

13. Thurgood Marshall interview with the Columbia Oral History Project.

14. Walter White to the Board of Directors, Sept. 9, 1946, NAACP Papers, LC; Passport Application for Thurgood Marshall, Sept. 27, 1946, U.S. Department of State.

15. Vincent Tubbs, "Implications . . . ," *Baltimore Afro-American*, Oct. 12, 1946, p. 2.

16. Ibid.

17. Vincent Tubbs, "Believed to Show . . . ," *Baltimore Afro-American*, Sept. 28, 1946, p. 1.

18. Author's interview with Paul Bumpus.

19. Tubbs, "Implications," p. 2.

20. Transcript of closing arguments in *State of Tennessee v. Pillow and Kennedy*.

21. Author's interview with Flo Fleming.

22. Winfred Hopton interview with Constable Archibald Butts, Feb. 2, 1947, FBI file 44–78.

23. *Pittsburgh Courier*, Dec. 7, 1946, p. 1.

14. *Jim Crow Buster*

1. Walter White to Thurgood Marshall, Apr. 24, 1946, NAACP Papers, Library of Congress.

2. Speech of Robert W. Kenny, NAACP Papers, LC.

3. Spingarn Award speech of Thurgood Marshall, NAACP Papers, LC.

4. Ted Poston, "On Appeal in the Supreme Court," *The Survey*, Jan. 1949, pp. 18–21.

5. "Mother Considered Power . . . ," *Baltimore Afro-American*, July 13, 1946, p. 17.

6. Author's interview with Alice Stovall.

7. "Supreme Court to Review . . . ," *Baltimore Afro-American*, Feb. 9, 1946, p. 17.

8. "Supreme Court to Hear . . . ," *Baltimore Afro-American*, Mar. 9, 1946, p. 1.

9. Walter White to Thurgood Marshall, Mar. 30, 1946, NAACP Papers, LC.

10. Robert Watts to Franklin Williams, Feb. 5, 1949, NAACP Papers, LC.

11. Garrett Power, "Apartheid Baltimore Style: The Residential Segregation Ordinances of 1910–1913," *Maryland Law Review*, vol. 42, no. 2 (1993), pp. 310–12.

12. Thurgood Marshall to National Legal Committee, June 13, 1945, NAACP Papers, LC.

13. Carl Murphy, "President Truman . . . ," *Baltimore Afro-American*, Jan. 24, 1948, p. 1.

14. Lem Graves, "Housing Decision Awaited," *Pittsburgh Courier,* Jan. 24, 1948, p. 4.

15. Carl Murphy, "President Truman . . . ," *Baltimore Afro-American,* Jan. 24, 1948, p. 1.

16. Ibid.

17. Notes from Richard Kluger's interview with Philip Elman, Aug. 19, 1971, Brown Collection, Yale Univ.

18. "They said . . . ," *Baltimore Afro-American,* May 15, 1948, sec. 2, p. 4.

19. Jack Greenberg, *Crusaders in the Courts* (New York: Basic Books, 1994), p. 259.

15. *Groveland*

1. "Posse 'Lynches' Fla. Case Suspect," *Baltimore Afro-American,* Aug. 6, 1949, p. 2.

2. "Three Prisoners Tied to Pipes . . . ," *Pittsburgh Courier,* Aug. 6, 1949, p. 4.

3. "Fla. Judge Bars . . . ," *Pittsburgh Courier,* Dec. 15, 1951, p. 1.

4. Thurgood Marshall interview with the Columbia Oral History Project.

5. Jack Greenberg interview with the Columbia Oral History Project.

6. Ibid.

7. "Guard NAACP Chief," *Pittsburgh Courier,* Dec. 22, 1951, p. 1.

8. "NAACP Rallies to Aid Moore," *Pittsburgh Courier,* Jan. 5, 1952, p. 4.

9. Buddy Lonsome, "Marshall Reveals . . . ," *Baltimore Afro-American,* Feb. 23, 1952, p. 9.

10. *Baltimore Afro-American,* Dec. 24, 1955.

16. *Lessons in Politics*

1. Thurgood Marshall to Tom Clark, Dec. 27, 1946, FBI file 61-3176-364.

2. J. E. Hoover to Tom Clark, Jan. 10, 1947, FBI file 61-3176-364.

3. J. E. Hoover to Walter White, Jan. 13, 1947, FBI file 61-3176-367.

4. J. E. Hoover to Walter White, Apr. 4, 1947, FBI file 61-3176-367.

5. Clyde Tolson to L. B. Nichols, Jan. 10, 1948, FBI file 44-1854.

6. D. M. Ladd to J. E. Hoover, July 21, 1948, FBI file 61-3176-462.

7. Michael Carter, "Meet the NAACP's . . . ," *Baltimore Afro-American,* June 3, 1944, p. 2.

8. "National Affairs," *Newsweek,* June 26, 1967, p. 35.

9. Ibid.

10. Stephen Spingarn to Mr. Clifford, May 16, 1949, Truman Papers, HST Presidential Library.

11. Eleanor Roosevelt to Paul Fitzpatrick, Aug. 9, 1949, Eleanor Roosevelt Papers, FDR Presidential Library.

17. *On the Front Line*

1. Thurgood Marshall to Walter White, Oct. 7, 1948, NAACP papers, LC.
2. Thurgood Marshall to Robert Silberstein, Oct. 25, 1949, NAACP Papers, LC.
3. Daniel Byrd to Donald Jones, Apr. 25, 1949, Byrd Papers, Amistad Research Center, Tulane Univ.
4. James Hicks, "NAACP Boots Reds," *Baltimore Afro-American*, July 1, 1950, p. 1.
5. Thurgood Marshall, Draft of "Report on Korea," undated, NAACP Papers, LC.
6. V. P. Keay to A. H. Pelmont, Dec. 15, 1950, FBI file 61-3176-573.
7. Thurgood Marshall, 1951 Diary, NAACP Papers, LC.
8. D. Clayton James interview with Gen. George Hickman, Douglas MacArthur Library.
9. Thurgood Marshall, "Report on Korea," NAACP Papers, LC.
10. Cliff MacKay, "Courts Martial Hasty," *Baltimore Afro-American*, Feb. 24, 1951, p. 1.
11. "Mission Accomplished," *Pittsburgh Courier*, Feb. 24, 1951, p. 22.

18. *Direct Attack*

1. *Time*, Sept. 19, 1955, p. 26.
2. Michael Gillette, "Heman Marion Sweatt: Civil Rights Plaintiff," in *Black Leaders: Texans for Their Times* (Austin: Texas State Historical Assn., 1981), pp. 163–64.
3. Heman Sweatt to Walter White, Sept. 3, 1948, NAACP Papers, Library of Congress.
4. Heman Sweatt to Walter White, Nov. 8, 1946, NAACP Papers, LC.
5. A. Maceo Smith interview with Fisk Univ. Black Oral History Program, Nov. 13, 1972.
6. Author's interview with James Stewart.
7. Author's interview with Constance Baker Motley.
8. Walter Gellhorn interview with the Columbia Oral History Project.
9. Author's interview with Ada Lois Sipuel.
10. Author's interview with Joe Greenhill.
11. Richard Kluger, *Simple Justice* (New York: Vintage Books, 1975), p. 263.
12. Statement of Thurgood Marshall, Sept. 5, 1947, NAACP Papers, LC.
13. Robert Carter interview with Caroline Stevens, Dec. 19, 1988.

14. Statement of Thurgood Marshall, Denison, Tex., Sept. 5, 1947, NAACP Papers, LC.

15. Charles Houston to Thurgood Marshall, Apr. 20, 1949, NAACP Papers, LC.

16. "U.S. Enters Schools Cases," *Baltimore Afro-American*, Feb. 18, 1950, p. 2.

17. W. 1. Gibson, "Equality Impossible . . . ," *Baltimore Afro-American*, Apr. 15, 1950, p. 6.

18. As cited in Genna Rae McNeil, *Groundwork* (Philadelphia: Univ. of Pennsylvania Press, 1983), p. 199.

19. As cited in ibid., p. 200.

20. As cited in Jack Greenberg, *Crusaders in the Courts* (New York: Basic Books, 1994), p. 4.

21. "NAACP Board Grieves . . . ," *Baltimore Afro-American*, May 6, 1950, p. 7.

22. Louis Lautier, "NAACP Lawyers . . . ," *Baltimore Afro-American*, June 10, 1950, p. 2.

23. As cited in Gillette, "Heman Marion Sweatt," p. 178.

24. Heman Sweatt, "Why I Want to Attend . . . ," *Texas Ranger*, Sept. 1947, p. 40.

19. *Number One Negro of All Time*

1. Charles Jones to Thurgood Marshall, May 1949, NAACP Papers, Library of Congress.

2. Carl Murphy to Eleanor Roosevelt, Aug. 30, 1949, Eleanor Roosevelt Papers, FDR Library.

3. "Leaders Ridicule . . . ," *Baltimore Afro-American*, Aug. 27, 1949, p. 12.

4. Ibid.

5. Thurgood Marshall interview with the Columbia Oral History Project.

6. Jack Greenberg interview with the Columbia Oral History Project.

7. Henry Lee Moon interview with the Columbia Oral History Project; author's interview with Herbert Hill.

8. Richard Kluger interview with Herbert Hill, Brown Collection, Yale Univ.

9. Arnold Aronson to Thurgood Marshall, Apr. 26, 1951, NAACP Papers, LC; author's interview with William T. Coleman.

10. Author's interviews with Claude Connor and Elizabeth Monteiro.

11. Author's interview with Evelyn Cunningham.

12. James Poling, "Thurgood Marshall and the Fourteenth Amendment," *Collier's*, Feb. 23, 1952, pp. 29–32.

13. Ibid.

14. "New Federal Judge?" *Baltimore Afro-American*, Apr. 12, 1952, p. 1.

20. *Planning a Revolt*

1. "End of JC in Sight," *Baltimore Afro-American*, June 17, 1950, p. 1.
2. Author's interview with Spottswood Robinson.
3. Robert Carter interview with Radio America.
4. *Mendez v. Westminster School District* (1946).
5. Thurgood Marshall interview with the Columbia Oral History Project.
6. Radio America interview with Kenneth Clark.
7. A. P. Tureaud to E. A. Johnson, July 15, 1950, Tureaud Papers, Amistad Research Center, Tulane Univ.
8. Franklin Williams to Thurgood Marshall, Sept. 9, 1948, LDF Papers, Brown Collection, Yale Univ.
9. Author's interview with Robert Carter.
10. Caroline Stevens interview with Kenneth Clark, June 21, 1988.
11. Author's interview with Kenneth Clark.
12. J. Waties Waring interview with the Columbia Oral History Project.
13. Thurgood Marshall and Robert Carter, "Real Heroes in S.C.," *Baltimore Afro-American*, June 16, 1951, p. 4.
14. J. Waties Waring interview with the Columbia Oral History Project.
15. Victor Gray, "S.C. School Case . . . ," *Baltimore Afro-American*, June 9, 1951, p. 2.
16. Ibid.
17. Ted Poston, "Time Running Out . . . ," *New York Post*, June 3, 1951, p. 22.
18. Ibid.
19. Hugh Speer, *Case of the Century* (Kansas City: Univ. of Missouri Press, 1968), p. 91.
20. Tinsley Yarbrough, *A Passion for Justice* (New York: Oxford Univ. Press, 1987), p. 195, from opinion in *Briggs v. Elliott* (1951).
21. "S.C. Case . . . ," *Baltimore Afro-American*, June 30, 1951, p. 19, dissent in *Briggs v. Elliott* (1951).
22. William Henry Harbaugh, *Lawyer's Lawyer: The Life of John W. Davis* (New York: Oxford Univ. Press, 1973).
23. As cited in Yarbrough, *Passion for Justice*, p. 199.
24. Marjorie McKenzie, in *Pittsburgh Courier*, July 7, 1951, p. 1.
25. Richard Kluger interview with Marjorie McKenzie, Brown Collection, Yale Univ.
26. Franklin Williams to Thurgood Marshall, Sept. 9, 1948, LDF Papers, Brown Collection, Yale Univ.
27. Richard Kluger, *Simple Justice* (New York: Vintage Books, 1975), p. 411.
28. Speer, *Case of the Century*, p. 49.
29. Ibid., p. 78.

30. Robert Carter to Thurgood Marshall, June 29, 1951, LDF Papers, Brown Collection, Yale Univ.
31. *Davis v. County School Board of Prince Edward County* (1952).
32. Author's interview with June Shagaloff.
33. Richard Kluger interview with Tom Clark, Oct. 8, 1971, Brown Collection, Yale Univ.

21. *Case of the Century*

1. Richard Kluger interview with Charles Black, July 29, 1971, Brown Collection, Yale Univ.
2. Thurgood Marshall interview with the Columbia Oral History Project.
3. Thurgood Marshall speech at Howard Univ., Apr. 16, 1952, NAACP Papers, Library of Congress.
4. James Freedman, Speech at Washington Univ. Law School, Feb. 16, 1994.
5. Radio America interview with Kenneth Clark.
6. "The Fading Color Line," *Time*, Dec. 21, 1953, p. 19.
7. Excerpted in *Baltimore Afro-American*, Dec. 13, 1952, p. 14.
8. Richard Kluger interview with Philip Elman, Aug. 19, 1971, Brown Collection, Yale Univ.
9. Caroline Stevens interview with Julia Davis Adams, July 20, 1988.
10. Caroline Stevens interview with Taggart Whipple, May 19, 1988.
11. "Supreme Court Hears Final . . . ," *Baltimore Afro-American*, Dec. 20, 1952, p. 6.
12. Oral arguments in the consolidated cases of *Brown v. Board of Education* (1952).
13. "600 Laud Marshall . . . ," *Baltimore Afro-American*, Feb. 21, 1953, p. 22.
14. Jack Greenberg, *Crusaders in the Courts* (New York: Basic Books, 1994), p. 177.
15. As cited in Mark Tushnet, *Making Civil Rights Law* (New York: Oxford Univ. Press, 1994), p. 187.
16. As cited in ibid., p. 190; and Richard Kluger, *Simple Justice* (New York: Vintage Books, 1975), p. 606.
17. Author's interview with Warren Burger.
18. Richard Kluger interview with Alfred Kelly, Dec. 28, 1971, Brown Collection, Yale Univ.
19. Alfred Kelly to Thurgood Marshall, Oct. 19, 1953, LDF Papers, Brown Collection, Yale Univ.
20. George Stevens interview with John Hope Franklin, May 25, 1988.
21. NAACP brief from *Brown v. Board of Education* (1953).

22. "All Citizens . . . ," *Baltimore Afro-American*, Dec. 5, 1953, p. 2.
23. Author's interview with William T. Coleman.
24. Richard Kluger interview with Louis Pollack, Brown Collection, Yale Univ.
25. Author's interview with William T. Coleman.
26. Paul Wilson, *A Time to Lose*, (Lawrence: Univ. Press of Kansas, 1995), p. 188; William Coleman to Thurgood Marshall, Dec. 10, 1953, LDF Papers, Brown Collection, Yale Univ.
27. Thurgood Marshall, Jan. 23, 1954, Brown Collection, Yale Univ.
28. Thurgood Marshall, Mar. 30, 1954, NAACP Papers, LC.
29. "The Tension of Change," *Time*, Sept. 19, 1955, p. 27.
30. Radio America interview with E. Barrett Prettyman.
31. John Geiger, "Mr. Civil Rights . . . ," *Pittsburgh Courier*, May 29, 1954, p. 13.
32. "Segregation . . . ," *Baltimore Afro-American*, May 29, 1954, p. 1.
33. Author's interview with Joe Greenhill.

22. *No Radical*

1. Author's interview with Herbert Hill.
2. Radio America interview with Kenneth Clark.
3. Author's interview with Alice Stovall.
4. Author's interview with John A. Davis.
5. Luther Huston, "1896 Ruling Upset," *New York Times*, May 18, 1954, p. 1.
6. "Ruling Gets Rebel Yell in South," *Washington Daily News*, May 18, 1954; *Baltimore Afro-American*, Nov. 14, 1954, p. 1.
7. "Editorial Excerpts," *New York Times*, May 18, 1954, p. 19.
8. William Henry Harbaugh, *Lawyer's Lawyer: The Life of John W. Davis* (New York: Oxford Univ. Press, 1973), p. 511.
9. Herbert Brownell oral history, Eisenhower Presidential Library.
10. James Hicks, "NAACP Warns . . . ," *Baltimore Afro-American*, May 29, 1954, p. 1; "School Plan Set . . . ," *New York Times*, May 24, 1954, p. 19.
11. John Geiger, "Mr. Civil Rights . . . ," *Pittsburgh Courier*, May 29, 1954, p. 13.
12. Speech of Thurgood Marshall, Jan. 23, 1954, Brown Collection, Yale Univ.; speech of Thurgood Marshall, undated, Amistad Research Center, Tulane Univ.
13. Speech of Thurgood Marshall, June 30, 1954, Brown Collection, Yale Univ.
14. William Coleman to Thurgood Marshall, Oct. 14, 1954, Brown Collection, Yale Univ.
15. Richard Kluger interview with Anthony Lewis, Brown Collection, Yale Univ.
16. Transcript of phone conversation between Carl Murphy and Thurgood Marshall, Nov. 29, 1954, Brown Collection, Yale Univ.
17. Author's interview with John A. Davis.

18. Author's interview with Mildred Byrd.
19. Ken Gormley, "Justice Thurgood Marshall," *ABA Journal*, June 1992, p. 66.
20. Author's interview with Claude Connor.
21. "Buster Marshall," *Baltimore Afro-American*, Feb. 26, 1955, p. 4.
22. Jack Greenberg interview with the Columbia Oral History Project.
23. "Roy Wilkins Seen Succeeding . . . ," *Pittsburgh Courier*, Mar. 26, 1955, p. 4.
24. Oral argument in *Brown v. Board of Education* (1955).
25. Thurgood Marshall interview with the Columbia Oral History Project.
26. Author's interview with Robert Carter.
27. Transcript of conversation between Thurgood Marshall and Carl Murphy, June 2, 1955, Brown Collection, Yale Univ.
28. *Time*, June 13, 1955.
29. "Junior Page," *Baltimore Afro-American* magazine, July 9, 1955, p. 4.
30. "The Tension of Change," *Time*, Sept. 19, 1955, pp. 23–27.
31. Samuel Hoskins, "Thurgood: Time's Portrait," *Baltimore Afro-American*, Sept. 24, 1955, p. 22.
32. C. Tolson to L. B. Nichols, Oct. 19, 1955, FBI file 61-3176-1076.
33. *New York Times*, Oct. 16, 1955; *Baltimore Afro-American*, Oct. 8, 1995.
34. L. V. Boardman to A. H. Belmont, Oct. 21, 1955, FBI file 61-3176-1076.
35. Author's interview with Gloster Current.
36. Author's interview with Cecelia Marshall.
37. Author's interview with Arnold DeMille.
38. "Thurgood Loses Heart," *Baltimore Afro-American*, Dec. 17, 1955, p. 1.

23. Martin Luther King, Jr.

1. Thurgood Marshall interview with the Columbia Oral History Project.
2. As cited in *Eyes on the Prize* (New York: Penguin Books, 1987), p. 76.
3. Bernard Taper, "A Reporter at Large," *New Yorker*, Mar. 17, 1956, p. 88.
4. Author's interview with Harris Wofford.
5. Author's interview with Evelyn Cunningham.
6. Mark Tushnet, *Making Civil Rights Law* (New York: Oxford Univ. Press, 1994), p. 239.
7. Oliver Allen, "Chief Counsel for Equality," *Life*, June 13, 1955, p. 148; Taper, "Reporter at Large," p. 84.
8. "Thurgood, Junior?" *Baltimore Afro-American*, Mar. 3, 1956, p. 1.
9. "Mrs. Marshall Is Expecting!" *Pittsburgh Courier*, Mar. 17, 1956, p. 6.
10. Taylor Branch, *Parting the Waters* (New York: Simon & Schuster, 1988), p. 190.
11. Speech of Thurgood Marshall, June 26, 1956, NAACP Papers, Library of Congress.

12. Author's interview with Herbert Hill.
13. David Garrow, *Bearing the Cross* (New York: William Morrow, 1986), p. 80.

24. *Machiavellian Marshall*

1. J. E. Hoover to Dillon Anderson, Jan. 3, 1956, Eisenhower Library.
2. "Probe of South's FBI . . . ," *Baltimore Sun*, Sept. 26, 1955, p. 28.
3. J. Edgar Hoover to Thurgood Marshall, Sept. 30, 1955, FBI file 61-3176-16.
4. Thurgood Marshall to J. Edgar Hoover, Oct. 7, 1955, FBI file 61-3176-10568.
5. J. Edgar Hoover to Thurgood Marshall, Oct. 13, 1955, FBI file 61-3176-1054.
6. Thurgood Marshall to J. Edgar Hoover, Jan. 24, 1956, FBI file 61-3176-1202.
7. L. B. Nichols to Tolson, Feb. 8, 1956, FBI file 62-86660-12.
8. Rosen to Price, Feb. 9, 1956, FBI file 62-86660-11.
9. L. B. Nichols to Tolson, June 15, 1956, FBI file 62-86660-16.
10. Speech of Thurgood Marshall, June 26, 1956, NAACP Papers, Library of Congress.
11. "The Thurgood Marshall Story," *Pittsburgh Courier,* July 14, 1956, p. 13.
12. Taper, "Reporter at Large," p. 91.
13. Samuel Hoskins, "NAACP Defies . . . ," *Baltimore Afro-American*, Aug. 4, 1956, p. 1.
14. Jack Greenberg interview with the Columbia Oral History Project.
15. Author's interview with Ed Dudley.
16. Jack Greenberg interview with the Columbia Oral History Project.
17. Author's interview with Gloria Branker.
18. Henry Lee Moon interview with the Columbia Oral History Project.
19. Jamye Coleman Williams, *The Negro Speaks* (New York: Noble and Noble, 1970).
20. "A Policy of Gradualism . . . ," *Newsweek*, Sept. 17, 1956, pp. 36–37.

25. *The Second Civil War*

1. Juan Williams, *Eyes on the Prize* (New York: Penguin Books, 1987), pp. 97–101.
2. Orval Faubus to President Eisenhower, Sept. 4, 1957, DDE Library.
3. Thurgood Marshall interview with the Columbia Oral History Project.
4. Wiley Branton interview at Moreland-Spingarn Research Center, Howard Univ.
5. "U.S. Court Denies . . . ," *New York Times*, Sept. 8, 1957, p. 66.
6. Ann Whitman Diary, Aug. 14, 1956, DDE Library.

7. Ibid., Oct. 8, 1957.

8. Thurgood Marshall to President Eisenhower, undated, DDE Library.

9. Thurgood Marshall interview.

10. Williams, *Eyes on the Prize*, pp. 105–6.

11. Woodrow W. Mann to President Eisenhower, Sept. 23, 1957, DDE Library.

12. Daisy Bates to Gloster Current, Sept. 23 and 24, 1957, NAACP Papers, Library of Congress.

13. Woodrow W. Mann to President Eisenhower, Sept. 24, 1957, DDE Library.

14. "President Eisenhower . . . ," *Congressional Quarterly*, Sept. 27, 1957, p. 1146.

15. Wiley Branton interview.

16. "Senators, Governors . . . ," *Congressional Quarterly*, Sept. 27, 1957, p. 1147.

17. "Mike Wallace Asks Thurgood Marshall . . . ," *New York Post*, Sept. 30, 1957.

18. Thurgood Marshall interview with the Columbia Oral History Project.

19. *Baltimore Afro-American*, June 28, 1958, p. 1.

20. Claude Sitton, "Little Rock Case . . . ," *New York Times*, Aug. 5, 1958, p. 1.

21. *New York Post*, Aug. 28, 1958.

22. "New Arguments . . . ," *New York Times*, Aug. 29, 1958, p. 8.

23. "Power of U.S. Court . . . ," *Pittsburgh Courier*, Sept. 20, 1958, p. 3.

24. Mark Tushnet, *Making Civil Rights Law* (New York: Oxford Univ. Press, 1994), p. 266.

25. Judge Carter refused to comment on this episode despite several phone calls and a letter requesting his input.

26. Jack Greenberg interview with the Columbia Oral History Project.

27. Author's interview with Marietta Dochery.

28. Michael Singer, "GOP Bars Negro . . . ," *New York Post*, Feb. 8, 1956.

29. *New York Post*, May 15, 1958.

30. *New York Post*, May 16, 1958.

26. *Marshall and the Militants*

1. Thurgood Marshall interview with the Columbia Oral History Project.

2. *New York Post*, July 16, 1959.

3. "Muhammud Hits . . . ," *New Jersey Herald News*, Dec. 5, 1959.

4. Kenneth O'Reilly, *Black Americans: The FBI Files* (New York: Carroll, Graf, 1994), pp. 458–59.

5. Memo from Office of the Director, May 11, 1959, FBI file 62-86660-23.

6. SAC, NYC, May 21, 1959, FBI file 100-111437-14.

7. SAC New York to Director, June 5, 1959, FBI files 100-111437 and 100-111437-16.

8. Robert Williams, *Negroes with Guns* (Chicago: Third World Press, 1973), pp. 58–63.

9. Louis Lautier, "Suspension Given OK," *Baltimore Afro-American*, July 25, 1959, pp. 1–2.

27. *Exit Time*

1. Murray Kempton, "The Diplomat," *New York Post*, Jan. 26, 1960.
2. Thurgood Marshall interview with Columbia Oral History Project.
3. *Baltimore Sun*, Jan. 22, 1960.
4. Robert Ruark, "Africa . . . ," *New York World-Telegram and Sun*, Feb. 3, 1960.
5. "Tomorrow's Too Late . . . ," *Baltimore Afro-American*, Jan. 30, 1960, p. 9.
6. Derrick Bell, "An Epistolary . . . ," *Blackletter Journal* (Harvard Univ.), Spring 1989, p. 55.
7. Robert Clark, "Behind the Sit-ins," *Washington Star*, Apr. 21, 1960, p. A-5.
8. *Baltimore Sun*, Mar. 30, 1960.
9. "Patience No Virtue . . . ," *Baltimore Afro-American Magazine*, May 28, 1960, p. 4.
10. Author's interview with Donald Hollowell.
11. Irwin Ross, "Thurgood Marshall," *Baltimore Afro-American*, Aug. 27, 1960, p. 4.
12. Carl Murphy, "Thurgood Marshall Next?" *Baltimore Afro-American*, Mar. 11, 1961, p. 4.
13. William Coleman to Frank Reeves, May 5, 1961, JFK Library.
14. Emanuel Celler to Robert Kennedy, May 24, 1961, Justice Dept.
15. Thurgood Marshall interview with the Columbia Oral History Project.
16. Jack Greenberg interview with the Columbia Oral History Project.
17. Ramsey Clark to Byron White, Aug. 4, 1961, Justice Dept.; author's interview with Louis Martin.
18. Jack Greenberg, *Crusaders in the Courts* (New York: Basic Books, 1994), p. 295.
19. Ibid., p. 294.
20. Jack Greenberg interview with the Columbia Oral History Project.
21. Author's interview with John Hope Franklin.
22. Author's interview with Robert Carter.

28. *Black Robes*

1. Thurgood Marshall interview with the Columbia Oral History Project.
2. "Judge Marshall Now," *Baltimore Afro-American*, Nov. 4, 1961, p. 4.
3. Felix Frankfurter to William Coleman, Jan. 2, 1962, Frankfurter Papers, Harvard Univ.
4. William Coleman to Felix Frankfurter, Jan. 4, 1962, Frankfurter Papers, Harvard Univ.

5. Author's interview with J. Edward Lumbard.

6. Author's interview with Ralph Winter.

7. *New York Post*, Apr. 5, 1962.

8. Victor Navasky, *Kennedy Justice* (New York: Atheneum, 1971), p. 285.

9. J. Edward Lumbard to Sen. James Eastland, Apr. 5, 1962, Justice Dept.

10. *Baltimore Afro-American*, Apr. 30, 1962.

11. Nomination of Thurgood Marshall, Senate hearing, May 1, 1962.

12. Berl Bernhard interview with Thurgood Marshall, JFK Library.

13. Nomination of Thurgood Marshall, Senate hearing, July 12, 1962.

14. Thurgood Marshall interview with the Columbia Oral History Project.

15. Jackie Robinson, "Birth Only Crime," *Philadelphia Tribune*, 1962.

16. "The Marshall Delay," *New York Post*, Aug. 26, 1962.

17. Nomination of Thurgood Marshall, Senate hearing, Aug. 17, 1962.

18. Ibid., Aug. 20, 1962.

19. Ibid., Aug. 24, 1962.

20. "Senate Unit's Decision . . . ," *Washington Star*, Aug. 30, 1962.

21. Thurgood Marshall interview with the Columbia Oral History Project.

22. "Senate Confirms . . . ," *Washington Star*, Sept. 12, 1962; Eric Sevareid, "Thurgood Marshall . . . ," *Washington Star*, Sept. 25, 1962.

23. Malcolm X to Judge Thurgood Marshall, July 1962, Marshall Papers, Library of Congress.

24. Gary Hengstler, *ABA Journal*, June 1992, p. 59.

25. Ralph Winter, Second Circuit Judiciary Conference speech, Sept. 6, 1991.

26. Author's interview with James Freedman.

27. Author's interview with William Coleman.

28. Author's interview with Monroe Dowling.

29. Author's interview with Berl Bernhard.

30. *Baltimore Sun*, May 16, 1964.

31. George Dugan, "Marshall Quits . . . ," *New York Times*, Oct. 22, 1964, p. 23.

32. "The Impact of the Constitution," undated, Marshall Papers, LC.

33. Walter Gellhorn interview with the Columbia Oral History Project.

34. Thurgood Marshall interview with the Columbia Oral History Project.

29. *Johnson's Man*

1. Thurgood Marshall interview with T. H. Baker, LBJ Library.

2. Author's interview with Ramsey Clark.

3. Randal Bland, *Private Pressure on Public Law* (Port Washington, N.Y.: National University Publications, 1973), p. 129.

4. Lady Bird Johnson Diary, July 2, 1965, LBJ Library.

5. Author's interview with Nicholas Katzenbach.

6. Marshall interview with Baker.

7. *New York Herald Tribune,* July 30, 1965.
8. Testimony before the Senate Subcommittee of the Judiciary, July 29, 1965.
9. Statement of President Johnson, Aug. 24, 1965, LBJ Library.
10. Thurgood Marshall interview with the Columbia Oral History Project.
11. Marshall to Johnson, Sept. 14, 1965; Johnson to Marshall, Sept. 20, 1965, LBJ Library.
12. Author's interview with Grafton Gaines.
13. Author's interview with Ralph Spritzer.
14. Author's interview with Louis Claiborne.
15. Joseph Mohbat, "Marshall Finds . . . ," *Washington Star,* Dec. 26, 1965.
16. *Baltimore Sun,* Mar. 21, 1966.
17. Author's interview with Monroe Dowling; Sidney Zion, "Thurgood Marshall . . . ," *New York Times Magazine,* Aug. 22, 1965, p. 69.
18. Ponchitta Pierce, "The Solicitor General," *Ebony,* vol. 21, no. 1, pp. 67–77.
19. Zion, "Thurgood Marshall . . . ," p. 71.
20. *New York Times,* June 14, 1966; John MacKenzie, "Would Be . . . ," *Washington Post,* June 14, 1967, p. A13.
21. J. Edgar Hoover to Mary Watson, FBI files, Hoover O. and C., May 27, 1966.
22. C. D. DeLoach to Clyde Tolson, June 6, 1966, FBI file Hoover O. and C.
23. C. D. DeLoach to Clyde Tolson, June 14, 1966, FBI file Hoover O. and C.
24. Supplemental Memo to the Supreme Court [*Black v. U.S.*], FBI file Hoover O. and C.
25. Author's interview with Harry McPherson.
26. *Jet,* Dec. 1, 1966.
27. Transcript of conversation between acting Attorney General Clark and President Johnson, Jan. 25, 1967, LBJ Library.
28. Transcript of a conversation between LBJ and Ramsey Clark, Jan. 25, 1967, LBJ Library.
29. Author's interview with Jack Valenti.

30. *Justice Marshall*

1. Hoover to Marshall, personal copy, June 13, 1967, FBI file 77-88227-150.
2. "The Distorters," *Lynchburg News,* Aug. 22, 1967, p. 6.
3. James Kilpatrick, "Marshall's Appointment . . . ," *Washington Star,* June 18, 1967.
4. "Mr. Justice Marshall," *Newsweek,* June 26, 1967, pp. 34–36; *Washington Star,* June 14, 1967.
5. Nomination of Thurgood Marshall, Senate Committee of the Judiciary, July 13–24, 1967.

6. Author's interview with Grafton Gaines.

7. Author's interview with William Brennan.

8. Thurgood Marshall's interview with Dennis J. Hutchinson, Univ. of Chicago.

9. Black to Marshall, Nov. 11, 1967, Marshall Papers, Supreme Court, Library of Congress.

10. Author's interview with Ramsey Clark.

11. Notes of the President's Meeting with Negro Leaders, Apr. 5, 1967, LBJ Library.

12. Larry Still, "President Warns . . . ," *Washington Star,* June 2, 1966.

13. Thurgood Marshall's interview with the Columbia Oral History Project.

14. Bruce A. Murphy, *Fortas* (New York: William Morrow, 1988), p. 299.

15. DeLoach to Tolson, Sept. 23, 1968, FBI file 77-88227-160.

16. Lady Bird Johnson Diary, Dec. 18, 1968, LBJ Library.

17. *Baltimore Sun,* Dec. 18, 1968.

18. Speech of Thurgood Marshall, May 4, 1969, Brown Collection, Yale Univ.

19. "Anarchy Is Anarchy," *Washington Star,* May 6, 1969, p. A8.

20. *Stanley v. Georgia* (1968), Marshall Papers, Supreme Court, LC.

21. Author's interview with Thurgood and Cecelia Marshall.

22. Author's interview with Monroe Dowling.

23. James Welsh, "Justice Marshall Buys . . . ," *Washington Star,* Nov. 13, 1968.

24. Author's interview with Tyrone Brown.

25. Roland Evans and Robert Novak, *New York Post,* Jan. 31, 1970.

26. Tkach to Nixon, May 19, 1970, and Chapin to Nixon, May 22, 1970, RMN Library.

27. "Justice Marshall, 'Not Feeling Well,' " *Washington Star,* June 14, 1971.

28. "Justice Doing Better . . . ," *Baltimore Sun,* July 18, 1972.

29. Thurgood Marshall to Simeon Booker, Nov. 20, 1972, Marshall Papers, Supreme Court, LC.

30. *Washington Star,* Nov. 30, 1972.

31. Author's interview with Aubrey Marshall, Jr.

32. *Swann v. Charlotte-Mecklenburg,* Marshall Papers, Supreme Court, LC.

33. Author's interview with Stephen Saltzburg.

34. *Furman v. Georgia,* Marshall Papers, Supreme Court, LC.

35. Author's interview with Ralph Winter.

36. Thurgood Marshall interview with the Columbia Oral History Project.

31. *Backlash on the Court*

1. McCorvey would later recant that story, admitting that she had become pregnant by her boyfriend.

2. Thurgood Marshall to Harry Blackmun, Dec. 12, 1972, Marshall Papers, Supreme Court, Library of Congress.

3. William O. Douglas, *The Court Years, 1939–1975* (New York: Random House, 1980), p. 251.

4. *Procunier v. Martinez* (1973).

5. *San Antonio Independent School District v. Rodriguez* (1973).

6. John Oakley to Thurgood Marshall, Mar. 30, 1973, Marshall Papers, Supreme Court, LC.

7. *Milliken v. Bradley* (1974).

8. Antero Pietila, "Marshall '25 Talks . . . ," *Baltimore Sun*, June 5, 1975.

9. *Gregg v. Georgia* (1976).

10. Author's interview with William Brennan.

11. John MacKenzie, "Marshall: Ready . . . ," *Washington Post*, Sept. 5, 1976, p. D6.

12. Lyle Denniston, "2 to 3 Weeks in Bed . . . ," *Washington Star*, July 7, 1976.

13. *Beal v. Doe* (1977).

14. Richard Smith, "Clerks of the Court," *Washington Post*, Aug. 29, 1976, p. 15.

15. Author's interview with Griffin Bell.

16. Author's interview with Doris McCree.

17. Author's interview with Daniel Friedman.

18. Author's interview with Louis Claiborne.

19. Author's interview with Phillip Spector.

20. Author's interview with Byron White.

21. T. M. to Conference, Apr. 13, 1978, Marshall Papers, Supreme Court, LC.

22. *Regents of the University of California v. Bakke* (1978).

23. Stuart Auerbach, "Blacks Told . . . ," *Washington Post*, Nov. 19, 1978, p. A2.

24. Remarks of Thurgood Marshall, Second Circuit Judicial Conference, May 1979.

25. Bob Woodward and Scott Armstrong, *The Brethren* (New York: Simon & Schuster, 1979), pp. 258, 429.

26. Author's interview with Karen Hastie Williams.

27. Author's interview with Phillip Spector.

28. Author's interview with Susan Bloch.

29. Author's interview with Warren Burger.

30. Author's interview with Lewis Powell.

31. Author's interview with William Rehnquist.

32. T. M. to Conference, July 31, 1980, Marshall Papers, Supreme Court, LC.

33. Author's interview with Cecelia Marshall.
34. "The Supreme Court Is a Life Term, Period," *Washington Post*, Jan. 25, 1981.

32. *Hangin' On*

1. Author's interview with Martha Minow.
2. Thurgood Marshall, "Outside Counsel," *American Lawyer*, Aug. 1981, p. 37.
3. "Court's Rulings Hinged . . . ," *Washington Post*, July 4, 1983.
4. Author's interview with William Brennan.
5. Michael Reiss and Al Jean, "How to Write . . . ," *National Lampoon*, Feb. 1982, p. 60.
6. William Webster to Thurgood Marshall, Mar. 4, 1982, Marshall Papers, Supreme Court, Library of Congress.
7. *Fullilove v. Klutznick* (1980).
8. Thurgood Marshall interview with the Columbia Oral History Project.
9. T. M. to Toni House, June 24, 1986, Marshall Papers, Supreme Court, LC.
10. *New York Times*, September 20, 1987.
11. *Life*, July 7, 1986.
12. T. M. to William Brennan, Feb. 28, 1986, Marshall Papers, Supreme Court, LC.
13. Author's interview with Lewis Powell.
14. Author's interview with Byron White.
15. Author's interview with Monroe Dowling.
16. Remarks of Thurgood Marshall, Maui, Hawaii, May 6, 1987.
17. Thurgood Marshall interview with Carl Rowan, June 1987, WUSA-TV.
18. "Judicial Lockjaw," *Baltimore Sun*, Sept. 13, 1987.
19. "Reagan Rejects Criticism . . . ," *Washington Post*, Sept. 10, 1987, p. A7.
20. Terry Eastland, "While Justice Sleeps," *National Review*, Apr. 21, 1989, pp. 24–25.
21. Jacqueline Trescott, "Making Marshall's . . . ," *Washington Post*, Sept. 15, 1988, p. C1.
22. Author's interview with Susan Bloch.
23. Tony Mauro, "Rowan Drops . . . ," *Legal Times*, July 18, 1988, p. 12.
24. Thurgood Marshall interview with the Columbia Oral History Project.
25. Author's interview with Antonin Scalia.
26. "Marshall: Brennan Is Irreplaceable," *Washington Post*, July 27, 1990, p. A16.
27. "Marshall: Speaking Ill of the Dead," *Newsweek*, Aug. 6, 1990, p. 18.
28. Ruth Marcus, "Plain Spoken . . . ," *Washington Post*, June 29, 1991, p. A1.
29. Author's interview with Jack Valenti.
30. Author's interview with Gloria Branker.

33. *Resurrection*

1. *Washington Post*, Jan. 29, 1993.
2. Author's interview with William Pregnell. "I just read the Episcopal Burial Service, with no comment," Rev. Pregnell recalled. "Sometimes saying less is better with a person whose presence is so commanding. I said to myself, 'God look at this. I'm a white, middle-class kid from Charleston, South Carolina, where the Civil War started. And here I am, committing what I think is the greatest Afro-American in history to his grave, at his family's request.' I was really much moved by it."
3. Author's interview with Sandra Day O'Connor.
4. Author's interview with Thomas Krattenmaker.
5. Author's interview with Lewis Powell.
6. Author's interview with William Rehnquist.
7. Terry Eastland, *Baltimore Sun*, July 1, 1991.

RESOURCES AND BIBLIOGRAPHY

Interviews

Author's interviews: Willie Adams, Victorine Adams, Terry Adamson, Cliff Alexander, Jesse Anderson, Kevin Baine, Griffin Bell, Cel Bernadino, Berl Bernhard, Sue Bloch, David Bogen, St. Clair Bourne, Gloria Branker, William Brennan, Scott Brewer, Leslie Brown, Philip Brown, Tyrone Brown, William Bryant, Paul Bumpus, Warren Burger, John Butler, Franz Byrd, Mildred Byrd, Cab Calloway, Nixon Camper, Walter Carr, Robert Carter, Stephen Carter, Julius Chambers, Louis Claiborne, Kenneth Clark, Ramsey Clark, Frank Coleman, William T. Coleman, Henry Steele Commager, Claude Connor, Archibald Cox, James Crockett, Evelyn Cunningham, Gloster Current, Sam Daniels, John A. Davis, Drew Days, Arnold DeMille, Marietta Dochery, James Dorsey, John Dorsey, Monroe Dowling, Ed Dudley, Ada Lois Sipuel Fisher, William Fisher, Owen Fiss, Flo Fleming, John Hope Franklin, James Freedman, Daniel Freidman, Grafton Gaines, Jill Garrett, Jim George, Paul Gewirtz, David Glenn, Ronald J. Greene, Joe Greenhill, Jack Greenberg, Kathleen Hauke, Julia Woodhouse Harden, Donald Hollowell, Leon Higginbotham, Jr., Herbert Hill, Oliver Hill, Benjamin Hooks, Sam Hopkins, Alfreda Hughes, Essie Hughes, Carrie Jackson, Vernon Jordan, Nicholas Katzenbach, Damon Keith, Randall Kennedy, Martin Kilson, Whitman Knapp, Thomas Krattenmaker, Earl Kroger, Lena Lee, Lennie Lewis, John Raymond Lockridge, Peter Lockwood, Jack Lovett, J. Edward Lumbard, Aubrey Marshall, Jr., Burke Marshall, Cecelia Marshall, Goody Marshall, Thurgood Marshall, Louis Martin, Doris McCree, Enolia McMillan, Genna Rae McNeil, Harry McPherson, Martha

Minow, Frank Mitchell, Michael Mitchell, Parren Mitchell, Elizabeth Monteiro, Constance Baker Motley, Michael Murphy, William Murphy, Rosa Murray, James Nabrit III, Helen Nelson, Sandra Day O'Connor, Agnes Patterson, Pat Patterson, Etta Phefer, Theodore Phefer, Louis Pollack, Lewis Powell, William Pregnell, Margery Prout, William Rehnquist, Chuck Robb, Spottswood Robinson III, Stephen Saltzburg, Dick Sanders, Antonin Scalia, John Segenthaler, June Shagaloff, Charlotte Shervington, Phillip L. Spector, Ralph Spritzer, Jordan Steiker, James Stewart, Teddy Stewart, Alice Stovall, William Thompson, Douglas Turnbull, Jr., Mark Tushnet, Jack Valenti, Mike Wallace, Gil Ware, Robert Watts, Robert C. Weaver, Warren Weaver, Byron White, David Wilkins, Maxine Wilkins, Minnie Wilkins, Ethel Williams, Karen Hastie Williams, Vinnie Williams, Ralph Winter, Rose Wiseman, Harris Wofford, Biddie Woods, Andrew Young

Amistad Oral History: Daniel Byrd

Columbia Oral History: Sam Battle, Walter Gellhorn, Jack Greenberg, Thurgood Marshall, Henry Lee Moon, James Nabrit II, J. Waties Waring

Howard University Oral History Program: Wiley Branton

George and Caroline Stevens, American Film Institute: Julia Davis Adams, Robert Carter, Kenneth Clark, John Hope Franklin, Jack Weinstein, Taggart Whipple

Fisk University Black Oral History Project: A. Macio Smith

Maryland Historical Society: Juanita Mitchell

Public Broadcasting Corporation: Constance Baker Motley

Radio America: Robert Carter, Kenneth Clark, Walter Dellinger, Randall Kennedy, E. Barrett Prettyman, Jr.

WUSA: Thurgood Marshall

Archival

American Film Institute, The Kennedy Center
Amistad Research Center, Tulane University
Carter Presidential Library
Emily Bissell Sanitarium
Eisenhower Presidential Library
Federal Bureau of Investigation
Ford Presidential Library
Harvard University, Frankfurter Papers
Harvard University, Hastie Papers
Library of Congress, NAACP Papers
Library of Congress, Marshall Papers
Lincoln University Archives
Johnson Presidential Library

Kennedy Presidential Library
MacArthur Library
Moreland-Spingarn Research Center, Howard University
National Archives
Nixon Presidential Library
Reagan Presidential Library
Roosevelt Presidential Library
St. Katherine's Episcopal Church, Baltimore
Truman Presidential Library
United States Department of Justice
United States Department of State
Yale University, Brown Collection
Yale University, Legal Defense Fund Papers

Newspapers

Annapolis Evening Capitol, Buffalo Courier Express, Chicago Defender, Chicago Sun-Times, Columbia Daily Herald, Baltimore Afro-American, Baltimore American and Commercial Appeal, Baltimore Sun, East Africa Standard, Las Vegas Sun, Legal Times, Lynchburg News, Nashville Banner, Nashville Tennessean, New Jersey Herald News, New York Daily News, New York Herald Tribune, New York Mirror, New York Post, The New York Times, New York World Telegram and Sun, Norfolk Journal and Guide, Oklahoma Black Dispatch, Philadelphia Tribune, Pittsburgh Courier, St. Louis Post-Dispatch, Texas Ranger, Toledo Blade, Washington Afro-American, Washington Daily News, The Washington Post, Washington Star, Wilmington Morning News

Journals/Magazines

ABA Journal, American Lawyer, B&O Magazine, Collier's, Congressional Quarterly, The Crisis, Ebony, Harvard Blackletter Journal, Jet, The Journal of Negro Education, Life, Maryland Historical Magazine, Maryland Law Review, National Lampoon, National Review, The New Yorker, Newsweek, The Survey, Time

Dissertations/Theses

Freedman, Elaine. *Harvey Johnson and Everett Waring: A Study of Leadership in the Baltimore Negro Community, 1800–1900.* Master's thesis, George Washington University, September 1968.
Gardner, Bettye Jane. *Free Blacks in Baltimore 1800–1860.* Ph.D. diss., George Washington University, May 5, 1974.
Hawkins, Mason A. *Frederick Douglass High School: A Seventeen-Year Period Survey.* College of Education thesis, University of Pennsylvania, 1933.

Marth, Andrea L. *The Fruits of Jim Crow: The Edgewood Sanatorium and African-American Institution Building in Wilmington, Delaware, 1900–1940.* Master's thesis, University of Delaware, Spring 1994.

Skotnes, Andor. *The Black Freedom Movement and the Workers' Movement in Baltimore, 1930–1939.* Ph.D. diss., Rutgers, May 1991.

Books

Anderson, Jervis. *This Was Harlem: A Cultural Portrait, 1900–1950.* New York: Farrar, Straus & Giroux, 1982.

Argersinger, Jo Ann E. *Toward a New Deal in Baltimore.* Chapel Hill: University of North Carolina Press, 1988.

Bland, Randall, *Private Pressure on Public Law.* Port Washington, N.Y.: National University Publications, 1973.

Branch, Taylor. *Parting the Waters.* New York: Simon and Schuster, 1988.

Brown, Philip. *A Century of Separate but Equal Education in Anne Arundel County.* New York: Vantage Press, 1988.

Brugger, Robert J. *Maryland: A Middle Temperament.* Baltimore: Johns Hopkins Press, 1988.

Callcott, George. *Maryland and America: 1940–1980.* Baltimore: Johns Hopkins Press, 1985.

Callcott, Margaret. *The Negro in Maryland Politics: 1870–1912.* Baltimore: Johns Hopkins Press, 1969.

Caro, Robert. *Means of Ascent: The Years of Lyndon Johnson.* New York: Vintage Books, 1990.

Charns, Alexander. *Cloak and Gavel.* Urbana: University of Illinois Press, 1992.

Davis, Michael, and Hunter Clark. *Thurgood Marshall: Warrior at the Bar, Rebel on the Bench.* New York: Birch Lane Press, 1992.

Dorsen, Norman, ed. *The Evolving Constitution.* Middletown, Conn.: Wesleyan University Press, 1987.

Douglass, Frederick. *Life and Times of Frederick Douglass.* New York: Collier Books, 1962.

Douglas, William O. *The Court Years, 1937–1975.* New York: Random House, 1980.

Fee, Elizabeth, Linda Shopes, and Linda Zeidman, eds. *The Baltimore Book.* Philadelphia: Temple University Press, 1991.

Fields, Barbara Jeanne. *Slavery and Freedom on the Middle Ground: Maryland during the Nineteenth Century.* New Haven: Yale University Press, 1985.

Foner, Eric. *Reconstruction: America's Unfinished Revolution, 1863–1877.* New York: Harper and Row, 1988.

Forbush, Bliss. *Moses Sheppard: Quaker Philanthropist of Baltimore.* Philadelphia and Toronto: J. B. Lippincott and Co., 1968.

Friedman, Leon, ed. *The Justices of the United States Supreme Court.* New York and London: Chelsea House, 1978.

Gallen, David, ed. *Black Americans: The FBI Files.* New York: Carroll & Graf Publishers, 1994.

Garrow, David. *Bearing the Cross.* New York: William Morrow and Co., 1986.

Gillette, Michael. "Heman Marion Sweatt." *Black Leaders: Texans for Their Times.* Texas State Historical Association, 1981.

Goldman, Roger, and David Gallen, eds. *Thurgood Marshall: Justice for All.* New York: Carroll & Graf Publishers, 1992.

Graham, Leroy. *Baltimore: The Nineteenth-Century Black Capital.* Washington D.C.: University Press of America, 1982.

Greenberg, Jack. *Crusaders in the Courts.* New York: Basic Books, 1994.

Hall, Kermit, ed. *The Oxford Companion to the Supreme Court of the United States.* New York: Oxford University Press, 1992.

Harbaugh, William Henry. *Lawyer's Lawyer: The Life of John W. Davis.* New York: Oxford Univ. Press, 1973.

Jack, Robert. *History of the National Association for the Advancement of Colored People.* Boston: Meador Publishing, 1943.

Kluger, Richard. *Simple Justice.* New York: Vintage Books, 1975.

McNeil, Genna Rae. *Groundwork.* Philadelphia: University of Pennsylvania Press, 1983.

Murphy, Bruce A. *Fortas.* New York: William Morrow and Co., 1988.

Navasky, Victor. *Kennedy Justice.* New York: Atheneum, 1971.

Poinsett, Alex. *Walking with Presidents: Louis Martin and the Rise of Black Political Power.* Lanham, Md.: Madison Books, 1997.

Radoff, Morris, ed. *The Old Line State: A History of Maryland.* Annapolis: Hall of Records Commission, 1971.

Rampersad, Arnold. *The Life of Langston Hughes.* New York: Oxford University Press, 1986.

Reef, Catherine. *Buffalo Soldiers.* New York: Twenty-first Century Books, 1993.

Scharf, J. Thomas. *Chronicles of Baltimore.* Baltimore: Turnbull Brothers, 1874.

Sides, Joseph C. *Fort Brown Historical.* San Antonio: The Naylor Co., 1942.

Speer, Hugh. *Case of the Century.* Kansas City: University of Missouri, 1968.

Tushnet, Mark. *Making Civil Rights Law.* New York: Oxford University Press, 1994.

Waskow, Arthur. *From Race Riot to Sit-ins, 1919 and the 1960s.* Garden City, N.Y.: Doubleday & Co., 1966.

Ware, Gilbert. *William Hastie.* New York: Oxford University Press, 1984.

White, Walter. *A Man Called White.* Bloomington: Indiana University Press, 1948.

Williams, Jamye Coleman. *The Negro Speaks.* New York: Noble and Noble, 1970.

Williams, Juan. *Eyes on the Prize*. New York: Penguin Books, 1987.

Williams, Robert. *Negroes with Guns*. Chicago: Third World Press, 1973.

Wilmer, L. Allison, J. H. Jarrett, and George W. F. Vernon. *History and Roster of Maryland Volunteers, War of 1861–5, Vol. II*. Baltimore: Guggenheimer, Weil, 1899.

Wilson, Paul. *A Time to Lose*. Lawrence: University of Kansas Press, 1995.

Wofford, Harris. *Of Kings and Kennedys*. Pittsburgh: University of Pittsburgh Press, 1992.

Woodward, Bob, and Scott Armstrong. *The Brethren*. New York: Simon and Schuster, 1979.

Yarbough, Tinsley. *A Passion for Justice*. New York: Oxford University Press, 1987.

Manuscripts

Bogen, David. "Black Lawyers in Maryland in the Forgotten Era."

———. "Race and the Law in Maryland."

PRINCIPAL CASES CITED

Adams v. U.S. (1943)
Ades v. Maryland (1934)
Ake v. Oklahoma (1984)
Alton v. School Board of City of Norfolk (1940)
Angelet v. Fay (1963)
Batson v. Kentucky (1986)
Belton v. Gebhart (1954)
Benton v. Maryland (1969)
Black v. U.S. (1966)
Bolling v. Sharpe (1954)
Bowers v. Hardwick (1986)
Boynton v. Virginia (1960)
Briggs v. Elliott (1954)
Brown v. Board of Education of Topeka (1954)
Buchanan v. Warley (1917)
Bush v. Orleans Parish (1960)
Clark v. CCNV (1984)
Connecticut v. Spell (1940?)
Cooper v. Aaron (1958)
Davis v. County School Board of Prince Edward (1954)
Dove v. Parham (1959)
Dred Scott v. Standord (1857)
Faubus v. Aaron (1959)
Sheperd v. Florida (1951)

Ford v. Wainwright (1986)
Fullilove v. Klutznick (1980)
Furman v. Georgia (1972)
Garner v. Louisiana (1961)
Gayle v. Browder (1956)
Gong Lum v. Rice (1927)
Green v. County School Board of New Kent (1968)
Gregg v. Georgia (1976)
Hale v. Kentucky (1938)
Hall v. DeCuir (1878)
Harper v. Virginia Board of Elections (1966)
Harrison v. NAACP et al. (1959)
Herbert v. Lando (1979)
Hetenyi v. Wilkins (1964)
Hocutt v. Wilson (1933)
Holtzman v. Schlesinger (1973)
Hurd v. Hodge (1948)
Katzenbach v. Morgan (1966)
Keyishian v. Board of Regents (1964)
Lucy v. Adams (1955)
Lyons v. Oklahoma (1944)
Maher v. Roe (1977)
Maryland v. James Gross (1934)
Maryland v. Virtus Lucas (1936)
McCleskey v. Kemp (1987)
McCready v. Byrd (1950)
McGee v. Sipes (1948)
McLaurin v. Oklahoma State Regents (1950)
Mempha v. Rhay (1967)
Mendez v. Westminster School District (1946)
Metro Broadcasting v. FCC (1990)
Milliken v. Bradley (1974)
Mills v. Board of Education of Anne Arundel County (1939)
Miranda v. Arizona (1966)
Missouri ex rel. Gaines v. Canada (1938)
Morgan v. Virginia (1946)
Moses, Harvey v. Dr. W. Aubrey Marshall (1936)
Murray v. Maryland (1936)
Patton v. Mississippi (1947)
Payne v. Tennessee (1991)
People of New York v. Galamison (1964)
Plessy v. Ferguson (1896)

Procunier v. Martinez (1974)
NAACP v. Alabama ex rel. Patterson (1958, 1959)
Regents of the University of California v. Bakke (1978)
Richmond v. J. A. Croson Co. (1989)
Roe v. Wade (1973)
San Antonio Independent School District v. Rodriguez (1973)
Shelley v. Kraemer (1948)
Sipuel v. Oklahoma State Regents (1948)
Smith v. Allright (1944)
South Carolina Electric & Gas Co. v. Flemming (1956)
Stanley v. Georgia (1969)
Swann v. Charlotte-Mecklenburg Board of Education (1971)
Sweatt v. Painter (1950)
Taylor v. Alabama (1948)
Tennessee v. Pillow and Kennedy (1946)
U.S. v. Classic (1941)
U.S. v. Gilbert (1950)
U.S. v. Nixon (1974)
U.S. v. Price (1966)
U.S. v. Yazell (1966)
Virginia v. Crawford (1933)
Ward's Cove Packing Co. v. Atonio (1989)
Watts v. Indiana (1949)
Williams v. Zimmerman (1937)
Wygant v. Jackson Board of Education (1986)

INDEX

NOTE: TM refers to Thurgood Marshall; LBJ refers to Lyndon B. Johnson.

Abortion, 355, 361–62, 370, 393,
    400–401
ACLU (American Civil Liberties
    Union), 105, 111, 124
Ades v. Maryland (1934), 67–68, 82–83
Affirmative action, 364–68, 384, 388,
    389, 392–93, 399, 401, 402–3
Afro-American: TM's use of term, 387
Afro-American Co.: 42, 70–71. See also
    Baltimore Afro-American; Murphy,
    Carl
Ake (Glen) v. Oklahoma (1984), 379
Alabama: civil rights movement in, 313;
    King in, 309; NAACP in, 258–59; and
    NAACP membership lists, 258–59;
    school segregation in, 248–49. *See also*
    Montgomery, Alabama
Alexander, Clifford, 8, 9–10, 11
Allred, James, 103, 104
Alpha Phi Alpha, 41, 46–47, 56–57
Alton v. School Board of City of Norfolk
    (1940), 91
American Bar Association, 12, 57–58,
    214, 334, 390, 395
American Civil Liberties Union
    (ACLU), 105, 111, 124
Angelet v. Fay (1964), 309
Antilynching lobbying, 81–82, 95–
    96
Apollo Theater (Harlem), 275

Archer, Roy, 180, 181
Autobiography of TM, 385–86

B & O Railroad, 28, 41, 213
Back-to-Africa movement, 25, 276
Baker, Josephine, 190
Bakke, Allan, 364–68
Baltimore Afro-American, 42, 83–84, 125;
    and *Ades*, 67–68; and black soldiers,
    170; and boycott in Baltimore, 72, 73;
    and Carter lynching, 69; and
    communism, 169; and equal pay
    issues, 89–90; and federal judgeship
    for TM, 290; and graduate school
    segregation, 75; interview of TM's
    parents in, 144–45; and Little Rock,
    269; man-of-the-year award for TM
    by, 218, 234; and *Murray*, 79; and race
    relations in Baltimore, 26; and race
    riots during World War II, 134, 138;
    and racial stereotyping, 105; and
    school segregation, 201, 216, 226–27,
    286; and *Sweatt*, 195; and TM's
    marriage to Cissy, 244; TM's
    reputation enhanced by, 82, 163, 218,
    232, 234; and TM's Spingarn speech,
    144; and TM's trip to Kenya, 286; and
    voting rights, 111
Baltimore City Bar Association,
    70

Baltimore, Maryland: "Cake Walk
    Homicide" in, 30–32, 66; equal pay
    issues in, 89–91; housing in, 148–49;
    Jews in, 15–16, 27, 29–30, 45, 73;
    justice system in, 66–68; legal circles
    in, 70; NAACP chapter in, 26, 66–67,
    71, 72–73; NAACP conference in
    (1936), 84; police in, 30–32, 35,
    66–67, 89; politics in, 19, 22–23,
    26–27, 33, 88–89; race relations in,
    15–16, 22–23, 26–27, 30–33, 52–53,
    67–68, 71–73, 79–80, 399–400; school
    segregation in, 79–80; TM leaves, 85,
    86; TM statue in, 372; TM's
    childhood/youth in, 15–16, 23, 24,
    25–39, 399–400; TM's legal practice
    in, 62–74, 75–85, 166; union
    organizing in, 67, 69–70, 82–83
Baltimore Sun, 347, 372, 383, 402
Bates, Daisy, 263, 264, 267–69, 273
Batson v. Kentucky (1986), 380
Bazelon, David, 345
Bease, Charlie, 191
Beldon, Stanley, 115, 116
Bell, Derrick, 287
Benton v. Maryland (1969), 345
Bernhard, Berl, 307–9
Billington, James, 394
Birmingham, Alabama, 309
Bishop, Shelton Hale, 235
Black, Charles, 210, 211
Black (Fred) v. U.S. (1966), 323–26, 328,
    333
Black, Hugo, 7, 184, 190, 317, 338,
    339–40
Black: TM's use of term, 388
Black athletes, 164
Black colleges, 232. *See also specific
    institution*
Black media: and *Brown*, 230–31, 232;
    and housing issues, 149–50; and *Irvin*,
    157; and *Morgan*, 146; and NAACP
    fund-raising, 225; reputation of,
    239–40; and sit-ins, 287; and *Sweatt*,
    181–82; in Texas, 109; and TM's
    consideration for federal judgeship, 5,
    193; TM's reputation enhanced by,
    187. *See also specific person, paper, or
    journal*
Black Muslims. *See* Nation of Islam
Black nationalism, 321, 387, 393. *See also*
    Nation of Islam
Black Panthers, 342–43
Black Power, 7, 342–43, 359, 388

Black soldiers, 32–33, 128, 148, 169–73,
    321. *See also* Military: segregation in
Black teachers, 89–91, 200, 232, 381
Black vote, 289, 340
Blackmun, Harry, 347, 353, 354, 355,
    360, 361, 372, 375
Blacks: as clerks for TM, 377; in
    Congress, 399; as middle class, 399;
    and scientific treatments to look
    white, 188–89; youth culture of, 359
Bloch, Susan, 370, 386
Blossom, Virgil, 265
Bluford, Lucille, 98–99
Bomar, Lynn, 134, 138
Bombings: of Cambodia, 355–56; and
    civil rights movement, 155, 206, 248,
    249, 268
Booker, Simeon, 348
Boulware, Harold, 198–99
Bowers v. Hardwick (1986), 383
Boycotts: in Baltimore, 71–73; and
    Lincoln Memorial ceremony, 306–7;
    in Montgomery, 245–48, 251, 252,
    253, 254, 258; TM's views about, 241,
    341, 378
Boynton (Bruce) v. Virginia (1960),
    288–89
Branker, Gloria, 261, 396
Branton, Wiley, 264, 265, 268, 269,
    363–64, 368
Brennan, William, 372, 375, 391, 397;
    and abortion, 355, 361; and
    affirmative action, 365, 389; and *The
    Brethren*, 371; and broadcasting
    licenses, 389; and conservatism, 353,
    360, 374; and death penalty, 351, 359,
    360; defends TM, 371, 384; health of,
    350; Nixon's views of, 355; and
    peremptory challenges, 380; pressures
    to retire on, 380; retirement of, 389,
    390; and school segregation, 349–50;
    and TM's confirmation to Supreme
    Court, 333; and TM's criticisms of
    Supreme Court, 381; and TM's
    relationship with other justices, 376;
    TM's relationship with, 339, 345, 351,
    374, 378, 379, 381, 384, 390, 392
The Brethren (Woodward and
    Armstrong), 369–71, 385
Brewer, Scott, 391
Brilliant, Hyman, 66–67
Broadcasting licenses, 389
Brotherhood of Liberty, 23
Brown, Daniel, 30–31

Brown, Scrappy, 73
Brown, Tyrone, 347
Brown v. Board of Education of Topeka
(1954), 5, 8, 335, 391; backlash
against, 230, 260; black reactions to,
230–31, 239–40; and Fourteenth
Amendment, 213, 218, 219–25;
impact of, 232, 239–40, 284;
implementation of, 230, 231, 232–33,
236–39; and Justice Department,
213–14, 222; media reactions to, 226,
230–31; NAACP reactions to, 228–29,
253, 261–62; oral arguments in,
215–18, 223–25; preparations for,
209–12, 213–15, 220–23; Reed's
dissenting opinion in, 339; and school
district boundaries, 357–58; and
separate but equal, 209, 225–26, 230;
and social science methods, 209–10,
216, 220; Supreme Court decisions in,
225–26, 237–38; Supreme Court
questions for, 219–25; Supreme Court
reaffirms decision in, 271; tenth
anniversary of, 309–10; TM's brief for,
397; and TM's impact on American
society, 239–40, 400, 401; TM's
reactions to, 226–27, 228–30, 231–32,
240–41, 264–65. *See also specific person*
Brownell, Herbert, 231
Bumpus, Paul, 136, 138, 139
Bunche, Ralph, 218, 237
Burger, Warren: and abortion, 354; and
affirmative action, 366; appointed
chief justice, 346–47; and bicentennial
of Constitution, 382; and *The
Brethren*, 369, 370; and *Brown*,
219–20; and conservatism of Supreme
Court, 347, 353; and crime issues,
374, 375; and death penalty, 360; and
homeless, 378; resignation of, 379;
and rumors of TM's death, 372–73;
and school segregation, 350; TM's
relationship with, 374, 375; and
Watergate, 358
Bus boycott: in Montgomery, 245–48,
251, 252, 253, 254, 258
Buses: segregation on, 145–46, 245–48,
251, 252, 253, 254, 258
Bush, George, 387, 389, 390–91, 392,
393, 395
Bush, Paine, 102, 103, 104
Busing, 350, 355, 356–58, 401
Butler, Richard, 269
Byrd, Daniel, 107, 234

Byrd, Franz "Jazz," 41–42
Byrd, Mildred, 107, 234, 236
Byrd, Robert, 14, 332

Cairo, Illinois, 206–7
"Cake Walk Homicide," 30–32, 66
Calloway, Cab, 37, 39
Calvert Whiskey, 163, 225
Cambodia, 355–56
Canty v. Alabama (1940), 116
Capital punishment. *See* Death penalty
Carmichael, Stokely, 13, 341
Carr, Jimmy, 28–29, 36
Carr, Walter, 71
Carswell, G. Harrold, 347
Carter, Jimmy, 361, 362, 368, 372, 383
Carter, Michael, 163
Carter, Robert, 164, 183–84, 212, 317;
and *Dove*, 272; and federal judgeship,
291, 292–93, 294, 297; Greenberg's
relationship with, 295; Hawaii dinner
with, 382; and implementation of
Brown, 238, 242; and LDF-NAACP
split, 260–61; and Montgomery bus
boycott, 245, 247, 252; NAACP
resignation of, 349; reputation of, 294;
and school segregation, 196, 197, 199,
201, 203, 204, 205, 213, 216, 228, 272;
and sit-ins, 288; TM hires, 125; TM's
relationship with, 259, 260–61, 272,
291, 292–93, 294–95, 349; and TM's
replacement on Supreme Court, 348,
349; and TM's successor at LDF,
294–95
Carter, Stephen, 377, 385, 393
Carter, William, 69
Catonsville High School (Maryland),
79–80
Chaney, James, 319–20
Cheatwood, Vernon, 114, 117
Chemical treatments: for turning blacks
into whites, 188–89
Chesnut, W. Calvin, 91
Childers, J. R., 116, 117
Civil disobedience, 142, 310, 341
Civil liberties, 192–93
Civil rights: definition of, 378–79;
integration as foundation for, 5
Civil Rights Act (1964), 343
Civil rights bills (1940s), 165
Civil rights movement: as Civil War,
268–69; on college campuses, 6–7; and
communism, 254–48, 255–58, 280–83;
emergence and expansion of, 136,

Civil rights movement *(cont'd)*
142; as fast-changing, 246–47; and
FBI, 280–83; and JFK, 5, 291, 307,
308; and LBJ, 313, 326–28, 330, 343;
leadership of, 5, 246–47; and Reagan,
383–84; TM as symbol of, 300, 317;
TM's alienation from, 252, 282–83,
288–89, 311; and TM's appointment
as federal judge, 5; TM's commitment
to, 370; and TM's reputation, 7, 8,
130, 142, 187, 239–40, 271, 272, 377;
TM's views about, 343–44, 377–78,
385, 387; transformation of, 274. *See
also* Militancy, black; *specific person,
organization, city, state, or legal decision*
Claiborne, Louis, 318, 322, 338, 364
Clark, Georgia, 315, 346
Clark, Kenneth, 197, 199, 202, 209, 210,
212, 215, 220, 229
Clark, Ramsey, 338, 346, 385;
appointment to Justice Department
of, 328–30; and federal judgeship for
TM, 293; and King's assassination,
340; LBJ's relationship with, 328;
personal and professional background
of, 7; and TM's appointment as
solicitor general, 315; and TM's
confirmation to Supreme Court, 334;
and TM's nomination to Supreme
Court, 6, 7–8, 9, 328–29; TM's
relationship with, 328
Clark, Thomas, 184, 317, 338; and
Hoover, 158, 159–61; and housing
issues, 151; as NAACP supporter, 161;
and Reed's dissenting opinion in
Brown, 339; retirement of, 3, 4, 8–9,
329, 330; and school segregation, 208;
and Tennessee race riots, 135, 141;
and TM's arrest, 141; and TM's
nomination to Supreme Court, 329;
TM's relationship with, 163; and
Truman, 331
Clark v. CCNV (1984), 378
Clerks: of TM, 305, 362, 369, 370, 371,
377, 384, 386, 397. *See also specific
person*
Clinton, William, 395
Coleman, James P., 316
Coleman, William T. Jr., 191, 297, 392,
394; and *Ades*, 67, 68; and *Brown*
decisions, 209, 223, 224–25, 233; and
Frankfurter's comments about TM,
297; on LBJ-TM relationship, 320; as
possible Supreme Court nominee, 8,

361; and TM as federal judge, 291,
305–6; and TM's marriage to Cissy,
243
Collier's magazine, 192–93
Collins, LeRoy, 155, 157
Colored: TM's use of term, 388
Colored High and Training School
(Baltimore, Maryland). *See* Douglass
High School
Columbia, South Carolina, 247, 248
Columbia, Tennessee, 131–42, 247
Communism: and *Ades*, 67–68, 82–83;
and black soldiers, 321; and civil rights
movement, 254–48, 255–58, 280–83;
and FBI, 124, 169, 255–58, 280–83;
and labor organizations, 257; and
NAACP, 161, 166, 167, 168–69,
170–71, 241–42, 255, 257, 282–83;
and segregationists, 257; and selection
of NAACP defendants, 176; and
Tennessee race riots, 136; and TM's
confirmation to federal judgeship,
300, 301; TM's identification with,
241–42; and TM's
nomination/confirmation to Supreme
Court, 14, 332, 333, 336–37; and
TM's possible run for Congress,
82–83; TM's views about, 255–58
Confessions: and *Lyons*, 113–18; and
Miranda, 323, 325, 334–35, 375
Confirmation hearings, for TM: for
Second Court of Appeals, 296–97,
298–303, 317; as solicitor general,
316–17, 331; for Supreme Court, 7,
14, 331, 332–38
Congress, U.S.: and antilynching bill,
95–96; blacks in, 399; and *Irvin*, 157;
and march on Washington, 309; and
"Southern Manifesto," 248; TM
considers running for, 82–83, 273–74;
TM's lobbying style with members of,
81. *See also* House of Representatives,
U.S.; Senate, U.S.; *specific person or
committee*
Connecticut v. Spell (1941), 119–20
Connor, Claude, 191, 235, 243
Conservatives: and Fortas' nomination
for chief justice, 342; and TM's
confirmation to Supreme Court, 333;
and TM's impact on American society,
398–99; and TM's nomination to
Supreme Court, 13. *See also person or
specific decision*
Constitution, U.S.: bicentennial of,

381–82; Thomas' views about, 393; TM's views about, 382, 400–401. *See also specific amendment*

Contracts: set-asides for, 377, 388, 389, 399

Cooper v. Aaron. See Little Rock, Arkansas

Corporate law, 304–5, 353, 370

Cox, Archibald, 314, 316, 320, 362

Cox, W. Harold, 299, 301

Crawford, George: murder case of, 58–59, 147

Crime, 317, 334, 374–75, 387. *See also specific decision*

The Crisis (NAACP), 47, 48, 49, 69, 94, 118, 167

Cruel and unusual punishment, 359, 379, 381

Cummings, Harry, 26–27

Cunningham, Evelyn, 191–92

Current, Gloster, 242–43, 281

Daily Worker newspaper, 131, 139, 190

Dallas, Texas: Porter case in, 101–4

Davis, John A. (Lincoln professor), 230

Davis, John W. (South Carolina lawyer), 214–15, 217–18, 222, 223–24, 230, 236, 296

Davis, Julia, 215

Death penalty: as cruel and unusual punishment, 359, 379, 381; and *Ford*, 379; and *Furman*, 350–51, 359; and *Gregg*, 359–60; and *Gross*, 66; and *Irvin*, 156–57; and *McCleskey*, 381; public support of, 387; and racism, 359–60, 381; reinstatement of, 360; Thomas' support for, 393; TM's opposition to, 66, 350–51, 355, 359–60, 370, 375–76, 379, 380, 381, 391, 392, 401; and TM's reputation, 120; and victim impact statements, 391

Debating teams: TM on, 36–37, 43

Delaney, Hubert, 203, 238

Delaware: school segregation in, 207, 208, 218, 219

Dellinger, Walter, 400

DeLoach, Cartha, 325, 326, 343

Democratic Party: in 1940s, 160; and antilynching bill, 95; and elections of 1960, 289; in Harlem, 212; in Maryland, 22, 23, 26–27, 33; in New York, 166; primary system in, 108–10; and rumors of TM's retirement, 361;

in Texas, 108–10; and TM's confirmation to federal judgeship, 303; and TM's consideration for federal judgeship, 166; and TM's retirement, 352

Denniston, Lyle, 361

Detroit, Michigan, 126–28, 247, 277, 357–58

Direct-attack strategy, 174–86, 195–208

Dochery, Marietta, 273

Dodson, Clarence "Boots" (uncle), 24, 25, 87–88

Dodson, Denmedia "Medi" (aunt), 88, 244, 294; and TM and Buster in New York, 86, 87–88, 95; and TM's childhood/youth, 24, 25, 276; TM's relationship with, 145, 193, 250–51

Doe v. Bolton, 354–55

Dole, Robert, 390

Dollarway, Arkansas, 271–72

Donaldson, Sam, 389–90

Double jeopardy, 312, 345

Douglas, William O., 7, 219, 333, 339, 353, 355–56, 358, 359

Douglass, Frederick, 18, 31, 386

Douglass High School (Baltimore, Maryland), 34–39, 359

Dove v. Parham, 271–72

Dowling, Helen, 95, 126, 234, 250

Dowling, Monroe: on birth of Thurgood, Jr., 250; and Buster's illness and death, 234, 235; at Lincoln University, 46, 48, 49, 50; reputation of, 95; and Thomas' confirmation hearings, 393–94; on TM and Cissy's marriage, 250; and TM's criticisms of Supreme Court, 381; and TM's health, 50; on TM's lifestyle, 306, 322, 346; and TM's marriage to Cissy, 243; TM's relationship with, 95, 126; and TM's style, 385; on TM's Texas voting rights case, 109; on TM's travels in South, 106

Dred Scott v. Standord (1857), 138

Du Bois, W.E.B.: and benefits of segregation, 217–18; and communism, 167, 168; as *Crisis* editor, 48, 49, 69, 94, 167; and elections of 1948, 168; and faculty integration at Lincoln, 49; and labor organizing, 69; NAACP ouster of, 168, 188; Spingarn Medal awarded to, 143; TM's relationship with, 167–68; White's relationship with, 168

Dudley, Edward, 125, 260
Due process, 138, 153, 208, 382, 389
Dunjee, Roscoe, 113, 115, 117, 118, 176,
    177, 178, 179
Durham, W. J., 109, 110, 175

Eastland, James, 10, 230, 268, 297, 298,
    299–300, 302–3, 334, 335–36, 337,
    342
Eastland, Terry, 384, 402
Eavesdropping: on Black, 323–26, 328,
    333; on Faubus, 266; on King,
    310–11; on TM, 162–63, 242, 310
Ebony magazine, 322
Eckford, Elizabeth, 263–64
Economic inequity, 403–4
Eighth Amendment, 359, 379, 381
Eisenhower, Dwight D.: and *Brown*,
    219–20, 222, 231, 233, 237–38, 266,
    383; and elections of 1956, 237; and
    elections of 1960, 289; and Little
    Rock, 264, 266–67, 268, 269, 271; and
    NAACP, 222; TM's views about, 222,
    383; Warren nomination of, 221
Elections: of 1936, 82–83; of 1940, 108;
    of 1949, 168; of 1952, 212, 219–20; of
    1956, 237; of 1960, 289–90; of 1968,
    7, 13, 321, 328, 329, 331, 337–38, 340,
    342, 343; of 1972, 352; of 1976, 361;
    of 1980, 372; of 1992, 395
Ellington, Duke, 110–11
Elliott, J. Robert, 299, 301
Elman, Philip, 151, 214
Episcopal Church, 37, 144, 310, 398
Equal pay issues, 89–91, 200
Equal protection, 149, 151, 216, 218,
    287–88, 357, 364–68, 381, 389
Equal rights, 222, 344, 382, 399, 400,
    403, 404
Ervin, Sam, 303, 332, 335, 337
Evers, Medgar, 307

Fair Employment Practices Committee
    (FEPC), 123
Farrakhan, Louis, 399
Faubus, Orval, 263, 264, 265, 266–67,
    269, 271
Faubus v. Aaron. See Little Rock,
    Arkansas
Federal Bureau of Investigation (FBI):
    and civil rights movement, 192,
    280–83; and communism, 169,
    255–58, 280–83; and King, 310–11;
    and NAACP, 169, 242, 254–58; and

race relations, 192, 253–58; racism in,
    161–62; and Shagaloff situation, 207;
    and Tennessee race riots, 135, 141;
    and threats against TM, 343; TM
    investigated by, 14, 124–25, 169, 171,
    242; and TM's nomination to
    Supreme Court, 14; TM's secret
    meetings with, 254–58, 278–80, 281,
    282–83; Willie Marshall as janitor for,
    145; and Woodard, 158–59. *See also*
    Eavesdropping; Hoover, J. Edgar
Federal Housing Administration, 148
Federal judgeship: Hastie nominated for,
    184; JFK nominates TM for, 290–94;
    rumors about TM getting a, 258, 274;
    TM considered for, 164–66. *See also*
    Second Circuit Court of Appeals, U.S.
Fifth Amendment, 208, 323, 339
Figg, Robert McC., 201, 202
First Amendment, 345, 356, 368–69
Fisk University, 49, 185
Fleming, Billy, 132, 141, 142
Florida: death penalty in, 359–60;
    Groveland case in, 152–57; lynch
    mobs in, 152–57
Ford, Gerald, 359, 361
Ford v. Wainwright (1986), 379
Fortas, Abe, 7, 14, 325–26, 332, 333,
    342, 343, 347
Fourteenth Amendment: and *Brown*,
    213, 218, 219–25; and D.C. code of
    laws, 57; and graduate school
    segregation, 77; historical arguments
    concerning, 220–23; and housing
    issues, 149; and jury service, 102; and
    school segregation, 196, 207–8, 213,
    218, 219–25; and sit-ins, 287–88, 289;
    and status of Washington, D.C.,
    207–8; and TM's confirmation to
    Supreme Court, 336, 337; TM's views
    about, 389. *See also* Equal protection
Fox, Albert, 44, 45
Fox, George, 90–91
Frankfurter, Felix, 150, 216–17, 224–25,
    238–39, 297, 307
Franklin, John Hope, 220, 221, 295
Frederick, Maryland, 68–69
Free speech, 311–12, 400–401
Freedman, James O., 305, 306, 307
Freedom of the press, 368–69, 400
Freund, Paul, 223
Fried, Charles, 383
Friedman, Dan, 363
Friedman, Samuel, 119

Friendly, J. Henry, 305
Frivolous lawsuits, 284
Fulbright, William, 269
Fullilove v. Klutznick (1980), 377
Furman v. Georgia (1972), 350–51, 359
Futch, Truman, 154, 156

Gaines, Grafton, 318, 338, 354, 386
Gaines (Lloyd) case, 96–98, 175, 176, 218
Garland, Charles, 94
Garner v. Louisiana, 288–89
Garvey, Marcus, 25, 276
Gayle v. Browder (1956). *See* Bus boycott: in Montgomery
Gellhorn, Walter, 178, 311
Georgia: abortion in, 354–55; death penalty in, 359–60; sit-ins in, 289–90; sodomy in, 383
Gibson Island Club, 43–45, 51, 52, 59, 64, 83, 145, 214
Gilbert, Leon A., 170, 171, 173
Goldberg, Arthur, 296, 307, 332, 334
Gong Lum v. Rice (1927), 77, 80
Goodman, Andrew, 319–20
Gore, Al, 395
Government-funded abortion, 361–62
Graduate education, 75–79, 96–99, 175–79, 180–85, 192, 195, 364–68, 399
Gray, Fred, 248
Green v. County School Board of New Kent (1968), 349–50
Greenberg, Jack, 235–36, 249; and Carter-TM relationship, 261, 292–93; Carter's relationship with, 295; and dissension within NAACP, 154, 190, 260, 261; and *Dove*, 272; and LDF-NAACP split, 260, 261; and school segregation, 204, 208, 218, 223; as TM's successor at LDF, 294–95
Greenhill, Joe, 180, 227
Greensboro, North Carolina, 286–87
Gregg v. Georgia (1976), 359–60
Griswold, Erwin, 178
Gross, James: murder case of, 65–66
Groveland, Florida, 152–57
Gun control, 387

Hale v. Kentucky (1938), 101–2
Hall, Amos T., 177, 179
Hall v. DeCuir (1878), 145
Harden, Julia Woodhouse, 29, 30, 35
Harlan, John Marshall, 334

Harlem: black migration to, 24, 25; Democratic party in, 212; lifestyle in, 275; Marshall (Willie) family in, 24–25; Nation of Islam in, 275–76; politics in, 166, 273–74; race relations in, 13, 25, 247, 303; Renaissance in, 24, 25, 47; Special Commission about, 13; TM and Buster's homes in, 87–88, 164; TM and Cissy live in, 272
Harper v. Virginia Board of Elections (1966), 320
Harvard University, 8, 43, 54–55, 61, 62
Hasgett (Sidney) case, 108–10
Hastie, William, 218, 235, 296; and Carter-TM relationship, 261; and drafting of TM, 123–24; as federal judge nominee, 165, 184; and federal judgeship for TM, 292; and graduate school segregation, 75; and housing issues, 149; and Houston's death, 184; and Howard Law School, 54, 111; as possible Supreme Court nominee, 7, 8, 307, 330; reputation of, 56; and *Smith v. Allwright*, 111; TM's relationship with, 183, 250; as Virgin Islands governor, 137
Hayes, George E. C., 226, 230
Haynsworth, Clement, 347
Herbert v. Lando (1979), 368–69
Hetenyi v. Wilkins (1964), 312, 345
Hicks, James, 170, 195
Hill, Herbert, 190, 251, 252, 334
Hill, Oliver, 56–57, 58, 59, 80, 205–6
Hocutt v. Wilson (1933), 75, 76
Hollings, Ernest, 299
Hollowell, Donald, 290
Holtzman (Elizabeth) v. Schlesinger (1973), 355–56
Homeless, 378, 404
Hoover, Herbert, 241–42, 383
Hoover, J. Edgar: and Clark (Tom), 160–61; and eavesdropping on TM, 162; and federal judgeship for TM, 293; fiftieth year party for, 326; and Katzenbach, 324–25; and Kennedy (Robert), 323–26; and LBJ, 323–26; NAACP letter of, 161; and Nation of Islam, 278–79; power of, 159–60; and race relations in America, 253–58; and TM's Korean trip, 170–71; and TM's nomination/confirmation to Supreme Court, 14, 332–33; TM's relationship with, 157, 158, 159, 160–62, 163, 170–71, 252, 253–58, 278–79, 325–26;

Hoover, J. Edgar *(cont'd)*
  and TM's swearing in as solicitor
  general, 317; and wiretaps, 323–26.
  See also Federal Bureau of
  Investigation
Horne, Lena, 188, 273
House of Representatives, U.S., 82–83,
  95–96, 399. *See also* Congress, U.S.;
  specific person or committee
House, Toni, 379
Housing, 148–51, 228, 258, 346
Houston, Charles Hamilton, 54, 69,
  228; and *Ades*, 67; and Carter lynching
  case, 69; and *Crawford*, 58–59, 147;
  death of, 183, 184, 236; and federal
  judgeships, 165; and forced
  confessions, 116; and graduate
  education segregation, 75, 76–77,
  96–97, 98, 182–84; and housing issues,
  149, 150; as Howard Law School
  dean, 53–54, 55–56, 57–58, 79; and
  jury service, 101–2; and lynchings, 82,
  96; and military segregation, 123; and
  Murray, 76–77, 78; as NAACP lawyer,
  4, 5, 79, 84, 94, 95, 99; personal and
  professional background of, 54–55;
  and *Porter*, 102; reputation of, 56; and
  school segregation, 80, 174, 181, 194,
  208; style of, 93; and *Sweatt*, 182–84;
  TM as assistant to, 93, 95; and TM as
  law student, 56–60; and TM's possible
  run for Congress, 82; and TM's
  pressures for NAACP appointment, 4,
  5, 83, 84–85; TM's relationship with,
  56, 57–58, 59, 63, 93–94, 100, 183,
  184; TM's southern travels with,
  59–60, 63–64; and voting rights, 112;
  White's relationship with, 99; in
  World War I, 122
Houston, William, 54, 99
Howard, T.R.M., 254–55, 256
Howard University, 10, 76, 305, 327;
  accreditation of law at, 57; Aubrey
  Marshall at, 46, 52; awards honorary
  degree to TM, 232; faculty at, 49, 83;
  LDF sit-in strategy conference at,
  287–88; and preparing for *Brown*, 213,
  223; TM as student at, 53–60; and
  TM's clerks, 377; TM's speeches at,
  333, 368. *See also specific person*
Hruska, Roman, 299, 300
Hughes, Essie, 34, 35, 36, 39
Hughes, Langston, 47–48, 49, 395
Hughes, W. A. C., 62

Hugo, Oklahoma: *Lyons* case in, 113–19
Humphrey, Hubert, 10, 340, 343

Illinois: school segregation in, 206–7
Immigration, 402–3
Individual rights, 311–12, 387, 400–401,
  403, 404
Integration: with "all deliberate speed,"
  237–38, 249, 265, 349–50; and black
  colleges, 232; and black teachers, 232;
  and *Brown* aftermath, 253, 261–62,
  265, 284; as foundation of civil rights
  movement, 5; gradualist approach to,
  233, 236–37, 262; implementation of
  school, 213, 232–33, 236–39; as key to
  equal rights, 64; as means of ending
  1960s racial strife, 7; resistance to
  school, 230, 233, 236, 350; slow pace
  of, 269, 271–72; TM as model of, 244;
  TM's commitment to, 5, 13, 232, 304,
  357–58, 387, 401; and TM's impact on
  American society, 398–400, 401,
  403–4. *See also* Affirmative action;
  Busing; *specific city, state, or legal
  decision*
International Juridical Association, 171,
  301, 336
Interracial marriage, 188, 242–44, 250,
  387, 402–3
Interstate commerce, 288–89. *See also*
  Transportation
Irvin, Walter Lee, 153–57
Israel: TM as Truman's representative
  in, 328

Jackson, Jesse, 378, 399
Jackson, Juanita, 72
Jackson, Lillie May, 71, 72, 73–74, 79
Jackson, Robert, 153, 219, 223, 226,
  322–23
Javits, Jacob, 296, 300, 316–17
Jet magazine, 7, 328, 347
Jews, 15–16, 27, 29–30, 45, 73, 239, 342,
  367
Johnson, Lady Bird, 4, 315
Johnson, Lyndon B.: and civil rights,
  268, 313, 317, 326–28, 330, 343; death
  of, 352; farewell party for, 343; and
  Fortas' nomination for chief justice,
  342; and Hoover, 323–26; personal
  background of, 4; returns to Texas,
  346; style of, 6; and TM's
  confirmation to Supreme Court, 334,
  337–38; and TM's nomination to

Supreme Court, 4, 6–7, 8, 9–11, 312,
328–31, 356; and TM's
nomination/confirmation as solicitor
general, 313–16, 317–18; TM's
relationship with, 9, 11, 313, 320–21,
327–30, 331, 340, 343, 352; and TM's
swearing in to Supreme Court, 338;
TM's views about, 383; and wiretaps,
323–26, 328
Johnson, Mordecai, 55, 232
Johnston, Olin, 299, 300, 301, 303
Jones, Charles, 187–88
Jones, Essie Mae, 187–88
Jones, Maude, 234, 235
Jordan, Vernon, 385, 398
Judges: TM's relationship with white,
67, 68; TM's views about, 181. *See also*
Federal judgeship; *specific person or
legal case*
Judiciary Committee (U.S. House), 95,
291–92
Judiciary Committee (U.S. Senate): and
Thomas hearings, 393; Thurmond as
chairman of, 374; and TM's
confirmation as solicitor general,
316–17; and TM's confirmation to
Second Circuit Court, 294, 297,
298–303; and TM's confirmation to
Supreme Court, 10, 332–38
Jury service, 101–4, 136, 139, 147,
380
Justice Department, U.S., 124, 254, 318;
and *Brown*, 213–14, 222; and
Columbia riots, 141; and
eavesdropping, 323–26; and
Fourteenth Amendment, U.S., 222;
and *Irvin*, 157; and King, 290, 340–41;
and school segregation, 213–14, 222,
266; separate but equal briefs of 183;
and *Smith v. Allwright*, 111; and
Sweatt, 183; TM as civil rights
consultant to, 307; TM's criticisms of,
383; and voting rights, 111. *See also
specific person*

Kansas: NAACP in, 204; school
segregation in, 198, 204–5, 207, 216,
219. See also *Brown v. Board of
Education of Topeka* (1954)
Katzenbach, Nicholas, 7–8, 316, 324,
325, 326, 328, 329, 330
Katzenbach v. Morgan (1966), 320
Keating, Kenneth B., 299–300, 301
Keith, Damon, 364

Kelly, Alfred, 220–21, 301–2
Kelly, Michael, 371–72
Kennedy, Anthony, 385
Kennedy, Edward, 336, 337
Kennedy, John F.: assassination of, 309;
and civil rights, 291, 309; and
elections of 1960, 289–90; and
Frankfurter's replacement, 307; and
King's arrest, 290; and Lincoln
Memorial ceremony, 306–7; and TM's
nomination/confirmation to federal
judgeship, 5, 291, 294, 296, 299, 302,
303; TM's views about, 291, 308,
383
Kennedy, Lloyd "Papa Lloyd," 139, 141
Kennedy, Robert F.: assassination of,
342; and civil rights, 307, 309; and
elections of 1960, 290; and elections
of 1968, 340; and Frankfurter's
replacement, 307; and Hoover,
323–26; and King's arrest, 290; LBJ's
relationship with, 13, 321, 323–26,
328; and TM's nomination as solicitor
general, 316; and TM's
nomination/confirmation for federal
judgeship, 5, 290–94, 299, 302; TM's
relationship with, 290–91, 292, 293,
308, 321; TM's views about, 302–3,
383; and wiretaps, 323–26, 328
Kennedy, Stephen, 277–78
Kennedy administration: and civil rights,
307, 308; and federal judgeships,
290–94; and foreign affairs, 307–9;
and NAACP, 307; TM's views about,
308. *See also* Kennedy, John F.;
Kennedy, Robert F.
Kenny, Robert W., 143
Kenya, 284–86, 307–9
Kenyatta, Jomo, 285, 308–9
Kilpatrick, James J., 333
King, Ivor, 39
King, Martin Luther, Jr.: arrest of,
289–90; assassination of, 340–41; in
Birmingham, 309; bombing of house
of, 248; eavesdropping on, 310–11;
and elections of 1960, 289–90; and
FBI, 310–11; fund-raising by, 251;
memorial service for, 341; and
Montgomery bus boycott, 245,
247–48, 251, 252, 253; NAACP's
relationship with, 251–52; personal
and professional backgroud of,
245–46; popularity of, 272; and sit-ins,
286–87; and TM's impact on

King, Martin Luther, Jr. *(cont'd)*
American society, 400; and TM's
nomination/confirmation to Supreme
Court, 13, 333; TM's relationship
with, 341; TM's views about, 248, 251,
252, 255, 256, 282, 311, 392
Konvitz, Milton, 125
Korean War, 169–73
Kraft, Joseph, 13
Kramer, Reuben, 372
Krattenmaker, Thomas, 400
Krech, David, 201
Kronheim, Milton S., 345
Ku Klux Klan, 108, 133, 134, 138, 279,
301, 343, 368

Labaree, Robert, 48–49
Labor unions, 41, 67, 69–70, 82–83, 122,
257
Ladd, D. M., 162
Lake Barcroft (Fairfax, Virginia), 346
Langston Law School, 177
Lautier, Louis, 98
Law: TM's views about, 404
Law practice: TM's Baltimore, 62–74,
75–85, 166
Lawyers: responsibilities of, 59; as social
activists, 60; statistics about black, 55
Layoffs: of teachers, 381
LDF. *See* NAACP Legal Defense and
Education Fund, Inc.
Legal Times newspaper, 386
Lehman, Herbert, 261
Lemley, Harry, 268–69
LeViness, Charles T. III, 77
Libel, 368–69
Liberal Party, 273
Liberals: and federal judgeship, 292–93;
and housing issues, 151; and NAACP,
160; and TM's impact on American
society, 399; and TM's
nomination/confirmation to Supreme
Court, 6–7, 13, 333; and Truman
administration, 151; and Vietnam
War, 13. *See also specific person or
decision*
Liberia, 340
Liberty Lobby, 336
Library of Congress, 394
Life magazine, 249, 380
Lincoln Memorial ceremony, 306–7
Lincoln University: Aubrey Marshall at,
37, 38, 40, 41–42; faculty integration
at, 48; TM as student at, 41–51; TM's

honorary degree from, 163; TM's
struggle to attend, 39, 40–41. *See also
specific person*
Lincoln University (Jefferson City,
Missouri), 97
Little Rock, Arkansas, 262, 263–71
Lockridge, Raymond, 134
Looby, Z. Alexander, 131, 132, 135, 137,
138–40, 141
Look magazine, 188–89
Los Angeles, California: riots in, 317
Louis, Joe, 144, 151, 218
Louisiana: school segregation in, 198;
voting rights in, 110, 111. *See also*
New Orleans, Louisiana
Lovett, Edward, 80
Lovett, Jack, 133, 141
Lucas, Virtis: murder case of, 66–67
Lucy (Autherine) v. Adams (1955), 248–49
Lumbard, J. Edward, 296, 297, 299, 304
Lunch counters: sit-ins at, 286–89, 378
Lurie, Isabel, 198
Lynn, Conrad, 281
Lyons (W.D.) v. Oklahoma (1944),
113–19, 147, 176, 386

MacArthur, Douglas, 171, 172, 173
McCall, Willis B., 153–54, 155, 156
McClellan, John, 298–99, 300, 303, 332,
334–35, 337
McCleskey (Warren) v. Kemp (1987),
381
McCree, Dores, 363
McCree, Wade, 7, 362–63, 364
McDaniels, Gough, 36
McDonald, Patrick, 30–32
McGuinn, Robert, 62, 79–80
McGuinn, Warner, 61–62, 70–71
McHale, Jane, 386, 394
McKenzie, Marjorie, 203, 204
McLaurin v. Oklahoma State Regents
(1950), 176–79
McMechen, George F., 26
McPherson, Harry, 327–28, 330
Maher v. Roe (1977), 361–62
Mahoney, Colleen, 391, 392
Malcolm X, 276, 277, 278–79, 281, 282,
283, 303–4, 313, 393
Mann, Woodrow, 267, 268
Mansfield, Mike, 10
Marches, protest: of Black Muslims, 277;
TM's views about, 241, 341; on
Washington, 309. *See also* Protests
Margold, Nathan, 75–76, 94, 228

Margold report (NAACP, 1930s), 59–60, 174, 184
Marshall, Annie Robinson (grandmother), 17–18, 20
Marshall, Cecelia Suyat "Cissy," 296, 308, 330, 338, 349, 354, 370; background of, 242–43; and Carter-TM relationship, 382; and McCree dinner, 363; and Souter appointment, 390; and threats against TM, 278; and TM as solicitor general, 314; TM's courtship and marriage with, 229–30, 242–43; and TM's "death," 373; and TM's lifestyle, 305, 345–46; and TM's nomination to Supreme Court, 3, 8, 12; TM's relationship with, 250, 272–73, 346; and TM's retirement, 361, 372, 392; and TM's style, 384–85
Marshall, Cyrus (uncle), 35
Marshall, Helen (sister-in-law), 349
Marshall, John (son), 272, 296, 310, 312, 345, 346, 353–54, 372
Marshall, Norma Williams (mother), 64, 85, 218, 244; *Afro-American* interview of, 144–45; and ambitions for TM, 42–43, 51, 86; and Aubrey's care, 86, 87, 89; birth of, 19; and Buster's death, 235; courtship and marriage of, 21–22; death of, 294; and equal pay issues, 89–90, 91; in Harlem, 24–25; as mother, 23, 25, 27, 29, 33, 37, 39, 40, 144; and race relations, 30; as teacher, 21, 22, 33, 37, 39, 88, 89–90, 163; and TM in law school, 52, 53, 55–56, 59; and TM's move to New York, 86, 87, 88; and TM's name change, 26; TM's relationship with, 33–34, 144, 250–51
Marshall, Sadie Prince (sister-in-law), 46, 64, 86, 87
Marshall, Thorney Good (grandfather), 18, 19–21, 22, 26
Marshall, Thoroughgood (uncle), 22
Marshall, Thurgood: ambitions of, 5, 35–36, 39, 42, 51, 193, 296, 315, 331; autobiography of, 385–86; birth of, 22; birthday parties for, 363–64, 385; childhood/youth of, 15–16, 23, 24–39, 399–400; courtroom style of, 77, 80, 145, 180, 215, 320; "death" of, 372–73; death of, 396; early jobs of, 15–16, 29–30, 38, 41, 43, 44, 45–46, 51, 52, 56, 59; elementary/secondary education of, 28–29, 34–39; family background of, 16–22; funeral of,

397–98; as genuine American revolutionary, 402; health of, 49–50, 136–37, 209, 212, 235–36, 249, 347–49, 353, 358–59, 360–61, 362, 368, 371, 379, 386, 390, 392, 394–96; honorary degrees for, 163, 232; impact on American society of, 397–404; as lazy, 8, 13, 330, 369; legal complaints to bar association about, 82; lifestyle of, 171, 177–78, 185, 190–93, 212, 223, 273–74, 305–6, 321–22, 345–46, 353–54, 362, 386; lobbying style of, 81; as man-of-the-year, 218, 234; management style of, 203–4, 209–10, 211, 212, 220–21; military drafting of, 123–24; as model of integration, 244; name change of, 26; nicknames of, 36, 56; papers of, 394; passes Maryland bar exam, 61; personal style of, 163; as prankster, 34–35, 42, 46–47, 56; salaries of, 94, 99, 164, 314, 338, 386; tributes to, 397–98
Marshall, Thurgood, reputation of: as black hero, 347; as black Horatio Alger, 333; black press enhancement of, 82, 163, 187, 218, 232, 234; and *The Brethren*, 369–71; and *Brown*, 231–32, 239–40; and civil liberties, 192–93; and civil rights, 7, 8, 130, 142, 187, 239–40, 271, 272, 377; as criminal lawyer, 67–68, 120, 130; as diligent lawyer, 68; and federal judgeship, 292, 293; and graduate education segregation, 187, 192; and housing issues, 149, 151; and lifestyle, 190–92; and *Lyons*, 118–19; and military drafting of TM, 124; and *Murray*, 78; and NAACP power, 160; as national hero, 391–92, 399; and power of TM, 218–19; as senior black leader, 149; and Supreme Court appearances, 164; and *Sweatt*, 187; and TM's confirmation to federal judgeship, 302; and TM's confirmation to Supreme Court, 333; and voting rights, 112; among whites, 192
Marshall, Thurgood, speeches by: at Apollo theater, 275; and *Brown*, 231–32; and civil disobedience, 310; about communism, 257, 321; about crime, 375; at eightieth birthday party, 385; at Episcopal convention, 310; FBI report about, 124; and fiftieth

Marshall, Thurgood *(cont'd)*
anniversary of high school graduation, 359; and fund-raising, 288; and Groveland, 154; at Harvard, 8; at Howard, 368; and militants, 342–43; and military segregation, 172–73; and Montgomery bus boycott, 251; at Mount Zion Baptist Church (Miami), 154; at NAACP conferences and conventions, 84, 108, 126, 143–44, 257; and NAACP fund-raising, 179, 212, 225; and Nation of Islam, 278; in New Orleans, 142, 343–44; on nonviolent protest, 142; and possible congressional run, 273–74; on race relations, 241; and radicals, 257; and school segregation, 182, 225; on separate but equal, 185; and sit-ins, 288; about Supreme Court, 375, 381–82; on *Sweatt*, 185; and TM's appointment as solicitor general, 315; and TM's confirmation to Supreme Court, 333; and TM's reputation, 151; about Vietnam, 321; to youth groups, 210

Marshall, Thurgood, as symbol: of best of American society, 317; of civil rights movement, 300, 317; for equal justice, 293; of peaceful racial progress, 8, 13, 313, 328

Marshall, Thurgood, threats against: and *Ades*, 69; in Columbia, Tennessee, 131–32, 139–41; in Detroit, 127; and Groveland, 155; and *Lyons*, 115–16; and militants, 342–43; and Nation of Islam, 276–77, 278; and *Porter*, 102, 103–4; and TM's arrest for drunken driving, 131–32, 139–41; and TM's travels in South, 106–7; at University of Alabama, 248–49; at University of Wisconsin, 342–43

Marshall, Thurgood, Jr. (son), 243, 250, 296, 310, 312, 345, 346, 347, 353–54, 372, 391, 392

Marshall, Thurgood William (grandson), 392

Marshall, Vivian Burey "Buster" (wife), 86, 87–88, 94–95, 99, 218; attacked in boycott, 73; birth of, 50; courtship and marriage of, 50–51; family background of, 50; illness and death of, 229, 233–36, 249, 261; law suit initiated by, 65; and TM as beginning lawyer, 61, 63; and TM in law school,

55–56; and TM's health, 137; on TM's health, 193; TM's relationship with, 64–65, 125–26, 163–64, 191, 212–13, 215; and TM's Supreme Court appearances, 146, 215

Marshall, W. Aubrey (brother), 126, 144, 145, 294, 317; birth of, 22; childhood/youth of, 25, 28, 29, 34, 36, 38, 39; in college/medical school, 37, 38, 46, 52; death of, 349; illness of, 83, 86–87, 88, 89; marriage of, 46; medical practice of, 64, 65; TM's relationship with, 41–42, 64, 349

Marshall, William Aubrey, Jr. (nephew), 64, 87, 349

Marshall, William C. "Willie" (father): *Afro-American* interview of, 144–45; birth of, 20; childhood/youth of, 21; death of, 163, 236; drinking of, 36, 37–38, 64, 86, 88, 89, 145; fascination with legal system of, 35; as father, 29, 34, 35–36, 38, 39, 145; in Harlem, 24–25; illness of, 37, 40–41, 43–44; jobs of, 21, 23, 25, 33, 44–45, 64, 83–84, 145, 213; marriage of, 21–22; and police, 30, 32; and race relations, 15, 30, 32–33, 392; TM's relationship with, 35–36, 64, 145

Martin, D. D., 171–72

Martin, Louis, 6, 7, 9–10, 11, 150, 293, 327, 329–30

Maryland: equal pay issues in, 89–91; TM as civil rights lawyer in, 5; TM passes bar examination in, 61. *See also* Baltimore, Maryland; *specific legal decision*

Maryland v. James Gross (1934), 65–66

Maryland v. Virtus Lucas (1936), 66–67

Masons, 179–80, 223, 225, 289–90

Mboya, Tom, 284–85

Media: and *Brown*, 226, 230, 239; reaction to TM's nomination to Supreme Court by, 12–13; and TM's reputation, 239, 240. *See also* Black media; *specific person, newspaper, or journal*

Meese, Edwin, 383

Mempa v. Rhay (1967), 339–40

Mendez v. Westminster School district (1946), 196–97

Mentors: of TM, 45, 59, 60, 100, 184, 188, 236, 305

Metro Broadcasting v. FCC (1990), 389

Militancy, black: in civil rights movement, 253–58; and communism, 280–83; growing strength and influence of, 249, 254, 313, 343; and NAACP, 280–83; and TM's alienation from militants, 256–58, 282; TM's opposition to, 7, 334, 343–44. *See also specific person or group*
Military: and drafting of TM, 123–24; segregation in, 121, 122, 123–25, 128–30, 169–73
Mills (Walter) v. Board of Education of Anne Arundel County (1939), 90–91
Ming, Robert, 177
Minority businesses, 377, 388, 389, 399
Minow, Martha, 374
Miranda v. Arizona (1966), 323, 325, 334–35, 375
Mississippi: civil rights movement in, 319–20; protest marches in, 241
Missouri: graduate education in, 96–98, 175, 176, 218
Missouri ex. rel. Gaines v. Canada (1938), 96–98, 175, 176, 218
Mitchell, Arthur, 82, 95–96
Mitchell, Clarence, 72–73
Monteiro, Elizabeth "Penny," 29, 191
Montgomery, Alabama: bus boycott in, 245–48, 251, 252, 253, 254, 258
Monumental City Bar Association, 70, 218
Moon, Henry Lee, 190, 261
Morgan (Irene) v. Virginia (1946), 145–46
Morton, James, 133, 134
Moses, Harvey v. Dr. W. Aubrey Marshall (1936), 65
Motley, Constance Baker: 178, 183, 185, 248–49, 295
Muhammad, Elijah, 254, 276, 278, 304. *See also* Nation of Islam
Murphy, Carl: complains about Wilkins, 74; and federal judgeship for TM, 290; and housing issues, 150; and *Murray*, 78; NAACP relationship with, 71; professional background of, 71; and racial stereotyping, 105; and school segregation, 79, 80, 233, 239; style of, 71; and TM's possible run for Congress, 82, 83; and TM's pressures for NAACP appointment, 84; TM's relationship with, 100; and TM's views about race relations, 240; and White scandals, 188. *See also Baltimore Afro-American*

Murphy, Frank, 112
Murphy, James, 42, 50, 70
Murphy, John H., Jr., 67–68, 70–71
Murray (Donald) v. Maryland (1936), 76–79, 90, 180

NAACP (National Association for the Advancement of Colored People): black criticisms of, 251–52; board of, 168; and *Brown* aftermath, 253, 261–62; and communism, 161, 166, 167, 168–69, 170–71, 241–42, 255, 257, 282–83; dissension within, 181–82, 189–90, 251–52, 258–62; expansion of, 94, 106, 136; and FBI, 169, 242, 254–58; formation of, 23; and Kennedy administration, 307; King's relationship with, 251–52; LDF split from, 259–62; left-wing/liberal influence in, 105, 160; lobbying by, 95; membership lists of, 258–59, 272; membership of, 94; and militancy, 280–83; opposition to violence by, 280–83; political power of, 160; Spingarn Medal of, 143–44; tax-exempt status of, 104–5, 168, 258–59; and Thomas nomination, 393; TM as head of legal department of, 99, 100; TM on leave from, 137–38; TM as Maryland representative of, 69; TM as point man in Washington for, 81; TM resigns as special counsel to, 260; TM's alienation from, 281, 282; TM's appointment with, 83, 84–85; and TM's confirmation to Supreme Court, 334; TM's early days with, 90–92, 93–100; and TM's impact on American society, 402; and TM's reputation, 81; TM's responsibilities with, 106; and TM's southern travels, 59–60, 63–64; TM's views about, 377–78; and White scandals, 188–89; Wilkins appointed head of, 236; Williams suspended by, 280, 281, 282. *See also* NAACP Legal Defense Fund and Education Fund, Inc.; *specific person, legal decision, topic, city, or state*
NAACP (National Association for the Advancement of Colored People)— conventions/conferences of: in 1954, 232; in Atlanta (1946), 174–75; in Baltimore (27th), 84; in Boston (1950), 169; about *Brown*, 231; in Chicago (1945), 149; in Cincinnati

NAACP *(cont'd)*
  (1946), 143–44; in Detroit, 126, 127,
  261–62; on housing, 149; in New
  York, 175, 242, 281–82; in
  Philadelphia (1940), 108; in San
  Francisco (1956), 251, 257; and school
  segregation, 195–97; in Washington
  (1947), 181
NAACP Emergency War Conference
  (Detroit, 1943), 126, 127
NAACP Legal Defense and Education
  Fund, Inc. (LDF): board of, 261, 295;
  and Carter-TM relationship, 272,
  294–95; and communism, 282–83;
  creation of, 104; dissension within,
  209–10, 211, 271–72; expansion of
  staff of, 125; fund-raising by, 288;
  Greenberg appointed head of, 294–95;
  and social science methods, 209–10;
  splits from NAACP, 259–62; tax-
  exempt status of, 259–62, 272; TM as
  head of, 4–5, 6, 104; TM's control of,
  261–62, 279, 295; TM's leave of
  absence from, 284–86; and TM's
  management style, 203–4; and TM's
  strategy for criminal cases, 147–48;
  TM's strategy for, 107–8, 195–208,
  259–62; TM's successor at, 294–95.
  See also specific legal case
Nabrit II, James, 177, 179, 181, 208,
  226, 230, 272
Nation of Islam, 254–58, 275–80, 281,
  303, 304, 399
National Bar Association, 57–58, 70, 82
National Lampoon, 376
National Lawyers Guild, 105, 111, 169,
  171, 241–42, 300, 301, 336
National Negro Labor Council, 257
National Review, 384
National Urban League, 341
Nativist backlash, 403
Negro: TM's use of term, 388
New Orleans, Louisiana, 107, 142,
  343–44
New York City: Democratic Party in,
  166; Liberal Party in, 273; police in,
  277–78; politics in, 273; race relations
  in, 277–78. *See also* Harlem
New York Post, 166, 273, 279–80, 322–
  23
New York State Board of Regents, 273
The New York Times, 345, 379; and
  Brown, 230; and civil rights, 165; and
  graduate education segregation, 195;

and Little Rock, 270–71; and *Miranda*,
  323; and Pentagon Papers, 351–52;
  and TM's death, 398; and TM's
  nomination to Supreme Court, 12,
  323
New York v. Galamison (1965), 311–12
Newsweek magazine, 12–13, 262, 333,
  390
Nichols, Lou, 255, 256
Nixon, E. D., 245, 246, 247, 251
Nixon, Richard M., 289–90, 343, 346,
  347, 348, 351–52, 355–56, 358
Nonviolent protest, 246, 247, 248, 251,
  255, 256, 282
Norfolk, Virginia: equal pay in, 91
North Carolina: militancy in, 280–82;
  sit-ins in, 286–87

O'Connor, Sandra Day, 375, 376, 391,
  398
O'Dunne, Eugene, 69, 77
Ogunlesi, Adebayo, 377
Oklahoma: graduate education in,
  176–79; *Lyons* case in, 113–19, 147,
  176, 386; NAACP in, 177
Oklahoma Black Dispatch. See Dunjee,
  Roscoe
Omega Psi Phi, 47, 56–57
Owens, Buck, 162, 310–11

Papers of TM, 394
Parker, John, 200, 202
Parks, Rosa, 246
Patterson, Agnes, 28
Patterson, John, 258
Patterson, Pat, 29, 64, 65–66
Patterson, William L., 189
Patton (Eddie) v. Mississippi (1947), 147
Payne v. Tennessee (1991), 391
Pentagon Papers, 351–52
Peremptory challenges, 380
Perlman, Philip, 151
Philadelphia, Mississippi, 319–20
Philip (prince of Great Britain), 286
Philips, Leon Chase, 114, 115, 116, 117,
  119
Pierce, Samuel, 348
Pillow, William "Rooster Bill," 139
Pittsburgh Courier, 125, 144, 173,
  231–32, 236, 250, 271
Plessy v. Ferguson (1896): and *Bakke*, 365,
  366; decision in, 22; and interstate
  commerce, 146; and school
  segregation, 196, 202, 203, 205, 215,

216, 219, 226. *See also* Separate but
equal
Pollack, Louis, 223, 305
Pornography, 344–45, 355, 376, 400
Porter, George, 101–4
Poston, Ted, 322–23
Pound, Roscoe, 57, 61
Powell, Adam Clayton, 267, 273–74, 306
Powell, Colin, 385
Powell, Lewis, 353, 354, 365, 366–67,
370–71, 372, 381, 400
Primary elections, 108–12, 176, 200, 313
Prince Hall Masons, 179–80
Prisoners' rights, 356, 378, 379, 401
Protests: antiwar, 6–7, 340; and free
speech, 311–12; nonviolent, 246, 247,
248, 251, 255, 256, 282; and TM's
confirmation to Supreme Court, 334;
TM's views about, 241, 341–42,
343–44; and transformation of civil
rights movement, 274. *See also*
Marches; Race riots; Sit-ins; Urban
riots

Quotas, 364–68

Race riots: during World War II,
126–28, 132–42; in early 1900s, 23,
32–33; and elections of 1968, 340; in
1960s, 13; TM's investigations into,
277; TM's views about, 247. *See also*
Bus boycotts; *specific city, state, or legal
decision*
Racial stereotyping, 105–6
Racial transformation, 188–89
Racism: and TM as racist, 301–2,
335–36
Randolph, A. Philip, 122–23, 309
Ransom, Leon Andrew, 58, 80, 83, 137,
138–39
Rape, 119–20, 128, 147, 152–57, 281
Raymond, Harry, 131, 139
Reagan, Ronald, 372, 373, 374, 375,
379–80, 383–84, 392, 398–99
Redding, Louis, 208, 218
Reed, Stanley, 226, 322–23, 339
*Regents of the University of California v.
Bakke* (1978), 364–68
Rehnquist, William: and abortion, 354;
appointment to Supreme Court of,
353; and *Brown*, 219; as chief justice,
380; and death penalty, 360, 375–76;
and TM's funeral, 397–98; and TM's
impact on American society, 401, 402;

TM's relationship with, 371; and TM's
retirement, 391
Religion: TM and, 37, 144, 310, 398
Republican Party: in Maryland, 19, 23,
26–27
Resegregation, 398–99
Restrictive covenants, 148–51
Resurrection City, 341–42
Richmond v. J. A. Croson Co. (1989), 388
Richmond, Virginia, 288–89, 388
Right to counsel, 339–40
Rising Sun, Maryland: TM's accident at,
49–50
Robeson, Paul, 47, 143
Robinson, Jackie, 164, 218, 277, 301
Robinson, Spottswood: and *Morgan v.
Virginia*, 145; and school segregation,
196, 197, 199, 205–6, 209, 210, 211,
218, 223; TM's relationship with, 205
Roe v. Wade (1973), 354–55
Roosevelt, Eleanor, 129, 130, 165–66,
188, 189, 261, 301
Roosevelt, Franklin D., 82, 108, 122,
123, 127, 383
Rowan, Carl, 383, 385–86
Ruark, Robert, 286
Russell, Richard, 230, 288

Sailors: mutiny by, 128–30
Saltzburg, Stephen, 350
Scalia, Antonin, 379–80, 388–89, 394
Schoen, Mr., 15–16, 45
School district boundaries, 357–58, 401
School segregation: amalgamation of
Supreme Court cases about, 207–8;
benefits of, 217–18; and criticisms of
TM, 203–4; and direct-attack strategy,
174–86, 196–208; and due process,
208; and equal protection, 216, 218;
and equal rights, 222; and Fourteenth
Amendment, 196, 207–8, 213, 218,
219–26; and Justice Department,
213–14, 222; and management of
desegregation, 213, 219; NAACP
conference about, 195–97; NAACP
dissension concerning strategy about,
181–82; and revolutionizing American
race relations, 174, 194; in secondary
schools, 79–80; and social science
methods, 197–205, 209, 216, 220;
Supreme Court's power to abolish,
219, 223; and TM's impact on
American society, 401; and TM's
southern travels, 59–60, 63–64, 95;

School segregation *(cont'd)*
TM's strategy concerning, 181,
195–208, 209–10. *See also* Busing;
Graduate education; Integration;
Separate but equal; *specific city, state, or
legal decision*
School spending disparities, 357,
401
Schwerner, Michael, 319–20
Search and seizure, 309
Second Circuit Court of Appeals, U.S.:
annual conferences of, 369; and
Cambodia bombing decision, 355–56;
confirmation of TM to, 296–97,
298–303, 317; TM as judge on,
297–98, 304–5, 309, 311–12, 351; TM
sworn in as judge for, 296; TM as
visiting judge for, 394–95; and TM's
confirmation to Supreme Court, 332;
and TM's criticisms of Supreme
Court, 381
Segregation: benefits of, 217–18; direct-
attack strategy on, 174–86, 195–208;
NAACP challenges constitutionality
of, 200; schools as means of
eradicating, 174, 194; and social
science methods, 197–205, 209, 216,
220; and TM's impact on American
society, 402, 403–4; TM's NAACP
strategy for, 107–8; as unfinished
business, 194. *See also* Bus boycotts;
Graduate education; Housing; Labor
unions; Military: segregation in;
School segregation; Segregationists;
Transportation; *specific person, legal
case, city, or state*
Segregationists: and communism, 257;
and elections of 1960, 289; foot-
dragging by, 284; and implementation
of *Brown*, 233; racist backlash among,
249; and sit-ins, 288; and TM's
nomination/confirmation as solicitor
general, 316; and TM's
nomination/confirmation to federal
judgeship, 5, 294, 303; and TM's
nomination/confirmation to Supreme
Court, 7, 13, 333. *See also specific person*
Self-incrimination, 323
Selma, Alabama, 313
Senate, U.S., 14, 95, 296–97, 298–303,
316–17, 337, 399
Separate but equal: and *Bakke*, 365; and
Brown, 209, 225–26, 230; death knell
for, 230; and graduate education, 76,
96–99, 176–79, 180–85; and
Houston's NAACP strategy, 94; as
illegal, 175; new version of, 403–4;
and Reed's dissenting opinion in
Brown, 339; and school segregation,
80, 174, 175–86, 202–3, 205, 206, 209,
225–26, 230; and TM's impact on
American society, 401, 403–4. *See also*
Segregation; *specific legal decision*
Separatism, 304, 343, 344, 399, 404. *See
also* Nation of Islam
Set-asides, 377, 388, 389, 399
Sevareid, Eric, 303
Sexual harassment, 393
Shagaloff, June, 206–7, 211, 213,
215
Shelley v. Kraemer (1948), 149–51
Shepherd (Samuel) v. Florida (1951). *See*
Groveland, Florida
Shervington, Charlotte, 34–35
Shores, Arthur, 174–75, 199, 248
Short, Anita, 36, 39
Sierra Leone, 291
*Sipuel (Ada Lois) v. Oklahoma State
Regents* (1948), 176–79, 180, 203,
221
Sit-ins, 274, 286–90, 378
Smith (Lonnie) v. Allwright (1944),
110–12
Smith, Maceo, 108–9, 110, 176
Smith, Tom, 88–89
Social science methods, 150, 197–205,
209–10, 216, 220. *See also* Clark,
Kenneth
Solicitor general: TM as first black, 4,
314; TM sworn in as, 317–18; TM's
cases as, 318–20, 323; and TM's con-
firmation to Supreme Court, 332, 333;
and TM's nomination to Supreme
Court, 4, 315, 317, 322–23, 328; TM's
nomination/confirmation as, 313–17,
331; and TM's reputation, 6
Souter, David, 389, 390, 397
South: backlash about *Brown* in, 230; and
implementation of *Brown*, 233, 237,
239; NAACP fund-raisers in, 242; and
NAACP membership lists, 258–59;
school segregation in, 176, 233, 237,
239; sit-ins in, 286–89; TM's travels to
schools in, 59–60, 63–64, 95, 106–7.
See also Segregationists; *specific city,
state, or legal decision*
South Carolina: bus segregation in, 247,
248; NAACP in, 198–99; school

segregation in, 198–204, 207, 214–15, 216–18, 219, 236
Southern Christian Leadership Conference (SCLC), 286–87
"Southern Manifesto" (1956), 248
Spector, Phillip, 365, 370
Spell, Joseph, 119–20
Spingarn, Arthur, 104–5, 165
Spingarn, Stephen, 165, 166
Spingarn Medal, 143–44
Sports: TM's interest in, 164
Spritzer, Ralph, 318
Stanley v. Georgia (1969), 344–45
State Department, U.S., 307–9
States' rights, 252, 335
Stay of executions, 147–48
Stephenson, Gladys and James, 132, 133, 141–42
Stereotypes, racist, 105–6
Stevens, John Paul, 359, 360, 369, 372
Stevenson, Adlai, 212, 218, 306–7
Stewart, James, 177, 180
Stewart, Potter, 353, 354, 359, 360, 365
Stewart, Teddy, 38, 44, 88–89
Stovall, Alice, 145, 163, 164, 165–66, 177, 200–201, 211, 234
Strubing, Eleanor, 119–20
Student Non-Violent Co-ordinating Committee (SNCC), 341
Supreme Court: backlash against, 356–58; conferences of, 376, 377, 381, 388–89; conservatism of, 347, 352, 353, 360, 374–75, 379–80, 381, 384–85, 388, 391; image of, 347; march to, 341–42; Nixon's assessment of, 355; powers of, 219, 223; pressures on TM to retire from, 352, 361, 362, 368, 370, 372–73, 380; replacements for TM on, 361, 362–63; rumors about TM's appointment to, 322–23; rumors about TM's resignation from, 347–48, 361, 372–73; TM sworn in to, 338, 349; TM as symbolic black on, 356; TM's alienation from, 352, 360, 368, 371, 378, 380–81, 387, 389, 398; and TM's appointment as solicitor general, 315, 317, 322–23, 328; TM's confirmation to, 331, 332–38; TM's criticisms of, 375–76, 381–83, 384; TM's first loss in, 118–19; TM's nomination to, 3–14, 312, 328–31, 356; TM's record of cases argued before, 6, 10, 11, 187, 284; and TM's relationships with other justices,

338–39, 344, 345, 364–69, 374, 375, 376–77, 381, 388–89, 390, 394; TM's retirement from, 391–92, 394; TM's visits as law student to, 57. *See also* *specific justice or decision*
Suyat, Juan, 242, 250
Swann v. Charlotte-Mecklenburg Board of Education (1971), 350
Sweatt (Heman) v. Painter (1950), 175–76, 180–85, 195, 203, 218, 221, 227

Talmadge, Herman, 230, 233
Tammany Hall, 166, 193, 273
Taylor (Samuel) v. Alabama (1948), 147
Teachers. *See* Black teachers
Tennessee: graduate education in, 96; race riots in, 131–42, 247
Tennessee A & I University, 96
Tennessee v. Pillow and Kennedy (1946), 131–42, 247
Texas: abortion in, 354–55; bad debts in, 319; death penalty in, 359–60; graduate education in, 175–76, 180–85; jury service in, 101–4; NAACP in, 108–10, 176, 182; primary elections in, 108–12, 176, 200, 313
Thirteenth Amendment, 150, 336
Thomas, Clarence, 392–94
Thornburgh, Richard, 390
"Thurgood Marshall, Mr. Civil Rights" (song), 239–40
Thurmond, Strom, 248, 332, 336, 337, 374
Tilghman, Sue "Little Bits," 62, 63
Till, Emmett: murder of, 241, 254
Time magazine, 5, 176, 239, 240
Timmerman, George, 200, 202
Tkach, Walter, 347
"To Fulfill These Rights" (conference, 1967), 327–28
Tobias, Channing, 235
Tolson, Clyde, 343
Toney, Charles, 149
Toomer, Jean, 47
Topeka, Kansas: school segregation in, 204–5. See also *Brown v. Board of Education of Topeka* (1954)
Transportation: segregation in, 145–46, 228. *See also* Buses: segregation on
Truman, Harry S., 148, 151, 331; appoints Hastie governor of Virgin Islands, 137, 184; and consideration of

Truman, Harry S., *(cont'd)*
  TM for federal judgeship, 165, 166;
  and elections of 1948, 168; and
  MacArthur, 172, 173; and military
  segregation, 169–70, 171; and
  NAACP political power, 160, 168;
  TM as stand-in in Israel for, 328;
  TM's support for, 165; TM's views
  about, 383
Tubman, William, 340
Tureaud, A. P., 174–75, 198
Turnbull, Douglas C., Jr., 28
Tuskegee Institute, 225
Twenty-fourth Amendment, 320

Underwood, J. J., 133–34, 135
United Nations, 168, 317
United Negro College Fund, 232
University of Alabama, 248–49, 307
University of California at Davis,
  364–68
University of Maryland, 52–53, 61,
  75–79, 371–72
University of Mississippi, 307
University of Missouri, 96–99, 175
University of North Carolina, 75
University of Oklahoma, 176–79
University of Tennessee, 96
University of Texas, 175–76, 180–86
University of Wisconsin, 342–43
Urban League, 126
Urban riots, 7, 13, 23, 326–27, 342–43.
  See also Race riots; *specific city*
U.S. News and World Report, 366
U.S. v. Classic (1941), 110, 111
U.S. v. Denno, 351
U.S. v. Gilbert (1950), 170, 171, 173
U.S. v. Nixon (1974), 358
U.S. v. Price (1966), 319–20
U.S. v. Yazell (1966), 319
USA Today, 398

Valenti, Jack, 330, 395
Vaughn, George, 150–51
Victim impact statements, 391
Vietnam, 13, 321, 327, 340, 341, 351–52,
  355–56
Vinson, Fred, 147–48, 184–85, 213, 214,
  221, 365
Violence: NAACP opposition to,
  280–83; TM's views about, 304, 344.
  See also Militancy; *specific event*
Virginia: *Crawford* murder case in,
  58–59; and frivolous lawsuits, 284;

poll taxes in, 320; school segregation
  in, 205–6, 207, 218, 219; sit-ins in,
  288–89
Virginia v. Crawford (1933), 58–59
Voting rights, 108–12, 313, 320, 382
Voting Rights Act, 317, 320, 343

Walker, W. W., 40–41
Wallace, George, 342
Wallace, Henry, 168
Wallace, Mike, 269
Ward's Cove Packing Co. v. Atonio (1989),
  388
Waring, J. Waties, 200, 201, 202–3, 204
Waring, J.H.N., 34, 35
Warren, Earl, 341, 344; appointment of,
  221–22; and *Brown*, 221–22, 225–26,
  231, 237; Eisenhower lobbies, 237; as
  liberal, 7, 333; and Little Rock, 269;
  and Reed's dissenting opinion in
  Brown, 339; resignation of, 342, 346;
  and TM's nomination to Supreme
  Court, 10, 11–12, 333; TM's
  relationship with, 375
Warren, Nina, 223
Washington, D.C.: civil rights
  conference in, 327–28; code of laws
  for, 57; as federal territory and not a
  state, 207–8, 219; and Fourteenth
  Amendment, 207–8, 219; housing in,
  149; NAACP chapter in, 32; race
  relations in, 32–33, 162; riots and
  marches in, 309, 341–42; school
  segregation in, 176, 207–8, 218, 219,
  226; TM and Cissy move to, 318; TM
  as NAACP point man in, 81
The Washington Post, 32, 323, 351–52,
  373, 386, 398
The Washington Post Magazine, 386, 387,
  388
Washington Star, 287–88, 302, 344, 346,
  361
Watergate, 358, 359
Watson, Marvin, 10, 324–25
Watts riots, 317
Watts (Robert) v. Indiana (1949), 147
Weaver, Maurice, 131, 135, 137, 138–39,
  141
Weaver, Robert C., 149, 150, 317
Webster, William, 376
Wechsler, Herbert, 111
Weinstein, Jack, 210
Wesley, Carter, 181–82
Whipple, Taggart, 215

White, Byron, 14, 293, 332, 338–39, 353, 354, 359, 360, 365–66, 372, 381

White, Lulu, 175

White, Walter: and antilynching bill, 95; and Baker (Josephine) law suit, 190; and *Brown*, 228–29; and communism, 167, 169, 171; and *Crawford* murder, 58, 59; death of, 236; Du Bois' relationship with, 168; and elections of 1948, 168; and *Gaines*, 98; and graduate education segregation, 175–76; and Groveland, 154; and Hoover-TM relationship, 160–61; and housing issues, 149–50; and Houston's death, 184; Houston's relationship with, 99; influence on TM of, 101; interracial marriage of, 188, 243, 244; and Justice's recruiting of TM, 124; on leave from NAACP, 168, 169; and lynchings, 81, 82; and *Lyons*, 115, 116, 117, 118; and military drafting of TM, 123–24; and military segregation, 123, 129, 170, 172–73; and *Morgan*, 146; and *Murray*, 78; and racial stereotyping, 105; scandals about, 188–89; and school segregation, 203, 211–12; and *Spell*, 119; style of, 99, 105, 190; Supreme Court visits of, 189–90; and tax-exempt status for NAACP, 104; and Tennessee race riots, 135, 138; and TM's award of Spingarn Medal, 143; and TM's consideration for federal judgeship, 165–66; and TM's health, 137; and TM's pressures for NAACP appointment, 84–85; TM's relationship with, 81, 106, 146, 154, 188, 189–90, 228–29; as U.N. delegate, 168; and voting rights, 108, 112; Wilkins' relationship with, 189, 190; and Williams-TM disagreement, 154

Whitman candy company, 105

Wilkins, Roy, 218, 296; as acting director of NAACP, 168; Baltimore visit of, 74; and *Brown*, 229, 230; and Carter-TM relationship, 261; Carter's relationship with, 349; and communism, 171; death of, 377; defends TM against communism, 241–42; and FBI, 254; as godfather to Thurgood, Jr., 250; and graduate education segregation, 97; as head of NAACP, 236; and Houston's death, 184; and implementation of *Brown*, 238; and King, 251, 341; and LDF-NAACP split, 259, 260; and Montgomery bus boycott, 246; and NAACP suspension of Williams, 280, 281, 282; as nominal head of NAACP, 189; and school segregation, 211–12; and sit-ins, 288; and tax-exempt status for NAACP, 104; and TM's confirmation to Supreme Court, 334; and TM's marriage to Cissy, 243–44; and TM's pressures for NAACP appointment, 84; TM's relationship with, 74, 106, 190, 236, 258, 334; and White, 189, 190, 236

Williams, Ethel, 29, 37–38

Williams, Fearless Mentor, 27–28, 30, 33, 38–39, 52, 69, 87, 236

Williams, Florence (aunt), 29, 76

Williams, Franklin, 153, 154

Williams, Isaiah O.B. (grandfather), 17, 18–19, 21, 22, 24, 27–28, 30–32

Williams, Karen Hastie, 370, 377

Williams (Margaret) v. Zimmerman (1937), 79–80

Williams, Mary Fossett (grandmother), 17, 19, 25, 27, 29

Williams, Robert, 280–82

Wilmington, Delaware, 208

Wilson, Paul E., 216, 224–25

Winchell, Walter, 190

Winter, Ralph, 297–98, 300, 305, 351, 395

Wiretaps. *See* Eavesdropping

Wofford, Harris, 247

Women: as clerks, 377; and TM, 43, 306, 346, 376; voting rights of, 382

Woodard, Isaac, 158–59

World War I, 32, 54

World War II: and drafting of TM, 123–24; and labor unions, 122–23; and military segregation, 121, 122, 123–25, 128–30; race riots during, 126–28, 132–42

Wygant v. Jackson Board of Education (1986), 381

Yazell, Ethel Mae, 319

Yerba Buena Island (California), sailors' mutiny at, 128–30

Young, Whitney, 341